KU-339-434

HC

A STRANGE MOTHER

HARTLEPOOL BOROUGH

WITHDRAWN

LIBRARIES

1681199 2

A STRANGE
MOTHER

M. L. REID

Copyright © 2015 M. L. Reid

The moral right of the author has been asserted.

Apart from any fair dealing for the purposes of research or private study,
or criticism or review, as permitted under the Copyright, Designs and Patents
Act 1988, this publication may only be reproduced, stored or transmitted, in
any form or by any means, with the prior permission in writing of the
publishers, or in the case of reprographic reproduction in accordance with
the terms of licences issued by the Copyright Licensing Agency. Enquiries
concerning reproduction outside those terms should be sent to the publishers.

Matador
9 Priory Business Park
Kibworth Beauchamp
Leicestershire LE8 0RX, UK
Tel: (+44) 116 279 2299
Fax: (+44) 116 279 2277
Email: books@troubador.co.uk
Web: www.troubador.co.uk/matador

ISBN 978 1784620 851

British Library Cataloguing in Publication Data.
A catalogue record for this book is available from the British Library.

Typeset in Aldine401 BT Roman by Troubador Publishing Ltd
Printed and bound in the UK by TJ International, Padstow, Cornwall

Matador is an imprint of Troubador Publishing Ltd

Dedication

I would first like to dedicate this book to my partner who has been supportive in my life; he has been more than a rock and an angel in disguise. After reading this book you will have a better understanding about him and why he is paramount in my life during this unusual journey; also to my beautiful daughters Rachel and Rebecca who endure the difficulties.

My journey is a combination of paranormal activities – spiritual wickedness, child abuse, poverty, neglect. As I write this book it is still on-going and has escalated. I was inspired to share my experience with the world because I know there are many others who are suffering in silence because nature or culture has dedicated that a mother is caring and someone you always trust almost like a shadow of yourself so people may be afraid to come out and share their experiences. I cannot comprehend my life and relationship with my mother and this is why the book is called *A Strange Mother*.

Chapter 1

I was born in 1971 in the United Kingdom in a town called Hackney, which is densely populated with ethnic minorities such as Caribbean people and Africans as well as orthodox Jews. I was born to parents who emigrated from the Caribbean – Jamaica. My father came to the UK in 1962 to find work and study. He worked in the post office for some time before my mother joined him in 1963. He was very much attracted to her, and after a difficult marriage previously he thought this was the woman that would make him settle again. They got married in 1965. My mother always had unpleasant things to say about my father; he was a wicked man and he physically abused her and was jealous because she was attractive.

The real story is that my father fell in love with a stranger – a 'holiday romance'. He did not know this woman very well. He was attracted to her and decided that he wanted to spend the rest of his life with her. He was from a wealthy background: my grandfather had inherited a legacy of acres of land with crops and farms from my great-grandparents, which they inherited during the time of slavery. My mother suffered hardship and saw an opportunity to be swept off her feet and brought to the UK. She kept a very private life in as much that I lived with my mother for 15 years and I do not know much about her life.

It was not long before my father made the true discovery, when he sent for her in 1965, that she was not all that she seemed. They had constant fights and arguments because she wanted to live the life of partying, shopping sprees and was not ready for family life as she promised; just carefree. My father was very disappointed, he had planned for years for her to join him; he felt at the age of 33 that this would be the perfect time to start. At the same time, she left my three-year-old brother behind in Jamaica with her mother, who also had four young children of her own. My mother was more interested in living the dream life, even though her mother insisted she would not take the responsibility of looking after her child. My father told me he was not interested in taking care of another man's child, but I questioned this decision; surely he knew she had a child, so why not? It would really be up to my mother to decide. The arguments and fights became severe; my mother was throwing blows as well as my dad. The next door neighbours had no peace as the walls were so thin, you could hear every sound. I had the opportunity of meeting one of the neighbours, Mrs Jacob, who told me about the noise. My mother always told me how much she hated my father.

"You are just like your stinking father," she said.

The change had really started now because the plan my father had – to settle and live the family life – was not her plan. It was all a sham: she did not love my father at all; to this day she calls him short, ugly and mean. What does that do for me? He is my father; I express my frustration and pain, how I hate them arguing all the time. I have told her many times not to speak about my father in this way. She always looked at me in disgust and spewed more abuse.

My father was heartbroken to know he had been played. He told her that he refused to carry on with the relationship unless he had a child. At this point, my father had no idea that my mother came to the UK to use him. Her behaviour had changed from when they met in the Caribbean; she started to make demands for money that she had to send to her mother and other family members. This went on for a while: all sorts of demands, even for the church her mother attended in Jamaica. My dad refused to furnish this lavish spending and stated that he wanted out of the relationship. My mother always had her way and the battle turned really dark. She started to return home and disappear at odd times in the evening. My father realised she had met some friends that had a huge influence on her. She ignored him; she went to church almost seven days a week, he was not introduced to these people. They would collect her outside of the house in a van filled with others and then drop her home, sometimes at 2am, and she started to wear a strange uniform from head to toe. My father was concerned that he had brought this woman to a country where she didn't know anyone and suddenly he was kicked to the kerb and she had started a new life in this society. She performed rituals which involved candles and incantation, then he started to experience really horrific nightmares, which involved coffins, being buried alive and snakes attacking him in his dreams. Her behaviour had changed: she had developed extreme confidence, and was very overpowering. On the other hand, my mother told me that my father was one of the biggest *Obeah* workers (a Caribbean dialect word for Voodoo). She told me that my father sent talismans through the post on many occasions, but she was always lucky enough to detect them before opening the letter. One day, a friend of hers didn't believe her about these odd letters and decided to be brave and open it: she coughed for days and not long after she passed away.

"He will never be able to conquer me," she said.

"What do you do to overcome?" I asked her.

"God can do great things; all I do is pray to God."

My father started to have strange things happen to him, bad dreams and strangulations in these dreams. One day when my mother made dinner, he was convinced his food was spiked. He felt the room turning around and at the same time like he was going down to hit the floor. She said,

"You brut you," meaning 'good for you'.

She developed this power and confidence and wanted to be in full control. Dad decided to investigate and secretly followed her one evening to see where she was going and who her new friends were. He discovered she was attending a ritualistic church in Tottenham, London. The members wrapped their heads and wore long skirts; the uniforms were in various colours, depending on what rituals were performed. The leader conducted spiritual healing. My father could hear them from the outside window groaning strangely and calling the devil. He later said,

"I heard from others who were attending this organisation that the leader did good works as well as bad."

He saw some of the members unconscious on the ground. They had been possessed by the devil, and my mother was part of the ritual.

He confronted her about it. She said he was mad, it was not her. Then that same night, she told him she was pregnant and wanted a divorce. Dad wanted to know how she had suddenly took an interest in this organisation, so he conducted an investigation by going back to Jamaica to really understand her background. To his surprise, her mother also was a leader of the same type of organisation; his donation was used to build the church. A family friend from the same district came to visit my dad in his confusion and told him,

"If I hear what I am about to tell you again, I will deny it. The family your wife is from are *Obeah* workers and you need to be careful."

On his return, he would experience hell; she was ready to declare war. My dad said that in spite of what he heard, he was cautious because he knew a child was on the way. She deliberately created unnecessary arguments, being physically abusive by hitting him with anything to get him in trouble with the law. My mother told me that my father was so vindictive that he slit his wrist to prove to her friends that she was abusive. Her story was that she bought a new bedspread and because my dad was jealous he cut his wrist to smudge it with blood, as well as being really violent.

"The *Obeah* was getting really strong," he said.

Fortunately for him, when the man from the district gave the warning, he went to seek protection from a spiritualist in the mountains of St Catherine, Jamaica. The leader from her church was set to inflict pain and cast many spells upon him, which were not effective. She started to put potions in his food and drink. One evening after dinner, he realised a powder-like substance was seeping out of his body through his pores like fish bone. Shadows were passing as if someone else was in the house; all sorts of entities were strangling him in his sleep. On another occasion, she appeared to be really pleasant and told him she had made him Guinness punch. He later said,

"I was so desperate for a change; I wanted my marriage to work. I fell for deceit."

He sat down for the meal and as he was about to lift the glass, it exploded, followed by a ripple shattering the house windows. It seemed another potion was set but deterred; he was always exhausted, but his protection was obviously working. Now that he realised her intentions, he started to retaliate with the instructions from home to drive the demons back to their sender. She was still denying it was her. One evening, he returned from work to find the same experience he had with the powder, all the powder she had sprinkled was coming through her legs and face like tiny fish bone. My mother told me about this story, but a different version. She explained that my dad had cast a spell on her and powder was seeping out of her body. A spirit frequently visited the home at midnight; a house that was peaceful had suddenly turned into a haunted house. My father was now fighting back, her brethren were giving her a lot of support and unprofessional advice on the legality of custodial rights and divorce proceedings – how she could benefit from the divorce, with the child. She had convinced them of the abuse by my father and of his wicked ways. The divorce was certain. She left their matrimonial home to stay with her friend until the divorce. My dad refused to let her have full custody of his child. He was going to put up a hell of a fight and was concerned for my wellbeing, if I were to be brought up in such an environment.

I was born while the divorce proceedings were already on the way. During the separation, my father had custodial rights for me to stay with him on weekends. My aunt told me that my parents were not at peace enough even to keep the arrangement. They were competing and fighting over who bought the best clothes and the most expensive chocolate. My mother was trying to turn me against my father, not to go with him on the weekend, but for children, simply mention ice cream or chocolate. I was young; I cannot remember, but it was obvious to me from what I have been told the impact this would have had on me.

In 1972, at the Old Street Magistrate Court, London, my parents attended the court hearing. The arrangements were breached and my father refused to let my mother have custody. The battle was fierce, my mother used the abuse scenario to claim that my father was violent and she had to run for her life on several occasions – of course in a court of law, especially in the UK, battery is a serious crime. My father used the witchcraft scenario; that she was an irresponsible mother who indulged in witchcraft and that it would not be safe for a child to grow up among such practices. My father had brought a very strong case to the court and proof: after all, he was claiming that he had sent for this woman to join him to create a family and that he had been used and tormented by her and her friends. Her peers advised her that if she went down this route it would be beneficial to her, and she would be entitled to child support from him. My father decided there was no way he was going to allow her to use him again, because had he not given her the ultimatum she would not have considered having a child.

The verdict: my father won custody. The judge found that such practices of witchcraft were unsuitable for a child; it would have been unusual for a father to have won custody in that period. I learned this from my father with documented proof from the courts. My mother, like always, did not discuss the outcome with friends and family, not even me. She kept this secret and had made a decision that would change my life. I was never to see my dad or know him. My mother decided to emigrate to the Caribbean with me at the age of two years, unannounced to my father. My mother took off to the Caribbean with no finances or place to live; her intention was to escape the law and take revenge on my father.

These were the stories I was told all my life by my mother and father about my childhood. I am about to tell and embark upon my own journey and discover the truth.

My Journey

My mother immigrated to Jamaica; to a village called Williamsfield, situated in the parish of St Catherine. I am unable able to recollect my arrival, as I was so young, but what I do remember was that I suffered ill health for a while. I constantly had fever and broke out from allergies: my system was finding it difficult to cope in the heat. National Health Service is not available there, unlike in the UK. She only took £100 for us to survive on – medical fees are a must there, so what was my mother's plan? We didn't have a home; we had to share with other relatives in a room at my grandmother's house. My diet as a three-year-old had to be adjusted very quickly to the native food, which I really disliked, and it made me very ill. I now have children and it is a real problem to even get them to eat it at that age.

We stayed at my grandmother's for a while. Mum went home unannounced without telling her – it was not long before we were given the marching orders. My step-grandfather would not tolerate this and asked us to leave. My mother decided it would be better if we moved to Kingston, where it would be much easier to find work. In the UK, my mother was a tailor; this type of job would be difficult to find. Out of desperation, she found a job as a house help, which would pay enough to rent a room and buy food for us to survive on, as I was struggling with adjusting to the climate. Until this day I cannot understand the logic of her decision. When I asked her as a child, my mother's excuse was, "If I had not run away from that man, I would have been a dead woman."

There is no other fairer justice system, the United Kingdom is known for this, especially for women and children and moreover in cases of abuse. The system goes to the extreme on such crimes so they would have provided protection for us in a safe home and even supported us. I grew up as a little girl believing that my father was some kind of a monster who wanted to hurt us. I am still waiting for an explanation of the real motive to her decision, because I could have lost my life from an allergic reaction. I suffered severely acclimatizing. I was told by an aunt that I had to be rushed to hospital once; my reaction was so serious I was lucky we got to the hospital on time and received the correct treatment. I still have some of the scars on my body. Was her decision revenge, to get back at my father?

We were living in Kingston, experiencing real hardship there with not enough to survive on. She had a very bad temper, where she threw tantrums when things were not going her way. Frustration was setting in, which turned into verbal abuse, words used such as, "You're just like your father; just as ugly as him."

As I grew older, that anger was getting more terrifying for me. She would shout at me so fiercely. I was treading on eggshells for her not to be angry, but I don't know what triggered it. Even if I tried to be affectionate towards her, she barked like a hound. The church she attended in the UK had affiliations in Jamaica. It was a successful business; the healing and miraculous works had raised huge sums of money to buy acres of land and houses and the pledge promised to the members who donated money was that they would all live together on this land forever. This is where she now resides and lives in fear of being thrown off. The promise was obviously not true, for the members are not the sole proprietors, even though the promise was to pensioners that had given their last penny. Because of the influence and power to commit *Obeah* that could kill or destroy, no one dares to challenge and seek justice to retrieve their contributions or enquire about this unlawful deceit; they just wept aside in sorrow and disbelief. Many of those pensioners have now passed away and were not able to go home and retire as planned. The subordinates had so much fear to stand up or confront the senior members that possessed extreme power. Young girls were molested, even the parents knew about this and turned a blind eye; this was going on in the UK. If any damage was caused, depending on the age of the child, the treatment would be to anoint the affected area with healing oil. I also knew of a teenager that was impregnated. It was my inquisitive nature that led me to learn about the atrocities, getting part of the puzzle from different associates, piecing them together. I found this disturbing. Why was my mother a part of this and knew of the horrific acts and did nothing?

Although this society had its reputation, not all the individuals were the same. I grew up amongst some of the most loving and caring people; I wanted to know what had driven them to this society. There were a number of reasons. The husband or wife would marry, to unfortunately discover that the ex-partner from a previous relationship would be carrying a grudge and cast spells to destroy the marriage. The most common were to prevent them from having children or being prosperous, or the disapproval of the bride's or groom's parents. The partner sometimes indulged in bad omens in the past or had cast a spell due to jealousy or done a person wrong in retaliation and a spell was cast for eternity. Married women took revenge on mistresses. A bad past exists when parents have indulged in evil. A family that had cast a spell and retribution was often passed on to the next generation, but whatever the problems this would be the reason to initiate into this society.

There was one member from the society who was very caring to me as a child before I left the UK. She had taken the place of my biological grandmother. She immigrated to Jamaica in 1975 after her retirement. She was a lifesaver, because at this point my mother had lost the will to live. With no plans in place to take care of me, we were now suffering real hardship. She was unable to pay the rent on time, we could not afford to buy clothes and her anger had now grown into physical abuse. She would just start shouting and telling me many times that I didn't do this or that properly. When I appeared, she would give me a great slap across my ear and face; it echoed like a major treble from a microphone in my eardrum, followed by, "Didn't you hear me calling you?"

I had to answer by the first call. Mealtimes were also another problem. It was taking me a long time to adjust to the food – I hated it. I would sit there for a while playing with it, then I would be in for torture, another slap for each spoon I refused.

"Why don't you eat the food?"

"I don't like this; I don't like this horrible Jamaican callaloo."

"You better eat it, for there is nothing else!"

Sometimes I vomited. The beatings became so constant, I would be afraid every time she came in from work. She would pick on me for no reason, followed by a strike, always on my head. If I asked to play with the other children, it was not allowed, always no; it was as if I was not allowed to have any fun while she was unhappy. I found comfort in sucking my thumb. I constantly wet my bed and that would result in more slapping and shame as she would embarrass me in the yard, saying that I should take the wet sheets out so that the tenants would know I wet the bed again. I was ordered to take them out and wash them. I understood from this point my mother hated me. She would humiliate me by saying how the other children next door were beautiful and well-spoken and I spoke like an 'old nigger' (like the locals). This was a lot for a child to take on. I assumed I was the cause of ruining her life. She kept telling me how ugly I was and about my wicked father, who I had now forgotten because I was taken away from him at the age of 2. Who do I turn to? There was no one to defend me; the tenants in the yard would look in disgust or sometime plea for me, but she would say, "Don't mind her; she is a difficult child to deal with."

Mrs Archie arrived from the UK, how great it was. She lived in the same tenement yard as I, and she wanted to stay there for a little while, until her house was completed on the Promised Land. It was as if my real mother had arrived; she was affectionate, kind. My mother was struggling to find a sitter after school, Mrs Archie volunteered immediately. She had brought down my treats that I loved in the UK, my favourite pudding and custard. I was now becoming a happy child again. This was the year I had my first birthday party. I didn't have many friends to invite, but I met a few from the church and Mrs Archie arranged the cake and my mother organised the catering. I had a great day. The abuse was less now; I was only experiencing verbal abuse – maybe because Mrs A was there. She came home one evening and saw the delight in me and Mrs A; how happy I was, laughing and joking. She suddenly took a turn; she started to shout at me that I had been at home all evening after school and had not done my chores. Mrs A tried to explain that we had so much fun, it was her fault. My mother did not accept her explanation, she went outside in a mighty speed and came back with a piece of plank and started to batter me with it. What had I done? Mrs A was so shocked and tried to console my mother. She really had a go at Mrs A. She said that Mrs A was spoiling me and she would not allow it. Mrs A said sarcastically, "After all, there's nothing I can do, what do I know about children? I never had a child, I am sorry, my love."

She did not want to cause any rift between my mother and me. I could see her face; her grey eyes lit with anger and she was going red, she was so horrified. From that day, she was always careful and kept a distance when mother was due home, so as not to cause any problems. During the time we had together we would play, laugh and sing, but as soon as my mother got home, Mrs A would pull into her shell. It didn't take me long to understand what was going on.

I remembered one day in particular: it was really hot during the mango and guinep season, fruits I really enjoy. I was playing out in the yard when a white van pulled up at the gate, my mother was home. I saw some men get out of the van towards the gate, they looked official. I ran to my mother to tell her there were these men at the gate, one of the tenants told my mother that they were asking for her. She said, "Tell them I don't live here and then come, let's hide in the back room."

I could hear them talking and going around the yard, I dared not ask. For years I wondered whom we were hiding from. It was immigration; my father had a summons to find me because he had full custody from the courts. I always remembered this day but never fully understood what was going on until 17 years later.

My mother's behaviour started to change, she was getting happier. In the tenement yard where we lived there were about five other tenants. My mother started dating one of the tenants, Longman. He was very pleasant, we had regular chats and he would bring me sweets sometimes. Mrs A's house on the Promised Land was completed now and she was due to move out. There was a change – my mother and Longman were due to be married. I really don't know how long they had been dating, but things were really moving fast. Mrs A would not be far away – I could visit her but it wouldn't be the same without her. The wedding was scheduled. I was not told about the new life from my mother. Longman told me that he would be my new father and my mother asked how I would like to be a mini bride. That was it.

The wedding took place. I was so excited being a mini bridesmaid, it meant I wore a white dress with a veil; a little girl dreams to be a princess. It was quite a day and well attended by the church members' families. I was excited that I would finally have my own bedroom, as I was nine years old. They rented a bedsit situated in the Rock Fort area; it was 5 minutes' walk from the seaside. I had to walk four miles to school every day; it was quite a distance in the baking heat of the sun. I was disappointed, even though I had this new life, things were not much better, apart from I had my own bed in the dining room. We were still struggling for food and clothes; I needed a school uniform, shoes, and school books. I had to share with children in my class when they allowed me. I was given 6 pencils and 6 exercise books every September, the same stationery given since kindergarten. School shoes were hard to come by; my mother would beg her employer Mrs Cook to buy sneakers if she went to America. Mrs Cook was very generous, and she would buy me shoes and other gifts. When she left this job, we had to find another source to beg from. I asked myself, what is happening here? If you are married, surely things should be better, not the same. There were also some nights that we would not have a meal. I would attend school without proper breakfast, just lime leaf tea and crackers, and for lunch I had $1. This would purchase a pack of biscuits and a frozen bag of juice called suck-suck. Concentration at school was difficult. I had to sit and listen to the children read their books and at the same time I was often hungry. It got worse near to lunchtime. I could sometimes smell the sweet aroma, chicken and rice especially, coming from the canteen. I would see the children waiting in line with their shiny aluminium plates and cup.

"I wish I could taste that lunch," I said to myself. Instead I would purchase my lunch from the vendors outside the school gate. They would make and sell homemade snacks, but my money was never enough to buy anything substantial. I was satisfied because I was quite feisty. I would not beg, and I pretended I was fine.

At this age I had very low self-esteem. I was told by my mother we could not fit into society, for the rich people were special people. I didn't understand why I had to be poor and miserable, why did we have to live like this? I was quite lonely, I did not have friends because I felt I could not fit in with children who had the luxury of even a bicycle. I was unable to go on school trips, and I didn't have presentable clothes to wear to class parties nor spending money. Whenever there was an event at school I knew I could not attend, I would go to school on my own, go to lunch on my own, and go home on my own. It was noticed by one of the bullies in the school. She attacked me one day on the staircase. She grabbed my bag, but I pulled it back from her and walked on. She said something in the distance – I didn't take any notice. The next day she waited for me, but this time with a gang of friends, about four of them. They blocked me on the staircase. The ring leader was a lot taller than I, and she put her leg across the way. I would not let them take my bag because I had seen what they did to other children, taking all their stationery, and that was all I had. I said to her, "Move your foot."

The others stood by looking surprised. I told her again, "Move your foot."

She did not, so I barged past, walking over her feet. She pulled my hair vigorously from behind and at the same time the others took my bag from me. It was at this point that all the rage and anger within me exploded. I closed my eyes and I threw my fists and kicked in every direction. A crowd of schoolchildren gathered around to see what was happening; I caused mayhem. I was taken to the principal's office and received a warning. Those girls never tried it again and suddenly I made a friend with this girl called Candy. Somehow my outburst changed me; I felt confident after standing up to the bullies. Candy became my best friend; we would walk home together and have lunch, which she would share with me. Her mother was in the United States. She was well taken care of and I was able to share her books. I had potential academically, as I could read and write very well, but education was not a priority to my parents. I don't know what my mother had planned for my future. No one was interested in my reports or progress. Whatever was to be the next step after primary school was entirely up to me. I had a desire to one day be someone who was accepted in society.

Things were getting worse at home; my parents were physically fighting, my stepfather was becoming an alcoholic, and my mother started directing her abuse toward me again. The physical abuse was every day: she used belt buckles, planks, and when it seemed these where not inflicting enough pain she would invent her own weapon. She gathered pomegranate sticks and plaited them, then left them in a corner by her bed and told me to go and fetch one when she was ready for torment. The next door neighbours could not understand what could be causing the uproar. I heard the neighbour say over the fence, "Why does that woman beat the child every day?"

But I had become immune to the beating and verbal abuse, so that when she hit me, after a while I just stood there and took it without crying, I just turned my back and received it. On my back especially I had a lot of scars. This was from the striking and my skin was dreadful for healing; it scarred very easily and took a long time to clear. The chastising was not working anymore. I accepted that she was going to hit me – it was going to be over in a few minutes anyway. She realised and started to use more hefty force. The studio flat had steps leading to outside the yard; one day I did not complete my chore to her satisfaction, which was to polish the floor on my knees and then use the coconut brush to shine it. She said, "The floor must be as shiny as looking glass."

As she shouted and hit me with the whip, I kept on walking towards the step. She kicked me off the stairs and I landed on my stomach. My hands and legs were bruised; it burned like fire because of the sandy ground. After, she told me to wash the clothes. The soap and water getting into the wound was excruciating, because we washed our clothes by hand. My mother never apologised or gave me a reason for my punishment; I just had to do what she asked properly. I never lived in a yard where there were parents carrying out such acts on their children. I felt I had a wicked mother and there was nothing I could do about it; it was no one's problem but my own. When he was at home, my stepfather Longman disliked what my mother did to me. He would shout at her when she started, but as soon as he went out she bullied me, saying that I was trying to get her husband on my side.

The rent was now in arrears, the landlord had taken out notice against them. My mother's behaviour was at the extreme. This was the worst punishment I have ever had: I was not allowed to have friends to come by and play. I was told I should meet and greet outside and never bring them home, and sometimes after school, Candy and I would play skipping or dandy-shandy (dodge a ball that is thrown at you). I started to have other friends – even boys – who would walk the four mile journey with me to my gate. When they came she was pleasant and she invited them in, but that was as far as they went, as long as she was in control. It had now reached the stage where I was afraid to come home. I hated going home; it was hell. So this time Candy and I decided to do some sightseeing, which made me late. I was timing how long the journey home should take for me, because my mother actually walked the journey herself and timed it. Candy and I explored some places that we had heard about in the news, where criminals lived and there was a shootout which was being investigated – we were just children being curious. We wanted to explore what this life was about, was it for real? I also stopped by her house and her grandmother made us dinner. I should have reached home about 4:30pm – I got home around 5:45pm. Unfortunately for me, she was home early from work that day when I got in. I wanted to run away but I thought, 'what's the worst that could happen? She will beat me again and it will all be over'. I went home to meet her sitting on the steps, waiting for me. I knew she was angry. I said, "Good evening, mum."

"Where are you coming from?" she asked.

"School," I said.

"What time is this? You are coming in from school? I bet that you were with those bad friends. You are a disgusting child and you are going to tell me, where you have been?"

I didn't answer and walked past her into the house. As I went in, so did she. She picked up the wooden clothes brush which was heavy and solid. I saw her waiting for me. I knew she was going to use it. I tried to run outside but she caught me before I could get out. She repeatedly hit me on my head with all her anger and force and I could feel this warmth running down the back of my neck. I missed a step, my leg folded under my body and I fell down the steps. I could feel warm drops dripping on my neck. I crawled on my hands and knees in the dirt, crying, I was so fed up. I sat and leaned my back and head against the wall by the outside bathroom. I could see the blood oozing out like a heartbeat in the shadow on the wall. I started to feel lightheaded and I could see how the blood was gushing on the wall like a pulsation. I screamed with fear. I collapsed on the ground from frustration, anger, and fright. I had decided at this point that if I could have just died then I would be better off. She too was shocked; she had gone too far. If I was taken to a hospital she would have to explain, and the consequences would not be pleasant for her, so she quickly ran in and put a compress on my head. My heart was beating so fast. She gave me some sweet drink. The cut was quite deep. She kept this secret and she couldn't even tell her husband about what had happened. I went to bed that night in so much pain. My head and body were aching and the graze from the fall in the dirt was burning. The next morning, I was told my mother was admitted to the hospital during the night. I wasn't told the reason, but I assumed her blood pressure had gone up. Years later, during a conversation with my mother at the age of 25, she stated the reason she went into hospital was due to a miscarriage as a result of the incident. She said, "You know why you did it. You wanted to be the only child."

What the hell was she talking about? I didn't know she was pregnant. The only conversation we had was that she asked me in the presence of Mrs A whether I would like a brother or sister and I said to her no. She didn't tell me that she was carrying a child, this was insane; she was putting the blame on me. I was innocent. I told my father about this conversation as I was speechless to know someone could fabricate such a lie and have the nerve to confront me with it. I cannot explain how angry I was. He said, "You need to really investigate her allegation, as she exaggerates to the heavens, for in order for your mother to conceive you she had to undergo several treatments for years. She might have made this up because Longman was desperate for a child and she was unable to reproduce."

I also found out from her husband that she told him the same story. I had no idea, but if he had a grudge against me he kept it hidden well. Longman never showed any resentment; he was always caring, even during his drunken states. She also told the same story to my eldest daughter, Rachel. One morning while she was having breakfast, she asked her dad, "Is it true that Mummy killed Grandma's child?"

GA was shocked to know my mother had told the child this story. He knew it was unfair to lay this on a child. I confronted her about it in 2009, but she denied ever saying such. I said, "Rachel asked her dad a very disturbing question and I want to clarify this with you, as this is not the first time you said or I have heard you say that I killed your unborn child."

She replied, "I don't know what you are talking about." Completely oblivious.

"I want to know why you insist on this ridiculous story when you know it is not true."

Then she said, "Maybe the child might have misconstrued something she heard me talking about with a friend!"

I said, "So you were talking about it!"

"No! Ahh! Yes! Ah, no."

"Don't go around telling fibs on me; don't use me to cover up your misfortune. How wicked are you?"

The situation financially had escalated. We were about to be evicted, Longman lost his job, her aggression festered. Regardless of the incident we had, that did not deter her from continuously hitting me. When I heard her footsteps, fear was upon me. If I was in a place that was peaceful, as soon as she made her presence known it ruined everything. I hated her and I started to retaliate because I couldn't understand what I was punished for most of the time. When she called me, I answered extremely loudly because I was angry. She would be sitting beside a cup and call me all the way across the yard to pick it up and give it to her, just to be spiteful and annoying as I might not be busy enough at the time. I just wanted some free time as a child to play, even though I had no friends. She called me one day and I answered really loudly with a strop. This made her really mad. When I went to her, she gave me an almighty punch in the face. My left eye swelled so much I could barely see through it. I had to go to school with this the next day. I tried to hide it by avoiding my classmates, but my teacher Sir Johnson noticed, and he asked me, "What happened here?"

I told him a wasp had stung me. I am not sure if he believed me. The abuse continued; it was like a hobby for her and she used all her strength to hit me or kick me as she pleased. The fear was intense, I was still wetting the bed and really clumsy. We had Christmas dinner one year, and she took out her special plates she brought from the UK. After the meal, it was always my chore to wash the dishes. She warned that if I ever dropped those plates she would beat the hell out of me. I carefully packed them to take to the kitchen. On my way I missed my step up and all the plates – it was like slow motion – were disappearing out of my hands to the floor. My heart skipped a beat, from the fear of having broken the plates. She heard them from the other room and flew around. She said, "Jesus have mercy, this stupid child – after I told her, she broke my expensive plates."

She lifted her hand and punched me on the head. The same step I missed to break the plates, my head ended up hitting. I always remember darkness when this occurred; I think it is because I closed my eyes. I could hear in my head when she hit me, a loud bang and crunch. It was so loud that sometimes my ears would be ringing for a while, as if I heard loud music. Sometimes the area where she inflicted the lashing, for instance my arm, would be a struggle to lift for days. When I mentioned it, she said, "It is because you are too out of order."

There were occasions where after a slap on the face, my lip would get caught. It would bleed and become swollen and there was no one to help or seek help on my behalf. They all looked away.

With Longman out of a job and the eviction notice served, where were we going to live? My mother must have been discussing the situation with Mrs Archie. She suggested we reside on the Promised Land; after all, it was rent-free. It didn't take much convincing, we were on our way. She was entitled to a room; we had gone back to square one even after the supposed new life. I did not have a room of my own. What was really good about this move was I had the opportunity to live with my best friend Mrs A again. I insisted that I would not stay in my parents' room, but with her; she accepted. She was only a pensioner, but she was beyond generous. Mrs A was riddled with severe arthritis which prevented her from walking unless assisted by a walking stick. She had no immediate family and was a widow from a very young age. She was the Good Samaritan for all the children in the area. Those without food would be welcome; the parents also came to her when they had financial crises. I am not sure of the arrangement, but my mother had decided to give up work. I was happier; I had someone I could talk with, someone who showed me motherly love, who took an interest in my education and what I wanted to do in the future. This was the Promised Land. Where the church is situated is called the Mount Zion Revival Church. It was at this point I really started to understand what my mother's society was all about. The same practices my father mentioned that occurred in the UK continued here.

I was by now at an age where I was very observant, and the most brilliant thing was that I could ask Mrs Archie any question, and she was so thorough in her answers. She was the senior member in charge of the church, which explains how advanced she was in this society.

Chapter 2

As I grew older, I realised that this society is frowned upon by many Jamaicans. It is given all sorts of names: *Puko* church, *Obeah* workers, Zion church, wrap-head church. As a result, many children, including myself, were embarrassed to mention the church we attended. People would stay far away as if we had some sort of contagion. It was not only what took place there, but the community believed it was illiterates and witches who attended this church or that it was a safe haven for those who had lost touch with reality. They were perceived as uneducated and most of the time unemployed. There were frequent services every day; it was like a medical surgery for those who required healing from spiritual entities or were possessed with demons, and also those who were seeking deliverance from evil or general problems would attend. The remedy would be prayer or rituals that were carried out. The church members dressed in various uniforms depending on the occasion; the colours were blue, red, khaki, green or purple and they also wore a turban on their head to match. Some members, depending on their power, would have their turban in a shape at the front like the beak of a dove. The women had to have the crown of their head fully covered and the men partially covered. This uniform originated from West Africa. The turban was worn for protection from any evil passing on to them during deliverance. As I understand, the first place to receive an attack is from the head through to the brain. The demons speak to the mind and then travel to the soul, gradually taking over the body. I was born into this society; I didn't have a choice. I still attend on occasions when invited, despite not being part of it.

There is still a lot I don't understand, because I choose not to. I possess some gifts which, if I am initiated, could be quite powerful. I want to remain as I am in the world because I prefer not to be committed. This society is a full-time job and at every service there is never a dull moment. I was at the heart of the experience growing in Jamaica, which from time to time had a history of witchcraft. All sorts of unusual things happened. I didn't know much until I was about 10 years old, when I encountered the first sighting of the leader from the UK. He had passed away when I was about eight and I was at the Promised Land; the church building was nearly completed. I stood on the veranda one fine, sunny day. There was no one at home except for Mrs A. I was playing with some grasshoppers that I caught on the veranda. The building windows were incomplete; you could look through to the other side. Suddenly I went into a trance. This man appeared very briefly from nowhere in a green and white floral shirt with frills around the neck, and sleeves. I could only see half of the body from the side and then it disappeared. I ran around to the area to have a closer look; it was gone. I even looked inside the church to see whether the person went inside, but there was no one. There were a lot of activities on the Promised Land with this same character. That man haunted my friend; she screamed frantically one evening when we were playing hide and seek inside the church just before dark, it was so frightening for her. She had convulsions and gave the same description of the man I saw. The revivalist had to resolve this issue because it was getting very dangerous; he was attacking girls in death as he did in life. This is not a horror story; it is extremely difficult for anyone to convince me on such matters. I tell you the story as it really occurred. I also realised I developed feelings and sensations on the Promised Land; there was a scent that usually passes by every day at 6.00pm and I said to Mrs A, "There is smell that passes."

She confirmed, "Yes, it is called *Ioda* from a purple medicine used back in the day to heal sores. The spirit passing was a man who suffered from wounds."

The other experience I have encountered until this day is the head rising. I feel my head growing in size like it is swollen, with goosepimples on my arms and legs. This tells me there is an entity around.

A typical service in the Revival Church is the beating of the goat skin drum to call angels. The colour of the candles depends on the occasion, but they are typically white. A glass of water and bouquet of flowers are set up on a white table cloth and decorated with one red flag with a white cross in the centre, used for clearance to cut any destruction such as bad spirits that may enter. The service would start with singing and the beating of the drum. Revivalists are Christians – they would pray to God and read the Bible. During the service, the singing, which is a slow a cappella theme with various melodies, is astonishing. It sounds as if there is music or angels present. This, with the concentration of the table, would attract the Holy Spirit, which travelled through the body of one or a few members. The transition would react with a sudden shout or groaning sound. They would spin around and speak in tongues. The spirit may give specific instructions about what they should do, or reveal some hidden darkness within someone present. They would take the person out from the congregation and follow the instruction; this may be to heal, give a warning or to uplift, it depended on how intense the spirit was within the individual. They would go into a trance and use their feet to stamp in a rhythm and chant in an unusual sound. I have never experienced personally what it is like to be in the spirit, but I do get some sensation. I have never seen heavy rituals in the UK, but I have in the Caribbean. There was an incident with a lady who lived a few yards from the church in a tenement yard. Ethel was said to be possessed with demons and I saw this lady totally unconscious on the ground. The relatives were seeking help and carried her to the church. As a novice, I wondered is this person dead, or just unconcious? The lady apparently had stolen her next door neighbour's money. She was suspected and denied it and went as far as swearing an oath on the Bible and key. The consequence if she lied would be to fall into a coma. She wanted to prove her innocence and believed the curse was a load of rubbish, but she stole the money and three days later her boyfriend heard her scream and say, "Mi head," and collapse. The doctors were called in; they were unable to assist the lady. I was quite inquisitive; I wanted to see if this was some joke. She looked as if she was asleep.

They called her by her name, "Ethel! Ethel! Wake up!"

This was fascinating. The residents from the whole community heard about the story. They were congregating in amusement, all staring through the window at Ethel's thin body on the floor, and everyone was concerned whether this woman was going to recover. As the doctors were unable to help, the revivalist was called in. They made their diagnosis that the lady was possessed. They started by gathering around and they prayed and prayed; the lady did not respond. I hated the secrecy by the members; I wanted to know what was happening.

"What are you going to do?" I said.

Mrs A told me the lady was possessed and it was very serious; they had a limited time to resurrect her from her sleep. I was not going to miss this. The ritual took three days. Ethel had been sleeping for this while; no food, not even the toilet. She slept on the ground in the church with candles placed around her and a white basin of water within the circle, with a sword. A member was on guard throughout the whole time.

On the third day, the service for healing commenced. They had selected their uniform for the occasion: red turban, red skirt or trousers for the men with white blouse. They all gathered around Ethel. The crowd of people from the community returned on the third day and were bursting with anticipation. I had to move seats because I was not going to miss this. They started to chant, calling up healing angels by singing these wonderful hymns. I expected the lady to rise from the floor. She was barricaded by the members; I couldn't see the whole body, just her feet. The spirit took over, they started to speak in various tongues, a lot of chanting and stamping of feet; they were spinning around very fast. The drilling of the bands began, which is a rhythm made by stamping the feet in a timely procession while everyone chants, even the onlookers. I got up and started to stamp my feet also, then a coconut was thrown down to the floor with a smash. Every individual present must then turn in a 360 degree angle; the men then lifted Ethel to her feet. She was still in a coma. Then the women started to anoint her head with oil from her head to her feet; her eyes were opening! This went on for hours, and then eventually Ethel was able to stand on her feet, but with her eyes shut. They commanded her, "Woman, walk in the name of Jesus."

She slowly rose, looking bewildered, with the red cloth that they had tied onto her head. They sat her down. She looked completely lost, probably embarrassed. She was kept at the church for a few days and then returned home. This was just a synopsis of the type of work revivalists perform; their motto is 'from dead works to righteousness'. Revivalists have a bad reputation as being witches and wizards, but in fact they help those who are in distress, depressed, possessed and do so for no monetary rewards. The true believers dedicate their lives to help people from all walks of life and they are not all unemployed and uneducated. There are professionals who help during their spare time. Some clearances are vile and contagious, which could result in death or serious illness, that are called by the revivalist (destruction). The procedure can sometimes take months: this is one of the reasons they are unemployed, as this service is so time consuming and demanding. There are good and bad people, and some of these revivalists use the gift they have in the wrong way to hurt others, due to jealousy, to prevent success or inflict death or illness to break up marriages, greed to steal land or someone else's possessions, or to steal and ruin a brethren's power or gift.

On the Promised Land, there were living other church members, it now meant that I would have to attend all the services. Sometimes they finished at 12am; the children would have to be put to sleep on the back benches to get some rest for school. I disliked it, I would have preferred sometimes to go to the beach or have fun with other children, rather than constantly attending church. I started to experience repercussions from the bad reputation of my society and would pretend that I attended the Methodist Church across the road. I wanted to fit in and make friends or else they would mock me. My mother was fine for a while in our new home, but started again to be abusive. I think the pressure was upon her as I grew older. It was time for real decisions; what was I going to do in the future? That wasn't the only problem, I realised she left my brother with her mother when she left for the UK. He was abandoned on the street at the age of 9 years. His grandmother was using him as a goat herder, and he never attended school. He slept on the floor in the kitchen. He would be quite fortunate to have a decent meal every day. I wanted to know why my mother left her three-year-old son with her mother who refused to take responsibility. She should have called for him to come to the UK, and her response was that my father would not allow it. My brother was a teenage pregnancy; I have never met his father and my mother refuses to speak about him. My brother is placid, quiet and very handsome; we got on quite well. I was always happy to see him. He would tell me about this great big truck he was going to buy and we would cruise around in it together. I would relish the fantasy. My mother hated him; he was an embarrassment for her. She said, "He is a bad boy."

My brother was neglected from such an early age with no one to turn to. He was the outcast of the family; he was treated worse than an animal. He wasn't allowed to sleep in their house. With no education or skills, he was unemployed, had a criminal record and smoked weed. I suppose when he was hungry he stole to get by. What sort of mother and grandmother could treat their own flesh and blood in this way? My mother had returned to Jamaica and continued to turn a blind eye, not taking responsibility, ignoring the needs of her son. The grandmother refused to take care of him when she left for the UK because she had her own children and life to live. Maybe my mother did not expect my grandmother to treat her grandson this way, but she showed no hostility or disappointment towards her mother. I would want to know what she had done to my son; instead my mother retaliated, throwing her frustration on my brother every time he came to see us, shouting abuse, "Dirty, stinking boy."

The worst was when he came by one weekend to see us. He was growing dreadlocks. My mother was not happy about this, it made her angry. He was 22 years old and she took the machete from the kitchen and chased him out of bed in his underwear and around the yard in the early hours of the morning. She said, "Why are you sleeping until this time of the day when you should be finding work?"

I felt sorry for my brother. I knew he was crying out for acceptance and help. As a mother, she should have been helping him. I think he came by looking for affection, and there she went, slagging him off, embarrassing him in front of the tenants. He was humble, unlike other young men. It could have been a different story, he could have retaliated.

We had breakfast in the morning. I smiled to him, he smiled back. I could see the pain in his eyes; I felt it for him. I hugged him and I had the feeling he would never return. He realised that he was not welcome in our home. After the incident that morning, he packed his bag ready to go. There was not a lot I could say because she might start on me. I am not sure, but I think he wanted to come home and live with us. He was on curfew. He had an order from the court to sign in at a police station at a particular time, and on his way back he had gotten himself in trouble. It was very disturbing when the officer asked him to sign and he said, "I don't know how to write my name, I only can do an X."

This was the day that I found out my brother was unable to read or write. To this day I get very upset. Why bring children into this world for your own convenience and when it doesn't suit you, give up on them and throw them aside like a bag of rubbish? I also noticed that my brother was edentulous at the age of 22; all 32 teeth were removed due to cavities. No one cared for him as a child, what kind of life would he have had? My brother suffered, it was like living in hell. He lived with a friend in the hills of Williamsfield, St Catherine. They survived on the basic essentials in a zinc house on captured land. I met a lady from the district, Aunty Nurse, who told me of the conditions when she met my brother at the age of 13. She took him in and allowed him to use her facilities to clean up, and prepared meals for him every Sunday. There was a rumour that my brother was also dating this woman, who would have been 30 years his senior. My brother never came back to see us in Kingston, but whenever I went to the countryside I would greet him with such delight.

I don't know what was causing the frustration again. I was always the victim. She kept shouting and giving me ridiculous chores, that I should clean all the toilets and go on my knees and polish the tile floors, "Like looking glass," she said.

I was tired of the anger and abuse. We were not the only ones living in the house.

"Why should I be a slave to everyone? Why am I cleaning other people's mess? Why am I constantly tortured and picked on?" I asked.

She started to punch me on my head because I refused. Mrs A heard the commotion and intervened, and she was very rude to Mrs A. She told her, "Get out of it. You wouldn't know, you don't have children. She is a difficult child to deal with."

Mrs A sarcastically agreed and kept quiet. I said to Mrs Archie, "I am fed up and I am going to run away."

She pretended as if she hadn't heard what I said. I had now reached a stage in life where I felt I would be better off dead. I couldn't see how I was ever going to get out of this. I had been pounced upon and I didn't know the reason most of the time. I was not having any fun as a child, was constantly in fear and battered as if I was imprisoned. I was not allowed to have friends. Then she shouted, "I regret the day I gave birth to a sh** like you, you are as ugly as your stinking father."

In my rebellion I replied, "You had nine months to make a decision, you could have aborted me. And what were you looking at, not to see my father was ugly when you dated him?"

Mrs A started to sing and it got louder and louder; she was rejoicing, for the day had come when I retaliated. My mother became so angry when I told her this that she took up the zinc wash pan and struck my head repeatedly. The ground was wet and muddy and I slipped and hit my head on the ground. Mrs A got really angry and told her, "If you continue with this, you will never see your grandchildren."

She walked off in hysterics. My clothes were covered in mud and my lip was bleeding; my bottom teeth were red with blood. I knew at this point that something had to be done and Mrs A saw a change in my persona. Mrs A and I were very close after all, we were like best friends. She knew my mother was unpredictable. I thought she was not attentive to my conversation, but she was very careful not to show affection and started to advise me on my plans. I wanted to leave but where would I go? If I knew where my father was it would have been better, maybe he would love me, but how would I contact him? I am British after all. Mrs A spoke about the British High Commission in Kingston. If I packed my bag and sought refuge from them, they would send me back to the UK. This was plan A. Mrs A told me how wonderful Britain was, how the NHS was a blessing for those who were poor and unemployed, and how the HMRC never failed in sending her pension.

"God bless Britain, God bless Mrs Maggie Thatcher," she said each month when she received it. I told her that I was serious with my plan, would she advise me?

She said, "I would prefer if you went to a friend or relative than a children's home or foster parenting; only use this option if everything else fails. When you return to the UK, remember: go to your god-sister. That is the house where you were born, if you have any problems – plan B."

My mother realised I was now standing up for myself. She began to report me to Longman, my stepfather. He was always highly intoxicated with rum. When I went to him for discipline, he would give a long lecture which was nonsensical. One day she reported to him that I was so out of control, I was not listening and very rude. He grabbed me on my chest and pulled me towards him, "Why don't you behave yourself?"

In his rage he ripped my dress, exposing my breast. I was not happy, what was he doing? I was a young girl, going through puberty: I didn't want to be exposed. Another occasion when he did the same thing, I told him, "Don't lay your hands on me again. You are not my father. If you do, I will report you to him and it would not be pleasant."

He hit me with his belt and said, "Now, go and tell your father."

I had made up my mind at this point that if he tried this again, there was going to be hell. I would not accept a man tearing off my clothes. He got the message.

The beating of the drum and the continuous services I had to attend were daunting. I had finished primary school and was now into secondary school. There was still a major problem with my education; even at this stage my parents did not see the necessity of books, extra lessons, or visiting the library, like the other pupils. I was not allowed to take on activities at school, as this would seem an opportunity to visit boys. My school uniform would last for two years. The green colour tunic would be burnt out by the sun and grow short, my shoes would be worn until the bottoms gave way, and my parents had decided not to work anymore. Longman had lost his job three years before and didn't bother to find another job. My mother explained that he lost his dream job and would not find another like it; as a result it had put him in a permanent state of depression. My mother's excuse was that she was caring for Mrs A. I was older and needed more essential things, like clothes or shoes. They were not able to afford this, and Mrs A – we could not expect her to do this, to maintain my mother and her family plus the children in the community. Why was her frustration directed at me and not at her husband? He should have been finding work. Instead she treated him so delicately, he didn't have to work or wash his clothes and still was able to have a decent meal daily without providing for it. I couldn't understand the logic here, how was this allowed? Instead of applying pressure on her husband, she found an alternative – to put the responsibility on others. I had to write to my godparents in the UK for the things I needed. My godparents attended the church in the UK. I cannot express how faithful they were. Without question they would send the items I required every September. Without fail, every birthday to this day my godmother sends my birthday card and £10, and to think they have their own children to maintain. Proactive as I am, I asked my mother what plans she had.

"What am I going to do after graduation?"

She muttered, "I will asked Mr Chinkwee if he will allow you to join his typing school."

He was her ex-employer, who owned a private school; did she expect this man was going to give me free lessons? Her answer had no substance. It was as if she made it up just to keep me quiet. I accepted it; it seemed my life was in my own hands. My future would be dull, I needed help. I didn't want to get trapped in this society. I was not aware of any real role model and I wanted to be a professional; a doctor or a nurse. I wanted to travel the world and rub shoulders with influential, well-spoken people. Mrs A would laugh when I got on my soap box; she was immensely supportive and encouraged me. She said, "I know you will be a remarkable woman in the future in whatever you do, I believe in you."

I have never heard such words from my mother. Instead, she would talk about the girl down the road who was very bright and beautiful.

"I am your child, why would you patronise your own child?"

My strange mother is the same today. If and when I give her advice she ignores me and listens to someone else's guidance that is completely to the contrary. She tells her companions negative things about me. We never hug each other like mother and daughter unless she receives a gift or money, then she makes the effort, a pretend appreciation only to encourage more. She is never satisfied, she always wanted what I have and more, even though she doesn't work for it. She deceives herself that she is my mother and whatever belongs to me is hers. I fail to comprehend the logic to her mindset. Our personalities clash; I am completely the opposite of her. I cannot be around my mother without an outburst within half an hour. Her tone is very abrupt; she is a control freak and intrusive. I cannot explain enough how strange she is. She seeks friendship with people who are jealous of me and joins in to criticise and make friends with them. I met my best friend at school in the UK; we had a quarrel. After 16 years of friendship she decided to get married in Jamaica without telling me. We were very close; I thought we shared everything with each other. Six months later, still no explanation. I decided to end our friendship when I asked her. She replied by saying, "It is my life. I don't need to explain to anyone."

My mother knew how upset I was about the situation. She hypocritically agreed it was very disappointing, but behind my back my mother invited my friend and her husband to lunch and kept in full contact. She criticised me with them and then she had the nerve to tell me about the lovely friendship she had with them, only to annoy me. They had no idea who they took for a friend. They found out later that my mother's behaviour wasn't genuine. When the gifts and money expected were not forthcoming, she turned against them.

My mother was getting desperate for money. She started to do some embarrassing odd jobs whenever anyone from abroad visited; she would offer to wash their clothes, cook and clean for them. This was embarrassing for me, why didn't she find a decent job? If I gave her the opportunity, she would control my household and my family. She spoke to my partner in a condescending way and at the same time tried to convince him that I was not a good mother and he was a great father, "If you weren't here, my grandchildren would have rotted," she said.

She also tried to turn my children against me. I have never experienced a mother in this lifetime that so detested, despised, and envied, and was condescending and vindictive to her child. What had I done? I didn't choose to be here. She never celebrated my success; instead, she would tell me about someone else down the road that was better. In later chapters, the truth will come to light as to what she is about.

As a lonely child, I found comfort in sucking my thumb. I tried reading books I borrowed from friends at school, but I didn't have enough time to enjoy the novels. Most of the time, I was preoccupied with chores or being shouted at, "What are you doing? Find something to do."

As I grew older, my mind was constantly far away, daydreaming. I had no time to think about boys, but there was a boy from church who saw my distress and loneliness and decided he wanted to be my friend. He visited the yard often. I had a lot of hurt and although I relieved the heartache with Mrs A, this was different. I was very snappy at first when he asked me my name. I said, "Why are you asking me for my name?"

He told me his name and the school he attended, and I reciprocated, hoping that he would not ask me any more questions. Yet in spite of my abruptness, he was calm and friendly. One evening I saw him waiting for me at the school gate with a box of jam doughnuts. I was surprised. I walked past him in shyness and shock. He said, "Wait for me."

I walked on speedily – I think I was embarrassed – and he came with his friends. I had a real fear of making friends with boys after the threat and warning of danger which my mother inflicted. She told me that boys were bad. If I was ever seen with a boy she would remove my genital organ. He kept on following me along the way with the box of doughnuts and I really liked them. I thought to myself that it was safer to dismiss this guy; I didn't want any further problems. I started to run, losing him in the short cut by Rollington Town and headed home. On Sunday he approached me. I thought why doesn't this guy give in? I was not interested. I told him never to embarrass me again or turn up at my school because I would ignore him. He laughed and said, "OK, I brought something for you."

I said, "Again?"

"I told my mother that I really like you and she helped me to select the gift."

I knew his mother. She had a great sense of humour, but I did not believe him and refused his gift. He respected my wish and never waited for me at school again, but instead came by the yard to see me, which was worse. I couldn't believe it, was this boy insane, what was he doing here? He greeted my mum and Mrs A and then started to make conversation with me. I knew my mother was pleasant, but when he was gone I would be in serious trouble. I did not invite him here. He told Mrs A if she needed any assistance he would come and help her and my mother. As he left, she started.

"Do you think I don't know that you and that boy are up to something? I don't want him back here. Tell him don't come back."

On Sunday in church I told him, "Don't come back to my yard, my mother is not happy."

He ignored me and returned back on Saturday, offering to help my mother and Mrs A accepted. He did so many chores for them willingly. They were impressed and he won their hearts, but my mother was still cautious of him. I felt a little more confident and we talked about school and the church members; what they did during the rituals. During this time my mother kept barking that I should find something to do as I was not allowed quality time to myself. He turned up almost every day by now and my mother was getting agitated. She had one of her turns and started on me while he was there. She hit me in his presence and said indirectly to him, "If other people have nothing to do in their house, you have got to work."

I saw the shock and helplessness in his eyes. He sat under the mango tree in disbelief at what he saw take place. He said, "I didn't mean to get you in trouble, are you OK? I have this money I brought for you because you told me that you did not have enough money for school dinner."

He reached out to me and in his hand was $50. I said, "Where did you get this?"

He said, "Don't worry about it; I earned it from selling in my parents' shop."

"I cannot accept this; if my mother sees it I will have to explain."

He said, "Then hide it and buy yourself a good meal."

I took the money, and for the first time I had a really good school meal. I was also able to buy the sweets I always saw in the shops. At the time this was a lot of money for a decent school meal; I was very happy and guilty at the time, for I felt I was being deceitful to my parents. I started to like my friend. I didn't realise that he was affected by my situation. I told him about my life and he wanted to do something about it, to make me happy. I think he felt sorry for me. I started to open up to him about how my mother treated me and how I didn't know the direction my life was going. He became affectionate and would give me hugs sometimes, but I still held on to my emotions; don't come too close to me. Mrs A became very concerned about his frequent visits; she believed this boy was up to no good. I now enjoyed his company; in a strange way he was my friend, then he told me one day in the kitchen, out of the blue, "I love you and want you to be mine."

I was not happy, why did he have to ruin it? Then slowly he tried to put his arm around me and tried to kiss me. I couldn't take part in this; he was treading on dangerous ground. If my mother ever caught us, I would be dead meat, and it was as if he was oblivious to the fact. I said, "What's wrong with you? My parents have trusted you to this point and you want to destroy it."

He couldn't help himself and it was making me angry, for I was terrified of the consequences. He would not be facing them, but I would.

I looked forward to Sundays. We had a lot to talk about. He confided in me regarding one of his deepest secrets: that one of the church members, a female, was trying to molest him by touching him in sensitive areas. He felt he could not disclose this to his parents or the leader of the church. I was stunned; this lady had a husband and children, and she was 15 years his senior. At first I must admit I thought it was an exaggeration, until another boy and my cousin also disclosed it to me. I had to swear not to tell. I think this particular person was deprived and so turned to the boys in the church for pleasure and dominated them entirely. They were so afraid to speak as they could be punished through *Obeah* or rejected and it could cause severe problems in their family.

My friend realised how strict my parents were and I was not allowed to leave the yard unsupervised. We wanted to meet up at an ice cream parlour at Devon House in Kingston, but how would we do it? He told me about the various flavours and my favourite, grape nut ice cream. I was tempted and for the first time in my life I was having some fun. We had a plan; my classmate next door and I pretended that I was visiting her church for a concert. Our plan worked, she also came along. On our arrival at Devon House I was ecstatic, but at the same time nervous in case someone might see me and report to my mother. I was constantly in fear, watching the time. I wanted to be here, but now I was worrying about being in trouble. I told them let us quickly have the ice cream and go before we got caught. My friends were annoyed with me, calling me paranoid, "She can't know, man."

But I couldn't help it, I wanted to go home. I was afraid. I didn't want to be beaten for the night. We bought our ice creams and left. When I got home, it was fine. My friend and I became so close now and it was noticeable. We were together all the time when he visited and my mother was throwing verbal abuse, "What is this boy finding around here again? Tell him to go back to his yard, because those riff-raff are only after one thing and do you think if he gets you in trouble he can help you?"

The person that my friend confided in me about was not happy about our relationship, as he was spending more time and attention with me. She went to report lies to my mother, that she saw us on Sunday night and we were locked in a corner. What a liar! I was so annoyed. I wanted to tell about her dirty little secret, but I had promised my friends not to. I would now lose the company of my friend. My mother blatantly told him not to come back, forgetting all the chores he did for her on Saturdays. So I had to continue with my imaginary friend and loneliness again. I didn't know if a female friend could understand like he did without being bitchy. I couldn't stand any more isolation and torture. I said to Mrs Archie, "This evening, when you are free, I would like to call a meeting between ourselves."

She said, "What time?"

"6:00pm, after dinner."

"OK," she said.

"I want to talk to you; I believe you are my mother."

"Don't say that."

"Why not?"

"Don't let your mother hear that."

"I want to get out of this place as soon as possible, can you help me?"

She laughed in hysterics, did I say something funny? Thinking back what I said to her next I must have been naïve, this was not Mrs A's responsibility. I said, "I am going to give you 4 weeks to find someone for me to live with in the UK, or else I will go to the British Embassy in New Kingston."

She laughed even more and we left the conversation at that. Did she take me seriously? Weeks had gone by and there was a sense that came over me that I was going to leave Jamaica very soon and go home. I visualised happiness and success, and as I gazed into the sky there was a beautiful sunset and from then on a sudden hope and a sense of freedom came over me.

Two weeks later, Mrs A said, "I want to talk to you about a matter."

She seemed serious, but I was never afraid of her; she had such a wonderful heart. She expressed her love for me like a mother, everyone knew of her affection towards me. I sat down. She said, "You made a proposition two weeks ago and I have been searching for your new home. I have found a church sister who would be willing to accept you into their home as part of their family."

I couldn't believe it, I was right! My vision was spot on.

"When do I leave?"

"Next week."

I told my friends and best friend. He went into a major depression; he couldn't imagine me not being there. He said, "You will be gone forever."

He wrote me a poem and made a tape with all his best love songs. His mother told me he hadn't eaten or been outside for days.

I felt sorry, but I was more ecstatic leaving this hellhole. Then it hit me: I wondered if these people were going to like me? I wondered if they would change their mind – I might not have been pretty enough. As my mother always said, I was ugly, just like my father. I started to imagine my future, would I get married someday? What kind of life would it be? I hoped to have a profession, travelling the world. My mother had no input into the arrangement. Mrs Archie wouldn't have to do much convincing to get help for someone to receive me. She was a dignified character and respected by many of the members. When my mother heard the news she was pleased, as if relieved to see the back of me. I was like a monkey on her back. She said, "You can go to the people's house and misbehave so them can throw you out, you better behaviour yuself."

I looked at her in disgust and thought, if I get off this island, this would be the last she sees of me. I hated this woman.

Mrs A sat me down and spoke like a real mother. She said, "I am going to miss you very much, but I want the best for you. I might never see you again because I am old and riddled with pain, but in case it doesn't work out, I told you Britain is a fabulous place. You are British, they will take care of you, go to your god-sister if you are in trouble. I will write to her to be on the lookout."

I said to her, "I will see you again and you will be very proud of me."

She kept saying, "I hope you behave yourself when you get there."

Chapter 3

Home

It was finally time to go. I felt relieved, but at the same time nervous, not knowing what to expect when I got there. It was not a direct flight; I had to transit at Miami. And being under age at the time (15 years old), I was taken as an unaccompanied minor. I waited for four hours in transit. It was fine, I was amused with the surroundings so I didn't notice the time, but unfortunately my baggage went missing during transit.

I arrived in the UK without the few pieces of clothing and the one pair of shoes I treasured. The flight attendant announced, "One hour until landing."

My heart started to beat fast and I became nervous and agitated, wondering what the family would be like. Would they like me? They might have had a change of heart and not accept me into their home; it was peculiar all these thoughts were in my mind. I was escorted to Immigration and waited to be collected. They made an announcement for Miss Reid at the information desk. I waited for two hours and then I saw the beautiful lady who I was going to live with. She hugged me and asked about my flight; then we walked out to the lobby to meet the rest of the family, the father and two young girls. I greeted them; they seemed very friendly and told me I was part of the family, and to accept them as Mum and Dad. It was reassuring, I felt really comfortable with this. On our way from the airport, it was extremely cold that year (1987); there were icicles hanging off the roofs. The snow was high on the ground. I was amused; I wanted to feel it in my hands. I was fascinated. Although there was ice on the ground, the sun was shining. It must be hot outside, I thought. I came out of the car to explore, but had to run back in the house at full speed as the cold was excruciating. My ears were frozen, my fingers were burning; my little body had just received an experience that it was not ready for, at least for the next few weeks. We were living in Tottenham. We went inside the house and I was shown to my room. The children made me a welcome sign, it was a lovely gesture. I thought that all my worrying had been pointless. I had my first meal and I found it difficult for a while to adjust to the flavours. Mrs Burnet was organising my new school and I was excited to meet new friends. I started school two weeks later. Although these people were hospitable, I felt isolated. It was as if I didn't belong here. I had nothing to offer, my parents were not going to support me. I was different. I was not up to their level – the children attended private school and Mrs Burnet was a professional. I didn't fit in. I felt inferior and out of touch, my background was mediocre in comparison to this way of life. I kept away most of the time in my bedroom. I spoke with an accent and all the family and friends visiting came by to see what I was like and asked me patronising questions. I was like a stray animal in a cave. My guardian decided that the property was small and so we moved to another house. It was at this point that my life in the UK began. I was pleased to have a bigger room. These people were so accommodating and I wondered why my parents couldn't be like them. I felt like I had been sold. I was right; I wasn't aware of the arrangement, but later I realised I was the house helper. Obviously – where would you find such a Good Samaritan that would give you such a life for free? It was only a matter of time before I had to maintain myself. It was my responsibility to ensure that the house was clean at all times, the children got their breakfast and were ready for school, and the clothes were washed and ironed. I was not a good cook at that time and that was frowned upon. This was quite a new experience for me, a huge change. I was attending my new school and the journey to school was challenging because we had moved about 23 miles further away. I would sometimes get a lift as the children were commuting to London as well. Also at this time I was going through puberty, GCSE studies and the method of teaching as well as the language barrier was strenuous and I struggled. I was also required to make the beds and do the laundry, a full-time job. I was finding it hard to organise everything. I was responsible for the children if they required anything. Mrs Burnet had set out the chores for me to do on a daily basis; I was always busy from one minute to the next.

I had forgotten about my mother at this point. I failed to let her know my situation; she was not interested anyway. She never wrote to me and I knew I was on my own. I just had to get on with it, until one day I would be free. It was now clear to me that I was a helper; apart from the usual chores, again I had no free time and had to look busy at all times. Mrs Burnet worked really hard and frequently came in late – twelve midnight, sometimes later. If the house was not up to her standard, I would be called to get it done. The children were hard work, they knew I was different and sometimes they made my job even harder, and what could I do but just clear up behind them and be pushed around? They had no regard for me. After a while, they were abrupt and said very unkind words, "You are so greedy. You just came here to eat up all our food and get big, fat and ugly."

This really hurt my feelings. It was not the first time I was told I was ugly and for a seven-year-old to make this statement meant I was truly ugly. I became self-conscious. The parents did nothing about the children's abuse to me and it became worse. I felt intimidated. I would discreetly eat when everyone had gone to bed, so not to be insulted. After all my effort to be pleasant and accepted and work hard for these children, I was now a victim. I had to accept that I was an intruder and not blame them; I felt rejected and had no real value in society. Mrs B confirmed this one day when a visitor came to the house and asked me, "What would you like to be when you grow up?"

I said, "I would like to be a doctor."

Mrs Burnet hastily interrupted, "She cannot be a Doctor!"

The lady said, "Why not?"

"Have you seen her background – where she is from? She will never make it."

And that was the end of the conversation. I felt worthless and defenceless; it was as if I had dropped in a massive hole. Some encouragement would have been appreciated. As a result I grew up with a lot of pain and lack of confidence. I now knew that the dream I hung onto with Mrs Archie was all over. I was worthless, fat and ugly. I would never make it in life. Who was going to help me, my parents? I accepted this and would lie low, where I belonged. I took on a new perception of life. I would admire other children anywhere, on the street, in the park at school and imagine how fortunate they were for being born into the right family. At fifteen I was experiencing severe depression, which I kept to myself, no one was interested. The only consolation was when I met a friend, who also returned from Jamaica. She lost her mother and had to return to live with her dad. I was delighted to meet her as we shared similar memories of Jamaica during our school days. She resided in St Mary, Jamaica. She was very kind and friendly, she shared her lunch with me and sometimes I would visit her. At first I didn't disclose my life or situation to her as it was embarrassing for me to talk about my background, but as the relationship developed and she saw the situation, she became very sympathetic. Later, however, she used the hidden secret I confided in her as a weapon to patronise me. She created a stereotype that there was only a certain level I would reach and she was higher. My future was predicted condescendingly; I was not as bright as her and my background inhibited that. I would be a subordinate to her.

With the chores, the depression, and the isolation in the family, it now appeared I was like a sore. I sensed it; the time was near for me to be kicked out. I was constantly in trouble, not doing enough or not being good enough, I was useless – unable to iron a shirt properly or cook a meal.

I still hadn't contacted my parents in Jamaica. I didn't want Mrs Archie to be disappointed; I wanted to stick this out and I certainly would not have liked to return to that place. I would go up to my bedroom sometimes and pray to God to please make it possible one day to leave this house. I was sometimes afraid to come downstairs and associate with them, as I was certain I would be picked on or sent by Mrs Burnet or one of the children to find something to do, or if any guest arrived I would be called down to make the tea or drinks. There was no time for me to study or relax unless they were not at home. I had predicted this would happen – unless you are the Good Samaritan – with someone's child living in your home with no support from the parents, who are alive and well and useless! The pressure was really getting to me, but I kept all the anger and frustration to myself. The cracks were also reflecting in my schoolwork; I was constantly tired and tardiness was a problem at school. My tutor noticed that something was wrong and called me into his office for a meeting. He wanted to know what the situation was at home – how could I be this late to school daily? I didn't want to tell him no one really cared and I didn't want any uproar. This could be very uncomfortable for me. He said, "I will have to contact your parents."

I said, "They are not my parents but my guardians. I am living with them for a little while until I am old enough to defend myself."

"Is this the reason why you are late for school?"

"I get really tired because I stay up late – that is the only time I have to myself. I help out with my sisters and the household."

"Are you here for domestic purposes?"

"No."

"Were you born in this country?"

"Yes."

"I will have to contact them; this is affecting your career and future."

I said, "No, you don't have to. It is fine."

By the next day, a letter was sent. Mrs B was on the phone to her whole family and friends about how ungrateful I was, and her mother called me a wicked child. The children were even ruder. The eldest said, "I don't know why you are here. You are just destroying our family. You are so ugly."

Mrs Burnet was there, she heard and said nothing. I lashed out and I told her, "Don't speak to me like that."

She continued and I smacked her on her bottom. The next day the child came to me and said, "My mummy said you should not hit me."

I said, "Your mummy said I am your big sister, so if you choose to be rude to me I will not accept it and I will stop when mummy tells me not to."

This was the controversy that the school had created; I should have kept this to myself. I felt even worse, like I was the instigator. It would have been better if I was punished like my mother would have done, smack me around the ear or punch my head, then it would have been over. The silent treatment was ghastly.

I had now reached the age where I could apply for part-time work. My first job was in a fast food restaurant that is well known around the world. I wanted to learn how to drive, so I started to save. I was also required to pay £5 per week keep to my guardian. It had been nearly a year since I arrived in the UK and my mother had used no initiative to find out my wellbeing. Telephone calls then were extremely expensive, so I decided to write her a letter.

Dear Mum,

I can see how you have sold me away, you couldn't even be bother to find out how I am. I have realised that you have sold me as a slave to get rid of me. I am not enjoying it here, give my love to Mrs A.

Maria

A month after this letter, a friend of the family visited from Jamaica. Gifts were sent from my mother and Mrs A – my favourite fruits and cake, and underwear which I heard about but was not given to me. The letter from Mrs A was opened and I saw some of the food sent for me had been thrown in the bin. There was nothing I could do or say, just accept that nothing lasts forever.

My life was miserable as a teenager. I didn't even have interest in boys. I felt unattractive and sad. There was so much to think about. I had just one friend living 20 miles away. We sometimes had brief conversations on the telephone, and I was always at home looking after the children and fulfilling my domestic duties.

One gloomy winter's evening, I arrived home and everyone was sat in the living room, as if they were waiting for me. I knew something was wrong. I got changed and went downstairs immediately. I thought the children had told Mrs Burnet some exaggerated story of something I did wrong. I was quite apprehensive, could this be what I had been anticipating – to be sent home? I went downstairs and Mrs B began, "There has been terrible news from home."

I immediately thought Mrs Archie had passed away.

She said, "Your brother has been killed in a terrible accident."

It was like a sudden rush of sharp pain in my heart, I took a deep breath.

"What type of accident?" I asked.

"He was shot in the chest due to trespassing on land in Williamsfield."

It was like the whole world had come upon me. I was hurting, it was like my chest was ripping out. I would never see my brother again, why was this happening? I went to my bedroom and reflected upon the good times we had; how he was going to buy a big truck for us to cruise around in. The next morning Mrs Burnet told me that I would be allowed to go to Jamaica to the funeral. I was extremely grateful; she didn't have to do this. I understood the financial burden I had caused, God bless her, and this would also be an opportunity to see Mrs A and my friends from church again.

I was on my way to Jamaica the following week. I had mixed emotions of joy at going home, but also sorrow over my brother. I didn't know what to expect. I was nervous, but at least I would have a break. I landed at the Norman Manley International Airport and my mother and other family friends came to meet me. My mother looked older, her grey hair was shining in the sunlight. She greeted me with a hug. I asked her on the way about the tragedy. She said the week before my brother died he was acting strangely, as if he had a premonition of his death. He took a photo and visited her as if it was the last time. He said, "When you see my sister give her this photo."

His death occurred when he was walking with a group of friends through a farm near his captured land. The ranger on the farm had given strict warning that trespassers would be shot. They were stealing oranges from the farm and unfortunately on their escape he was the one who took the bullet. I was so annoyed that he had lost his life for a bag of oranges. Our grandmother has a farm with the same fruits. This is inconceivable, he died of hunger? Nothing had changed and this was inevitable. I asked, "What are you going to do about the murderer?"

She said, "Nothing, the Lord will fix them."

I insisted, "This must be taken to the court of law."

She was not interested in pursuing the case. I was delighted to see Mrs Archie. She had aged considerably, her hair was fully grey and her walking had deteriorated. I gave her a big hug and kisses.

She had instructed my mother to make my favourite meal, rice and peas with jerk chicken and sorrel drink, delicious. I had called for my first meeting with Mrs Archie, just like the old days. I wanted to give her a synopsis of my life in the UK, the chores and the behaviour of the children towards me and how I didn't feel secure. I said, "They may want to send me back."

She told me not to worry, she understood and wished it could have been better because she had been reassured that I would be a part of that family. She gave me a few words, "Remember this always, 'kiss ass before you kick it'."

This was clear enough to understand. Then we caught up with all the gossip and I wanted to know what happened to my boyfriend; he had left the church and visited occasionally. I couldn't afford a gift for him, but I thought I would give him one of my toiletries as he was so vain and would wear any fragrance, male or female, as long as it was pungent.

The funeral was already scheduled and we had to travel from Kingston to Williamsfield for the burial. Due to the experience I had as a child, the allergies and bad reaction to the atmosphere, I was very cautious. I disliked the darkness at night in the village as there weren't any street lights and electricity was scarce. Some roads were in need of serious repair. Transports were unable to drive by and pedestrians would have to walk the rest of the journey on the stony hill. Sanitation was a real issue for me with the pit toilets, made from wood and bamboo, which were outdoor – a haven for frogs and insects to take residence. Although I lived in the Caribbean for 13 years, I was unable to adjust to the environment, and the allergies were emerging again in such a short time. I realised I was not immune. I broke out in sores all over my body, which were like blisters. Mosquitoes and sand flies were having a feast. I spent more time dressing my sores than enjoying the sunshine.

It is tradition to host a ninth night: a celebration of the dead on the ninth night after death, with singing, dancing, feasting and reflecting. There were many family and friends. My brother was to be buried in my grandmother's yard in front of the house; this was unjustified, he was not allowed to live in the house when he was alive but was buried there. At these events the truth always appears. Another concern was how the funeral would be financed. Nothing had changed for my parents, they were still unemployed, and my brother did not leave any legacy. Throughout this time, my mother showed no initiative about how to organise the church service or the coffin for the body; it was my Great-Aunt V who took the initiative to organise the funeral. At age sixteen, I was unable to contribute. My step-grandfather was a coffin maker. He was the one who despised my mother's decision to leave my brother with his wife. He refused to make the coffin. His excuse was that he did not have the material to do so and if he did he wanted to be paid. Great-Aunt V pleaded and promised she would provide the material – it was the only cider board left on her property. She wanted to use it to make her furniture. He finally accepted, otherwise we would not be able to buy a coffin. The food was contributed by family and friends; this should have been my mother's responsibility, not her aunt's. She showed no emotion throughout. It was sad. I didn't know enough about my brother or how he grew up. My mother never spoke about his birth and how he was as a child before she left for the UK. What a waste of life. I never heard about his father, though I met him briefly at the funeral. He was a lot older than my mother, and he was also a married man. Could this have been one of my mother's gold-digging tactics that had gone wrong? I worked out her age: she would have been 17 years when she conceived. Because of his life and certainly budget, the body was not committed in a church. The funeral took place in the yard next to where he would be buried.

The morning of the funeral I was so emotional. I didn't know what to expect. I saw the hearse coming down the hill slowly into the yard, playing gospel music. The people from the village followed along. It stopped, my eyes filled up with tears, and then they took the small, velvet, purple coffin with gold screws out of the hearse and placed it on a stand in front of the house. The undertakers removed the cover; he was visible from head to toe with his arms crossed over his chest. He seemed asleep; I just wanted him to wake up. I had to be strong. I struggled to hold back the tears, but I broke down uncontrollably. This was not to be, we were to meet again, this was inconceivable. People in the village were gossiping about the arrangement. It was an embarrassment, as in the Caribbean funerals are important, almost like a major celebration. You are expected to wear your best and the coffin to be drawn in fine mahogany wood. People would claim how lovely the dead appeared in their final clothing and how pretty the house is which would be the tomb or sepulchre. They would be buried on the most expensive cemetery plot, or if it is the family estate, the sepulchre should be exquisite. The pastor conducted the service. It was a hot, sunny day. We sang hymns. He read scriptures and preached about winning souls. It was peculiar that my mother was a singer in her church and she sought out every event to show off her talent, especially funerals, but not her son's. I regret not giving a farewell. It was like a dream. I didn't know my brother enough; I was so young when we were together. There were questions I would have liked to ask, about his life when he was rejected. His friends who witnessed the murder attended the funeral, but kept their distance. It must have been devastating for them to lose their close friend. The sermon was very short and people were allowed to pay their respects by passing around the coffin in an anticlockwise march. There was a myth about the dead of passing young children across the coffin for protection, this also took place. Then six men came and lifted the tiny coffin to its final resting place. I could not bear to see it going down. I ran away to my Aunt Lily, a very affectionate aunty to me. I loved her dearly, she treated me as her own child. She comforted me and told me not to worry. I went back later in the evening to the graveside. His name had been engraved with his date of death in the cement before the concrete was set. I reflected and stared at his grave; I laid my flowers, cut from the garden, then I walked away. I just didn't understand why this had happened to my brother. We left for Kingston that evening, after the funeral. My mother seemed to have taken it well. I reported to Mrs A about my feelings of how I missed my brother and would never see him again. With my inquisitive nature, I wanted to know all the stages of decomposition that would happen. Mrs A explained thoroughly.

I woke the next morning at approximately 8am. The heat was intense. Mrs A had a long bench on her veranda that was abandoned by the church. We all sat down and reflected on the experience the day before, then Mrs A asked, "How are you getting on in school?"

I didn't even get the chance to answer the question before Mother sarcastically barked, "You better be behaving yourself because all these nice shoes and outfits you are wearing, you won't get them here."

I said, "I don't want to go back to be a slave. I want to come home."

She said, "Come back where?"

I said, "Home."

"You must be mad," she said.

"I am fed up of hanging out people's dirty laundry and cleaning and ironing."

She got up in rage to hit me. I rushed off the bench; I decided if she hit me, I was going to defend myself by throwing a stone at her head. I told her, "If you hit me, I will throw this stone."

She backed off. I couldn't believe it, what had I done? I was now 16 years old and she wanted to treat me like my brother, threatening to hit me. By God it was not going to happen. I said, "I am better off going back anyway, what is the point being around aggressive people? I'd rather be a slave than put up with this. Since I have left this yard there is no improvement, still the loyal church attenders." I really had a go. She went into her room and I stayed on the veranda with Mrs A. Then the telephone rang; it was Mrs Burnet ringing from London. She extended her condolences and explained that there was no need for me to return to the UK, because I was not much help to her, I could not do basic house chores. She was sorry and wished me all the best.

When my mother gave us the news I was delighted; my mother was extremely frustrated and explained how condescendingly Mrs B spoke to her on the telephone. Mrs Archie said, "Let us all calm down here, I will give it 24 hours and call her and apologise for any trouble or disappointment."

I said to Mrs A, "I don't want to go back."

She sat me down as a parent would. Calmly, she said, "I understand the difficulties you are experiencing, but nothing lasts forever. Remember, kiss ass before you kick it and remember plan B. If you are evicted, go to your god-sister in Hackney and she will support you. If that fails, go to Social Services. I can foresee that when you return, you will not be there for long. The inevitable is going to happen, promise me that you will try your best and do the best you can, there is no other way. There is not a future here for you; return and fulfil the dream we have been rehearsing over the years."

I said, "I will only do this for you, Mrs A. You are my mother, make no mistake. I don't know what would have happened to me if you were not in my life. When I return on the next trip, I am going to buy a flashy car and drive you all around the island."

She said, "By God's grace, but unfortunately I will not see you again."

I said, "Of course you will."

The next morning Mrs A rang Mrs B; she accepted for me to return back to the UK. My mother said, "You can go back and create problems again, so that they can chuck you out of their house."

What did her comment mean? Would she accept me in her home if that was the case? I would find a way: I had made a promise to Mrs Archie, my second mother, and I would honour that promise. It was clear – all that my mother wanted was to see me gone. She didn't want to take on the responsibility. She could have spared the time to give me alternatives rather than continuing to be hostile. I hated being around her, she spoiled the air. I was not sure if Mrs B planned to dismiss me and used this opportunity of my brother's death to send me home, but it was very inconsiderate. The day after the funeral she gave us such disturbing news and it was a time when we were grieving. The visit was short; I was not sure if it was a return ticket. I wanted to see my friends, but it was time to go.

Chapter 4

I returned to the UK. Mr Burnet came to collect me at the airport. He was very supportive, but he didn't say much.

"How was your trip, how are your parents?"

I asked how the family was, he said his wife Mrs B had gone to work and the children were at school. I told him thanks for collecting me. I envisaged it was going to be a rocky road. I felt uncomfortable deep down – I was lucky, they could have dismissed me. I humbly got out of the car and went up to my room – the furniture was taken out. The children must have used it for their playroom. I had some clearing up to do. Mrs B came in quite late that evening. I waited up for her. I knew she would be morose, but it was best to face it, like treading on eggshells. I spoke with her; she didn't say much about her decision to send me home. I could hear a few arguments about finances – maybe things were hard? I might be a contributor to the distress. Pressure was applied for me to contribute, which was reasonable, but the atmosphere at home had changed. I was hanging on by a limb, I could feel the tension. I had to try and make this work. I owed it to these people; if they had not accepted me into their family I would probably have been in trouble.

It was summer, school was out on holiday. I had a shower and came downstairs to have lunch. Mrs B went on a business trip to the USA. Mr B was in the kitchen and I greeted him. He was very pleasant. We started to talk about some old friends and relatives that I met at the funeral and then about the different types of fruits that Jamaicans love, then I went into the cupboard and he grabbed my bottom. I was not sure, maybe I misunderstood – I was confused but at the same time frightened. He said, "You shouldn't wear these types of skirts."

"I always wear this skirt."

He was making advances on me; I didn't believe this! I was speechless and shaking, and then he said, "Did you know that I was the one who allowed you to come back?"

I said, "I didn't know." Was this to soften me up so he could have his way? It was not going to happen. He came towards me and I pushed him and ran to my bedroom. He later apologised, but said that I should never tell anyone, I had to be civil. If this matter got out, it would be catastrophic. This would be worse than the incident at school. Mrs B would have me through the door immediately. That night I held the door in my bedroom closed with a chair and hid there for the rest of the evening. I watched during the night to see if the handle of the door was to turn. I watched, waited and waited. I was lucky – he didn't harass me. After this incident, I felt very uncomfortable. I was unable to keep eye contact with him; it was difficult being in the same room with him. I don't know why I was uneasy, I wasn't the one who had caused this. It was as if I had done something wrong. Mrs B may have thought I wanted to ruin her home. I had to get out of here soon, I didn't want any trouble. Since my return it was a real struggle to get back into a routine; everything changed.

Mrs B was the main breadwinner and I suspected that business was not going well. She was constantly morose and threw the odd tantrum at me. The tide was about to turn this day. I was watching television. I wanted to relax, being on school holiday. The children were out playing. I expected her back at the usual time of late evening, but this day she was back by lunchtime. This was not good. I should have been busy at all times, relaxation was out of the question. It was the shock of seeing her – I didn't know how to adjust myself to be busy. I greeted her and carried on watching the television, even though I knew there was going to trouble. I said, "Hello."

She ignored me and went into the kitchen with a strop, and then the sitting room and then upstairs and back downstairs. I didn't get up, maybe I should have got up and got busy. Then she burst into the room and asked, "Haven't you got anything to do?"

I said, "Oh, I have done all my chores this morning."

"Do you know what? I am sick and tired of all this. I think you should pack your things and go to your godmother."

Was she throwing me out because I was watching television in the afternoon? I didn't do anything! Her reaction was that this was my opportunity to leave this house. Was she serious? I asked her if I could borrow her travel bag to pack my belongings. She dismissed me before I could say the word. She said, "Don't think you can beg me to stay, please pack your things and go."

I was delighted, I would be free. Let me hurry before this opportunity passed. I ran upstairs and started packing. She allowed me to borrow her travelling bag. I also packed another ten carrier bags with personal items. I told her goodbye and she said, "Bye."

I had so many bags to carry on the bus. As I went through the door I saw her friend getting out of the car to visit us. I dodged because if she knew, she would not allow me to leave. I must use this opportunity. I had plan A, to see my god-sister as instructed by Mrs A. If that failed, plan B: I would borrow my friend's sleeping bag and sleep rough for a while, until I found a job. If that failed, Social Services was the last resort.

I was heading to Tottenham, London, to see my friend first, as the bags were many. Then I would have to locate where I was going to sleep for the night – although Mrs B said I should go to my godmother, it was inconvenient. There she had a young baby in a one-bedroom flat; it would not be fair and this would lead me back to that house. Moreover, I believed I could take care of myself and get on with my life. My friend empathised with my situation, but she explained it would be difficult for me to stay at her house. That was not part of my plan anyway. I was so confident I didn't need her help for I had plans and one would succeed.

I got to the house. It was weird; this was the house I grew up in as a child in Hackney. I was so young when I left but I remembered the flight of stairs at the front door. This was my godmother's second house; she died many years ago and my god-sister was residing there. I knocked on the door and she opened.

"Hello Mrs Gardener, it's me, Maria."

She was delighted to see me. She said, "How's Reid?" referring to my mother.

I replied, "She is fine."

"I heard you came over some time ago, Mrs Archie wrote to me. Is everything fine there?"

I said, "Not really. I was thrown out today and I'm looking for somewhere to stay. Will it be OK if I stay here with you?"

She said, "Of course, you are welcome. This is your godmother's house, she would turn in her grave if I refuse you and I would be pleased to have your company as I am a lonely old woman with a useless husband. He is never here, we don't really get on."

I went back to collect my bags. I had a roof over my head the same night. I did not contact my godmother or Mrs B. I was determined never to return. I also gave my friend strict instructions not to tell where I was if Mrs B called. I had to sleep on the sofa that night but my god-sister was very warm and affectionate to me. She was very disappointed when I explained to her how I had been living. She was angry. She was appreciative of how my mother helped her to check on her disabled son in Jamaica. My deceased godmother was very wealthy. She had left a legacy for me: when the house was sold a percentage should have been mine. I never received it; I was more grateful to be rescued. My god-sister announced the following morning,

"I want you to have your godmother's room. It is vacant. I will go out today and we will choose the furniture together."

I was astounded, all this for me? She would also cook my meals. It was like going back home to my parents. I felt secure and loved for the first time, I was not expected to be a house help. I became so relaxed and happy. I wanted to now concentrate on my studies again. I applied to Tottenham College to study to become a dental surgeon's assistant; five days a week practical and paid with two evenings learning the theory. The pay was enough to survive on. My god-sister wanted me to concentrate on my studies; she would provide for food and my accommodation. There was one major hiccup – her husband. My godmother apparently did not approve of their marriage to this man. He had a lot of skeletons in the closet, with four failed marriages to wealthy women who all passed away mysteriously. I was warned to keep far away from him as he performed witchcraft and may have wanted to seduce me with his magic charms. I didn't believe in such anyway, but stayed clear as instructed. One morning he knocked on my door to offer me tea. I pretended to drink it; his wife saw him and all hell broke loose, the arguing and shouting. I felt responsible and helpless, I stood at the kitchen door in silence, listening.

My god-sister and I got on so well, we would sit and talk for hours on end. It was like second nature. I enjoy older company; there is a lot to learn. I also find the Jamaican dialect entertaining. Being so contented, I had the time to take more pride in myself. I was now 17 years old. I started to make new friends. I was allowed to have sleepovers. A friend I met at college was supportive and her mum and dad accepted me as a daughter, so I had the best of both worlds. I would sometimes go round for a real, proper English Sunday roast with homemade apple pie and custard – luscious – or Jamaican rice and peas with jerk chicken.

On my way home from a party one evening, I saw a guy admiring me as I walked past his car. I didn't want him to know I had noticed, so I hung my head down and sped up. He called out to me, but I ignored him, and then he shouted louder, "Excuse me."

I turned around. "How can I help you?"

"I was just admiring you walking down the street so elegantly. You look very smart."

I said, "Thank you. May I ask, what your name is?"

"My name is Steve. I would like to get to know you. Here is my number. I visit my friend on upper Clapton Road here every week, here is my number."

I said, "Sorry, I don't have a number." Mobile phones were not as popular as these days. I felt really good, this was a surprise. I was always told that I was ugly from my mother and others; this must be a wind up, so I didn't call. I told my god-sister about him. She said if I wanted to meet him that was fine, as long as she met him first. My mother would not have trusted me to go on a date, and after all, I had never had a real boyfriend intimately. I thought about it for days and dismissed it; then one evening as I got off the bus, I saw him walking up the road. I thought 'oh no' – too late to escape. He said, "I have been waiting for your call."

"I have been very busy with studies."

"I was trying to figure out where you live around here."

I said, "I live with my guardian."

"Can I walk you home?"

"It's fine. I will definitely call you this week."

He said, "I insist, let me walk you home."

I was only two doors away. I hesitated for a while and then gave in. He walked me to the gate and then I waved bye. Every time I saw this guy I seemed to like him a bit more, but our meeting would all be a fantasy. I was reluctant to call him. I would explain to my friend about him; how I liked him, it was a teenage crush. My friend bought me a teddy and we named it Steve.

I came home one evening and I could hear a man's voice speaking in the kitchen. I crept around the corner to see who it was – it was him, deep in conversation with my god-sister. I was not happy – who invited him in? I didn't believe it, what was he doing in my house? I pretended I was fine with this. He smiled and gave me a peck on the cheek. My god-sister was saying how handsome he was and that he had asked her permission for us to go out on Friday evening. She gave permission, but I had to return home by 10pm. I was put on the spot; it was difficult to decline. They seemed to have arranged a date without me. I accepted the invitation, which left me feeling nervous and worked up the whole week. What was I going to wear? Where were we going? I had my hair done and my friend helped me to choose a dress. The engagement was at 6:30pm, and he was on time. He complimented me on my appearance. I was so nervous that I had sweaty palms and my stomach was rolling like a ball. I tried to impress him with good behaviour and a posh accent. We firstly went to the cinema, followed by a meal. I didn't know anything about this guy and this would be an opportunity. He was originally from Jamaica and in the early stage of a career as a middleweight boxer. He was 8 years older and not involved in a relationship at the time. He had no children. I told him about my experience growing up in Jamaica. We had a lot in common to talk about. He kept saying about how young I was and reminiscing about how old I would have been when he started school. It was a surprise, how much older he was. This made me have less interest in him. I wasn't sure if I would continue the relationship and also, I couldn't put my finger on it, but there was something peculiar about him. The conversation throughout the evening improved; I became more relaxed. He was very confident to give me a kiss, but I was very shy and pulled away. I thought it was too early and I was still not sure about us. I looked at my watch and reminded him it was time to go. I told him I would call him, there was no need to come by the house. My god-sister didn't approve of me inviting visitors. That was my first date. It was interesting. I felt I didn't know enough about him, but it might be OK, knowing that my god-sister, Mrs G, had met him. I called him, not hearing from him in over two weeks. He was delighted to hear from me and wanted us to meet again. It was to be a surprise for the next date. I was excited, going out again, but this time I was going to ask him more about himself. I had to break out of this shyness – after all, he said we were in a relationship now.

Our date was on a Friday evening, after work. I was curious as to where our date would be. This time he said it was going to be an exquisite place – I couldn't wait. He was 30 minutes late – he apologised for his tardiness and explained he hadn't had the time to go home, he would stop home first to freshen up before we went out. I thought OK, so we went to his place. He had a number of trophies and he sat down for a while watching a match. I thought 'what is he doing? Are we not going out?' I was polite, waiting in anticipation; he seemed relaxed. Time was going, I said, "Are we not going out?"

He smiled and leaned over to hug and kiss me. We had not discussed intimacy – sex. I was not ready. I moved over to the right of the settee, but he came closer. I was feeling uncomfortable because it seemed he was in the mood for something else. He didn't even show me around the house. I wondered if he lived with someone else. I asked to use the toilet, but I discovered nothing. I tried to stare in one of the other rooms, the door was ajar; it was difficult to see inside the room. I was bored – I didn't spend the whole evening getting dressed for this. After two hours, he said, "I am going to get ready now."

He went into the room. This was my opportunity to observe. I was not convinced that he lived alone; he might have a flatmate, I just couldn't prove it. Then he called me in the room. He said, "Sit down."

"I will wait for you in the living room."

"Don't be silly, I won't bite you. Just keep me company."

I sat on the edge of the bed. He was talking about a fight he had lined up and how he was training hard for it. I asked him about his fitness level and what stage he was at, but I was uncomfortable in the bedroom with a naked man. Then he lay down on the bed and pulled me towards him. What was he doing?

I said, "Are we going anywhere this evening?"

He said, "No. We are going to make out tonight."

I said,

"No, I am not ready for this. I am a virgin and I want to do this with the right person and when I am ready."

I don't know if he thought I was lying. He grabbed hold of me and I found myself in a struggle with him. He was so damn strong, I couldn't fight him.

"Get off, stop it, stop it!" I said, "Let me go!" He held me down with force. He was on top of me and at this point I knew I was in trouble; no one could hear me screaming. The struggle was endless, he was so strong. I could feel my clothes being ripped off while he used his body to pin me down. I used my legs to try and kick about, but that was useless. I tried to bite his face or ear. I was losing this fight. I was frustrated; he was not listening to me. I could feel the huge force penetrating inside of me, it was like steel being shoved up inside. I lost the battle. He raped me. There was blood everywhere, the sheet was soaked; my clothes, his clothes. So this was the big surprise. He had achieved what he had planned. He was in shock and I was angry. He sat by the side of the bed looking at the blood and all he could say was, "I am sorry."

There was immense shock on his face. I was so upset. I ran to the bathroom. I was in so much pain; I couldn't believe what had just happened. I went to the living room and said, "Take me home."

I was just astounded. I should have been more furious with him. On my way home I didn't talk to him. He kept looking at me but I just wanted to get home. I hated him. I got home, and he said,

"I will call you."

I walked off. I have never told my story until now. I felt foolish. I should have been more careful; this guy took advantage and I would regret this for the rest of my life – how my virginity was taken away from me in such a brutal way. I was upset all night. I couldn't tell Mrs G, she would have called the police – she was not one to mess with. This guy had done this to me. I don't know much about him, I don't even remember where he lived. If this is what sex was about, I didn't think I would ever have sex again. Two weeks later, he visited but I was very pleased not to be at home when he did.

There was a sudden change in Mrs G – she had become uncommunicative, aggressive and impolite. What was happening to her? I could not believe this. Was she senile? I really wanted my friend back. She went to the extreme of accusing me of sleeping with her husband. A friend from college came to visit me and she told them the same. There were other unusual things happening in the house. I started to get these weird dreams of a little Indian boy in a turban standing by my bedroom door, just looking at me, and when he was there the force would be so strong that even though I tried to wake up, I would be pinned to the bed. I was told her husband disapproved of our relationship because I might have inherited the house if his wife changed the will. He cast a spell to disturb our friendship. If this was the case, it was working because Mrs G was completely different. Her behaviour was so atrocious – she accused me of sleeping with her husband, ignored me and snapped at everything I did or said. I was so hurt. I couldn't understand what I had done to her for her to react this way and all that she accused me of was a lie. I tried exhaustively and failed. I had to find somewhere else to live; this was difficult without a deposit for rent or an income. I had started a part-time job with one of Britain's leading supermarkets. A friend I met there invited me to come and live in their house. I would only need to contribute towards food and was not to worry about paying rent. This sounded great, and risky, but I would rather take the risk than be branded a homewrecker. This was also the perfect opportunity to see the back of Steve. He would have been visiting the next week. I wanted to get away before he returned – I didn't ever want to see him again. I never wanted to be in a relationship after what happened with Steve, men could not be trusted. My friend helped me to pack. I was very unhappy to know that the relationship between my god-sister and I had disintegrated. I offered to accompany her to the doctor's or shopping. Even though I left the house, she refused and this was the end.

I couldn't endure her abuse. I promised I would come and see her again someday.

Chapter 5

This was the real beginning of my journey. I was officially on my own. It was daunting at first – I earned enough to buy a decent meal a week, but I was content and happy that I was in charge of my life for the first time. The property was a four bedroom house. My housemates were men and it was intimidating for me, so I kept a low profile. It would be fine, I reassured myself. We shared all the facilities together. I was also the youngest. The household was multicultural – there were English, African, Swedish and Asian. As I knew them better, we got on like a house on fire. We made up a rota for cooking and house chores, which meant various dishes depending on the cook for the evening. It was so hospitable there, like family. I could knock on any door and have a conversation. Help was at hand if needed, whether for moral support or financial. We also protected each other. The next door neighbours were envious of the relationship. They couldn't comprehend how we got on so well because it was unusual to see a house with such variety, and some were racist – they gave us a hard time, complaining about noise. The real story of the house was that the landlord was fraudulently acquiring these houses and collecting rent; the tenant would pay their rent, but would eventually find themselves on the street, evicted by the mortgage company, and the landlord was nowhere to be found. I didn't realise that until it happened to us, or I would never had taken such a risk. I had finished my studies at college; I did very well, which motivated me to consider higher education, which was difficult financially. I continued studying other courses that were more affordable. I decided to find additional work to increase my income, but was unsuccessful due to lack of working experience. Living at Mrs G's proved to be a real luxury. Now I could not afford to buy essentials like clothing, not even a decent coat to keep me warm in the winter. There were particular days on my job hunt when it was so cold. My cardigan that I wore every winter was not able to withstand this particular winter. I walked for twelve miles in the bitter cold; my feet and fingers were lifeless. I couldn't afford the fare to get the bus. I was also very hungry; it was like the cold had taken the last bit of strength from my body. I couldn't even afford lunch. When I got on the bus with the one-way ticket I reserved with the last penny in my name, I was unable to stretch my fingers out to the driver to pay. He saw my distress and helped me. When I got home, I thought I was going to have permanent damage to my leg. My body was frozen. I was lucky my flatmate saw the distress and helped me to rub my fingers and prepare a hot drink.

As life became more difficult, my health was affected. I began to lose weight rapidly and felt unwell most days. I was fortunate to have friends who cared and sometimes prepared hot meals for me. I was a loner, blind to what the future held in store. If something had happened to me, no one would know and I didn't think they really cared. I was determined to fight for life regardless. There was only one problem – my flatmates. They saw a vulnerable young girl who was so naïve. It was like a rota after a while – they were all trying their luck to sleep with me. I had to be on my guard. I had to show aggression as my defence. If I appeared weak, this situation could have spiralled out of control and I didn't want a repeat of what happened six months before with Steve. I was afraid sometimes, especially when male friends were invited round. They flirted and sometimes banged on my door. They would sometimes patronise me when I was introduced as the baby of the house. I tended to hide away, not to cause any attraction. I was not ready for a relationship, much less sex; I had made a promise to myself never to get involved.

I had no one to call on – I had to face the music on my own. It was very risky. It would have been really comforting if I had a mother or family member to call on. I knew I was a reject and decided to get on with life on my own, regardless of the outcome, life or death. I was 18 years old, alone, distressed, ill. The inevitable happened and I was admitted to the hospital for anaemia. Unable to inform the hospital of a next of kin when they insisted for a parent or guardian, I asked a friend from work to assist me, which failed. I had no choice – I had to call for Mrs Burnet or else I would not be discharged. She refused anyway; but thank goodness for her brother, who consented on my behalf.

At this point, my guardian and parents did not know where I was. I wanted to block them out of my life. I felt at one point when I was getting really ill that if I died I would be better off; at least I would not be a burden or relying on anyone. But reality was setting in, I needed help. I had no money for food, no work, no pay and being off work due to illness prevented me from making any money. I would plan how many meals to prepare from four cans of baked beans for two weeks. My recovery took a lot longer than expected – unfortunately, after the anaemia, I had another operation. I was very fortunate to be rescued time and time again by my friends. I had enormous pride – I would pretend that everything was fine and reminded myself I could do this on my own.

There was one flatmate who was loving and caring. He was more concerned about my health and how young I was to be left in such a vulnerable situation. He was like a big brother. He was curious, because of my age, as to why I was alone. Where were my parents? He had just returned from Nigeria after leaving the UK at the age of 9 for 18 years. I always enjoyed his company. It was a platonic friendship. He worked very hard. He would come by my room once in a while. The worst that I feared happened – we were going to lose our home, and to add to that the landlord did not pay once for the utility bills. It all started when the authorities came one day and disconnected the electricity. Two weeks later, the gas was disconnected. We managed to apply for a meter system. Some of the tenants were still paying rent and were appalled about the service. We had to cook our meals in the microwave and boiled the kettle to have a bath. The house was freezing cold. I borrowed a portable heater from the next door neighbour to keep warm. The landlord was threatened with health and safety issues by one of the tenants. Obviously, I could not have a say in the matter because I didn't pay the rent; I was really a squatter.

We discovered the house was to be repossessed very soon. I was very worried, where was I going to this time? The housemates called a meeting and gave advice about what I could do when the situation arose to contact the local authorities. I had become so thin that people were worried that I had a serious illness. There were dark circles under my eyes and my head was almost bigger than my body. My Nigerian friend GA (Guardian Angel) saw me one evening and offered to buy me a takeaway. Maybe he realised my condition and thought I had lost weight due to hunger, but it was stress. I accepted and we ate that evening and watched television. We ate so much that he fell asleep in the warmth on the floor in my room. It was not unusual to crash out in a flatmate's room, sometimes through drunkenness – we were that close. GA was more attentive to me; he even offered to share his shopping should I need anything. I had a lot of pride; even in my condition I preferred to satisfy myself with what I had rather than receive. That was the way I was brought up. I really enjoyed his company. He was very patient and encouraging. I had no interest in him sexually, nor did he in me. He recognised the loneliness and danger I was in, particularly with my health, and began to keep a close eye.

One night after a long chat I went to sleep. I had a dream I went to Jamaica to visit Mrs Archie to give her an introduction to my partner; it was surprisingly GA. She was sitting on the veranda. It was as if she was beaming like a bright light. I spoke with her and heard her voice, but I did not see her face. I woke from the dream. I was so angry with myself, how could I introduce my best friend as a partner? We were not even attracted to each other in that way. I had to run away from him now or the friendship would never be the same. I was sick, why would I think such a thing? I avoided him for a few days. He noticed I was acting strangely, but I pretended to behave normally. He was visiting more frequently – I felt like he was watching over me. We had our normal long chat about back home, how he grew up, and exchanged the differences in culture. Time was never enough. Whenever he mentioned my parents, I would dismiss it. I told him about how abusive my mother was to me, but he was confused. He thought I didn't understand that I was wrong. He lay back on the bed in exhaustion and I curled up at the side of the single bed. We both fell asleep later in the night. I thought I had this dream again of him stroking my toes and I wanted to jump from the bed. I realised this was not a dream. I said, "What are you doing?"

He said, "I like you very much."

"How long have you felt this way?"

He said, "A very long time."

I said, "I like you too, but I never knew you felt this way about me."

I will say no more about what took place that night, but that was the beginning of our relationship. My nineteenth birthday was in two weeks and our love for each other was blooming. I couldn't have enough of him. I was his first love. He was kind and gentle; I was really happy. The other flatmates were disappointed. It caused mayhem, but it was my life and I was entitled to choose who I wanted to share my life with. There was jealousy, not only at home but among my friends from college. A mate I met at college was staying with me for a while – she had run away from home due to her culture. She was rebellious and would not accept an arranged marriage with an older man from India. She wanted to be free to choose and go about her life without being imprisoned. She told me of her unhappiness and I had a lot of sympathy for her. I could imagine her grief and frustration. Regardless of the kindness and love I showed her, she tried to seduce my boyfriend by wearing revealing clothing and flirting at every opportunity. My intuition was spot on. I caught her red-handed in the kitchen, smiling and being really friendly, sitting in a way that left nothing to the imagination in a see-through dressing gown and underwear, seducing GA! I went into the kitchen in a rage and asked, "What the hell is going on here?"

She quickly adjusted herself, "Nothing."

"I can see what you are doing."

She got up from the chair and headed for the bathroom, grumbling, "I was just talking with him."

I said, "Do I look stupid?" and then I turned to GA. "What are you doing chatting with her in her condition?"

She had a reputation from the time she resided there. I heard after she left that she had slept with all the housemates and she was just preying on this one to complete her mission – but she had no idea what she had started. I told her to leave immediately. I was not going to take any chances – as nice as GA was, he was extremely naïve at times, and what is it with friends? We planned to go out on a date on my birthday. He was still learning the geography of his hometown after being away for such a long time in Nigeria, so I had to choose the venue and do most of the arrangement. He was so shy.

It was my birthday and my friends came around to celebrate with me. I was so happy for the first time in my life. I was in my own world. I never thought of my mother, who didn't even try to contact me to find out about my wellbeing – I suppose to avoid any burden I may cause. Anyway, I was contented. Life was better and I didn't want to see or hear from them. It would just resurrect bad memories and it would be a total embarrassment amongst my friends when they realised my background, from parents that had no value to society. GA came home from work early that evening. He had a huge box. He said, "Happy birthday," and gave it to me. Before I opened the box I was speechless at the size of it – what did he get me? I opened it in anticipation – he had bought me a stereo.

"Oh my god, this is the best present I have ever had in my life."

I was shivering all over. It is hard to explain this feeling – it was happiness and like I was entering a new dimension in my life, but at the same time I couldn't help thinking or fearing how long this would last, or being hurt by GA. I was getting to know him so well – it was a feeling both bitter and sweet. I just didn't want it to end. GA made me feel so special that day. I could not imagine that someone would think so much of me after all the names I had been given and the way I had been treated in the past. I chose the restaurant for our date. He asked me to choose his meal, but I was also naïve to the menu so I asked the waiter to explain the dishes. We ate and talked and had a wonderful time. I felt more relaxed with him than the awful experience of the last time I visited a restaurant, with Steve. He was such a bastard, he didn't love me. He was just after one thing, but one day hopefully I will see him again and really tell him where the sun does not shine. Our relationship escalated and we were more of a couple now, shopping together. I was unable to cook a decent meal in the microwave, but we managed. We continued to talk for hours. I would wait anxiously for him to get home from work and we made love. He was gentle and sweet for hours until we were exhausted. I couldn't stop thinking that this was going to be short-lived – I couldn't believe my luck that we were getting on well. Our relationship had blossomed and GA was concerned about my future. He had adopted the role not only of my boyfriend, but he also offered to pay for the higher education that I had interest in. I was delighted; I believed this would enable me to get better jobs in the future.

Education was paramount to me because I believed this could break the boundary of poverty. The first course I embarked upon I passed; then I moved on to others and was also successful. I learned how to drive – I was dreadful to start with but GA had the patience, even though we argued a lot during the practise. I had become more confident in myself and I felt I could work much harder to achieve my goals. It was evident that what Mrs B had suggested – that I would never do well because I was from a poor background – was not true: I just needed to work hard and I did. The atmosphere in the house with my housemates had changed; some were moving out to get on with their lives and we didn't spend as much time together as before. Everyone was in the process of being committed to their loved ones or changes in their life.

The time had come. At around 5am there was great, almighty banging on the door. Everyone was startled. I peeped through the curtain – my room was by the front door – and I saw six men in plain clothes standing by the door, looking for any sign of movement. I wasn't sure, but I thought one of the guys in the house must have been in trouble. I stood still and they continued to bang on the door. The next door neighbours were out to see what was going on; they would have been thrilled to see the troubled house being raided. I couldn't bear it anymore, they really meant business. I would just have to tell them that whoever they were searching for was not available. I opened the door and this huge force pushed forward.

I said, "Hello, may I help you?"

The gentleman explained he was the sheriff and was here to repossess the house.

I said, "What! We were not informed that this would take place today."

He replied, "You must remove your belongings this day as we are instructed to barricade this house."

I didn't have a suitcase; I had a television and stereo – where was

I going to store my things? Where would I sleep? What was I going to do? It was very helpful that we had our meeting and had put in place some contingency plan. I had to quickly contact the homeless unit to be rescued or I would sleep on the street with all my possessions at risk. I was so afraid. I was comfortable where I was. I didn't know what to expect at the next level in my life. GA was also confused with nowhere to go. I had an advantage because of my age and being female – at the time I was considered a higher priority by the authorities. Thank God, I was saved late that evening. All my belongings were packed on the street into an old, abandoned car where I planned to sleep. GA was not given a place and he was not allowed to share my room, so he slept with some friends for the night. It was really frightening, things had changed drastically within 24 hours and I was missing him.

At my accommodation, a bed & breakfast hotel, there were all sorts – from drug addicts, prostitutes and thieves to battered wives and ex-convicts. It was a frightening experience – it was as if I was in another world. I avoided interacting with these people. My personal documents had to be hidden in a safe place. A decent meal was hard to come by as the kitchen was three floors down in the basement, with four cookers. I had to queue up and travel two floors down with the ingredients from my room to the kitchen. There was strong advice from one lady to watch over the cooking, as the whole pot could be stolen off the fire or sabotaged. It was incredible; there were various cultures and there could sometimes be miscommunication and physical fights in the kitchen over who had been using the facilities first or for how long. I had to find an alternative the moment I saw threatening behaviour with a knife and the aggressive manner of some of the ladies.

I was told the leader was an ex-convict at Holloway Prison, charged with attempted murder, and one of the residents was attacked with boiling water poured over her. I started to cook meals in my bedroom, for health and safety reasons it was unsafe, but I had no choice. The hotel was situated in Finsbury Park, London, in the heart of the red-light district. The prostitutes used this hotel as their brothel and I could sometimes hear what was taking place. It was almost as if I was in the same room. I could hear the screams, groaning and vibration of the bed and ceiling, as the walls were so thin. I turned my television up high to block out the sound and the resident below would bang the ceiling for me to turn it down, then you would hear the noise of screaming young children, the sound of footsteps and squeaking floors and beds. I would have liked to go out for a walk most nights because of the noise and disturbances, but it was so dangerous; there were always incidents of young women being raped and robbed on the street.

The hotel was not safe either. There were reports of attacks where room doors were kicked down or families were robbed. My time at the hotel was temporary, until suitable accommodation was located, but this could be months or years. The hotel manager informed me that the accommodation was not suitable for me as I was not a priority. He said, "You are not suitable for this hotel; it is for people in priority – ex-cons, pregnant teenagers, battered wives. Therefore you must contact the authorities."

With pleasure, I thought, anything to get out of this hellhole, but the authorities declined and suggested I seek private accommodation. How would I afford this on a low wage, which was not enough to buy a decent meal for the week? I could just about manage to feed myself. I was devastated. I imagined I would now be homeless and my health started to deteriorate again. I lost more weight and felt very anaemic. I had constant sleepless nights. Not able to have a decent meal, I lived on bread and butter; that was all I wanted, as well as bags of gelatine sweets. I became extremely tired and most days I had no strength. I was bedridden, with my bones protruding from my chest and ribcage. I was also missing GA; he visited each day, but it was not enough. I was in hell. This matter needed to be resolved or I might not live. The doctor also had concerning results about my health.

GA was worried and took matters into his own hands. He supported me by ensuring that I had a decent meal daily and whatever I needed. He was staying with his brother. He saw the danger of my deterioration and was prepared to take the risk of sneaking in at night to watch over me in the B&B. He was really disturbed, but I didn't know this until he later told me. The caretaker who wanted me out caught me one evening inviting him in. I knew I was in real trouble and I was expecting him to evict me, but it was fine with him. He remained oblivious to GA staying there; I think he realised how terrified I was of the place. When GA was with me I slept peacefully, it was like the sounds disappeared. The barricades I placed behind the door at night were fewer. The arrangement was that GA had to leave early in the morning, before the other manager took the shift – this was quite challenging.

I was given notice to leave as I was not a priority. I went back to the local authority and found a staff member who was like a Good Samaritan. They advised me on what to do, that due to my age it was best to go to a hostel and they wrote a letter of recommendation. Within two months I was rehoused – what a relief. It was safer, cleaner and I was living with my age group. I shared my bedsit with one flatmate. I was so happy when I received the news, but there was only one concern – I wanted GA to be with me, but he was not allowed to stay in the hostel. It was difficult not having him by my side, he meant everything to me. I had no family and hardly any friends; I was so grateful to have such a partner. Determined and strong-headed as I was, we were not in a position as a couple to afford a house or flat, but I found a way to invite him to stay with me in the hostel. The advantage here was that we were not supervised by a caretaker 24 hours a day. The youth workers would only appear once or twice a week for maintenance. My flatmate was great; she also had the same plan which worked well. We had our own facilities to ourselves, a kitchen and bathroom; and the location was two blocks away from Tottenham Hotspurs' ground. It was so close you could hear the cheer of fans during the matches.

One day, I met with the youth worker who was processing my application for a permanent accommodation. I realised he was very friendly, but I imagine that he was doing his job. I didn't take much notice of him, but he started to watch my flat and movements, and at one of our meetings he told me that, "I know you are living with a man in your bedsit."

I said, "No I am not."

He said, "I have seen you."

This was a shock, as I made sure that GA came into the flat past office hours. I denied his accusation and carried on. I was in my flat one morning at 6am, getting ready for work, when I noticed someone turning the door handle to come in. I called out to my flatmate, but I knew she had gone to college and GA had not stayed over as he had gone to Nigeria. I was half-naked and ran to find cover, calling out, "Who is there?"

The person didn't answer, so I wrapped a towel around myself and ran to look through the key hole. Oh my God, it was the caseworker – what was he doing at my door, and with a key in his hand? I would expect him to knock on the door especially at this time of the morning, but he turned up unannounced. All the students in the entire block had gone to college. I kept quiet for a while, hoping he would go away. I knew the answer now – he had been coming into my room when I was not here. I was lucky, my keys were left in the lock, or else he would have come in. I was so annoyed and frightened. I went straight to the office and complained. The staff tipped me off that it was not the first complaint they had had and that this was under investigation. He stalked girls he fancied and invited himself in to their premises; the result was instant dismissal.

I had made a superb recovery, my weight increased and my haemoglobin level had improved. I felt happier as life took a turn for the better. I passed my driving test and had a car, I finished my course at college with distinction, and GA had a good job; we were planning for the future and the next agenda was to get married. All this time I was not missing my parents. My mother was probably quite pleased to see the back of me – less responsibility for her. I began to experience strange dreams and quite horrific nightmares – I was attacked by small, monstrous creatures, it was so real but it made no sense. This went on every night for a week and what was strange about it was that Mrs A was in the dream. Then the following week, I was sent a message that Mrs Archie was poorly. I now understood this must have been the sign. I located the telephone number from one of the church members and called Jamaica. Mrs A was dying. I immediately made arrangements to see her because she was my best friend. It was important to me to be there for her; there was so much I wanted to tell her, especially about GA, and commend her for all the guidance, advice, comfort and care she had given to me as a child. I was reminiscing about the promises I made to her about how I would drive her around the island and the meetings. I was very anxious to get there. I went shopping and bought her favourites and I was all packed to leave in two days. Unfortunately, it was too late. I was told she wanted to leave a message for me, but was discouraged as I was on my way. They told her she should deliver the message herself, but it was not to be. When my mother told me the terrible news, the pain was unbearable. I sobbed uncontrollably all the way to Jamaica – just as I was getting on my feet, I had lost her.

On my way to Jamaica, I was extremely apprehensive, especially about the dreams that I had been experiencing. I felt great fear that she might haunt me, like the terrifying feeling I had when I lost my brother. I remembered the mental torture, how difficult it was for me to see my brother gone and now this again. The 9 hour flight felt like 24. I could not face this. I got off the aircraft and waited at immigration. My mind kept wondering how badly I was going to react when reality set in. My mother and a few others came to meet me. My mother looked stressed. She was Mrs Archie's carer and I was anxious to know what happened to her – did she suffer? Apparently she was ill for some time. I should have been told much sooner. I assumed she gave specific instruction for me not to be told as I would worry. God knows, she knew me so well from the incident when at age 5 I screamed in hysterics. I think that experience lived within her, and thinking about it, my reaction to seeing her dying could have been catastrophic. When I entered the Promised Land, it was as if I was in a trance. I couldn't imagine her not being there, I was in disbelief. I went to look for her on the veranda where she usually sat. Her chair was there and her walking stick was put aside. I stood and reflected on the good old days. I walked towards her room, but as I stepped up there was an overwhelming presence; it was like something invisible blocking me mentally and maybe spiritually from entering her room. I just could not go in.

My mother and I were to plan the funeral. She had to wait for me to arrive for us to identify her body. I have never spoken of this experience; I prefer to write it in this book. We arrived at the hospital and a porter led us to where her body had been laid. Her body was waiting for us in the lobby on a stretcher, covered with a white sheet. This is where I discovered my supernatural gift for the first time. As soon as we entered the door, her spirit came to me and spoke within. How pleasant it was! I was not afraid, it said, "Oh Lou, you came!"

I spoke to her inwardly. I said, "Oh Mrs A, how are you? I am really sorry I couldn't be here to see you earlier."

I could feel the spirit leading me with delight to her body as I approached it; so delightful, as if she were just waiting for me. I recognised her legs and was able to stroke them, and then it said inwardly, "I am so glad you made it."

I did not look at her face. As we sat and waited for the post-mortem to be done, there were bodies being carried in in the most brutal way: the most disturbing was a baby, probably a still-birth, being put on a trolley and dangling from the side. The body might have slipped off; it was so disturbing. I started to feel really ill, like I was going pass out. My head and body were feeling weak, as if I were going to fall to the ground. The heat was not helping. My head was spinning, I was going to faint! I thought I needed some water. This was the experience I was dreading, not pleasant at all. After the post-mortem, the doctor invited us to come in. I peeped through the half-closed door into the room and there were about seven other bodies being operated on and some waiting – some covered, some uncovered. I refused to enter the theatre. I knew I would not make it, so my mother went in alone. She was strong, so she coped, but it must have been hard and I was sorry about not being much help.

I was quiet throughout our journey back home. We were not alone – she was with us. I felt her presence all the way; it was like a feeling that someone was behind me, with occasional hair raising and goosepimples. We got home and I was so distraught that I preferred not to eat. I went to bed, it was like I had been on a month's marathon. When I woke up, it was just the beginning. I decided to go into her room because we had to gather documents for the funeral. The overpowering feeling in the room was still there. I could sense the exact location where it was, by the bedside table. I couldn't see it, but it was so strong; it was like a huge invisible force and so powerful. I thought I had some rest – maybe I was jetlagged. I wanted to dismiss that it was the spirit of Mrs A. I struggled to ignore it, but I was now afraid. I managed to keep away from the area that the presence was in and continued my search. What I found disturbing was that others came in the room and had not experienced what I felt. I needed clarity, so I went to my mother and whispered, "Mum, there is something weird happening to me. I can feel a strong presence in Mrs A's room – am I being stupid?"

She said, "No, I am touched by it as well."

I said, "But what about the other people in the room? They seem to be fine."

She said, "It's your spiritual gift that has kicked in."

I said, "I don't like the feeling. It makes me afraid and ill, moreover I don't know how to dismiss it."

She said, "There is nothing you can do until the appropriate time."

What did that mean? I struggled for a week before the funeral. I sought clarity on this matter; remember Mrs A was the leader of the revival church – obviously she possessed extreme powers in life and possibly in death. I was experiencing severe nightmares where I was in a graveyard, chased by the devil and being alone. I would wake up at the same time, 3am, and everyone would be asleep. I imagined odd things, like what if she wanted to take me with her? I remember she specifically told me when I was young, "When I die, do not feel sorry for me."

I don't know why she said that. I just could not wait for it to be over and to go home. In the evenings, especially after 6pm, as her room door was near the kitchen, if the door was left open when I passed it was like a huff of a volcanic whirlpool bellowing in the room. As soon as I got close to the room, my energy connected to it. I felt powerless and afraid following the sensation. It appeared that I possessed the gift to sense spirits as my mother said. I hoped that after this I would never encounter such an experience again – an unknown territory, the dark side of this world.

The week of the funeral went slowly. The arrangement was

made in an orderly fashion thanks to the organised nature of Mrs Archie, who had planned her own funeral. I was asked to help dress her. At first I accepted, but on the morning, after all that I had been through, I declined; it would have been difficult. I chose her clothes and casket and the order of the service. The day had come. She was a popular person: people were arriving early in busloads from all around the island – it was a full house. One of the members shouted out, "She is here."

I walked toward the hearse to help carry the casket into the church. I wanted to be involved as much as I could – this was the last time. I looked at her for the first time. She was peaceful. I walked away to get dressed, then the service commenced. Words could not describe what she meant to me. I wanted to do something she would have enjoyed – my singing as a child. At the end of the service, I met some old friends and thanked them for coming. There was a procession to the cemetery, the farewell. At the graveside, people were singing as the grave diggers prepared and there was also preaching. This was the most difficult part, to see the casket slowly disappearing into the ground. My friend was gone. I was glad we met because she had an incredible impact in my life, a true friend – so caring and truly remarkable. I often dream of her. She gave protection and guidance and if there was something in the yard that was not pleasing to her, she appeared in my dreams. I would call my mother because she would relate to what was happening; for instance, Mrs A came in a dream and said there was a problem and she was soaking wet in her house. I rang my mother to ask what the problem was and she told me that due to the storm a tree had fallen on the house and damaged the roof, which led to severe leaking into the room. That was odd. This might be another gift, seeing danger coming in my dreams or if someone was trying to hurt me, which I discovered later. After the funeral, whatever had been done to release the force, her room was free. No one wanted to divulge to me what ritual was performed to release the spirit, but I knew from a young age that after the person dies, the room must be rearranged and their clothes removed.

I returned to the UK that same week. I was very sad and quite taken aback about the experience I had, but I was glad to be home at least. I had left all the fears behind. GA met me at the airport and I was so pleased to see him. This was the first time I had been away for so long from him. He was so supportive and showed empathy. It was good to be home. I was tired from restless nights and continuous nightmares, so I was looking forward to a peaceful sleep. I lay down to rest that afternoon and what do you know, whatever it was had followed me to the UK and the nightmares continued. I called my mother and asked her why I was haunted. What had I done to deserve this? My mother replied, "It is not Mrs A, it is the devil. She would not have tried to hurt you."

I said, "I don't understand, I am seeing her in my dream."

This went on for two months. The dreams became so real. I was having a conversation in my dream asking her what it was like to be dead. I would like to declare that this is not an exaggeration. I have conversations in my dreams with dead people – Gran, Aunt, Grandfather – unfortunately I never get the answer. When I acknowledge that they are dead, that would always be the end of the dream. I started to enjoy the dreams about her, as long as they were not the frightening ones. It was as if this was the opportunity to catch up with what I had missed. I began to realise this could be dangerous, it was not real. There was a significance, it was as if she was inviting me to come along into her world, but something held me back. I said, "I will not follow you over to that field,"

She insisted but somehow reality set in that it was not a place for the living. I woke out of my dream and called my mother straight away and explained the dreams. Mrs A had gone to another dimension, she was calling me over to a land that is not for the living. My mother said, "Don't worry it will be fine."

That was it? No explanation, no reason? All I know was that the dreams stopped. It was years later when I had a dream from Mrs A again. She came to introduce a male companion and I was very pleased to see her. That same day I received a letter, I had been granted my permanent flat in Wood Green, London. This was exciting news – it meant GA and I would be able to live in the comfort of our own home without sneaking to see each other. We went to view the flat and it was amazing. We started to make arrangements to furnish and paint. The flat was peaceful and very secure with very friendly neighbours. The surroundings were perfect as we lived on top of the shopping centre – how exciting. I celebrated my 21st birthday there and invited friends. My health was back to normal, I started considering higher education, and I also started a new job. Life was good. I changed my appearance – more fashion-conscious, elaborate hairstyles. GA and I were happy and very much in love. We would go out for meals and travel sometimes across Europe for sightseeing. We were blessed. We were exploring and doing things we had never imagined after going through so much in the past. We were doing well and GA thought that it was time for me to bury the grudge with my mother and create a better relationship; he suggested this because we were planning to get married soon and he wanted my mother's blessing. I didn't think it was that important for him to receive approval from her, but I wanted him to be satisfied. It was tradition, so I arranged to see my mother in Jamaica. I never travel light, even when I try – there are so many presents to take for friends and family. As a result, I missed the flight and was diverted to Barbados. Hopefully from there I would get a connecting flight to Jamaica. I arrived in Barbados – such beauty, but I was more concerned about the connecting flight. I later discovered that I would have to stay over two nights for my connecting flight. I stood in the lobby in dismay with a huge suitcase – I didn't have enough money for accommodation and I was so worried. The airline manager must have seen the worry on my face, he was so courteous and asked, "Can I help you?"

I said, "I missed my flight from London and I have not made arrangement for a place to sleep tonight, can you please advise a local hotel – something cheap?"

He said, "Don't worry, we will sort something out. Please take a seat," and 30 minutes later he returned with a hotel booked and transport to take me there. I was amazed and taken aback. How would I pay it back?

I asked, "Please tell me how much will it cost, I just have to know."

He said, "No charge!"

I was still puzzled. I was really lucky, I supposed. I also felt relieved but uneasy about the arrangement. I kept thinking I had to pay something. Then he said, "I will see you tomorrow."

What did that mean? Anyway, I stayed in the hotel – very good service – and then he turned up the following morning. I said, "Thank you very much for assisting me, how much do I owe you?"

He said, "No, the bill is on me."

I thought 'just like that?' Maybe it was the airport's funds – how naïve I was to think that. He took me around sight-seeing. I trusted him as he was a grown-up. I rang GA and told him about what was happening and he found my little adventure fascinating – two holidays in one. The manager dropped me off and told me he would take me to the carnival later that evening. I must admit that I felt at home: he was like an old friend and introduced me to his friends. We had a good night out. I was unable to understand his intention – did he fancy me or was he just being helpful? He was respectful and pleasant. I called GA to give me his opinion on the situation; he thought it was OK, maybe he was just a nice man. We continued with the sightseeing in Christchurch, into the craft market where we made more friends and received gifts from people I had just met, then he said, "I will be busy today so you can take the car and we will meet later."

I thought, he trusts me with his car? Maybe I reminded him of his daughter. After his shift, he came by the hotel and we went for dinner with his friends. We left late that evening as it was my last night before moving on to Jamaica. He was behaving strangely: he would always wait for me by the lobby, but this time he knocked on the room door. I didn't like this and said, "I am not dressed; I will meet you in the lobby in 10 minutes."

He said, "That's OK I can wait inside for you."

This was when I realised that this was weird.

I said, "No, it's OK. I will meet you there."

I looked through the spy hole on the door as he went. From that moment, everything changed – I was more conscious what I wore and how I approached him. It also felt uncomfortable knowing an older man had an interest in dating me. I felt obligated because he had paid for my hotel and all expenses, but by then I knew it was not genuine. I started to panic – how would I pay him back if he asked? I went down to the lobby. I was embarrassed – were people noticing what was going on? I held my head high and he kissed me on the cheek. I cringed. I gave no eye contact, to discourage him. My apprehension was intense. We sat down for a meal and his friends came and joined us. They were sarcastic towards him, saying how young I was. I don't know what he told them about me – obviously I was supposed to be his girlfriend. I had put myself in a very awkward position. We had a good time after they left us at the restaurant. He took the opportunity of expressing how he felt – I was astounded and unimpressed when he said,

"I think you are very attractive. I like you very much and I would like to see you again. I will pay for the next flight for you to come over when you are free."

I said, "I have a boyfriend – that will not be possible."

He said, "That's fine. I attend an annual conference in the UK every year – it would be nice to see you anyway when I come over."

I said, "OK," I was treading on eggshells here. I had received a massive favour from this man and on an island where I was a stranger. If anything, I was an easy target. We exchanged phone numbers.

"Goodnight," I said. He began to walk with me to my room. I stopped and hoped that he would realise and go, but he continued and opened the room door with a duplicate key to let me in. Oh no, this was not happening! The last time a guy tried this I was raped and I would not take this chance. I politely said, "If you don't you mind I am feeling very tired. I would like to go to bed now as I have a flight to catch in the morning, and I would prefer if I see you at the airport in the morning."

He said, "What do you think I am going to do?"

"I don't think you are going to do anything, but I will have to know you better before you can enter my room. I am scared."

He said, "OK," pulled me towards him and kissed me on the lips, then stood there.

I said, "Bye," and closed the door quickly, grabbed the chair and barricaded the door.

I sat up very late that night as I believed he was coming back. Maybe I should have paid him back. I felt uneasy that this might be the cause. I waited and waited until I fell asleep and woke up early the following morning in the clothes I wore to dinner. Thank God he stayed away. I got ready to disembark and saw him at the airport in the morning, organising the flight. He walked me to my seat on the aircraft – that was helpful with all the bags I had. I thanked him; I really appreciated all he did, but I was not attracted to him at all. I was in love with someone else. I kept in contact with him and even attended one of the conferences in Brighton. He was not willing to accept I was with someone else, that I couldn't be his lover, and our friendship disintegrated.

Chapter 6

I arrived in Kingston, Jamaica – this trip was one of the happiest, no funerals! My mother and cousins were waiting for my arrival. The sun was boiling hot; it felt like Barbados was cooler. On the previous trips to Jamaica, I didn't have the chance to appreciate the beauty and scenery, such a beautiful island. I was always fascinated as a child with mountains. I don't know why – maybe I had climbing in mind. We drove back to the Promised Land, as I called it. I went to Mrs A's room: the last visit I had was quite an experience with heavy and dark forces around, but now it was really calm and peaceful. I was able to go in and lay down on her bed, it was as if she had never existed. My mother and I spoke and caught up with all the latest gossip in the community – who got married, who had children. My mother seemed to have changed; we were having a better relationship, her condescending and controlling behaviour seemed to have vanished. I was glad, but not for long. I was excited to meet with friends from church. I also had a friend who emigrated from the UK. We met up and did some sightseeing and went to quite a few parties. We had a wonderful time, such fun, but all this was about to change. My mother saw the happiness and returned to her old self, making rules about what time I should return home. I was not allowed to stay out later than 10pm – I asked why.

"Why are you so happy? You just want to go out and have a good time, am I too ugly for you?" she said.

What was she talking about? I went away for a few days out of a four-week holiday, during which we spent most of the time together, visiting her family, sightseeing and at the beach. Although I tried to create this new relationship between us, something was not right; it was not working. Her behaviour started to resurrect the past. There were still scars from my childhood. It would never be 100% between us. She seemed to believe she had a right to treat me the way she did. I asked her to explain her actions; why she abused me so much as a child, did she think that laughing and joking and ignoring the past would heal everything? Wasn't now the time to make things right? But instead she wanted to continue controlling me – even how I spent my pocket money and where I should and shouldn't go unless she was present. It became embarrassing; at times my friends were wondering why she was there. I can understand this possessiveness – it is possible for a child who is very close to her mother, but our relationship was far from that. The vacation became a nightmare. We constantly argued and she made me angry with some of her suggestions and conversations we had. This was a trip gone wrong. She refused to accept that I was an independent adult. She could not treat me like in the past – I was not a child. Our conflict was about ridiculous matters – to have children. I was only 21; she should have been encouraging me to finish my education. She also used innuendos about children taking care of their parents when they are old and buying them a house. I supposed that was her wish but by the way it was mentioned, it was like dictation; command and force. I was not afraid of her anymore, what would she do? Kick me down the stairs or use her pan to whack me over the head? Her wishes are the responsibility of her husband. I was also to buy elaborate gifts for her mother – this was the woman who neglected her grandson and as a result his life ended tragically, with the help of my mother. I was angry and I told her, "I will not sacrifice my future to sit with you when you are old and dying, and please refrain from mentioning a grandmother. I lost her already – Mrs A. This woman is not my grandmother. When I needed food, love, comfort, guidance for the future, Mrs A was there."

This was the time for her to explain, but she kept quiet.

I said, "I am still waiting for an explanation – why did you abuse me as a child?"

She replied, "You were a difficult child and the licks didn't kill you did they?"

That did not answer my question.

I was hating my vacation. I respected the fact I was in her house and she had her rules, but I wanted the days to go quicker, to go home. I lived with my boyfriend GA, he didn't set curfews. There is a saying, 'you give an inch they take a yard'. I could understand if I brought friends to the house to disturb her – it would be disrespectful. I simply wanted to create a relationship for the sake of GA and to enjoy my holiday. Because I had obeyed her rules, the bullying, patronising, and controlling turned worse. She even dictated that I should eat only her food. I rang GA and told him it was not worth me going to see her, she was a control freak. The relationship did not improve, I became her personal chauffeur and drove her to church and her friends and family, which she enjoyed. How selfish, I was not interested in her family – we were not acquainted before, why now? It was as if she was being pompous, she pretended to become this superstar overnight while I was in the background. There was another side to her that I had not experienced. My success had nothing to do with her, but she wanted to take the credit. Sometimes the way she looked at me gave me the creeps, as if I was a stranger. I didn't know what her thoughts were. There was hypocrisy amongst my family; even if they were aware a parent is irresponsible, they would give advice on how you should take care of them in the name of God and love them, as they are irreplaceable. No one wanted to listen or accept that there are bad parents, so the victim suffered in silence, and if you tried to express your feelings you were deemed rebellious or abnormal in that society. For instance, if I spoke about my experience, the abuse and how unloved I was, I would be ignored. Is this what life is about? I wrote this book because I want to express my feelings and hope that if anyone is experiencing the same, it should be exposed and not wrapped under the tongue.

In my view, irresponsible parenting should be penalised so that children and others can identify and accept this to be true in the black society. The victims should not feel embarrassed or less of a person, worried of rejection or called insane; it is life, it happens. In the Western world, children are taken away from irresponsible parents and placed in care. I have experienced so many strange mothers and yet the victims have to pretend that it is acceptable. For instance, a mother who was a nymphomaniac that had seven children with various men. When the eldest, the 14-year-old daughter, was approached by the mother's ex-boyfriend with an offer she could not refuse – to live with him and he would support her and the daughter, even the rest of the family – history repeated itself. The daughter carried on the same role, having children with various men. She too had seven children and now had to support herself and her mother. Obviously for the man who made the request it was only temporary, but her life became difficult, as did the future of her children. There is also the mother who had separated from the father in anger and mentally and physically abused this child against men. That child is now a 48-year-old lonely woman caring for her mother who continues to be manipulated; she is also an only child. I tried to explain my mother's behaviour but was ignored and deemed insane. I had to pretend, even though I knew my mother had not done her duties, and she took advantage. She knew that in our society, no one would believe me – they would always be on the mother's side. The request my mother had laid on the table, she did not deserve it. She obviously had made plans with her husband, Longman; moreover they were still at an age to fend for themselves. Her excuse was that she never had the opportunity, luck was never on her side. I sat my mother down in spite of her behaviour and asked what she wanted to do with her life and how she could help herself. I asked, "Do you have an idea what you would like to do?"

No answer. Her reaction was as if I asked her a ridiculous question, it seems she planned to depend on me but I hadn't achieved anything yet. Obviously she had no plans. I called a meeting with her and her husband; I was not prepared at such an age to take on a huge responsibility when these people could help themselves. My plan for the future was to be responsible for my children and I would not be able to afford all this on our income. I refused to have this hanging over me. Her suggestion was to seek work in the United States and for her husband to become a taxi driver. Their situation was hopeless since Mrs A had died; the basic essentials in the household needed replacement and I thought I would help – after all, she was my mother.

Time to go home, and I was pleased to return. GA knew how I felt, but he thought that as I was the only child he wanted to prove to my mother that he was the right man for me and for her to accept him as her son-in-law. He wanted to prove to her that he had my best interest at heart and wanted me to climb to the highest height. He believed in me so much and suggested that rather than doing these small courses I should aim for higher education. I thought we could not afford that, but my real setback to this suggestion was psychological. I was told by my guardian back in the days, Mrs B, that people like me would not be able to reach this level due to my background. GA insisted, "It's a load of rubbish, just try."

I pursued a BSc degree and my God, I came out with honours. This enhanced my CV and I started working for one of the most prestigious banks in the UK while I completed my Master's. I kept in contact with my mother and I started to realise that her intention was to constantly demand money. I worked really hard that year to return to Jamaica to fulfil my promise.

GA and I for the first time started to have rough times in our relationship. I wanted to do so much more travelling and studying, but as he was 10 years older he was experiencing peer pressure. His friends were settling down and having children and he wanted to start a family. I was so young and not ready. This would slow down the plans I had. We started to have arguments and disagreements about starting a family. I respected him for his honesty and giving me the option to choose; I know of situations where women do not get a choice, they find themselves pregnant by deceit, but in my case I was given the option to choose whether I wanted to start a family now or for him to move on. I loved GA and wanted to spend the rest of my life with this man, but I was afraid of being surrounded by bad advice and stories of how men change – once a child is involved you will be trapped, your free paper is burned, life will not be the same, your body will change and your partner will not have the same interest. This was the discouraging advice, all negative. I had to sit back and think, the advice was from people who did not have a relationship, most of them had bad experiences and some were jealous. It is my life, I must choose, I have been with GA now for five years; he is very loyal and I trust him. He promised me that he would be there to support me as always, and he told me, "I will give up my job to be with the child until it is old enough while you continue your studies." Obviously I would do my part, but it was reassuring to know how much he cared. Moreover, I could not afford to lose such a friend; he meant everything to me – he was my confidant, my father, my brother. This is the person who took an interest and restored me when I was near to death and abandoned like a piece of furniture thrown in the bin. Sure, he may change after our child is born, but the child will be mine – that is a risk I will take. I want him to be happy like he wants for me always. I am not selfish; he was honest to give me the choice. We sat down over dinner one evening and I explained to him how I felt and the advice that was given. I told him how much I loved him and gave him my decision for us to start our family. We were really happy and started to plan and shop for the baby. Within two months I was pregnant. The early stage of the pregnancy was difficult and I became so ill with morning sickness that my health deteriorated. GA was there to give me all the support and tender loving care that a pregnant mother would need. We visited the clinic together; he would massage my back and feet when they were tired and swollen. There was one issue during my pregnancy – I decided not to tell my mother straight away since I didn't want any dictation or interfering.

I was thinking about my father a lot. I had this sudden urge to meet him. I don't know if it was triggered because of the pregnancy or because we were also getting to the stage of planning the wedding date. My mother always told me how violent he was. She said, "There is no point knowing that bastard; he is a wicked man."

I wanted to meet him anyway and for years I thought of ways to do it. I asked my mother on several occasions and she said she had lost contact, but I didn't believe her. I applied pressure and demanded her to find him or else, and to my surprise she brought his address to me. When I received it, I sat on the bed thinking he might not be interested to know me, he may refuse. All I could do was try, so I wrote to him in New York where he was residing. I had lost contact with my father for 21 years. My mother chose to deny me that right to be in contact with my him. I wrote

Dear Dad

This is your daughter. You might not be interested to meet me, but if you would like to I would very much like to meet you. I think of you all the time and what you would be like. And if I have siblings, I would also like to meet them. Please see my telephone number xxxxxxx
    Your Daughter,
    M Reid

I honestly didn't think he would be interested anyway and there was no response I waited and waited. I was now four months pregnant and decided now was the time to tell my mother that her grandchild was on the way. I always got this overwhelming feeling of fear whenever I was about to tell her, like someone was whispering in my ears dictating I should not tell her. I decided it would be best to let her come over to the UK. It was weird, I cannot explain why I was not allowed to tell my mother. It was peculiar – it was like there was a spirit that was leading or instructing me in my mind. The morning sickness or rather day sickness was upon me when the phone rang. I answered and the person said in an American accent, "Hello is that Maria?"

I said, "Yes speaking."

He said, "This is your dad."

I went quiet in shock for a few seconds. I said, "Hello Dad. How are you? Thank you very much for contacting me."

He sounded really intelligent and was interested in my education and what I was doing. His main concern was my mother and whether she was living with me. He was probing a lot about our relationship, asking how often did I see her. Then this was the biggest surprise of all – he said, "I will come over and see you in two weeks."

I could not believe it! Everything was happening so fast, I did not tell him I was pregnant. I thought it might not be a good first impression. I was really excited, but nervous. Finally I was going to meet my dad. GA and I started to make preparations; he was also excited to meet him. The days could not pass quickly enough. The day had come: he told me that he would make his way to the station and he described what he would be wearing and the colour of the travel bag. I was to meet him at the station. I tried to look my best. I waited at the spot where we agreed to meet for 20 minutes and there was this small man coming up the escalators. I said, "Dad?"

He said, "Maria?"

We hugged – he was delighted to see me. Remember, the last time my father saw me, I was 2 years old. I had prepared him one of my special meals. We talked on the way home about basic things like the climate and he spoke about how some of the areas and buildings had changed since his time in the UK. I don't know what he might have been thinking as he met me pregnant. I was hoping he would be happy to meet my partner and would see that we were a couple together. We reached home and GA greeted him and he shook his hand, but he was not very polite with him. I tried to keep the conversation going and after a while he was slightly agitated. I was feeling uncomfortable; I was not sure what the problem was, but he would not give GA any eye contact or talk with him. He only kept requesting for him to bring him cups of tea. I didn't like this one bit and I had to put a stop to it. Why should he give GA the cold shoulder. I started to ask him questions about the relationship between him and my mother and the reasons for all of the violence. He told me my mother was the wickedest person he had ever come across. I was now confused here – I was like piggy in the middle. They were both slagging off each other using the same terminology, 'wicked'.

I said, "What do you mean dad?"

He said, "She performed witchcraft on me to an extent that I had to run for my life." I looked and thought this man was mad. I had never seen my mother carry out any ritual. If she did I would have noticed. Then this was the final straw when he went on to say, "Any day I catch that woman, I will punch her in the head."

I shouted frantically, "Don't you ever speak like that about my mother again! What kind of man are you! My mother told me about you and how vile you are." This man had huge bitterness for my mother and I wanted him to explain to me why he was so violent with my mother that she had to run away with me to Jamaica where I really suffered. There were nights I had nothing to eat, nowhere to live.

He said, "I will prove it to you, give me a minute." He went into his suitcase and reached for a folder. He said, "This is a copy for you." I examined the document stamped Old Street Magistrate; it seemed genuine. I read on, it explained in 1973 my father had won full custody for me and all the arrangement put in place for me to be with my father. I was taken aback by this and mortified; my mother had not explained this to me ever, so I was right when I saw those men, when we hid that day in Jamaica. It was immigration searching to return me to my father; it was not what I was originally told by my mother, that I was not allowed to leave the UK because I was a British subject. Why did she lie? This information was disturbing; it turned my whole life upside-down. I know the British law typically protects mothers' custody of their children, and for her to lose custody, something must have been very wrong. He started to explain his relationship with my mother, how they met and how he fell in love with her.

"She was a beautiful girl," he said. "I believed this was the woman I would spend the rest of my life with." She was kind and calm, and he had decided to send for her to join him in the UK in 1963. But it was not long before her behaviour became erratic; she wanted to constantly party and demanded money for shoes and clothes and irresponsible spending sprees. That was not the plan – they were to work hard and return to Jamaica. I was finding it difficult to comprehend what he was saying, because the person he was describing, my mother, did not fit. However my mother never explained to me until this day how she lived her youthful days – everything about her is a secret. I don't know the father of my brother, who was her first love interest. What I realised was her whole interest was her religion and every scenario was in the name of God.

This was the time my father explained the experiences he had when my mother joined the revival church as mentioned in Chapter 1. There seemed to be a lot of skeletons in the closet and when I asked her about her youth she would reply, "I was always a decent girl you know."

This did not answer my question, but I dared not probe.

During my father's visit he was always on edge, as if he was always nervous and he didn't trust me. It felt like I was going to attack him or steal from him. I just couldn't work out what was going on. I realised he thought that my mother had used me to find him to demand inheritance, and strangely, even though that was not my intention, my mother was laying on pressure to demand money from him saying, "That wretch, he left us for years without a penny. Make sure you get some money from him. He has money. Don't let him come here without giving you something."

I was furious and I told her, "If you need money you should contact him direct. Do not use me to swindle money out of my father, I don't need anything from him."

That was the reason she released the contact details of my father – to benefit from it. My father knew my mother more than I did. His prediction was right, but he couldn't trust me. It was frustrating trying to prove myself. As the days passed, our relationship deteriorated. All the memories of my mother and what he had gone through created a lot of bitterness in him. I was not to be blamed that it didn't work out. Why did he bother to come? He would say, "Do you know if your mother had not messed me about we would have done better than you. All the plans we had to build an empire, all the dreams I had just scattered. My life just disappeared before me."

He told me how much he loved me when he saw me last. It broke his heart when my mother decided to use me and blackmail him with threatening behaviour and divorce, saying he had better pay up or else she would not allow me to see my dad. Sometimes my mother would try to discourage me from meeting him on the weekends agreed by the courts. I knew he was telling the truth because I heard my mother bragging on many occasions to her friends how she would deny him access to his daughter because she hated him so much. My dad would desperately try to win me over with the most delicious sweets and exciting fun days out. My father had nothing good to say about my mother. My father's visit was becoming stressful. My mother, on the other hand, was also being abusive.

"He should get lost," she said.

I was piggy in the middle. All I wanted was just a normal life like everyone else. I wanted to know my mother and father and have a relationship with them both for the benefit of my children in the future. My parents, after decades of separation, are still at each other's throats. They do not realise I am hurting. I don't care now; I have gone through so much in my life. I just want to fix it and they just kept going on.

I went on to Wood Green high street and sat by the park feeling sorry for myself. I wondered how many people who passed by had experienced a similar situation. I admired every individual that went past that day and thought they were so blessed to have a mother and father; their life could not be as complex. It was nearly time for my dad to return to New York. The visit did not quite work out how I planned – to go out for meals and sightseeing with him, to show me the places we had been. The fights continued between my mother and father. They were not listening to me and I had to put up with it. My dad eventually calmed down, but my mother just kept igniting the flames. The proof my father brought made me more scrupulous and the witchcraft scenario was an exaggeration. I cannot be sure I knew my mother better than I knew my father, and I believed in my mother more. I can understand his point of view. His child had been taken away from him, and that would make any parent angry. He had brought the evidence that he was a responsible father. He won custody and he came to see me when I contacted him. I should allow him the opportunity to tell his side of the story. He sent for her to start a family together. She took the opportunity, but she didn't love him and she played him. He didn't know her well but claimed that she practised witchcraft, as mentioned in Chapter 1. I have never seen my mother carry out any rituals personally. I didn't believe him and all my life my mother convinced me that my father was insane, but he was fine. I didn't approve of her religion; the rules were very restrictive regarding what you can do with your life, what to wear, how to live and the devotion of your entire life not to be amongst the world, e.g., not to go to the cinema or theatre or to a party – everything must be done in the name of God. I listened and most of his explanations were contradictory to what my mother explained, but I reflected on my separation from my father and why my mother was so loyal to this type of religion. Why not be Catholic or a member of the Salvation Army or Anglican Church?

He returned to the States and we kept in contact. My mother was very cross at the fact that he had left me empty-handed, but that was not my plan. I didn't need anything from him. I just wanted to know my father. She was really angry and said I should have demanded money from him.

"Why? You had my father's details all this time. When we were suffering you failed to contact him and now you are having a go at me?"

Could my father be right about the gold-digging? When I needed shoes, school books, help with my education, or clothes why didn't she contact him as she has done now? This makes me angry. This is using, and I didn't like it.

My bump was growing and six months into the pregnancy the morning sickness was not easing. I was so weak most mornings. My mother was due to come over in couple of weeks. GA and I were relishing the experience of the pregnancy, my cravings and mood swings were growing bigger by the day. I was not looking forward to having my mother be around me. We could manage fine without her dictating and her controlling manner, but it was just polite to have her here – unfortunately for six months. It appears there was a rivalry between her and my father, since he was here before her – how petty and ridiculous.

Chapter 7

Hell begins

The day had come. GA and I went to the airport to meet her. He met her for the first time, although they had spoken on several occasion over the telephone. She was happy to meet him, and hugged and kissed him. She really knew how to put on a show. We hugged, and on the way home she was amused at how the weather had changed since she left the country in the seventies. It was not foggy and bleak and icy as it was back in those days. I was pleased to see her, but I knew I would not be for long. I prepared everything to make her comfortable; being away in the tropics for such a long time meant it would take some time for her to adapt again. We made sure she was warm and well looked after. Her reaction to GA was better than Dad's. She had conversations with him. Her friends knew she was here and they came to visit. She started to rearrange my flat. I told her not to and that I was happy with the way it was. The patronising soon started.

"It was a good job I came so that the baby will get good food to be strong and healthy," she said.

She began to cook meals I would not eat anyway. I accepted that mothers always worry about their children's health and that in my condition she was probably genuinely concerned, until she said, "I brought along my gloves. I knew how nasty you were as a teenager. I didn't know that you would be able to keep your house clean like this. I imagined rats escorting me out of the flat." Some people may think I am overreacting, but this certainly was not a compliment, especially when my partner GA was hearing this. He was very tolerant and nothing seemed to really bother him. It is just his nature, and he felt that my mother was to be respected regardless. She took a turn on GA.

"Can you cook? I don't see you in the kitchen, how are you going to take care of the baby when it is born if you can't do anything?"

He was so polite in explaining what he could do. I refused to let her patronise my partner – we were fine. As a mother and grandmother to be, I received no support or instruction on what to do as a new mother. We had not been on visits together to the clinic or to nursery or shopping as grandmothers do. She was more interested in going out with her friends, regular visits to church, and itemising the goods to cargo back to Jamaica. It was as if she was on a business trip. I was getting fed up with the constant visits and disturbance. She received numerous presents, but it came at a cost to ship and who would be paying the bill? I encouraged her to find a job. Obviously she assumed I had a bag of money to buy her clothes, and gifts for her family and friends back home.

I was heavily pregnant, we had good days which ended when she asked me to help her pack. It was only six weeks into the visit. I helped her and was so exhausted. The next day, her friends came by. They had their items to fit in and had to dismantle the work I put in from the night before in my condition. I was so annoyed to come home and again find a group of people, without my permission, taking over and doing as they pleased in my home. It was like an invasion. I asked her, "If you knew that the packing was not OK, why did you let me spend over three hours last night packing only to now find your friends here in my home pulling it down again?"

She replied, "Don't tell me about any bloody barrel. If it is going to cause you any problems, I will take it and your stuff and fling it out the door."

I said, "I refuse to accept this. You better leave. I don't have to put up with this. I invited you to my home, as you showed an interest to be here for the birth of your grandchild. I paid your fare and made arrangements for you. What have you done for me, but to dictate and patronise, pass condescending remarks towards me and my partner and run my house?"

She answered, "I didn't beg you for anything." I just could not imagine how ungrateful, cold and rude her attitude was. She believed she owned me and could do as she pleased. It was only week six out of six months. If we were fighting this much only a quarter of the way through her visit, what was going to happen? I went to the clinic with GA one morning and she decided to rearrange the flat again. She continued to entertain her friends on a daily basis and ignored my rules to inform me when she would be entertaining her guests. Why does she have this much confidence and power? Longman kept ringing her, crying about how he had nothing to eat. It surprised me how attentive she was to his needs. She would be so caring to him over the telephone and would arrange for him to have what he wanted. He was like her child. I don't remember my mother being this affectionate with me as a child. She would not make such an effort to ensure I ate for the night. His cost would be mine. It appeared he was struggling without her, and was unable to fend for himself. As a result, she decided to return home to care for him. It meant that I had to pay for the early return flight and her cargo at a time when we would have liked to save towards the baby. Nine weeks into the visit, she was on her way back to her husband and left me with all the bills to pay. I was relieved that she was gone. I rang dad as usual, but I heard no reply. I kept trying; it was really odd not to hear from him.

This was the day that my life changed into horror forever. I was felling unwell, but I was pregnant. I thought this must be part of the symptoms. I was so tired that I slept most of the day. I would wake up and within minutes was exhausted again and went back to bed.

I had this weird dream that I was travelling in a graveyard all by myself at night. I could see some people I recognised that had passed away from the revival church committing a burial. I woke and thought 'what an odd dream,' but went back to bed. After sleeping for so many hours, I decided to prepare a meal. I went into the kitchen. GA was at work and I was surprised by a sudden rush in the form of a dark shadow behind the kitchen door. It frightened me and I reacted in shock. It bothered me for the entire day. I knew I saw something. Oddly, after the experience I started to become afraid and I didn't understand why. To relieve the fear, I put the television on loud and opened the blinds for more sunlight, as it was a summer's evening.

I dismissed what had happened until GA came home from work. I told him what had happened. He laughed and thought maybe my bump was deceiving me. I found his idea humorous. We went to bed, only I had another dream. This time, I was in a church and every bench I sat on was collapsing in a domino effect. I was going down and I called out to the people for help, but they could not hear me. I was invisible to them. I woke up from the dream really disturbed, thinking that this was the second time I was having dreams about a cemetery and dead people. I got up and I had this immense fear. GA was fast asleep, but I stayed up for hours. When I tried to rest again, it was the same cemetery again. This time, I saw dead people carrying a black coffin on their shoulders in the night. It seemed they couldn't see me – I was invisible to them – but where they were taking the coffin I was unable to get there. I couldn't get past the gate. The following morning I explained to GA that throughout the night and the day before I had been experiencing really weird dreams. We decided that we would observe over the next few days to see if it was just a myth. I decided that it would be best if I slept in the day and kept awake at night because I was so terrified. The dreams continued in the day and at night; at this point I was getting really tired. Each time I had a dream I didn't want to go back to sleep. Another morning, I went to prepare my breakfast. As I walked towards the bedroom, the big shadow moved again. I screamed, but no one could hear me. I was trembling, my heart was beating so fast, my palms were sweating, and I started to cry. I telephoned GA to explain, "I have seen the shadow again; it is in the bedroom."

I was afraid to go in the bedroom. I had the sensation something was in my room. I called my friends round pretending it was for a social call. I was truly embarrassed to tell them that I was afraid to live in my own flat, riddled with nightmares and dark shadows moving about. It was peculiar; I had been living there for four years and never experienced any phenomena. I was desperate for help and decided to tell one of my friends the difficulties I was experiencing. She had some experience interpreting dreams, and she explained, "You are definitely under spiritual attack. Be careful; you are in a vulnerable condition. Someone has sent a curse upon your home; you must contact your mother, let her know in order that she will be able to seek help for you."

My mother was the last person I wanted to speak to about this. We were not getting on and I didn't want to ask her for any favours. However, this was a matter I couldn't handle myself. I don't believe in curses, witchcraft, or the paranormal – I believe it is a load of rubbish, just idle conversation. Moreover, who had I offended to inflict such a plague? I carried out my plan to eat well and rest more, especially in the days. I went to sleep that day and behold I had a dream of my unborn child, lying on the bed beside me when the head came off from its body, bounced off the bed and landed on the floor. I got up in frustration and I started to believe there was something wrong with me. Were these signs that I was not going to have a successful birth? I went to my midwife and explained to her that I was hallucinating. The midwife suggested a relaxation technique. It had now been nearly a week and I had not slept properly; my distress was affecting the baby. The fright became more prevalent, even when GA was home. We would be having a conversation and then the dark shadow would pass in a quick flash from the corner of my eye. I would see it and then react in hysterics: "Oh my God!" Sometimes, I tried my best to be quiet about it, trying not to upset him or be seen as insane. GA was not sure; as it was my first child, this may be a natural reaction. I lived in constant fear in my home. The effects were visible – around my eyes were dark circles, I started to get anaemic again, and the worry would not allow me to eat well.

GA began to get really concerned. He said, "This is not good for you or the baby; you will have to contact your mother immediately."

I rang my mother and told her the situation – the nightmares day and night and the shadows and movement in the flat. I rang her every day for hours explaining the dreams. She said, "Don't worry just eat and relax; you will be fine."

I was now in this situation where I was fine before, suddenly I was haunted in my own home and no one could help me. I was worried for the safety of my child. My mother was not helping me or making any realistic suggestions, saying, "You will be fine" just like everyone else.

I had two weeks to the delivery. I was exhausted. The baby was not moving as usual because of the bad dreams and health issues. I became paranoid visiting the midwife, visiting my doctor and then the hospital. The entity in my flat was taking over. I had become weak with the pregnancy, and was losing the fight. I didn't know what to do about it. I asked my mother and she suggested lighting a red candle, praying, and reading a psalm – any one. The religion and background she was from was the revival church, whose motto is "REVIVING FROM DEAD WORKS TO RIGHTEOUSNESS." That is a very powerful mission statement and she was very useless. What was the point her being there? I tried to help myself by researching I became even more confused. Could I be hallucinating due to the pregnancy? Or was I under attacked by the force of the devil?

The dreams were getting worse. I frequently dreamt of walking on a bridge and falling into the river and dying. This dream was so frequent that when I visited the bridge in my dream, I would get down on all fours and crawl across, but I would still manage to fall off and be defeated. I would also dream of a dead member from the revival church rising from his grave to frighten me in a hide and seek frenzy. I was sometimes having up to five different dreams a night, one after the other, not making any sense. I realised I was not mad or hallucinating. I wanted to prove this to myself by confronting the issue. When I had a dream, I would get up, go to the toilet, have a snack, watch TV, and go back to bed, yet the dream would continue like resuming a movie placed on pause. When the phenomena of the dark shadow scaring me moved in the flat, I would try to confront it in the direction it went. But this was challenging, as the sudden fear that arose as soon as this happened was overwhelming. It was the same sensation of the head rising and goosepimples as when Mrs A died and I was not able to enter the room. I decided I would take the Holy Bible and read the psalms my mum suggested while entering the room. I tried to be brave and sat on the bed with the Bible in my hand. As I sat there confronting the demon, my legs were shivering with cold shooting up my leg and at the same time my head was expanding – a really weird experience. I quickly ran out the room and called my mother and said this was really happening. She said, "I am praying for you. The lord will help you. Just make sure you say a prayer before you go to bed."

I said, "Is that all you can recommend? All this time you have been telling me to pray and read my Bible and nothing has changed."

I didn't want to talk about it with friends anymore. They were talking about me going mad. I was now convinced evil existed. I had to do something about it. I didn't know where to go and I preferred not to get involved with anything that could affect my child. I went to Seven Sister's Road market and there was a man there who sold incense. I asked him what it was for and he told me for clearance in the house. He recommended incense to drive out the evil spirit. After receiving the lecture about the paranormal, it was like going through one ear and coming through the other. I was just desperate for normality in my home. I couldn't continue to be tortured anymore. It felt as if something was trapped inside my body and I was desperate to rip it out. I opened up to him about my dreams and the dark forces in my home. He confirmed that there was definitely the sign of an entity in my home. I asked, "How would it have entered?"

He said, "It was planted or sent."

I asked, "Could you recommend where I can get assistance for clearance?" He gave me contacts, but I was not comfortable with this. I was entering into something I knew nothing about and it was weird. I prayed and hoped that what I bought would be sufficient. I was very anxious to get home that day. I lit the incense smoke in every corner and room of the flat at 6pm in the evening and the procedure was to be carried out for seven days. I went to bed that night hoping for a difference – no difference. I dreamt of a girl about seven years old standing in the corner of the room. It seemed we were somehow related. This was followed by a black bull chasing me. Over the next seven days – nothing. The shadows were still rampant and the fear I experienced was dreadful. I was constantly on edge; every sign of movement caused my heart to skip a beat. It was even more terrifying as I was heavily pregnant and I couldn't defend myself.

The baby was due in a week. I was so nervous that I started to pray every day leading up to the birth. The time had come, but the baby was not ready. I was induced two weeks later; my gorgeous baby girl arrived. I had some minor complications, but it was fine. She was alive and well. I was worrying about nothing. I thought that definitely it was a myth due to the pregnancy. I was admitted in hospital for three days. I was looking forward to going home and being a mum. GA was ecstatic with his daughter and was so emotional. Everything seemed to have gone back to normal. I was so busy the first few days adapting to this new way of life, what a relief. It is Nigerian tradition to have a baby naming ceremony in seven days. The ceremony is similar to a christening. We had decided to name our daughter Rachel. I was exhausted and weak. I was more worried about the baby – she was so tiny. GA rang his parents with the good news. He had not told them I was expecting a child, so it was a real surprise for his parents. They celebrated the arrival of their first grandchild. I rang my mother and told her the news. She said, "I wish I was there to hold my granddaughter and look after you."

I ignored her comment; she must imagine me as a real fool, wasting my money for her to be here in the first place for the birth. She ran back to her husband to babysit him because that was more important and now she had the nerve to mention she would have liked to have been here? She had no discretion, and was inconsiderate and heartless. Obviously she thought we had a lot of money to waste. I was able to have dreamless sleep and no fear. I was confused; it could have been a hallucination, but I felt fine now. I just had to wait and see what happened when we returned home.

We arrived home as proud parents. GA was such an expert, he knew how to wash the baby and fed her instantly. He also took care of me and prepared the meals, as I was still recovering from the sedatives. That night I slept well, but not for long; the dreams started again. The most significant dream of all occurred in the morning on the seventh day of the ceremony. The dream was set in Jamaica. Next door to the Promised Land, I saw a hut made from wood. These are frequently used in the marketplace; it had a huge opening to the front like an open window, and I could see everything. A slim man appeared inside the hut. I could see him all the way to his knee in a strange attire. It was like an African native that I have seen before; it was a brown cloth with one sleeve decorated with feathers and odd looking beads. He was very slim and was preparing something for me – he was a bush doctor! What was he doing? I wouldn't accept anything from this strange man, but then my mother appeared. I thought this shop was odd in the dream. There were various different dried dead animals, possibly for sale, hanging from the window. A dead dried snake hung from the ceiling. The man used a knife and cut a piece of the flesh and presented it to me to consume from the tip of the knife.

I said, "I am not having that."

The man laughed. He tried again and I said no.

This dream was so real. He gave it to me again and I refused for the third time and then woke up from my dream. I wanted to rest as much as I could as the naming ceremony was in the evening. I fed the baby and fell asleep and continued that same dream; it was as if they were waiting for me. They knew I would not accept eating that muck, so they used GA to trick me and persisted by showing that the medicine was good. If GA was having it, then it would be fine for me. I watched GA tasting it and he said try it. I did; it was weird. I tasted it and it had a flavour like salt and the meat was gritty on my tongue. I never until this day had a dream where I could taste and feel, unfortunately I gave in. The next day after the ceremony, I remembered the dream and told GA that I had a weird dream and he was involved in it. I had to eat a snake and the dream was so real that I tasted the salty flavour on the tip of my tongue. Is this part of the African tradition? He replied, "No." This was unusual, so I rang my mother and asked her what it meant and why was the dream so real? She said, "Oh that is a good sign. It means GA's parents are protecting you and the baby from the evil forces."

She seemed really pleased and I thought that's really good of them to do this. I hoped I would be cured from whatever the spell was that I had been experiencing. GA was very concerned about this dream; he too had some experience from Africa about voodoo and he told me that the protection my mother mentioned was definitely not from his parents. Snake was not used for that type of ritual. It was more for bonding together, and moreover he had not told his parents of my experience or that he was expecting a child – it made no sense. I believed my mother was useless anyway; she hadn't a clue what she was talking about. The dreams continued to appear, but since I had the baby they seemed less frequent. Maybe I was very busy and forgot most of them. I was not seeing the shadows, but my instinct told me they were not far off. As a result, I wasn't prepared to take any chances. I would not leave the baby through the night on her own. I watched her at all times, just in case I was unsure about what was happening.

GA and I were coping quite well. We had a routine that worked really well for us; the plans were as soon as the baby was old enough, I would complete my Master's. The dreams were getting stronger again, but strange. Before it was more about a graveyard and dead people, now it was about me having sexual orgies with various women. I would meet a woman but I could not see her face completely. She would caress me and I would be fully aroused to the point I was gyrating until I woke up. When I woke up, I would be so disgusted with myself. I wanted to know where the hell this type of thought was coming from. I would examine what I watched on the television, read or ate. I started to check myself. Was I losing control of myself? I found it difficult and embarrassing to explain in full detail to my mother and GA each time I got these dreams.

The more intense the dream became, my mother would also appear in some of them controlling me, trying to hit me, threatening that I must do as she says or else what she would do. In most of them I would swear at her and tell her where to go. She had no right to tell me how to live my life, but it was more of an intimidation technique. I refused to be told, especially by her, how to live my life and it was just a dream. The dreams were obviously not going away. It was not a hallucination due to the baby. As I write this book and remember some of these atrocious experiences, it makes me cringe in horror. It was like I was living in two worlds – one in my dreams and then reality. I prefer reality; at least I can understand and ask questions. With the other side, no one could give me a straight answer. This part of my story is so emotional for me. The more I tell the story, it is like stirring the darkness in my subconsciousness. It brings out extreme frustration. I have to clasp my hands tight to avoid explosion and pain. I am so tense going back; it is disturbing. I now realise this was one of the worst parts of my life.

Things were happening to me that a doctor could not cure. I didn't know where to turn and there was no help, not even from my mother. It was as if I had an unusual disease in my head. I started to notice a slight change in mine and GA's relationship, but as explained from other experienced mothers, your body will change and you will be more bonded with the baby and have less time for your partner sexually and in other ways. I started to feel irritated when he tried to make sexual innuendo. My love for him had not changed; I still loved him as always. He was very patient and understanding. He thought it was the changes and coped really well, until months passed and things were not improving. Whenever he tried, I would be so angry with him and found it repulsive. I was dreaming a lot more about the sexual orgies. It escalated not only with women, but also men. I detested this experience. It was sort of forced upon me. What was wrong with me, was I losing sexual direction? This put me in a foul mood, for the rest of the day, shouting at GA. Obviously, I couldn't share with him what was going on in my sick dreams all the time. I didn't know how to stop these dreams. It was now affecting my relationship. I started to behave really aggressively and angry all the time, especially with GA

– everything he did was wrong and stupid to me. I constantly kept throwing verbal abuse and I don't know why. I was so out of control. He put up with it for a long while and then would retaliate.

"What is your problem?" he said. "I am trying to make you happy, I help you with the baby so not to stress you out and you are pouncing on me continuously."

There was something on my mind which was making me depressed, irritable, and anxious. It was like I had been given a prescription from the doctor that was having an adverse reaction. I couldn't identify what it was, then it became worse. I was also pouncing on people I didn't know, like road rage. I would get out of the car and bang on some driver's window for overtaking me. I also became antisocial to my friends. I didn't want to see anyone. This erratic behaviour carried on for a while. The only consolation was my daughter. I enjoyed every moment, and I was certain it was not postnatal depression. It had been nine months – my behaviour had not changed. I loved GA the same, but not sexually. I would dismiss the subject entirely. When we tried, I would tell him how useless he was at it; however, he was perfect before. I told my mother everything – how irritated I was.

I decided that the baby was old enough to attend nursery in order for me to return to university to complete my Master's degree. My mother made a suggestion that she was available at the moment and instead of wasting all that money on childcare, it would be better for her to take care of the baby during this time. She promised she would do her best. I thought no, we will manage. I couldn't imagine sending my baby far away and I didn't trust her to take care of her. GA was delighted with the idea. I was not convinced. I didn't like the environment. I told him the history of my mother and when I was a child, but he insisted, I was overreacting. He said my mother loved me and she would certainly love her granddaughter. We could always visit; after all, she wouldn't be there for long – just a year. I still was not sure. My mother seemed so caring and helpful over the telephone. She suggested that we could use this time to save and complete my studies, which would help us towards the future. I thought long and hard and we decided we would take her to my mother. It was so hard; I had sleepless nights.

We went together and during our visit, we decided to invest. We bought a truck, hoping that this would help us towards retirement and an emergency plan now that we had a child. This was GA's first time to Jamaica; I introduced him to Longman and some of the other relatives. We all sat on the veranda on the Promised Land one evening. My mother brought up the conversation about how brilliant some children were who had done well and who loved their parents to the extent that they bought them anything they wanted. I didn't understand, but GA did and was furious. She was suggesting we buy her a house.

GA replied, "How old is this girl you are suggesting to buy a house? Where do you expect her to get that sort of money from at her age? As parents you should still be supporting her, not demanding."

She dismissed the subject after GA told me that he was very disappointed with my mother, especially her situation. What was the role of her husband? I was very embarrassed. I brought GA to introduce him to my family and enjoy our holiday. There my mother was flexing her muscles again, and I believe she thought GA was an easy target to use as she liked, but I would have none of it. She wanted to be in control as usual. She managed to get her brother to be the driver. He had the same greedy traits as her and most of the money from the contract was squandered in the betting shop. He also committed fraud by cashing the cheques that were written in our names and then had the audacity to call us in the UK to maintain the truck that should be parked, i.e. new tyres, broken axle, while he ran his errands. We thought if the truck was not profitable and parked, why are we paying for all these maintenances? And he was a real good liar. Before we entered into an agreement when my mother created this business, GA was not interested because he felt we might be conned. My mother was very abrupt with GA and said, "What are you talking about, my brother is not a thief. He is just trying to help you, don't talk about my brother like that again."

GA was still seeking my mother's approval by adhering to her wishes. She got away with it all. That was how we started the business and it ended disastrously. We didn't plan to start such a big business, but my mother had made an arrangement with her brother that we would give him a job. The truck was wrecked, we were robbed, and my mother turned a blind eye. I asked why she kept the truth from us, as the business was on the verge of collapse because of her brother's actions. We could have employed someone else before it had come to this, and she said, "After all, I didn't tell you to go and buy a truck, not my problem."

It was only God that saved me from lifting my hand to strike her down. She had the audacity to deny her involvement when she was the one who arranged this for her loving brother. I don't know what was wrong with me, but I kept falling into ridiculous traps. After the truck, I tried another business to assist her husband in order that they would be able to fend for themselves. I didn't want to take on the responsibility. I could only assist them, but after what had happened why did I bother when the husband wasn't in a position to drive a car. He was constantly intoxicated. We bought the car and asked GA to go on a test drive with Longman. When they returned, he told me he was fine. It was years later that GA confessed that he was so happy to return to the house alive. His experience with him was dangerous. Longman was highly intoxicated with alcohol, but he knew if he told me I would not have allowed Longman to carry on with the job and my mother would have been angry with him and probably hurt him. The same result occurred with the taxi – it was wrecked and abandoned, and mother did nothing to protect or consult me, even though I did this for her own interest to put food on her table. It was as if she was instigating all these businesses to be pompous to her friends and family. The love that GA had for me, meant he was trying desperately hard to please my mother. He told me from this point he realised she was secretly manipulating him. There was nothing he could do, she would not accept him and our relationship was in danger.

GA was in a battle with my mother, which I had no idea about. When I spoke with her about him, she would say: "That boy is such a loving and lovely guy I know he really loves you and I know he is one of the best sons-in-law, thank God for him."

GA one day explained to me that my mother did not approve of our relationship. I said to him this was a load of nonsense. She accepted him as her son. He said "No."

I couldn't believe what he was saying. Was he being paranoid? I asked myself the question over and over. I was not close to my mother, apart from telling her every dream I had and we talked about my health, and the latest gossip. I didn't have any feeling towards her, no love, so why did I leave my only child with her? What had changed for me to trust her with the life of my only child after the history of my childhood with her and the demands she was making? I was going over and above to fulfil them. Remember, this was a mother who could not care less how I lived my life when I returned to the UK. I was not important to her. The physical abuse I suffered as a child, she had no care in the world for my future. Doesn't this make me stupid? I searched deep into myself. I felt trapped all of a sudden. My life of happiness and exuberance came crashing down. I was laid down with my mother's burden. It was about buying her a house, and I was tied to her through my child. How in God's name did I get myself in this position? It was like a nightmare and I was not sleeping. I found myself constantly depressed without a reason on a daily basis. I sat and searched my thoughts, asking myself why am I depressed? Was it because my child was staying with her? My thoughts would always go to how my mother was going to manage when Rachel returned. She also constantly gave innuendos about the Promised Land being repossessed by the government and I would have to find her a place to live soon. The pressure was so bad that I would wake up in the middle of the night out of my sleep just thinking about this. It was weird, because it was not important to me. This was not my problem. I needed to be thinking about my home and life first. What had been her plans? Why did her problem become my burden? When we talked together, she would tell me how the house was depressing, the government was coming to take away the Promised Land. It was as if she was trying to paint a picture that I needed to hurry and get a place or my child would be on the street. She understood I would do anything for my child and she was using that. I had also been taunted in my dream about how she would be thrown out. I was so young, I couldn't afford all this. She told me that if I assisted her, which was what I did when we had two failed businesses, she would be able improve her life.

It was now affecting GA. He had to get involved. He accepted that we had to do something as she was my mother and was trying to help us with our daughter. This was unfair on him. We began enquiring about a new home that we might be able to afford. My mother was using my child to manipulate us and take everything she desired in her life. The next agenda – she wanted a visa to travel to the States to find work. That was a great idea. She would become independent and enjoy her life, and this would also be the perfect opportunity for my daughter to return home. I arranged to take Rachel so that she could get on with her life. I knew she would miss her granddaughter, but at least she would be improving the standard of her life. I applied for the visa and when she arrived in the USA it was different a story. She appeared to be on a holiday and shopping spree at my expense, visiting friends and family and receiving gifts to cargo back to Jamaica, and of course I would be paying. I was very annoyed and rang her. I asked, "What is your plan or has it changed? I heard, which you did not discuss with me, that you were on holiday."

She said, "Oh, I changed my mind. Things have not worked out as planned."

I asked, "What are you going to do, give up?"

She replied, "I am just going to take the baby back home with me."

I didn't argue. She obviously had made her decision, but I began to feel like she was taking my child away from me and using my child to swindle whatever she wanted from me. Some of the demands were just ridiculous. It had been a year and now I had finished my Masters' degree. It was time for Rachel to return, but things had taken a turn for the worse.

Chapter 8

During this time, the nightmares were now becoming a reality. GA thought that my intense behaviour was probably postnatal depression and my mother taking the child may have resolved the situation, but in fact it became worse. I was more aggressive towards him. We had really bad fights. I kept throwing a lot of verbal abuse at GA and sometimes physical abuse. Only God knows how he was putting up with it. I can remember some of the incidents. The rest GA tells me the stories of what he was experiencing. I felt terrible about my actions, but I didn't understand what was happening to me – I had no control of myself. The dark shadows seemed to have gone, but the nightmares were at their worst. The new phenomena were during the dreams. There were times I would be pinned down. I drifted off to sleep and then I would be struggling to get up. My eyes were open and fixated on the ceiling. Every muscle and limb in my body was lifeless. I tried to speak and the words would not come out. I recited every prayer I knew under the sun and I would not be released. Someone told me a theory once that it is more scientific than spiritual when this happens – "your body is ahead of the brain." It made sense to me at the time, because I was unable to give a real explanation for what was happening. This strangling became frequent and I decided to journal the encounters. There wasn't a pattern to forecast the next attack – sometimes it was twice a week, once a month, or two months later. Then GA had an encounter with the same experience.

"It was horrific. I have never experienced anything like this in my life," he said.

This proved I was not a complete lunatic. He described to me how dreadful it was to be pinned down to the bed. He had just decided to have a nap, and it wasn't long before he realised he was struggling in broad daylight to get up.

"I felt like I was suffocating, I was struggling to get up and every limb in my body was weakened, then eventually I was released."

The dreams kept coming. It was as if it had gone to another black cat or black cow charging towards me. The most upsetting ones seemed so real, like when at the scene of a tsunami I can see the sea rising as high as the mountain – I know that I am going to die so I clench my fists and close my eyes tight in preparation for my death, which is when I would wake up. There have been countless times I died in my dreams. When I woke up from such dreams I would become paranoid throughout the day and cautious of everything I do – how I crossed the street or drove extremely carefully. I developed this peculiar sense as if there was an invisible guide interpreting the dreams, like someone protecting me and saying, "you need to be careful today."

I would hear this in my subconsciousness and for this reason I would be extra careful and vigilant. Blood on my hands or fire was also extremely significant. This guaranteed for that day that there would be conflict and it could be anyone. This would be my warning. Sometimes it revealed the person I was going to have the altercation with. By now, I had experienced 100's of dreams – I had learnt so much that I could now detect a warning or danger. I was unaware of the hidden spiritual gift. I discovered that the dream I had been experiencing was a warning of spiritual danger that was happening in my life and what was to come. Because I was inexperienced, I was confused and lacked a guide to train me in order to fully develop my gifts. The anger and rage was because of the spirits that had been sent to attack me in the flat; it gave me the feeling of unease and irritation I had no experience as to how to fight back, even though I had the gift. Moreover I was not interested and

I didn't want to get involved. There is no doubt that spiritual wickedness does exist. I was under attack and it has taken years for me to accept that. I sought to find a minister to come to the flat; I explained to him all the paranormal activities, when it started and the type of dreams. He was accompanied by his brethren and he prayed and prayed. After, he told me the result.

He said, "Something spiritual has been buried in this flat, and we need to locate it in order to remove the entities."

I thought 'what is he talking about? No one stays in my flat to have the opportunity to carry out such an act.'

I instantly distrusted him. He gave me a prescription and that was it. I carried out the instruction he left. The dreams continued, but with a difference – I was no longer afraid. I felt I was in control. I was confronting the demons and defeating them, sometimes with a sword in my dream or in tongues (speaking in an unknown language that affected the entity and it understood) or with my bare hands. I continued to tell my mother all that was going on in my dreams. She was interested to hear all of them, but did nothing to help. This new development evolved into seeing others in the dream, with Mrs B was frequently appearing. I thought how odd. I dismissed it, there was no way she was involved in such things. However, our parents were from the same society, she was converted in the past and now retreated. And what would be her motive? I assumed I had left her house never to return. She had done me a favour and I should have been submissive, although I was rejected from the family. It was my success – "I will not be able to go to university due to my background" as suggested. What had been predicted as an excuse for my departure – partying, drinking, drugs – had caused a huge embarrassment in as much as I was confronted by a letter from her to pay back my fare when I returned to the UK. I can honestly admit I did not hold a grudge, I really appreciated what they had done when they took me into their home when I was on death's door. If they had not accepted, I probably would not have had the opportunity to escape my corrupted background. I cannot blame Mrs B for her actions. She had children of her own. She was a fantastic mother to them. But I was not her child, my mother was responsible for my life. I would not have been in this situation had she carried out her role. They had given up on me. They had all right to; after all, it was a favour, no obligation. It was up to my mother to resolve the fallout between Mrs B and I. It had left a bad taste and an apology or forgiveness would have eased the grudge. Instead on my visit, my mother condemned me and like she does best, ignored the situation, pretended that everything was fine without resolving the issue with Mrs B. My motive could've been wrong. I had been having dreams about how I would go back to her house, how it was when I returned to the UK. I saw myself slaving away by washing her floors on my knees and running around being her servant. When I woke up, I would be really upset. Why was I revisiting the past and each time, the dream was the same. I don't even think about this woman. Why were these dreams continuously reoccurring?

The most peculiar thing happened one day out of the blue. I heard my doorbell and to my surprise it was her. She explained that she had run out of change and was wondering if I would lend it to her. This was shocking – if you did not have enough change, wouldn't you find the nearest cash machine or the sweetshop? Anyway, I didn't have any coins either. I had a five pound note, which would mean she needed to find change. I gave it to her, but this was still bizarre to comprehend. GA was there that morning as my witness. A month later, she returned to repay the five pounds. When she approached me, I had this overwhelming inner voice loud in my ears saying, 'do not accept it.' I said to her, "It's fine, you don't have to pay me back." She insisted strongly.

I refused, "You can use it for your bingo, on me." Two weeks later as I was on my way out, we met by the entrance door to the flats. She was again still offering to pay back the five pounds. As she reached in her handbag to get the money, the weirdest thing happened – it was as if she turned into a different person before my very eyes. It was happening in slow motion, like a dream. I said, "No thank you, don't worry about it," and moved away swiftly.

As I walked, I pinched myself. What on earth just happened there? I held my head straight without looking back. Was I going crazy? What was that? My protector, the inner voice, had shown me she was about to hand me a five pound note that would have harmed me. I started to think about the incident intensely and remembered the dreams. In one I went to her house for tea and she invited me in. When I sat down and had a sip of the tea in this white cup and saucer, I realised I was tranquilised. I tried desperately to escape, heading for her front door in slow motion and I struggled to escape. It seemed forever. I fought long and hard; my inner voice warned me not to enter her house. The dreams about me being her slave continued. I was not afraid I accept that she had a grudge and there was nothing I could do about it, but I will never be her slave – that is for sure. Nine years later, we met up again at a friend of the family's 60th birthday party. I remembered our last encounter and was very sceptical of her, but remained very polite and respectful. She responded well. I suddenly realised she was extremely agitated as if she was finding it very difficult to make eye contact with me during our very brief conversation. I asked, "How is the family?" That was it. I was there first and she came after. Within 10 minutes of us meeting, she decided that it was best for her to leave.

She said, "It is best I come another time." She left in a flash. What was wrong? Conscience perhaps, or something I was not aware of.

My sense of spiritual danger began to grow stronger. I was driving down Wood Green high street on my way home from work one evening. I saw two people that were affiliated with the revival church and that inner voice spoke again, and when this happened it was like the world paused or was in slow motion.

I heard the voice say, "You see those people crossing the street – be careful! They practise iniquity."

Strangely, I remembered I replied in amazement, "Hmmm?" The question I asked myself was how did I get myself involved in these spiritual shenanigans? I haven't done any rituals or been to see a bush doctor. This unusual phenomena that was guiding me, where has it been all this time and why me? How was it activated? Then I gathered it was always there – the warnings, the endless dreams, the dark shadow, the sensations felt – it had always been there. The attacks sent to me were revealed in the dreams. I am oblivious to how powerful my gifts are and what I can do. I really don't want to know. I am satisfied with my life so far and feel really blessed to have such a guide, but I don't want to commit myself to a society which involves rituals and ceremonies. It would seem like having a life of the living dead. Although I am alive, my frequent encounters are with the dead in the spirit world. I want to be in the real world without any chains or shackles, free-minded and able to express myself in a way I please, not living under any rules or subjection.

The strangling and suffocation had become frequent. I put up such a fight that sometimes when I woke up I was in pain and had lost strength in my body. I hated this experience – I was completely defenceless. I continued to tell my mother about these experiences and her advice was to pray and she would continue to pray for me as well.

She said, "God is good and he will deliver you." I was really missing my daughter Rachel. I made frequent visits to Jamaica to see her. On my visits, most of the time I would be very depressed. I was not happy with the environment; although she was taken care of, I felt I wanted more for my only child and it was my responsibility to provide it for her. The decision to take her home was daunting. All the excuses in the world would appear in my head: my home was not big enough, we needed to make more money, and private education was more affordable in Jamaica. I had to really think about this. What was my problem? I could look after my child without my mother's patronising comments. GA and I were managing. When I suggested Rachel's return to my mother, it was negative. We had an agreement for the child to be there for a while. My mother would say, "Anyway I know that is what GA wants, to take her from me!"

I said, "It is not his choice only, I want my daughter home."

She would show such a dominating attitude, and be really nasty and patronising saying, "Anyway that is how people always use me, and dump me."

What was she saying? This was my daughter – I would not have allowed her to go in the first place if GA hadn't insisted. Now I was having a problem to get my daughter back.

This was my only child. She suggested as a grandmother to help us, like most grandparents genuinely would, and I thought it was a good idea. So in return I offered to pay her a wage to look after her grandchild, instead of her running around doing the most ridiculous odd jobs. I realised she had other plans. This was the way she would use me to get what she wanted from us. My mother cannot be satisfied. She would dig and dig endlessly, was greedy without a conscience and had no love for anyone but herself. My brother had passed away 8 years before at this time. My mother never spoke about him or visited his grave. I knew of families where mothers had lost their children, even at a young age, many years beforehand and they still remembered the date of death and had a picture for memory or something else. My mother did not have a picture of her son, even from birth. The week before he died, according to the story I heard, he had a premonition of his death. He took a picture and gave it to her and said, "I took this picture for you to remember me." He was also subdued and distant like someone who was in trouble. I asked for the picture when I attended his funeral. Unfortunately, it was lost during the move from Mrs B's. That was the only memory we had. My mother told everyone I was the only child she had. Why did she hate my brother so much? I asked her for my brother's date of birth and she struggled to remember. She had forgotten and told me to enquire from Aunt V, as she was the person who registered his birth when she left him at age of two so she could be with my father in the UK. I had dreams of my brother. It was weird – I was so happy to see him. He said, "Beg you for a drink."

I said, "What type of drink?"

He told me. I called my mother for the interpretation. She said he was asking for a memorial called (*Tombing*) in Jamaica. It is a period of time after the burial where you would have a gathering at the graveside to add a headstone or modification and clean the area. On my next trip, I arranged for it to be done.

Chapter 9

Mine and GA's relationship took a turn for the worse. I loved him with all my heart and I knew the feeling was mutual. My inner voice and dreams were suggesting we were going to have great difficulties in our relationship, in which we were going to be separated. I was devastated that I was conscious of the warning. I kept imagining this was a myth. Why would we break up? Everything was fine at the moment. I became agitated and protective. This man was my rock; I didn't believe this. My tantrums and arguments had escalated. Deep down, I felt something was going wrong. I didn't know what it was and it was making me really angry. I became withdrawn, and kept to myself. The thoughts were growing stronger each day. I was observing, but GA's behaviour had not changed towards me – he was the same. I believed in what my inner voice suggested. I was devastated to know that this was the man that I had been through so much with, and I was going to lose him. He also told me that he was having a weird feeling about the future of our relationship. He believed we were rock solid and had nothing to worry about. He said, "I am not going anywhere babe, from the day I became committed to you, and now we have a child together. It is not possible to split. I promised you that I would always be there for you."

I would ask, "Where are you going? What time are you getting back?"

Calling him more frequently, I wanted to be with him wherever he went. I had become overprotective. I was sometimes very annoyed with myself. I felt like a nuisance watching over him. He had done nothing for me to distrust him. I didn't understand this ridiculous thought. I was happy with him; I didn't have eyes for another man and he was loyal. As always, it was the fear of the unknown.

I told my mother about the fear and anxiety in my relationship. She did not express much concern, but encouraged me to make frequent trips to Jamaica. She said, "Your daughter is missing you; you need to come and see her."

She was not interested in how expensive these trips where. It would be sensible for my daughter to come home. Then I began to realise when I got there that it had nothing to do with my daughter. My mother was using the opportunity to receive gifts and be ostentatious to her friends on my expense. I realised she had no conscience. The amount of expenses that were accumulating was having a negative impact, as well as leaving GA sometimes four times a year because of my daughter; and I fell for it all the time.

I sat on the beach alone one day and reflected on my life. It wasn't going the way I had planned; it was like entrapment – my daughter was taken from me. Every emphasis was about Jamaica. I didn't plan to live in Jamaica; I was very happy staying at home in the UK. I would embark upon some ridiculous programmes like enquiring about citizenship, businesses in Jamaica, etc. I didn't have any interest in any of this. I felt like my soul or body was on autopilot and being remotely controlled. I was embarking upon a territory that I had no interest in. My trips were as if I was forced. I was only going for the sake of my daughter. Once I arrived, I would say to myself, "What the hell am I doing here again?" My mood changed and I would get into a strop. I hated being around this woman. I would meet my mother at the airport, we would be fine for at least an hour, but it was guaranteed we would get into a fight not long after. It was like my daughter was the only connection that kept us together. When I returned to the UK, I would discuss my frustration with GA. He wanted me to make the decision, but I was confused every time I got back. The strangling entity continued and there was no improvement in our sex life. The dreams were now as plain as day, like watching a movie. I dreamt that I was involved in a threesome with GA in our bed. I woke up freaked out; I didn't need an interpreter to tell me what it meant. I knew there was a third party in our life. I immediately asked GA if was he having an affair. He told me, "No, who would be interested in somebody like me?"

I didn't notice anything unusual; he came home on time and followed a normal routine on Friday night to the pub with friends. When I would call him he was always there. One Friday night, GA went out with friends as usual and would normally return at about 3:00am. He came back on time, but in those days smoking was allowed in most amenities and the stench on his clothes was horrendous. I told him, "Go and have a shower or put your smoky clothes outside on the balcony."

He was drunk and replied, "Oh… don't worry I will sleep on the settee," and he dragged himself and lay there.

I thought that has to be better than sleeping beside smoke fumes. I never went into a deep sleep when he was out. I lay back down to sleep. It took me a long time to sleep, especially when I had already had a nap. I turned the light off, then I saw a figure move at the doorway in the reflection shining from the outside light and it was instant – no human being could move that quickly from the bedroom door to the bed and then the strangling began. This time I was not asleep and I felt the sensation. The entity was trying to kiss me and I could feel the lips on my cheek; I was defenceless. I struggled to keep one eye open. I wanted to see what it was. I was pinned down on my side. I fought it, but it had the strength of a man and was overpowering; it was like being suffocated. I called out to GA, but he couldn't hear me. When it decided to release me, I tried to lift my head, but my body was still lifeless. I was upset and ran to GA. I told him, "I saw him!"

I was afraid to sleep alone on the bed. "Please come back to bed," I pleaded. I didn't mind the smoke, I was afraid to go to sleep. I stayed awake until the morning. Weak and tired and fed up, I rang my mother and told her about it. As usual I received the odd comment. I was annoyed with her and I said, "You are no help and you are in that society."

Then she said, "Read a psalm and light a red candle."

GA's movement began to change. He was very busy throughout the whole weekend from Friday to Sunday and when I suggested I come along, he was abrupt and refused. I asked, "Are you seeing someone?"

He said, "Just because you cannot come along with me doesn't mean I am having an affair."

But I was feeling his distance and I couldn't be sure. He had never hurt me in this way and I knew that I had been overprotective for a while, so I gave him the benefit of the doubt. But his movements where changing drastically – he would be late for Valentine's Day or in a hurry to be somewhere else on our dates. I was convinced he was having an affair. I was devastated. My warning was correct; he was like a completely different person. This was not the same GA. He became so cold and I couldn't say anything to persuade or change his mind when he was going out. He would just smile and leave me shouting. I was in so much pain it was like my whole world was crashing down.

It was difficult to prove the affair. I couldn't keep track of his movement. I tried to do things that he enjoyed, made nice meals, and invited him out, which most of the time he declined because he had a busy schedule. The only consolation was that he came home every night. I wondered to myself, what I have done to make him change? I thought maybe it was my attitude, the constant tantrums, and worst of all our intimacy, which was zero. It has to be the lack of physical relationship. So I decided to improvise and make the effort to seduce him and something terrible happened.

Whenever he touched me, I was very irritated and barked and when we tried to have sexual intercourse, it was as if sand was poured inside of me followed by blood oozing out of me. I knew I was in trouble. I went to the hospital for an examination to find out what was wrong with me. I was told I had endometriosis and was referred to have an operation, which did not cure my symptoms. I had a further two operations and it became worse. I was stressed out and the usual remedy was to go to Jamaica to see my daughter. It was also convenient to be my Aunt Lily's chief bridesmaid; she was getting married after 28 years with her partner. She was my favourite aunt, and was like a best friend to me as a child. I was very pleased for her and was delighted to be her chief bridesmaid. I hadn't told her of my problems, but deep down the pain was unbearable. I knew while I was out of the country, he would have the opportunity to get on with his infidelity, which was now out of control.

I confided in my mother about the anguish and what I was going through. She was more interested in whether GA was continuing with the upkeep and maintenance of his daughter. As long as he was continuing to do this (and by extension continue providing for her), she was fine. My aunt suspected something was wrong; I was not my usual chirpy self. One evening when I visited her after the wedding, she called me aside and we had a one-to-one chat. She spoke about my mother, her sister. She was very disappointed with the way she chose to live her life. She believed my mother should be more responsible, as I was her only child, and come back to UK to live with me. She said, "I wish I had the opportunity she had, my life would be so much better."

I felt my aunt wanted to tell me something, but she was not clear. She gave me advice to continue my life with GA and gave us both her blessings. She had such a good heart. "GA is a good man and if you need assistance with anything I would be glad to help." On this same day on my way to my aunt, I had an accident in the car where I was haemorrhaging. I called my aunt and said, "I don't know why this has been happening."

She quickly ran inside, gave me a wash, cleaned the car, and gave me her special herbal tea. I looked at my aunt and in my mind I thought, I wish you were my mother, even though she had four girls of her own. I felt well when I left the house. I had a real good time with my daughter, but I was still unwell. I kept spotting and losing so much blood. I though maybe the coil that was administered during the last operation had not settled. On my return to the UK, GA was still living at home. I went to see my friend about half a mile down the road as I was so lonely. Immediately upon stepping into her flat, she said, "You don't look so good."

I told her about my symptoms. She insisted that I should visit casualty right away, "You have gone grey."

I said, "Oh, I will go to the doctor's tomorrow."

She said, "Now!"

I went to hospital and had a test done. I thought it was the return of the anaemia. I waited and waited and the nurse and two other doctors returned. I needed to have a pregnancy test. I said, "I cannot be pregnant because I have an implant."

I did the test; the result unfortunately, was that I was seven weeks pregnant, but it was ectopic. My tube was ruptured severely. The doctors could not comprehend how I was able to travel without excruciating pain. I was told another day longer would have been fatal. I was admitted and an emergency surgery was performed to remove the foetus and the damaged tube. GA rushed to the hospital. He was in shock and supported and took care of me through my recovery. I was hoping this would be the breaking point, where he would get back to his senses, but as soon as I well enough, we were back to square one. This other life or whatever he was doing kept going on. I didn't know how to stop him. I threatened to leave him. I shouted and screamed. His reaction was what can she do; she cannot leave me. The dreams were still continuing – the orgy and this other woman that I kept seeing in my dream. We were sharing the same bed and sleeping with GA. This was so disturbing. Every weekend he would be gone. I would sit on the sofa watching television until 6am, just hoping to hear when he would put the key through the front door. Sometimes I would be in tears, terrified he may never return one day.

The same routine continued, but on this particular Friday I decided that I was going to sit in his car and he would have no choice but to take me. He told me, "It's OK, you can keep the car," and walked off.

I ran after him, but being 5 feet 4 inches and running after a man at 6 feet 2 inches was very challenging. I felt so frustrated; I wanted to be loved again. It was like he turned into a monster. I didn't understand him anymore. He was a new person. I didn't know what his intentions were. Lonely and low, I was looking for any opportunity – something that would make me feel like I existed again. As I was driving through Hackney high street one glorious summer's evening heading to Greenwich, this guy – a real show-off with his convertible Mercedes – stopped and started to have a conversation with me at the traffic light. To be honest, it took me by surprise. He asked how I was and I said "Fine." Usually I would've ignored him. He asked me what direction I was heading. I said, "Greenwich."

He said, "Oh, I am heading that way as well." The light changed and I thought does he think I am going to follow him? He was pompous anyway. I carried on down through the black wall tunnel and drew nearer to my destination. I ignored him, overtook him and headed off; this should have been an indication to him that I was not interested. I looked in the rear-view mirror and saw he intended to follow me. I increased my speed to get away, but he was determined. I reached my destination in Greenwich at the college where I was studying. Searching for a parking space, he was very persistent following me, just waiting for me to get out the car. Eventually I found a space. I thought 'what is his problem?'

He said, "Do you have far to walk?"

I said, "No," abruptly. He was trying to have a conversation.

I said, "I am running late for a lecture."

He said, "Take my number."

I took his number in anticipation that he would go. Although I was not interested in this guy, the experience made me feel like a woman and put me in a great mood – at least someone had interest. GA had lost interest and was attracted to someone else. The weekends were the same; by Friday evening off he went. I refused to put up with the rejection and called the persistent friend. I wanted to be with someone having a social life as well. I picked up the telephone. I felt nervous and confused: was this the right thing to do? I was almost hoping that it would have been the wrong number. The phone rang and he answered almost instantly. I said, "Hi it's me, the one you met by the traffic lights."

He was delighted; you could hear the excitement in his voice. We arranged to meet up in Greenwich for a meal that evening. I was nervous, my stomach kept turning. I wanted to look my best. This was a novelty, making the extra effort to go on a date. I couldn't remember what he looked like. At one stage, I almost turned back. On my arrival he was running late. As I waited I desperately tried not to look nervous. I forgot his name. Then he came up to me from behind and said hello. I said "Hi." He was so confident in himself; he looked at me as if I was undressed. He remembered my name. During our long conversation about Jamaica, which we had in common, I had to ask his name, which was embarrassing. His name was Mark. I wanted to know about him. He told me he was single at the time and I told him I was with someone. I didn't want to divulge that my relationship was in turmoil. He wanted to know more, but I decided not to talk about it. He was a cheerful character. I was happy to be in his company, but I knew it would be for a short while. I was not attracted to him. We had our meal and I set off for home. He insisted that he would call me. I told him that he should wait for my call, because I don't want him to call me as GA might be there. Unfortunately he had stored my number when I first called him. On my way home, he talked with me over the phone until I reached home to make sure I was safe. When I got in, GA was not home. I didn't feel lonely or sad. I'd had good evening and went to bed.

I now felt I had a solution to my problem when GA disappeared on the weekend. I had found a friend, but he was obstinate. He ignored my instruction to wait for my call and sometimes he called ten times a day. I wanted to hide this secret from GA. I still loved him. I didn't want to lose him, but I was looking for anything to keep me living. One day, GA was home and I forgot to turn the phone off. It rang several times. GA knew this was odd as I hardly received or made calls. I became nervous; I couldn't think of how to switch off the phone or ringer quick enough. GA asked, "Are you going to answer the phone?"

I said, "No it must be a sales call; it's not important." I was furious. It was as if Mark was intentionally trying to create problems for me. The more I told him to wait, it was like he couldn't help himself. I wanted to be in control, I told him I was involved with someone else. His explanation was he thought I would be at work. We met again two weeks later. GA was suspecting I was having an affair, but I could tell he wasn't sure. I wanted to know more about Mark. This would have been our second date. I believed he was lying about being single.

I said to him, "I find it very peculiar that a successful man is single, no commitment what is your past life?"

He paused.

"Do you have children?"

"Yes two."

"And where is their mother?"

"She's around."

"What does that mean?" I asked.

"I prefer not to talk about it."

I couldn't put my finger on it; there was a dark side to him that I didn't think I was going to like. It was deceitful and cold. My feelings toward him had not improved. I was just meeting with him to pass time when I was lonely. I eventually told him about the problems at home with GA. It was a relief to share the heavy burden I had on my shoulder; he showed empathy and gave me advice. Mark was getting worse, he was calling constantly throughout the day and would spend a long time on the phone. I just couldn't get rid of him. Then he told me one day he was cohabiting with his two children and I should not fall in love with him. I almost laughed – he should have noticed that I was not at all in love with him.

GA had had noticed that my routine had changed. He stayed in one weekend. When I returned home, he wanted to know where I had been. I said, "Out."

"Out with who and where?"

"With friends."

It was now like an interrogation. I said, "I don't know where you go every weekend, you don't tell me. Why are you interested?"

The phone rang and GA rushed and grabbed the phone before I got to it and heard Mark on the line saying, "Hello."

GA kept quiet for a while and then said, "So you are having an affair?"

I said, "Yes. What did you expect, treating me the way you do?"

GA asked, "How long has this been going on?"

I said, "A while."

"Tell me about this guy and how far gone is this relationship." I told him about Mark and the relationship and how I felt about him. GA was devastated to know I was seeing someone else, but I was glad that he found out. Maybe it would bring him to his senses. GA started to come to the realisation that the relationship was surely coming to end. It was awful we were both living a double life and we both knew about it. It was bizarre – this should have separated us, but instead we still cared for each other. I didn't hate him and he didn't hate me. I knew this was not the ideal life or relationship and I had to stop this nonsense. GA and I had a meeting and we decided that we had both been ridiculous and decided to end our third-party relationships and lead a normal life again. I had enough of this. I called Mark and told him that GA knew about him and I would like to end our relationship. I knew this would be hard for Mark to take in, as we had become very close. I called him and gave him the news. He was very cross with me for telling GA. I immediately thought, 'did Mark think I would be his playmate forever?' What kind of woman does that make me, living a double life which was only for convenience and I was not enjoying it? He also had a life. GA was considerate and thought if I had been seeing this guy for so long, we would have been close and he would give me some time for closure. Mark told me that same day I gave him the news that he understood and we should meet by Hackney where I planned to do some shopping for a quick chat for 'the last time.'

I agreed because I had to get back to make GA a meal. When I got there he was on time. He said, "Park up, let's talk in my car."

I sat in his car. I had rehearsed everything I wanted to say to him. We greeted each other knowing it would be the farewell. It was weird – it was like attending a funeral. Before I uttered a word, suddenly he said, "I won't be long, let me quickly dash over the river and collect something. We can talk on the way."

Without me even approving, he drove off.

I said, "No. I have to get back; you said we are having a discussion."

But he continued driving erratically and kept going. He went inside a shop in Hackney to collect I don't know what it was, and was there for such a long time. Then we got caught up in traffic. Before I knew it, time had gone and GA was at home waiting for me. It was Mark's plan all along to run off and ruin it for me. There was no way GA would believe that I had got over this guy. What he had done made me dislike him. GA would not accept my explanation; I couldn't convince him I had ended our friendship. He returned back to his double life. It was like moving five steps backwards. Even though GA was having an affair, it appeared as if I was the guilty one. This is always the case – it is acceptable when men have affairs, women are seriously ridiculed for such an act in my community. The reaction I had from friends and family was I shouldn't have had an affair to get back at GA; I should have broken off the relationship and started fresh with someone else or put up with it until he saw sense. As long as he came home that's fine; "that was a man's trait." So this made me a bad woman. I told my mother all that was happening. She was not happy with the situation, but her concern was about money. As long as he was paying his due, that was fine. I now knew that the chance I had to get back with GA was over. He would never believe me or forgive me – I had failed. Mark was like a pest. He had no sympathy for me. He knew I was heartbroken and wanted to get back with GA, but he was like the devil. Every move I made to make my relationship work, he found a way to destroy it and wanted to make sure that GA knew he was there for him to be gone. Mark decided to confess the truth. He had something to tell me. He was a married man living with his family. I was not surprised, but the most annoying thing was he wanted to crumble my relationship so I would be his mistress. I thought, 'enough is enough, I don't need this. I am going to break this off. I don't love him and the best way to see the back of him is to disappear for some time.' I rang him and said, "I am going away. I am now breaking off this relationship. Do not try to contact me again, even on my return to the UK."

The pain was unbearable. The entity in the flat had changed, it was like something else was added, a new phenomenon apart from what was there. Amongst the dreams and shadow there was a new sensation. It was like something came in revenge. It was hurting me, my body was aching with emotions. It was as if someone with very large feet had stepped on my heart and crushed it. I remember at one point it was so bad that I went down on my knees on all fours. I wept, no one could hear me. Something was controlling my mind, telling me that the other woman GA was seeing was fighting me spiritually. That night, as soon a GA got in, I told him.

"The woman you are seeing is performing witchcraft to inflict pain. I feel like I am physically fighting a spirit."

He shouted, "You are saying a load of rubbish!" and stormed out and didn't return until two days later. I had reached the pinnacle of this problem. There was no going back – the only solution was to book a flight to Jamaica.

Chapter 10

I arrived in Jamaica in so much pain. I had lost a lot of weight. I stayed in bed most days. I was so angry, especially towards my mother. My aggression spiralled out of control; it was so bad one day that I almost got arrested when an officer tried to use his authority on me and I thought I have a lot to think about other than to worry about where was appropriate to park in a car park. The parking bays are not clearly marked. The man in plain clothes told me in an abrupt way to get out of the car park. I did, but with a great mud splash from head to toe on his clothes. My mother was there. It was a scene like something in a movie. All the residents were crowding around and looking in anticipation of what the officer was going to do to me. As I was told by one of the residents, since that man was a police officer, he had the right to slap me across my face for my action. The muddy officer was furious and confronted me with great urgency, as if he was going to shoot me or hit me with his gun. I was not afraid because I was so wound up by everything in my life; I didn't care. I felt that the officer was exerting his authority and how was I to know he was a cop. He could have dealt with the situation more professionally. As he came towards me, I said, "If you lay your hands on me this day, I will make sure you are exposed to the whole world and especially to the British authorities."

He said, "I am Chief Constable Brown," and he told one of his officers to escort me down to the station. I was not sure what the charge would be, but I had made up my mind, whatever. My mother pleaded on my behalf. The officer spewed a lot of verbal abuse to me that I had no manners and my shoes were too big for my feet. Did I know who he was? I replied and said two things in return.

"Firstly I buy all of my shoes and never fail to purchase the incorrect size, secondly you were not in uniform. I felt the way you dealt with the situation was as if you were exerting power."

We argued for a while. It ended on a good note. I apologised to the officer and even offered to wash his clothes. The great thing was I did not get arrested. I reflected on that day. I just cannot understand what could have made me tip over the edge so badly.

Throughout my stay, I don't know whether it was exhaustion or the stress, but my body felt so weak. I found it difficult at times to go out. GA was still in contact. He rang to find out how I was. I rang him a few times when I needed a friend; he failed to pick up his phone most of the time. It doesn't take Einstein to figure out his intentions. He had all the time in the world. During a conversation with my mother about the situation, she interrupted with this huge outburst, "You stay there. You should have locked him out of your flat. Don't you know he is bringing his woman there?"

I disagreed with her comment. She wasn't there; how could she make such an allegation? GA would not be that disrespectful to do such a thing. It had been two weeks and the depression had lessened, but whenever I thought about GA, I would get sharp pains in my chest. It hurt so badly from my broken heart. I lost interest in everything. To even try another relationship would be impossible, with what had gone on.

I decided to get out of bed and drag myself to soak up some of the beautiful sunshine, while I did some grocery shopping in New Kingston. I walked around the aisle and met the friendly Jamaicans. As I walked around again, I saw this tall and dark guy. He looked at me and I walked on uninterestedly. He followed me and I thought 'oh not now. I am going to be really rude to let him go away.'

He said, "Hello."

"Hi."

"What is your name?"

I said, "I am really sorry, but I don't want to get into a conversation. Sorry."

I walked on, but he followed me. I quickly moved to the other aisle. The hide and seek went on for a while. I was uninterested. I wished this guy would leave me alone and let me get on with my shopping. He continued to be polite and persistent. Somehow I was attracted to this guy, his personality and sense of humour; I don't know why.

"I am going to keep stalking you until you talk to me."

The way he said it made me laugh. "I can hear an accent. Are you from England?"

I said, "Yes."

He lived in the UK for many years also. We started to talk about locations around London which he was familiar with. We spoke for a while. He was keen to catch up on the changes. Then the inevitable – he gave me his telephone number. He wasn't pushy; he was a real gentleman. I told him I would call him. This put me in a really good mood for the rest of the day, but I really had to be careful here. I was just pulling myself out of catastrophe. I needed to stick to my plans and be free from relationships.

I called GA several times, but he did not respond. My mother kept nagging about how I was making her place untidy and cluttered, but she was the one who was inviting me home. She was really getting on my nerves. What did she want me to do? If I was in a good mood, that made her unhappy. It was almost like she enjoyed seeing me miserable. One evening I went out with my friends. I was on a curfew to be in by 10pm as usual. I got in on time. I was really pleased to see my friends and was happy. I came in and I could see that she was annoyed, not for the fact I had done something wrong, but because I came home singing. She said,

"You're happy. I wonder why you are so happy?" The moroseness set on her face; it was as if she was about to explode with envy, her face was so distorted with anger. What was her problem? She was giving the impression that I went out to enjoy myself and left her to babysit my child, but that was not the real reason. I now realised my mother was envious of me and my life, and there was nothing I could do about that. We had a huge argument that night and we exchanged words to the deepest point; it really came out.

She said, "Yes I know I am not rich like some people."

I asked, "What are you talking about?" I let her know the position she was in was due to her religion or setbacks and has nothing to do with me. Rachel being here was her suggestion and quite frankly GA and I were in a position to look after our child. Rachel was only there as she had suggested. My child was not an excuse or burden for my enjoyment to abandon her. The only reason she had the opportunity to be with my daughter was because she was her grandchild and when she suggested to help I considered because the petty job of slaving for others on such a low wage, it would be a privilege as she said, to care for her.

"Don't try and control me, I am responsible for myself. GA does not control my life; neither can you."

She was throwing all sort of abuse.

I said, "I will move out of your room tonight." And I started to pack with my child. She sat down on the bed pretending to cry. I stayed for the night, by the next day I found accommodation and thereafter whenever I visited.

This was not the first altercation I have had about her room. I heard her before muttering under her breath that I made her room smell and I have too much junk cluttering her space. I had had enough; I wanted to share my feelings with GA. I tried calling him, but he was unreachable. I wondered to myself why did I feel I was in submission to my mother? Anywhere I went I was compelled to take her. I had to be home at a certain time. She was really controlling my life. When would I be able to take my daughter home, for I now feel threatened somehow? Why do I feel this way? Why should I be guilty? I owe my life to my daughter and want to give her the brightest future. I was just sitting there with no one to talk to. In my frustration, I decided to call the guy I met shopping – Ali.

I was very nervous. I thought if he didn't answer or remember me, that was my opportunity to move on. I called him. He remembered me and said, "I was looking forward to your call. How about we meet for lunch tomorrow."

The next day I was excited, but almost returned home. I came back to my senses a little late though; this was not what I should be doing. I should not be going on a date so soon. As I was about to walk out, I turned around and he was walking towards me looking very smart. He said, "Did you find the restaurant OK?"

I said, "Yes." I sat at the table.

We spoke about London again and he asked about my relationship. I was so glad he asked. I really let my hair down with all my troubles, I felt so much more comfortable talking to him than my mother. He was a fantastic listener and gave me sound advice. He even offered that if I ever needed to talk, I should call him anytime. I was so happy. He was like a real friend. I called on him whenever I wanted to talk and he was always there whether in the UK or Jamaica. His advice was to take my daughter home. That would resolve the issue and as a result it would create the bond again and make the family stronger. He invited me home for a meal one evening. It was impressive. We sat by the pool afterwards and I kept going on about my problems and he just sat there admiring. It never occurred to me that he had feelings for me. I just thought with all these problems and he knew I was still in a relationship that it would put him off and if he did have some affection, it would just be the heat of the moment, because I didn't think I was his type. Then he reached over and kissed me – that changed everything. How naïve was I, to think that our friendship was platonic and simply based upon advice? I ignored it; what was happening here? I carried on talking, then he pulled himself forward in the chair. We were sitting opposite each other. He stared in my eyes very closely and told me, "I am serious about you. I want you."

This freaked me out, this guy was in a position to get the most beautiful girls. He was playing. That evening I was confused. I had a great time and he wanted me to stay the night but I wasn't ready. I felt like my mother was watching me or had some kind of influence on me even though I had my own place. Deep down the altercation we had about my child affected me. I felt guilty because my child was with her. I knew that this would be the only time we would see each other again and I was fine with it. I had to control myself. My life would be different when I returned to the UK. I would forget about it all and start afresh.

When I returned, GA was acting strangely. I felt guilty – maybe he found out about Ali. He was still living his double life. I needed to confess my sin to him. I couldn't find the appropriate moment. I went to Jamaica to get rid of Mark and start afresh and I ended up again in another tangle. He would think that I had turned into a nymphomaniac. Every time I tried to correct this problem, it got worse. His phone was ringing constantly and it was difficult for him to answer. I knew it was her.

I said, "I bet it is your woman calling."

He answered sarcastically, "Yes."

I said, "You have no intention of getting rid of her, do you?"

"How do you expect me to get rid of her when there is one thing after the other happening in this relationship? I don't know if I am going or coming. I had a terrifying dream two nights ago. It was so bad that I think I would have gone out of my mind."

I said, "Tell me the dream."

"Your mother came into my dream and threatened me. She was strangling me like she was going to kill me."

I said, "Are you sure of what you are saying?"

He said, "Yes." I thought that was weird. No it was not my mother, it was the devil in disguise. I rang my mother immediately and asked her for the interpretation, as I normally did.

She said, "No, not me; it was Mrs Archie who came to threaten him, that wretch."

I replied, "Why? She is dead. She doesn't even know him or where we live. It doesn't make any sense."

I told him that it was Mrs Archie. She probably was not happy with the double life we were living. I couldn't explain why he would have such a horrid attack in his dream. I decided to confess to him that I met this guy when I went home. I didn't mean to, but it was just a fling and now it is over. He wanted the full details of this guy. I told him how we met and how the guy was responsible and single. He was taken aback and believed he could lose me. He was under immense pressure to end his relationship with his woman, but it was proving difficult. Obviously she didn't want to let go. He told me she was threatening him. I also had an argument with her one day over the telephone when he accidently left his phone home. It kept ringing nonstop.

I answered the phone, "Hello?" No answer. "I know you are there, what do you want? Why don't you get lost?"

She said, "Well if you were treating him good, he wouldn't want to be with me."

I shouted back, but she hung up. I redialled, but she ignored me. I was so annoyed. I told him about our quarrel, but he defended her and started to use the affair I had against me. I called Ali for advice. He told me I should be patient. Every man cheated; it depended on how a woman dealt with it.

I said, "So you are a cheater."

He admitted, "Unfortunately, and I got myself in a lot of trouble, which led to my divorce. But I have now learnt my lesson." As I was about to say, "thank you, goodbye," he said, "Why don't you come down and spend some time with me and ease some of the stress?" I was surprised at his suggestion.

I replied, "Maybe," but I knew that it would be impossible. "That is not a good idea."

He said, "Do you know, since your return to the UK, I can't stop thinking about you; I think I love you."

I said, "Say that again." He repeated it. I said, "Sorry, I can't afford it."

"Don't worry, I will take care of that," he said.

I couldn't believe he had feelings for me in that way. It was a real surprise. I had doubts. Is this for real, my best friend is in love with me? This was hard to take in. Although I found him attractive, I had created a barrier within my mind that I would not have a relationship with him. Although the invitation was tempting, what would I say to GA? Within four weeks of my return, I am going back again? No! This was way beyond me; I was walking in dangerous territory. I could lose GA forever and couldn't be sure of Ali; he could simply be frolicking.

The nightmares were out of this world. They were getting stronger and were revealing that GA and I were over. The strangling was still occurring in the dream. The strange thing was whenever I visited Jamaica, I did not have these dreams. I only had them at home. And what was interesting was as soon as I arrived in Jamaica, within a couple of days, I would become very weak as if I had lost all the strength in my body. I wouldn't be able to get out of bed sometimes until 3pm. I was really concerned. Maybe I had a serious illness or it could be all the sleepless nights. After the conversation with GA, I couldn't get Ali's suggestion out of mind. It was haunting me that I had to go. The rows between GA and I had escalated to another level. It became physical – he was throwing me around and I was giving blows with anything I could find. Furniture was being thrown around the flat during our tantrums, yet we still slept in the same bed, I still prepared his meals, washed his clothes, and he took care of me. There was no indication of us separating, although the dreams were to the contrary. I was fed up with the daily arguments. I could actually hear voices in my head cheering me on to go take the trip to Jamaica. It was really overpowering. It put me in a bad mood; I became aggressive and irritated by GA if he talked or tried to touch me or even sitting quietly having a drink I would get angry and pounce on him. He put up with it, but there was only so much he could take. I had to question myself most of the time when I had calmed down. I didn't mean to be annoyed. I hugged him and apologised for my behaviour, but by the next day it would start all over again, being irritated and finding fault with everything he did. I was fed up with the whole situation. GA carrying on with his woman on the side and with the overwhelming persuasion going on in my head, I decided to accept Ali's invitation. I told GA I was going back to Jamaica because I wanted to start a new life with Ali. He realised this time I was serious. He was concerned and tried his best to prevent me from going by hiding my passport and being difficult. I was determined and I left for Jamaica.

Ali came to meet me at the airport. I was delighted to see him. We hugged – it was weird because now it wasn't pure friendship; we were entering into a relationship, which was daunting for me. I was apprehensive as to what was to come. How serious was this guy? I had to guard my heart for the moment so as not to get hurt because this had taken me by surprise. He sensed I was cautious. We had a wonderful time together. His personality was similar to GA's – compassionate, caring, and a real good listener. I watched every move he made just to see if he was genuine; I don't know why. I believed that I was not good enough for him. It was the lifestyle he lived. I started to discover his constant partying and flamboyance, all the beautiful girls he could have, what did he see in me?

Although I started to have some happiness by not staying with my mother anymore, I was still under curfew. She would physically expand in anger for me going out with friends and having a great time. She insisted I had to have my breakfast, lunch and dinner with her. Most of the time, I would have to end a nice quite evening out to get back to her, just to sit down and do nothing interesting and be miserable. I couldn't understand the fear and control I was under. It became embarrassing. Even my friends were confused about the hold my mother still had on me. They thought I was a grown woman living like a teenager. My mother didn't provide for me. I sent a substantial amount of money to her, which was more than her wages, for her and my child to be comfortable. I was manipulated through her influence of my child. If my child was not here, there would be no need for me to hang around. I would have been gone. After all, I didn't really have the bond that I saw most mothers and daughters have. Even so I was an adult and GA couldn't dictate – I had my own free will, so what was the reason, why should I put up with this control? If I was guilty of leaving my child with her, as she said to 'have a good time' that was a lie. I really enjoyed just being with my daughter. I took her to the hotel to stay with me. We would go to the beach with my friends and their children.

My mother was still upset by the fact she was not invited. On one occasion, my friends and I planned a trip with the children to the beach. This was to be a reunion with friends and our children. I told my mother about the trip and instantly she was angry that she had not been invited. I couldn't believe how childish a grown woman could be. No other grandparents were invited. She behaved so atrociously. She said, "Is it because I am ugly, why am I not invited? I don't have any luck; people always use me." She had to be there at the beach. I took her along and everyone was disappointed. What was this woman doing here? When she got there it was embarrassing for her as she realised it was not appropriate for her. There were only young people there. She started to suggest that it was time to go before I was ready and she ruined my day.

My mother wanted to live her dream through me and also at my expense. Everywhere that I went and everything I had, if she didn't get her way she would use her tongue in such an abusive way, accompanied with blackmail and patronisation? It was as if whatever life I was living she should be living the same, in fact better. The envy had become overwhelming. I couldn't believe how blind I was. She even wanted to date the men I met. I was pulled over by the police one evening. My mother and I were together; it was a routine check. The guy was very polite and we got to talking as I discovered that he attended the same school and knew friends that I wanted to keep in contact with. We exchanged numbers and he appeared by the house uninvited one day. My mother thought it was fine, but I never understood how it worked back home, that people can invite themselves without invitation. I wasn't interested in dating him.

I knew my mother well, if she disapproved, her behaviour would change to moroseness and cold shoulder. It was not the case; she even invited him in for a drink. He was an handsome man, but not my type and I didn't give him the impression I wanted a date. I told my mother I had no interest in him and there was no need to keep up this entertainment, after all my mother knew I was in love with GA. One evening the telephone rang. I received a call in the UK, it was the policeman. My mother had given him my home number and presents for me on his visit to the UK. I thought is my mother going insane? Does she want to end my relationship? GA was sitting by the phone when I answered; it was no surprise to him as he already knew about this guy, and suspected that my mother disliked him. I dismissed my mother's action and thought she was very naïve. I gathered years later that my mother was going out with him; I knew this from photos that were taken of her, him and my daughter. I kept the photos and asked her what was going on and she pretended as if she couldn't understand my question. This may seem a coincidence, but it happened again.

My mother had made an arrangement with Mark, who I had broken up with, to come to her home. They had a meeting behind my back. I didn't want this guy to know where I lived or have any contact with my family, because he was not in my life, but my mother took the opportunity. She thought I would have been pleased to know that Mark came to visit her and spoke with her about me, because he was so in love. She told me the news in a way, as if we had a relationship of keeping our dirty little secret together. I was livid! I am not in a culture of arranged marriage. In fact, I had not told my mother I ended my relationship with GA. Why would she have the nerve to call a meeting and reassure this man without my consent? He was an hypocrite. When I asked him what was discussed, he avoided the question. I wanted to know what was said. He replied, "You should listen to your mother."

I had the impression she had made him a promise that we would be together. This woman was stepping in my shadow. She wanted to be me. I thought she had gone too far interviewing who I should date. In addition, she just couldn't be satisfied – pure bitterness and envy. It was astounding and deep down I had this fear that when I took my child, I was going to face a huge challenge. I began to notice how she was covetous of my personal items that I left in her possession for safe keeping. She would admire and compare things to her time, what it would have been if she had all that. She would brag about her time and how she dated the best guys and how men were still noticing her. That was not something I was interested in hearing. I was not comparing or keeping score with my mother. I wanted a parent to give sound advice and ideas on how to mend my broken relationship and a plan towards the future. She wanted to let me know that I could get any man I wanted and at the same time uttering how marvellous her son-in-law was and that she was happy with him; this is confusing. Her motive was for me to enter into various relationships or meet different men. That was not my intention of a promising future for myself or my child. I was happy with GA, but it was going wrong. There was no one I could trust like him. I spoke with GA about the situation and he wanted me home. He had made his mind up to end the affair, but I didn't believe him.

Ali and I became very close. He fell in love and I loved him, but it could not compare to the relationship with GA. Ali tried on numerous occasions to steal my heart entirely from GA, but it was not the same. Deep down, I knew he was not the man. I couldn't trust him enough. After a while, I found out he was a philanderer. It started with the lies and excuses. One night he went out with friends and didn't return home. His excuse was that all four tyres of the car were punctured and so he had to sleep at a hotel until the morning. He tried to change his lifestyle to suit me, but it was not good enough for me. The cracks started to show. The skeletons in the closet were bursting out. I didn't want a miserable life in the future. I had to make up my mind to end this before it was too late. My heart could take only so much; GA was very disappointed. Although he wanted us to be together, he wanted me to be happy with whatever decision I made. I began to feel frustrated, a failure, I just wanted my life back. The constant rollercoaster in my life was draining. I wanted to be with GA. There was a blockage and Ali was now bad news. My mother disliked Ali. He was the only one she confronted me about, and she had never met him. I went to pay some taxes in downtown Kingston at the tax office. I had forgotten a document, so I returned home. On my arrival, I headed straight into my mother's room. I realised Ali's picture was on her bed. I knew I did not put it there; it was kept in my camera bag. I was confused and sensed something was not right here. I immediately called GA and told him. He was not interested because he was fed up with me and the whole situation anyway. I was puzzled as to why she had the picture. The position it was placed on the bed was as if she panicked when she heard me come into the house. She quickly exited out of the room. Moreover, I had not introduced or shown her where I had kept them. Maybe she wanted to see what he looked like.

The very same week, everything was going wrong. The diamond fell out of my engagement ring. I searched everywhere. My mother told me that it was a sign that my relationship with GA was now over. "Once dat happen your relationship is done."

I knew that GA and I had separated but not broken. My inner thought was telling me our relationship was not over, but how can that be? We were both living a double life and I could not feel closure. I was confused. Ali and I had an argument; he was less committed. I figured there was a third party. I tried frantically to find out, but his friends and family covered up for him. Even the housekeeper who I tried to bribe was coerced not to tell. It was over and as soon as I had ended it with Ali, another guy turned up – Doctor Brown.

He was there when I went to collect my medication. There was something wrong here. I was not the most beautiful woman in the world – far from it – but the way these men were appearing it was ridiculous. This was not good for a decent woman's reputation. I took off to the UK and ended all contact with these guys. I threw my mobile SIM card down the toilet and flushed it away. On my return to the UK, I came home to find GA had moved. All the furniture from the flat, including the bed, was gone. He had told me he would do it. I couldn't believe it, but I didn't blame him. I had to sleep on the floor. He still had access to the flat and he came back home to gloat at my distress. I was determined not to be disgraced. This would be a new beginning. It was best to be alone and reflect. The trauma had left me with so many emotional scars. I vowed to myself that I never wanted to get into a serious relationship again. I bought new furniture.

GA had gone to set up home with his mistress. I was angry with myself. I was now a complete loser. She had taken away my man. At the same time, Mark was trying to get his revenge. He claimed that I had dumped him and broke his heart in pieces, how ridiculous. He hid the fact that he was a married man. I was open with him that I was in a relationship and was not serious, and he also gave me the same impression. Was I to be blamed that he fell in love? He had lost control and his wife gave up on him. He told me he was not in a steady relationship. She was his children's mother, so why was it my fault? I learned from my mother by the slip of her tongue that during Mark's visit to see her, he said he was deeply in love and would end his marriage. He had decided to discuss his intention with my mother behind my back, but surely if he had told me I would have declined anyway. It just wouldn't have worked. He was so vengeful. He knew the situation I was in and used it to his advantage.

GA had left and I had broken things off with Ali. The whole idea was to crush my emotions like an avalanche, insulting me about this ghetto I came from and blackmailing me by saying: "Can't you see there is no one there for you now? I can be your friend if you do as you are told."

That was to be his piece on the side and answer to his beck and call. I was broken in pieces, distraught, and in a situation I never imagined. However, Mark was ahead of himself. I didn't tell him I wanted him back, but he was so nasty. It was a real celebration for him to see my downfall, and he waited to drop me into the gutter for his benefit. As low as I was, he could not patronise me or bring me down.

I told him, "If you were the last man on this planet, I would never go out with you again."

He thought it was a joke and I ignored his phone calls. He called at least twenty times a day for two weeks. He was more desperate than I was. He wanted to make sure that GA did not return in my life – how selfish. Although he was going through his divorce, greed would not permit him to let go. I had made up my mind to get on with my life, but it was annoying as GA had left me and held onto the keys, where he could drop by anytime. I was furious and told him if you had moved out to be with your mistress, what the hell were you doing here? Please leave the keys and get out of my life completely; leave me alone! I would survive. But he kept appearing and watching over me, refusing to go, stoking me and calling me. I was really struggling to replace the bed, much less to change the lock. The furniture finally came and as the nights passed, reality was setting in – I was truly alone.

Some nights were scary; everywhere was so quiet and spooky. It was difficult sleeping alone after so many years. GA was always there. My main fear was if the riding of the sprit appeared. I left the lights on all night and the television on constantly. I was really afraid to be in the flat on my own. I also found that I started to find comfort in the bottle more than usual. My main concern was my daughter. I kept my mother informed, but she wasn't concerned. I became antisocial and hid away to avoid the disgrace. They were keen to hear my misfortune to gloat. There was a lot of jealousy among them since I met GA. The loneliness proved daunting and I was struggling. I needed to speak with someone about my troubles. I would walk sometimes for miles late in the evening to exhaust myself into sleep. The weight issue started again and the anaemia. It was like the pain was consuming my insides. In my desperation, I called a friend from university who I was acquainted with. I was happy to share with a distant fantastic mate from Gambia. She listened attentively and gave sound advice and support. She was like a real sister, Jawara. This helped me to become stronger. GA still tried to call me and I just didn't understand why. This guy should leave me alone. He was living with his woman. What was wrong with men? I ignored him; it had been three weeks now. GA was persistent in calling and one day I decided to answer the phone to tell him for the last time where to go.

I said, "Hello."

He said, "How are you babes? I just want to let you know that although we are not together, I want to support our daughter and for you to carry on with your career."

"Why do you care?"

He said, "I don't want to keep a grudge. By the way I am downstairs."

"What are you doing downstairs? Shouldn't you be with your girlfriend?"

"Come down let's talk."

I was missing him and he sounded sincere. I went to see him and sat in his car.

I said, "But you have moved on with your life. You are living with another woman, you have taken all the furniture, why do you bother?"

He said, "You have it wrong. The furniture is in storage and I have been sleeping rough. I did this to give you a wakeup call. We cannot continue living this double life the way we are. There has to be a stop. I still love you and I miss you."

I broke down uncontrollably. I couldn't believe all this time I had been suffering and ignoring his calls that he was trying to get through to me. I told him to come home. We went to the storage and took back some of the furniture that same day. I was so happy to see my friend again. Now I could have a real good rest without fear. I went and prepared his favourite meal and we had a good time. I now knew this guy truly loved me. After all that had happened, he waited for me. The following night I went to bed around 8pm. I laid down to rest. There was a patio door in the living room which can be seen from the bedroom. As I was about to close my eyes to sleep, I could see a man in the form of GA hopping along into the bedroom, plain as day. He wore a striped jumper and blue trousers. I thought it was GA. I was also in a trance – it was like tunnel vision. My eyes were fixated on the object and everything else around me was blurred. The figure was approaching towards me and I realised it was not him and not human. Instantly, I tried to push myself off the bed, but it was too late. I was under attack. I saw the face of the spirit; it was a resemblance of GA. This was the same person I saw in my dream. I was really annoyed that this nonsense was starting again. I rang my mother and told her.

She said, "Don't worry. No one can do anything to you. It is just the devil."

I was so frustrated. How do I stop or get rid of this menace? My mother took this problem very lightly. I was still having the problem with sand inside and the blood oozing during intercourse. I had no symptoms with Mark, but with Ali it was even worse than GA. I had to endure another operation to see what was wrong. The result was unclear – they were unable to decide on a prognosis. GA and I were back together. We really wanted to try again and correct any mistakes. I told my mother and she insisted on our marriage. After what had happened, I just couldn't understand it. I loved GA very much and after all that we had been going through, my inner thoughts were deterring me from walking down the aisle and apparently GA felt the same. If there was no other decision we were sure of together, this was it; we both agreed that we were not ready to get married. GA told me during our separation that he knew for sure my mother was not interested in our relationship. I don't think he understood her well. Why would she be praising her son-in-law and showing concern for us to be married? He was very sure my mother was a hypocrite during our quarrels. He rang my mother for advice and support in confidence, asking how we could resolve the altercations and her reaction was not pleasant.

I said, "But if you had this conversation with my mother she would have told me."

He replied, "I rang her the week you arrived in Jamaica. I was so fed up of the life we were living. I knew about Ali and I could see he was in love with you. I knew he could take you away from me. I didn't know what to do, but I thought if I confided in my mother-in-law, she would help us to resolve this nightmare. I told her the way Maria is going on, she is not thinking about you mum and my daughter, how will you cope financially? I know what I did was wrong, but we can sort this out."

My mother replied in extreme anger, "What are you talking

about! I don't blame her. I don't need anything from you. I have my source to support me, and what about your woman?"

I replied to GA, "She would have been angry after all that I have been going through, but I still can't understand why my mother has not told me about this conversation."

If I knew GA wanted to call her, I would have discouraged him as my mother behaves atrociously when she is angry.

Chapter 11

GA and I had fallen in love all over again. He had changed; we were going out together more often and did some travelling across Europe together. He had ended his relationship with the other woman; we wanted to start building our life again to take our daughter home and live the life we had planned. I was so happy – I felt on top of the world. Again, all my troubles had gone. We didn't split up after all. The only problem was the dreams were coming back again and this time even stronger. I could now visualise the spirit that was sleeping with me. Apparently they were two men – the one that tried to replicate GA and the other was a lighter skinned guy. I thought, 'so these are the sprits that are raping and strangling me; now I can see them.' This was a terrifying experience. I went back into watchful sleep, as you can never predict when it was going to happen. I told my mother about it and as usual she did nothing. This was really irritating. I know what it's like being a woman being raped by a real person – you are defenceless. It is like someone is taking away what is yours without your permission and you watch as they do it and there is nothing you can do. I started to share my problem with friends and they had no idea what to do but refer me to their mother or grandmother. The same remedy would be suggested: pray, go to church, read a particular psalm before you go to bed, burn out the house with incense – all the above did not work. A relative in Jamaica even suggested I visit a bush doctor (reader man). He told me there was a woman disturbing my life, but I was not sure who the woman was. I suspected GA's ex-girlfriend. If the advice was true, she could be my enemy now that they had broken up. My mother was useless. I decided to help myself. She strongly forbade me to go back to such a place; however, she wasn't helping.

I went to bed that night and this was the most peculiar dream. I saw my Aunt Lily. I was all alone in the graveyard at night. The graveyard was descending down a hill. When I looked ahead, I could see all the headstones up above me at a far distance, far beyond and even under a huge tree. I was standing alone and my aunt appeared in a beautiful green gown I bought for her wedding. I was delighted to see her as I had missed her so much.

I said, "Hello Aunty, how are you?" She did not speak.

She looked very angry standing in front of me, then she gave me a beautiful baby girl to hold.

I said, "Is this your baby, Aunty?"

She still did not reply and as I happily took the baby to hold her, the baby slipped out of my hands. Fear of the baby falling overcame me – I knew it would not survive. She would have fallen on a concrete grave. I screamed out in the dream to try and catch it, but my aunt swiftly grabbed hold of the baby and gave her to me and pointed to the exit up the hill where I saw the big tree. She was giving direction for me to take the baby and go. The dream made no sense to me. I rang my mother and she said maybe my aunt was pregnant when she died, but I thought 'how odd.'

I decided to sleep on the sofa because the trouble – all these weird dreams and attacks – seemed to happen in my bed.

One Sunday, I prepared a delicious meal. We ate and decided to have dessert later: my favourite treat, apple pie and custard. We snuggled up on the sofa watching our favourite soap. I was really cosy. Then the doorbell rang. GA's friend had come to visit him, but he would meet him in the downstairs car park.

He said, "I won't be long, just going to see my friend."

I said, "OK."

As GA left, the overwhelming tiredness came upon me like

being tipsy and I started to fall asleep. I could feel GA's hand fondling me and I started to enjoy it. I don't know how or what gave me consciousness that GA had just left for the car park, but I immediately thought it cannot be him! I jumped from the sofa and as I looked through the patio door, I saw GA returning from the car park. I was so upset; this thing would not go away. What have I done? Who have I harmed? To be haunted by a spirit that was having an affair with me, this was an invasion – this was preposterous. When GA returned, I ran and hugged him. He didn't understand what had happened and I explained. He was so fed up with it.

He said, "This is not good for your health. You have to call your mother and she will have to find help."

I called my mother. She told me to read a psalm and light a red candle. I sat down that night and concentrated hard on who I had done wrong. I thought of all the people I knew who I may have offended. I came up with one person, and after all the shenanigans that happened in the past, it had to be Mrs B. I frequently saw her in some of my dreams, where I was returning back to her home and serving her as the housekeeper. I had heard through the grapevine that she was very disappointed with my success because she had predicted that I would live a flamboyant lifestyle of drinking and smoking. To this day I have never smoked and a glass of wine knocks me out. The following day, I rang my mother and told her.

"I cracked it. I suspect Mrs B."

She replied, "Don't worry. They can't do anything to you. I am sure they regret what they did to you."

What did that mean? Did she know that this woman was the culprit? Or did she know something I didn't? I found it bizarre; it was really hard work to get a clear explanation – it was like cracking a secret code. The attacks had reduced and my mother told me she was praying for me and GA, but although the dreams had reduced, the arguments between GA and I started again. The inner voice was tormenting me to return to Jamaica. I didn't know why. I was compelled to go home. Everything GA said was to stop me, and I was more determined. I would physically fight him if need be. He was concerned that if I returned to Jamaica, I might rekindle the past with Ali. I had lost contact with him for a year, and it was very unlikely I would find him. Moreover that was now in the past. I had seen my daughter six months before, as she was now of the age to travel. GA was over his relationship and we were getting on really well. I felt there was no need to worry. Everything changed overnight as soon as the trip was instigated. The troubles would start with arguments. I would get really irritated and angry when I saw him; everything he said to me was nonsense. I hated him touching me affectionately, yet I couldn't live without him or sleep without him. I worried about him if he was not at home on time. Deep down, I knew I wanted to spend the rest of my life with him.

I don't remember how I usually got my way, but I would be on that plane to Jamaica within a week and before landing I would consider, what am I doing here again? It was going to be so boring sitting down with her. On my arrival when I saw her I would be so angry. She irritated me as well. I looked in her eyes for the first time and it was hypocrisy. The relationship between us was not there; there was no affection. I really didn't need to be with her or see her. Our conversation was based on gossip; our relationship was about material things, what new shoes or utensil she could get, etc. I discovered my daughter was used as a cash cow. I booked this trip for a month as it was December. I wanted to be with my daughter for Christmas, and whenever I called GA I would feel regret and guilt over how I left him alone at Christmas when we should be together as a family. Boring as usual, the only pleasure was being in the company of my daughter. I felt the urge to see Ali as GA feared. I stayed away from trouble this time. I was not interested in meeting or seeing anyone. I would stay and enjoy time with my daughter, family and friends and go back home to the United Kingdom. Well that was the plan. Three weeks later, I started to have a strange urge.

It was as if I was losing my mind. I just had to be with a man and I wouldn't want to be with any strange man. I started to think about Ali uncontrollably. I found myself desperately seeking him; it was like something inside of me was bursting to come out and it drove me insane, like something was urging and controlling me and I had the pain like I had the last trip. I went to knock on his gate. I was told he no longer lived there. That was it – there was no way I would know where he was. I had lost contact with him. I was in emotional pain, it was excruciating, like a knife was piercing my heart, but I had been fine for three weeks. I had forgotten about this guy in this way. What was happening to me?

The following day I was staying at a hotel in New Kingston. I decided to go for a walk and clear my head. Something was not right with me. Did it mean every time I went to Jamaica I would be having an affair? I was never like this; it would not happen again. I had put on my control armour. The same repetition I heard in my head when I need to go to Jamaica I was hearing the same calling for Ali – this was crazy. As I walked towards a well-known bank in New Kingston, I saw this BMW car and my inner voice said to me that's him. I saw him – everything was in slow motion. This would be the third time this had happened to me. I was so shocked by what was revealed. I quickly ran into the arcade and hoped he would be gone when I came out. The car was heading the opposite direction. He was close enough that if I had waved he would have seen me, but I chose not to. I didn't know how he would have reacted if I had tried to stop him. I went back to the hotel, had some lunch, and went back to see my mother. I didn't mention anything to her and somehow I was relieved that I saw him and he seemed to be doing well. I went back to the hotel that evening. I had an early night in preparation for a meeting the next day.

The next morning as I walked into the lobby to have breakfast, I heard someone call out to me. It was Ali's niece. I was delighted and also disappointed at the same time. We had breakfast together.

She was curious about my disappearance and wanted to know what had happened. She also told me how devastated Ali was. I didn't say much and we exchanged numbers. She was also staying at this hotel. I tried my best to ignore my feelings to see him; it was too much of a coincidence. It was like everything was thrown at me to tempt fate and the feelings were growing stronger. The more I resisted, the more it dawned on me that it was in my head. I looked to the bright blue sky. I closed my eyes to relieve the crushing pain. It was piercing as if my heart was pounding through my chest. I called GA and told him that I met with the niece, and I was having this overwhelming uncontrollable feeling to meet up with Ali.

GA was furious, He said, "After all we have been through, you want to see him again?"

I said, "I don't know. I just have to see him." I felt as if I was led to him.

His niece had contacted him and told him I was on the island. He called me and we planned to meet at the club. I was so nervous about how this was going to work out, with GA already upset. We met up at the club. He was excited to see me, but I was disappointed for the urge was an anti-climax. We hugged and he wanted to know when I arrived. I told him three weeks ago. He was surprised and disappointed I didn't try to reach him sooner.

I said, "I did but you had moved."

He said, "You didn't try hard enough."

I said, "It's fine. We have both moved on in our lives anyway, it has been a year."

"I really miss you. I can't believe how you disappeared without even looking back. I travelled to the UK to find you. I went to your favourite store in Green Lanes London. I hung out for days to see if I could locate your car passing by… and nothing. I didn't have your address. I went through so much pain."

I was in shock because I remembered a time when I had strong feelings that Ali was in the area. I thought 'what madness he doesn't even know where I live.' I confirmed it was around the same time when GA moved out of the flat. The time the inner voice was speaking as I drove down Green Lanes. I was taken back. I didn't know he felt so strongly about me. He also asked if I ran away from him because I had his child, as he was so desperate for me to bear him a child. He told me he was with someone that evening and we should meet up the next day. Now that I that had seen him I could not understand where the urge and passion had gone. It was as if I was satisfied and I really couldn't care less what was going on in his life. GA and I were back together. I would not live that life again. It was as if I was seeking closure. We met up the next day for lunch. One thing lead to another and GA was frustrated, trying to prevent a repeat of what had happened a year ago. He rang my mother for support. She replied against him in fury. He told me she was very rude to him. I found this strange because again my mother had not told me when they had this conversation. GA was so frustrated; he kept calling me and spouting verbal abuse, hoping that it would prevent me from falling in the same trap again. Strangely I do not remember most of these events that have taken place and I have a very good memory. I just cannot remember this part of the story. I do remember I had an affair with Ali and after committing such a betrayal I knew that this would definitely be the end of my relationship with GA. What had I done? I would have to lie to GA and hope to get away with it. The night of the affair, I spoke with GA on the phone as usual. I was due to return New Years, January 2004; we spoke on the phone for three hours. I felt guilty. Ali was showing all the love and affection; he wanted to make sure that this time he would not lose contact again. He was very serious to start a relationship and move to the UK, but it was too late. I had already devoted my love to GA and I explained that to him, but he was oblivious to my reasoning. Besides, there were many changes and bad habits in his life that were not suitable for me. I had to play along. I knew I would not continue this. We said goodbye and I was terribly worried – I knew what I had done was wrong and I felt I was intentionally hurting GA.

I arrived back in the UK very nervous; lying doesn't really work for me. I played along as if GA was making a big deal about Ali. After all, nothing happened between us.

We made love and during the process GA reacted very oddly. He said, "Hmmm," and I knew straight away he had caught on. I was in trouble.

I asked, "What's wrong?"

He said,

"I knew that if you did anything with that guy I would know."

"I didn't do anything," I replied.

"Let me tell you. I went to bed early to meet you at the airport this morning and in my dream I was told that if you had done anything, when you returned I would know. I wasn't sure, but before I woke up there was like a hand fondling my privates. I jumped out of the bed in hysteria. And now I know what it meant."

I begged him to please forgive me. I didn't know what came over me.

He refused and said, "I told your mother that this time I will not take it easy because you have overstepped the mark."

His behaviour was bitter towards me. He continuously tormented me at any opportunity for what I had done. The crushing and sickening pain in my chest returned. How was I going to fix this? I had ruined my relationship.

There was no need for me to return to Jamaica for Christmas. I had to decide that this relationship was over. He threw abuse and I accepted it. I tried to explain to him that I didn't understand what had happened to me. Maybe it was revenge with Ali because I had lost the feeling for him anyway. This had become a regular pattern out of my control – every time I put one foot forward, I ended up taking three steps backward. Something was wrong somewhere. I went down on my knees and said, "God! What is happening here?

What can I do to resolve this problem, because there is nothing that will save this relationship, now please give me an answer."

I waited and waited; ten days later, I heard that inner voice say 'you will need to have a child in order to solve this problem.'

I immediately called GA, sat him down, and told him the plans. He asked me if I was sure this was what I wanted. I was unsure how long it would take me to become pregnant or if I would be able to after the near death experience I had with the ectopic pregnancy, where one of the fallopian tubes was completely removed. Fortunately within a month, I was pregnant. GA had advised me that due to the experience we had in the past when we were having severe problems, I fell pregnant. It was not planned. I couldn't believe it. To be sure I took three pregnancy tests and all were positive. I was furious because I wasn't sure if GA was deceiving or trapping me, to keep me and the other woman. There was nothing I could do. I called my mother, who was so furious, telling me that I should not go down that road. GA was sitting beside me and heard her uproar. We sat down together and planned for the birth of our child. It was odd that I finally accepted to have the child after weeks of contemplating what to do, and as I decided to tell my mother the news later that evening, I had a miscarriage. I became so confused about the issue that I kept asking GA if I was really expecting? I was disappointed and the grief I experienced was as if my mind was playing tricks on me. I was getting confused about whether I was pregnant or not.

This time we planned not to tell anyone about this pregnancy until the foetus was at least six months. GA strongly suspected foul play from the last experience. I decided that I would work throughout the term to keep active. GA was over the moon and we finally believed that this time we would start all over again. The arguments had ceased, he was back to normal, and very attentive to me, especially with my cravings and the back massages. I telephoned my mother, but would not mention a word about the pregnancy; this went on for four months until I received a phone call from her.

She said, "I had a dream that I saw fishes." Shock registered on my face.

I asked, "What does that mean?"

"It means someone is pregnant," she replied.

"I don't know anyone who is pregnant."

She insisted. "Someone definitely is."

She was going on about it so much with real certainty, as if someone had told her I was pregnant. I gave in and told her. I hate to lie to my mother.

She said, "Really? Oh congratulations!"

I was not happy with myself. I had given in too easily. I promised GA that we would not tell anyone until six months. I felt very upset that my mother had forced me in such a situation; it was intrusive. However, I could have kept my mouth shut. But at the same time, I had a compelling feeling that I had to tell her the truth. I admitted to GA that I had broken the promise. He was fine about it; he believed it was far gone, so it should be fine.

Five months pregnant, I was very excited to start baby shopping. It was slightly tedious as we were not told the sex due to the hospital's policy. I wanted to have a boy this time and then that would be my lot. My bump started to show, but I was pleased, as it was winter. The joys of wearing a coat just concealed it.

The severe and horrendous nightmares returned, mostly about the baby. The head of the baby came off the body, rolled off the bed, fell to the floor and smashed in pieces. This spiritual madness was going to start all over again. It was like a vicious circle. I would have relief from the nightmares and conflict with GA, and then it would return again. GA was planning positively about investing in order to secure our family's future. Apparently, I was discouraging him. Most of what I said to GA at this time I don't remember, but he always gets upset when he talks about it. I do remember developing this sudden guilt towards my mother, even though I had told her about the pregnancy. It was haunting me in my thoughts, returning back to the days when I was young and she brutally attacked me for telling a lie. The sense was so strong I had committed a betrayal; this intense pressure was pinning me down. I had to find a solution to please her. The remedy suggested in a supernatural form was to get married, as she had been suggesting. It was as if she was my controller somehow, and I was submissive to her. The advice from friends and colleagues was the same – I owed it to my mother for not informing her of the pregnancy. They had no idea of the history and that there wasn't a genuine relationship between us.

The feelings were so overwhelming – crushing pains in the chest – why was this a big deal? After all, it was my life. Should GA and I decide to get married made no difference. The arguments were intense again. I can only write what GA told me at this point. I somehow cannot remember what I said or did – it's weird; I never had a diagnosis of amnesia. I can only remember some sequences of events. I suddenly decided to return to Jamaica at five-months pregnant. He was frantic as to why I wanted to travel in my condition. I told him that I had to go to Jamaica to see my mother. What I can remember was I had this uncontrollable urge to go home because of that guilty feeling, as if I needed to apologise or beg forgiveness from the master and mother was also compelling me to come home over the telephone. GA begged me not to go on the trip. I replied, "I want to see my mother and child." We had a huge row. When he insisted that my decision was wrong, I told him I planned to leave the unborn child in Jamaica and that it would be for the best, and I was going to start building a house on the land for the children. They would get a better education, as private education was more affordable there. He said, "Where has this sudden plan come from? Did you change your mind overnight without telling me? Why do you have to go now in your condition? I don't believe you want to do this for your children, it is for your mother." I remember this part because I was very upset. Why should I sacrifice my hard work for my mother more than my children. She did nothing for me all through my childhood. I genuinely believed this was for the benefit of my children? They meant everything to me. We argued and argued and the same – within a week, I was in Jamaica again. What was I doing here? This was risky; if I became ill it would be a nightmare. I didn't approve of the medical practices there, and also for my safety the airline might not allow me to return at this stage of the pregnancy.

I greeted my mother at the airport. She seemed pleased to see me, but ignored or failed to ask me about the baby. I would try to bring up the subject, but somehow it would be lost or avoided in the conversation. I wanted to be sure before I made accusations or assumptions – maybe I was paranoid because of the guilt, but I was right. She failed on every occasion to notice my pregnancy. Did that mean when she gave her congratulations it was misguided? She was distant; she couldn't be bothered if I ate or not. All attention was the usual, what she could get, the gifts, and she was very keen for me to get the house sorted. I sensed that was the main priority.

I felt victimised, bullied by my mother. It was as if she couldn't care less about me; as long as she got what she wanted and in a hurry. I thought this child that I was carrying has ruined a lot of her plans, whatever they were. I started to enquire and got the ball rolling, but something had changed in my persona. I began to realise that this project I was about to embark upon was not right, but I couldn't put my finger on it. The architect was an absolute crook – he overcharged and tried to manipulate me because of my condition. I was getting weaker by the day and heavier. The sun was beaming down at me at about 100 degrees. I was tired and my mother was still indirectly pushing. I took Rachel for the weekend at the flat where I was staying.

Even though I was far gone, I couldn't get rid of the morning sickness. Nothing would stay down; as a result it aggravated my dehydration. This particular morning, I had my first sickness of the day. I sat on the bed recovering. Rachel was asleep; my inner voice came.

She said, "This project you are performing, you are on the wrong track. You are in a position to take care and look after your children. Look around you – you have achieved so much more than your friends. If you complete this house, it will never be yours nor will you have any control over it, for your mother will take over and push you out and all you will do is work to maintain it. You will not achieve any success, but rather extreme frustration."

This was the morning that changed my life. It was like I once was blind, but now I could see. I couldn't believe what I heard. I have been a fool all this while. Everything opened before me like a closed chapter that I had reopened. I realised my mother was just using me; she had no love for her daughter. The hatred she had for my father was extended to me. This was frustrating; I had wasted so much time and my hard-earned money, and most of all, GA was on his way from the UK to meet and oversee how the project was progressing. How was I going to tell him that the project was a waste of time, and risk the health of my unborn child to be in Jamaica for nothing? This was a horrific discovery and I didn't know how GA would react when I explained to him that I had made a serious error. I was so angry with myself for being so naïve to be used, I didn't get it. I was always careful, methodical in my decision making. How could a mother look me in the eye and be so cold to use me to settle her life with her husband, who bless him, could not even put a roof over our heads or a meal? I have experienced many women with children, where the father had left and they found a man to help. In this case, it was the other way around – the obligation was thrown at me, with no remorse. She saw my success and decided to transfer her load of burden on my head and live a luxurious life. She wanted a mansion with a fancy car and to travel the world. I am certain I do not love my mother more than myself, so why would I give her more than I deserved? She failed to do her job as a parent.

I had to tell GA the bad news. This poor man had been going through so much. I had wasted his money and put him through all this stress. I called him and I started the conversation gently. I told him I would understand if he left me after what I was about to say, "I realise I have put you through so much unnecessary stress. I know you are coming to see me tomorrow and check on the project, but I just have to let you know that we are on the wrong track with this project. I wish I had told you before things had gone this far. I am really sorry, I know there is nothing I can do now."

GA said, "I can't believe it. I am sitting here with my best friend this very moment, discussing how you planned to use me to build a house for you and your mother and take my children away from me, then get rid of me. I could have retaliated against your decision, but I feared anything that would cause harm or distress to my child. I couldn't afford to lose our baby, so I allowed it. I proceeded with the plan anyway, for the sake of the children and have already considered that after that project, I was certain that this would be the end of us this time."

I went to see my mother that day. I was a different person; I felt sick of stupidity. How could I possibly build a five-bedroom house within a month and in my condition. I noticed that morning that she was exceptionally happy.

"Hello my daughter."

Every time she opened her mouth, I became so angry. I could see the hypocrisy. She was so fake. Why wouldn't she be? I also felt like she was patronising me cunningly. It was almost like when you have a conversation with someone and you can tell that it is sarcasm. They are going to laugh as soon as you turn your back – that was her attitude. I had to do all the organising, running around in the baking sun and heat. My bump had just sprung out so big overnight. It must have been the good food and wonderful sunshine. I started to feel really exhausted, followed with an uncontrollable bladder. I developed a cough that was irritating. I couldn't sleep. As the days went by, I was getting worse. I had to see the doctor and explain my symptoms. Luckily, I had some knowledge about prescribed medical drugs. The doctor prescribed a drug that could have been fatal for me and my unborn child. I asked the pharmacist to double-check the prescription and she was in shock. I saw her running back into the surgery and later she returned, apologising for their incompetence. I demanded a refund. I left the surgery in disgust and I decided to make my own home remedy. My mother wasn't interested, even though she saw how I was suffering – not even a recommendation of one of her home remedies or advice about what I could do about my illness. I had to help myself. It was apparent my mother was just pretending to be happy about my pregnancy; she showed no affection towards my child. After a few days, my remedy worked – garlic, honey and lime. The cough was under control, but after so many days of coughing, I was evidently weaker.

On top of that she had the nerve to demand I chauffeur her to the village to visit her mother. I knew this would have been an impossible task, dodging potholes and reckless drivers and driving the distance. She insisted with real pressure, as if it was so important that I had to go. I said, "I am not feeling well and I am happy to pay a driver to take you there."

She insisted, "No!" I should take her.

She behaved as if I was being unfair and mean. This really upset me and I called GA and told him the situation. He was furious; he couldn't understand what could be so important that I had to take her in my ill health. He forbade me to go. She was ridiculous. My inner voice also told me not to go – I could be in danger. My mother was sarcastic; she applied all the pressure she could, insisting for me to go. I couldn't believe it. Doesn't she worry at all about my health and the unborn child? What could be so important? I refused to go.

GA had arrived on-site. The project was not going to plan. My mother decided that a sacrifice would be essential as this was the old tradition for new buildings to chase or satisfy the spirits. A goat was slaughtered and then she carried out the procedure with the blood, which was poured at the four corners of the land. GA and I could see disaster approaching. The contractors were deceptive and cunning with our materials. We were dictated to and in my position I couldn't stress myself anymore. I had to be careful. From the vision and warning that was given, I decided not to push any further. We abandoned the project. GA's visit was short and he was due to return within the week. He preferred to return without me, so that he could arrange and prepare for my return. The evening of his departure, we went to my mother's. He wanted to spend some time with her and especially his daughter. My mother had bought a present for him and he wished her farewell until he saw her again. She said, "Don't worry to tell me now. We can say our farewell at the airport."

He said, "Mum there is no need to bother to come to the airport. My daughter and wife will just drop me off as it is a late flight."

Instantly, you could see the disappointment on her face. She was so annoyed we wanted to be together that evening. I was only to take him to the departure lounge and exit. I didn't want to risk being out late. I couldn't understand why it was so important for her to be there. We had planned to have this private moment together; she failed to accept our wishes and behaved like a spoilt child. What was really irritating was she kept on hugging GA repeatedly, but I knew it was pretence. It was an encouragement, being friendly to him to return and complete the project – the 'house' she has been demanding. Her actions were over the top.

I said, "Stop hugging him you hypocrite. You are only doing this because of what you want."

She replied, "What! Do you think I want to take him from you? I have a drunken husband of my own you know."

I said, "Hug him then."

She ignored me and then still carried on doing it.

Then she said, "I thank God for my son-in-law. If it wasn't for him I don't know how I would live with what you do hahaha."

I said, "I didn't realise you were the reason GA was involved in this family and you seem to know him a whole lot more that I do."

I was really angry. I felt used. She spoke to me in such a condescending way and here I was risking my child and my life for this woman and she had the nerve to spit in my face. I couldn't cope with the pretence; it was right in my face. GA couldn't see it. He thought I was overreacting but it was all coming to roost. My mother used me to get what she wanted from GA. I was always careful not to be a tricked; what happened here? And now she behaved like a champion patronising and humiliating. My spiritual guide was right. We hadn't completed the project and this was her reaction. What will happen if it was done? After our confrontation about her insincerity, it was like a demon was released; she attacked me viciously. GA realised her disappointment and anger for not inviting her to come along to the airport and was about to allow her.

I said to him, "No. It is our decision. There is no need for her to be there. Anyway, her behaviour to me is atrocious. I am not afraid of her. I am an adult. What is she going to do next? Use abuse?"

He said goodbye to her. I couldn't care less. She was still in a rage – I could see it in her eyes. There was nothing she could do. Her tantrum would not deter me. I now realised who she was and what she was about. We must make decisions about our life, without a third party dictating, which was causing damage financially and also to our relationship. We went and left her behind. When I returned from the airport with Rachel, I went back home to see my mother to report to her everything went well. As soon as I walked into her room, she was huffing and puffing, lying down on her side in the bed with the light off. I looked at her and thought, 'is she seriously still carrying a grudge because she didn't go to the airport?'

I asked her, "Is there anything to eat?" to break the tension. She didn't answer and turned her face to the corner.

Then she said, "If you want something, go and help yourself."

She always prepared my food. I helped myself and she continued the silent treatment. I just couldn't understand how this could be so upsetting to her. GA was spending so much on the project, where she would eventually be living, and he made one simple request. I was fed up with her attitude and drove back to flat I was staying at that night.

It was Christmas Eve. The atmosphere in the Caribbean this time of the year was uplifting. It was celebration to another level. I loved how they shared the love. Although I was in the right place, Christmas 2004 was the beginning of my nightmare. I started to hate being around my mother even more. She wanted me to leave GA every Christmas to be with her, but this was going to be the last time. Christmas morning was ghastly: Longman had drank more than he should have the night before; however, this was traditional from him. I was told he started from 4am, swearing, shouting and disturbing the children and the neighbours. When I arrived, he also attacked me verbally and then tried physically. He was pulled away by one of the tenants. I had found myself in a situation where there was nothing I could do. My mother had made a mess of her life and I wasn't prepared to try anymore. It was far beyond me; it was a load that my back was not fit to carry and a vicious circle of disaster. There was no stone that was unturned since I returned in their life. I had tried business after businesses for them to try and get them on their feet and every one failed. Since my childhood until then, there had not been a shred of improvement. How useless they were as parents, and as they got older it became even worse. What were their plans, to live like scroungers? Then the phone rang. It was GA wishing me a Merry Christmas. I discussed my reflections about the situation with him, and told him that I was furious and couldn't wait to return home.

He told me to be careful. I asked him how he was coping for dinner. He said he spent it alone and was making eggs for his breakfast. I felt sorry for him putting up with this nonsense of me being away from him at Christmas. I don't know what came over me. That was it, I went for round two with my mother. She reacted with sarcasm. I told her how useless she was. She married a man who had no use, for her own selfish gain, just to prove to the world she had a husband. I wanted her to tell me since she packed me up and sent me off to someone else to take her responsibility for what she had done in her life. Well I can answer, 'nothing' but now she wanted to use my fiancé, while she kept hers on the mantel piece buffing and polishing him. He didn't work; he has never even bought the clothes on her back. I didn't want her to put any pressure on my partner. 'From this Christmas, I will never leave my partner ever again to spend Christmas on his own.'

I meant every word, because since 2004 I have not returned to Jamaica. My mother did not retaliate, but you could see in her eyes that she had other plans and they were going to be vindictive. I knew it would be a while before I returned to Jamaica. I wanted to make sure that I organised and ensured the safety of the project, as it was incomplete, to prevent any squatters and land theft. I would be returning to the UK in the next few days. I asked my mother to accompany me to the land for the final view. We left at around midday. The sun was in its prime. As we reached the Mandela highway, the glorious sunshine had disappeared. The sky became overcast. I thought, 'I don't want to be on-site during the pouring rain.' We carried on for another two miles and the highway was gridlocked with traffic. And even though it was overcast, the heat was still piercing. We queued for an hour and a half, then I followed some cars that were taking a shortcut to Spanish Town. But when we reached a point, again bumper to bumper traffic. I was getting really tired and I had to get to the land today, only this time it was really jammed. I can neither go left or right and my inner voice said to me, 'you must abandon the journey, you will not get there.'

It was like a deterrent, not a warning, but I was determined. My mother was very anxious to get there. Two and a half hours later, we were still waiting. I was exhausted and extremely uncomfortable. As we got to another point, I tried again to escape, but the same result. We were held in traffic for six hours. The contractors waited and gave up eventually. It was now dark. There was no point going to the site when it was pitch black. I decided to head back home. I told the workmen to meet at a point on the high road. What I found strange was they travelled from the same location, and they told me there was no indication of an accident or traffic because they left at the same time and took the same route. It was like I was crazy. My mother was there, she saw what had happened. I later discovered that my spirit had prevented me from going to the land that day. I couldn't explain it, but I felt there was something spiritual happening, but I couldn't be sure. Anyway, it was too late. Now I was going back to the UK to have the baby – there was nothing I could do about it.

I was so pleased to return home. GA had done a fantastic job tidying up. It was time to prepare for the birth. The experience in Jamaica was real. I had realised that my mother was spineless, and there was a lot that was said. This woman's intention was to use me to scrape all she could from GA. I remembered a comment she made.

"Doesn't he know this is Jamaica. Let me see how he is going to come and take his place."

I asked her, "What do you mean by saying that? You have no right! GA's property has nothing to do with you. How ungrateful, this is the man who did your job, educated me, clothed and fed me, and gave me a chance in society so that I would not be inferior and this is the gratitude you would like to repay him with?"

I said, "I will tell you now, no one will take GA's property. Over my dead body. Why don't you use your husband?"

This woman was greedy beyond all belief. It was as if she wanted to jump into my boots and run my life for me. The insane thing about this was she didn't have a clue about life. She was extremely far removed from reality. This dream world of hers that she had been imagining had affected her – just sitting and dreaming about living in a mansion and travelling the world without working for it. I had now realised a pattern in my dreams. I only got them in the UK. They were back again. The dreams were directed at the baby, how disfigured the child would become and how it would not survive. The head of the child was at one point on the ground; it was dismembered from the body, rolled off the bed and bounced and rolled on the floor like a doll. I woke up terrified – my child was going to be ill or it was going to die. I rang my mother and told her.

She said, "Expectant mothers tend to have weird dreams."

I only had a few weeks left until the birth. I was fretting a lot about it and the intense dreams were really frustrating. I was so freaked out that I might not survive the delivery that I almost planned for my funeral as well. I had passed the due date. The baby normally moved in my stomach like there was a rugby team you could visibly see the tiny figure moving through my stomach. I was fascinated how amazing Mother Nature was, then noticed for three days there was no movement. I panicked – I began to think the worst. I rushed to the hospital, because at this stage it was advisable to check if there was less movement. The examination was carried out; the baby was fine, but they wanted to keep me under observation for a few hours. I stayed in hospital for the day and was discharged. I was over two weeks overdue when finally I went into labour the Saturday morning at 4am. We went to the labour ward; the pain was excruciating as expected. I went into the labour room and this overwhelming emotion took over. I looked at all the equipment and the cot to place the baby in, and I broke down in tears. I imagined this was where it was all going to happen, the death of the baby or me or maybe both of us. I was so terrified I couldn't let GA know. I would depress him with the way I was feeling. I just had to act normal because whatever happens will be horrifying. I felt there was nothing I could do now. I just had to pray and hope that God would deliver me from whatever these dreams had been revealing. The labour was really intense; it went on for twenty-four hours. The child was to be delivered and the nurse was extremely anxious after trying her best. On the last push she shouted, "Oh my God!" and for a while she seemed very nervous. I knew something was wrong; she kept quiet and just kept monitoring carefully.

Then she said, "I am so glad that I was careful."

I said, "What is happening? Is the baby OK?" My heart started to beat so fast, it was as if it was about to explode or I was about to pass out.

"The umbilical cord had wrapped around the baby's neck in such an unusual way. Had I applied even the slightest pressure it would have hanged the child," she said.

I said frantically, "Is it OK? Is it OK?"

No answer. I couldn't hear the baby cry. GA said when he saw the baby come out, it was as if she smiled to him. The nurse would not answer, she was busy cleaning up the baby and ignoring me. I believed something went wrong. After a few minutes, she turned around from the table and said, "Congratulations! You have a baby girl."

I could have sworn it was a boy after all that vigorous football going on in my stomach. GA was so delighted; she was so beautiful and fair. What a relief. The labour was intense and when we arrived the Saturday morning, the nurse that received me on the ward went home and came back on duty the evening to find us still struggling. She decided to help us. We were told that she was one of the most senior midwives – a real expert at her job. She was extraordinary. I was so pleased she helped us because of what could have happened to Baby Rebecca, Nurse Brown told me afterwards, "If an inexperienced nurse had done the delivery, the consequences could have been devastating." I was so relieved to know God helped me; my worst fear was over for the delivery. I took the baby home. We named her Rebecca.

Although I felt I had passed the worst, I was very cautious in the flat. I refused to allow the baby to sleep alone in her cot. I wanted to be sure that I could see her every move. As a result, I had less sleep than I needed as I was constantly in fear for the baby's life. I called my mother and told her the news of the birth of her granddaughter. We had the naming ceremony like we did for our first daughter Rachel.

I had decided to take six months maternity leave. It was important that I spend as much time as I could with my daughter. I was really concerned about Rachel in Jamaica. Now that her sister had arrived it would be unfair to raise them apart. I started to develop this anxiety within me. What would now be the plan for Rachel? I had no plans to keep my children apart and what would be the reason? I had discovered a lot on the last trip. My mother's intentions were clear to me; she was not interested in me. It was about her, all about her. I couldn't imagine how foolish I had been allowing myself to be deceived. How did this get so far without me realising? I always have a sharp eye to detail. From the last altercation I had with my mother, she had revealed another real nasty side she couldn't hide. What really bothered me was the deliberate verbal abuse, patronising me that if it wasn't for her son-in-law, when she knew damn well it was a lie. For without me she wouldn't have been in the position she was in now. This ungrateful woman had the nerve, telling me I was nothing. It was weird that my mother was envious of my life and even the relationship between GA and me. My persona towards the whole charade had changed for I started to have a different feeling. I wanted to never return back to Jamaica. I had enough of this nonsense. The feelings were getting stronger every time I thought about it, as if this immense hatred had developed between me and my mother. Even though we spoke regularly on the phone, the feelings were changing. It felt so insincere. When we communicated I could sense the feeling from her was mutual. Her reaction was to have no interest in what I said. The sound of my voice irritated her. She struggled to be genuine and sometimes pretended the bitterness between us was covered up with the odd gossip. It was as if I was forcing myself to keep a relationship with her. In our conversation, her reaction would be to just hurry and say what you had to – she was busy now.

GA told me one evening that he had something to tell me. It had been on his mind for a while and he was wondering if he should tell me, as it was so disturbing.

I said, "What is it?" anxiously.

He said, "Remember the night when you took me to the airport in Jamaica? Well as soon as we took off, it was less than an hour that I was so tired I fell asleep. Then I had the most disturbing dream. Your mother appeared to me in a dream this time. It was not as bad as the first dream where she pinned me down. In this one, she told me that if I knew what was good for me I should leave her daughter alone. It was a warning and I replied, 'I am not holding down your daughter.' Then I saw her change into you lying on the bed and inviting me to lay down with her. I said 'No!' She said, 'if you cannot love me the way you love her, then it will not work out' and I woke from the dream."

It was so disturbing he was unable to sleep throughout the whole duration of the flight. I was outraged, after all the belittling comments she made to me in regards to him and the gratitude he showed to her, building to accommodate her and husband, she appeared in the dream, wanting to take my life. That was beyond greed and ungrateful and a real sign of mental illness. What does she want, blood? But the dream was so spot on. It showed that she turned herself into me. If she could take my soul and live my life, I guess she would.

There was an odd sense that trouble was ahead. There was a new feeling I wasn't sure what it was. The dreams were appearing even more real, I started to see myself in some of the dreams dressed in full white with a turban like the revivalist and groaning in the spirit, speaking in tongues as if I was a member of a ritual taking place. There was a long table covered with a white tablecloth with various coloured candles – red, blue, green, purple, yellow, white, and gold. I also had this overwhelming power to conquer all. I woke up not sure what this dream was about, but it felt good. The dreams ranged from strangling and falling off a bridge to being attacked by some of the most deadliest creatures, like large scorpions, surrounded by black cats, black cows charging or attacking me. I knew I was definitely under attack, but I had other matters on my mind – my eldest daughter. The inner voice had spoken again, 'Rachel must be home by age ten years.'

The burden became heavier. I didn't know where to start. I had not made preparations for her and she would be ten years in a few months. I also had to care for a young baby. We had to find a bigger place, it was just not convenient. I also realised that the day Rachel returned home would be the biggest challenge of my life. I would have to turn back the clock for all the years I had lost that bond, which was not going to be easy. I felt my own daughter was a stranger to me. This really hurt me and was one of the biggest regrets I had in my entire life so far. There was something wrong and I couldn't put my finger on it. This was definitely a spiritual matter. I had to try and correspond with my guide, but how did I do it? Meditate perhaps, so I did.

I asked, "How bad is my situation. I know there is a danger to Rachel. Would it be death?"

She replied, "Not death, but severe problems and hardship."

I accepted and replied, "That is fine."

I was prepared to go through that, but it was my child who shouldn't go through hardship. The message was telling me that my mother had no intention of releasing my child. If I tried to take my child, she would challenge me. Deep down, I was prepared to go to the death and how could she challenge me? She could never succeed. Would she challenge me by witchcraft? I dismissed that. I knew she was vindictive, but no parent would perform rituals to harm their child and my mother was not involved in such acts anyway. I had no choice – I had to bring my child home. I kept recalling what my mother had said, the suggestion to snatch GA's property from him and the other sequence of events. My mind wanted to break free but was clouded. There was something not right. I tried my hardest to figure out the answer. What was preventing me from thinking straight? What was this enormous fear? For no particular reason I would gear myself up to tell my mother I was going to take Rachel home. As soon as I heard her voice, I would back down because of this overwhelming fear. There was more to come. It was like a big cloud of darkness over me and I was not sure what the weather forecast was going to be.

I struggled to come terms with this mental fight. How could it be so daunting to protect the future of my own flesh and blood? It was like mental torture followed by a severe headache, and sometimes blurred vision. I could feel this was going to be an extremely bumpy ride. I had to fight it to the end. I made up my mind that if I passed away in the process, I would be happier for my children to be in the UK. They would be looked after and would have a better opportunity in life. I went along with my plan – Rachel would return during the summer holiday. I had strong feelings not to inform my mother of my intention. I just felt so fed up of having to explain everything and getting nowhere. At the end of the day, it was my child and I could never live with myself if her life went wrong. I had told my mother several times that I wanted my child to return home and she found all the excuses in the world – the child was living in conditions that I was not happy with, she needed to have her own bedroom, and the yard was full of young boys. She was also developing and the only girl there – I could see danger. One night the inner spirit came to me and said, 'Rachel is in danger.'

As I received the message, I called my mother and said, "I am not happy with the conditions my child is in. She is in danger. She is going to be molested and it is now time for her to come home."

She replied, "What do you think can happen, for if I go to the toilet she is there with me."

Her response was unacceptable. From that day, that was it. The mental torture continued. I knew that whenever I got the warning, I must pay attention. I started to put GA under pressure. We had to find somewhere fast to put the children.

He said, "How can we make such a decision in a hurry?"

But it was like something inside of me was tearing me apart. GA started to look around for somewhere we might want to live.

I prayed and said, "God if I am going to die soon, I don't want to pass away and leave my daughter far away from her father. Please give me a solution to my problem. I have tried everywhere to get rehoused and no joy. Please give me a solution to this problem. I will wait on you."

I searched my thoughts about what to do and waited and waited and then it came to me – to sell the asset that my mother had been threatening GA about. This was painful, for we had invested towards our future and this would be distressing to lose our dream. I explained to GA. It was very upsetting for him, but he thought his child must come first, and it was now well overdue for his daughter to return. Friends and family gossiped that we were useless parents; we had gotten rid of our only child to gallivant around. All this was not true. It was at this point I realised I had been entrapped. I felt a host of pressure on me – it was like being tangled in a web. My child was important to me, but I also had the whole responsibility of my mother to think about – how she eats, sleep, medical bills, if she became seriously ill – and at the same time she was blackmailing me, that if I took my daughter could I see how I set out to use her?

Now that she had done all the work on her, given up her job in America and put her life on hold, then now I wanted to take all the glory; just use her and dump her. Whatever tactics she was going to use, I was sorry; I couldn't trade my child like a commodity. I couldn't sacrifice my child to furnish her desire of a luxurious life, a mansion and to live like royalty, squandering money to please the people that condemned her. After all, I must think about myself and the children first. She did not deserve more than she already received. She was a strange mother; she abused me as a child and was selfish. With no plans for my future, she abandoned me and sent me off to complete strangers while she arranged her life for the comfort of herself and her husband. When I returned to Jamaica to visit her, there were no signs that she had any plans or I was involved in her life anymore. She was satisfied with her position. She went to church and begged anyone who came from abroad for money and clothes and did the most degrading jobs for them, like cleaning their home and washing their clothes. All this was because she was lazy and had no ambition or vision in life; she was comfortable living this pitiful way until I turned up.

All the memories suddenly came flooding back. As a child she found all the excuses she could why I was not able to have books for school or shoes on my feet when I needed a pair of shoes, which was once a year or two. I had to write to my godmother and godfather in the UK, God bless them. I had to take my chair and sit on the neighbour's veranda to watch their television. The intense heat I endured without a refrigerator or even a fan and her excuse was we were not blessed like some people. The fact that I went to bed most nights without a decent meal and when it was time for my school uniform to be replaced, which was every two to three years, by this time the green tunic would have been bleached out by the sun and the thread under the armpits of my white blouse would be broken from continuous washing and wear and tear and growth. I would sew it so many times that eventually I would have to be careful to keep my arms down due to the embarrassment of friends noticing this huge hole. As for lunch, I went to school with hunger most days – a pack of cream biscuit and bag of juice to keep me for the whole day. I heard a lot of children complain about their childhood and poverty; I can sympathize as it was genuine, but for me it was not. My misfortune was about bitterness, revenge, selfishness, and greed. It was a marriage that had gone wrong and I was made to suffer for it. I was a British citizen and my father was wealthy. If she cared any at all, she could have made better decisions. I thought, moreover, that we were not alone. She had a partner, but it was always about her. I met friends who have found themselves in similar situation to my mother – the marriage failed, then divorce. They returned to their hometown to release the pain or get away to start a new life and when they found themselves in a difficult situation, the children were their priority. Drastic decisions had to be made like returning home to the UK and sometimes the United States, just anywhere to survive. I was obviously not important to her. She had the nerve to look me in my eyes and watch me suffer and spew abuse about how much I looked and behaved like my 'stinking father.' I didn't know what came over me, but I should have listened. If only I knew and understood this inner voice warning me never to get involved. Hypocritical friends and family that surrounded me knew the history of this woman and what she was capable of and they confused me that I was the one who was cold and I should be there for my mother. I should take care of my mother because I was the only child, because she really suffered. How did they know that? My mother was a master in deceiving people. When she realised she would be caught out that she was hopeless, the blame would be shifted onto my father – how he abused her and she had to escape with me, or how she had no luck in this world. I realised later that I was surrounded by people who were deceivers. They knew the problems about how useless she was and dangerous and they kept it to themselves. But what I found so disturbing was they were still encouraging and interfering, attaching us together. There was also jealousy; they would not or could not tell me the real problems or the history about my situation and pretended that every mother on the planet was responsible when they knew very well she was not. They were so conceited and led me into danger and later accused and ridiculed me about how stupid I was for what I had done. For instance buying a truck to help my mother's family, which was orchestrated by my mother. These people had abused my brother while he was in their care. It damaged his life so much it lead to his early death. And they caused me to leave my only child with the woman who physically and mentally abused me throughout my whole childhood.

Chapter 12

The real truth

I realised I had been used for nine years. Rebecca was a blessing – all was to be revealed because of this child. It was now evident my mother was very bitter towards the decision I had made to set up my life and live as a family with GA. She was unable to hide her dark and mysterious mind and heart. It became clear what her plans were and what she wanted. She knew I would decline, therefore she took an unusual approach to get what she wanted, after all: "I am not an easy nut to crack," she said.

GA and I were busy searching for a home to accommodate our daughters. It was not long now until Rachel's arrival. Our life was like a ship that had been sailing in the wrong direction and we turned it around to go in the right direction, away from the stormy seas and huge waves and tide. We put the property up for sale and the house sold instantly – we were amazed. We also had found a home. Everything was going so fast; it was as if there was something unusual speeding things along. We were holding back; it couldn't be this easy. But even so, the processing of the house for us to move in and the sale of the property was all completed and waiting for us to make the final move. I was apprehensive about this massive change that was about to take place in our lives. What if it didn't work? We were so worried that we didn't move into the new property until four months later.

We finally moved to our new home. I decided not tell my mother of the sale of the property or about our new home. Somehow, deep down, I felt I didn't want to tell her because she would be unhappy and make me feel guilty for moving on with my life without her, which was not the case – she was just selfish. The year 2006 was the biggest change in our lives. I had been living in the new property for months and I never experienced a single dream. Whenever I went to sleep, I would sleep peacefully and in a really deep sleep. I was so happy that this curse had gone away. I started to really love this new life; however, I was very worried of what the outcome would be when I told my mother of my new home. I had decided I would tell her when Rachel returned home so that she would not have any plans.

The day had come for Rachel to return home. We had arranged her bedroom for a little princess. I had another problem – even though I made several trips a year to see my daughter, we were still distant, like the bond was dismembered between us. I knew it would take some time for us to bond again; it was really peculiar. Rebecca was only one year old when Rachel returned. On their first meeting at the airport, Rebecca kept looking at her sister. I was concerned that if there would be any problems with them bonding together that Rachel might feel left out, but on that same day when they got home, Rebecca just changed. She was so delighted; it was as if she was examining her sister and suddenly realised, 'it must be my sister and I'm going to have a lot of fun with her.' The child was bursting with so much excitement she almost injured herself. Rachel was also very attentive to her younger sister. I decided now that Rachel had returned to tell my mother about the move. It was also complicated for me to tell her that Rachel would not be returning to Jamaica. I only told her about the move. She seemed delighted; not what I expected. I was afraid to tell her the other news. I believe that she had an idea that Rachel would not be returning, Rachel told me she suggested it to her at the airport, and in her spiteful vendetta, she sent Rachel back with only a dress in this huge suitcase. Things were really hard. We had to quickly adjust to family life. We were struggling financially, child care was an issue for the youngest, and my job was miles away. It meant I would leave home at 6am and return at 8pm. GA had a real challenge to get the children ready when I had gone and then get himself to work. Our struggle became unmanageable. I had to work so hard to support the family and also support my mother. I was desperate for help only for a little while. I called my mother and told her that I would be very grateful if she would help me for a while, as things were so difficult.

She replied, "I'm sorry mi love. I am too old to be coming over that cold place, sorry."

I thought how cold and ridiculous was that, here I was, busting my ass in the cold to support you and your partner and I just needed a hand with her grandchildren and she was refusing? GA was very angry with me for asking her for help. He figured that my mother was deliberately hoping that we would fail. He had a grudge after he overheard her comment to me the time when I had the miscarriage, that I should not go down that road and give GA any more children.

He promised me he would do it all on his own, after all, "They are my children," he said.

I knew this situation was far-fetched. We had to seek help. I started to look out for home help. The first person we had was so inexperienced she fed the baby with tin fish left in the can overnight and the baby's milk was warmed up in a water kettle. On many occasions I could smell burning and hear the fire alarm going off. We tried training her for a while, but there was no improvement. We had no choice – we had to dismiss her. I was getting really frustrated. I searched endlessly to get help, but was unsuccessful. I told my manager about the difficulties we were facing and she promised to help us find someone. A week later she told me that she had found someone who was very interested and ready for an immediate start. I couldn't believe my luck. By the weekend, I went to collect our au pair. I was delighted; she seemed very friendly. Rebecca loved her. We had some inexperience issues as well, but there was room for improvement. GA showed a sigh of relief; he was also tired. We started to make plans for how we were going to work really hard again to secure our future. GA was very protective of the children and even though we had the au pair, he wanted to be sure that the children were safe with this stranger in our home for a while. On Day 5, I returned home and GA seemed disorientated.

I asked, "Why do you look so depressed?"

He said, "Something happened here today that cannot be explained."

I said, "What?"

He said, "The nanny has gone."

"What happened?"

He said, "The nanny woke up as usual to feed the baby. They played together and she gave her a bath, then they both went upstairs for the baby to have her rest. They lay down together on the bed and within ten minutes I heard the au pair screaming. When I ran upstairs she was crying and clutching her Bible and a cross. She immediately demanded to leave the house. I begged her to explain what had happened and she refused. The woman was terrified and started packing her bags to leave. I asked her, 'why are you leaving in such a hurry?'

She said, 'I can't stay here not even another night in this house.'"

After what she had experienced, I couldn't believe what I was hearing. How could this disaster be; what happened to this woman? I really wanted to know. I rang her to tell her thanks for all she did and to find out what really happened.

She said, "No, I cannot tell you."

She seemed terrified. Was there something in my house that had attacked this woman spiritually or was she just pretending? I felt so sad to know she had gone. I sent her a gift; she returned it in the post saying that she was sorry, she couldn't accept anything from me. This was odd. We were back to square one within a week. GA believed that what had happened to the lady was spiritual and whatever it was meant to deter anyone from helping us, so we decided we would have to work out a plan and take on our own responsibilities and we did and managed quite well. The telephone rang one Saturday evening and out of the blue my father was on the line. I had not spoken to my father for over three years and here he was.

I said, "Where on earth have you been?"

He said, "I had some issues to resolve."

Apparently my father was going through the process of another divorce at his age. I just couldn't understand why he was going through these challenges, and he didn't think that I would want to support him. He didn't have to go through it by himself. He was very vague as to the situation. He didn't talk much about it, but he was anxious for us to meet. I was very busy with the children and work and told him it would be best for him to come and spend the Christmas with us. The children would also have the opportunity to meet their grandfather for the first time. He accepted my invitation. We would see each other for Christmas, which was months ahead.

The long hours and excessive travelling to work were taking their toll. I was very tired and hardly had any time for the children. I decided I had to look for a job that would be close to home or work from home, and I found both. I applied for two jobs and was successful in both. There was the job that was close to home and the other which was the career I studied for, which would enhance my finances and growth for the future. I accepted both jobs because the one close to home was a temporary position and the processing for me to start the other job would take over three months. I was so pleased with myself – there seemed to be light at the end of the tunnel, I thought. The job close to home was so convenient; I could spend more time with the children. I kept in contact with my mother and financed her, even though she refused to help me. It was like I was bullied into what I did for her. She showed such confidence that I was obligated to her and I didn't know why I thought I was. There was a new concept towards our relationship and the insincerity was at its worst. I was struggling to even pick up the phone to call her; her attitude on the telephone was abusive, sometimes rude and sarcastic, and most of the time it was about money. She would describe how things were hard in Jamaica. Things were hard everywhere and even worse when you decide not to do anything about your life. This was frustrating – here I was struggling, and I was still trying my best to support her. And then sarcastic remarks like these appear, that she would rather go and be a nanny to a cousin in America than help her grandchildren. I was confused as to where this conversation was going.

I said, "I am not sure. Are you saying that you prefer to go and work for your cousins than help out with your grandchildren?"

I didn't know what satisfaction she got out of winding me up, but maybe she thought that by saying this I would dole out some more money for her out of the money fountain I have here in the UK. I was annoyed. I told her she was welcome to go, but I knew deep down when she had gone to beg and be a slave to family and friends again after all that I had done. I would refuse to have anything to do with her ever again because I was now seeing greed beyond measure. I think she was expecting me to send the same amount of money to her as if Rachel was there and that was impossible, especially as I was struggling. The amount she received was the same amount her peers got from the UK for their pension and they survived very well. What was her problem?

The pressure for money was getting obscene. One day, she had the nerve to make requests for other family members as well. Whenever I called my mother to greet her, it seemed like she found all the problems on the whole island to dump on me, and it was guaranteed that they would be financial. It was like a bitterness to let me spend my money. When I spoke to her, she wasn't even listening to my conversation and hers was based on gossip because that was the only way she could have a conversation with me. When she asked about her granddaughter Rachel, she totally ignored Rebecca's existence. I corrected her on several occasions, but she failed to correct herself. My regular calls to her had reduced significantly. I used to call her twice a week. Now that the distance was clear, I called once a month or sometimes every five weeks. I was just fed up with the hypocrisy and constant demand for money and the doom and gloom. That was not my weight to carry; that should be between her and her husband. Once she came up with a ridiculous request again for money, I was really angry and she was being forceful about it, as if I was obligated. I put the phone down on her. I didn't think she had the audacity to be controlling me, like she did when I was a child. The dreams were no more, but there was still that problem of the invisible grains that were embedded inside me during intercourse and the blood was oozing out profusely. I started getting severe headaches with disturbed vision and the worst was I felt like my eyes were forcing out of their sockets. I couldn't understand; it was so painful. I arranged to have an eye test; maybe I needed glasses. My vision was fine and the opticians did additional tests to determine the symptoms I was describing, yet nothing was found. My eyes were being plucked out of my head. I would sit in my room alone in the darkness pressing my hand on my eyes to push them back in. The problem started to affect my attendance at work. I visualised dark red spots inside of my eyes. It appeared like blood floating around in my vision. I decided to revisit a famous London hospital for eye complaints, as I'd had an operation there in the past. They carried out the most rigorous test; I went a few times and they found nothing. I called my mother and told her what was happening and she suggested I was just tired. Although our relationship was not sincere, I still called her and supported her in any way I could. Dad and I kept in regular contact. My mother was so bitter towards him that when I mentioned to her that I spoke with him, the abuse she would spew was vile: "that dirty stinking wicked man, Obeah worker. I have nothing to do with that man."

I said, "Excuse me, that is my father you are talking about and moreover you call yourself a true child of God. Where is the forgiveness that you preach? Don't you ever speak about my father like that again. He is my father and I love him the same as you. I am not taking sides."

She continued, "I don't care what anyone says."

I thought, 'she's a fine one to talk after kidnapping me from my father and her lame excuses.'

It was only God who saved me from becoming the next drug addict or the girl down the stream who had to survive through prostitution and later end up with many children from different fathers. Now she was condemning my dad. I decided that I would have a relationship with my father anyway; she had no right to dictate to me what I do, especially with my own flesh and blood. My dad also has his say; he warned me about how dangerous she was and that I shouldn't let her know where I lived or give her my money because she would use it to harm me. I was fed up with this verbal bashing, from the left and right he said this all the time, but how would I prevent my biological mother from coming to my home, and I am the person that fed her for years. I was not interested; they both had issues between them and they needed to sort it out after thirty odd years.

The second job I accepted. Once all the processing was completed, I would start my dream job as a financial adviser for one of the UK's top financial services firms, which also had chains of supermarkets, pharmacies, and funeral services. The training would occur over two years. I felt really proud of myself. I rang my mother and told her the great news. I started the job in October 2007. It was intense, as I expected. It was really what I wanted to do and I was getting on really well. The headaches persisted with the piercing in my eyes and other symptoms started to develop when I lay in bed.

I could feel a cold sensation running up my legs, like ants crawling up my arms and legs, but cold and tingling. I thought that it was weird, maybe it was menstrual. But it became frequent and always when I lay down in bed. I had had a sensation like this before. I remembered years ago when I visited my grandfather's grave. It was peculiar, a gradual cold sensation moving up from my foot, and at the same time I felt my head growing. I didn't have to ask any questions as to what it was. I thought my grandfather was probably pleased to see me, but I was not at a burial ground, so why was this happening in my bed? I told GA about it. We believed it was spiritual and it continued. I coped with it for a while, but it was as if that was not enough. Something else was added; for no reason, I would feel deeply depressed. One minute I was fine and the next disheartened. This was also quite frequent, as well as the other symptoms. I just couldn't understand how I could be depressed without a reason. So whenever it happened I would meditate and think about what had triggered this and I still couldn't find a reason. In the next stage, I started to become morose and threw tantrums. We would end up having an argument over something really stupid, for instance: "I don't like your question, why are you asking me what time I will be back?" he said.

I always asked what time he would be back, how odd.

The job was also getting more demanding. There were constant examinations which I needed a lot of time to study for and I was now working, also having targets to meet. I started to really struggle and GA had this weird pattern. He would be fine most of the time, but guaranteed, whenever I had an examination he would create the worst morning for me. Without a reason he would throw the biggest tantrum and speak the most ridiculous nonsense. We would end up arguing and away I went, to take the exam. I realised the pattern and whenever I had an examination, I would keep it to myself. But that never worked; we would still have a nasty argument.

I asked him, "Why do you always deliberately try to ruin my exam? Don't you want me to pass?"

He said, "It is not really me who causes the problem – it is you."

"But how could it be me? I have an exam; why would I want to upset myself before taking it?" I didn't understand this, and it went on and on. It was like torture sometimes. I hated to go home. As soon as I got in, GA would attack me verbally about how I had ruined his life, I had put him in a difficult situation and now he would never do well, his life was over, my mother and I used him and wasted so much of his money and now things were impossible. This was really painful for me to hear, because I was sincere and I wanted to spend the rest of my life with GA. I didn't believe in deceiving or using anyone. I realised my mother did; she had been a user all her life. She did it to my father and I would be damned to adopt such behaviour. After all that had been done, I couldn't blame GA for what he said because it seemed as if I was a user – using him to build a house for her and her husband whilst our one and only child was left with her for many years. My mother used my daughter as her money tree. I get really frustrated when I get accused, but how do I explain it? I failed to believe how I could be so carried away and stupid and not seeing what was happening. I took it on my chin for I knew it was my fault that my family ended up in this situation. Unfortunately, I struggled to give reasonable explanations, but what was for sure was that I wanted the world for us and not for anyone else.

My home started to turn into chaos – Rachel was misbehaving at school, GA and I were constantly arguing, and I felt really exhausted. I couldn't see how things could get better with the dreadful conflicts. I was living such a miserable life now. It was as if I had made five steps backward. To add to the deterioration of my health, it was as if I was moving, but I didn't know where I was going. The relationship between me and mother had broken down. I was sensing bitterness and hatred, so I didn't want to tell her what was happening at home; it didn't feel right. I started to have this weird feeling about my mother. It was as if she had turned her back on me. I would call her and she would respond in an unresponsive way and when I reported to her about Rachel's performance and behaviour, she reacted in such a rejoicing way. She would say, "Do you think you people can handle her?"

I replied, "What skills do you possess to handle her that her mother and father do not?"

It was the sign of the bitterness all coming out. She had a massive grudge. I didn't care, my child's future was more important. The tension was so high that sometimes I would have to prepare myself for the next round of blame, torture and be haunted with verbal abuse from GA. It was the same thing over and over on a daily basis – how my mother and I used him. There were times I felt I didn't need this; I was going to run away. I was exhausted in this fight. It would have been easier if children were not involved. But for the children's sake, deep down I knew something was wrong here. During the times we were not arguing I realised GA was still in love with me and I loved him.

I had an assessment on this particular day; this had become routine. I prepared myself for another round of verbal torture. It was about 6am that morning. Rebecca came to our bedroom, as young children do – they tend to enjoy the warmth of their parents' bed. She came to my side of the bed. I hugged her to have a snooze. After about 5 minutes, she removed herself from my arm and sat up on the bed.

I said, "Are you OK, Becky?"

Then Rebecca sprang off the bed, screaming frantically. She looked at me like I was her enemy and ran away from me. I was so shocked, frightened and confused. What was happening? I reached out to hold her, but she ran away from me to her dad. She was fine when she came in the room.

We asked her, "What is the problem?"

She kept screaming hysterically.

Then she said, "There was a white cat and the cat went up through my bottom and it is inside me."

I asked, "Is it in the dream?"

She said, "Yes."

Then she started again. When she looked at her hands, she screamed, "The cat's paws are inside my hands. It's inside my hands!"

She kept stamping and screaming. When she looked at her hands, it seemed to her that it was the paw of the cat and she kept touching her bottom and looking behind her and every time she would scream even more. I thought it was a nightmare because Rebecca suffered frequently from them. Her sister rushed to the room to console her. I believed that she would snap out of it when we explained to her that it was just a dream, but as the morning went on the terror this poor child was going through grew worse. Rebecca loved cats, I couldn't understand it. This was the time I should be on my way to work to take my exam. We were unable to control the situation. I hysterically screamed out, "Oh my God, my child has gone crazy!"

I was shaking, I was frustrated. I took off all her clothes to show her it was just a dream. There wasn't anything that had gone inside her body. My child did not look the same; it was as if she was someone else. My three-year-old stood in the corner naked and frightened. I was so afraid. Her dad took her for a bath and we all watched to see if there were any changes. No one could leave the house that morning, after her bath. She settled for a little while and then the screaming started again. It was now 12pm. I rushed her to the hospital. The doctor assessed her, determined that she had a disturbing dream, and put her under observation for the next 24 hours. That day when I returned home, I knew that this was going to affect me severely; how could I go on? What happened to my child? The incident led us to be put under investigation with social services. They asked if any of the parents took drugs or performed black magic. I couldn't believe it.

This carried on all day. I had to call my mother. I was convinced the problem was spiritual. For the first time in my life, I started to realise and believe that this was for real – I had seen it with my own eyes. My mother told me to light a candle and read a psalm and she should be fine. I did it anyway – it was not going to work – she knew nothing. The fear I had encountered for my child disturbed me. I would be on alert, constantly listening to see if she was fine. She slept well that night and the following morning. It was as if it hadn't had happened, from that day on I did not allow Rebecca to sleep in my bed.

It was almost Christmas. I was looking forward to having the first Christmas with my father since we reunited. Due to my mother's relentless bitterness, I did not tell her about my plan. After all he was my father; she would try to discourage me from inviting him. I was not going to take sides. The first meeting GA had with my father was in 1994. My father seemed distant, but over the years, he realised the commitment GA had and they became close. GA told me not to inform my mother about my father's visit.

"I don't trust her," he said.

I said, "What do you mean, what can she do to Dad?"

He kept silent. The time had come to meet Dad. The children were very excited to meet their grandfather. I had not seen Dad for a while and was anxious to see if there were any changes. When I saw him, I could see myself in him. We were delighted and anticipated it was going to be one of the best Christmases. There were many things Dad wanted to discuss. He had this idea that the telephone was never the best place to have a discussion in regards to private matters. Someone was always listening. This would also be the opportunity to ask questions about my parents' relationship, how it deteriorated, and to resolve this ridiculous conflict between them. What I enjoyed most about my father's explanations was that they were sincere. You could understand and get an honest reason. My mother was always vague and when I pressed for clarity, it would be brushed off with, "You have no idea how wicked that man is."

Dad came on that trip because he wanted to warn me about my mother. He also wanted to show his love to his daughter that my mother had taken away from him. He expressed the pain he went through for years when she took me away.

He said, "I remember every birthday, and the thought of how much I loved you and you were very proud of your daddy as a little girl when we took the bus. You would tell everyone this is my daddy. I am getting old now. I can die at any time. I want you to know I would never have abandoned you. Your mother is not what she seems to be."

I said, "What do you mean Dad?"

"She performs evil and wickedness."

To be honest, I thought he was saying a lot of rubbish.

Then I asked, "What has she done, for you to be able to convince me?"

He said, "The spell she cast upon me, my health deteriorated so badly that the bones in my body went to a serious stage – every tooth fell out; I collected them one by one in a kerchief – due to the amount of potion she used to destroy me. You must never give her your money, you must never let her get a hold of your clothes, you must never allow her to come to this house – she will destroy you."

I said, "Well if she did all these things you have mentioned, what did you do?"

He said, "I had to seek spiritual help in Jamaica; I had to protect myself. When she sends a blow I take revenge and also send her a blow."

I found all that my dad was saying baffling. The other thing that struck me was my mother always complained that my father was a witchcraft worker and when I asked her how she overcame it, she would say, "If it wasn't for my prayers to God."

And I believed that because of the society she was involved in, but my inner spirit was telling me there was more to her story.

We had a wonderful Christmas. Dad really enjoyed himself. We ate and drank. There were two days left until his return and I thought, 'I hate to play the hypocrite.' I was wishing Mother a Merry Christmas over the telephone while Dad was spending Christmas with us. I decided I would tell her. GA was in the living room and Dad was outside with the children.

I said, "I have something to tell you; Dad is here."

She said, "Really?"

I said, "I wanted to see him. He has been telling me some dreadful things. Anyway, the reason I am telling you is because I want you both to get along."

After we spoke about her Christmas, she sounded fine to me. Then I asked, "Would you like to speak to Dad?"

She said, "Yes I will. I am a child of God you know."

I said OK and I went to fetch Dad.

I said, "Dad, Mum is on the phone. Would you like to speak to her?"

He said, "Yes, that's OK."

It would have been over 34 years since they had seen each other. I was really excited. I listened as they greeted each other. It was civil, until my dad started to ask some weird questions.

He asked, "So where do you live and which church do you attend? What does your husband do?"

I just didn't want a fight; for the first time maybe peace would reign. Their conversation lasted for ten minutes. I wasn't sure if some of the conflict had been resolved. I was hopeful and was very pleased my mother had cooperated. I asked how he felt the conversation went.

He said, "It was OK, but nothing has changed about her."

I am sure I share the same experience with many individuals where parents have separated and you are like the referee in a boxing ring; you just want your parents to acknowledge your feelings and respect that no matter what, you are hurting when they are continuously at war. That same evening, my dad called me to his room. He wanted to have a one-to-one chat. He told me the history of my grandfather and his conversation was concerning. He spoke as if he was going to die, talking about plans after his death.

I said, "Dad is there anything I need to know? Are you dying?"

He replied, "Everyone has to die. You must take the instructions I have given you seriously."

I asked, "Dad, the first time we met, you were extremely uncomfortable. Is it because of the experience you said you had with my mother – the witchcraft and gold-digging – maybe you thought I was the same?"

He said, "Yes, because I know without a doubt your mother is useless and conniving. If I knew my granddaughter was going to be with her, I would have forbid it. She has very bad habits, not suitable for a girl, and that's why when I met you I thought you might have inherited her persona."

I pretended I understood what he meant; I really wish I had asked him to elaborate when he made that statement. Dad had only a few days left; the week had gone so quickly. We planned to go out the next day and see his side of the family, but when Dad woke up the following morning, he didn't seem happy. I thought maybe he was not feeling well and he didn't want to make me worry. Then later that evening, GA called me into the bedroom. He said he had something to tell me.

"Your father told me in confidence that I should not tell you, but I told him you should know. He had a terrifying nightmare last night."

I said, "Really, what about?"

"He was attacked. Whatever it was tried to strangle him, can you see! When I tell you things, you don't listen. I told you not to tell your mother he was here."

I was so disappointed and desperate to prove my innocence. Dad had been here for five days and had no problems until he spoke to my mother. How did I know he was not making this up? I immediately went to Dad.

I said, "Dad, GA told me what happened. What was this dream about?"

He said, "They came to worry me. I asked, 'who sent you?' Don't worry, I conquered them when they tried to hold me down."

I had a problem with this for I had been having the same experience for years, until I started living here. How he described the experience was the same.

I said, "Dad, please don't think I had anything to do with this."

He said, "I know it is not you."

I couldn't believe it; here I was trying to build a relationship with my father and it was about to end. I was trying to be as nice as I could before he went home. I was still confused. Was it my mother? She told me she was 'a child of God.' She seemed to be fine with Dad being here, but I didn't think that was truly the case.

We drove Dad to the airport on his return to New York City. He seemed fine, but I had a feeling this might be last time he would visit us. I kept in contact with Dad for a while until 2010. I lost contact and he disappeared. I couldn't help being cautious with my mother after what had happened to my father. It was as if she was threatened by him and wanted him gone. She was jealous of him getting close. After a while, I didn't talk about him with her anymore. She tried to get information, but I would tell her I hadn't heard from him.

She replied, "That's good he is where he belongs, that filthy man."

I said, "I have told you many times, do not speak about my father like that."

She replied, "I don't care."

This mysterious depression was like something piercing my heart and was constant. I didn't know what brought it on. I had to check back with myself – what had I done today to trigger this? Most of the time, I didn't know the reason. Another symptom started: at about 3am I would wake up tormented with the piercing eye pain. I would try desperately to go back to sleep, but I would be up until I was ready for work. This went on for weeks. I tried going to bed later, drinking hot chocolate, and exercising in the evening to make myself more tired. I told my mother about the symptoms I was experiencing. She suggested I was just tired. I sought medical advice, but there was nothing much to do, as the doctor could not make a diagnosis.

The demand for money was less now, but there was a new problem developing in our conversation. Her mother had taken ill – she was senile and had other complications that resulted in blood loss. To be honest, I was not interested. I sympathised with the family, but I never got on with her, so I didn't know why I would now. It was not my problem and I let my mother know that. What did my mother want me to do? She put all of her burdens on me and this was one I would not carry. Whenever this was mentioned, I would ignore her. This depression was growing stronger; it was so overwhelming it made me miserable and drained every ounce of strength in my body. GA started to realise that I was becoming so sad. I started to have the thought that I should see my mother, but I did not have time due to the intensity of my job training.

I was getting to the final stage of my course. One morning at 3am this brilliant idea appeared that I should invite my mother to visit us. I discussed it with GA and he was uncertain. I told Mum the great news and she was delighted. My inner voice was contradicting itself – one minute it said I should let her come and the other that it was a bad idea. There was also another problem – I discovered that processing her visa was complicated. When Rachel returned, my mother went to apply for a visa with the intention of inviting herself on my behalf. She took all of my personal documents as well as GA's to get a visit. As a result, the embassy was dissatisfied with her claim as it appeared fraudulent, and denied her access to the UK. I was furious for that was a silly thing to do. I left her in care of my documents and trusted her not to take them out and make applications in my name. I had to appeal on her behalf for them to allow her back into the UK. All through the process, I had this battle indecisively. I thought – don't her allow here, allow her here. I went to GA.

I said to him, "Do you think I am doing the right thing to let her come here?"

He said, "Of course you are doing the wrong thing. When she sees how well you have done, especially our new home, she will be jealous. But I have no problems, it is your mother."

I kept thinking about it and thought, I will explain that if she is not happy with the way I have set up my life and the better future I have created for her grandchildren, then there is nothing I can do if that is not acceptable to her. Deep down, I wasn't excited about her coming to see us. This trip had to happen. It was in my head for days and nights. It kept playing on my thoughts. We didn't get along – she was a control freak and a bully. I predicted there would be conflict throughout the whole visit. There was no way out. Why did I feel this way? It took me three weeks to make a decision. She would arrive in July 2009. GA and I were tense, so many weird things had been happening. This was test of faith; she was due to arrive the Monday morning.

The day had come. I left home on time to meet my mother at the airport. There was a delay on the motorway, which set me back an hour. I got there and quickly made my way to the departure lounge. There she was sitting in the lounge waiting. I was not as excited to see her as I should be. There was something in her eyes that was insincere. I hugged her and asked, "How was the flight?"

She replied, "It was nice."

I apologised to her for the delay and took her luggage. She instantly started to patronised me, mentioning how much I had put on weight.

She said, "I almost didn't recognise you."

I was not happy with the backhanded compliment as I was still fighting to get rid of my baby weight. We went to the car park – and this had never happened to me before, but I forgot where I had parked the car, perhaps in the rush. I had my mother walking around with me for forty minutes. Then I decided, it was best I let her have a seat in the lounge whilst I tried to locate the car, which was another twenty minutes later. On our way home, she was making conversation, but it was so disingenuous. I knew she had a lot on her mind, but I was waiting to hear it. Her main concern was Rachel not being at the airport. I knew the journey home was going to be a long one. I hoped when she got home that she would be impressed with all the preparations I had made for her and then at some point we would have a serious talk.

We finally got home. I made her comfortable and showed her some of the programmes on the television I knew she would love, so she would be entertained. I wanted her to tell me if she liked our new home. She made no comment, but just kept looking in admiration. She carried on with the usual gossip. I sat with her while she relaxed and we were in deep conversation. As soon as Rachel arrived from school and entered through the front door, she sprang from the chair in excitement, hugged and kissed her, and told her let's go upstairs and talk. I thought, 'wait a minute!' She was only buying time until Rachel came home. She had no interest in me or what I had been saying. She played that really well and what was she discussing with Rachel that I shouldn't hear? After all, it was my house and daughter. I was left alone in the living room while they had the bedroom door shut in my own house. I felt belittled and rejected. I was hurting. I went into the kitchen to prepare the meal. They were upstairs for hours. I could hear them laughing and joking. I went to collect the youngest, this would be the first time my mother would meet her granddaughter. I sent her upstairs to interrupt the conversation, I heard her say,

"Hello, you are a sweet little girl, how was school today?"
Rebecca reacted shyly and said, "OK."

And then my mother said, "Bye," and shut the bedroom door, leaving her outside the door. Rebecca was always close to her sister. My mother was reacting like the child was a neighbour or friend, and I was very disappointed. I called Rebecca downstairs and consoled her. I wanted to see how long these shenanigans were going to go on for. When GA returned from work that evening, I told him about the experience I had and worst of all, how Rebecca was treated in her own home. I couldn't blame Rachel, she was a child. I could see that my mother's intention was to create division in my family. It was like I had been bullied all over again. This went on for three days and I was really upset how Rebecca had been rejected. I had had enough of it and stormed upstairs in a rage. They had locked Rebecca out again. I opened the door and said, "What the hell do you think you are playing at? Why do you lock Rebecca out of the room? What are you discussing that she cannot hear or for her not to be there? You have no right to do this. This is her home. Is it your plan to come here and create division in my home? I know you hate Rebecca – that's fine, but don't you dare take my daughter Rachel and have private conversations behind closed doors in this house."

There was a great silence in the house; GA was also annoyed about my mother's behaviour. Then she came downstairs – no explanation or apology – it was like nothing had happened. I could see her beckoning to Rachel like a signal or mocking. She was planning to carry on. Rachel started to behave strangely. It was like she was influenced and coerced into being a different child. She became disrespectful to her father when she misbehaved, throwing tantrums and abuse and I watched my mother from a distance celebrating it and encouraging it. GA took Rebecca to the nursery that morning. I had a feeling I was going to hear bad news. The telephone rang – it was GA; he had had an accident. I was so anxious that I quickly drove down to see them. The airbag was deployed and the car was a write off. This was the second accident in two weeks. The first time he was hit by the neighbour's car. Thank God they were fine; we had only bought the car over the weekend for work. I had to use the spare car that evening to go to work. My appointment was very late that evening. I was very concerned about leaving Rebecca in the care of my mother because of the way she behaved towards her and GA also would be coming home late. I called and said I didn't feel comfortable with Rebecca being in my mother's care and if possible could he please try and get home sooner. I drove out that evening and on my way down the A6 I had a premonition I was going have an accident, so I went slowly. As I approached the roundabout, I felt a big push forward. A van had run into the back of my car. I couldn't believe it. I asked the driver what had happened. How could he not see me? He said his foot slipped. The car was driveable and I managed to get to work. How bizarre – two accidents in one day; there was definitely a problem here. I thought my mother had serious bad luck with her. Very rarely did we experience any type of collision, much less so many in such a short space of time.

I came in from work one day and as I entered the front door, the vibes in the house had changed. I thought what the hell! I had told my mother many times that I had the gift to detect spiritual entities if they ever entered my territory. She said my father was a witchcraft worker; however, when he came here, there weren't any vibes. His spirit was calm and sincere, but on this day something had gone wrong in my house. It was like a ball of fire containing confusion, with conflict floating about. I was not happy. I didn't want whatever crap she possessed to be off loaded in my house and for a member of the revival she should get it sorted out. I didn't like this one bit, not around my children. When we moved into this house three years ago, I was attracted to the house because of the peace that dwelt there. It was like someone with a good heart. I went upstairs, got changed, and came down for dinner. I was still trying to understand the change. It was making me angry, for I sensed there was a big problem. Every time I looked at mother, she made me cross. Even when she opened her mouth to talk, I pounced on her. There was something in her eyes that was dark and mysterious. She had a lot of vengeance. She even had the nerve to start her verbal abuse again about my father. I was not going to listen to this. I lashed back at her and told her how ungrateful she was.

I said, "My father, who took you out of the slum when even your mother abandoned you, brought you to the UK. How ungrateful, how could you ever have had the opportunity to return to the UK without the influence of him through me?"

She said, "I don't care, he is a wicked man."

I said, "That's all you can say. I haven't ever seen what good you have ever done in your life or mine – just vile verbal and physical abuse. Answer this: why did you leave the UK and let me suffer so much, no food sometimes, begging my godparent for clothes when you had a husband?"

She replied, "But that is their job; that is what godparents do."

I said frantically, "You must not say such crap. I can't believe you haven't even sat down to give me a reasonable explanation. They have their children; they don't ask godparents to provide for theirs; only you did and that is using. Answer this: you have never asked me how I coped when I was thrown out on the street at age 16, have you? Where were you? My godmother was the only person who cared to look out for me whether I was dead or alive."

She replied, "I am sure they regret what they did."

I got up and left her in the kitchen. This conversation was going nowhere. The rage in me was getting more intense towards my mother. GA told me off for picking on her, even though he disapproved of her visit. I just couldn't help myself. It was as if I was out of control. I had lost all respect for her. GA was also getting irritable with me with that same bad temper when I wanted to do my exams. He just started pouncing on me for no reason.

I asked, "Why are you having a go at me?" He looked at me in confusion; he couldn't give me a genuine answer.

He said, "I don't know. I am in a strop. It is because of your mother. I am not happy with her."

My mother insisted on using Rachel as her ally to cause havoc in the house, whispering to each other, still having private meetings; she was determined. I came home early one evening to find that Rachel was allowed to introduce her boyfriend to her. I didn't know my daughter had a boyfriend. I heard my mother saying at the door, "Let me see him," jokingly, completely oblivious to me. This was my home and family and she was taking over and being a pain and annoying me. She was trying to prove to me she owned Rachel and there was nothing I could do about it. In order for her to win her trust and love, she would allow and suggest to the child to get up to some ridiculous things. I was living with a bully in my own house. I went to my bedroom one evening. I couldn't wait for GA to come home, being the squatter in my own home I laid on my bed, wide wake and my inner voice came to me louder than ever with a warning.

It said, "You should not eat her food when she cooks." Immediately GA came through the door, I told him as he was about to enter the kitchen.

I said, "Listen; do not ever eat her food."

He looked at me in astonishment; he understood immediately and smiled in acceptance, nodding his head. She realised we were not interested in her food. I could see the disappointment. She asked me to eat. I told her I was not hungry. The argument and pouncing on my mother had reduced. I realised something significant after a while. Whenever I got angry to tell her off, I struggled to get the words out and my anger would change. I tried it on several occasions and I couldn't.

I said to GA, "My mother has used something so that I will not be able to confront her when I am angry."

He looked at me peculiarly; he probably thought I was crazy.

I was dumbstruck and confounded; she could now have her wicked way.

I took my mother shopping and to meet her friends in London, five miles away from home. As I drove towards the roundabout, this car was oblivious that we were on the road. It sped to overtake us and couldn't avoid the oncoming car and smashed into my door, literally pushing us off the road into some bushes. What was peculiar was that the car I was travelling in was the courtesy car from the recent accident. I was in so much shock. I felt nauseated. The police and ambulance came to our rescue and now I really had to believe that maybe somebody was going to get killed. This was the third accident in three weeks. I overheard my mother in the car telling Rachel, "Yes, the reason why she is having these problems is because she does not give her heart to God."

Rachel replied, "I don't think so Grandma. My mother is an excellent driver. I have never known her to have an accident ever."

I looked at my mother repulsively; she would find any excuse and put the blame on anything or anyone to escape herself. I was finding it difficult to cope with my mother, her behaviours were appalling, the deceitfulness and immense greed – she could not be satisfied. She started to contact all her friends and family that we had lost contact with to receive gifts. I refused to do a repeat of the last trip, so she spitefully developed an illness overnight, in which I had to call the emergency doctor, which turned out to be a routine check, nothing serious was wrong. It continued with dental and optical; she was on a mission to take everything she could get at my expense. I also realised the purpose of the trip was paramount to her mother. She was dying. I discovered when I overheard a telephone conversation with her sister; she knew the only way to get support for the funeral was this trip. I was pondering what had changed her mind, since when I asked her to help me with Rebecca and she gave all the excuses such as the weather and her health, once again I had been used and fallen into her trap. She really took me for a fool and her cash cow. She had become overpoweringly confident. It was as if she had accomplished what she had set out to do. I was submissive, she could release whatever verbal abuse she liked and I would be dumb to answer. For instance, we were having breakfast and she made this sarcastic comment:

"I don't know, but I love boys, I prefer boys more than girls," with a smirk on her face.

This was aimed at me to patronise me. Because I didn't have boys I was less than a woman. GA realised that she was out of order and started to retaliate.

One morning I came downstairs into the kitchen to greet my mother. The children had already gone to school. She was washing up and I stood by the door as I was on my way out. I remembered a story from my childhood that I wanted to remind my mother about, then suddenly as I got closer to her, my head was expanding with the tingling cold shooting up my legs with goosepimples. It made me cross.

I said, "Mum, there is an entity right here."

She said, "Really?"

I said, "Yes."

"Maybe it is something you sense is coming," she said, looking up to the sky through the kitchen window.

I said, "No, it is right here in front of me."

And I left the kitchen in a rage and went straight through the front door. I sat in the car on the drive. She didn't realise I could see her silhouette through the glass door, running hastily upstairs. I gathered that something was odd. I started to investigate in her room when she went out to church on Sundays. I was hoping to see bottles of oil or an ornament. Unfortunately nothing. Could it be she was carrying a very deep and dark destruction and if so why doesn't she seek help from the revival workers? Whatever she was carrying was contagious and it was affecting my home. I became more curious about her movement. I think she caught on. I was concerned about leaving her in the house. I was not sure about her. We had a huge row again. This time, I wanted answers to some of the things she had done and said about me. There was a comment she made that 'she regrets the day she gave birth to me,' told by her husband. Of course, her answer was, "The man was highly intoxicated; it is a load of rubbish."

I wanted to know why she was physically abusing me.

She replied, "It didn't kill you did it? Look at you now."

I said, "You nearly did. The day I left school late and you hit me on my head with the wooden clothes brush, my head burst open and the blood was oozing out."

She instantly denied it and said, "Jesus have mercy! When? I don't remember anything about that."

I was horrified to realise how cold and callous my mother was as well as being a compulsive liar.

I said, "How can you look me in the eyes and deny your malicious act? And on top of that, you lied to my daughter, that as a result of this same incident I killed your unborn child."

She said, "I didn't tell Rachel that. She must have overheard something."

I said, "Ah so you did say it from your own lips. I didn't even know you were pregnant. I learnt this years later. Your anger that day, because I came in from school late, led to your miscarriage and I have heard this same accusation from your husband."

In the evening when GA returned, she started to bring up the conversation, looking for him to intervene and defend her. She was complaining she didn't like the way I confronted her. He didn't want to get involve and ignored her. She pretended everything was well with her and continued with the private meeting with my eldest daughter Rachel. It was as if she was training the child to become a terror. I could hear them together in the house making signals and code, laughing out loud together, and we were not a part of it. The atmosphere was intense. GA returned home one evening in distress. He had an accident again, in the replacement car, only this accident was different.

He said, "As I was coming along the dark road, I was in good spirits and enjoying the stereo. I decided to cruise as I was near home. The car behind overtook me. I remember looking in the mirror at the time. I though he's in hurry and then out of nowhere there was a deer. It stood still in front of me. I couldn't break in time. I couldn't not swerve as the other car was overtaking at the same time. I collided with the deer; unfortunately it did not survive."

He managed to get home. He was so upset about the deer.

He said, "I saw its face and I couldn't save it." The car was a write-off. In one month, we experienced four accidents. We were lucky not to sustain any injuries. I felt sad too.

I was getting fed up with my home being invaded. It was not pleasant. The hypocrisy was blatant. She suddenly gained so much power. She ignored what I disliked most – bringing people into my house. She did it even more to prove there was nothing I could do. She would just get on with what she wanted, calling my ex-friends that I didn't get on with on my phone and having conversations behind my back.

GA and I had become very cautious about staying in the house after the experiences. He would get in very late in the evening to avoid her. Something odd was happening to him. He developed this uncontrollable urge of consistent arousal and erection. I just didn't know what was going on with him. We would be sitting with the children watching the television when he would have this urge to go to bed. I thought he had taken Viagra or some sort of aphrodisiac, but he didn't need it. I was really concerned. He was so embarrassed to talk about it. He felt out of control, and it was happening always when he saw me. There was a time he was so frustrated, it was like he would rape me. My inner voice was telling me that she was interfering with my private affairs in my bedroom. I thought, 'no! I am going absolutely crazy.' I knew she was strange, but I don't think she was capable of that, and what would she gain from it anyway? It didn't make sense. I had another appointment for an operation to resolve the on-going haemorrhage and stone-like sensation I had been experiencing for nearly a decade. I had been telling her about it for so long. As she seemed uninterested, I didn't bother to mention it until the morning of my appointment. I could see the fear and worry in her eyes. As I went through the door, she hurried, calling me back inside for prayers.

I said, "Why?"

Did she not realise it was serious before now? I refused to accept her prayers.

I told her, "No thank you."

Obviously unconcerned for all the years I had been reporting this, she didn't take it seriously. What was new today?

I said, "If I die, so be it."

I was tired of carrying a problem that the doctors couldn't even solve. She stood by the front the door, and watched GA and I get into the car. I was very nervous that morning, but it had to be done.

I woke up from the sedation. A nurse was calling out "Miss Reid" repeatedly. What a relief, I was alive. The operation was a success, and the doctors predicted the problem should be resolved. When I returned home, I was in a great deal of pain, I lay in bed and Rachel attended to me. My mother, who was so concerned in the morning, did not show any care. She appeared briefly and asked, "How do you feel?"

Then she went downstairs to watch television, and sent my eldest daughter to attend to me. That was fine, I preferred GA and my daughter looking after me anyway. I didn't trust her. I told GA how she had been responding to me. He was not surprised, but what upset him most was the pretence, the insincerity towards the youngest, the hugging and kissing pretend grandmother affection she started to show towards Rebecca. He was so outraged. One morning, he confronted her and said, "Do you really love your granddaughter?"

She said, "Yes, of course."

He said, "But if it was for your sake only, she would not have been on this planet today."

She replied, "I was just trying to protect my daughter."

I don't know from what, I had been on the street from a very early age. She wasn't bothered then, why now? She started to explain to GA how it was for her in her youth. She wished my father was like him. He was so controlling and jealous, he wouldn't allow her to go anywhere, he would not share his money with her, it was always about the future and saving for a rainy day. Was this her excuse for becoming such a bitter human being? This was a confession to jealousy.

My recovery from the operation was taking longer than anticipated. I was getting towards completing my training as a financial adviser. The deadline was already set and not recovering on time was causing difficulties. My manager was very supportive and wanted to see me through. He had been a real support for the last eighteen months. During that time he visited and showed his concern. My mother met him and immediately created her own misconception and said, "He is a really nice man; do you know he would marry you?"

I was confused.

I asked, "What did you say? Are you for real? Here I am living with my partner and you are proposing for me to get married to my boss? I didn't tell you I had problems with my relationship or fancy my manager. You are insane."

I couldn't understand what went on in my mother's head and whenever I tried to understand she concealed her thoughts. But I felt that I had been down this road before. In a strange way, it was as if she wanted me to live an adulteress's life and she was trying to instigate the move.

It was a Sunday evening. My mother had gone to church. I received a telephone call from her sister. Her mother had passed away. I didn't see much remorse; it was as if she had already known. When she returned from church that evening, I told her the news and we had to make preparation for her to return to attend the funeral. The pressure was now on for real, for the mission she initially came on had to be accomplished to prevent shame when her mother died. She had to make her contribution. She always had something to prove to this family. There were hidden secrets between her and her mother and one day I would find out. It was as if she needed to buy back her mother's love, trust and forgiveness. Whatever she had done was obviously damaging. All this was not necessary. The funeral was already taken care of, her sister told me. All she had to do was show up for the funeral, but she obviously had a plan and I also later discovered that it was to do with her inheritance. The same pattern emerged in 1995. Her intention was to go on a shopping spree, so that when she arrived, the whole island would know. She was pleased her plan had worked, for she knew her mother was dying and the only way not to be a shame was to get to the UK to collect all she could from friends. Ostentatiousness was her speciality. We went to the shops and she would select the most expensive items, like a sort of revenge and the final farewell. She was relentless, she wanted everything, as if I was not doing enough. I retaliated and refused; she would throw tantrums like a child, and then move on to the next item on her list. When that was not enough, she turned to GA, asking for more and more ridiculous favours and that's where I drew the line. She has no right to put GA under pressure for anything – that was her husband's job. I didn't do it, so I would not allow it.

I had returned to work. The recovery was not a hundred per cent, but I had targets and a deadline to complete the course. I was finally approaching the end. My mother had a few days to go. I came in from work. I went shopping and as I opened the front door, there was a weird sensation again. It was like the soul of my house had been tampered with. It was a dark instead of a light sensation. My mood changed instantly. I was really annoyed; it was the same feeling I had when Mrs A died and I entered her room.

I said good evening to her. She was in the living room sewing. Then I went upstairs to call GA. I told him there was something wrong in the house; evil was in my house.

He asked, "What happened?"

"I came home and was hit with a nasty presence and it is very dominant. I don't know what my mother has gotten herself involved with, but from the accidents we have been experiencing and the presence I felt in the kitchen with her the last time, she is carrying a huge omen and it is affecting my home and by God, she will take it with her. She will not leave it in this house. I will confront her now and find out what is going on and ring you back."

I went downstairs. She had this plastic smile. I knew a fake smile when I saw it. My head felt strange, especially coming down the stairs; it seemed to be a lot more there.

I said, "Mum, I find it very strange that you call yourself a revivalist and you cannot feel the presence that is in this house."

She said, "No, not really I don't feel anything."

I looked at her in disgust and thought to myself, 'she has no idea how spiritual I am, because I am one hundred per cent certain an entity is present in my house, and it must leave my house today or else.' She continued sewing. I went upstairs for a while to consider what I could do. I said a prayer because from the last trip by my mother in 1995 and ever since the bad experiences that I had, I refused to go through that again. I now understand where those spirits came from in the previous flat. She was the one attracting them and I didn't know why or what she had done. My inner sprit spoke. I should go back downstairs and tell her to do something and remove the bad omen present in the house. I went back downstairs in a rage.

I said, "Mum, I don't know what is going on in this house, but I want whatever is here to be removed now."

She looked at me as if I was confused.

I said, "Now or I will call a revivalist here to help."

She quickly leapt from the sofa chair and told me to bring a bottle of rum, and as we know, Jamaican rum is very strong. She recited a psalm and put some of the rum in her mouth and sprayed it over the wall and staircase as we came down the stairs. I was behind her. After her performance, she said she was pleased that I had such a gift. God was good. I was still not convinced she was totally innocent with what had happened. She claimed to be spiritual and was unable to detect such an aura was present; instead she sat there not knowing? That was odd. The presence was lifted that very evening. She didn't explain what it was and I didn't ask either.

Thank God the day had come for her to return back to Jamaica – January 2008. I couldn't wait for my home to return to normal again. We took her to the airport and said our goodbyes. I couldn't say that I would miss her, for it had been a real rollercoaster ride. The funeral was to be the next day after she arrived in Jamaica. I rang her to find out the situation and how she was getting on. My next agenda was to get on with my career and become fully qualified. It was the New Year and I always had a new year's resolution – to go on holiday was one of them. I was considering investing. It was going to be an exciting year for me and I started on my plans. My mother was gone for two weeks and we were back into our routine. I had an early night to bed. For the first time in this home after three years, I had a dream. It was very disturbing. One of my work shoes was in a public toilet and all the people were staring and looking at it. I was trying to retrieve it, but it was kicked around. I was frustrated and embarrassed. I said in the dream, 'what the hell is my shoe doing here!' I felt exposed and humiliated. I woke up during the night. That was odd, I hadn't had dreams for many years and this one was peculiar. I told GA about it and he also thought it was peculiar. The very same week I dreamt again that all my clothes were thrown into Wood Green high street in London. They were soaking wet in public. Again I felt humiliated. What was all this about? Was this telling me I was going to experience a scandal of some sort and I would be ashamed? The following week the dreams were even more frequent, like the previous ones they consisted of me walking butt naked in public. I would try to cover myself, but it was not enough. I called my mother and told her there were some really odd dreams appearing again, it was like an eye was placed to watch me and because I moved it became blind. Somehow it had found me and it was starting all over again. Some of the dreams I was experiencing were ones that I used to have in my past that were revisiting me all over again. I couldn't believe it, the operation I had to resolve the problem was now worse. I had to attend the clinic again and this time they advised me that they needed they remove my womb. I also started to really struggle with my studies. It didn't matter how persistent or hardworking I was, with all the support I received from work, my manager would spend hours in training with me for the exams but I kept failing. After three failed attempts I could be fired. I was really a hard worker when it came down to studying. This time I felt it was out of my hands. I started to imagine the worst. What if I didn't make it? This would be the final exam until I was qualified. It would be a complete waste of time if I failed, and this would dent my morale and confidence. I might not be able to practise as a financial adviser because a record will be kept to incriminate me for every application when asking for a reference. I was devastated. I asked my mother to please pray for me. Her reaction was odd – she showed no interest. She was more interested in knowing when I would send her the batch of money. On the last attempt, I studied endlessly. I called my mother again and asked her to please remember me in her prayers and her reaction was even more placid. She didn't ask me when I was taking the exam or express any urgency.

I said, "Mum it is really strange. Even though I am telling you how stressed out I am about this exam, you don't care. You didn't even ask me when it was."

She said, "OK, then when is it?"

I told her. I knew how keen she was before when I attended university. She would ask when and what time my exams were and gave huge encouragement. Now it was like she was bitter.

I went for the exam the final time. It was not hard; there was nothing surprising on the paper, but somehow I was getting confused and for the final time I failed and was sacked from my job. I was escorted off the premises. It was the very humiliating situation that explained the meaning of the dream. The experience I had dented my confidence. I became self-conscious. I started doubting myself and felt like a dullard, a loser, and an idiot. It took me a long time to pick up myself. I had ruined my chance to ever work in the financial industry again. I was out of work for six months.

During this time, my mother was still expecting me to support her. Her attitude towards me was much colder than before. It was like her visit made her more jealous and vindictive. GA warned me this would happen. He believed that she was not happy with our life or relationship. She had her own agenda which I failed to honour. Well I wish I knew what it was, because she had not told me and because I had not fulfilled her wishes, I would pay by her revenge. But what could she do? Kill me? How would she be cared for?

The dreams were endless; the tsunami that I encountered at the last property returned. I was always covered by this great flood of sea. I would see it coming. I was defenceless and I would stand there as it rushed towards me. I turned my back in surrender. I could feel myself being covered and I knew I was going to drown... then I would wake up. I hated these dreams. They were the worst and quite frequent. After the first warning with the job, I honestly had to pay close attention to every dream. I didn't know what the meaning of this one was. It was really difficult to interpret my own dreams. It could mean death I thought, but I didn't know.

I finally found a job that was way out of my remit, but I had to survive. I managed to return to a job that I had done years ago. The employer was very generous to offer me a job again and it was close to home. The money wasn't great, but I was able to pay the bills and put away some savings for a rainy day. I started to have weird experiences and heart palpitations, as if I was scared that something dreadful was about to happen. For instance, I would hear the ice cream van outside and I would have a premonition that Rebecca would be run over by this van and be killed. So I would be in the kitchen and would run outside, so worried to protect her, but it would be a false alarm. She would be playing with her friends. I could hear voices in my head saying that GA was having an affair and he was going to leave me and the children, so I would be paranoid and check to see where he was. If his phone was off at the time or I couldn't get a response, I would be heartbroken that he had gone. I would have all these senseless ideas appearing, followed by sleepless nights. I went to bed and guaranteed I would be awake at 3am in the morning for the whole week and would not go back to sleep with the same ridiculous thoughts haunting me. I could hear GA snoring and enjoying his sleep while I was wide awake until it was time for work. The eye problem I had returned even worse; it was as if someone was poking their finger in my eyes. the depression I was experiencing without a reason was creating a hole in my heart. I became miserable and exhausted. I couldn't carry on like this. My health was deteriorating and the problem I had was a spiritual one.

I decided I would never ask my mother for her prayers or assistance again. She was uninterested and bitter in my affairs. I had now seen that clearly from her response during my exams. I was now going to seek spiritual help. I needed to know where the problem was coming from. I didn't even know where to start. I didn't want to seek help from the same environment of the revivalists – I wanted to go as far away as possible. This was a very embarrassing situation and I couldn't ask just anyone. I had to be careful. I tried to seek help but could not find any.

I sat down one day and tried to contact my guide or inner voice. I asked where could I seek help? I received an answer while I was having a conversation with GA. She told me a colleague from my previous job might be able to help. I hadn't seen this guy for at least four years. I had his telephone number in my phone book. At first I didn't know how to approach the subject, as he might have thought I was mad. We spoke about work and his family and eventually I said, "I have a problem. I wonder if you will be able to help me."

He said, "What kind of problem? A spiritual problem? I don't understand, what you are talking about?"

"I am sorry. I have put you in an awkward position asking you for such an odd favour, but I overheard you in the office when you spoke about the experiences you had in Nigeria and I was wondering if you would be able to recommend a spiritual person who will be able to help. My problems are severe. I am having sleepless nights and terror in my dreams."

He said, "Oh my God." He hesitated and then asked, "Have you got a pen?"

I said, "Yes."

"I am going to introduce you to my pastor in Nigeria. He is a real man of God. You don't need to get involved with those juju people or bush doctors. This pastor is one of a kind. He is honest and believes in nothing more than prayer. He will get you through it."

I said, "Thank you very much."

I immediately called the pastor in Nigeria and introduced myself and mentioned who had recommended me to him. I told him what was happening to me. Most of all, I was determined to pass my exam although I had lost my job. I had taken the same exam six times. I would study relentlessly as I always did during my studies at university. These exams were similar or even less intense than before. I would look at the questions. I got really excited as usual, but as I was about to attempt the question, I would become completely blank and overwhelmed with panic and worry. I knew the answers, but I got confused. The crazy thing was that I had been taking these exams for the last two years. This should be no surprise. I told the pastor I would like him to pray for me. I knew my mother was not interested and I promised myself that I would never ask her again for her prayers or blessings in anything I do. He said, "Don't worry. God is good. You will pass. There is a disturbance spiritually; someone is trying to ruin your success. I will pray for you and whoever it is that is disturbing you will appear in your dream over the next few days." He prayed for me and dictated some prayer point I should recite. I went in the morning to take the exam. I looked at everyone else and thought, 'I am dumber than everyone else here.' I used to look forward to the challenge in exams and now I feared it greatly. They called me into the room and I prayed briefly before I looked at the questions and thought, 'this will be the last time.' As I started, all the topics I had reviewed appeared. The first question I attempted I knew well and there was a surge of confusion and confidence at the same time, like a fight going on in my brain. I said it out loud in the room, "It is happening again!"

I gave in and decided I would just sit until time was up, and then the inner voice came to me. It was like a very peaceful moment and it started to teach me and correct me on the answers I had made. I felt I was back to my old self. I had thirty minutes to correct the nonsense and carried on to complete all of the questions. As the exam was electronic, I waited for the result. I felt different on this day and the lady came to me with the results – congratulations! I couldn't believe it. I waited until I got into the corridor and I went down on my knees and said, "Thank you God." I rang GA and gave him the news. He was extremely delighted. That was an experience of a lifetime. It was like the angel from heaven came to assist me. I would not tell my mother about the news; she didn't care anyway.

One week later, I spoke to my mother to see how she was and to send her keep. We were having the usual chit chat and then she interrupted our conversation with a different topic.

She said, "I don't know why, but I think you are going to pass your exam the next time you go."

I didn't answer her, then she said, "For you know why I said that. I met this man. He was walking through Rollington down to Kingston, Jamaica, like the prophet of old in the Bible, praying and healing people and I remembered your problem and I told him. He prayed on a red piece of cloth I gave him and he just kept moving from town to town and went to the church across the road."

But to me something about this story didn't add up. It was like a fairytale and the church she mentioned across the road was Catholic. They would not accept such a character to preach or heal in their assembly. I ignored her and changed the subject. I didn't want to discuss it with her. She managed to bring up the subject again to let me believe that she had sought help for me towards my exam. I didn't even know why this was an issue now; I was not going to tell her. In her frustration, she started to preach about how I needed to go and get myself to church to sort out my problem with the exam. I became really cross and said, "I don't know why you are showing any concern about my exam now, I have passed and I am already attending church."

She said, "Which church?"

I replied, "Don't worry about it."

It was only after I thought, 'what a fool I am. This woman always uses tactics to get information from me and I always fall for it.' She used the same method to get the information about my pregnancy with Rebecca. Was this just a coincidence that she always knew, even if I didn't tell her what was going on in my life? That was weird. I continued to contact the pastor. He was always so humble and happy to hear from me. He prayed with me and I carried out his instruction to read and pray. He promised me that I would see within the next few days who the perpetrator was. I was anxious on the first night. I started to expect this dream, but nothing. The second night – nothing. The third night – the same. I gave up; it was not going to happen, but I carried on anyway reciting and reading the psalms.

On the fourth night, I had a dream that the same spirits that were raping me at the previous home returned, only this time it was both of them at once. I was pinned down to the bed. I fought with every ounce of strength in my body. While the first one was carrying out the act, I saw the other behind him waiting patiently and my mother was lying on the opposite side of the bed with her legs crossed as if she had instigated it or was waiting patiently for her turn. The second one came on top of me. I recognised the features – I know you! It was the same spirit that was haunting my life before. I struggled to get up, but was pinned down. When I was eventually released, I was hysterical that early morning. I couldn't stop crying. This dream was the most disturbing I had ever had. GA was very concerned. I told him that the demons had returned; this time it seemed they had come to create more damage.

He said, "It seems to me that they have come to finish something."

I said, "No, I refuse to have this happening to me again. I have to do something. This is the most disturbing dream, so my mother is involved in this. She is the one performing all these atrocities. This is wickedness beyond comprehension. For years I have been calling my mother and telling her about all these things, my dreams, everything about my life and she is the one behind it."

My dreams were never wrong; it showed me plain as day who my perpetrators were. I couldn't find the courage or confidence to confront her about it. I couldn't even tell her the dream. What was I going to do? It was as if I was about to lose my mind. I refused to have these things mount on top of me again. I had already booked a flight to visit GA's mother in Nigeria. I couldn't wait. While on my visit there, I had to find someone to help me. I couldn't go through this again. I explained to my mother-in-law what was happening to me, but not where it was coming from. We went to her church, but I knew prayers alone could not solve this problem. She was such a loving mother, she was gentle and attentive and showed real concern. We had no luck finding someone. The pastor who had been praying for me came by. He prayed and told me, "All will be well."

On my return from Nigeria, I was not satisfied. I didn't find the help that I had hoped for. I imagined I would meet a spiritualist in the village with a shrine and he would use a third eye to confirm what I had seen and I would give him instruction on what to do. It didn't quite work out that way. I returned to the UK a few days later than anticipated. My flight was delayed due to the natural disaster of volcanic ash which was spreading throughout Europe. That dream was the beginning to all my answers. I was curious to know what the meaning was. I had asked all the pastors and elders and the answer was not correct. I carried out my own research. I found the spirits that were having an affair with me were called a spiritual marriage. They are used to cause mayhem and destroy relationships, causing separation, divorce, and impotence. When they attacked, the victim would experience withdrawal from their partner, resulting in being irritated physically as well as with verbal conflict. And in severe cases, bleeding and disturbing sensations during intercourse with their partner could occur. There are also cases were the woman becomes pregnant with a completely deformed child. Mrs A told me once of a case where she was called to pray for a lady that was possessed and in child labour. The delivery time was dangerously overdue. The woman was in so much pain and growling like a lion and they prayed and anointed the stomach with holy oil and continue to pray. When the lady delivered the child it came out in the shape of an iguana lizard. The symptoms mentioned in the research were so similar, especially the bleeding, the stone-like sensation, and the irritation. It meant my mother was pretending she approved of my relationship with GA but in reality she wanted to destroy it through Obeah. This all began from a very early stage with my first pregnancy.

'My God! No one will believe me,' I thought.

GA said, "I told you, before our daughter was born that your mother does not approve of this relationship. I realised she was spiritual, but I believed she was protecting you, as you are her only child. From the time I saw her in the dream when I had the affair in the flat, and she strangled me and warned me and then lied to you that it was Mrs A, I knew then what I was dealing with. I am not afraid of her because I understood what I had done was wrong, but the way she approached it was deadly. I wouldn't try to hurt you again. I realised how powerful she was. Apart from that, she will not be able to harm me otherwise, because I am already heavily protected."

I was deeply disturbed. I was finding it hard to come to grips with it. It was like I had fallen into a deep dark pit, with all the bad experiences at the bottom. I just couldn't see myself coming out of this. I would have to get to the bottom to investigate. The terrible experiences I tried to block out were going to be resurrected. I was terrified, but I must be certain as this was a huge accusation. My confusion was at the fact that my mother had deceived me, that she didn't believe in Obeah and forbade and condemned anyone who even mentioned it. This proved the sensation I had in the house and this woman pretended that she was innocent. The only person I could talk to was my father; all this time I thought this man was saying rubbish.

He said, "I warned you about her, but you didn't believe me. She is a very wicked woman."

I wanted to know what he had uncovered when she had started.

He said, "I realised that she came from a generation of witches. You have no idea how dangerous she is. Your mother has cast many spells that even I am too embarrassed to discuss with you. I lived in hell with her for years. She put potions in my drink that would make me dizzy and white substance would be oozing out of my body. I didn't realise that she was involved in such acts until it was too late, when a man from her village saw me with her one day and asked me how I was related to that woman.

He said, 'I will warn you that those people are the wicked people in this village.' I saw later what he meant. If she doesn't get her way, she would cast spell on your life to destroy you. As I told you, stay far away from her."

I was still experiencing sleepless nights at 3am. It was as if someone woke me from my sleep. I would be thinking about ridiculous things, like my job and money until it was time for work. I was finding it difficult to confront her with my discovery. It was as if I had a fear of asking her about it and I didn't normally have such a problem. I pretended to have a relationship and continued sending her maintenance, but I would have to be careful not to let her know about any future plans. I applied for another job in my chosen career with another top financial service. The pay was very satisfactory, and it was as a result of the exam I persisted with.

We decided to go on holiday and take the children to Disney in Florida. It would be one of the most enjoyable holidays we had as a family. On my return to work, I was faced with the sack. Apparently because I went on holiday, things had changed and I had missed the training. They had to let me go. I couldn't believe it. I had never heard such lame excuses. I had booked my holiday weeks in advance – the holiday was approved. My whole world came crashing down. The lovely holiday we had became a nightmare. GA also lost his job. I didn't tell my mother about our holidays because I realised her jealousy and bitterness. I told her I had lost my job and she started the same tactics, asking probing questions as she does, it was like confirmation. Then something else really weird happened – a friend of my mother kept calling and asking me how I was and how was my job. I thought, 'why was she asking me about my job?' The following week again I saw her at an event. She was so desperate to know if I had a job and was asking about my children discreetly. I didn't have any dreams on holiday, but I realised when I returned that the dreams had started again about nakedness, tsunami, faeces, and blood – these were the signs of great trouble and disappointment. I knew deep down that this atrocity was to do with my mother. I had an idea that my mother would be jealous. She felt that she should be part of our life and control everything. She became bitter and cast spells for me to be unsuccessful to lose my job and to create unhappiness in the home. I was devastated. My life had become a vicious cycle – every time I made one step forward it was as if I was going five steps back. The nightmare was the worst and she was applying more pressure for money for all sorts at a time. She knew I didn't have a job. I wasn't prepared to inflict this type of pressure on GA, as he was the only one working. Things started to get really tough. GA and I were at war again, the mental torture was back again how my mother and I had used him and ruined his life. The curse or spell was quadrupled, the conflict was so intense. GA was constantly angry. Rachel was misbehaving again, even at school. And the vicious cat Rebecca saw in her dreams for over a year reappeared; this time not in her dreams, but on the road. On their way back from school, I receive a distressing call from Rachel one evening. I could hear her sister in the background. She was screaming and pulling away in fear from her sister from a cat that her sister could not see. I could hear her on the phone screaming frantically, "It's there! It's there! It's looking at me."

And Rachel was screaming saying, "There is nothing there!"

My heart started to skip a beat. It was happening again. I had to race home to find out what was happening to my child. When I got home, I asked her to explain what she saw. It was a brown cat with frightening big yellow and red eyes that was sitting at the corner of the street looking at her. I asked her to draw a picture of what it looked like. At the age of four she tried, but I wanted to see for myself the emphasis of the creature. She concentrated on the eyes, which I believed were more frightening for her, and the cat's coat, dark brown and orange. I was furious. I paced all night watching over my daughter considering where to go and what to do. I wasn't speaking with my mother about these matters anymore. This issue needed more than prayer. I just didn't know what was preventing me from doing so. I continued praying with the pastor. The dreams were getting really intense. I dreamt I was getting married, all dressed in white with the bridesmaids dressed in purple, and then after the ceremony I found myself barricaded in a hall with these strange people I didn't recognise. They were dancing and celebrating while they ignored me. I anxiously tried to find a way out. There were no doors. The only way out was through a small rectangle window next to the ceiling. It was as if I was underground in a castle and had been given away to the spirit world. I managed to escape by squeezing through the tiny window I saw when I looked up. I told the pastor about the dream.

He said, "Don't worry; someone is trying to take your soul."

I was off work for months. It was difficult finding a job. The little I had I shared with my mother and the children, and she refused to understand my circumstances and made all these demands. What was I to do? My children were more important to me. She was still healthy and strong, and she should help herself and husband. I could feel the bitterness and vindictiveness. It was as if she was angry that I was not doing enough and I had disappointed her setting up my family, and she was going to apply huge pressure demanding money using sarcasm about other children who were taking care of their parents. Not once did she mention any sympathy or encouragement or prayers for me to gain a job. My body felt as is if it was laced with some sort of foreign body like kerosene. My skin was discoloured and when I looked in the mirror at myself, I was a different person in appearance and also overweight. I prayed and prayed, I just wanted to feel better. The horrific bad feelings were taking a hold. I would sometimes have to lay on my back on the floor due to the discomfort I would be feeling. After months of experiencing that horrific dream of my mother and the creatures, I had another. This time, I dreamt I was sitting outside in the yard. I could see the skeletal bones inside my feet. Six small tiny sardine creatures embedded on top of my cuboid bone four on the left and six on the right. I was going through a gruesome surgery done by my mother, removing two from the left foot. It was so real; I could feel the pain like a scalpel making the incision. I screamed in agony while she removed them, I said to her, "Why are you removing only two, what about the rest?"

She smiled and shook her head in disapproval and I woke up. I was stunned. How did these get inside my feet? I asked one of the elders. He said it would have been given to me through food or drink over a period of time. So all the trips I made to Jamaica, I was called home to be given a cocktail of potions, each sardine had its purpose for tracking my movement, to prevent arousal – that was the unpleasant experience during intercourse – and the on-going operations I had to endure. A few weeks later, the bleeding I had been experiencing was gone. Also the sand-like sensation and bleeding for over ten years went away. Months later the irritated feelings I had towards intercourse were fading. GA noticed and was amazed.

He said, "All this time I thought you had retired early. I cannot believe this, I gave up."

I got up on the Friday and decided that whatever forces were preventing me from seeking help only death would stop me today. I was very determined and nervous. I decided it was now time to speak with the elders from the revival church about my troubles. My main concern was that I would be rejected and they would not believe my story. I made an appointment and told them I would like to speak with them about a very private matter. As I was on my way, I could feel a presence in the car travelling with me, but I was determined. I told GA before I left home that if anything happened, he knew what to do.

I made the journey cautiously. Thank God everything was fine. I rehearsed over and over how I would approach explaining this matter. They greeted me and I sat down. I could see the anxiousness in their faces. They asked how I was and how the family was. Then I started to explain about the experiences of the horrific dreams, the encounters of strangulation, the encounters my daughter had and the disturbance of my career. Finally I said it was all done by my mother. They leapt out of their seats and said, "Never, how could you say such a thing? When you are the only child and without you this woman would be lost."

"I can give you the answers – my mother took me from the UK when she lost custody."

I was interrupted immediately. "No," he said. "That was not the case. Your mother had to flee this country because of the physical abuse from your father."

I said, "That is what she told you. I have the evidence from the court that she had lost the case and my father won."

There was a great silence, then they started to probe further, asking questions like which court was it? What year was it? They became puzzled.

"I was abused as a child by her and suffered hardship and I managed to fend for myself, and reached a point in life that she had not anticipated. My first visit to the UK, my mother was requesting for me to have many children at the age of 21. I didn't realise she was looking out for her own interest. She also spoke about buying her a house when she first met GA. I couldn't explain how and why I left my only daughter with a woman I hated. I realised that she wanted to use my child as her money tree. She used every ritual or spell to hold on to her and when I decided to take my child back to get on with my life, she had cast a dreadful spell on my life. I had asked her on numerous occasions what her plans for the future were and she deceived me and played mind games. When she realised it wasn't going to go her way for me to get rid of my fiancé and live a life of adultery, she crushed me. I am here to please ask for help to deliver me from this wickedness. My life is a misery and I haven't harmed anyone. I just want to live my life."

He asked, "How do you know for sure it is your mother, because sometimes the devil comes in the form of the person closest to you."

I said, "It may be hard for you to believe because I am not fully committed to the church, but I possess a spiritual gift that I was awarded from childhood – the third eye – and whoever is in my domain I will see unless there is a blockage, as my mother did for a while."

They whispered to themselves and said, "OK. We are going to carry out an investigation to see what is happening and let you know by Sunday."

I had the impression after the meeting that they didn't believe me and thought I don't know what I was talking about. I waited anxiously the whole weekend. On the Sunday I waited and waited and finally the evening the call came – now for the result.

I said, "Hello."

He said, "Hello, we have checked and your case is extreme. It is very bad, the blockage is so much that it would take years to resolve."

I said, "So what do we do about it?"

They arranged to come to my home to start the clearance from there.

On their arrival, they came in the house and we had a meeting. They brought a bag with various remedies – lemon, sea salt, sage, candles of various colours and a type of herb in a bottle and some charcoal. I was curious. What the hell was going to happen here? I wanted to confirm if what I had told them was correct.

He replied, "Yes, you have been tampered with by spells, but it is not your mother."

'Bullshit,' I thought.

"How much damage is there?" I asked.

"It is very bad; it could be cured with a lot of work."

One of the elders said, "I was very surprised to see the amount of obstacles present because the last time I visited you in the previous home, it wasn't as bad as this."

Somehow I felt deceived, like I had not been told the whole truth, yet they wanted to try and help me. What was really peculiar was that they didn't contact my mother and give her the bad news or ask her permission – they just got on with it.

I asked, "Why are you carrying out a ritual on my behalf without consulting my mother?"

He replied, "Your mother does not believe in these things."

Was this for real? A woman that was a revivalist, who was supposed to be filled with what they called the 'holy ghost' did not believe? This was laughable. The ritual consisted of candles, incense burning, baths, and reading psalms for two weeks. My family had to endure this smoking. I felt guilty putting them through that. After I completed the two week course, I felt like a brand new person. For years I had not felt so good, followed by two huge jobs at the same time. I couldn't choose – they were both high up in the financial services industry. The pay was perfect and they were both contending to give me the job. I was so excited and at the same time confused as to which to choose. I finally made my decision to choose the one closer to home. I felt so proud of myself.

The dreams had gone for a month and surprisingly, I dreamt Mrs Archie appeared and gave me back my passport. I knew it had to be a good thing. I asked the pastor; he said that was a significant breakthrough in respect to my life being given back to me. Then I had another peculiar dream. My mother was sitting in a yard with various animals nurturing them, black & white and multicolour cats, like the one Rebecca experienced, dogs, and there was a particularly strange one. It was like a miniature reindeer (I researched and discovered that the animal is called a lama), but with three eyes, and it was slowly moving towards me. I could see it had an intention to attack me while she sat looking. I gave it a violent punch on the head and it fell to the ground unconscious. I looked over to the right and I saw a place with various doors that were locked and she gave me a bunch of keys and instructed me as to which key I should use to open this particular door. I wondered why she had all these keys and why the doors were locked. They were the doors of my life that she has prevented or locked and she would only release them on her command.

I started the job, it was amazing. I felt so proud and I knew I was on the way to success. Within a month I was granted an extension and promoted as trainer. I wanted to shine and I started to feel overwhelmed, like I had to work harder than anyone else. I was determined to be successful, for this was the beginning of a successful life.

As the weeks went by, there was change. I had a dream that I was at a strange airport and they asked me for my passport, but I was not sure if I got it back. I found I was going through about seven various passports and when I looked at the photo it was of someone else. I was not sure if I gave them the right one. I didn't pay much attention to this dream. My brain felt as if it were deteriorating. I was unable to meet targets. My manager was brilliant; he tried to help me, but he just couldn't understand the problem. I had a premonition that I needed to work harder, as the contract may not last long, so I started to put in extra effort, working longer hours. The problems had started again at home. GA had tantrums about the amount of hours not spent with the children and all sorts of nonsense and I could feel that sensation, when the devil is about to strike. It was like a cycle – GA's mood followed by Rachel's behaviour. I didn't take any notice, for I was on a mission. I went to church on the Sunday to tell one of the elders that things were changing. He promised to check and give me the result which was, unfortunately, the spell was returning and the person who was committing these atrocities was determined to bring me down. This person checked my status on a regular basis, to see my progress. He told me to read some psalms to keep it at bay, which I did religiously. Then I had this dream the following week, I was at work in the foyer speaking to a colleague and I saw this peculiar dog, a wolfhound with a leopard coat walking towards me and I thought 'what the hell is a dog doing in here?' It looked, then as it moved closer it charged at me and I dodged to avoid it. Instead of hitting me, it landed on the glass window, smashed it and fell four floors down. I looked out of the window and saw the dog had transformed into a snow leopard and was climbing up the gutter to come back in and I woke up. A week later an incident happened at work. A new manager had arrived, a female, and I knew she despised me. A colleague noticed and I tried to be friendly with her, but through the third eye I saw darkness. She sacked me using a ridiculous excuse, which shocked the entire staff. I went home that day ripped to pieces. I cried night and day for a week with gruelling nightmares. The chest pain returned, this time so bad that I held the right side of my chest and was on my knees in agony. Every night I dreamt about people mocking me or I would go to work and be at the front door, but I was trying to get in using the wrong key. All the dreams were about me revisiting the workplace every night for a month. The excruciating heart ripping became worse. I would be rolling on the floor sometimes. I had to pretend that I was fine most of the time to give my children attention, as it was too much for them to understand, and while I was playing with them the attack would start with this loud voice repeating in my head: the job, the job, the job, and at the same time, the torture on my body.

GA was really concerned; he could see the hell I was experiencing.

He said, "You cannot continue; this is going to kill you."

I had been praying, used the clearance and it was getting worse. I went back to the elders and they said it had returned in full force and it was beyond their capability. They couldn't do any more. This meant I would have to go and seek help elsewhere. For three months I went through the worst hell of my life. I decided that I would do some cold calling on the streets of London, and just ask anyone who might know where I could go. I struck luck one day – I was recommended to a healer in Brick Lane, London. I debated what the point was; it was not going to work. I believed it was going to be another ritual with candles and a bath. GA encouraged me to try it. I went and the lady was very calm and attentive. We sat down for over an hour talking about my experiences. The room had some type of equipment covered up under a white cloth. I looked around apprehensively wondering what was going to take place. She explained I would lay on the table and she would pass her healing hands over me while I listened to some soothing music. I could hear her breathe deeply as she passed her hands along my body, beginning from my legs. I could feel a sensation. That was odd, she was not even touching me and then she moved to my stomach and it was amazing. It was like a period pain – how miraculous; and then she moved all the way up to my neck, then she gave me a report.

She said, "You have a huge amount of blocked energy and your aura is one of the worst I have seen in a while."

When I got off the bed, I felt very tipsy all the way home. It was a relief that I didn't drive on that day, it was an experience. I went back a few times and that sickening feeling had disappeared: as a result and I felt wonderful. I even got back the job in the bank that I had lost – the one after my holiday – but with a higher position. The same pressure and intensity for taking an exam returned. I had gone through the training for three weeks to take my assessment to be placed on the floor. The same sequence – GA being angry in the morning for no reason to upset me. I began to develop overwhelming fear before commencing the test. I was determined to fight this. I answered all the questions and for no reason I hesitated until the computer timed out. I had to do it all again, this time with no confidence. I now believed I was going to fail.

A colleague I met was very spiritual and she realised there was an odd problem. She took me into the prayer room and prayed intensely for me to pass on the third attempt, or else I would be sent home. I couldn't believe what was happening here – the disgrace was about to return. I took the test and passed. I was delighted, but still tense. A week later I was in the process to be signed off. Two managers came to me and said that there were some discrepancies with my references, but how could there be? I worked for this company less than a year ago – and the inevitable, I was escorted off the premises. I was sacked within three weeks of the job. I didn't get a dream this time, but the morning when I was to be dismissed I left GA in the worst mood again, for no reason. It doesn't matter how many times I had told him, "when you get these urges to be angry, calm yourself and think, 'why am I angry?'" He just cannot help himself.

When I got back the same evening, he said, "I remembered what you said, but this morning I don't know why I was out of control again, I am really sorry."

I said, "Don't bother now, I have lost the job again."

I was now realising the concern of that family friend who came and enquired about my job. It seemed they had a premonition that something was wrong, that the door to my finance career had been obstructed; it was now very clear. The only relief was that the side-effects from this one were not as intense, with the constant dreams and sickness. I was a fighter and would not give up.

I applied for many jobs. My CV was unhealthy with the numerous dismissals for no reason having become detrimental. I could accept if my career was over due to committing fraud or misconduct. It made me realise that my mother intended to cripple my future because she could not have her way. I was convinced since I had the healing done that it was as if my eyes had opened and my mind was more alert. I had become very forgetful about a lot of things I had done in the past. I had to ask GA to remind me what I had done at a particular time or event and he would tell me things I had said which I couldn't remember, like amnesia. I tried very hard to examine this problem; I didn't want to be seen as a confused woman. I haven't reached that age yet. It seemed that my mother was using every spell in the book. She was determined to destroy me; my job loss and the pain she had inflicted were not enough. Of course she was frustrated, as I was not reporting to her my dreams anymore to see if her spells were working.

Another trick was tried. I noticed this peculiar pattern – I would be woken up at 5am, then go back to sleep within minutes and normally have dreams with three different scenarios. This was the new pattern. In October in the UK, the clock goes back an hour and reverses in April. The wakeup call changes with the time difference. For instance if I am woken at 5am every morning when the clock goes forward, I should be woken at 5am not an hour later. I was convinced that the culprit was from another country. It also coincided with the time difference in Jamaica. I continued to observe the time and the dreams. A very particular dream involved a cobra snake. I was in the yard in the village. It was so long. My youngest Rebecca was with me. I saw the danger so we crept silently to pass to the other side. It snapped at us. We were in such an awkward position that it was impossible not to get bitten. I am certain that I saw my mother in disguise instigating the attack. I shielded Rebecca behind me while this reptile was so furious that it snapped again. I am not sure if I got bitten. I woke up. Another outrageous dream involved all my dead aunts. I loved them dearly and my grandmother appeared in the dream.

I was so pleased to see them, but they were attacking me. It was as if they were set upon me. I stood there defenceless and they took turns to frighten me and push me, saying, "Why do you behave like this to your mother?"

I was so terrified. I could see my grandmother did not want to take part in it. They were pouncing on me and my mother was in the background instigating. I knew she was involved. How was she doing these things? She knew when GA brought a woman into the flat while I was with her in Jamaica. She knew when I fell pregnant with the youngest. She knew when I passed my exam and I refused to tell her about it. She knew when I went on a holiday that I didn't want her to know about and now that I had sought help, I was seeing a very big picture. So all along she was behind most of this horror and played the hypocrite using me and my family while she was the deadliest demon in my life. All the spells and atrocities – it would really have to be someone who was indulged fully in the supernatural. Was my mother a witch? Casting spells in revenge because she didn't get what she wanted, she decided to destroy my life.

Chapter 13

Confrontation

The healing and the various help I had received surely was working. My power was restored; I was blind and now I see, for by telling her my dreams I was allowing her to see my destiny through my eyes. I always wondered at how curious she was to know what dreams I had. I thought maybe she was impressed with my gift, but it was the contrary. There was only one hurdle. It was always like a mental and physical fight to confront her. As soon as I picked up the phone, what I want to say to her diminished and I was also overcome with fear. This particular morning would be the confrontation. My inner spirit said as soon as I had the dream, "Call her."

Another said, "You don't have credit."

My inner voice insisted.

I was determined and I was going to obey my inner voice. I told GA good morning. I didn't tell him what I was about to do because the plan would have been destroyed. I dialled her number. I was surprised she answered within 2 rings – this would have been 1am Jamaican time. My mother did not go to bed late. By 10pm she would be asleep normally.

I said, "Hello Mum."

She said, "Good morning my daughter."

I said, "What are you doing?"

She said, "Praying for you."

I said, "Why? Do you think I don't know the spiritual crap you are inflicting on me?"

She said, "What? But you are raving mad."

"I know you are the one behind all these atrocities, sending monsters to sleep with me, trying to spilt up my relationship with GA, planting trackers in my feet. Why don't you leave me alone and let me live my life?"

She said, "But Jesus have mercy, you have gone mad!"

I said, "If you don't stop this, I am going to expose you."

"Don't call my name in your mouth, you need prayer," she said.

I said, "I don't need your prayers." She started praying and then I put the phone down.

When I placed the receiver down, GA was in shock.

He said, "I can't believe it, you have finally been released to confront her."

I felt a massive relief. Hours later I received a phone call from one the elders that my mother had called and was very upset. She said I almost gave her a heart attack, because I accused her of working Obeah.

I said, "You have no idea."

He said, "She wouldn't do such a thing."

I was convinced and certain, and as much as they tried to confuse me, they had little luck. I was hoping that by confronting her she would realise she had been caught red handed and stop her wicked ways. I decided to end my relationship with my mother. I didn't want to communicate with her. I was still experiencing dreams. GA was very optimistic that she would stop. My inner voice had suggested it was now time for me to give her back her burdens. I shouldn't carry them anymore. All the wickedness and damage she had caused to other people in her lifetime had put her in the position she was in. I decided to attend church every Sunday. I prayed that God would help me to regain my job and my life that had been tampered with. I continued praying with the pastor from Nigeria; he was so faithful. And I returned back to the elders for help. This time I was rejected. The clearance from the last time had returned, but in order for them to help again it was another level which was outside their remit. My mother was not giving up; she was determined to destroy me. I continued to seek help, some were a waste of time, but what was consistent in the readings was a woman was the perpetrator and I had three children. I had two children not three, but the one that was removed spiritually was showing up as the third. I started to have the premonitions again. One day I was taking the children to music lessons and I wasn't feeling great that day. As I approached the traffic light the inner voice said, "You are going to have an accident," like a whisper.

It was raining. For that reason I proceeded carefully. I made the right turn. I believed it would have been at the junction where I was told. I passed it and I felt I had escaped, so I waited for the lights to change with the hand break up. I could hear a skid in the distance. I looked across the street and I couldn't see it and as I turned around to look, there was a great bang in the back of the car. A van had lost control and hit us. I suffered for months. It was peculiar there was hardly any damage to the car or van.

The cloud over my eyes was completely gone. I began to see even clearer pictures in my dreams. One evening after prayer with the pastor he told me that I should look out for a revelation in my dream. Two nights later I had a dream that I was in the village in Jamaica, and there was this house made from wood with zinc covering on the roof. The house was at the edge of the hill and the stone from the hill at the side had been paved away; it appeared as white as chalk. It was GA, myself, and the youngest. Rebecca was playing by the hillside and I told her to get away from there, it was not safe and GA said in the dream that he wanted to free himself behind the building and as he reached towards the building there was a loud bang from a wooden gate, flown open onto the concrete wall like a rage with all these people coming out. As they got closer, I recognised them, they were the spirits that had been haunting me in my dreams. I started to attack them. I had some unusual power.

When I struck them they disappeared in a puff of smoke. There was only one; a tall man. His clothes were ragged – he escaped. I thought what an odd dream and all those spirits. Was this some indication that I had conquered them all? A few weeks later, I had another dream of the same house on the hill. This time I went inside the house. I went through some doors that led me into a room and I saw a group of men sitting on church benches and a table with candles. It was a church! And they tried to confuse me by speaking with a Nigerian accent, but I couldn't be deceived. I detected the Jamaican accent; it was as if I was taken or invited there, I asked, "What am I doing here?" morosely.

It was as if I was taken by force. I woke from the dream. This was the dream that partially completed the puzzle. I was walking in the village and it was an early morning. I could tell by the mist rising from the green grass on the right side of the road and the bright sunlight and the green lush grass in this small field. As I glided up the hill I looked towards the left and there was that church house on the hill again. This time my mother was standing by the door as if she was expecting me. As I walked towards the house, the concrete steps were polished red. She was inviting me to come in; it seemed insincere to me as she was about to hold my hand. I shrugged from her and went into the house. On my approach I saw to the right from the corner of my eye a table set with seven wine bottles used as candle stands for seven black candles, a white table cloth with black patterns of half-moons and stars. I knew this was a ritual set up for me and whatever ritual they had planned for me it would be done over seven days. I decided not to sleep for the next seven days. At around 5am I would become sleepy and the cold sensation from my feet to my head would began. I turned on my lamp and the television, got out of bed to stay awake. I knew they were waiting for me, but I would not appear. So this is the place my mother had been attending to perform these rituals. I was not familiar with this society. It seemed like a church, but I know it was nothing like revival. I didn't understand why I was invited there. I spoke to my pastor and he interpreted that they were trying to convert me into the society which would follow by incantation. How could I join a society without consenting to it, and why me? Three weeks later, I was present there again, in another service at the church on the hill. There was this young woman sitting in the congregation to the left, very dark, looking at me and smiling. I was very hostile towards her. I didn't know what I was doing here again. I was very apprehensive. GA was sitting beside me on the bench. A man came to me with the big black book which resembles a Bible and asked would I like to join.

I said, "No thank you."

He said, "Why?"

"Because I am already a member of another church."

He went to the front of the congregation praying, then I turned to GA and said, "Do you think I should have joined?"

I noticed that as I asked the question, GA began to change from fat to slim, dark to light, with a hat, without hat. I looked him in the face and my God! It was not GA; they were trying to use the form of GA again to confuse me. I couldn't understand why I was considered to join this society. I was not interested in such practises. Was my mother trying to nominate me to be converted? I was now convinced my mother's hands were dirty with witchcraft. God only knew how long she had been doing this and I didn't have a clue. I had never seen any odd object or image; however, she had a table in her room with dry coconut and olive oil. I was forbidden to touch anything there, but I thought it was so I shouldn't lose her documents. Mrs A had a similar table, but anyone could access it. At this time, I hadn't spoken to my mother for five months and she was bitter. I had lost all feeling for her. I had no interest to call also.

Although I was still struggling to find a job, I felt relief. She was out of my life. My inner voice was right – it was time for me to stop carrying her burdens. She created them and she would carry them. The sensations were getting stronger and it was as if she was trying to prove that whatever help I got or wherever I went, she was more powerful and we were fighting a war. Most days I was made to feel like a failure. I would go out and it was like the whole world knew my problems. I would feel ashamed of my downfall and go out mostly at night. I was getting by for a while, but gradually I was worse off financially; I could imagine how some people become so fed-up and commit suicide. This overwhelming feeling started to affect my thoughts. I became forgetful of what I had said, what I had done due to stress. The only joy and accomplishment was when I looked into my children's eyes.

I was persistent, and even though the elders had dropped their swords, I went back again to ask for help. I just wanted to live my life in peace. I suffered on my own as young girl. I didn't foresee this cobweb in the future. I had planned a life of happiness with the family I had created. I just wanted it gone.

I was given another remedy to try, because all the others had failed. It was a remedy to call upon God and his angel for protection over seven days. I carried out this procedure for a while. I knew deep down it was not working quickly enough. I had one more card on the table – to expose my mother. I planned to let all her family and friends know of her little dark secret. I sent emails and made telephone calls. The responses I received from them were shock and disbelief. I made a discovery of others who had tasted the venom of witchcraft from my mother to ruin and end their relationships because of envy. Some were so afraid to tell the truth that they went into denial. I decided to contact one of the elders in Jamaica. I knew him from when I was a child. He was a very kind man and spiritual. My inner voice told me it was now time to contact him. I called him; he was surprised to hear from me. I started by telling him my dreams and the attacks of shadows passing the unpleasant experience sexually. I had to break it to him gently. He was shocked that these things were happening and my mother did not utter a word about it to him, even though they were close. The same conclusion came from him which really annoyed me.

He said, "It is not her, but in the form of her."

He told me not to worry. He would look into my case. He found out that a very bad spell had been cast upon me because of the promise to build the house for my mother to live in. He told me to call him back in seven days.

I asked, "Is there anything I can do during this time?"

I was told to read psalms every morning for the next seven days. I carried out the procedure and to be honest I wasn't sure if I could trust this man, for I didn't get a dream or any indication that he had done anything. I knew I had a gift but I needed to know for sure if it was for real or if I was going bonkers. I needed to prove it. On the fifth morning, I started to read the psalms and I noticed this cold sensation travelling from the soles of my feet up to my arms with goosepimples and I thought, 'oh yes' he has kept his word. The following morning I didn't feel the sensation again. I went back to sleep and I dreamt that this man and another old patriarch who had died many years ago had come to visit me in my kitchen around the table. We were having a meeting. She tried to hide her face, but I knew who she was. He also tried to disguise himself by hiding his face in the dark, but I knew it was him. After they reviewed my situation, there was an unusual spell that he was not familiar with and had to call her to help. He wrote the symbol down in a book and asked her to clarify. I got up to have a closer look and I saw it was the number 66 turned around and facing in an odd way. The curve on the sixes were both facing each other.

She said, "This has happened to me before."

He said, "What did you do?"

She said, "I can't remember, but I did resolve it."

Immediately I remembered what the symbol 66 meant. Mrs A had told me from childhood that it was the symbol of revival and 61 was the darker side which dealt with witchcraft. So why is it bent or turned around? It meant that the protection that was placed on me under the revival was tampered with in order for the perpetrator to cast her spells. This was even more profound than I imagined. My mother had gone through all that to destroy me? I wanted to know if my dream was true. I rang the elder as he requested after the seventh day and let him explain firstly what he had found out.

He said, "I travelled in the spirit to England for the very first time. What a beautiful place, the landscape and houses, I also met some people. I couldn't quite understand their accent, but eventually it was clear to me."

I asked, "When?"

He said, "Yesterday morning."

I was in disbelief and relieved. I didn't want to ask how he did it or whether it was on a broomstick. I wanted to try and cooperate to understand and figure out what this organisation was all about and how they did things.

I said, "I saw you, with the senior elder."

He didn't answer.

"What was the meaning of the symbol she couldn't find a remedy for?"

He said, "It wasn't that she couldn't find a remedy. She was just explaining it had happened to her before. Don't worry everything will be fine. I had no idea you were so spiritual," he said.

It was alarming to him. I had seen too much. I had trod into an area that I shouldn't be because I am not committed or converted. The sworn secrecy in that society could be exposed. He became cautious and explained in parable. What I really respected about him was that he was the only elder that was ever honest.

So, I had proved it. I could see, and my dreams were not nonsense. The protection placed on me was from 66 and dismantled. That explained the dimness of my spiritual eye. It had been interfered with. I always wondered why I had lost memory in some situations and made foolish decisions. I could remember some of the past and the rest is vague. The spells were way beyond Mount

Zion. She realised my gift; that was the reason she showed so much interest in my dreams. It helped her to construct her wicked plans. It also showed how much my mother was involved in witchcraft. After this revelation, I was waiting to feel relieved and experience a massive change where my life would return to normal instantly, but this was not the case. Somehow the jigsaw puzzle was unravelling even more. I had another dream two weeks later that I was back at the Promised Land and it appeared GA and I went together to confront my mother about the ridiculous things she has been performing, but before we entered her room I saw Mrs A and another elderly lady dressed in the general uniform – white turban white blouse and skirt – as if they were attending a meeting, but most of these people were dead and there was only one living person I could see. She was like an aunt to me, greeting us with empathy.

She said, "Are you guys OK?"

I said, "Yes, thank you." She was also getting ready to put on her full white for the meeting, which was on my behalf. I was not allowed to attend. GA and I went into my mother's room to confront her. She was not there. My plan was to go into her room and destroy her table that I suspected she used to cast her spells, but as I entered the table was already cleared – there was just a white table cloth. I was disappointed, because I wanted to catch her red handed and destroy her charade. I was told when I was a child that one of my eyes represented a third eye and had a mark above it, so I used it in the dream to take a closer look and my God! The table that appeared empty had a candle in the sign of a cross burning on the left of the table and on the right was the dried coconut chopped in half with the three dots representing the eyes, facing the ceiling. The most disturbing was the black velvet hat with an X symbol that was placed on the left side of the table in front of the candle. I somehow could interpret the setup. The candle for deliverance for me, the coconut is the watchful eye she used to communicate with the spirit, but the black hat represented she was attending a secret dark cult. This was where the spells were sent from. I pulled away from the table – nothing; went close to it again and there it was. The meeting was called for her to lay down her malicious act; it was as if she was put on a warning. The black hat explained, as I figured, that the spells were not revival. It was from the church on the hill revealed in my dream. She had become a fugitive hiding and running away from me in the dream. We waited for her to return and explain. I went to explain my dreams to the elders for them to confirm my interpretation; did I really know what I was talking about? They confirmed the candle as suggested, it was for clearance and deliverance. They were very vague about the coconut and the hat. It was laughable, the hide and seek explanation. I decided to put the record straight, I knew.

"I am not committed to this society, but that hat is not revival, it is from another organisation."

They went silent, and then it was broken by, "Yes, that's right; this is where the spell derived from."

I said, "Do you have an idea who or where?"

He said, "No."

I knew at this point I was pushing my luck. They would never tell me. It was amazing how these people could keep a secret unto the death. I could tell they were not happy that I was catching on. I could only tell by my feelings if I have been delivered or not. Since the confrontation, I felt a lot better. My health had been restored and the depression and palpitation I suffered from have gone. The unpleasant experience of the sand during intercourse with the excruciating stomach ache is no more. I was now waiting for my career to be released for me to live the life I have worked so hard for.

In November 2012, I was feeling really frustrated. Christmas was approaching with no sign of a job. I did the usual chores on a Saturday and decided to relax and have a quiet evening to myself. As I lay down on the bed, I could feel this odd presence in the house.

I thought maybe I was just tired or hormonal. I was struggling to fall asleep. I laid on my right side with my body across the bed. I saw through my left eye a shadow had moved in the spare room. The silhouette seemed like a man. I ignored it because I desperately believed everything was over now. I didn't want to take any chances anyway that night, so I prayed and read my Bible before bed. I remembered it was approximately 12.30am after watching a film. My God, I was under attack. This male figure had come to strangle me. This time I was going to put up a big fight. I repeatedly recited, "The blood of Jesus." The amazing thing was that I was getting the upper hand in this fight for the first time. I fought, then I felt my body rising off the bed. I was going higher and higher. I could feel the power of this man, quite tall around 6ft 4inches. I found my body was going around in circles during the fight. It wasn't my physical body, but my spirit; it felt so real. Then I slowly descended to my bed. I got off the bed that morning and I checked the time – it was 1am. GA woke up and realised I was very upset. I just wanted to know how long I would have to carry on with this fight. I had to be constantly looking over my shoulder, scrutinising every dream or scenario. My life has not been the same; I must be on guard at all times, reading my Bible and trying to be conscious in my dreams in order not to be defeated. I go to bed every night and think, 'what will happen in my dream tonight?' Sometimes I just want to lay down, watch television, and fall asleep but I might find I am vulnerable because I haven't said a prayer or read the Bible.

Chapter 14

I find my situation unimaginable. The Revival Society that I was born in and was a part of throughout my childhood I grow up to be embarrassed about it. I stay far away. It just did not appeal to me because I wanted more out of life and throughout my childhood the reputation was damaging. Although the revival had a reputation, I find the members were like family to me. They would show love and care towards all the children born there and wished the best for our future. The scrumptious cakes and the most popular dishes – rice and peas with chicken – were made by the elders religiously at every occasion. Although I chose to move on in life, I would visit occasionally. There were great mysteries and magic, especially for sick people. I think deep down I knew there were some capabilities of powers to destroy from what has been said from members in parables and people from the outside. I wouldn't have known unless I joined. I realised I could sense things and see spirits as a child more than the others, maybe because I was very inquisitive. I could never imagine that my background would come back and haunt me. There were many questions I asked as a child about the foundation of this society and the answers were always vague. The relationship between my mother and I was unusual. Although we lived under the same roof during my childhood, I know nothing about her nor do I have any love for her. I felt I had to please society and pretended to be an obedient and wonderful daughter. I knew from a very early stage when I returned on the first trip that she had not changed. I was not paranoid as others had suggested. I wanted to be as far away as possible from her. I saw her as a disturbance. I knew she despised me; a simple question would incur an aggressive barking response or a kick, so I had learnt as a child from this not to even bother speaking to her or asking her for anything. I would ask Mrs Archie. I am still asking myself this question: if I didn't get on with my mother, what on earth would have possessed me to leave my only child with her? Even after my visit, I sensed the greed and insincerity. Was I trying to pass on my responsibility to her to have an easy life as she suggested? I know that was not the case. We planned for our child and GA is a huge support. He had decided to sacrifice his life for his child and was supportive for me to continue my studies; we were not struggling for help. I am always in control and make sensible decisions, but I have to say in this scenario I still feel like a fool. I cannot explain most of what I have done. I sometimes find it hard to believe that witchcraft can take such dominance. I consider hard each day. I just cannot recollect, understand or justify why I made these decisions. For instance, I sent my daughter to my mother to care for her, when I knew my mother was abusive to me as a child. I had nothing to prove to her, she had moved on with her life without me.

The dreams I had I just could not interpret or understand why they kept appearing. The dream in the cemetery when my Aunt Lily gave me the baby girl and sent me out of the cemetery, she had discovered a real dark side and tried to shout out beyond the grave how to resolve my troubles by handing me the baby. I was to have a child and that would send me out of the hellhole I was in or break the spell. I told my mother this dream; she knew what it meant and confused me that my aunt was just trying to let me know she was pregnant. After speaking with interpreters, it meant rebirth, new life.

For years I have been experiencing theses dreams; I just couldn't understand why. When I ruminated on my life, every dream was significant. It was a guide about the past, present and future. There are so many dreams as they occurred on a daily basis, some threefold. I chose the ones I believed were significant. The head of the baby rolling off the bed, this indicates how bitter she was towards the child and threatening to harm her. My passport returned to me from Mrs A was my freedom to success had be taken and returned. At the same time the dream with all the doors that I saw locked and my mother had the keys, that was all the doors for my success in my life. She was in control and had locked them up. She would only open the doors if she got her desires. The dreams of constant orgies was a spell cast for me to lose interest in GA and vice versa. Eventually the irritation should have led him away as he was a threat to her and a disturbance to her evil plans, but the love between us is so pure that it was difficult for her spell to break us apart.

She cast every spell in her book to separate us including the sand that was to drive him away to another woman because he had no pleasure. She went even further by creating the attraction for me to see these men – Steve, Ali, the doctor – this was to frustrate him. This should have led to the inevitable. How many men would put up with this? The worst I think, were the spells to call me home and at the same time administering cocktails of potions in my food and drink that would enhance her activities. That was the reason she dictated I should be fed by her. This explains the draining feeling when I couldn't get out of bed in Jamaica. I thought I had a serious reaction to the sun, but this was the deadly effect to control me like a puppet to get all she wanted through me. And the deadliest, which was the beginning of her Obeah, the snake eating from the tip of the knife in my dream because my mother was convinced I had no love for her. She carried out this ritual to create a bond by taking away the love I have for my daughter for herself. The relationship we had was spellbound and could only be broken by having another child, that was the reason for her bitterness towards Rebecca, for her plan had gone seriously wrong. My clothes in public showed the disgrace and permanent failure and damage I was going to face and she was truly angry and turned her back on me for what I had done. So the only damage was to put me out of my job, crumble my success forever – that was my work shoes in public in the dream. The dream of me falling from the bridge was a strong indicator there was going to be a disturbance for me to get to where I need to in my life. I would experience great troubles – this was the pushing off the bridge into the river; so was the tsunami where I was covered over by the sea. I was buried in sorrows, distress, problems and I was so deep that I surrendered by turning my back as there was nothing I could do – this represented failure in the exam and losing my jobs. The dream of my mother and the animals in the yard – the cats and dogs – these are her workers she sends to attack by biting or charging at me to bring me down.

This woman's insecurity, selfishness and childish behaviour has led her to this spiritual world. She is so involved that she has lost contact with reality. Anyone who hurts her feelings she retaliates against with black magic to ruin their lives. She went as far as to set up the spiritual eye in my flat to watch my every move. Those were the dark shadows I saw in the flat, that was the beginning and how she knew GA brought the girl in the flat. The small sardines that were embedded in my foot had various purposes, a tracker to find me wherever I went and also to prevent my success and my relationship. The sand-like sensation I suffered for years was also among this. When she came in 2009 and I experienced the gruelling and horrific pain I suffered after my operation, she decided to relieve me by removing the two sardines from my left foot as I was at death's door. I witness this because of my gift. I saw what she had done in the dream – she planted it. The black candle set upon the seven bottles where she was inviting me to come into the church on the hill, I always wondered about this dream. It didn't make sense, for this was the same place she was casting the spells upon me and yet she was inviting me to come in and join. The real truth was that after the confrontation my mother discovered that the gift I had inherited was more than she anticipated, because although she tried her best to cover my sight, I found out her wicked act and that she was the culprit and I could see beyond. That wasn't to be – I was never to discover that it was her, so she arranged with her group to take my gift away from me. That was the ritual that was set up. That is why the 66 symbol was twisted facing each other in the attempt to remove it and fully destroy me. This is the same cult I saw where the man kept changing his features to trick me to join. The black hat I saw on the table in the dream when GA and I went to confront her shows the rank of my mother in the spiritual world in that society. The poking of the eyes I felt, my picture was used to inflict pain by removing my eyes in vengeance. The bad feeling which brought me to my knees was used by my clothes and also my picture, inflicting pain to my heart in revenge from the way I have broken her heart by failing to carry her burdens and give her my child as a sacrifice.

GA and I are convinced we were joined together by a spiritual bond, from the very first dream I had with the bright light and Mrs A on the veranda as the witness. What we have gone through, God only knows how we manage to still be together. There is something very peculiar about us. I knew evil existed by the experiences I saw and heard as a child, but I wasn't curious to find out how to cast a spell or get involved. My perception was, if you don't get involved then there is no reason for evil to confront or attack an individual. When it happened to me, it made me change my view. There are some seriously disturbed people on this planet, who will cast spells for jealousy, greed, or envy on an innocent, defenceless individual. It was from my experience that I realised my perception was incorrect and started to understand other people suffering with this problem. I had the privilege to meet some people that claimed spells had been cast upon them. In most cases I discovered that it was done by family or rivals in businesses or when relationships break down; sometimes it is even friends, but I have not come across one that mentioned their mother or father. Surely I cannot be the only person in the world. Is it because individuals are afraid that society would not accept it? Maybe they have been spiritually blinded as I was, or are we so afraid to confront it? I wanted to open up to the individuals I met at this church. I asked questions about their experiences, I told them about my problem and before I did, I had to prepare myself that they were going to disapprove. I would feel real tension and fear; like a tortoise slowly pulling out of her shell cautiously. When I mentioned my mother the expressions on their faces said it all, "It cannot be, no mother would do such a thing."

This woman carried me for nine months, how could a mother be so selfish and cruel to her own flesh and blood? Could it be spiritual madness? But I have discovered her profanity has been done to every individual who was close to her, like my father, brother and stepfather. If she cannot have her way to control and manipulate, she will seek revenge and destroy whoever gets in her way. What is really disturbing for me is the deceit. I trusted my mother, confided in her, believed she was my friend, tried to show her the love I could to make her happy. She looked me in the eye and said how much she cared and wished the best for me, when behind closed doors she used her supernatural powers to intimidate, patronise, control and destroy me, hoping that I would never find out until it was probably too late. What she had not realised was that in spite of her vendetta, there are some people on this planet who are gifted and destiny will prevail. You don't have to possess supernatural powers or be a witch, God truly exists. I have never cast a spell on anyone nor would I know how to start. My mother has done a lot of appalling things to me from my childhood, mainly because of her hate for my father and her miserable life which no one knows about, not even her husbands. From the information I have gathered from great aunts, my mother has been carrying bitterness since her childhood because she had been rejected by her mother from a young age. My grandfather was not approved of by my grandmother's parents and they tried frantically to deter the relationship, which resulted in six miscarriages and the seventh survived – my mother. As a child, the relationship I noticed between my mother and grandmother was peculiar; it was as if the mother was guilty of what she had done to her daughter, yet my mother also was trying really hard to get her mother's forgiveness or approval for whatever dark secret they had between them. My grandmother had moved on and started a new life with her husband. They had four children and worked in the UK for some time and then returned to Jamaica. My mother would not accept being an outcast and retaliated. It was very important to her to be part of the family, she was labelled the child out of wedlock so she developed extreme hatred and envy of the other children who lived with their parents, and she became so vindictive and created a lot of havoc between her stepfather and her mother. My mother had created so much uproar just to be noticed and to destroy her mother's happy home that she deliberately turned to the stepfather and caused a rift. What she had done was so severe her mother kept it a secret. It had caused my grandmother huge pain. That was the reason why mother was trying to buy back her mother's love at my expense. I didn't know this until now. My grandmother died in 2009 and never told the story. My mother's strangeness was to do with her childhood and the environment, apart from her hurt, she was surrounded by superstition and spiritual wickedness. According to what I found out relating to my mother's background, the witchcraft was mostly for the poverty stricken. Religion was paramount and had driven a lot of families to turn to witchcraft to make a better life by either stealing land, to marry a wealthy man or woman, revenge for what they have had stolen or taken away by others. Education was not paramount and is carried on for generations. Some of these people know nothing else other than to rely on spells to hurt or destroy for their own personal gain.

My mother obviously had an extremely difficult childhood and was brought up in an environment of such practises. After conducting my investigation, I realised that many children had suffered psychologically due to polygamous relationships. Women could have up to 14 children from five men and vice versa and this was up to four generations ago. I have learnt how disturbed my mother is, but it still doesn't justify her actions to me. I cannot be blamed for her life. Moreover, I should have brought happiness into her life; I have tried. I have had a hard life after being released into the world at the age of fifteen. I struggled and have come across challenges, but I am not bitter nor envious of others. If the opportunity is there in this life, you grab it with both arms, work hard and the result will be there. We just have to take life sometimes as it is; we cannot just sit and feel sorry for ourself and bring everyone down with our pessimism.

I am trapped, my life is on hold. There is no progress, my career is ruined. I try desperately to seek help, yet as soon as I am released my mother is determined and it comes right back. These dirty hands of my mother will not leave me alone. I tried to tell my friends and family; it has now reached a stage where everyone is avoiding me, running away as if I have a contagious disease, afraid that if they help, my mother might retaliate and harm them. Some are avoiding me in disbelief. They don't call me or associate with me. I understand, I had always been alone until GA came and my children. I will continue to lick my wounds and hope the day will come when all will be revealed.

A family member recently told me in confidence that my mother has been broadcasting how wicked I am, just as she did with my father when I was growing up. Now I have lost him maybe forever, but wherever he is I want him to know I love him and I hope he can forgive me for not believing him about my mother's atrocious acts. I really appreciate after all he has been through that he took the risk and still found the courage to come back and see me. I hope it will not be too late for us to see each other again; I am her current victim. Through thick and thin GA is the only person there with me through the storm, fighting together. He is everything to me. I don't know how I would have made it this far without him. GA is more than a partner to me, he stands beside me through all the storms and never gets tired. He would prefer if he could put the blame on himself. He met me as a young girl all alone who had been thrown in the rubbish, he took me out, cleaned me up and the culprits who had got rid of this rubbish can now see it was good and want to claim it back in such a brutal way. I don't care about my mother, how she lives or dies. I am a mother and it doesn't matter what my children do or say – they are my flesh and blood. I could never be so cold to inflict a curse on them and watch them fall in life. To do so, one would have to be a *strange mother.*

The SAGE
Handbook *of*

Economic
Geography

The SAGE
Handbook *of*
Economic
Geography

LIS LIBRARY

Date	Fund
2-8-13	g-che

Order No

2434362

University of Chester

Edited by
Andrew Leyshon,
Roger Lee,
Linda McDowell
and Peter Sunley

Los Angeles | London | New Delhi
Singapore | Washington DC

Editorial arrangement © Andrew Leyshon, Roger Lee, Peter Sunley and Linda McDowell

Chapter 1 © Jürgen Essletzbichler 2011
Chapter 2 © Trevor Barnes 2011
Chapter 3 © Ron Martin 2011
Chapter 4 © Richard Peet, Ipsita Chatterjee and
   Elaine Hartwick 2011
Chapter 5 © Neil M. Coe 2011
Chapter 6 © Peter Sunley 2011
Chapter 7 © Martin Jones 2011
Chapter 8 © Neil Brenner 2011
Chapter 9 © Phillip Kelly 2011
Chapter 10 © Susan Christopherson 2011
Chapter 11 © Paul Routledge 2011
Chapter 12 © Jonathan V. Beaverstock, James R.
   Faulconbridge and Michael Hoyler 2011

Chapter 13 © Michael Samers 2011
Chapter 14 © Gavin Bridge 2011
Chapter 15 © David Demeritt 2011
Chapter 16 © Michael K. Goodman 2011
Chapter 17 © Ray Hudson 2011
Chapter 18 © Nick Henry and
   Stuart Dawley 2011
Chapter 19 © Michael Pryke 2011
Chapter 20 © Louise Crewe 2011
Chapter 21 © Andy C. Pratt 2011
Chapter 22 © Linda McDowell 2011
Chapter 23 © Louise Johnson 2011
Chapter 24 © Roger Lee 2011
Chapter 25 © Andrew Leyshon 2011

First published 2011

Apart from any fair dealing for the purposes of research or
private study, or criticism or review, as permitted under the
Copyright, Designs and Patents Act, 1988, this publication may
be reproduced, stored or transmitted in any form, or by any means,
only with the prior permission in writing of the publishers, or in
the case of reprographic reproduction, in accordance with the
terms of licences issued by the Copyright Licensing Agency.
Enquiries concerning reproduction outside those terms should
be sent to the publishers.

SAGE Publications Ltd
1 Oliver's Yard
55 City Road
London EC1Y 1SP

SAGE Publications Inc.
2455 Teller Road
Thousand Oaks, California 91320

SAGE Publications India Pvt Ltd
B1/I1 Mohan Cooperative Industrial Area
Mathura Road
New Delhi 110 044

SAGE Publications Asia-Pacific Pte Ltd
33 Pekin Street #02-01
Far East Square
Singapore 048763

Library of Congress Control Number: 2011920328

British Library Cataloguing in Publication data

A catalogue record for this book is available from the
British Library

ISBN 978-1-84860-114-7
ISBN 978-1-84860-115-4 (pbk)

Typeset by Glyph International
Printed in Great Britain by MPG Books Group, Bodmin, Cornwall
Printed on paper from sustainable resources

MIX
Paper from
responsible sources
FSC® C018575

Contents

Acknowledgements

This book has taken much longer to produce than was originally intended and we are grateful to all those authors who delivered by their original deadlines, and who have demonstrated remarkable patience, and to the authors who stepped in later when others dropped out. They too have also showed considerable forebearance. We are particularly grateful to Robert Rojek at SAGE who originally suggested the idea of this book, provided initial support to enable the editors to meet and plan this project, and who has stood behind it during its various iterations, including periods when it seemed to to be almost as far from the end as when we started.

List of Contributors

Trevor Barnes is Professor and Distinguished University Scholar at the Department of Geography, University of British Columbia. He has written or edited nine books including *Logics of Dislocation, A Companion to Economic Geography,* and *Politics and Practices in Economic Geography.* His most recent research interests are in the history of American geography during World War II and the Cold War period, and in Vancouver's new economy, particularly its video game and film and TV industries.

Jonathan V. Beaverstock is Professor of Economic Geography and Director of the Integrating Global Society Research Priority Group at the University of Nottingham, UK. He has published widely in the fields of human, economic and urban geography, in journals such as the *Annals of the Association of American Geographers, Environment and Planning A, Geoforum, Journal of Economic Geography, Transactions of the Institute of British Geographers, Urban Geography* and *Urban Studies.* His research interests span globalization and world cities, international financial centres, professional services and highly-skilled migration and mobility. His latest book is *The Globalization of Advertising: Agencies, Cities and Spaces of Creativity* (Routledge), written with James R. Faulconbridge, Peter J. Taylor and Corinne Nativel.

Neil Brenner is Professor of Sociology and Metropolitan Studies at New York University. His research and teaching focus is on critical urban and regional studies, comparative geopolitical economy and sociospatial theory. He is the author of *New State Spaces: Urban Governance and the Rescaling of Statehood* (Oxford University Press, 2004) and the co-editor of *Cities for People, Not For Profit* (with Peter Marcuse and Margit Mayer, Routledge, forthcoming 2011); *Henri Lefebvre, State, Space, World* (with Stuart Elden, University of Minnesota Press, 2009); *The Global Cities Reader* (with Roger Keil, Routledge, 2006); *Spaces of Neoliberalism: Urban Restructuring in North America and Western Europe* (with Nik Theodore, Blackwell, 2003); and *State/Space: A Reader* (with Bob Jessop, Martin Jones and Gordon MacLeod, Blackwell, 2002). His current work focuses on the reinvigoration of critical urban theory under conditions of planetary urbanization.

Gavin Bridge is Reader in Economic Geography in the School of Environment and Development at the University of Manchester. His research explores how the economic and political institutions of commodity production and consumption shape the ecology and society of resource producing regions. At the core of his research is a desire to understand and explain the spatial and temporal dynamics of natural resource development. He is interested in the economic processes and cultural practices through which nature becomes enacted as resources, and subsequently proliferates through the economy in the form of commodities. Through its focus on natural resources and energy, his work problematizes the treatment of 'nature' within modern economic geography, a field which has largely defined itself by bracketing out nature as an object of inquiry. His research has been funded by the US National Science Foundation, the European Commission and the National Geographic Society.

Ipsita Chatterjee is Assistant Professor in the Department of Geography and Environment, University of Texas at Austin. She completed her PhD. in Geography at Clark University Massachusetts. She has a Masters and M.Phil. in Geography from Jawaharlal Nehru University, New Delhi, India, and a Bachelors in Geography from Loreto college, Calcutta. Her research interests are in three main areas: (1) the economic, cultural and geopolitical implications of globalization in the First and the Third worlds. She is particularly interested in the contradictions of globalization, capital-labor confrontations, class-identity negotiations, market-state reorganizations, hegemony-counter-hegemonic contestations, Fordist-post-Fordist transitions, and space-place dialectics; (2) urban transformations, landscape changes, segregation, ghettoization, and other forms of urban exclusions in the context of a Neoliberal entrepreneurial turn in urban governance all over the world; (3) conflicts and violence revolving around issues of re-distribution and recognition. More specifically, she engages with justice and social movement literature to investigate class exclusion, othering, Islamophobia, religious fundamentalism, identity politics.

Susan Christopherson is an economic geographer whose research focuses on economic development, urban labor markets, and location patterns in service industries, particularly the media industries. Her research includes both international and U.S. policy-oriented projects. Her international research includes studies in Italy, Spain, Canada, Mexico, China, Germany, and Jordan as well as multi-country studies. Her current projects include studies of phoenix industries in old industrial regions and a comprehensive economic impact analysis of natural gas drilling in the Marcellus Shale in New York and Pennsylvania.

Neil M. Coe is a Reader in Economic Geography at the University of Manchester. His research interests are in the areas of global production networks and local economic development; the geographies of local and transnational labour markets; the geographies of innovation; and institutional and network approaches to economic development. He has published widely on these topics. He is also a co-author of *Spaces of Work: Global Capitalism and the Geographies of Labour* (SAGE, 2004) and *Economic Geography: A Contemporary Introduction* (Blackwell, 2007), and a co-editor of *The Globalization of Retailing* (Edward Elgar, 2009) and *The Economic Geography of the UK* (SAGE, 2010).

Louise Crewe is Professor of Human Geography at the University of Nottingham. She works on questions of consumption, retailing, commodification, value and disposal. She has a particular interest in the fashion industry. She has co-authored a book entitled *Second Hand Worlds* that focuses on car boot sales, retro retailing and charity shops. She has recently published articles on disposal and devaluation; on the desire and value of domestic objects and on fashion and architecture in the contemporary city.

Stuart Dawley is a Lecturer in Economic Geography at the Centre for Urban and Regional Development Studies (CURDS), Newcastle University, UK. His research interests focus upon local and regional development, TNCs, corporations, sectoral dynamics and labour market and skills issues. His work has been published in leading international journals and edited collections. He has considerable experience of working on policy-relevant research projects funded by the EU, UK Central Government and a wide range of local and regional agencies in the UK and Australia. His most recent work has examined the regional implications of the restructuring of the Northern Rock bank; the local and regional development dynamics of migration in the UK and Australia, and; the evolution of the Offshore Wind sector in the North East of England.

David Demeritt is Professor of Geography at King's College London where his research focuses on the relationships of environmental science and politics and policy. He is member of the Grants Assessment Panel of the Economic and Social Research Council as well as of the Peer Review College for the Natural Environment Research Council and recently co-edited the *Blackwell Companion to Environmental Geography* (2009).

Jürgen Essletzbichler is Senior Lecturer at the Department of Geography at University College London. His work with David Rigby attempts to contribute to the conceptual development of evolutionary economic geographies and employs large micro-data in the US and UK to examine empirically the regional evolutions of plant technologies, productivity and employment. The results of this work have been published in various outlets including *Economic Geography*, *Journal of Economic Geography*, *Regional Studies* and the *Handbook of Evolutionary Economic Geography* edited by Ron Boschma and Ron Martin.

James R. Faulconbridge is a Senior Lecturer and Economic Geographer at Lancaster University, UK. His work examines the globalization of professional/business services, the spaces of learning and knowledge within firms, and the role of world cities in professional/business service firms' activities. He has published extensively in journals including the *Journal of Economic Geography*; *Urban Studies*, *Global Networks and Work, Employment and Society* and is the lead author of *The Globalization of Advertising: Agencies, Cities and Spaces of Creativity*, published by Routledge.

Michael K. Goodman is a Senior Lecturer in the Geography Department at King's College London and is interested in the cultural material politics of 'alternative' foods and environment and development. In between his 'star gazing' of celebrities, munching on cans of Pringles, sipping organic, bird-friendly, fairly traded coffee, thinking about insurrection-driven consumerist 'interventions' with his students and (thus) subjecting them to Rage Against the Machine, he has recently co-edited two books (*Contentious Geographies*, Ashgate, 2008, with Max Boykoff and Kyle Evered; *Consuming Space*, Ashgate, 2010, with David Goodman and Michael Redclift), has a third in the works with Colin Sage (*Transgressive Food*, Ashgate) and has a monograph in preparation with David Goodman and Melanie DuPuis (Routledge) on alternative food networks.

Elaine Hartwick is Professor of Geography at the Department of Geography, Framingham State University, USA, where she teaches Population, Food and Technology; Political Geography; Cultural Geography; Globalization; Geography of Latin America; and World Regional Geography. Recent publications include *Theories of Development* (2nd edn) (co-written with Richard Peet, Guilford Press, 2009).

Nick Henry is Principal Consultant for the employee-owned policy research and evaluation consultancy, GHK Consulting Ltd (www.ghkint.com). He is also a Visiting Professor at the Centre for Urban and Regional Development Studies (CURDS), Newcastle University, UK. As an academic he has published widely on (new, diverse) economic geographies, acted as Series Editor for the re-launched RGS/IBG Book Series and spent much of his time empirically testing the myriad conceptual offerings of the time. As an evaluator of public policy he continues to test policy positions and interventions across economic and social policy at European, national, regional and local level, utilising his 20 years experience of research, analysis and evaluation.

Michael Hoyler is Senior Lecturer in Human Geography at Loughborough University, UK, and Associate Director of the Globalization and World Cities (GaWC) Research Network. His research interests are in urban economics and social geography with a focus on the transformation of European cities and metropolitan regions in contemporary globalization. His current research investigates inter-city relations on the eve of the financial crisis (ESRC), cities in economic expansion since 1500 (The Leverhulme Trust), and the emerging global geographies of higher education. His latest publications include *Global Urban Analysis: A Survey of Cities in Globalization* (co-edited with P.J. Taylor, P. Ni, B. Derudder, J. Huang and F. Witlox, Earthscan, 2010) and *The International Handbook of Globalization and World Cities* (co-edited with B. Derudder, P.J. Taylor and F. Witlox, Edward Elgar, 2011).

Ray Hudson is Professor of Geography and Pro-Vice Chancellor at Durham University, UK. He holds the degrees of BA, PhD and DSc from the University of Bristol and an Honorary DSc from Roskilde University. His research in economic geography has focused on the relationships between corporate geographies, state policies and territorial development, much of it carried out in north east England and similar regions in Europe and North America. More recently, he has become interested in the relationships between economy and environment and in the role of the social economy in the regeneration of economically distressed places. His most recent books are *Digging up Trouble: Environment, Protest and Opencast Coal Mining* (with Huw Beynon and Andrew Cox, Rivers Oram, 2000), *Producing Places* (Guilford, 2001), *Placing the Social Economy* (with Ash Amin and Angus Cameron, Routledge, 2002) and *Economic Geographies: Circuits, Flows and Spaces* (SAGE, 2005). His research has been recognised by the award of Victoria Medal by the Royal Geographical Society and election to Fellowships of the Academy for the Social Sciences, the British Academy and Academia Europaea. He has advised numerous local and regional organisations on economic development issues, served as Specialist Advisor to the House of Commons Select Committee on Coalfields Regeneration and as Invited Expert to the National Audit Office Examination of Coalfields Regeneration Programmes.

Martin Jones is Pro Vice-Chancellor and Professor of Human Geography at Aberystwyth University. His research interests are in: economic development and economic governance; the regulation approach and strategic-relational state theory; regional spaces/spaces of regionalism; work–welfare programmes; state spatiality and the geographies of state power; nature and the states; space and spatiality in geography. Author and editor of four books and over 50 journal articles, his current research is with the Wales Institute of Social and Economic Research, Data and Methods (WISERD), where he is Co-Director and Coordinator of the Locality Research Programme.

Louise Johnson is Associate Professor in Australian Studies at Deakin University, Melbourne, Australia. A human geographer, she has researched the gendered nature of suburban houses and shopping centres, changing manufacturing workplaces as well as the dynamics of Australian regional economies. She has published on Australian cities and suburbs (*Gaslight Sydney*, Allen and Unwin, 1984 and *Suburban Dreaming: An Interdisciplinary Approach to Australian Cities,* DUP, 1994) and on gendered Geography in Australia in *Placebound: Australan Feminist Geographies* (Oxford University Press, 2000). Her most recent work has been examining

Geelong, Bilbao, Singapore and Glasgow as *Cultural Capitals: Revaluing the Arts, Remaking Urban Spaces* (Ashgate 2009) looking at how the arts have been revalued and urban spaces remade by the creative economy. She is currently researching the nature of master planned suburban communities, waterfront renewal and post-colonial planning.

Philip Kelly is Associate Professor of Geography at York University in Toronto, Canada. His research focuses on transnational migration and immigrant labour market integration, and the economic and cultural effects of migration on migrant source countries, especially the Philippines. He currently directs a community-based knowledge mobilization project – the Toronto Immigrant Employment Data Initiative – and a new research project on the role of immigrant youth identity in processes of intergenerational class reproduction. He is the author of *Landscapes of Globalisation: Human Geographies of Economic Change in the Philippines* (Routledge, 2000), and co-author (with Neil Coe and Henry Yeung) of *Economic Geography: A Contemporary Introduction* (Wiley-Blackwell, 2007).

Roger Lee is Emeritus Professor of Geography in the School of Geography, Queen Mary University of London. His economic geographical interests lie in the socio-material constructions of economic geographies with special reference to alternative systems of value and to the meanings and effects of money within economic geographies. Publications include *Geographies of Economies* (1997, edited with Jane Wills), *Alternative Economic Spaces* (2003, edited with Andrew Leyshon and Colin Williams) and *Interrogating Alterity: Alternative Economic and Political Spaces* (2010, edited with Duncan Fuller and Andrew Jonas. He has been an Academician of the Academy of Social Sciences since 2001.

Andrew Leyshon is Professor of Economic Geography at the University of Nottingham. His work has focused on geographies of money and finance, and in particular on the geographies of financial exclusion and inclusion and the formation of financial ecologies, and on the impacts of digital technology on the musical economy. Publications include *Money/Space: Geographies of Monetary Transformation* (1997, with Nigel Thrift), *The Place of Music* (1998, edited with Dave Matless and George Revill), *Alternative Economic Spaces* (edited with Roger Lee and Colin Williams, SAGE, 2003), *Geographies of the New Economy* (edited with Peter Daniels, Jon Beaverstock and Mike Bradshaw, Routledge, 2007). He was elected as an Academician of the Academy of Social Sciences in 2007.

Ron Martin is Professor of Economic Geography and a Fellow of the Cambridge MIT Institute. He is also a Research Associate of the Centre for Business Research attached to the Judge Business School. He holds a Professorial Fellowship at St Catharine's College. His research interests fall into five main areas: the Geographies of Work; the Geographies of Financial Systems; Regional Economic Development; Economic Theory and Economic Geography (and especially Evolutionary Economic Geography); and Geography and Public Policy. Recent key publications include: *Putting Workfare in: Local Labour Markets and the New Deal* (with P. J. Sunley and C. Nativel, Blackwell, 2005); *The Competitive Performance of English Cities* (with J. Simmie and P. Wood, DCLG, 2006), and; *History Matters: Path Dependence and Innovation in British City-Regions* (with J. Simmie, NESTA, 2008).

Linda McDowell is currently Professor of Human Geography at the University of Oxford and a Fellow of St John's College. Her main research interest is the interconnections between economic restructuring, new forms of work in the labour market and in the home and the transformation of gender relations in contemporary Britain. Her books include *Capital Culture: Gender* *at Work in the City* (Blackwell, 1997); *Redundant Masculinities?* (Blackwell, 2003); *Hard Labour: The Forgotten Voices of Latvian Migrant 'Volunteer' Workers* (UCL Press, 2005) and *Working Bodies* (Wiley-Blackwell, 2009). She is currently working on a project about recent EU migrants to Greater London as well as a study of South Asian women's involvement in workplace disputes in the UK and is planning a new book about women migrants' working lives in Britain between 1946–2006.

Richard Peet grew up in a working class neighborhood near Liverpool in England. Somehow he passed the 11+ exam and eventually received degrees from the London School of Economics (BSc (Econ)), the University of British Columbia (MA) and the University of California, Berkeley (PhD). He was a founding member of the 'radical geography movement' and long-time editor of *Antipode: A Radical Journal of Geography*, while later serving as co-editor of the more mainstream journal *Economic Geography*. He is now Professor of Geography at Clark University, Worcester, MA and is interested in development, global power and policy regimes, social theory and philosophy, political ecology and the causes of financial crises. He is the author of 17 books, 100 articles, and 50 book reviews. He is editor of a new radical journal called *Human Geography*. His recent publications include (with M. Watts), *Liberation Ecologies* First and Second Editions 1996, 2004; *Unholy Trinity: The IMF, World Bank and WTO* (London, Zed Books, 2003, 2009) and *Geography of Power: Making Global Economic Policy* (London, Zed Books, 2007). He has two edited books forthcoming: *New Economic Policy in India* with Waquar Ahmed and Amitabh Kundu and *Global Political Ecology* with Michael Watts and Paul Robbins, both to be published by Routledge in early 2011.

Andy C. Pratt is Professor of Culture, Media and Economy and Head of the Department of Culture, Media and Creative Industries Research at King's College London. His central research interest is with the cultural, or creative, economy: its location, operation, governance and policy. He has worked as a consultant or advisor for the UK London Development Agency, South East Development Agency, the Arts Council, the Department of Culture, Media and Sport, the Department of Trade and Industry and NESTA; and, outside the UK for the cities of Hong Kong SAR, Barcelona, Catalunya, Bilbao, Mannheim, Berlin; the EU, UNESCO, and UNCTAD. He has conducted research in the US, Japan, China, India as well as many European nations. His current research is concerned with the social aspects of the economic processes of agglomeration (institutions and networks), which involves both work on 'industrial policy, creativity and innovation' and economic organisation. He edited a recent book on this topic with Paul Jeffcutt (2009), *Creativity and Innovation in the Cultural Economy*, Routledge. He is currently working on a major book *London and the Cultural Economy* to be published by Princeton University Press.

Michael Pryke is a Senior Lecturer in Geography in the Faculty of Social Sciences, the Open University, England. His research focuses on the cultural economic geographies of money and finance. He has edited (with Paul du Gay) *Cultural Economy* (SAGE, 2002), (with John Allen and Doreen Massey) *Unsettling Cities* (Routledge, 1999), and (with Gillian Rose and Sarah Whatmore) *Using Social Theory* (SAGE, 2003). He is currently co-editor of the *Journal of Cultural Economy*.

Paul Routledge is a Reader in Human Geography at the School of Geographical and Earth Sciences at the University of Glasgow. His research interests include climate change; global justice networks; social movements; activism and geopolitics. He is co-editor (with Gearóid Ó

Tuathail and Simon Dalby) of *The Geopolitics Reader* (Routledge, 2006), and co-author (with Andrew Cumbers) of *Global Justice Networks: Geographies of Transnational Solidarity* (MUP, 2009).

Michael Samers holds a BA from Clark University, an MS from the University of Wisconsin, and a D.Phil from Oxford University. He is Associate Professor of Geography at the University of Kentucky, having taught previously at the Universities of Liverpool and Nottingham. His research has centred on the economic and urban dimensions of migration, immigration, and employment. Over the last five years, he has also undertaken research (with Jane Pollard) on Islamic banking and finance. He is the author of *Migration* (Routledge, 2010) and co-author with Noel Castree, Neil Coe, and Kevin Ward of *Spaces of Work: Global Capitalism and Geographies of Labour* (SAGE, 2003). Since 2006 he has served as co-editor of the journal *Geoforum*.

Peter Sunley is Professor of Human Geography at the University of Southampton. He has published widely on economic geography and spatial dimensions of labour. His research has focused on geographies of labour organisation and welfare policy, regional development, innovation and venture capital, design and creative industries, and questions of continuity and change in evolutionary economic geography. He has frequently co-published with Ron Martin and their joint publications include *Putting Workfare in Place* (with Corinne Nativel, Oxford, 2003) and *Critical Concepts in Economic Geography* (Routledge, 2009). He recently completed work into the geography of design agencies in the UK with Steven Pinch and Suzanne Reimer, and he is currently working on a project examining local aspects of social enterprise.

Introduction

Andrew Leyshon, Roger Lee, Peter Sunley
and Linda McDowell

Knowledge is always grounded in specific physical bodies and tangible artefacts, is always bloodied by its corporeal circumstances. In this way knowledge is always from somewhere. Furthermore, because it is always knowledge from somewhere, from one particular location, not all locations, it is necessarily partial knowledge. (Barnes, 1998: 100)

A recent international, interdisciplinary conference which focused on the intersections of economy, politics and culture, was attended by a politics scholar who had five years previously shifted discipline to take up a position in a Department of Geography. During a conversation he was asked by a geographer about the experience of moving from one discipline to another and how he enjoyed working within his adopted field. His response was extremely positive and, when pushed, identified the thing that he most valued about being located in his adopted discipline: 'What's great', he claimed, 'is the lack of a canon'. In other words, what he most appreciated about working within geography was the fact that there are no core texts or bodies of work that are generally considered by the scholars working within the discipline to represent the nature of a field. Compared to subjects such as politics and international relations for example, where there is most definitely a set of canonical texts and approaches, geography presented itself as an open and tolerant intellectual space. Geography provides a liberal and welcoming environment to new arrivals, and is receptive to new ideas. The lack of a canon means that there are no core readings to learn before one can begin practising and performing it. However, context is all. So while a refugee from politics may welcome the absence of an agreed field, many within geography – including, he admitted, some of his departmental colleagues – yearn for more agreement and fixity about what the field of geography constitutes. They would prefer some sense of standing on firmer and less consistently shifting ground. As an academic discipline geography can appear as, well, rather undisciplined. But, on balance, while the porous and diverse nature of geography can sometimes make it a challenging field in which to work, these qualities and its inherent interdisciplinarity are also a key strength and resource.

GEOGRAPHIES AND HISTORIES OF ECONOMIC GEOGRAPHY

This is a book about the ideas and modes of thinking that have shaped one important sub-discipline of geography, economic geography. It seeks to explore the connections between text and context in the production of economic geographies and the ways in which theoretical approaches to economic geography have influenced how key research questions and problems have been framed and approached. In so doing, we should stress that the book is *not* setting out to identify an economic geography canon. Rather, it seeks to explore why the focus of research in economic geography has shifted over time, and to contextualize the economic geography 'problematic' at different times and in different spaces. In doing so, we have been influenced both by the emergence of work on the sociology of scientific knowledge (for example, Latour, 1987; Latour and Woolgar, 1986; Law, 1994; Shapin, 1998), which has sought to place the production of academic knowledge within the economic, political and cultural contexts in which it was developed, and by the pioneering work of Trevor Barnes (1996, 1998, 2001a, 2001b, 2002, 2003, 2004), who has applied these ideas to the development of theories and practices in economic geography (see Chapter 2 and below).

Many scientists see themselves as the translators of nature, as detectives who reveal its hidden laws, and establish fundamental truths both about the world in which we live and about worlds we can only imagine, as is the case in disciplines such as astro-physics and studies of sub-atomic particles, for example. However, claims for the superiority of the scientific method can often be made with little self-reflection, and infer a degree of arrogance and unwarranted certainty. For example, consider the response of Lewis Wolpert, Emeritus Professor of Biology as Applied to Medicine, at University College, London who, when asked by a UK newspaper to identify the one thing that everyone should learn about science, asserted:

> I would teach the world that science is the best way to understand the world, and that for any set of observations, *there is only one correct explanation*. Also, science is value-free, as it explains the world as it is. Ethical issues arise only when science is applied to technology – from medicine to industry. (Wolpert, in *The Guardian*, 2005 emphasis added).

Although Wolpert's position can be seen as partly a performative and political gesture in the face of growing lay criticism of science, arising from debates over the validity of theories of evolution, the safety of genetically modified organisms and the degree to which climate change has an anthropogenic cause for example, his comments reveal a belief in the power and validity of the scientific method that more resembles faith than reason. Moreover, his assertion that science is value-free hardly stands up to scrutiny given that work in science studies has revealed how science is always partial, particular and political, and represents 'a view from somewhere' (Shapin, 1998). However, the power of such ideas and their ability to attract followers and adherents may enable them to become transcendent and, thereby, generally accepted as a consequence of their generative agency over space (Latour, 1987; Law, 1986; Shapin, 1975).

In their now famous ethnographic study of the production of scientific knowledge, based on ethnographic study within a research laboratory, Latour and Woolgar (1986) insist that while scientists consider themselves to be discovering facts they are, in truth, *constructing* facts by bringing together a range of resources and artifacts – scientific equipment, scientific methods, notes, conversations, and the writing of academic papers – within the space of the laboratory and its environs. As a result, while natural science is thought to be about nature, it is also an attempt to try to constitute such a reality, where the laboratory is both a workplace and a system of production that goes about constructing, and so internalizing, nature.

As in natural science, so too in social science. Contingency, effort and narrative play a key role in constructing the field and what we understand to be the knowledge of disciplines. The work of Trevor Barnes shows how such ideas may be applied to the history of economic geography and, in particular, to the rise and fall of the Quantitative Revolution in the 1960s and 1970s (see Part 1 of this volume, and especially Chapter 2). Barnes seeks to remove any notion of a hidden order in the evolution of the sub-discipline to dispel a normative understanding that the move first towards, and then away from, a statistics and model-based form of inquiry was the result merely of the emergence of 'better' theories and conceptual frameworks (Barnes, 1996). Applying ideas derived from social studies of science, and in particular from the Strong Programme of the Edinburgh School of science studies, to the development of economic geography during the past 50 years or so, he traces the ideas of key figures in the Quantitative Revolution, such as William Warntz, Walter Isard and Peter Haggett, back to their local contexts, and particularly to their backgrounds, career ambitions, training and experiences, institutional settings and the academic power relations in which they worked. Thus, the pioneers of the Quantitative Revolution promoted the adoption of quantitative methods based on a belief in the power of mathematics and statistics. However, as Barnes points out, mathematics itself is hardly a 'pure', unmediated set of ideas and practices, and is socially structured around a set of historically developed conventions. Similarly, the turn to mathematics in geography was not a product of its natural superiority as a mode of explanation and analysis, but a consequence of the desire by the protagonists of the quantitative turn to raise the status of geography in relation to other academic disciplines. In other words, as Barnes (1998, p 146) argues, 'The main point is that our [geographical] theories are not distillations of rationalist thought but

very much reflect the bias of those who have social power and authority'. They are, in other words, a product of the social, economic and social context within which research is undertaken and written.

TEXT AND CONTEXT IN ECONOMIC GEOGRAPHY

Responding to such interpretations, the contributions to this handbook seek to provide an overview of a changing and dynamic research field, but also to illustrate the wider social and political significance of thinking the 'economy' and the 'economic' geographically. An understanding of the ways in which economic geographies are socially constructed and sustained is vital not only to a critical appreciation of how people make – or struggle to make – a living but also in showing how economic practices and interactions are centrally important influences upon the multiple scales of contemporary geographical transformations. But the ways in which this has been done by economic geographers is not independent of the times and places in which they work. The structure of the book is intended to reflect key phases in the intellectual history of economic geography and, at the same time, to point up the emergence of themes that continue to circulate within contemporary research agendas within the sub-discipline and beyond. It is not, therefore, intended to be a history of economic geography – far from it. However, the relationships between text and context are especially significant within economic geography.

The dynamics of economy – often measured in seconds as much as in years or decades – reflect not only the speed with which economic activity is itself transformed in the face of multiple spaces of competition and technical change but the sensitivity of economy to geo-political events and cultural influence. Furthermore, the inescapable materialities of economies—not least in the sense that they are necessarily manifest in economic geographies—for the sustenance of social life have the implication that transformations in economic geographies spill over into, and shape, political, social and environmental relations. Economic geographers are, therefore, especially sensitive to the circumstances in which they work and are particularly sensitive to geographical and historical context. However, this is not to say that the diversity and development of different approaches in economic geography can simply be read off from the context in which they arose.

For one thing, whilst different emphases rise and fall in fashionability and in the intensity with which economic geographers engage with them, academic path dependence makes itself felt in terms of a kind of creative destruction as emergent paradigms are driven, at least in part, by what went before. Thus, debates within economic geography – such as those around different notions of the new economic geography (see, for example, the contributions in *Antipode* (2001)) – reflect real struggles over intellectual ideas. And beyond this, a number of verities continue to emerge with economic geography. A good example is the way in which nature threads its way through economic geography being treated in a variety of ways as the limitations and lacunae of past approaches become apprarent and as new and powerful contextual forces assert themselves (see Part 5). At the same time, amongst these diverse strands of academic development, ways of doing economic geography from the past continue productively to insert themselves into the present and the future. This reflects in part the nature of geography as an integrative discipline involved in thinking across conventionally separated spheres of environmental, social and economic life. And related to this integrative nature of geography, the lack of an economic geography canon prevents the kind of simplistic distinction between 'good' and 'bad' economic geography on the basis

of theoretical predisposition – a tendency which so bedevils economics and which was undoubtedly a contributory factor in the failure of economics to foresee the financial crisis at the end of the 2000s. Thus, diversity rather than a currently conventional singularity continues to characterize economic geography.

Given the complex intellectual history and geography of economic geography, no single approach to selecting and organizing its intellectual output is capable of capturing its diversity or of tracking its development through time and across space. And it is the proliferative and heterodox nature of economic geography which is central to the origins and structure of this book. Each of its eight parts addresses a key theme and problematic within the history of economic geography chosen on the basis of their formative (and continuing) contribution to the sub-discipline. Within that framework, individual chapters set out to illustrate the ways in which economic geography has developed contextually over the past 100 years or so. They do this by setting what they describe against the circumstances within which the subject matter of each arose.

Part 1: Location models and quantitative economic geography

The chapters in Part 1 consider different episodes in the study of economic geography and industrial location. Jürgen Essletzbichler provides an analysis of the development of German location theory from the early nineteenth century until the 1940s; Trevor Barnes explains the origins and the growth of the quantitative revolution in Anglo-American geography after the Second World War, and; Ron Martin concentrates on the development of geographical economics, tagged by such as New Economic Geography since the work of Paul Krugman in the 1980s.[1]

Despite the fact that these three approaches differ in terms of their history and consequences, all are involved in the development of formal, mathematical models of the space economy, and all raise difficult and highly significant questions about the attractions and limits of mathematical models and quantitative and statistical techniques. Indeed, the material in this section suggests that, throughout its history, economic geography has been torn by debates about the power and uses of numbers. A strong divergence of opinion between those who advocate rigorous formal models based on a series of limiting assumptions that seek to express regularities in mathematical terms, and those who deny that such models and technical tricks can explain why specific places change and develop in particular ways, runs through these debates. The former are convinced of the value of abstract, simple and parsimonious models of locational forces which can be used in an experimental and deductive manner. The latter, in contrast, insist that the excessive cost of such simplified and formalized abstractions lies in their unrealistic assumptions and limited vision, and prefer instead to use more inductive theories that can identify a broader range of contextual and institutional factors.

The chapters in this section address schools of thought that have been associated with the first position, although a close reading of the three approaches shows that they are based on somewhat different detailed aims and justifications. They also show that the emergence of periods of abstraction and formal locational theorizing is partly a matter of epistemic and academic context, especially developments in related social sciences and economics, but also reflects the influence of broader political and societal contexts. Ironically, then, they indicate that the rise, fall and rise again of formal abstraction in economic geography is the outcome of profoundly contextual processes.

Classical Germanic location theory has traditionally been interpreted as preparing the ground for equilibrium model approaches to economic geography. In this view, the formal location models of Von Thünen and Weber anticipated the potential of quantitative

economic geography and lit the way towards equilibrium models derived from rational choices by individual decision-makers. Essletzbichler, however, questions this view by arguing that it misreads the past and severs the models from their broader intellectual contexts. He argues that these location theorists saw idealized formal models of location as necessary but insufficient. They believed that models allowed the abstraction and isolation of key forces, such as transport costs and market potential, from the complexity of the world, but also understood the danger that models could artificially isolate forces that were in fact interdependent. They also recognized that such forces interacted in different ways in different places, so that idealized models should be accompanied by the historical geographies of specific places. Thus the chapter insists that Von Thünen and Weber both understood formal models as only the first step in understanding the evolution of any particular space economy. The tension between pure and abstract models and the desire to explain the historical evolution of real places continued in the work of Christaller and Lösch. Despite their move away from micro-economic process towards macro-patterns of demand and supply, both combined abstract general theorizing with concrete historical and empirical studies.

The chapter notes that the location theorists had only a limited impact on the development of geography until the decades after the Second World War. As their work became more popular during the resurgence of quantitative methodologies, it was reinterpreted as focusing solely on abstract formal models. Hence the price of their renewed popularity was, thereby, a selective appreciation of their merits and motivations. Their technical aspects were disembedded from their broader historical aims, so that important elements of their heritage were lost. This kind of reductive treatment parallels that frequently meted out to the work of Adam Smith (1776/1976), one of the founding scholars of Economics, who was as much interested in the moral and political aspects of economies as he was in the significance of markets as a means of economic and social order.

The chapter by Barnes throws more light on what happened in this era of quantitative revival. Specifically, it explains the origins of the 'quantitative revolution' in postwar Anglo-American geography. Barnes argues that we can trace the resurgence of quantitative and statistical approaches to the 'postwar regime' or the close interactions between science and the Cold War military-industrial complex. This assembly of interests promoted an instrumental view of knowledge and information, and emphasized the superiority of knowledge that appeared to be rigorous and mathematical, expressed in formal vocabularies and codes.

Barnes explains that the link is personified by the careers of many of the geographers who led the quantitative revolution. Quantitative geographers who had been employed by the American state during the war returned to academic careers full of new ideas and enthusiasm for statistical methods and made academic homes for their ideas The transformation of economic geography was led by key centres such as the University of Washington and Iowa, from whence it spread to Cambridge, UK and Lund, Sweden. In such centres, ambitious young male pioneers built new socio-technical networks by combining new computing technologies, statistical and mathematical practices and an underlying philosophy based on positivism. Above all, Barnes argues that the revolution stressed that theory should be expressed in a mathematical language and verified through quantitative empirical connections. It altered geography irreversibly. Thus, even when the quantitative revolution subsided in the face of a critical reaction in the 1970s, its foundational search for abstraction and systematic logic was bequeathed to geographical political economy. The recent resurgence of geographical economics also incorporates a similar impulse towards the development of generalized theory through formal rigour and modelling.

The third contribution addresses this resurgence of geographical economics, or New Economic Geography, over the past two decades. NEG uses formal mathematical models to understand how simple kinds of imperfect competition and increasing returns to scale in conjunction with factor mobility can produce spatial agglomeration. These show that the outcomes of the balance between counteracting agglomeration and dispersal forces depends on the level of transport costs and labour and capital mobility. Changes in these parameters produce varied spatial outcomes. This focus on simplified causal factors contrasts with the dominant approach in mainstream economic geography, or what Martin terms Proper Economic Geography (PEG), which is sceptical of high level abstractions and prefers to rely on place-based explanations. Martin argues that NEG models are not intended simply to be exercises of conceptual exploration but aim to throw light on real world phenomena. But how far can they do this when they are obviously built on unrealistic and simplifying assumptions? The key question, Martin argues, is whether the abstractions, and their underlying assumptions, offer grounds for making credible or plausible inferences about the real world. Do they cohere with what we know about processes in the real world? Martin delivers a mixed verdict as he claims that NEG models are typically a mixture of credible and incredible abstractions. The real weakness of the models lies not in their use of formalism itself, but in their lack of an interpretative context which evaluates the meanings, empirical plausibility and feasibility of the key mechanisms and assumptions. Indeed, as Essletzbichler's chapter suggests, classical location theorists had a stronger sense of the need for this interpretative context. Nevertheless, Martin is sanguine about the potential for conversations and exchange between geographical economics and other economic geographers. In this view, the tension between formal and inductive contextual approaches will continue to run through economic geography, but it can act as an important creative stimulant and irritant, just as it has in the past.

Part 2: Political economies of space I

Globalization was one of the most dominant buzz words at the turn of the twentieth and twenty-first century. It was so widely and frequently used that its descriptive and analytical purchase was often smothered and lost. This lack of clarity matters because globalization refers to a range of powerful and formative influences shaping life around the world. Indeed, it might be argued that contemporary human and non-human life is conditioned predominantly by globalization. The chapters in Part 2 of the book re-excavate the notion of globalization from the increasing mountain of commentary – popular, journalistic and academic – on the subject from those who make their living (including, of course, the editors and authors of this book) by thinking and opining. It reveals not just how complex a set of meanings are contained within the term but just how powerful and dynamic are the diverse relations and processes of globalization in shaping the contemporary world.

This subtlety, complexity and power arise because globalization is inherently geographical. That is to say that it takes place – literally *takes place* – across space and through time. It is not a condition somehow merely imposed upon the world but is made – consciously and unconsciously – through the thoughts and activities of people going about their daily lives. But, as with all social processes, globalization can never be neutral. The processes and relations of globalization reflect prevailing relations of power. And it is certainly not simple or uniform. Globalization is bottom-up as well as top-down. It is local and global. It is instituted in places such as major financial centres or the headquarters of globalizing corporations and it spreads – sometimes peacefully, at other times with extreme violence – across space and through place. It differentiates and, at the same time, it flattens difference. It integrates whilst also disintegrating places and societies. It enables places to cohere and simultaneously fragments them. It opens up possibilities and,

as it does so, it shuts others off. It subsumes but it also induces resistance. And, as all of these things happen, globalization serves not only to *take* place but to *make* place. Clearly, no understanding of globalization is possible without a full appreciation of these geographies necessarily inherent to it. So, while geographers may be relatively few on the ground in comparison with others in thinking and writing about globalization, their commentaries are, not surprisingly, more closely aligned with the diversities and contradictions of globalization and relevantly nuanced around its geographical complexities. They stand the tests of time and space far more effectively.

A major driving force of globalization is the economic geographies, legal and illegal, that compose and constitute the global economy. They institute the flows of capital, labour, ideas and things that swirl around the world. And, in turn, they carry ideas, religions, cultures, disease and politics with them. Further, the locational dynamics of these geographies – where and how production is organized, for example – reflect not merely questions of geographically variable opportunities and costs, including the geographically variable accounting of environmental costs of production, circulation and exchange, but the politics of attraction for, and resistance to, these geographies. And such geographies always involve the state – both national and international. States are involved not only in creating and sustaining the conditions in which economic geographies may take place or, alternatively, in encouraging the power of markets to shape these conditions but also in forcing globalization through intervention, both economic and military.

One of the significant geographical causes and consequences of globalization is the emergence of new geographies of power in which national and international states are both accompanied and challenged by centres of power based in the major financial centres of the global economic geography. The financial crisis which began in 2007 has challenged this relational geography of power, not least on the grounds that the system of beliefs and norms created in and through these close-knit places fed on itself and was virulently resistant to any critique or alternative views. The dire economic consequences that resulted from this introversion, heavily influenced by unsustainable and plain wrong accounts of finance from financial economics, necessarily induced the socialization of the crisis and the reassertion of nation states – and hence of a territorially-based loci of power – as the only financially credible institutions capable of rescuing the global economic geography from wipe-out. Meanwhile, however, the norms and beliefs of the actors creating financial geographies within these financial centres began to reassert themselves on the back of public money and public guarantees. Clearly, the politics of globalization – who is capable of exerting relations of power in shaping the course of globalization – remains central and crucial to its development. And this politics is, again, not merely simply there, inevitable and institutional. It too is created by those who live through and by it. Agency remains critical.

The three chapters in this part of the book explore the complexities, contradictions, advances and retreats of globalization in complementary ways. Political economy is central to all three in the sense that all recognize the complex of relations between the social, the political and the economic inherent to any economic geography. Richard Peet, Ipsita Chatterjee and Elaine Hartwick focus on the understandings of globalization rooted in the geographically expansionary but intensely uneven and exploitative economic geographies of capitalism. Geography (as discipline) and geography (as practice) play crucial roles in sustaining and resisting as well as understanding these dynamics. Neil Coe takes up this theme in showing how the dynamic geographies of globalization considered as a transformative set of processes are themselves constantly transformed, thereby highlighting the inevitable shortcomings of accounts relying upon only apparently stable verities of geographies of globalization.

Drawing at least as much on literatures from beyond Geography as from within, Peter Sunley offers a profound geographical critique of accounts of globalization that do not recognize the economic geographical incentives which drive it and the complex inequalities and contradictions that result from it.

Part 3: Political Economies of Space II

The chapters in this part of the book focus upon a particularly important theoretical approach within economic geography, namely the use of the concept of scale to explain the organization of economic activity of a geographical space. And in doing so they address a significant ontological debate on the nature of spatiality and the relationships between territorial and network notions of space. Whereas scale is associated with territory, verticality and a notion of hierarchy, network approaches are associated with horizontality and a 'flat ontology' (Marston et al., 2005). Martin Jones argues that the concept of scale offers something akin to a unique selling proposition for geographers within social science. Scale is an inherently geographical term that helps understand the real world economy and the relationship between places. However, similar claims are made by those who adhere to network approaches, although this term is less of a geographical preserve. Jones' chapter moves between these two approaches. He focuses on how to make connections between the local and global, and on how efforts are made somehow to 'hold down' the global in a fast-moving, volatile economic environment.

Jones illustrates that, over time, economic geographers moved from considering space as an absolute quality to a recognition that it is always relative. In so doing, their perspective has shifted to reflect the wider context of changing global-local economic relations. As he points out, during the qualitative revolution there was a form of ultra-localism in the nature of analysis. Neo-classical economics, which informed the economic geography of the time, assumed an isotropic plane and a hermetically sealed economy. This theoretical astringency may have assisted the development of arithmetic models, but did not really reflect the nature of the economy even then. However, Jones argues that to some extent this was understandable – if not forgivable – given the prevailing political economic context of Keynesianism within which the national economy was privileged above all else. However, with the breakdown of the Bretton Woods agreement in the early 1970s and the collapse of Keynesianism, a new neoliberal, global geopolitical regime emerged which forced national economies to engage with global competition. The crisis caused by this transition was the context for a shift within economic geography towards political economy and the embrace of what became known as the restructuring approach. The focus of research here was to explore and explain the way in which broader processes of economic change often had variable geographical impacts. In this context, the local was defined not in absolute terms but relationally, determined by geographies of social relations stretched across space. Thus, the fate of a local economy is as much – if not more – affected by issues such as investments/disinvestment by transnational corporations, the rise and fall of distant markets and the emergence/decline of new competition overseas as it is by events taking place within the region or nation of which the economy is a part. There was a need, in other words, to shift the scale of analysis.

The chapter by Neil Brenner picks up and takes further many of the issues raised by Jones, and in particular the relationships between scalar and network approaches, although in addition Brenner also draws attention to the importance of taking account of processes of place-making and territorialization. Brenner's focus is to explain the theoretical underpinning of attempts within economic geography to explain geographical difference, or what he describes more precisely as uneven spatial development. This line of enquiry has been strongly influenced by Marxist apprehensions of space and place, and, in particular, by key thinkers such as Henri Lefebvre and David Harvey, and has focused attention on the politics of space. Uneven spatial development is understood as a product of the social relations of capitalism. Inequality, therefore, is seen to be endemic and constant within such a system, although the geography of its distribution is not, and is subject to change and variation. Understanding and interpreting these shifts is a key objective of economic geographers working within this tradition. Brenner argues that the four-fold analytical distinction between dimensions of socio-spatiality – scales, networks, territoriality and place making – demand a combination of incisiveness and flexibility in order to comprehend the highly complex and multi-layered production of uneven spatial development within the contemporary global economy.

In the final chapter in this part of the book, Phillip Kelly provides a series of pertinent examples of the complexity of uneven spatial development through his analysis of contemporary economy geographies of space, place and labour (see also Chapter 13). Place is critical to the economy because, for the most part, employees and employers interact together within particular places. Moreover, as Kelly points out, place is particularly important for labour because employees are relatively immobile compared to employers: most people live their lives in particular places, and the bonds of family, friends and housing tends to make workers relatively 'sticky', particularly in comparison to large companies. But, Kelly points out, the ability of companies to be mobile tends to be exaggerated – not least by employers themselves, if only to keep employees, regulators and governments on their toes and ensure they are not taken for granted. Moreover, many companies are locked into particular localities because of the importance of concentrations of skills, knowledges and information 'spillovers' (see also Chapter 18). Nevertheless, employers tend on average to be more mobile than employees. This is particularly significant given that one of the other consequences of the relative immobility of labour is that being locked into particular places can engender camaraderie and solidarity which can be mobilized to counteract demands by employers to change terms and conditions of employment in order to improve profitability, efficiency or both. If resistance by labour begins to have an effect on the costs of production, then firms may relocate activities across space, divesting in one location and investing in another, thereby countering the power of labour in place.

Kelly here draws directly on work in the uneven spatial development tradition considered by Brenner, and on the concept of the 'spatial fix' developed by David Harvey. Firms may use space to attempt to escape the contradictions of capitalist social relations in place. But, in fact, they can only delay them because, after locating within a new place, the same tensions between labour and capital will develop over time. The tensions between place and the cementation of local solidarities, and space as the medium of the mobility of capital, may be resolved through the emergence of relatively coherent and stable forms of local or regional economic organization and the territorial politics which coalesce around them. An example is that of the local labour market, which has traditionally been defined in relation to journey-to-work times and spaces, and the proportion of people who both live and work within a particular area. However, such scales are in constant flux, as illustrated by the growing numbers of people undertaking long-distance commuting and growth of migrant labour. But, as Kelly is keen to point out, the reconstruction of scale is not just a product of the ability of capital and labour to move more easily over space. It is also a political project, as can be observed in the language used by national governments to represent globalization as an irresistible external force with, thereby, significant disciplining effects upon employees.

Part 4: Political economies of space III

The political economy approach is characterized by an interest both in analysis and in action. It emerged first in human geography in the 1960s in response to the quantitative revolution and its perceived political silence in the face of significant social economic and political transformations that were taking place during that decade. Contemporary political economy in geography is concerned with the possibility of a transformatory politics – and, in particular, with the implications of neoliberalism for global inequality – and with the gender dimensions and environmental consequences of the constant search for revenues and profits within capitalism.

Within this broad framework, the chapters in this section further develop ideas about globalization considered in Part 2 and do so in ways that link them to the political regime of neoliberalism which has held sway over large part of the world since the 1970s. As Robert Wade (2008: p 4) has argued, this regime is 'centred on the notion that all governments should liberalize, privatize, deregulate', prescriptions that have been so dominant at the level of global economic policy as to constitute, in John Stuart Mill's phrase, 'the deep slumber of a decided opinion'. As Wade points out, neo-liberalism earns its nomenclature and its distinctiveness from classical liberalism through the role of the state, the intervention of which was sanctioned 'not only to supply a range of public goods that could not be provided through competitive profit-seeking ... but also to frame and enforce rules of competition, overriding private interests in order to do so' (*op. cit*: p 4–5). But despite the critical role played by states in bringing the regime of neoliberalism and globalization there has, as Susan Christopherson points out in her chapter, been more than a hint of normative thinking about the ways, in which the state has been seen to shrink in the face of the rise of global capitalism. In so doing, arguments that make claims such as 'the end of geography', 'the death of distance' and the arrival of a 'flat' or 'borderless world', for example, seek to naturalize globalization as an inevitable and unstoppable process. These ideas are motivated by a belief in the convergence model of globalization, wherein the role of the nation-state, which is immobile and territorially bound, is one that ensures that governments and citizens effectively 'get with the program(me)' which requires that they accommodate and adapt to the imperatives of a globalizing economy.

However, even while many accounts of globalization aspire to this view, they are unable to write out geography altogether. Geography is recognized either as a barrier to be overcome or as what Christopherson describes as forming 'natural economic zones' – agglomerations, industrial regions, or city-regions – to which accrue economic activity and are considered to be demonstrable examples of success within an increasingly competitive and mobile global economy. But the recognition of such geographies is acceptable within laudatory accounts of globalization partly because they are not nation-states. Rather, they are celebrated as more appropriate sites of governance and political accountability than are traditional states.

But, as Wade reminds us – and as a vast body of work on neoliberalism has repeatedly pointed out – the turn towards markets from the 1980s onwards within the global economy was made possible only by states bringing them into being through legislation and re-regulation (Harvey, 2006; Peck and Tickell, 2007). Moreover, as Christopherson illustrates, there has been a critical reaction against attempts to write out the state through work that makes claim to a borderless world. This can be seen in the form of two key approaches that have challenged flat world or borderless world views of the global economy. The first is a set of scalar approaches which introduce the notion of verticality and the fact that globalization proceeds through a series of interrelated and constantly shifting set of boundaries and scales in terms of the operation of key processes (see, in addition, Part 3 of this handbook). The second is an array of network approaches which have been developed both in opposition to notions of scale but which also reveal limitations of popular 'spaceless' accounts of globalization. This work recognizes both the important economic roles played by the state – and especially the nation state – as well as the legacy effects of state action within particular spaces. Capitalist economies are typically geographically uneven – spiky or mountainous rather than flat (Gibson-Graham, 1996; Leyshon et al., 2003) – and in some places are decidedly weak and in need of support. Such supportive interventions continue to be provided by the state, particularly in times of crisis and emergency.

Moreover, while both scalar and network approaches represent significant advances from the flat or borderless world-view, limitations within these approaches are increasingly being recognized, a result in part of the stubborn refusal of the state to leave the stage. Moreover, states are important because they still represent the space within which most political struggle takes place and, as such, retain progressive potential organizing against the most egregious examples of exploitation through globalization.

Paul Routledge's chapter considers the possibility for social justice within a global capitalist regime. He also considers the role of neoliberalism and the development of key national and international institutions that provide a stimulus to, and support for, the extension of market relations across national economies. The chapter examines the structure of capitalist economies and their tendency to produce inequality and speculates on the possibility of opposing these outcomes through the development of oppositional and transformatory politics (see also Chapter 4). Routledge considers the development of the political economy approach, which emerged originally in the eighteenth century as a way of analysing government policy but which, through the work of pioneering figures such as Adam Smith and David Ricardo, moved on to focus more directly on the economy and its social and political implications. Smith and Ricardo developed far from narrowly economic-theoretical interpretations which were given a further analytical and political impetus by the work of Karl Marx.

One of the key sites of inequality within neoliberal capitalism, as Frederick Engels (1845/1969) showed so graphically, is the large global city. The chapter by Jon Beaverstock, James Faulconbridge and Michael Hoyler considers the city as a key nexus within capitalist globalization with a particular focus on the emergence of world or global cities as networks of connections. The authors chart the development of research on pre-eminent cities within the global economy, which over time has sought to come to terms with the growing significance and importance of cities within contemporary capitalism. They trace the origins of this work back to the early 1980s from the work of Friedmann and Wolf, through that of Sassen and of Hamnett, to that by the collective of researchers who work under the banner of the Globalization and World Cities Research Network (of which the authors of this chapter are a part).

Cumulatively, this work has recognized that cities are simultaneously key control points for the coordination of global capitalism, places of global inequality – producing both extremes of affluence and poverty – and sites which enable vital global networks through which economy, culture, society and politics flow. At the same time, the flows enabled by global cities also both sustain and transform them. As such, they are key sites of power and influence, creativity and innovation. The largest of the world's leading cities not only cast a shadow over the countries within which they are located, but in some cases their influence and power reach right around the world.

In the final chapter in this part of the book, Michael Samers looks at the development of economic geographies of workfare, which may be seen as the labour market expression of neoliberalism, and is a policy response that has deepened inequality within contemporary (mainly western) societies. Research on workfare emerged as part of wider attempts to understand broader socio-economic shifts within western societies and, in particular, the breakdown of the Keynesian welfare state. The rise of neoliberalism saw a focus on welfare replaced with one on workfare, a neologism which emphasized the individual responsibility of citizens to pay their way and earn their keep. Focusing in particular on the work of Jamie Peck and Peter Sunley and colleagues, Samers documents how economic geography research revealed the ways in which workfare was an engine of inequality, forcing low skilled people into poorly paid jobs, particularly in an era when jobs were relatively plentiful and when labour shortages might otherwise have occurred. Significantly, this work also drew attention to the ways in which geography was constituent of the production of workfare. While workfare was developed as a universal and generic policy solution to the 'problems' of welfare, it was perceived and deployed as a local solution within cities in the Anglo-American capitalist world, often with brutal consequences for those on its receiving end.

Part 5: Political economies of nature

Chapters in this part of the book consider economic geography's increasingly significant engagement with nature and the environment. Gavin Bridge shows how economic geography's approach to the natural world has moved in and out of analytical focus. During the early twentieth century economic geography considered nature as part of its holistic, description-based analysis of national and regional economies and the physical geographies of places were seen to be intimately bound up with their economic geographies. However, with the rise of the Quantitative Revolution (see Part 1) the natural world was re-conceptualized within economic geography. It significance came, reductively, to be defined through Von

Thünen's model of agricultural production, and in the role of raw materials in the industrial location models of Weber and Losch, for example. Nature was abstracted and reduced to the margins of economic geography interpretation and explanation. However, the turn towards political economy and Marxism from the 1970s onwards saw nature brought back into the foreground of economic geography. Through the work of people such as Neil Smith and Margaret Fitzsimmons nature was seen as a product of capitalist society. The natural world was reinterpreted as anything but 'natural' and seen as the outcome of economic processes, which constantly work to shape and produce the ecologies and 'natural' landscape of human life within which we live.

This 'production of nature' approach was significant for at least two reasons. First, it emphasized the way in which nature can be seen as a product of social relations. It had much in common with the parallel body of work on political ecology – which also became politically significant during the 1980s – in seeking to reveal the ways in which environmental problems – the classic example here being soil erosion – had as much to do with social change as with biophysical processes. Second it was important because it heralded the rise of a cultural reinterpretation of the role and place of nature, which accelerated during the 1980s and 1990s in line with the cultural turn within the social sciences more broadly. As such nature was considered a social construction, created and represented in particular ways to serve the political interests of different social groups. However, as Bridge points out, there is a limit to social constructivist accounts of nature – and, indeed, of everything else. Nature has an irreducible non-social agency. Biophysical processes need to be taken into account, because they have a noticeably uncooperative quality that refuses to be corralled by purely social interpretations. By acknowledging the importance of such unruly processes in their accounts, economic geographers have moved a long way from the

uncritical treatment of nature and from the reduction of nature first to a factor of production and then to a mere social construct. Contemporary analyses seek to engage simultaneously with both social and non-human agents.

In his chapter, David Demeritt charts the evolution of the concept of sustainable development, which was developed to overcome the seemingly irreconcilable tension between notions of environmental sustainability on the one hand and economic development on the other. Demeritt traces the origins of this term to the rise of the conservation movement which emerged in the nineteenth century as a result of concerns about the exploitation of natural resources and the despoiling of ecologies, and forests in particular. Over time, understandings of how best to preserve natural resources have moved away from a narrow focus on one crop or commodity to take on a wider ecological view. Focusing on just one aspect of the natural world to the exclusion of its environmental context was seen, in the long term, to have particularly problematic effects by failing to see the way in which particular species evolve in relation to others in place and over time. The creation of mono-species spaces was revealed as having damaging long-term consequences as the removal of complementary flora and fauna made it possible for opportunistic and invasive species to develop and thrive. This broadening of the concept of conservation to encompass more complex ecosystems was accompanied by an extension of the notion of sustainability, which moved beyond a narrow environmental focus to incorporate social and political dimensions. And here, by seeking to identify the winners and losers within the conservation movement, work in the political ecology tradition (see Chapter 14) was crucial in drawing attention to the equity effects of sustainability. Western concerns over conservation and the environment often led to a reclassification of land use in developing countries with severe consequences for the ability of the poorest in society to make a living and, thereby, generative of broader economic and political struggles.

If the idea of sustainable development has evolved for a century or more, the origins of contemporary usage may be traced to a 1980 World Conservation Strategy report. This, Demeritt argues, was a conscious attempt to reconcile the goals of economic development with environmental conservation, and was later institutionalized in the 1980s. This process of institutionalization is important, because as Demeritt points out, it enabled these ideas to sink into the political and economic background, so that they have become normalized, and notions such as the 'triple bottom line' – the combination of economic development, social development and environmental protection – have become part of the business mainstream. Moreover, these ideas have spilled over into the commodity chain itself, with ideas such as fair trade and environmentally sustainable goods which can be seen not only to discipline producers but consumers too (see Chapter 16). However, in his discussion of its latest transfiguration into a concern with the consequences of climate change, Demeritt questions the seemingly triumphant progress of this concept to global domination. The attempt to construct climate change within an economic metric that would make it possible for governments and citizens to consider forgoing current expenditure to ensure future sustainability has proved highly problematic and helps explain why progress along these lines has proved so tortuous. Moreover, the debate around climate change has also revealed deep geographical divisions. As the growth of CO_2 in the atmosphere is rooted in western economic development, are western states responsible for dealing with its consequences? Or is it the responsibility of emerging superpower economies such as China and India to cut down on their rapidly increasing carbon emissions, even though they had little to do with creating the problem in the first place?

Michael Goodman's chapter switches the focus to the economic geography of food which, as he points out, forces us to engage with aspects of the natural world on a regular basis through sheer biological necessity. Food is also a particularly useful device in helping us to think through global inequalities, faced as we are by the unedifying aspect of hunger and food riots coexisting alongside epidemics of obesity and global food corporations making fat profits. Goodman reveals how food is interlaced with all aspects of our being given that we draw upon its sustenance, and that large parts of the economy are orientated towards its production, commodification and consumption. The concern of political ecology with the geographies of food, and the inequalities upon which it is predicated, has encouraged research into the organization of agricultural commodity chains. It is significant that the products first associated with the Fair Trade movement are tea, coffee and bananas. These are banal enough to require regular and consistent purchases and, as a result, enable consumers regularly to demonstrate their support for more equitable exchange relations with producers in developing countries promoted by Fair Trade. Just as sustainable development has moved into the business mainstream, so the concept of Fair Trade has become a mainstream marketing category. But this development is also loaded with contradictions. References to fair trade may be found on many foodstuffs and is lauded within supermarkets which, at the same time, may also be accused of driving down farmers' incomes through the exercise of oligopsonistic power in the markets for food and agricultural commodities.

Part 6: Uneven development: geographies of economic growth and decline

The chapters in this section develop some of the ideas raised earlier in the book. In particular, they look in more detail at work which sought to account for the emergence of uneven spatial development. Ray Hudson documents efforts by economic geographers in the 1970s and 1980s to explain geographies of economic decline. He pays particular attention to the work of David Harvey and Doreen Massey who did much to make sense of the processes of deindustrialization which, from the 1970s onwards, were laying waste to the traditional economic regions of North America and Northern Europe. As companies closed and levels of unemployment increased sharply, theories that sought to explain the decline of older industrial economies abounded but, as Hudson points out, these theories were deficient in their scale of analysis, tending to be national rather than international in tone, focused on manufacturing to the exclusion of other kinds of industrial activity, and failing to acknowledge the role and interplay of corporations and states. What Harvey and Massey achieved in their work was to draw on the turn towards Marxism and political economy to explain the causes of economic decline that was having such significant negative impacts across Western economies.

Both Harvey and Massey emphasized that the crisis was a product of inherent tensions and contradictions within the capitalist economic system. But both also went beyond Marxist accounts in other disciplines by drawing attention to the fact that these crises were both founded in *place*, and that capitalist enterprises sought either to resolve them in place through reorganization – in particular, by bringing about technological change leading to efficiency gains – or to use space by divestment and relocation from one place to another. The insights of Harvey and Massey forced a critical revaluation of regional development policy. They revealed that, without proper attention to the kinds of institutions and infrastructures present or absent in struggling regions, new investment may combine with existing patterns of structural inequality effectively to lock-in such regions to weak levels of economic competitiveness over the long-term.

However, at the same time as economic geographers were mapping geographies of economic decline, work going on elsewhere

was beginning to identify the other dimension of uneven spatial development: economic growth. Nick Henry and Stuart Dawley focus on a body of work that, beginning in the early 1980s, began to draw attention towards spaces that were growing rather than subject to decline. This growth was based on high value-added sectors in manufacturing and services, driven by the accumulation of knowledge and learning and typically located in distinctive districts, clusters and regions. Moreover, as Henry and Dawley emphasize, there was a close link between theory and practice in the growth of such sectors, in as much as theoretical interpretations of the rise of agglomerations of growing industries has a distinctive narrative push attractive to businesses and governments alike (see Chapter 25).

However, there was more than a little irony in the fact that these leading edge and propulsive industries were initially interpreted though a framework deriving from the nineteenth century, namely the theory of industrial agglomeration developed by the English economist Alfred Marshall. It was economic geographer Allen Scott who provided the first systematic account of what he described as 'new industrial spaces', which were enjoying growth and expansion during a period when more traditional economic spaces were faltering and in decline. Whereas the prevailing industrial paradigm of the twentieth century had been based upon economies of scale, Scott drew on a range of examples to illustrate that factors such as agglomeration, transaction costs and economies of scope helped explain the success of industries and regions that were bucking the general problems of deindustrialization experienced elsewhere. As time went on, examples of such agglomerations and regions abounded and distinctive forms and types were identified, ranging from the 'Third Italy', through the City of London and Silicon Valley, to the motion picture industry in Hollywood. The formation and survival of these agglomerations was shown to be strongly dependent on the production, transmission and retention of knowledge in place. Despite broader attention to issues such as globalization and theories such as the 'space of flows' (Castells, 1989, 2001), agglomerations of leading-edge industries resisted being swept away in a technologically-driven 'end of geography' by their retention of knowledge and information in place. As Ann Markusen (1996) put it, knowledge made some places particularly 'sticky' within the slippery space of global capitalism.

This work on agglomerations was a highly significant development in the history of economic geography. Not only did it turn the discipline's attention towards a new field of study but was it also generative of some considerable interdisciplinary and policy attention – although much of this was contentious (see Chapter 3) – as national and local governments alike sought to learn the secrets of cultivating successful industrial agglomerations and clusters.

The power of these ideas was similarly apparent in a related body of work which also focused upon a dynamic and propulsive sector that had been studied only fitfully until the 1980s, the financial services industry, which is the focus of the chapter by Michael Pryke. Financial centres are agglomerations of financial activity, based on logics of transaction costs, economies of scope and sticky knowledges. But as Pryke points out, as the financial services industry grew from the 1980s onwards, it accumulated a cultural and political power to go alongside its undoubted economic significance. The financial services industry was capable of generating staggering amounts of money: for the firms that worked in the sector, for its more senior employees, for the city-regions in which the firms were based through the expenditure of employers and employees alike, and for the revenue income of the governments that encouraged its growth through sympathetic regulation.

However, as is all too evident in the wake of the financial crisis of the late 2000s, relying on the financial services industry to deliver economic growth is a highly risky strategy, given the endemic tendency towards

crisis. But for economies such as Britain, this proved to be a long-term strategy as finance was one of the few globally competitive industries that remained after the shake-out of deindustrialization. Since the 1980s, the City of London has been encouraged by both UK Conservative and Labour governments to compete for global pre-eminence with New York. Geographers began to study the financial services sector initially as part of a turn toward the service economy in general and then as part of more focused studies on the City of London and other financial centres, before broadening the scope of their work to look at the impact of the power of money and finance on uneven spatial development, including work on geographies of financial exclusion. In so doing, Pryke argues, geographies of money and finance have moved towards the centre of economic geography and, at the same time, has also pursued a theoretical openness which sought to combine economic and cultural accounts reflective of analytical shifts in economic geography over the past 20 years or so.

Part 7: Geographies of consumption and economic spectacle

The shift towards a more culturally-inflected economic geography is illustrated in Part 7 of the book. Louise Crewe focuses on geographies of retailing and consumption and, in particular, on the shift in emphasis from the former to the latter. Although retail geography had been around for many years, it remained something of a specialist pursuit. It was concerned with issues like store location and could trace its lineage back to the location models of the quantitative revolution. The complexion of this arena of economic geography began to change in the 1990s as part of the broader cultural turn which saw retail geographers become increasingly interested in the process of consumption. As a result, the research agenda moved away from the location of stores to an exploration of the things that were in them, and the passions, desires and emotions that drove consumers to shop for them. In this, economic geographers began to take inspiration from cognate disciplines such as sociology, cultural studies and anthropology, bringing techniques of qualitative research to an arena where quantative techniques had previously ruled. From this work, people began to pay attention to the ways in which companies use the power of affect and drama to create a sense of excitement within the act of consumption, as well as the consequences of consumption itself, through an analysis of the movement of goods and services along commodity or value chains (see Chapter 16).

Andy Pratt's chapter draws attention to the ways in which economic geographers began to pay attention to the cultural industries themselves which, like the financial services industries before them, began to generate a capacity for rapid economic growth, and also displayed a similar propensity to be located in urban agglomerations. However, as Pratt points out, as an object of analysis the cultural industries are problematic in that they do not appear in conventional industrial classifications and their association with consumption means that aspects of their production have tended to be neglected. Moreover, as many cultural industries are intimately connected to technology as part of their product, the speed of technological change means that the very boundaries of industries are constantly in flux. Nevertheless, there has been a growing interest in studying cultural industries as their economic, political and cultural significance has been recognized. Like financial services, part of the interest in the subject has been driven by public policy, as governments have been attracted by the jobs and revenues that cultural products can generate. But this field of study has also been significant in furthering our understanding of economic agglomerations, such as the importance of project-based work, for example, as well as the limits to agglomeration, as witnessed in research that has focused on the ways in which global centres for cultural industries have generated

a set of dependent, satellite agglomerations that pick up work relocated to cheaper locations (such as the relationship between Los Angeles and Vancouver in the motion picture industry, for example). This work has also drawn attention to the ways in which processes of production and consumption are increasingly blurred, as are the divides between what we might previously understood as 'the economic' and 'the social and 'the cultural'.

The final chapter in this part of the book, by Linda McDowell, focuses on the rise of service sector work and the ways in which this has prompted interpretations of the economy that draw attention to the importance of gender, identity, performance, embodiment and sexuality. Service work is dominated by women, and much of this work involves the worker embodying the service being sold in what has been described as 'body work'. As McDowell argues, recognizing the significance of the personal attributes of workers is not something that was previously undertaken within economic geography, which tended to frame employment within concepts such as supply, demand, skills and competencies (see also Chapter 9). However, as studies in cognate disciplines such as sociology and organizational studies revealed, how a worker looks, behaves and presents themselves is integral to many jobs, particularly in the service sector. McDowell illustrates the significance of this in a number of case studies, including her own research on gendered work in high status services work within the City of London during the 1990s. As these studies show, gender identity is important, although it is not fixed and permanent. It is performed in line with the demands of customers, managers and the employee's own sense of self.

Part 8: Rethinking the economic

The final part of the book extends the critique of the 'economic' in economic geography. In this regard. It may appear strange, therefore, that the section begins with a chapter by Louise Johnson on feminist economic geographies, which are hardly new, having been around since the dawn of feminism as a social movement in the late 1960s and early 1970s. However, it is instructive to be reminded by Johnson just how radical a perspective feminism brought to scholarship by insisting on the engendering social processes and relations which enabled the economy to be reimagined and rethought. Feminism has been productive of highly innovative and transformative modes of thinking based on the idea of a liberatory politics. During this time feminism has acted as an important bellwether for prevailing modes of thought within the social sciences more generally, and in economic geography in particular.

As Johnson illustrates, it has informed a range of approaches, from Marxism, through social theory, to the cultural turn. In so doing, it has advanced thinking in each of these areas. Take for example the case of work on uneven spatial development, informed by Marxism and political economy (see above, and Chapters 7, 8 and 17); the production of uneven spatial divisions of labour at national and international scales were frequently highly gendered, with new forms of investment being driven by an attempt to recruit a 'green' or a 'reserve army' of female workers who were for the most part cheaper and considered more docile and less likely to oppose management strictures than their male counterparts. Meanwhile, in The *End of Capitalism (As We Knew It)* (1996), J.K. Gibson-Graham produced one of the most innovative and startling re-interpretations of the economy of the past 30 years. Drawing on an eclectic mixture of Marxist and cultural theories, *The End of Capitalism* reveals the liberatory practices and methodologies emanating from feminist theory.

Some of the ideas developed by Gibson-Graham, and in particular that of 'diverse economies', are developed in Roger Lee's chapter which seeks to push the limits of the economic in making the case for an apparently non-economic economic geography. He does this by exploring the concept of the 'ordinary economy'. This is an attempt to reclaim economic activities from their reduction to the calculating and powerful but ultimately simplistic concepts and theories of non-social economies and the structural logics of capitalism. Whilst insisting on the material imperatives of economy, Lee attempts not merely to seek recognition of economic activities that are socially useful and go beyond the production of profit as a criterion of validity – and thereby makes a case in support of Gibson-Graham's later call for a post-capitalist politics – but argues for the inseparability of social, cultural and environmental relations and those of economy.

The problem for any analysis of economy grounded in material and social circumstances, and for any radical alternative, is to grapple with how the inherent social, cultural and environmental aspects of economic activity may be reconciled with the brute material imperative of producing at least as much value as is needed to sustain all those materially dependent upon it. Central to this reconciliation are the complex relationships between material value and the values – both moral and ethical – that guide and shape economic activity.

In the final chapter of the book, Andrew Leyshon approaches the idea of a non-economic geography from a different direction, exploring the concept of the cultural circuit of capital by way of an historical examination of work on the economic geography of firms and managers. The chapter seeks to illustrate the power of the cultural turn by drawing attention to the ways in which facets of social action that once would have been seen as uneconomic have, over time, been recognized as significant in understanding the production of economic geographies. The chapter reveals how new approaches make it possible to look at the same problem from different viewpoints, even though reconciling these viewpoints may be difficult. Leyshon argues that while new approaches may draw attention to weaknesses in earlier positions, it is important to recognize that newer ideas are not necessarily 'better' but will have their own problems and blindspots.

The final chapters of the book return us to the issue of the relationships between knowledge, thought and the places and times in which those thoughts occur and the construction of knowledge takes place. Given the profound contemporary challenges – both material and moral – to the functioning of the economy, it is perfectly predictable that economic geographers will begin to think of alternatives and begin to rethink the very concepts of economic geographies and the relationships that drive them. In this respect, the lack of a canon of thought and knowledge in economic geography is a massive advantage in trying to come to terms with contemporary economic and environmental dilemmas which strike at the heart of the sustainability of human life.

The chapters in this book show beyond doubt that modern economic geography is a vibrant intellectual tradition marked by strong controversies and shared concerns. As Scott (2000) argues, economic geography is best understood as a palimpsest of approaches and schools of thought, rather than a united front. Legacies from past schools of thought remain visible and influential even as they are written over, reworked and rejected. The chapters in this book show the profoundly contextual character of this palimpsest. They explain how intellectual contexts and schools of thought have shaped the economic geographical interpretation and understanding of the spatial differentiation of economy. As a consequence economic geography has been, and continues to be a genuinely critical and contested intellectual community.

But, as many chapters illustrate, intellectual thoughts and practices are not easily distinguished from, and nor are they more influential in shaping economic geography than, social and economic interested practices. These too shape the priorities, themes and theories, of economic geography. The constant differentiation of knowledge in economic geography reflects the profound significance of space, difference, mobility and dynamics in economic cultures, materialities and practices. The contested and partial nature of economic geographical knowledge does not therefore deny the hope that this knowledge provides critical and helpful understandings of its varied geographical contexts outside the academy. The goal of this text is to sustain and build that hope.

NOTE

1 However – and without getting involved in a terminological war – some economic geographers use the term 'New Geographical Economics' to refer to post-Krugman developments in economic geography. Others use 'New Economic Geography' to refer to the transformations of the sub-discipline following the so-called 'cultural turn'. For discussions and exemplifications of this latter work, see Parts 7 and 8 of this handbook.

REFERENCES

Antipode (2001) Debating Economic Geography: (More than) responses to Amin and Thrift, 33: 2.

Barnes, T. (1998) Envisioning economic geography: Three men and their figures. *Geographische Zeitschrift*, 86; 94–105.

Barnes, T.J. (1996) *Logics of Dislocation: Models, Metaphors, and Meanings of Economic Space*. New York: Guilford.

Barnes, T.J. (2001a) 'In the beginning was economic geography' – A science studies approach to disciplinary history. *Progress in Human Geography*, 25; 521–44.

Barnes, T.J. (2001b) Lives lived and lives told: biographies of geography's quantitative revolution. *Environment and Planning D-Society and Space*, 19; 409–29.

Barnes, T.J. (2002) Performing economic geography: Two men, two books, and a cast of thousands. *Environment and Planning A*, 34; 487–512.

Barnes, T.J. (2003) The place of locational analysis: A selective and interpretive history. *Progress in Human Geography*, 27; 69–95.

Barnes, T.J. (2004) Placing ideas: Genius loci, heterotopia and geography's quantitative revolution. *Progress in Human Geography*, 28; 565–95.

Castells, M. (1989). *The Informational City: Information Technology, Economic Restructuring, and the Urban-regional Process*. Oxford: Blackwell.

Castells, M. (2001). *The Internet Galaxy*. Oxford: Oxford University Press.

Engels, F. (1845/1969) *The Condition of the Working Class in England*. St Albans: Panther Book.

Gibson-Graham, J.K. (1996) *The End of Capitalism (As We Knew It): A Feminist Critique of Political Economy*. Oxford: Blackwell.

Harvey, D. (2006) Neo-liberalism as creative destruction. *Geografiska Annaler Series B-Human Geography*, 88B; 145–58.

Latour, B. (1987) *Science in Action: How to Follow Scientists and Engineers through Society*. Cambridge, Mass.: Harvard University Press.

Latour, B. and Woolgar, S. (1986) *Laboratory Life: The Construction of Scientific Facts*. Princeton, New Jersey: Princeton University Press.

Law, J. (1986) On the methods of long-distance control: Vessels, navigation and the Portuguese route to India. In J. Law (ed.) *Power, Action and Belief: A New Sociology of Knowledge?* London: Routledge & Kegan Paul. pp. 230–263.

Law, J. (1994) *Organizing Modernity*. Oxford: Blackwell.

Leyshon, A., Lee R. and Williams, C. (2003). *Alternative Economic Geographies*. London: SAGE.

Markusen, A. (1996) Sticky places in slippery space: A typology of industrial districts. *Economic Geography*, 72; 293–313.

Marston, S. A., Jones, J. P. and Woodward, K. (2005) Human geography without scale. *Transactions of the Institute of British Geographers*, 30; 416–32.

Peck, J. and Tickell, A. (2007) Conceptualizing neoliberalism, thinking Thatcherism. In H. Leitner, J. Peck and E. Sheppard (eds). *Contesting Neoliberalism: Urban Frontiers*. New York: Guilford.

Scott, A. (2000) Economic geography: The great half-century. *Cambridge Journal of Economics*, 24; 483–504.

Shapin, S. (1975) Phrenological knowledge and the social structure of early nineteenth-century Edinburgh. *Annals of Science*, 32; 219–43.

Shapin, S. (1998) Placing the view from nowhere: Historical and sociological problems in the location of science. *Transactions of the Institute of British Geographers*, 23; 5–12.

Smith A. (1776/1976) *The Wealth of Nations*. Chicago: University of Chicago Press

The Guardian (2005) Life lessons. *The Guardian*, Thursday 7 April 2005. http://www.guardian.co.uk/science/2005/apr/07/science.highereducation

Wade, R. (2008) Financial regime change? *New Left Review*, 5–21.

PART 1

Location Models and Quantitative Economic Geography

Location Models
and Quantitative
Economic Geography

1

Locating Location Models

Jürgen Essletzbichler

INTRODUCTION[1]

This chapter traces the evolution of location theory from Johann Heinrich von Thünen's (1826) *Der isolierte Staat* to August Lösch's (1940) *Die Räumliche Ordnung der Wirtschaft*.[2] Location theory, simply put, is concerned with two features of economic life: distance and area. It examines how transportation costs, the cost of overcoming distance, affect the price of products and the location of production facilities on the one hand, and the geographic extent of markets on the other. Although location theory evolved over a period of 113 years and location theorists focus on different aspects of the space economy (Barnes, 2003) their realist ontology, their method of isolation (abstraction), and their insistence on complementing abstract analysis with historical case studies tie them together.

Location theorists are generally known for their formal and abstract models leading to idealised patterns of the space economy (see Table 1.1). Their use of formal models has been emphasized by members of the quantitative revolution in geography (Chorley and Haggett, 1967; Abler et al., 1972), regional scientists (Isard, 1956) and economists

(Stolper, 1943; Ponsard, 1983; Samuelson, 1983). Because of their use of formal models, the works of Thünen (1826), Weber (1909), Cristaller (1933) and Lösch (1940) are highlighted while a large number of less formal research by economists working on spatial problems (List, 1841; Roscher, 1857; Schäffle, 1867; Engländer, 1926; Ritschl, 1927) is footnoted by conventional disciplinary accounts. In such accounts location theorists function as mere stepping stones on the disciplinary path to general spatial equilibrium analysis (Ponsard, 1983). The compression of disciplinary history into a few key texts and the emphasis on the formal part of their analysis has some important ramifications: First, general equilibrium theory emerges as natural outcome of an uncontested disciplinary history. Second, important alternative frameworks are buried and potential insights from those alternatives are lost.

Closer inspection of the classic texts reveals that location theorists applied abstract and formal analysis alongside detailed historical case studies. They are, therefore, not easily placed on either end of a spectrum of work ranging from purely formal, abstract and deductive at one extreme to purely empiricist, contingent and inductive at the other. Location theorists believed that they were able to isolate particular features of the real world in order to identify causal forces between these features (such as transportation costs and plant location patterns, for example). While they were aware that these abstractions were idealizations of the real word, they believed that the forces between the isolated features were real. Location theorists also believed that their models were necessary but insufficient for explaining the evolution of particular places that could be understood only through detailed historical analysis.

This chapter has two main aims. First, it highlights some of the common features shared by the classical location theories, including their realist ontology; their method of isolation (abstraction); and the fact that they were all German. These similarities existed despite the shifting economic, political and intellectual contexts in which the theories were developed. Second, the chapter examines the important relations and tensions between location theorists and the work of the German historical school. Members of the historical school emphasized geographic specificity and historical evolution and rejected the search for universal economic laws.

While location theory has been rediscovered through its incorporation in regional science and the New Geographical Economics (see Chapter 3), the historical-evolutionary approach to location theory employed by members of the historical school seems to have vanished from the disciplinary memory. This is probably the outcome of the rationalist reinterpretation of disciplinary history as explained by Barnes (2003): the shift towards formal modelling in economics in the 1930s, the entanglement of some of the members of the historical school with fascism, and the lack of translations of the vast majority of their work into English. This is unfortunate considering the vibrant dialogue between members of the historical school and location theorists. On the one hand, location theorists recognized the importance of contingency and historical evolution for understanding actually existing location patterns. On the other hand, work by the historical school was influenced in significant ways by the writings of the location theorists, and in particular by Alfred Weber. The discussion of the intellectual and institutional context in which location theory evolved also sheds light on some anomalies in disciplinary history, including the long lag between the publication of Thünen's (1826) *Der isolierte Staat* and Weber's (1909) *Standort der Industrie*, the apparent tension in the work of location theorists between formal and historical analysis and the insignificant impact of location theory on mainstream geography and economics. In order to get a sense of the importance of the changing institutional context for the development of location theory, the chapter is laid out in chronological order starting with Thünen's and ending with Lösch's contribution.

JOHANN HEINRICH VON THÜNEN (1780–1850)

Thünen's (1826) *Der isolierte Staat* is celebrated as the first serious treatment of spatial economics. It also contains the first formulation of the marginal productivity theory of distribution in a mathematically concise way (Samuelson, 1983), the interpretation of entrepreneurial profit as risk premium (Blaug, 1986), and a discussion of the natural wage (Barnes, 2003; Barnrock, 1974; Harvey, 1981). The work is remarkable because the geographic problems of economic activity had largely been ignored by classical political economy, the domain of English political economists.[3] It is therefore not surprising that the first abstract geographical model was developed by a German member of the landed class rather than an economist. When Thünen purchased the Tellow estate in Mecklenburg in 1810, he meticulously recorded prices of inputs and outputs over an extended period of time. The main task of Thünen was to run his estate as efficiently as possible and in opposition to his teacher

Thaer who propagated the universal introduction of English agricultural business practices in Germany, to demonstrate that business practices would vary in relation to labour costs, capital costs and product prices; that is, Thünen understood that efficiency can be determined only relative to the environment in which businesses operate and that best practice is geographically specific (Palander, 1935).

Running the estate led Thünen to the following general question: Assuming efficient producers, how does a change in product prices affect agricultural land use? Thünen assumes perfectly rational farmers who maximize profits. Evaluating all costs and possible revenues, farmers will choose those land uses that maximize the ground rent, the surplus emerging from working the land. The original question is then modified: What are the origins of the ground rent and what are the laws that govern the size of the ground rent? In order to answer those questions, Thünen develops an ideal state:

Imagine a very large town, at the center of a fertile plain which is crossed by no navigable river or canal. Throughout the plain the soil is capable of cultivation and of the same fertility. Far from town, the plain turns into an uncultivated wilderness which cuts off all communication between this State and the outside world. There are no other towns on the plain. The central town must therefore supply the rural areas with all manufactured products, and in return it will obtain all its provisions from the surrounding countryside. The mines that provide the State with salt and metals are near the central town, which, as it is the only one, we shall in future call simply 'the Town'. (Thünen, 1966: 7)

Table 1.1(a) provides the set of most important assumptions employed to formulate the basic model of agricultural land use in the isolated state. Assuming identical market prices in the Town, producer prices must fall with distance from the market. The original questions are transformed into: How must the farming system and land use change with distance from the Town? Thünen's location theory is a by-product of his analysis of the factors determining the comparative advantage of different land use systems. Given the assumptions of the model, Thünen is able to deduce the results right at the beginning of his book where he expects the emergence of:

fairly sharply differentiated concentric rings or belts [...] around the Town [see Table 1.1(a)], each with its own particular staple product. From ring to ring the staple product, and with it the entire farming system, will change; and in the various rings we shall find completely different farming systems. (Thünen, 1966: 8)

Mäki (2004) identifies *Der isolierte Staat* as:

one of the first systematic applications in social science of the combined method of isolation (sometimes referred to as that of abstraction) and de-isolation (decreasing abstraction or increasing approximation). On this method, theorizing proceeds first by stating a set of assumptions that are known to diverge from the actual characteristics of the real world and then by relaxing these assumptions one by one so as to approach a more concrete and complex picture of reality. At the first stage, one isolates a small selection of whatever are regarded as (perhaps the most) relevant factors – perhaps just one such factor – and at later stages one de-isolates by incorporating other factors and features of the actual situation in order to get a more comprehensive and detailed account of it. (Mäki, 2004: 1720)

In the preface to the second edition of *Der isolierte Staat*, Thünen is conscious of the significance of his method: 'This method of analysis has illuminated – and solved – so many problems in my life, and appears to me to be capable of such widespread application, that I regard it as the most important matter contained in all my work' (Thünen, 1966: 4).

Thünen is aware that in reality a large number of factors such as uncultivable land, unequal land fertility, industrial production, exchange taking place in non-urban settings and so on will influence the magnitude of the ground rent. Despite the unreality of the assumptions, Thünen does not believe that his theory does not provide real insights in the workings of the actually existing world.

The principle that gave the isolated state its shape is also present in reality, but the phenomena which here bring it out manifest themselves in changed forms, since they are also influenced at the same time by several other relations and conditions. Just as a geometrician performs calculations with dimensionless points and widthless lines, neither of which can be found in reality, so we may divest an acting force of all incidental conditions and everything accidental, and only in this way can we recognize its role in producing the phenomena before us. (Thünen 1910, translated in Mäki 2004: 1726)

Thünen is thus a realist who believes that there is an 'ontological reality with a definitive causal structure that exists independently of our theoretical and statistical representations of it; and the semantic thesis that our representations may be true of limited but significant aspects of that reality without having to encompass all causally relevant large chunks of it' (Mäki, 2004: 1726). In order to reveal an 'acting force' a theory has to be partial and idealizing and, hence, unrealistic in some respects. Thünen's interest in distance and transportation costs arose from the fact that Tellow was relatively isolated and markets accessible only via road transport that was expensive and slow at the time.

The locally specific condition of poor accessibility thus gave rise to Thünen's abstract model of agricultural land use that allowed him to isolate the impact of transportation costs on the ground rent. As a result Thünen's 'patterns of agricultural land use are shaped as if transportation costs were the sole real force acting upon them, in isolation from all other factors (even though we know it is not in fact so isolated)' (Mäki, 2004: 1726). Although Thünen was aware that isolation is a fiction and that in reality land-use patterns would manifest themselves in changed forms compared to the idealized situation in the isolated state, he was also convinced that the isolated force (of transportation costs on cultivation patterns) *does* exist.

The process of isolation and de-isolation has become the hallmark of location theorists since Thünen even if the subjects studied (land-use patterns, industrial location patterns, market areas) have changed over time. While the process of isolation is necessary to make sense of real-world complexity, the danger is that 'mentally we separate what in reality is interdependent' (Thünen, 1966: 229). The classic location theorists realized that there are theoretical limits on the process of isolation imposed by the structure of the real world and that abstract models have to be complemented by auxiliary hypotheses and historical-evolutionary analysis to account for real world complexity.

Despite the originality of Thünen's work, the emphasis on time rather than space in British classical political economy, and the move towards inductive, descriptive and historical analysis favoured by the emerging German historical school, meant that the contributions of Thünen were never fully incorporated in standard economic theory. In order to understand the long gap between the publications of Thünen's (1826) *Der isolierte Staat* and Weber's (1909) *Standort der Industrie*, it is thus important to discuss the intellectual context of German economics at the time.

THE OLDER GERMAN HISTORICAL SCHOOL[4] (1841–1883)

The German historical school appeared in a period of rapid economic, political and intellectual change (Gregory, 1981). The birth of the historical school is usually attributed to the publication in 1843 of the *Grundrisse* by Wilhelm Roscher in which he claimed to lay out the historical method, but should probably be predated to include the publication of Friedrich List's (1841) *National System of Political Economies* (Hodgson, 2001). Although some commentators argue that there are few common threads running through the work of the German historical school (Pearson, 1999), its members were unified by a rejection of the methodological individualism and deductivism of British classical political economy, and a concern to make economics sensitive to different social cultures and historical periods (Hodgson, 2001).

The concern with the problem of historical specificity started to appear in the 1840s. This problem is tied up with methodological issues and the empiricist claim that historical data are the source of truth. Roscher rejected universal theories in favour of particular theories based on simple description of specific phenomena. Facts should speak for themselves. Roscher also believed that it was possible by induction to establish general regularities and laws and emphasized comparative methods as means of theoretical study of the phenomena of the life of a nation. Unfortunately he never produced a coherent methodological framework. The emphasis on cultural and historical context united the members also in their rejection of methodological individualism. They believed that individuals are shaped by their social networks and the cultural environment in which they live. List assumed that the power of the national economy was more than the sum of the productive powers of the individual parts because of the productive benefits provided by national infrastructure and culture. He also emphasized the importance of learning and education in shaping productive capacities of individuals. Because of his emphasis on learning and education, he can be regarded as one of the early contributors to the literature on national and regional innovation systems.

Although location analysis was often implicit rather than explicit in the work of the members of the older historical school, the emphasis on historical specificity and cultural context is of obvious relevance for present day geography. The most relevant contributions to location problems by the older historical school were probably advanced in Wilhelm Roscher's (1865) *Studien über die Naturgesetze, welche den zweckmässigen Standort der Industriezweige bestimmen* and Alfred Schäffle's (1873) *Das gesellschaftliche System der menschlichen Wirtschaft*. Roscher sketched out a theory of stages of economic development and postulated that industries would appear only when some basic economic conditions are met.

Regularities in industrial location patterns were established through detailed case studies. Schäffle produced a more systematic version of Roscher's ideas and developed detailed classifications of industries that were primarily based on the input requirements (for example, skilled labour) of different industries. Specific locational requirements were deduced from those classifications. Both studies sought to generalize from detailed case studies and classification of empirical information. Although inductive reasoning led them to wrong conclusions in some cases, it also allowed them to speculate on the importance of agglomeration economies, highlight how different location patterns are related to different stages of development, write about the role of inertia and path-dependence, and discuss the impact of local differences of culture, history, environment and institutions on industrial location even if this discussion often lacked precision. Their work also influenced American location theorists such as Hall (1900) and Ross (1896).

A discussion of the older historical school is important for two reasons. First, because of the rejection of universal theorizing and deduction, Thünen's work had little impact on German location theory until the early twentieth century. Second, the rejection of methodological individualism and the emphasis of historical, cultural, and geographic specificity are important precursors for theoretical developments of modern geographic thought. Despite some important insights, the weak methodological position of the old historical school opened it up to criticisms culminating in the German *Methodenstreit*.

GERMAN METHODENSTREIT[5]: MENGER VERSUS SCHMOLLER (1883–1884)

In his *Untersuchungen*, Carl Menger (1883) launched his attack from Vienna on the historical school. Menger argued that it was impossible to derive social or natural laws solely from description or observation. He insisted that it was necessary to reach behind the superficial appearances and understand the underlying essences, to identify the typical and exclude the superficial and accidental. The historicists also tried to identify types and understood the importance of theory but falsely believed that they could arrive at those through description and detailed observation only. 'Having demonstrated the impossibility of description without prior theoretical concepts, Menger quite rightly saw the outstanding problem as one of the choice of relevant abstractions, by which to classify, analyze and begin to explain phenomena' (Hodgson, 1999: 82–3).

Menger tried to establish the following four methodological propositions (Hodgson, 1993: 93):

1. *Anti-inductivism:* Economics can proceed neither initially nor wholly from facts alone; even description relies on prior theoretical concepts and description cannot itself lead to an explanation of economic phenomena.
2. *Individualism:* The appropriate starting point for economic analysis is the individual, with given purposes and preferences, rather than the 'national economy' or any other higher level unit.
3. *Universality of economic principles:* Some economic principles, such as those relating to supply and demand, pertain to all economic systems. Economists must focus on the elucidation of such principles [on this point see Mäki, 1997].
4. *Relegation of historical specificities:* There is no need for economists to give priority to the problem of historical specificity.

Modern economists accept probably all four of the positions, but only the first proposition is really convincing. And it is this proposition that eventually sank the German historical school and with it all its attempts to develop context sensitive economic theories. For contemporaries of Menger the outcome of the *Methodenstreit* was not as clear cut as economic doctrine may suggest. While even most of the members of the historical school conceded defeat with respect to point 1, it was generally understood that Menger's propositions 2–4 were less convincing and both camps revised their views continually as a result of the *Methodenstreit*. The historical school continued to dominate academic positions at German universities (as they did in US universities), but the *Methodenstreit* forced its members to react to Menger's challenges and abandon their exclusive empiricist stance while still maintaining other positions such as the social embeddedness of individuals and in turn, the importance of the historical and geographic context in which they live. This view is very much expressed in the work of location theorists. With the abandonment of crude empiricism and inductivism, intellectual space opened up for location research to continue in the tradition of Thünen and develop abstract, general models that could serve as a basis for detailed historical studies.

ALFRED WEBER (1868–1958)

The first general theory of industrial location was advanced by Alfred Weber, whose work was influenced by the younger historical school[6] but who also absorbed the lessons of the *Methodenstreit*. Weber understood the limits of abstract theory in explaining historically and geographically concrete economic forms, but he insisted on the necessity of abstraction to uncover causal linkages and make sense of empirical complexity:

> By making use of the method of isolating analysis, we may ascertain, if not all, at least some, causal relationships, and prepare for a perfect causal understanding, and even for measurement. (Weber, 1929: 9–10)

The use of isolation and search for causal relationships makes Weber the true heir of Thünen[7] (Blaug, 1998).

Weber sets out to discover the pure laws of industrial location and identify abstract, causal mechanisms that are supposed to operate independently of historically specific modes of production. Once the pure laws are identified it is necessary to examine the '*particular form* these laws receive in the modern economic order, and what *additional* rules, or perhaps only regularities, enter' (Weber, 1929: 10, original emphasis). Like Thünen, Weber employs assumptions such as rational decision makers endowed with perfect information, perfect competition and a flat surface, to keep intervening forces constant [see Table 1.1(b)].

The main question Weber seeks to address is: 'What causes an industry to move from one place to another'? Because Weber believes that the goal of entrepreneurs is to minimize costs rather than maximize profits, he starts out to classify costs according to regional variability. Cost of land, fixed capital, cost of raw material and power source, interest rates and depreciation are assumed to be identical across regions, leaving transportation and labour costs as the only factor prices to vary spatially. Although Weber recognizes that cultural factors will influence prices, he does not consider them in the pure theory.

In the first stage of his analysis, Weber keeps labour costs constant and isolates the impact of transportation costs on firm location. Firms locate where they are able to minimize transportation costs. Weber demonstrates this with locational triangles [see Table 1.1(b)]. The point of least transport costs (P) depends on two factors: the weight of commodities required to produce a ton of output and the distance over which those commodities are moved. In order to establish P, Weber classifies industries as weight-gaining or weight-losing. For this purpose, Weber develops the material index, which is the total weight of localized inputs per ton of output. For weight-gaining industries (material index < 1), a market based location is most likely, while for weight-losing industries (material index > 1) a location close to the sources of raw material is most efficient.

Once P has been determined, the 'distorting' effects of labour costs are introduced. In order to evaluate whether locations of cheap labour are adopted, Weber develops the concept of the isodapanes (lines of equal total assembly and distribution costs). If a cheap labour location is available inside the critical isodapane (the isodapane where unit transportation costs equal unit cost savings through cheap labour), then the location will be adopted as a least cost production site. If the site is outside the critical isodapane, P is preferable. Weber also realizes the influence of agglomeration and de-agglomeration forces on the geographic distribution of industries in space and demonstrates how firms may be prepared to incur increased transport and labour costs if production rises sufficiently to lead to an overall reduction in the unit costs of production. Lloyd and Dicken (1977) and Smith (1971) provide empirical applications of Weber.

Weber (1909) acknowledges that his assumptions are violated in the real economy. In order to explain the particular forms in which the 'laws' of location are expressed in specific economic contexts, auxiliary assumptions are necessary. Brief empirical sketches are provided in Chapter 7 of Weber (1909) and in Weber (1914). Although Weber still uses isolation in this part of the analysis, he insists that it is impossible at that stage to employ deduction exclusively. Unfortunately, Weber never discusses in any detail the auxiliary assumptions nor provides a detailed historical analysis. He never succeeded in integrating successfully his location model of the pure economy with his historical studies. After the *Standort* he focused exclusively on real world problems, employing evolutionary and historical analysis of location patterns, before moving into sociology and later heading the academic movement against Fascism in Germany (Gregory, 1981).

Despite addressing some of the fundamental questions of economic geography such as the location of plants and industries, Weber's (and other location theorists') work did not receive a lot of attention from mainstream geography at the time. The inability of location theory to penetrate mainstream geography is probably the result of their use of abstractions and formal models that were out of tune with geography at the time which was dominated by descriptive, inductive and idiographic research (Hartshorne, 1939; Hettner, 1927).[8]

Weber's work was also criticized by economists for being a least-cost rather than maximum profit approach. Critics questioned whether even the pure theory is general enough to encompass all modes of production and whether the exceptional treatment of labour costs is appropriate. They also objected to the punctiform treatment of production and consumption, and the insufficient consideration of demand factors (Bortkiewitz, 1910; Schumpeter, 1910; Sombart, 1910; Furlan, 1913; Predöhl, 1925; Engländer, 1926; Ritschl, 1927; Christaller, 1933; Palander, 1935; Lösch, 1939). With the exception of Palander (1935), who found logical flaws as well as major omissions in Weber's model, those criticisms referred to specific points of the theory which, in principle, was accepted as a useful, though incomplete, model of industrial location.

Some contributions following Weber are of considerable interest for contemporary economists and geographers. Predöhl (1925) introduces substitution analysis and provides the first and rather limited attempt to merge Walrasian general equilibrium economics with location theory. Ritschl's (1927) paper on the pure and historical dynamic of industrial location takes Weber's (1909) strata to describe the development of activity layers during the periods of the village, city, territorial, national and world economies. Weigmann (1931) believes that distance creates monopolies such that the space economy cannot be studied with perfect competition models and that it is necessary to move from location analysis to spatial economics (*Raumwirtschaft*). For Weigmann (1931) the main purpose of spatial economics is the identification of subnational regions characterized by relatively dense flows of labour and capital. Those regions are understood as relational and dynamic spaces where various economic processes crystallize into temporary spaces

with an essential, identifiable form (*Gestalt*). Weigmann is also one of the few location theorists who build on the work of geographers such as Schlüter and Haushofer. Although critical of Weber's work, Tord Palander (1935), the first significant non-German location theorist, follows Thünen's and Weber's partial equilibrium approach and develops models of entrepreneurial behaviour in space. Palander does improve significantly upon Weber by introducing market areas rather than punctiform markets, relaxing some key assumptions and introducing more realistic transportation systems. Palander also insists that general equilibrium models cannot be successfully applied to location problems in any meaningful way, a view later echoed by Blaug (1998).

Weber and other members of the historical school took Menger's methodological critique of empiricism seriously and endorsed the use of abstract (although not necessarily formal mathematical) models while insisting on accompanying abstract analysis with historical-evolutionary studies of actually existing patterns of industrial location. This methodological position clarifies some apparent contradictions in Weber's work wavering between abstract models of industrial location on the one hand and historical case studies on the other (Weber, 1909, 1914). While it is true that his model of the 'pure' economy makes Weber the true heir of Thünen, Weber never returned to formal location analysis after the *Standorte* confirming Isard's (1956) assertion that Weber belongs to the historical school rather than the school of formal economic analysis, as Blaug (1979) and Ponsard (1983) incorrectly concluded.

WALTER CHRISTALLER (1893–1969)

Christaller was the first geographer among location theorists, although his ideas for his famous dissertation *Die zentralen Orte in Süddeutschland* at the geography department

Table 1.1 Geometry and assumptions of classical location theories

a. Thünen	b. Weber	c. Christaller	d. Lösch
Source: Thünen 1966	Source: Weber 1909	Source: Christaller 1933	Source: Lösch 1954
Geometry: Concentric circles	Triangles	Hexagons	Hexagons

Key Assumptions

a. Thünen

- The area is a plain, that is, there are no mountains, valleys, navigable rivers or canals.
- All communication between the area and the outside world is cut off by an uncultivated wilderness.
- The soil is throughout capable of cultivation and homogeneous in fertility.
- At the center of the plain there is a town with no spatial dimensions; hence it is represented by a single point. There are no other towns in the area.
- The town is the only market for sale of agricultural products.
- There is a uniform system of transport over a flat surface and transportation costs are proportional to distance and weight of goods.

b. Weber

- The area is a plain.
- Natural resources are distributed unevenly on the plain; raw materials are concentrated in specific sites.
- The size and location of markets are given at fixed points on the plain.
- There are fixed locations of labor where wage rates are fixed and labor is immobile and unlimited.
- Costs of land, structures, equipment and capital do not vary regionally.
- The area has a uniform culture, climate and political system.
- Entrepreneurs minimise costs of production.
- Perfect competition exists.
- There is a uniform system of transport over a flat surface and transportation costs are proportional to distance and weight of goods.

c. Christaller

- The area is a plain, homogeneous, unbounded limitless surface (abstract space).
- Population is distributed evenly.
- All consumers have a similar purchasing power and demand for goods and services and all consumers act rationally.
- No provider of goods or services is able to earn excess profit.
- There is a uniform system of transport over a flat surface and transportation costs are proportional to distance (only).

d. Lösch

- The area is a plain, homogeneous, unbounded limitless surface (abstract space).
- Resources are distributed evenly.
- All consumers have a similar purchasing power and demand for goods and services and all consumers act rationally.
- No provider of goods or services is able to earn excess profit.
- Technical knowledge disseminated throughout the plain and production opportunities available to all.
- There is a uniform system of transport over a flat surface and transportation costs are proportional to distance (only).

	a. Thünen	b. Weber	c. Christaller	d. Lösch
Supply:	Dispersed/areal	Localized/point	Localized/point	Localized/point
Demand:	Localized/point	Localized/point	Dispersed/areal	Dispersed/areal

□ City-rich
□ City-poor

at the University of Erlangen must have taken shape during his MA studies in macro-economics (Hottes, 1997). In this thesis, Christaller posed the following questions: 'How can we find a general explanation for the sizes, number, and distribution of towns? How can we discover the laws?' Like Thünen and Weber before him, he did not believe that historical investigation and statistical method are sufficient to uncover genuine laws. He sets out to construct a theory with 'validity completely independent of what reality looks like, but only by virtue of its logic,' which could then be 'confronted with reality, ... [to explore] to what extent reality corresponds to theory, to what extent it is explained by it, and in what respects reality does not correspond with the theory ... The unexplained facts must then be clarified by historical and geographical methods, because they involve personal, historical, and naturally conditioned resistances – factors which cause deviations from theory. They have nothing to do with the theory itself, and above all cannot be cited directly as proof against the validity of the theory'. He sets out to develop a 'theory of location of urban trades and institutions, to correspond with Thünen's agricultural production and Weber's theory of location of industry [...] derived deductively, by pure reasoning' (Christaller, 1966: 1–7, cited in Berry and Harris, 1970).

Following Thünen and Weber, Christaller (1933) builds his theory of the location of retail outlets on a set of assumptions to isolate the key relationships [see Table 1.1(c)]. Christaller excluded manufacturing towns and developed an idealized system of hexagonal market areas based on three basic concepts: centrality, threshold and range. Centrality is the draw to a particular place. Threshold is the minimum level of demand needed to maintain a service and range is the maximum distance a consumer is willing to travel to purchase that service. From these concepts, a hierarchy of service centres was envisaged, with a large number of small (low-order) centres providing the basic services and an increasingly smaller number of

high-order centres providing more specialized goods in addition to the basic services (Healy and Ilbery, 1990, Lloyd and Dicken, 1977).

From those assumptions and concepts, Christaller deduces a number of towns with different sizes endowed with hexagonal market areas [see Table 1.1(c)]. While Thünen and Weber were interested in the location decisions of individual producers, Christaller moved from the individual/firm level to the system level of cities and market areas. Thünen's and Weber's focus on the decision-making process, where aggregate outcomes emerge from individual decisions, shifts to an analysis of aggregate patterns with little concern for the micro-level. The link between micro-level decisions and aggregate location patterns disappears in Christaller's work.

Although his advisor Robert Gradman recognized the importance of the dissertation (Hottes, 1983), Christaller's work was never truly appreciated among German geographers who at that time were very much concerned with idiographic and chorological analysis (Hettner, 1927) and considered Christaller's work too abstract. As a result he never had a post at a German geography department throughout his career. However, his ideas travelled to the United States through August Lösch (discussed below), who introduced Christaller's work to Edward L. Ullman who was working on his 'Theory of Location of Cities', and as a result Christaller later became a cult figure among United States quantitative geographers. What is important but generally ignored is that Christaller revised his methods and adopted an inductive approach in his habilitation thesis, which was published as *Rural Settlements in Germany in their Relation to Community Administration* (Christaller, 1937) that has not been translated and is virtually unknown (Hottes, 1983).

While not influential in geography, Christaller's theories found considerable application in regional planning. Christaller joined the National Socialist Party in 1940, and took up a post in a government planning department headed by Himmler where he applied his theory to reorganize the Polish space economy according to his principles of central places. After the war he joined the communist party (in 1945) and then the social democratic party (1959). His brief episode with the Nazi party reflects the complex nature of the political context in which Christaller and other German scientists worked from 1933 to 1945 (Rössler, 1989). Christaller was reintroduced to German geography during the quantitative revolt (revolution would be too strong a term in the German case) in the 1960s and 1970s and through English-speaking textbooks, but he was never appreciated in geography during his own time.

AUGUST LÖSCH (1906–1945)

Lösch extends Christaller's central place hierarchy to include the location of agriculture and production. In a first step he summarizes the existing work on location theory from the perspective of a general equilibrium framework of the spatial economy. Lösch follows Launhart's and Christaller's concern with market areas of competing producers rather than the micro-economic approach of Thünen and Weber. Employing the usual assumptions [Table 1.1(d)], Lösch demonstrates that competition between different producers will result in hexagonal market areas. The size of hexagons will vary across industries dependent on the range and threshold of industry-specific products. Overlaying industry-specific 'honeycombs' and centering them on a single city (metropolis) expected to offer all commodities results in a complex economic landscape [Table 1.1(d)], Lösch demonstrates that production tends to bunch together and that abstract space divides into activity rich (core) and activity poor (periphery).

Lösch, like his predecessors, was still very much socialized in an intellectual environment dominated by the historical school where theoretical models were a means to

explain the evolving space economy and not ends in themselves. Lösch was also working with Schumpeter in Bonn who was influenced by Menger and appreciative of equilibrium economics but who was also convinced of the necessity of dynamic and historical analysis. Lösch's work embodies a similar tension between formal modelling of ideal, equilibrium landscapes in one section of his book and the desire to understand the historical evolution of real places demonstrated by the large number of examples in another. Like Thünen, Weber, Ritschl, Palander and Christaller, Lösch (1954: 4) is very much aware of the distinction between real and ideal location patterns:

> The question of actual location must be distinguished from that of the rational location. The two need not coincide... it would be dangerous to conclude that what is must also be rational since otherwise it would not exist, and that therefore any theoretical determination of the correct location would therefore be superfluous.

His ideal landscape entails that the greatest number of locations coincide, that a maximum of purchases can be made locally, that the sums of distances and consequently shipments between industrial locations are least, and that transportation costs and transportation lines are minimized (Lösch, 1954; Stolper, 1943; Valavanis, 1955). The ideal landscape is an efficient landscape that increases social welfare and that is preferable to the actual location patterns governed by 'illogical, irregular, lawless' forces. Lösch thus demands: '[Our] real duty ... is not to explain our sorry reality, but to improve it. The question of the best location is far more dignified than determination of the actual one' (Lösch, 1954: 4). Although Lösch's work was not translated into English until 1954, he had contacts in the United States and published a paper in the *Southern Economic Journal* in 1938 (Lösch, 1938).

Lösch was the last of a long dynasty of German location theorists that combined abstract, general theorizing with concrete, historical, empirical studies. While their impact on economics at the time was limited outside Germany and they had no influence on German-speaking geography immersed in the idiographic tradition, the shift of Anglo-Saxon economics and sociology towards universal theorizing and methodological individualism, coupled with a rapid spread of the use of mathematics, paved the way for the quantitative revolution in geography. But this took on board the idealized models of the classical location theorists without supplementing them with historical case studies.[9]

In economics, space remained an unnecessary complication in general equilibrium models and was thus mainly ignored. Those that did try to take it seriously reduced geography to the price of overcoming distance and as such, to one of many substitutable and given factors of production. Lösch himself took a step in the direction of general equilibrium analysis when he moved away from the micro-economic concerns of Thünen and Weber. His work points towards the macroeconomics of regional science that had lost a lot of the interesting insights into the location decisions of individuals and firms in a partial equilibrium setting and probably contributed further to the marginalization of location theory in economics (Blaug, 1998).

LEGACY AND SIGNIFICANCE

Probably the single most important contribution of location theorists was their early use of abstraction to isolate key causal relationships while at the same time recognizing that formal models were only the first step in understanding the complex evolution of the space economy (or aspects of it) in specific historical and geographic contexts. They were aware that the isolations were fictions, but believed that the relationships between the isolated acting force (such as distance or transportation costs) and the phenomena studied (land use, location of firms and industries) were real. They were also aware of the limits of the method of isolation

imposed by the causal structure of the real world. Assumptions are, to some extent, arbitrary and, in the case of location theorists, identified through their experiences with their respective local environments (such as inefficient transportation lines connecting the Tellow estate with its markets in Thünen's case) (Barnes, 2003). The general causal processes identified are thus based on assumptions influenced by the local experiences of the theorists. Because the isolated forces interact with other universal and local processes they crystallize in different forms in different geographical and historical settings. Location theorists thus believed that historical analysis has to complement abstract models if we are to explain actually existing spatial patterns and phenomena.

The influence of location theory on both mainstream economics and geography has been limited (Blaug, 1998). After 1800, British political economy was concerned with time rather than space resulting in complete disregard of Thünen's work. The concern with context, historical and geographical specificity was important for members of the German historical school and evident in the work of American institutionalists who were trained at German universities and dominated US universities until the 1920s (Hodgson, 2001). The long delay between Thünen and Weber has to be understood in the context of the domination of German economics by members of the German historical school rejecting abstract theorizing, generalizations and deductive reasoning while believing in empiricism and inductive reasoning. Weber's work was published only after Carl Menger's methodological critique of the historical approach in 1883 that forced German economists to abandon their empiricist stance and opened up German-speaking economics to alternative approaches. Since Weber, German economists had a virtual monopoly on location theory that was broken only by the rise of National Socialism and the impact of the Second World War.

However, the recasting of mainstream economics in a general equilibrium framework from the 1920s and the increasing formalization of economic theory put an end to institutional, historical and holistic economic analysis in the US and the UK. The search was on for general laws governing the exchange economy rather than detailed historical and comparative studies of particular industries and places. Contrary to location theorists who considered their abstractions as a first step to understanding complex causal relations, modern orthodox economists seem to take their abstractions at face value. Abstractions are interpreted as accurate representations of the essential aspects of reality, while cultural, historical and individual differences deviating from those essences are seen as unnecessary complications that add nothing to a better understanding of the real world.

Such ontological, epistemological and methodological changes have been repeated, to a lesser degree, in geography. With the quantitative revolution, the search for universal rules and laws started to compete with the descriptive and chorological approaches that dominated geography in Germany and the United States. Removed from their historical context and the larger projects of the location theorists, location theory has been reinterpreted through a positivist lens. The technical aspects of the work were seen as useful tools suited to the development of an equilibrium space economy, while the normative and idealistic intentions as well as the historical and empirical material accompanying and complementing the abstract models were deemed irrelevant.

Because regional science followed Christaller and Lösch rather than Thünen, Weber and Palander it quickly ended up in a theoretical cul-de-sac of spatial equilibrium modelling that had little to say about actual spatial patterns of production and consumption (Blaug, 1998). Neither location theory nor regional science had much impact on mainstream economics. The incorporation of space in a general equilibrium framework in a meaningful way has proved impossible. But since mathematical tractability was favoured over realistic representations of the real world, it was space rather than general equilibrium that was dropped from mainstream economic analysis (see Chapter 3). Geography instead moved on to embrace a diversity of ontological, epistemological and methodological approaches. In some respects it also moved back to the ideals of the German historical school and classical location theory, endorsing abstract thinking whilst recognizing the need for detailed historical, evolutionary and comparative analysis and avoiding the pitfalls of purely inductive reasoning. The old texts may therefore have just as much affinity with modern evolutionary economic geography as they do with formalized quantitative geography and regional science.

NOTES

1 Acknowledgement: I would like to thank Peter Wood for passing on his excellent collection of classic texts that significantly reduced the number of trips to the library and Peter Sunley for valuable comments on an earlier draft.

2 While Thünen is relatively uncontested as founding father of classical location theory, choosing Lösch as endpoint is more problematic. Because of Lösch's role in attempting to link location theory with Walrasian general equilibrium theory he builds a conceptual bridge to regional science (see Barnes, Chapter 2) and opens up the theoretical cul-de-sac in which location theory ended up (Blaug, 1998). However, because he was socialized in the tradition of the German historical school, his work contains all the ideas of the earlier work by Thünen, Launhart, Weber, Engländer, Ritschl, Weigmann, Christaller and Palander, he was fully aware of the limitations of his ideal space economy, and he failed to develop a fully-fledged general equilibrium theory of the space economy. Thus his ties with classical location theory are interpreted as stronger than with the general equilibrium space economy of Walter Isard (1956) justifying his inclusion among classical location theorists.

3 While Adam Smith (1776) had a lot to say about the role of distance and area for economic activity interest in spatial problems disappeared in economics after 1800. Space was not included in a systematic fashion by classical and neoclassical economists who become confined to a wonderland of no spatial dimensions (Isard, 1956: 25–6). There are no

straightforward explanations for this but Isard (1956) proposes that the explanation is related to the historical and geographical context of the British economy concerned with international trade and resource extraction rather than the spatial organization of its domestic industry.

4 Because the intellectual (and in particular the methodological) position of members of the German historical school shifted after the German *Methodenstreit* (see footnote 5) in 1883 and because this shift is crucial to understand the work of Alfred Weber in the broader institutional context it is useful to distinguish between the younger (after the *Methodenstreit*) and older (before the *Methodenstreit*) German historical schools. The methodological shift as a result of the *Methodenstreit* is reflected in the work on location.

5 The *German Methodenstreit* refers to an important exchange between Carl Menger (an economist from Vienna) and Gustav Schmoller (the leading German economist at the time) on the role of theory and the use of empirical facts in the development of theoretical arguments. Schmoller believed that theories have to emerge from empirical facts through induction, while Menger insisted that facts can never lead to an explanation of economic phenomena without prior theoretical concepts.

6 Weber's teacher was Gustav Schmoller.

7 The first industrial location model was probably provided by Wilhelm Launhardt (1882, 1885) who wrote before the *Methodenstreit*. As an engineer with an interest in transportation issues he was able to ignore the methodological positions advanced by mainstream, historical economists. Because his papers were rather technical and published in engineering journals, his work had little influence at the time. Weber does not cite Launhart, although his three-point-location problem is very close to Launhart even if Weber goes far beyond Launhart's simple model (Blaug, 1998; Lloyd and Dicken, 1977; Palander, 1935; Pinto, 1977).

8 George S. Chisholm, one of the leading British economic geographers at the time confesses that Weber's work is interesting but too abstract for him (Chisholm, 1910).

9 A good example of an economist's reading of Lösch is Stolper's (1943: 636) review of *Die räumliche Ordnung der Wirtschaft* in American Economic Review: 'But neither his unjust attacks, nor his expressed liking for Hegelian philosophy, nor other hardly relevant statements of a philosophical nature [such as 'It is impossible to understand fully the Swabian economy without an understanding of Swabian philosophy' (Lösch, 1940: 125)] for which this review has no use, touch the core of his contributions. His philosophical statements are apt to irritate the reader and to draw his attention away from the main arguments'.

REFERENCES

Abler, R., Adams, J.S., Gould, P., (1972) *Spatial Organisation*. Englewood Cliffs, N.J.: Prentice-Hall.

Barnes, T. (2003) The place of locational analysis: A selective and interpretive history. *Progress in Human Geography*, 27(1): 69–95.

Barnrock, J. (1974) Prolegomenon to a methodological debate on location theory: The case of von Thünen. *Antipode*, 6: 59–66.

Berry, B.J.L. and Harris, C.D. (1970) Obituary-Christaller, W-Appreciation. *Geographical Review*, 60(1): 116–19.

Blaug, M. (1979) German hegemony of location theory– Puzzle in the history of economic-thought. *History of Political Economy*, 11(1): 21–9.

Blaug, M. (1986) *The Methodology of Economics: or, How Economists Explain*. Cambridge: Cambridge University Press.

Blaug, M. (1998) *Economic Theory in Retrospect*. Cambridge: Cambridge University Press.

Bortkiewicz (1910) Eine geometrische Fundierung der Lehre vom Standort der Industrien. *Archiv fur Sozialwissenschaft und Sozialpolitik*, 30: 769–71.

Chisholm, G.S. (1910) The geographical relation of the market to the seat of industry. *Scottish Geographical Magazine* (April).

Chorley, R.J. and Haggett, P. (1967) *Models in Geography*. London: Methuen.

Christaller, W. (1933) *Die zentralen Orte in Süddeutschland*. Jena: Gustav Fischer.

Christaller, W. (1937) Die landliche Siedlungsweise in Deutschan Reich und ihne Beziehungen zur Gemeind organization. Stuttgart.

Christaller, W. (1966) *Central Places in Southern Germany*. Englewood Cliffs, N.J.: Prentice-Hall.

Engländer, O. (1926) Kritisches und Positives zu einer allgemeinen reinen Lehre vom Standort. *Zeitschrift fur Volkswirtschaft und Sozialpolitik*, Neue Folge, 5. Band: 435–505.

Furlan, V. (1913) Die Standortsprobleme in der Volks- und Weltwirtschaftslehre. *Weltwirtschaftliches Archiv*, 2: 1–34.

Gregory, D. (1981) Human Agency and Human Geography. *Transactions, Institute of British Geographers*. NS 6: 1–18.

Hall, S.F. (1900) The localization of industries. *The Twelfth Census of the United States 39*, Volume 7, Manufactures: xc.

Hartshorne, R. (1939) *The Nature of Geography*. Lancaster, PA: Association of American Geographers.

Harvey, D. (1981) The spatial fix-Hegel, von Thünen, and Marx. *Antipode*, 13: 1–12.

Healey, M.J. and Ilbery, B.W. (1990) *Location and Change*. Oxford: Oxford University Press.

Hettner, A. (1927) *Die Geographie: Ihre Geschichte, ihr Wesen*, und ihre Methoden. Breslau.

Hodgson, G. M. (1993) *Economics and Evolution*. Cambridge: Polity Press.

Hodgson, G.M. (1999) *Economics and Utopia*. London: Routledge.

Hodgson, G.M. (2001) *How Economics Forgot History*. London and New York: Routledge.

Hottes, R. (1983) Christaller, Walter. *Annals of the Association of American Geographers*, 73(1): 51–4.

Hottes, R. (1997) Leben und Werk Walter Christallers. *Standort-Zeitschrift fur Angewandte Geographie*, 1: 28–30.

Isard, W. (1956) *Location and Space-economy*. Cambridge, MA: MIT Press.

Launhardt, W. (1882) Die Bestimmung des zweckmäs-sigsten Standortes einer gewerblichen Anlage. *Zeitschrift des Vereins Deutscher Ingenieure*, 26: 106–15.

Launhardt, W. (1885) *Mathematische Begründung der Volkswirtschaftslehre*. Leipzig: Teubner.

List, F. (1841) *National System of Political Economy (Translated by Lloyd from German)*. London: Longmans.

Lloyd, P.E. and Dicken, P. (1977) *Location in Space: a Theoretical Approach to Economic Geography*. London: Harper and Row.

Lösch, A. (1938) The nature of economic regions. *Southern Economic Journal*, 5(1): 71–8.

Lösch, A. (1939) *The Economics of Location*. New Haven, CT: Yale University Press.

Lösch, A. (1940) *Die räumliche Ordnung der Wirtschaft; Eine Untersuchung über Standort, Wirtschaftsgebiete und internationalen Handel*. Jena: Fischer.

Lösch, A. (1954) *The Economics of Location*. New Haven, CT: Yale University Press.

Mäki, U. (1997) Universals and the Methodenstreit: A re-examination of Carl Menger's conception of economics as an exact science. *Studies of the History and Philosophy of Science*, 28(3): 475–95.

Mäki, U. (2004) Realism and the nature of theory: A lesson from J.H. von Thünen for economists and geographers. *Environment and Planning A*, 36: 1719–36.

Menger, C. (1883) *Untersuchungen über die Methode der Sozialwissenschaften und der politischen Ökonomie insbesondere*. Tübingen.

Palander, T. (1935) *Beiträge zur Standortstheorie*. Uppsala: Almqvist and Wiksells Boktryckeri-A.-B.

Pearson, H. (1999) Was there really a German historical school of economics? *History of Political Economy*, 31(3): 547–62.

Pinto, J.V. (1977) Launhardt and location theory – Rediscovery of a neglected book. *Journal of Regional Science*, 17(1): 17–29.

Ponsard, C. (1983) *History of Spatial Economic Theory*. Berlin: Springer.

Predöhl, A. (1925) Das Standortsproblem in der Wirtschaftstheorie. *Weltwirtschaftliches Archiv*, 21: 294–331.

Ritschl, H. (1927) Reine und historische Dynamik des Standortes der Erzeugungszweige. *Schmollers Jahrbuch fur Gesetzgebung, Verwaltung, Volkswirtschaft im deutschen Reiche*, 51(6): 1–58.

Roscher, W. (1865) *Studien über die Naturgesetze, welche den zweckmässigen Standort der Industriezweige bestimmen. Ansichten der Volkswirtschaft aus dem geschichtlichen Standpunkte*. Leipzig: Winter.

Ross, E.A. (1896) The location of industries. *Quarterly Journal of Economics* 246.

Rössler, M. (1989) Applied geography and area research in Nazi society – Central place theory and planning, 1933 to 1945. *Environment and Planning D*, 7(4): 419–31.

Samuelson, P. (1983) Thünen at two hundred. *Journal of Economic Literature*, 21: 1468–88.

Schäffle, A. (1873) *Das gesellschaftliche System der menschlichen Wirthschaft*. Laub'sche Buchhandlung: Tübingen.

Schumpeter, J.A. (1910) Review of Weber's Standorte. *Jahrbuch für Gesetzgebung, Verwaltung und Volkswirtschaft*, 34(3): 444–47.

Smith, A. (1776) (1993 ed). *An Inquiry into the Nature and Causes of the Wealth of Nations*. Oxford and New York: Oxford University Press.

Smith, D. (1971) *Industrial Location*. New York: Wiley.

Sombart, W. (1910) Einige Bemerkungen zur Lehre von Standort der Industrien. *Archiv für Sozialwissenschaft und Sozialpolitik*, 30: 748–58.

Stolper, W.F. (1943) Review of Die räumliche Ordnung der Wirtschaft. *American Economic Review*, 33(3): 626–36.

Valavanis-Veil, S. (1955) An econometric model of growth, USA 1869–1953. *The American Economic Review* 45: 208–21.

von Thünen, J.H. (1826) *Der isolierate Staat in Beziehung auf Landwirtschaft und Nationalökonomie*. Hamburg: Perthes.

von Thünen, J.H. (1966) *Von Thünen's Isolated State (Translated by C.M. Wartenberg)*. Pergamon Press.

Weber, A. (1909) *Alfred Weber's Theory of the Location of Industries (Translated from German by C.J. Friedrich, 1929).* Chicago: University of Chicago Press.

Weber, A. (1914) Industrielle Standortlehre: Reine und kapitalistische Theorie des Standorts. *Grundrisse der Sozialokonomik,* 6: 54–82.

Weber, A. (1929) *Alfred Weber's Theory of the Location of Industries (Translated by C.J. Friedrich).* Chicago: University of Chicago Press.

Weigmann, H. (1931) Ideen zu einer Theorie der Raumwirtschaft. *Weltwirtschaftliches Archiv* 34: 1–40.

2

The Quantitative Revolution and Economic Geography

Trevor Barnes

INTRODUCTION

The quantitative revolution represented a profound transformation in Anglo-American economic geography from the mid-1950s onwards, defined by the systematic application of scientific forms of theorizing and rigorous statistical techniques of analysis and description. In the process, the previous regional economic geography concerned with describing, cataloguing, and delineating the economies of unique places was pushed aside, replaced by the 'new geography' directed towards explaining, scientifically proving, and abstractly theorizing spatial economic phenomena and relations. Economic geography was no longer rote memorization of leading ports, major waterways, and principal products, but a science, spatial science.

As a result, the days were over when the American geographer, Clarence Jones (1935: v), could stand before his Northwestern University economic geography class in Evanston, Illinois, and say without his student audience either rolling their eyes or tittering: 'Everyone likes to travel. Most of us wish to visit distant lands. Some want to be explorers and learn the ways of the Eskimo or the forest Indians who gather Brazil nuts in the Amazon. Many wish to hunt lions and tigers in the forests and savannas of Africa'. Jones could no longer say those words, or at least not say them without being ridiculed, because the quantitative revolution fundamentally changed what counted as economic geography, and who could be an economic geographer. Under the new definition, Jones' words were unrecognizable as economic geography, and he was unrecognizable as an economic geographer. The practices of the discipline were deeply altered, and those who failed to adapt necessarily fell by the way.

The chapter is divided into four short sections. First, I discuss the wider historical origins of the quantitative revolution, which lay in the Second World War, and its aftermath, the Cold War. Both produced an academic turn to formalism and rigour that affected the social sciences as well as even some of the humanities. Economic geography was just another one of the disciplines affected, and if anything, it was a Johnny-come-lately (the gendering is appropriate) compared to several of the others. Second, I tell the story of the quantitative revolution in economic geography as it emerged during the 1950s within a set of fragmented geographical centres, each associated with a small group of believers who were young, bright, very ambitious, and exclusively male. These were the revolutionaries. Third, I characterize the kind of economic geography that was produced. It was theoretical, mathematical, reliant on machines, underpinned by an explicit appeal to the philosophy of science, particularly to some form of positivism, and reflected the peculiar set of social characteristics of its practitioners. Finally, by way of a conclusion, I discuss how the quantitative revolution turned out in economic geography, and its intellectual legacy.

In all this, my focus is on the tradition of Anglo-American economic geography, and much more American than Anglo. Partly this is because it is the tradition I know best, partly it is for reasons of brevity, and partly it is because the most sustained and systematic impulse toward quantification derived from post-war *American* social science and first entered American economic geography before diffusing elsewhere.

HISTORICAL ORIGINS OF THE QUANTITATIVE REVOLUTION

The Second World War, and later the Cold War, created the conditions for geography's quantitative revolution. The sociologist of science, Andy Pickering (1995), applies the term 'World War II regime' to understand this period. For Pickering, the regime is distinctive because of a close interrelationship among several institutions that previously were separate, but through their mutual interaction, created an entity that never existed before. Before the Second World War, science and the military in the United States were more or less decoupled:

> [During] World War II, [however, there emerged an] intense coupling of science and the military. In a series of open ended social, technical, material, and conceptual developments, the civilian/scientific and military communities redefined themselves around endpoints that were interactively stabilized against and reciprocally dependent upon

one another. The inner technical practices of both science and the military were radically transformed in World War II, science (especially the physical sciences) turning into object-orientated multidisciplinary 'big science', and the military moving from traditionally structured tactics and strategy to scientifically planned warfare deploying the new technoscientific objects. There transformations were tuned to and aligned with one another via the establishment of new institutions of surveillance and control, by the creation of new technoscientific artefacts (like radar) and their circulation into military practice, and by the development of Operations Research, a new conceptual apparatus that invaded military practice carried by a civilian vector (physicists and mathematicians)...What had been largely separate and autonomous institutions before World War II – science and the military – had become profoundly transformed and locked together as a complex, social, material, and conceptual cyborg entity by the end of it. (Pickering, 1995; 18)

For the purposes of this chapter, especially important was the new relation forged between science, including the social sciences, and the military. It was not just that they cooperated – that had happened before – but their aims and structure increasingly bled into one another, creating a new combined entity that stressed above all else scientific and quantitative forms of knowledge. Just as he was leaving office in 1961, US President Eisenhower famously spoke of the military-industrial complex, and, in 1967, Senator Fulbright talked of the military-industrial-academic complex. In both cases, they point to this new entity that joined academics, the government, the military, and private business.

The purpose of that entity was to achieve definite geopolitical ends, from eliminating Fascism in Europe to fighting communism in the Third World. Such ends were too important to be left only to the military. It was also necessary to involve non-military scientific experts. For example, physicists, such as those employed at the World War II Manhattan Project at Los Alamos under Professor Robert Oppenheimer, and who created the atomic bomb that fundamentally changed the character of not only the Second World War, but the second half of the twentieth century. Or, social scientists, such as American economists based at the Enemy Bombing Unit in Second World War London, who invented cost-benefit analysis that determined the most rational targets for aerial bombardment. The critical point for this chapter is that the kind of knowledge deemed useful for achieving immediate military purposes and the associated larger geopolitical ends emphasized rigour, mathematics, formal vocabularies and models, 'hard' data, cutting edge technology, and objectivity. This form of knowledge was instrumental. It got things done. Even physical sciences that already generated this form of knowledge changed to accommodate the new demands, moving towards a 'big science' model. But the transformation was even more profound for the social sciences and humanities. Carl Schorske (1997: 295) characterized the development of the human sciences during the period 1940–1960 as a 'passage … from range to rigor, from loose engagement with a multifaceted reality historically perceived to the creation of sharp analytical tools that could promise certainty where description and speculative explication had prevailed before'. This was new, but exactly what one should have expected once social sciences and humanities were set within the military-industrial-academic complex. Some social sciences like economics and psychology had a head start in their transformation. Others, like geography, especially economic geography of the kind Clarence Jones taught, had a much longer way to go.

Specifically, in the United States, the beginning of geography's revolution was its involvement in the Office of Strategic Services (OSS), later the Central Intelligence Agency. Established in July, 1941, the OSS provided the intellectual brawn for US military intelligence. It brought together a who's who of American academics in the social sciences and humanities as well as from outside. The key geographer during the wartime period was Richard Hartshorne (1939), a political and economic geographer. In 1939 he had written the most systematic and philosophically sophisticated monograph ever in

English of the history and definition of the discipline, *The Nature of Geography*. For Hartshorne, and this was the import of his 1939 volume, the mandate of geographers at OSS was assiduous, atheoretical geographical representation and description; in other words, rote memorization, Clarence Jones's version of the discipline. Such an approach, however, became increasingly out of synch with the practices of other disciplines represented at OSS such as economics, psychology, and even political science and sociology. They were becoming more like physical sciences, drawing on new methods, mathematical techniques, and in some cases even abstract theories, and contributing to the 'World War II regime'.

Against this back drop, against the impress of Hartshorne's view of geography, some younger geographers employed at OSS became increasingly frustrated. They could catalogue geographical information, insert it within classification schemes, and describe, but that was it; they lacked the vocabulary, and tools to use their knowledge for specific instrumental ends. Edward Ackerman (1945: 122), one of those younger geographers, wrote after he had been demobbed:

> Wartime experience has highlighted a number of flaws in theoretical approach and in the past methods of training men [*sic.*] for the profession. It is no exaggeration to say that geography's wartime achievements are based more on individual ingenuity than on thorough foresighted training.

The training he had in mind was the kind of preparation that some of the other social scientists at OSS undertook. Economists could draw upon mathematical skills, psychologists statistical ones, sociologists conceived their discipline from the beginning as a science of society defined by empirical and numerical methods, and even anthropologists possessed ethnographic and field techniques. Geographers had only the map. And even then they weren't always sure what to do with it.

Ackerman wasn't the only geographer at OSS to be frustrated (Barnes and Farish,

2006). Geographers need not have worried, though. Another war was just starting, this one under the shadow of the Bomb, with the geopolitical end of resisting communism, and asserting democratic forms of government and the virtues of the free market (although the assertion of democracy was at best selective). Such an end would offer plenty of opportunities for geographers to contribute because even more so than World War II it was to be realized in part by the explicit use of science and social science. Dwight Eisenhower, then Army Chief of Staff, said in 1946:

> The lessons of the last war are clear. The military effort required for victory threw upon the Army an unprecedented range of responsibilities, many of which were effectively discharged only through the invaluable assistance supplies by our cumulative resources in the natural and social sciences and the talents and experiences furnished by management and science.... This pattern of integration must be translated into a peacetime counterpart ... (quoted in Allison, 1985: 290)

And so it was, even though as President Eisenhower, he later had doubts about what he unleashed. In the process, Cold War American social science became ever more scientific, more mathematical, more rigorous, even incorporating some of the humanities.

Geographers like Ackerman, and others who had been with him at OSS such as Chauncy Harris and Edward Ullman (and all economic geographers to one degree or another), once they returned to academic geography began trying to shift disciplinary course in line with the new intellectual current. But it was hard work. The discipline was firmly anchored in the regional approach. But it could not stay put forever. The military-industrial-academic complex was becoming more powerful and stronger, drawing in fresh recruits, transforming them. As geographers like Ackermann returned to university teaching with their new contacts, new ideas, new institutions for research funding (like the Office of Naval Research), and new machines (like the computer), so geography, and especially economic geography, began to be

pulled and tugged, slowly but inexorably into the main stream.

While there were some direct Cold War linkages between economic geographers and the military-industrial-academic complex, especially in the form of research funding and contract work (and discussed below, but also see, Barnes and Farish, 2006), equally important were the indirect ones turning on an innovative intellectual climate defined by scientific rigour and mathematical modelling. This was the future, certainly economic geography's immediate future.

CENTRES OF ECONOMIC GEOGRAPHICAL CALCULATION

But it took time to realize. It was not until the mid-1950s that the first real pangs of conversion from the old Clarence Jones's version to a shining new spatial science were felt, even though the conditions for change were laid more than a decade earlier. At first, the change was highly localized, confined initially in the United States to two centres: the University of Washington, Seattle, and the University of Iowa, Iowa City.

Key actors at the University of Washington were two faculty members: Edward Ullman, an OSS alumni, and briefly at the Department of Geography at Harvard before it was shut down in 1951; and William Garrison, who served on US Air Force bombers in the Pacific Theatre before completing a PhD in Geography at Northwestern University. It was at Northwestern that Garrison as a graduate student co-taught with Clarence Jones in his economic geography course. Their intellectual sensibilities could not have been more different, however. As Garrison says about Jones's lectures: 'they led me to keep asking: "What's the theory? What's the theory? What's the theory" (Garrison, 1998). Specifically, '... a systematic approach was in order. ...' (Garrison, 1979: 119).

It was precisely a systematic approach to economic geography, one attuned to Cold

War science that Ullman and Garrison pioneered at the University of Washington during the early 1950s, making it the premier economic geographical centre of economic geographical calculation. Both were thoroughly embedded in Cold War projects, institutions and money (for details see, Barnes and Farish, 2006). The money was especially important, particularly from the Office of Naval Research (ONR). Both men held substantial and continuing ONR grants during the mid-to-late 1950s. They enabled them to fund graduate students, and who were to lead the quantitative revolution's charge.

Annus mirablis was 1955, when in the Fall of that year a remarkable group of graduate students serendipitously gathered at the Department of Geography, University of Washington, to study. Later labelled the 'space cadets', they were to change fundamentally economic geography, fulfilling Garrison's goal of a 'systematic approach'. That first term they were exposed to the first advanced course in statistics ever given in a US geography department, Geography 426, Quantitative Methods in Geography, offered by Garrison. Richard Morrill (1998), who was in that first class, observed that 'it wasn't just the introduction to beginning statistics but the whole gamut from beginning to all that was known in those days. So, it was a ferocious baptism'. But it was not only numbers to which they were exposed, but also machines. There were the large, thudding Frieden calculators, but more important was the recently acquired, even larger, computer. In an early advertisement for the Washington department, the Head, Donald Hudson (1955), boasted about the departmental use of an IBM 604 digital computer, also a national first. The programming technique of so-called patch wiring involving plugging wires into a circuit board was crude and inefficient, but it helped define and consolidate the scientific vision of the discipline.

And then there was theory. It came from economics, and, perhaps more unlikely, from physics. Economic geography up until then was renowned for its antipathy towards theory (see Chapter 1). The British geographer George Chisholm, one of the late nineteenth century discipline's founders, had even 'wish[ed] ... th[e] love of pure theory to the devil' (quoted in Wise, 1975: 2). But the University of Washington's programme was defined by the titrated drip of undiluted theory. Ullman's seminar on urban location theory provided the basics of Walter Christaller's and August Lösch's central place theory. Garrison offered the 'cadets' during their first year a seminar in economic theory, likely also a first in Anglo-American geography. He assigned as the text Walter's Isard's just published (1956) *Location and Space Economy*, a volume defined by differential equations, simplified abstract assumptions, and hard-headed neoclassical economic rigour and logic. There were no lions and tigers here, no forests and savannas of Africa. But Garrison and his students now knew 'what's the theory'.

The other centre at the University of Iowa turned on the work of Harold McCarty. Direct Cold War connections were less apparent, although even here much of the research funding derived from the Office of Naval Research. In 1940, McCarty had written *The Geographic Basis of American Economic Life*, a book propelled by a stiff economic logic not found in comparable contemporary texts by economic geographers. 'Economic geography derives its concepts largely from the field of economics' McCarty (1940: xiii) wrote in the Preface. This was his mantra. All of his subsequent work took economic concepts, and tested them on the fodder of regional geography. Importantly for our purposes, that testing was formal, involving for the first time in the discipline inferential statistics, in this case, correlation and regression techniques. It was an approach solidified in the collective report, *The Measurement of Association in Industrial Geography* (McCarty et al., 1956). Consisting of a multitude of regression studies relating industrial location to various variables, economic geography provided the case studies, economics the theoretical muscle.

A cantankerous colleague of McCarty's, Fred Schaefer, was another contributor, in his case, by providing a philosophical rationale: positivism. A political refugee from Nazi Germany, Schaefer (1953) published in the flagship journal of American geography, a pointed philosophical critique of Hartshorne's justification of regional geography. Schaefer's alternative was positivism, a philosophy based on the canons of natural scientific practice emphasizing explanation, logical deduction, stringent empirical testing, and the virtues of a formal, universal mathematical vocabulary. It was everything that Hartshorne's view of geography, and Clarence Jones's view of economic geography, were not. Schaefer's positivism gave those at the University of Iowa, but also at other later centres of economic geographical calculation, an intellectual rationale grounded in a body of seemingly unassailable analytical philosophical strictures and developed by the philosophical heavy weights of the 1950s: Rudolph Carnap, Alfred Jules Ayer, Saul Kripke, and Willard Quine.

Washington and Iowa were central to the quantitative revolution in the United States. Outside of it, two other centres deserve mention. The first was the Department of Geography at Cambridge University. In autumn 1958, Richard Chorley and Peter Haggett (with David Harvey as teaching assistant) began lecturing first year undergraduates for the first time in the history of the Department on 'statistical methods, matrices, set theory, trend surface analysis, and network analysis' (Chorley, 1995: 361). Then in 1960, Haggett (1965: v) began offering a lecture course in economic geography, the 'much-thumbed and much-revised lecture notes' for which became *Locational Analysis in Human Geography*, still perhaps the most elegant statement of economic geography as spatial science. However, as Haggett (1965: vii) says, *Locational Analysis* was less an original contribution, than 'a report from an active battlefront' occurring elsewhere, that is, in the United States. The second is Lund, Sweden, and associated with the iconoclast, Torsten Hägerstrand. Virtually on his own

back, Hägerstrand (1967 [1953]) developed and deployed during the early 1950s a set of statistical and theoretical techniques to understand innovation diffusion across the Swedish space economy. It was sophisticated and original, resulting in Hägerstrand visiting the University of Washington in the late 1950s, influencing several of the 'cadets'.

By the late-1950s, the elements necessary for the quantitative revolution in economic geography were assembled: statistical and mathematical techniques, machines, theory, and an underlying philosophy. They needed to be put together, though, and diffused to a wider audience. Exactly this happened during the 1960s. Partly, the diffusion occurred through the bodies of the revolutionaries themselves, such as the 'space cadets', as they left Seattle for new jobs. As they moved, they spread the word of revolution to new sites such as the University of Chicago, University of Michigan, Bristol University, and perhaps ironically given its past history, Northwestern University. Partly the diffusion occurred through seminars, special sessions at conferences, training camps in quantitative methods for the uninitiated (the first was held again ironically at Northwestern in 1961), and dedicated meetings such as the Madingley Hall lectures that Chorley and Haggett arranged at Cambridge for secondary school geography teachers in England and Wales (the first was held in July 1963, and subsequently published as a series entitled *Frontiers in Geographical Teaching*). And partly diffusion occurred through the circulation of purple mimeographed papers, various discussion paper series (the first originated at the University of Washington in March 1958), and later formal journals such as *Geographical Analysis* founded in 1969 (for details see Barnes, 2004a).

ECONOMIC GEOGRAPHY AFTER THE REVOLUTION

If this was how the quantitative revolution in economic geography happened, what was wrought by it? After the revolution, the

LIBRARY, UNIVERSITY OF CHESTER

discipline was utterly different. Disciplinary training, practices, forms of writing, places of research, venues of publication, the hierarchy of academic status, all changed. In particular, five characteristics defined economic geography after the revolution.

First, the discipline was characterized by the aspiration to a particular form of theory, the kind characterizing physical sciences and mimicked especially in economics. For this reason the quantitative revolution was perhaps a misnomer. What excited revolutionaries was less numbers (although they turned the crank of some), but abstract theoretical explanations couched as hypotheses, models, axioms, and, the pinnacle, laws. This view of what counted as theory derived from the philosophy of science, and in particular positivism (and first systematically articulated for geography by David Harvey, 1969). Theories were conceived as formal statements, expressed in the vocabulary of mathematics, positing causal connections among classes of phenomena, and capable of empirical verification. In Harvey's words (1969: 87):

> The quest for an explanation, writes Zetterberg, is a quest for theory'. The development of theory is at the heart of all explanation, and most writers doubt if observation or description can be theory-free. ... Some writers, Berry and Blaut among them, regard the evolution of a distinctive theoretical structure for explaining certain sets of phenomena as being the main justification for regarding geography as a distinctive and independent discipline within the empirical sciences. If this be true, then a clarification of the 'nature' of geography depends upon the prior clarification of the nature, form, and function of theory in geography.

The problem was that given the intellectual history of the discipline, the influence, for example, of George Chisholm, or Richard Hartshorne, no indigenous economic geographical theory existed. It was necessary to beg, steal, and borrow it. A recouped tradition of German economic location theory that included Johann von Thunen's (1783–1850) formulations of agricultural land use

and rent, Alfred Weber's (1869–1958) model of industrial location, and August Lösch's (1906–1945) general theory of the space economy, provided an initial set of core concepts (see Chapter 1). Added to these from orthodox neoclassical economics and an allied movement, regional science (Barnes, 2004b), were rational choice theory as well as general and partial models of market equilibrium.

Geometry provided network and graph theory as well as the mathematics of topological forms, and used to explain spatial patterns such as transportation routes and trip patterns. And finally, physics offered gravity, potential and entropy models that, in turn, were used to explain geographies of spatial interaction, for example, the relation between the location of consumers and the location of retailers. These last models likely represented economic geography's finest theoretical hour. Thousands of papers were published on spatial interaction producing (at least for some) the ultimate: an economic geographical law. Waldo Tobler (1970: 236) formulated the First Law of Geography in August, 1969: 'everything is related to everything else, but near things are more related than distant things'.

More generally, economic geographers of the quantitative revolution believed that shaping the economy were a set of autonomous independent spatial forces that could be discerned, represented, and explained by drawing upon formal theory. Theory made the economic geographical world transparent and understandable. While initially theory would be taken from others, the ultimate aim was to construct home-grown versions. David Harvey exhorted geographers on the last page of *Explanation in Geography* 'to pin up on our study walls ... the slogan ...' 'By our theories you shall know us' (Harvey, 1969: 486).

Second, there was the quantitative part of the quantitative revolution. Quantitative did not mean simply numbers. Chisholm's *Handbook of Commercial Geography*, published in 1889, and the first textbook in the discipline, was not short of figures. Rather, quantitative for the quantitative revolutionaries meant the use of formal statistical techniques both to represent numerical data, and to draw scientific inferences. The first forays were in descriptive statistics with use of the mean, and standard deviation. But inferential statistics, that is, drawing conclusions about the larger populations from samples, quickly followed. McCarty et al.'s (1956) use of bivariate and multivariate correlation and regression was an early illustration, and by 1959 the full range of inferential statistics was mobilized by Garrison et al. (1959) and his students in their collective volume, *Studies in Highway Development and Geographic Change*. Geography 426 had clearly left its mark.

It was a slightly different story in Britain, where the quantitative revolution was slower in disseminating. In 1964 at the Institute of British Geographers' annual meeting Peter Haggett showed a multiple regression equation. The next day he was summoned by his Head of Department at Cambridge, Alfred Steers, who had been in the audience. 'This kind of thing has got to stop', Steers told him, 'You are bringing the subject into disrepute' (quoted in Thrift, 1995: 381–82).

Of course, it did not stop, nor could it stop. Haggett, in fact, was promoted on the basis of his economic geographical quantitative efforts, becoming Professor of Urban and Regional Geography at the University of Bristol in 1966, and helping to turn that Department into another centre of economic geographical calculation. Haggett, along with others, continued to develop and refine statistical methods, making them more appropriate for economic geographical use. He advocated (1969: 278) a set of regression cycles:

One of the simplest models for the testing of hypotheses in human geography has been evolved by McCarty. He argues for a sequential approach to geographical research in which (i) problems are defined, (ii) hypotheses are applied, (iii) their effectiveness is evaluated, and (iv) new hypotheses evolved to explain the discrepancies. In specific terms we may frame McCarty's approach as a series of regression cycles, as those shown in Figure 2.1. In the *first cycle* (C_1) the problem is defined, data are collected, statistically analysed, and plotted as an isopleth map; we may term this

the problem distribution (Y). Analysis of the map of the Y-distribution leads to the formulation of a hypothesis (H_1) to account for the geographical irregularities in its form. This initiates the *second cycle* (C_2) with the definition of an explanatory variable, X_1, for which data are collected, are statistically analysed, and related to the problem variable through regression analysis. Using the regression equation ($Y = f X_1$), the derivations for the actual distribution of Y from the predicated distribution Y_c can be measured. The map of these deviations of *residuals* represents the end of the second cycle. Analysis of the map of residuals may lead to a second hypothesis to account for the 'unexplained' distribution. This initiates the *third cycle* (C_3), beginning with the definition of the second explanatory variable, X_2. As Figure 2.1 shows, this third cycle parallels the second cycle and may lead to further cycles (C_4 to C_n) until a satisfactory level of explanation is reached.

Initially, though, there was a problem in applying non-geographical statistical techniques to spatial data. Traditional inferential statistical techniques assumed that sample data was independent; that is, the value of one data point was not influenced by the value of another data point. Spatial data of the kind used by economic geographers, however, generally violated this assumption: the value of a variable in one location was related to the value of the same variable in a nearby location. Spatial autocorrelation, as it is known, thus undermined the assumption of independent sampling, thereby invalidating traditional inferential statistical techniques. Since the early 1970s, however, new statistical techniques appropriate to economic geographical data were developed. Ironically given Steers' fulminations, the writings of Andy Cliff, formerly at Bristol, but subsequently Professor of Geography at Cambridge, was formative (Cliff and Ord, 1973).

Third, to cope with the numbers, to compute statistical formulae, required machines. Revolutionaries needed to appropriate the means of calculation. Initially, numerical work was carried out either on mechanical calculators like the Monroe, or electric calculators like the Frieden. Brian Berry (2000), one of Garrison's 'space cadets', remembers

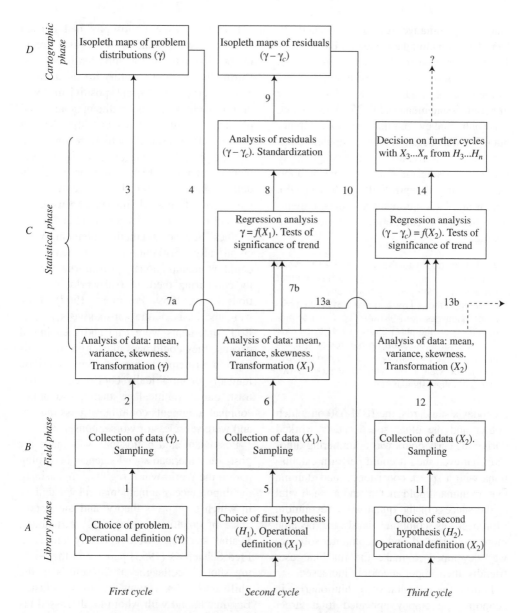

Figure 2.1 Model of regression cycles in geographic research, from P. Haggett, *Locational Analysis in Human Geography*, 1965, page 279.

'in his first semester [fall, 1955] learning statistics on these great big desk calculators that groaned'. But as calculations became more complex and fraught as multivariate statistical techniques, and increasingly large data sets were deployed, even the trusty Monroe and Frieden balked. Something bigger and better was needed. Fortunately, the military-industrial-academic complex came to the rescue. The first computer in the US, The Electronic Numerical Integrator and Computer (ENIAC), was first used to make calculations for testing ordnance at the Aberdeen weapons site, Maryland. Cohen (1988: 135–136) estimates that over the ten years it was in service ENIAC carried out more 'arithmetic than had been done by the whole human race prior to 1945'. This was exactly the kind of machine that the quantitative revolution needed. In fact, it got something even better. By the mid-1950s when ENIAC was decommissioned, computer development was already transformed (in large part because of Cold War imperatives and money). In 1954, IBM, which was contracted by the military as its computer manufacturer, began selling computers commercially to universities, the first going to Columbia. Using the computer meant bootstrap learning, though. Waldo Tobler (1998), one of the Washington space cadets, remembers his early computing experiences in Seattle:

> We had to go up to the attic of the Chemistry building at 2 a.m. so we could run the computer by ourselves. They didn't have any computer operators in those days, and that was before computer languages like FORTRAN. ... To cover programming on the [IBM] 650 you had to pick up two bytes of information on one rotation of the drum. It had a 2K memory which rotated real fast. And if you were clever, you could pick up two pieces of information in one rotation.

By today's standards, the IBM 650 on which Tobler and the other space cadets worked during the early hours was a lumbering dinosaur, but even then it could perform calculations with a speed, consistency, and stamina that no human could match, and as such vital to the success of the quantitative revolution. Moreover, as computer hardware became more sophisticated, and as computer software was developed to make the machine user friendly, their importance only increased.

Fourth, the quantitative revolutionaries in economic geography appealed to a larger philosophical project, positivism, to justify and legitimate. This was new. Economic geographers in the past rarely sought philosophical rationales, and when they did, their statements were murky. Chisholm's were (see Barnes, 2000). And Hartshorne (1939) spent well over 400 pages trying to make his philosophy of geography clear. But he later said that only one person other than himself understood what he had written. In contrast, positivism was a philosophy that prided itself on a scrupulous and transparent clarity.

Positivism as a philosophy had existed since its first formulation by Auguste Comte in the first part of the nineteenth century. During the twentieth century it was taken up and reworked as logical positivism by a group of philosophers, mathematicians, and physical scientists in Vienna (the 'Vienna Circle'). They argued there were only two kinds of true, meaningful (scientific) statements, each of which could be precisely defined and delineated. First, analytic statements were true by definition, and were the basis of the formal sciences, logic and mathematics. Second, synthetic statements were empirically verifiable, i.e. statements that could be unambiguously proven true or false by comparing them to real-world observations (Ayer, 1959; Passmore, 1967). They were the basis of the substantive sciences. Both statements were true and meaningful because they could pass muster on the 'verification principle'; that is, they could be logically or empirically confirmed. In contrast, moral, political, aesthetic, and philosophical judgments could never pass muster, and were senseless or worse, nonsense.

Positivism as a philosophy was made for post-war American social science, becoming part of the World War II regime, emphasizing the importance of a mathematical vocabulary in which to express theory, and the importance of quantitative empirical verification. Spatial scientists were certainly attracted. Fred Schaefer's (1953) paper was the opening shot. A colleague of Schaefer's in the philosophy department at Iowa, Gustav Bergmann, and with whom he discussed his paper, was a former member of the Vienna Circle. Further, it was Bergmann who finalized Schaefer's paper after Schaefer died from a heart attack in an Iowa City cinema before it was published. It was also Bergman who taught a philosophy of science course that all incoming geography graduate students at Iowa were compelled to attend (Amedeo and Golledge's, 1975, textbook in economic geography was written as a result of them taking that seminar, and in this sense, it is the heir to Schaefer's 1953 paper). If

Schaefer's paper was the opening shot, then David Harvey's (1969) *Explanation in Geography* was the closing one. Much more than Schaefer ever did, Harvey provided systematic accounts of both the analytic statements economic geographers could make in mathematics, logic, and especially geometry, as well as their synthetic statements, particularly the use of the verification principle embodied in particular statistical techniques.

Finally, there was a repositioning within the discipline's social hierarchy, albeit not without contestation. Young, male, very ambitious, very able graduate students and junior faculty primarily forged the quantitative revolution, and as it succeeded, they became the new top dogs. In some cases, their advance was rapid. Brian Berry completed both his MA and PhD at Washington in only three years, and by Fall, 1958, he was an Assistant Professor at the University of Chicago. Within seven years he was Full Professor (at the age of only 31). Or again, Haggett was appointed at Cambridge in 1957 as a Demonstrator (and below an Assistant Lecturer). Less than a decade later, he was Professor of Urban and Regional Geography at Bristol University.

Of course, there was some resentment of these 'Young Turks'. Steers' chastizing of Haggett was one example. Or again, Joseph Spencer, an old time regional geographer, and editor of the *Annals, Association of American Geographers* from 1964, vented his frustration by trying to block publication in the journal of quantitative/theoretical papers, suggesting that at best they be confined to a 'Research Notes' section. It was partly Spencer's attitude that led to the proliferation of alternative publishing outlets such as departmental discussion paper series, and culminating in the establishment of a journal dedicated to quantitative economic geography, *Geographical Analysis*.

Perhaps the most marked social characteristic of the revolutionaries was their masculinism. All of the early quantitative economic geographers were male. Moreover, they often acted typically male, tending to be competitive, pushy, playing practical jokes, and being sometimes boastful and evangelical in their beliefs. Michael Dacey, one of the believers at Washington, says 'we were very aggressive, very ambitious, and very appreciative. ... We were full of missionary fervour, and I imagine we were unlikable brats. ... In retrospect we must have been very disorientating to the establishment' (Dacey, 1997). Some of these characteristics come out in their writing, which could be brash and combative. It also made it difficult for women to participate. Susan Hanson (2002) when she enrolled at Northwestern University in 1967 says, 'We knew very well that we were entering male turf'. And ten years later, not much seemed to have changed in terms of gender relations. Pat Burnett who was a faculty member at Northwestern in the late 1970s sued the Department for its 'climate of sex discrimination' (Burnett, 2002).

The broader point is that the social matters, going all the way down. The quantitative revolution in economic geography did not happen at arm's length, as if theory, numbers, machines, and a positivist philosophy, entered the discipline autonomously, on their own volition. But they were always connected to a set of social relations. It was not spatial science in the abstract, but spatial science incarnate.

THE END OF THE STORY?

The year 1969 might have been the high-water mark of the quantitative revolution in economic geography: Harvey's philosophical bible of the movement was published, *Geographical Analysis* was launched, and Tobler announced the First Law of Geography. But it wasn't to last.

Harvey was a central figure in the subsequent unravelling. Even before he finished *Explanation*, he had doubts. In 1971 at the annual meeting of the Association of American Geographers in Boston, those doubts erupted. He announced there that:

[Geography's] quantitative revolution has run its course and diminishing marginal returns are apparently setting in as ... [it] serve[s] to tell us less and less about anything of great relevance. ... There is a clear disparity between the sophisticated theoretical and methodological framework which we are using and our ability to say anything really meaningful about events as they unfold around us. ... In short, our paradigm is not coping well. (Harvey, 1972: 6)

The rest of the 1970s was a decade in which various elements of the quantitative revolution within economic geography were in turn held up for scrutiny, and found wanting. Harvey (1972) began by attacking the usefulness of the theory and statistical techniques he celebrated only three years earlier, portraying them as at best irrelevant, and at worse, politically regressive and counter-revolutionary. Another beachhead was made on the internal logic of mathematics itself. Gunnar Olsson (1975), disgruntled with the spatial interaction models he had earlier triumphed, argued that their very formal reasoning, especially the invocation of the dreaded equals sign, undid any claim to empirical veracity. They were true only in relation to the language in which they were written, and not true, and could never be true, to the world. Doreen Massey's (1973) target was the use of orthodox economic theory, including the German location models, in understanding industrial location that, she argued, failed at every level: on logic, empirics, philosophy, and politics. And right at the end of the decade, the bastion of positivism itself, including its attendant mathematical and statistical apparatus of theory construction and verification was forensically dissected by Andrew Sayer (1979, 1982) who declared the body well and truly dead. Drawing on critical realism, Sayer argued that positivism failed to recognize the importance of causal mechanisms, and instead was content with the sop of mere association, and manifest in economic geography as an endless stream of correlation and regression studies that explained nothing.

Of course, for some, the announcement of the death of the quantitative revolution in economic geography was greatly exaggerated.

They were not willing to shuffle off to the other side. At least, not yet. None of the pioneer quantitative revolutionaries changed positions, and only some of those in the second generation did like Harvey and Olsson. But the latter were important, with status, and commanding attention. And in a small discipline like economic geography they made a difference, drawing allies to them, and to the new positions they held. There was no single death blow, but by the end of the 1970s, the quantitative revolution view of economic geography was fading. Interestingly, exactly the same trajectory characterized the allied movement of regional science. Rising meteorically from the mid-1950s, often in concert with quantitative economic geography, regional science's lustre dulled also from the 1970s (Barnes, 2004b). So much so that in 1995 the founding Regional Science Department at the University of Pennsylvania closed its doors to students, its faculty re-assigned to other Departments.

In its stead arose various stripes of a much more healthy and vigorous political economy based upon the writings of Harvey, Massey, and Sayer. While all three resolutely rejected positivism, number crunching, and any form of neoclassical theorizing, the quantitative revolution had nonetheless left its mark. All three, in fact, began as spatial scientists, and the kind of systematicity, logic, and abstraction that they brought to their new political economic theory was in many ways a carry over from their earlier lives.

More generally, the legacy of the quantitative revolution still remains potent For example, the contemporary interest in geographical economics, including the founding of the *Journal of Economic Geography* in 2001, is a clear continuation of the quantitative revolution's impulse toward rigour, a formal vocabulary, and modelling. Similarly, so is the continuing interest in GIS, and towards which some of the Washington space cadets later gravitated such as Duane Marble and Arthur Getis. The legacy also continues indirectly. Perhaps the most important has been the continued stress on theory. Even the most virulent 1970s critics of the quantitative revolution shared the belief that the discipline must be theoretical. This was the real watershed, separating economic geography of the last fifty years from economic geography of fifty years before that. When political economic critics attacked the quantitative revolution, and offered their alternatives, it was in a theoretical vocabulary made possible precisely by that revolution. The quantitative revolution enabled economic geography to become a mainstream social science, and to be taken as seriously as the others. For that reason, maybe there should be more praising than burying, and the realization that we are more the product of some defunct spatial scientist than we might imagine.

REFERENCES

Ackerman, E.A. (1945) Geographic training, wartime research, and immediate professional objectives. *Annals of the Association of American Geographers*, 35: 121–43.

Allison, D.K. (1985) US Navy research and development since World War II. In M.R. Smith, (ed.) *Military Enterprises and Technological Change: Perspectives in the American Experience*. Cambridge, MA: MIT Press. pp. 289–328.

Amedeo, D. and Golledge, R. (1975) *An Introduction to Scientific Reasoning in Geography*. New York: Wiley.

Ayer, A.J. (1959) *Logical Positivism*. Glencoe, IL: Free Press.

Barnes, T.J. (2000) Inventing Anglo-American economic geography, 1889–1960. In E.S. Sheppard, and T.J. Barnes, (ed.) *A Companion to Economic Geography*. Oxford: Blackwell. pp. 11–26.

Barnes, T.J. (2004a) Placing ideas: *Genius Loci*, heterotopia, and geography's quantitative revolution. *Progress in Human Geography*, 29: 565–95.

Barnes, T.J. (2004b) The rise (and decline) of American regional science: Lessons for the new economic geography? *Journal of Economic Geography*, 4: 107–29.

Barnes, T.J. and Farish, M. (2006) Between regions: Science, militarism, and American geography from World War to Cold War. *Annals, Association of American Geographers*, 96: 807–26.

Berry, B.J.L. (2000) Interview with the author, Pittsburgh, PA, April.

Burnett, P. (2002) Interview with the author, Cambridge, MA, May.

Chorley, R.J. (1995) Haggett's Cambridge: 1957–1966. In A.D. Cliff, P. Gould, A.G. Hoare, and N.J. Thrift (eds) *Diffusing Geography: Essays for Peter Haggett*. Oxford: Blackwell. pp. 355–74.

Cliff, A.D. and Ord, J.K. 1973. *Spatial Autocorrelation*. London: Pion.

Cohen, I.B. (1988) The computer: A case study of the support of government, especially the military, of a new science and technology. In E. Mendelsohn, M.R. Smith, and P.R. Weingart (eds) *Science, Technology and the Military: Sociology of the Sciences Yearbook*, volume 12, Dordrecht: Kluwer. pp. 119–54.

Dacey, M. (1997) Interview with the author, Evanston, IL, November.

Garrison, W.L. (1979) Playing with ideas. *Annals, Association of American Geographers*, 69: 118–20.

Garrison, W.L. (1998) Interview with the author, Berkeley, CA, March.

Garrison, W.L., Berry, B.J.L., Marble, D.F., Nystuen, J.D., and Morrill, R.L. (1959) *Studies in Highway Development and Geographic Change*. Seattle, WA: University of Washington Press.

Hägerstrand, T. (1967) *Innovation Diffusion as a Spatial Process (Translated by A. Pred)*. First published in Swedish in 1953. Chicago: University of Chicago Press.

Haggett, P. (1965) *Locational Analysis in Human Geography*. London: Edward Arnold.

Hanson, S. (2002) Interview with the author, Worcester, MA, May.

Hartshorne, R. (1939) *The Nature of Geography: A Critical Survey of Current Thought in the light of the Past*. Lancaster, PA: Association of American Geographers.

Harvey, D. (1969) *Explanation in Geography*. London: Edward Arnold.

Harvey, D. (1972) Revolutionary and counter-revolutionary theory in geography and the problem of ghetto formation. *Antipode*, 4(2): 1–13.

Hudson, D. (1955) University of Washington. *The Professional Geographer*, 7(4): 28–9.

Isard, W. (1956) *Location and Space Economy*. London: Wiley.

Jones, C.F. (1935) *Economic Geography*. New York: Henry Holt.

Massey, D. (1973) A critique of industrial location theory. *Antipode*, 5(3): 33–9.

McCarty, H.H. (1940) *The Geographic Basis of American Economic Life*. New York: Harpers & Brothers.

McCarty, H.H., Hook, J.C., and Knox, D.S. (1956) *The Measurement of Association in Industrial Geography*. Iowa City: Department of Geography, University of Iowa.

Morrill, R. (1998) Interview with the author, Seattle, WA, December.

Olsson, G. (1975) *Birds in Egg*. Michigan Geographical Publications, number 15. Ann Arbor, MI: Department of Geography, University of Michigan.

Passmore, J. (1967) Logical positivism. In P. Edwards (ed.) *The Encyclopaedia of Philosophy*, Volume 5. New York: MacMillan. pp. 52–7.

Pickering, A. (1995) Cyborg history and the World War II regime. *Perspectives in Science*, 3: 1–49.

Sayer, A. (1979) Epistemology and conceptions of people and nature in geography. *Geoforum*, 10: 19–44.

Sayer, A. (1982) Explanation in economic geography: Abstraction versus generalisation. *Progress in Human Geography*, 6: 65–85.

Schaefer, F.K. (1953) Exceptionalism in geography: a methodological introduction. *Annals of the Association of American Geographers*, 43: 226–49.

Schorske, C.E. (1997) The new rigorism in the human sciences, 1940–1960. *Daedalus*, 126: 289–309.

Thrift, N.J. (1995) Peter Haggett's life in geography. In A.D. Cliff, P. Gould, A.G. Hoare, and N.J. Thrift (eds) *Diffusing Geography: Essays for Peter Haggett*. Oxford: Blackwell. 375–95.

Tobler, W. (1970) A computer movie simulating urban growth in the Detroit region. *Economic Geography*, 46: 234–40.

Tobler, W. (1998) Interview with the author, Santa Barbara, CA, March.

Wise, M.J. (1975) A university teacher of geography. *Transactions, Institute of British Geographers*, 66: 1–16.

The 'New Economic Geography': Credible Models of the Economic Landscape?

Ron Martin

INTRODUCTION: THE NEW ECONOMIC GEOGRAPHY TWO DECADES ON

Traditionally, economists have paid scant attention to the role of space in their theorizations of the economy. Indeed, in standard neoclassical economics space and location are all but irrelevant since the assumptions of perfect competition, perfect information and perfect markets imply that geographical inequalities in economic growth and incomes would quickly disappear by virtue of the free movement of labour, capital and knowledge. Since the beginning of the 1990s, however, mainstream economists appear to have become increasingly interested in the significance of geography in the economy. At last there is an explicit recognition that the economy does not exist on the head of the proverbial pin, but is spatially distributed and organized, and that the 'geographical lumpiness' of the

economic landscape is intrinsic to how the modern economy functions.[1] The most determined attempt to introduce space and location into mainstream economic theory has been associated with the rise of the so-called 'new economic geography' (or NEG as it is typically referred to).[2] Building on the original pioneering work of Paul Krugman (1991a, b), over the past two decades this new subfield has developed apace, and now comprises a formidable corpus of literature, including several major books (such as Krugman, 1995, 1996; Fujita, et al., 1999; Brakman et al., 2001, 2008; Fujita and Thisse, 2002; Baldwin et al., 2003; Henderson, 2005; Fingleton, 2007; Combes et al., 2008), and hundreds of articles. The project of NEG, or 'geographical economics', would seem to be well and truly established.[3]

Economic geographers have not responded very favourably to this new 'geographical economics'. At one level, this is perhaps surprising, since NEG shares some common interests with 'proper economic geography' (or PEG as we might call it).[4] Both are interested in explaining the spatial agglomeration of economic activity, and both have emphasized the role of localized increasing returns.[5] But there, any commonality between the NEG and PEG stops, for the theoretical approach and explanatory method employed have been fundamentally different as between the two. The preferred method of the new geographical economists – in line with the methodology of mainstream economics more generally – has been to construct nonlinear mathematical models of spatial agglomeration and spatial dispersal forces and to examine the possible equilibrium economic landscapes these models imply. This approach is far removed from that typically employed in PEG, where theoretical exegesis is mainly narrative-based and discursive, or 'appreciative', typically emphasizing a range of socio-institutional and cultural processes as well as – or instead of – economic mechanisms, and where the interest is on 'actually existing' spatial economic landscapes, not on hypothetical and idealized ones. Thus, it has not proved easy to reconcile these two rather different versions of economic geography.

Indeed, an aversion to formal models and mainstream economics, together with a resentment that the new 'geographical' economists were threatening to encroach into geographers' 'academic space', laced with not a little irritation that economists should be so provocative as to call their neophyte field the 'new economic geography', quickly generated a wave of negative reaction by economic geographers (see Hoare, 1992; Johnston, 1992; Martin and Sunley, 1996; Boddy, 1999; Martin, 1999a, b) and even some economists (for example, Dymski, 1998). Just as Krugman (1995) had criticized economic geographers for abandoning their location-theoretic tradition, so economic geographers criticized NEG for the conceptual narrowness and limited geographical content of its revamped and highly formalized location models.[6] Neither camp seemed willing to engage constructively with the other: each, in its own way, regarded its approach as superior to the other's, with the geographical economists stressing the 'scientific rigour' of NEG, while the economic geographers highlighted the 'greater realism' of PEG.

In broad terms, this stand-off or *methodenstreit* between NEG and PEG still continues. Most economic geographers regard the formal models of NEG as 'reinventing the wheel', and most new 'geographical' economists probably dismiss the 'soft', qualitative approach that characterizes PEG as inferior to their approach. Meanwhile, NEG has become increasingly sophisticated, and numerous extensions of the basic models have appeared (for surveys of recent advances and new developments, see, for example Ottaviano and Puga, 1998; Brakman et al., 2003; Fujita and Mori, 2005; Fingleton, 2007). One only has to compare the scope and detail of, say, Fujita and Thisse's (2002) *Economics of Agglomeration*, Baldwin et al.'s (2003) *Economic Geography and Public Policy,* or Combes et al.'s (2008) *Economic Geography: The Integration of Regions and Nations*, with Krugman's (1991) *Geography and Trade* to appreciate how NEG has both widened and deepened its modelling framework in recent years. Many of the modifications and developments have been in response to self-awareness on the part of NEG theorists of the limitations and restrictions of their early models (Krugman, 1998; Neary, 2001; Brakman and Garretsen, 2003; Fujita and Mori, 2005). And a corresponding – albeit still small – literature is beginning to emerge that is directed at subjecting NEG models to empirical test (for example, see Brackman et al., 2004; and the contributions to Fingleton, 2007). Notwithstanding these developments, the adherence of NEG to the use of formal mathematical deductive models to theorize the economic landscape has remained its foundational and distinctive feature. It is this issue of formal models that is at the heart of the tension between PEG and NEG.

THE MODEL WORLDS OF NEG

Explaining the spatialities of capitalist economic development is not a straightforward undertaking. Two issues in particular stand out. First, there is the matter of what sort of economic (or other) theory we should use as the basis for our explanations. Second, there is the question of how far and in what ways it is possible to achieve the seemingly contradictory ambition of constructing general explanations given the spatial complexity and particularity of the economic landscape. David Harvey has expressed this latter challenge thus:

> Any theory of uneven geographical development must be simple enough to aid comprehension and complex enough to embrace the nuances and particularities that call for interpretation. (2006, p. 75)

The resolution of this challenge will depend on the position adopted towards explanatory generalization. On the one hand we may believe that beneath the apparent spatial specificity and chaotic complexity of the economic landscape, a limited number of general mechanisms and 'laws' are in fact at work, and that our task is therefore to render such complexity explicable by identifying that which is 'universal' or general in the particular. The quest for such universal or general causes typically involves high-level abstractions that ignore spatial particularities and specificities in favour of focusing on and emphasizing spatial similarities and commonalities. On the other hand, we might argue that spatial economic differentiation and specificity permit no universal explanatory generalizations, that the spatially particularizing aspect of economic processes and outcomes is the existence of infinitely diverse mechanisms and phenomena that concern us more for what distinguishes them than for what they share. In this approach, explanation is highly context dependent, constructed through place-based accounts (that is 'local narrative models'), and not via high-level abstractions. The options, it would seem, are that we must either downplay the locally-specific quality of economic life, or limit our scope to generalize across space.

Of course, to state the explanatory challenge in such stark oppositional terms is far too simplistic. Nevertheless, NEG can be seen as occupying a position towards the first extreme, and PEG a position nearer the second (see Table 3.1). This is not to suggest that all economic geographers are averse to theory, nor to the search for and use of general concepts. For Harvey, for example, the aim must be the 'possibility of general theory', though as he goes on to say, the nature of such a theory, and how it is to be derived, depend on the conception of 'theory' being advanced. However, he is sceptical that a general theory of uneven geographical development can be construed as a 'clean logical structure specified in direct propositional terms with law-like statements neatly derived from fundamental abstract categories' (*op. cit.*, pp. 75–76), mainly on the grounds that in the socio-economic realm the relation between the universal and the particular, between the abstract and the concrete, is dialectical and thus cannot easily be reduced to formal, logical relationships. Equally, those economic geographers who disagree with Harvey about the possibility of a general theory ('meta-narrative') of the economic landscape would also seriously doubt whether such a theory, even if one did exist, could be cast in formal (mathematical) terms.[7] But most economists take a very different view: not only do they firmly believe in general theory, their conception of the latter is precisely the construction of a 'clean logical structure expressed in formal propositions about the relationships among abstract economic categories'. It is this method that underpins NEG theorizing about spatial agglomeration.

Table 3.1   Theorizing and explaining spatial agglomeration: NEG and PEG compared

	'New Economic Geography' (NEG)	'Proper Economic Geography' (PEG)
Key aim	Construction of general equilibrium model ('universal grammar') of spatial economic agglomeration applicable at various spatial scales and various types of agglomeration.	To identify both possible general causal mechanisms and spatially specific processes and factors in explaining the genesis and development of particular spatial agglomerations and clusters.
Theoretical framework and causal mechanisms	Extension of mainstream (production function and utility function) theory to incorporate increasing returns, imperfect competition, transport costs, and location theory. Agglomeration driven purely by economic logic.	Eclectic and 'appreciative', drawing on neo-Marshallian localisation economies, social network theory, cultural theory, institutional economics, and evolutionary economics.
Form of economic space	Flat ontology. Economic landscape as absolute space, pre-given, and typically idealized and geometric.	Structured ontology. Space as not only absolute, but also relative and relational, and multi-scalar; socially and historically produced.
Epistemology	Deductivist, axiomatic, abstract theorizing. Theory as models. Analytical solutions as explanation.	Realist and pragmatic. Theory as explanation of process. General concepts used to frame explanations of specific cases.
Methodology	Formal mathematical model building. Numerical simulations dominate over empirical testing.	Discursive, empirically grounded, intensive and often local case-study and actor-network orientated.
Institutions and social context	Either ignored, or reduced to (subsumed under) 'initial conditions' and parameter settings of models.	Considered central, and basic to understanding formation and reproduction of specific spatial agglomerations.
Role of history	Recognized as important, but treated in terms of 'ad hoc dynamics', 'starting conditions' of model, and possibility of multiple equilibria.	Increasingly recognized as important; economic landscape regarded as inherently evolutionary, path dependent and adaptive.

Motivated by the empirical observation ('stylised fact') that spatial agglomeration – of different forms and at a whole variety of geographical scales – is a pervasive and persistent feature of economic activity, the key imperative of NEG is to devise a 'universal grammar' of spatial agglomeration in terms of formal models that have general applicability but also representational parsimony, that is as few basic causal factors and relationships as possible (Krugman, 2000a). The 'universal grammar' of spatial agglomeration proposed by NEG is based on four key features:

The first is the general equilibrium modelling of an entire space economy which sets the approach apart from traditional location theory and economic geography. The second is increasing returns or indivisibilities at the level of the individual producer, firm or plant. ... Increasing returns in turn lead to a market structure characterized by imperfect competition. The third is transport costs (broadly defined), which makes location matter.

Finally, the locational movement of productive factors and consumers is a prerequisite for agglomeration. (Fujita and Mori, 2005: 3)

Though stimulated by real world examples, the general equilibrium models constructed in NEG are not meant to represent or explain any *specific* real-world economic landscape. Rather they consist of hypothetical worlds built upon and defined by simplified assumptions and idealized geographical landscapes (see Table 3.2).[8]

Essentially, most NEG model-building is founded on a multiple location version of the Dixit-Stiglitz model of imperfect competition, in which workers are assumed to maximize the variety of goods they consume, and each profit maximizing firm produces only one unique variety of manufactured goods in only one location, and is assumed to benefit from internal economies of scale in production. In this model world, just three effects

Table 3.2   Key assumptions of basic NEG models

Consumption	Consumers assumed to have preference for variety of goods, and to maximize their utility according to a constant elasticity of substitution (CES) function defined over all such varieties. Consumer preferences assumed identical across space.
Producers	Assumed to be atomistic, single plant profit maximizing firms, with each plant producing only one (unique) good, and that production with a single plant is cheaper than with multiple plants. Firms are assumed to move to be near markets (demand).
Workers	Labour markets assumed to clear instantaneously. Workers assumed to move between locations (regions) in response to spatial differences in real wages.
Market structure	Two sector economy: competitive traditional (agricultural) sector, and manufacturing sector characterized by imperfect competition assumed to be of the Dixit-Stiglitz monopolistic type, with economies of scale purely internal to firms.
Trade (transport) costs	Assumed to be of 'ice-berg' type. Indicates a preference for location in regions with large market access.

drive the mechanics of spatial economic development (Baldwin et al., 2003). The first is the 'market-access' effect, which describes the tendency of monopolistic firms to locate their production in a large market (region, city) and export to smaller markets (regions, cities). The second is the 'cost-of-living' effect, which concerns the impact of firms' location decisions on the local (regional, city) cost of living. Goods are assumed to be cheaper in the region with more industrial firms since consumers in this region will import a narrower range of products and thus avoid trade costs. The third is the 'market-crowding effect', which is supposed to capture the fact that imperfectly competitive firms have a tendency to locate in regions with relatively few competitors. The first two effects encourage spatial concentration of economic activity; while the third discourages it (that is, encourages spatial dispersion). Combining the first two effects with factor mobility – firms are assumed to want to choose locations that have good access to large markets and to supplies of goods that they or their workers want, while workers are assumed to prefer locations that confer access to the greatest variety of goods at the lowest prices (high real wages) – creates a form of circular and cumulative causation in the model.

If market access or cost-of-living effects are stronger than the market crowding effect, then starting from an initial symmetry (equal distribution) of industry and workers between regions, a migration of workers into one region will trigger off a self-reinforcing cycle of migration that results in all industrial workers and thus all industry moving into that region, so-called 'catastrophic agglomeration'. If the dispersion force outweighs the agglomeration force, a shift of workers into one region will simply trigger off self-correcting shifts in real wages in the regions, and the initial symmetric distribution of industry and workers will remain stable.

What matters in NEG models then is the relative strength of spatial agglomeration (centripetal) and spatial dispersion (centrifugal) forces. The key factor here is taken to be transport costs (assumed to be of the simple 'ice-berg' variety).[9] Given the various assumptions of the model, it turns out that the dispersion force is stronger than the agglomeration force when transport (trade) costs are high, but the agglomeration force is dominant when trade costs are low. This means that at some level of transport costs – called the 'break point' – the agglomeration force overpowers the dispersion force and self-reinforcing migration ends up shifting all industry into one region. The tension between these forces, in combination with the level of transport costs, shapes the development of the economy's spatial structure:

These two ideas can give insights into a remarkable range of phenomena, from the broad division of national economies into manufacturing and farm belts, to the spontaneous emergence of highly structured urban economies, to the dynamics of the product cycle in international trade. What is more, the models we construct to analyse many different issues turn out to have similar 'deep structures'. The same equations reappear, albeit with somewhat different interpretations of the parameters and the qualitative behaviour of the model economy usually turns on a couple of repeated expressions reflecting the tension between centripetal and centrifugal forces. (Fujita et al., 1999: 345)

The basic NEG model – the two-region, so-called core-periphery model – assumes that both labour and capital (firms) are geographically mobile, and are mutually reinforcing in their interaction. This makes even this simple model very difficult to solve analytically, even for a two-region world. Thus a number of variants have been developed that hold either labour or capital immobile, but which allow other mechanisms to operate – such as local capital accumulation and depreciation, mobile entrepreneurs, vertical linkages between firms, and technological spillovers (see Table 3.3). Despite their specific differences, all such variants nevertheless embody the key fundamental assumptions relating to consumer utility, Dixit-Stiglitz type imperfect competition and increasing returns to scale, and iceberg transport costs. And all are used to derive spatial equilibrium outcomes – though the specific form and stability of the equilibrium may vary.

The model world of NEG, then, is a conceptually circumscribed and highly simplified one in which the spatial structure of the economy is shaped entirely by the specific interaction of labour mobility, capital mobility and transport costs. In one sense, none of this would come as much of a revelation to economic geographers, though they would argue that abstract mathematical models are not necessary to highlight the potential role and interaction of such forces. But they would also argue that the range of factors and processes that make for spatial agglomeration or spatial dispersion is far greater than allowed for in NEG models. For their part, NEG theorists would argue that their models are capable of incorporating several additional causal factors. Indeed, since the early-1990s, NEG theorists have continuously expanded the range of topics and factors covered by their models, especially so in the last few years (see Table 3.4), a trend that looks set to continue (Fujita and Mori, 2005; Brakman et. al., 2008).

Yet, economic geographers would still contend that many of the forces and factors they emphasize in their work – 'soft' social, institutional, cultural and political factors, various 'untraded' interdependencies among firms, and above all the character of knowledge creation and dissemination – cannot be meaningfully captured by or reduced to formal mathematical terms, and that this cannot be taken as sufficient reason to assume they have no significant impact. Actually, few NEG theorists would deny a potential role for influences of this sort, but argue that their goal is to show how even models based on highly simplified assumptions and a limited range of economic mechanisms can nevertheless generate results that seem intuitively reasonable.

Table 3.3 The four main classes of NEG model

Main mechanism	Type of model
Factor migration	Core-periphery models with mobile capital and labour; footloose capital models; footloose entrepreneur model.
Vertical linkages	Various models based on local input-output linkages between sectors.
Factor accumulation	Models that allow for *in situ* local construction and depreciation of capital.
Spillovers	Spatial endogenous growth models (inter-regional spillovers model; local spillovers model).

(Based on Baldwin et al., 2003 and Robert-Nicoud, 2005).

Table 3.4 Stages in the evolution of NEG

Stage	Main features
Early-1990s: First generation models	Initial development of NEG by Krugman. Basic core-periphery model, linking increasing returns, geography and new trade theory
Mid- to late-1990s: Second generation models	Elaboration of the basic model and its extension and application to regional development, the urban system and the emergence of cities, local economic specialization and the formation of the industrial clusters, and the geography of international trade
Early-2000s onwards: Third generation models	Several strands of further development to develop analytically tractable (including linear versions of) models, and to include endogenous technical change, knowledge spillovers, and various additional agglomeration and dispersion forces; growing attention to addressing recognized weaknesses (the unrealistic model of imperfect competition, the lack of a theory of the firm, oversimplified characterization of transport costs, etc.); integration with ideas from urban economics; use of models for theoretical policy analysis; beginnings of attention to empirical applications

Note: This is not intended to capture the evolution of NEG in full detail, but merely to indicate in broad terms the nature and direction of developments.

READING NEG MODELS: THEIR SCOPE AND LIMITS AS HEURISTIC DEVICES

How, then, should we interpret these NEG models? Are economic geographers right to reject NEG out of hand on the grounds that formal mathematical models based on unrealistic assumptions, that miss out a whole range of non-economic causal factors, and that treat 'geographical space' in an overly simplistic and restrictive way, tell us little about the real world?

The use of formal models to represent economic relationships and economic systems is, of course, the *sine qua non* of mainstream economics. Although the victory of formalism in economics can be dated back to the 1950s (Blaug, 1999, 2003), by the 1980s the use of mathematical models had become even more dominant. Advances in non-linear mathematics and associated analytical techniques and methods (including simulation procedures) have enabled the extension of formalism to an ever-wider range of economic topics. Such developments – what Krugman (1998) refers to as 'new technical tricks' – have been one of the factors behind the emergence of NEG.

According to Sugden (2000), model building in economics has serious intent only if it is ultimately directed at telling us something

about the real world. The phrase 'real world' is used here to distinguish the world within a model (the 'model world') from the reality outside it.[10] In broad terms, formal models in economics have two types of use: 'conceptual exploration' and 'empirical theorizing' (Hausman, 1992). Conceptual exploration investigates the internal properties and solutions of models, without necessarily considering the relationship between the world of the model and the real world. Certainly NEG models can be viewed as exercises in conceptual exploration, since a key interest centres on determining how changing certain of the model's parameters and assumptions (for example regarding the nature of the model's initial conditions, the degree of 'freeness of trade' or transport costs, the extent of firm or labour mobility, and the like), changes the relative strength of agglomeration and dispersion and the nature and stability of spatial equilibrium generated internally by the models. Indeed, a considerable degree of attention is devoted to such 'within-model' explorations (see Baldwin et al., 2003, for example).

But, as Sugden argues, theory becomes just a game when theorists work entirely in the world of models. A second type of use of models is that of 'empirical theorizing' or heuristics (Hodgson, 2006), where the aim is to identify some possible causal mechanisms that form part of a much more complex real-world system. The purpose of heuristics or 'empirical theorizing' is to establish a plausible or credible segment of a whole causal story, without necessarily giving an adequate or complete explanation of the phenomena to which they relate. NEG models are clearly intended to say something about real world phenomena. For one thing, there are constant references to real-world examples of regional and urban agglomerations, industrial clusters in the NEG literature. Krugman himself has often been quite explicit that his models are intended to help explain actually occurring examples of spatial economic agglomeration, as he states in his first major contribution that launched NEG, namely *Geography and Trade* (1991):

> To introduce the subject of divergent regional development, I turn to economic history to provide a particularly clear-cut example of the forces of economic geography at work. I then offer a simple model [the basic core-periphery model of NEG] that helps makes sense of that example. The example is the case of the US manufacturing belt: a relatively narrow stretch of territory within which the preponderance of US manufacturing was concentrated from the mid–nineteenth century until the 1960s. (p. 11)

Yet further, NEG models are also claimed to provide insight into how some of the key features of the contemporary economic landscape are likely to develop in the future:

> As the European market becomes more closely integrated, will the polycentric geography of its industries unravel, giving way to American-style concentration? Will high-technology industries concentrate in some European Silicon Valley? Will the financial services sector maintain its current polycentricity or will it concentrate in London (or Frankfurt)? These are questions about industrial clustering; and they are questions that can, we believe, be usefully addressed using our basic approach to economic geography. (Fujita et al., 1999: 283)

More directly still, although empirical work has been slow to develop within NEG, recent efforts in this direction have sought to test some of the models' key relationships and predictions. Typically this is done by comparing simulation results from NEG model runs against actual data on regional agglomeration patterns (for example, Brakman et at., 2004; Venables, 2005; Bosker et al., 2007) or testing for the predicted relationship between regional (or urban) wages and regional (urban) market potential.[11] Finally, and ambitiously, NEG models are now being used to assess the scope for and limits of regional and related spatial economic policies (such as Puga, 2002; Baldwin et al., 2003).[12] So, all in all, there would seem to be little doubt that NEG models are intended not just as conceptual explorations but also as exercises in heuristics or empirical theorizing aimed at providing 'first approximation' explanations and interpretations of certain observed features of actual economic landscapes.

But this brings us back to the central question: how can models like those used in NEG, based on unrealistic assumptions and simplified hypothetical worlds, purport to throw light on real world phenomena? Most NEG theorists readily admit that the assumptions on which NEG models are built – and which enter directly into their equations – are unrealistic, but justify such simplifications on the grounds that constructing a model on more realistic assumptions would render its solution extremely complex, if not impossible. Moreover, the argument of NEG is that even simple models that abstract from the full complexity of real economic landscapes are able to reproduce spatial patterns that resemble certain observed features: as Fujita, Krugman and Venables (1999: 45) argue, 'the Dixit-Stiglitz model of monopolistic competition is grossly unrealistic, but it is tractable and flexible … and leads to a very special but very suggestive set of results'.

This appeal to the virtue of simplicity in NEG models, which has a direct parallel in Harvey's call (cited above) for simplicity in theory construction in geography, is a common refrain in economics more generally. Simplicity is seen as desirable not only because it makes it easier to focus on what are thought to be some key relationships or processes (in NEG models the tension between certain centripetal and centrifugal forces), but also because 'complex models… are not necessarily more accurate than simple, *ad hoc* models' (Krugman, 2000b: 33). As Gibbard and Varian (1978: 672), in their discussion of models in economics, put it:

> Simplicity, then, will be a highly desirable feature of such models. Complications to get as close as possible a fit to reality will be undesirable if they make the model less possible to grasp.

In the case of NEG, as we have noted, even the basic two-industry, two-region (core–periphery) model is extremely difficult to work with, forcing numerical simulations for most results, so that it is often further simplified (for example by assuming one or other of labour or capital to be geographically immobile) in order to make it mathematically tractable (see Baldwin et al., 2003). Further, making models more complicated and 'realistic', it is contended, is beside the point, because it becomes obvious that similar outcomes could result from much more complicated models. Thus, unrealistic assumptions and structures are justified in NEG on the grounds that the models nevertheless are able to show that by assuming even simplified kinds of imperfect competition and increasing returns – rather than the wholly unrealistic perfect competition and diminishing returns beloved of mainstream economics – factor mobility alone can lead to pronounced spatial agglomeration and geographical unevenness of economic activity. The models, it might be argued, abstract from the full complexity of the socio-economy found in the real world in order to establish this key point.

The fact is that simplification is a strategy all theorists employ. This is as true of the descriptive and discursive theories found in PEG as it is of the formal theoretical models employed in NEG. In this sense, we all use 'models', since any theory – be it verbal or mathematical – necessarily abstracts some features or aspects of reality. According to Maki (1992, 1994), when we theorize or abstract a

given situation we necessarily 'isolate' certain features and causal factors from the influence of other, excluded, elements: the potential influence of those other, excluded, factors and elements is 'sealed off'. Such 'sealing off' makes a theory unrealistic, but the theory may still claim to describe an aspect of reality. However, some critics of formal models in economics take issue with this notion of 'isolation' on the grounds that it is not the same as abstraction. For example, Lawson (1997, 2003) argues that to assume certain aspects and features of reality exist 'in isolation' is to impose a closed model on what is in fact a highly open reality, and in effect assumes 'a world totally different from the one in which we live, and one that has no bearing upon it' (1997: 236). In his opinion 'there is a world of difference between leaving something (temporarily) out of focus [what he regards as abstraction] and treating it as though it does not exist [which he equates with isolation]. The achieving of an abstraction and treating something as though it existed in isolation are not the same thing at all' (1997: 236). For Lawson, formal models are guilty of isolation and thus rarely provide any explanatory insight.[13]

But is this a valid basis for dismissing NEG models? As Hodgson (2006) rightly points out, Lawson's attack on formal deductive type models in economics is largely misdirected: not only do models involve both isolation *and* abstraction, the distinction between these two is itself vague and difficult to sustain (see also Nash, 2004). Thus to adopt this line of attack on NEG models would be to miss the real target. As heuristic devices, NEG models have the paradoxical feature that they contain highly simplified and unrealistic assumptions yet seem to yield results that accord with certain features found in reality. However, because all such models are necessarily 'closed', in the sense that certain explanatory factors or processes are omitted, they can never clinch the argument concerning the causal mechanisms that actually exist in the real world. Thus, rejecting NEG models simply because they are 'closed' formal mathematical constructions that omit particular causal influences (especially 'soft' socio-institutional factors) is not of itself a decisive line of critique.

What matters is whether the particular causal factors and relationships isolated by NEG models, and the underlying assumptions that represent the workings of these causal factors, give sufficient grounds to make any plausible or *credible* inferences to the real world (Sugden, 2000). As Sugden notes, we make inferences from one part of reality to another all the time. Thus, to use his example, if we observe racial segregation in, say, the cities of Chicago, New York, Baltimore, Philadelphia, Detroit, Buffalo and Pittsburgh, then we might make the inference that segregation is a characteristic of large cities of the north-eastern USA, and so form the expectation that there will be segregation in, say, Cleveland. The thought behind this expectation is that the forces at work in the Cleveland housing market, whatever these are, are likely to be broadly similar to those at work in other large cities in this part of the USA. One way of describing this inference is to say that each of the housing markets of Chicago, New York, Baltimore, etc. constitutes a *model* for the forces at work in large north-eastern US cities. Sugden calls these *natural* models, in contrast to theoretical models created in the minds of social scientists. But, Sugden, asks, if we can make inferences from natural models, why not from theoretical ones?

However, for a model to have credibility, and thus serve as the basis for plausible empirical inferences, it is not enough that its assumptions and relationships cohere one with another within a deductive structure; they must also cohere with what is known about causal processes in the real world. It is not necessary that the assumptions and abstractions of NEG models correspond with – or even with a simplification of – any *particular* real world situation. But they must be adequately *representative* of firms, consumers, workers and spatial agglomerations in the real world. Only then can credible inferences

be made from the model world to the real world. The world of NEG models is much more uniform and regular than the real world, but clearly NEG theorists want us to believe that the processes represented in their models *could* operate in the real world, and are not just primitives in a formal deductive system. Some aspects of NEG models would indeed seem to be credible – for example the assumption that the economic landscape is shaped (in part at least) by the relative strength of agglomeration forces and dispersion forces, and that these forces are the outcome of (among other things) the interactions between transport costs, the mobility of firms and workers, and local and global technology spillovers. But other aspects are not credible – for example the assumptions that consumers are utility maximizers and are identical across space, that imperfect competition and increasing returns are of the Dixit–Stiglitz kind, that all firms are only single plant concerns, and that transport costs are of the iceberg type. These abstractions are obviously not representative of consumers, firms and transport costs in the real world.

Does this mean then that NEG's formal models fail as heuristic devices? Not necessarily. Some unrealistic assumptions are unavoidable in science. The main issue is the significance of these unrealistic and simplifying assumptions for the key processes and relationships that NEG models are meant to capture. The crucial point is that we cannot judge NEG models in isolation. The meaning of any model depends on an 'interpretative' or 'contextual' framework (Hodgson, 2006) that is not contained in the formalities of the model itself but which is needed to judge the scope and extent of the credibility of those formalities as a basis for inferences to the real world. The interpretative framework is crucial. An adequate interpretative framework would depend on the discussion of the genesis, meaning, methodological significance and empirical plausibility of the key concepts that relate to the model, and the qualifications that shape and limit the model's applicability to the real world. It would involve critical reflection on the nature of the definitions, assumptions and abstractions employed, detailed discussion of the empirical limits to and contexts of the model, the plausibility of its analytical solutions (such as equilibrium outcomes), and discussion of the possible role and significance of omitted variables and factors suggested by alternative explanations. All this is not a small task, and if done properly it will be at least as weighty as the formal content of any model, and will act to shape the content and realism of the model over time.

Bringing the interpretative framework of NEG models into the picture is, therefore, central to assessing their role and value in understanding the spatial structure of the economic landscape. Thus far in NEG, interpretative discussions of this kind have been wholly marginal and underdeveloped compared to the pursuit of mathematical sophistication. A diagnosis emerges in which the malady with NEG models is not the use of formalism as such, but the inadequacy and underdevelopment of the interpretative context in which they are placed. It is this lack of interpretative contextualization, and not the use of formal models *per se*, that should be a prime target of critical engagement by economic geographers. The highly abstract and grossly oversimplified nature of geographic space and place found in NEG models is an obvious key issue that needs interpretative interrogation; likewise the black-box nature of the firm, the simplified sectoral structure of the model economy (especially the neglect of services, now the core activity of advanced economies), and the neglect of a whole range of non-economic factors that shape spatial agglomeration. These are just some of the features of NEG models that require discussion. How far does their neglect undermine the plausibility of NEG models, and the credibility of any inferences that can be made from these models to the real world?

As mentioned earlier, NEG theorists might respond by arguing that their primary purpose is to demonstrate that even simple forms of increasing returns and labour and capital mobility can lead to spatial agglomeration and geographically uneven development, and that this is not to deny the role of other factors and forces. There are two problems with this argument. First, NEG theorists may well acknowledge that their models exclude many of the factors that economic geographers would argue are relevant in the real world, but they need to justify why these factors can be ignored, or why they are less important than the factors NEG models do include. A second and related issue is whether the limited range of factors and assumptions that NEG does include can be read as plausible claims or statements about the real world. As we have noted, most of the factors and assumption in NEG models cannot be so read. Or NEG theorists might fall back on the argument that the main role of NEG models is a counterfactual one, to show what the economic landscape would look like *if* consumers maximize utility, *if* increasing returns are limited to economies of scale within firms, *if* transport costs are of ice-berg type, etc. But even counterfactual worlds need to be credible worlds; otherwise what is the warrant for making inferences from model to real world?

At the very least we need some convincing demonstration that the simplifications and idealizations on which NEG models are constructed does not undermine their heuristic value: that is, a full discussion of the interpretative framework on which these models are based and the (limited) contexts in which they are likely to apply. Central to such interpretative discussion and debate is the issue of spatial equilibrium in the economic landscape since this is a fundamental feature, indeed key inbuilt presumption, of NEG models. How credible, or plausible, is it to assume that in the real world the processes of spatial economic development produce stable equilibrium outcomes?

EQUILIBRIUM VERSUS HISTORY IN NEG

Searching for the existence and stability of equilibrium is a prime objective in the use of formal models throughout mainstream economics. In mainstream economic models, equilibrium serves as a unique 'centre of gravity', or stable 'long-run' state, determined by the structure of the model and *a priori* assumptions and independent variables, to which the world in the model converges, regardless of initial conditions or the adjustment path taken. In this way traditional general equilibrium analysis reflects a curious absence for any role for history in the determination of economic outcomes.[14] NEG claims to break from this approach by producing model worlds – hypothetical economic landscapes – that are characterized by *multiple* equilibria, or multiple possible stable configurations of economic activity across regions. The possibility of multiple equilibria derives from the cumulative, self-reinforcing feedbacks between factor mobility, prices and consumer demand in NEG models, and the number and type of equilibria depend on the number of regions and initial conditions. For example, the basic two-region, or core-periphery, NEG model with factor mobility, yields five possible equilibria, of which three are stable. At high transport costs, the model yields a world in which manufacturing activity is dispersed equally between the two regions. For transport costs below a certain level, this dispersed pattern becomes unstable (a movement of one worker from one region to the other is sufficient to set off a cumulative self-reinforcing movement of workers and firms from the former to the latter). If transport costs fall below another critical level, two new stable equilibria emerge in which all manufacturing activity is concentrated in one region, or the other.

At the same time as focusing on equilibrium outcomes, NEG claims to recognize that 'history matters'. The notion of 'history' appears to be used in NEG in three ways. First, it is equated with 'initial conditions', the 'inherited starting position' of the abstract system represented in the model; initial conditions in this context might refer to assumed differences in consumer tastes or technology between locations, differences in the distribution of economic activity or factor endowments

between regions, number of regions, and so on. Because the precise equilibrium (out of multiple possibles) that emerges from the model is not predetermined but depends on these exogenous pre-given 'initial conditions' specified as part of the model's assumptions, NEG theorists claim that their models take history into account. Second, NEG claims to incorporate history by being able to simulate the 'evolution' of a spatial system by allowing key parameters to change 'over time'. In particular, much attention focuses on how incremental reductions in transport costs (incremental improvements in 'freeness of trade') lead to changes in the degree and pattern of spatial agglomeration:

> We address this question by carrying out the following experiment. We reduce transport costs in a series of small steps, and following each step allow the model economy to evolve until it reaches a steady state; then take the next step. ... As transport costs fall – in effect as the world gets smaller – the model eventually reaches a bifurcation point, at which the equilibrium structure of manufacturing regions changes. At that point the structure unravels, giving rise to a new structure with fewer (and therefore larger) manufacturing regions. As we continue to reduce transport costs, this new structure persists for a time, then it in turn collapses, and so on. ... We find then that even if the change in the underlying parameters is gradual, the evolution of the world's spatial structure is characterized by 'punctuated equilibrium'. Long stretches of stability are interrupted by episodes of discontinuous change. (Fujita et al., 1999: 319–320)

This 'evolutionary' pattern of punctuated equilibrium is also used as a basis for invoking the importance of history in a third sense, as 'hysteresis' effects – that is, the movement to a new equilibrium pattern following a shock, in this case a reduction in transport costs.

How meaningful are these notions of equilibrium and history in NEG? As geographers themselves have frequently documented, there is significant evidence of quasi-fixity in the economic landscape: patterns of spatial economic agglomeration and specialization, once established, often persist for extended periods of time, until shifts and changes in technology, markets, competition, regulation and other factors promote the emergence of new spatial configurations of economic activity. But NEG's notion of history and its preoccupation with equilibrium would seem to have severe limitations as descriptions of the real world. To equate 'history' simply with the possibility of multiple equilibria is to beg the question of whether the real economic landscape can ever be in equilibrium (Sheppard, 2000). The persistence of particular spatial economic patterns and features need not imply spatial equilibrium at all. Indeed, in a world where knowledge is constantly changing and evolving, and where innovation, learning and adaptation are key, the idea of an economic system ever being in a stable equilibrium seems most unlikely (see Metcalfe et al., 2006; Ramlogan and Metcalfe, 2006). Since knowledge is never in equilibrium, then neither can an economy nor its spatial structure ever be in equilibrium. The economic landscape may be structured and patterned, but structure and pattern reflect *order*, not equilibrium. To be sure, NEG models have a useful heuristic function in that they suggest that, under specific circumstances and assumptions, increasing 'freeness of trade' (or increasing economic integration) may promote shifts in the spatial structure of economic activity and greater spatial economic agglomeration. But their characterization of this possibility as 'evolution' is not convincing.

The notion of 'history' in NEG models is that of *logical* time, not *real historical* time. This is a distinction based on a substantive difference that is suppressed when the evolution of the economic landscape is interpreted as movement from one equilibrium position to another, as a sequence of equilibrium patterns. Recognition of this distinction makes it illegitimate to draw any inferences from the analysis of equilibrium in the world of the models to the events and processes taking place in historical time. Logical time is, in a sense, ahistorical. Time in NEG models is simply a solution sequence, following a change in a parameter, such as transport costs. It is reversible, since it is possible for

transport cost to rise (or freeness of trade to be restricted). Of course, transport costs (or other impediments to trade) may rise as well as fall; but history, as a social process, is not reversible. In contrast, historical time is based on the reality of actual experience. In the real economic landscape the past is embodied in the current situation and limits the range of actions that can be taken to bring about an adjustment to changing circumstances. The economic landscape, so to speak, is locked into the conditions existing today and inherited from the past. It is characterized by varying forms and degrees of *path dependence* of technology, knowledge, infrastructures and institutions. In such a real-world economic landscape there can be no necessary presumption that processes of technical change, knowledge acquisition, factor movements, consumer preferences and the like will lead to an equilibrium pattern in the spatial distribution of economic activity, if any exists, whether a unique equilibrium or one of several possible equilibria.

Conceptualizing and explaining the evolution of real economic landscapes is something that economic geographers themselves have only just begun to do (for example, Boschma and Frenken, 2006; Boschma and Martin, 2007; Essletzbichler and Rigby, 2007; Martin and Sunley, 2006, 2007). And while this new, emergent 'evolutionary economic geography', which draws heavily on evolutionary economics, does not eschew the use of models, it is wary of using any notion of equilibrium to explore the historical evolution of the space economy. NEG theorists would also benefit from engaging with evolutionary economics, where there is an explicit attempt to build 'history friendly' formal models (Malerba et al., 1999).[15]

CLOSING THE *METHODENSTREIT* BETWEEN NEG AND PEG?

What, then, are the likely prospects for greater interaction between NEG and PEG? There are several possibilities. As Overman

(2004) – a staunch and self-declared advocate of NEG – observes, NEG theorists are about as likely to give up their formal models as proper economic geographers are to undergo conversion to mathematical mainstream economics! As he remarks, it is unlikely that we will see methodological convergence between NEG and PEG anytime soon. For this reason, one might envisage continuing dissonance between the two camps. Yet, notwithstanding fundamental methodological differences, along with other commentators – both NEG supporters and others broadly sympathetic to the project (for example, *The Economist*, 1999; Goodchild, et al., 2000; Sjöberg and Sjöholm, 2002; Marchioni, 2004; Duranton and Rodriguez-Pose, 2005) – Overman suggests there is scope for and value in greater interaction, dialogue and 'cross-fertilization' between NEG and PEG. Each form of economic geography, he and others contend, can learn something from the other.[16]

Thus, Overman recognizes that NEG theorists tend to be 'rather imprecise' about what is a location, region or place, and that as a result often naively assume that similar processes and relationships apply at all spatial scales (see, also, Martin, 1999). Proper economic geographers are much more exercised about defining and conceptualizing space, and NEG theorists ought to be much more receptive to the ways space, regions and place are problematized in PEG (Environment and Planning, 2006). At the same time, Overman argues – admittedly with some justification – that PEG suffers from its own biases and weaknesses – especially its lack of precise concepts and definitions, its lack of empirical rigour and its frequent preferences for highlighting spatial idiosyncracies to the neglect of generalizations. Thus, in his view, PEG can learn from NEG in terms of the need ìto identify the core, ignore the trivial and deal with issues of refutability, causality and observational equivalence (2004: 513).

There is, therefore, a value in interaction for both camps (Monk and Monk, 2007). For their part, NEG theorists would benefit from engaging in dialogue with the arguments concerning the causal explanations of spatial agglomeration – and regionally uneven development more generally – found in the empirically-grounded, 'appreciative' theory of economic geographers. The empirically-orientated work found in PEG – on real-world agglomerations, clusters, cities and the like – addresses a whole range of explanatory factors, and conceptual ideas not found in NEG, and NEG theorists need to get much closer to the 'appreciative-theoretic' stories and local empirical models found in some quarters of PEG: it is not sufficient for NEG theorists to argue that the sort of qualitative and non-economic factors emphasized in PEG are 'too messy' to taken into account. Getting closer to the 'appreciative' theories of economic geographers would not only encourage NEG theorists to take such factors more seriously – if only in stylized form – but would also compel them to give explicit consideration to the interpretative structures behind their models.

But at the same time, economic geographers need to be more amenable to learning from NEG. Economic geographers may well be disinclined to take the formal models of NEG seriously. But NEG formal theory can be of help in thinking through appreciative theory: it can identify gaps in PEG explanations, and can lead to consideration of mechanisms and factors ignored or downplayed in the latter. Thus NEG theorists could encourage economic geographers to give much greater attention to the role of market forces, prices and other basic economic processes that seem to have all but disappeared from the appreciative-theoretic work in PEG. Further, NEG models and methodology could be useful in working through the logical implications of local explanations developed by economic geographers. In these ways, the model solutions produced in NEG could provide a useful stimulus to appreciative theory in PEG, though this will only happen if the formal models of NEG are recognized by economic geographers as representing an accurate version of their beliefs, and if, at the same time, the logic of NEG models is understandable by economic geographers.

This invocation resonates with the view taken by those who have proposed the forging of a 'third-way' or 'middle-path' between the two approaches (Fingleton, 2004), involving the development of clearly defined models and hypotheses concerning explicit relationships and interactions along NEG lines, but ensuring the inclusion of a range of important geographical variables and factors that PEG emphasizes but which NEG typically assumes away (Fingleton, 2007). And some economists and economic geographers have sought to do this explicitly by working together (Leamer and Storper, 2001; Storper and Venables, 2004; Corrado et al., 2005; Duranton and Storper, 2006; Garretsen and Martin, 2010). Though such alliances may still be few, interestingly (even if entirely coincidentally), they reflect what has been a growing call by certain economic geographers for PEG itself to recover some of its former interest in conceptual rigour, modelling, quantitative methods, and statistical analysis (for example, Markusen, 1999; Martin and Sunley, 2001; Plummer and Sheppard, 2001; Johnston et al., 2003; Scott, 2004).[17] Whilst such calls do not necessarily advocate close dialogue specifically with NEG – indeed, some of those involved have been staunch critics of NEG type models – the plea for a less negative stance towards quantitative methods within economic geography at least opens up potential space within which collaboration could take place.[18] In taking stock of the first decade of the development of NEG, Krugman (2000) observed that:

> The new economic geography, while it may be past its first rush of enthusiasm, has ended the long silence of mainstream economics on the whole question of where economic activity takes place and why; now that the conversation [within mainstream economics] has begun it is sure to continue. (p. 59)

The challenge is now to develop a corresponding conversation between NEG and PEG, and this will require flexibility on both sides if it is not to be a 'dialogue of the deaf'.

NOTES

1 Contrary to what Thomas Friedman (2005) has claimed, the world is not being rendered 'flat' by accelerating globalization.

2 Other strands of economics that have also recognized the regional and local dimensions of economic development include the new 'endogenous growth theory', the economics of innovation, and the new 'intra-national macro-economics'.

3 This is not to suggest, however, that the rise and growth of NEG has wrought a corresponding 'geographical turn' across mainstream economics as a whole. Whilst NEG represents an important movement within the mainstream economics canon, the great bulk of the latter remains resolutely aspatial. On the other hand, the award of the Nobel Prize to Paul Krugman in October 2008, in part for his work on the 'location of economic activity', may well lead to a new wave of conversion among erstwhile non-spatial mainstream economists.

4 In his review of NEG, Paul David (1999) contrasts NEG with what he calls 'plain old geography', or POG. Others (for example, Perrons, 2001) prefer the labels NEG-I and NEG-II, where the former is used to highlight the new institutional-cultural turn within economic geography and the latter refers to the new subfield of Krugman-style spatial economics. I used the phrase 'economic geography proper' in my earlier review of NEG (Martin, 1999), but this hardly makes for a digestible acronym, so here I will refer to 'proper economic geography' (or PEG for short).

5 Both, for example, have drawn on Alfred Marshall's concept of localization economies.

6 In many ways, NEG represents an updated, general equilibrium, version of the location theory developed in the 1920s and 1930s by German spatial economists such as Weber, Christaller and Losch. Though Germanic location theory was to exert a significant influence on PEG after the Second World War, by the mid-1970s economic geographers had all but abandoned this approach (see Chapter 1).

7 Certainly, most economic geographers would agree that no one single theory is capable of capturing the complexities of uneven geographical development.

8 Such as a two region core-periphery, a linear multi-region economy, a 'race-track' economy, a regular multi-location lattice, etc. Though Baldwin et al.'s (2003) book contains a number of different variants of NEG models (with and without worker and firm mobility, vertical linkages among firms, even technological spillovers), all assume a symmetric two-region ('North-South', or 'Core-Periphery') economy.

9 That is, it is assumed that a given fraction of the value of a good is used up – simply 'melts' away – per unit of distance transported.

10 What that 'reality' is, of course, is itself a problematic issue, since different scientific and social philosophies posit different ontologies of the 'real'.

11 This so-called 'wage equation' is a core relationship in NEG models. It gives the manufacturing wage at which firms in each location break even, given income levels and price levels in all locations and the cost of transporting goods to those locations (i.e. the market each potential for location). It is predicted to be higher the higher are incomes in the all of a firm's markets, the lower are transports costs to those markets and the less competition the firm faces in those markets.

12 One worrying aspect of this move into policy analysis is that NEG models are being used to argue that a trade-off exists between the spatial dispersal of economic activity ('spatial equity') and national economic growth ('national efficiency'), that spatial agglomeration fosters overall national growth, so that policies that seek to control spatial concentration or deliberately promote activity in less prosperous regions could well be nationally inefficient (Crozet and Koenig, 2005; Philippe Martin, 2005). In effect this a spatial reinvention of the old Okun 'equity-efficiency' trade-off.

13 The debate about the open nature of economic systems, and how this raises issues for the use of formal models in economics is also explored in Chick (1998), Nash (2004), Chick and Dow (2005), Hodgson (2006) and Pratten (2007).

14 The tension between equilibrium and history has been the subject of vigorous debate in economics (see the famous critiques of equilibrium by Kaldor (1972) and Robinson (1978)). Kaldor (1972: 1244), for example argues that '[i]t [equilibrium economics] assumes that forces operate in an environment that is 'imposed' on the system in a sense other than being just a heritage of the past – one could almost say an environment which, in its most significant characteristics, is independent of history'.

15 'History-friendly' formal models aim to capture the qualitative 'appreciative' explanations of the mechanisms and factors affecting the historical development of an industry or technology, put forward by empirical scholars of industrial economics, technological change, and business organization and strategy.

16 The discussion in *The Economist*, in response to my assessment of NEG (Martin, 1999), called for bringing together the 'top down' approach of NEG and the 'bottom-up' approach found in PEG.

17 As evidence of just how far the expurgation of modelling, quantitative methods and statistical analysis from PEG has gone, none of the major surveys and overviews of economic geography that have appeared in recent years make any significant reference (or any reference at all) to such methods (see, for example, Lee and Wills, 1997; Bryson et al., 1999;

Clark et al., 2001; Sheppard and Barnes, 2000; Leyshon et al., 2003; and Lawton-Smith and Bagchi-Sen, 2006; Martin and Sunley, 2007; Martin 2008).

18 The motivations for this call for a revival of quantitative approaches alongside the now hegemonic qualitative and discursive methods deployed in economic geography vary. For some it is the loss of conceptual and analytical rigour in economic-geographic study that has accompanied the cultural and institutional 'turns' in the subject. For others it is that the excessive emphasis on qualitative and textual methods overly restricts both the subject-matter and empirical reach of economic geography. Yet others see the problem as the loss of a set of basic intellectual skills, a loss that not only forecloses some interesting avenues of economic-geographic research but also prevents economic geographers from engaging in an informed way with quantitative data or the work of economists.

REFERENCES

Baldwin, R., Forslid, R., Martin, P., Ottaviano, G. and Robert-Nicoud, F. (2003) *Economic Geography and Public Policy*. Princeton: Princeton University Press.

Blaug, M. (1999) The formalist revolution, or what happened to orthodox economics after World War II? In R.E. Backhouse, and J. Creedy, (eds) *From Classical Economics to the Theory of the Firm*. Cheltenham: Edward Elgar. pp. 257–80.

Blaug, M. (2003) The formalist revolution of the 1950s. In W., Samuels, J.E. Biddle, and J.B. Davis, (eds) *A Companion to the History of Economic Thought*. Oxford: Blackwell. pp. 395–410.

Boddy. M. (1999) Geographical economics and urban competitiveness: A critique. *Urban Studies*, 36: 811–42.

Boschma, R. and Frenken, K. (2006) Why is economic geography not an evolutionary science? *Journal of Economic Geography*, 6: 273–302.

Boschma, R. and Martin R. (eds) (2010) *Handbook of Evolutionary Economic Geography*. Edward Elgar.

Bosker, M. (2007) Growth, agglomeration and convergence: A space-time analysis for European regions. *Spatial Economic Analysis*, 2: 91–110.

Brakman, S. and Garretsen, H. (2003) Rethinking the 'new' geographical economics. *Regional Studies*, 37(6 and 7): 637–48.

Brakman, S, Garretsen, H. and van Marrewijk, C. (2001) *An Introduction to Geographical Economics*. Cambridge: Cambridge University Press.

Brakman, S., Garretsen, H., and Schramm, M. (2004) Putting the new economic geography to the test:

Free-ness of trade and agglomeration in the EU regions. *Mimeo*, Faculty of Economics, Utrecht University.

Brakman, S., Garretsen, H., Gorter, J., van de Hoorst, A., and Schramm. M. (2005) New economic geography, empirics and regional policy, *Mimeo*, Faculty of Economics, Utrecht University.

Brakman, S., Garretsen, H., and van Marrewijk, C. (2008) *An Introduction to Geographical Economics* (2nd edn). Cambridge: Cambridge University Press.

Bryson, J., Henry, N., Keeble, D.E., and Martin, R.L. (1999) *The Economic Geography Reader*. Chichester: Wiley.

Chick, V. (1998) On knowing one's place: The role of formalism in economics. *The Economic Journal*, 108: 1859–69.

Chick, V. and Dow, S. (2005) The meaning of open systems. *Journal of Economic Methodology*, *13*: 363–81.

Clark, G.L., Feldman, M., and Gertler, M. (eds) (2001) *The Oxford Handbook of Economic Geography*. Oxford: Oxford University Press.

Combes, P.-P., Mayer, T., and Thisse, J.-F. (2008) *Economic Geography: The Integration of Regions and Nations*. Princeton: Princeton University Press.

Corrado, L., Martin, R. and Weeks, M. (2005) Identifying and interpreting convergence clusters across Europe. *Economic Journal*, 115: C133–C160.

Crozet, M. and Koenig. P. (2005) *The Cohesion vs. Growth Tradeoff: Evidence from EU regions (1980–2000)*. Mimeo, University of Paris I [http://team.univ-paris1.fr/teamperso/crozet/tradeoff_July2005.pdf]

David, P. (1999) Paul Krugman's economic geography of development: NEGs, POGs, and naked models in space. *International Regional Science Review*, 22: 162–72.

Duranton, G. and Storper, M. (2006) Agglomeration and growth: A dialogue between economists and geographers. *Journal of Economic Geography*, 6(1): 1–8.

Duranton, G. and Rodriguez Pose, A. (2005) When economists and geographers collide, or the tale of the lions and the butterflies. *Environment and Planning*, 37: 1695–1705.

Dymski, G. (1998) On Paul Krugman's model of economic geography. *Geoforum*, 27: 439–52.

Environment and Planning A (2006) Special issue on 'when economists meet geographers'. *Environment and Planning, A, 28*.

Essletzbichler, J. and Rigby, D. (2007) Exploring evolutionary economic geographies, *Journal of Economic Geography*. 7: 549–71.

Fingleton, B. (2004) Some alternative geo-economics for Europe's regions. *Journal of Economic Geography*. 7: 389–420

Fingleton, B. (ed.) (2007) *New Directions in Economic Geography*. Chichester: Edward Elgar.

Friedman, T. (2005) *The World is Flat: The Globalised World in the Twenty-First Century*. London: Penguin.

Fujita, M. and Krugman, P. (2004) The new economic geography: Past, present and future. *Papers in Regional Science*, 83: 139–64.

Fujita, M. and Mori, T. (2005) Frontiers of the new economic geography. *Papers in Regional Science*, 84: 377–405.

Fujita and Thisse, J.-F. (2002) *Economics of Agglomeration*. Cambridge: Cambridge University Press.

Fujita, M., Krugman, P. and Venables, A. (1999) *The Spatial Economy: Cities, Regions and International Trade*. Cambridge Mass: MIT Press.

Garretsen, H. and Martin, R.L. (2010) Rethinking (new) economic geography: taking geography and history more seriously. *Spatial Economic Analysis*, 5: 127–160.

Gibbard, A. and Varian, H. (1978) Economic models. *Journal of Philosophy*. 75: 664–77.

Harvey, D. (2006) *Spaces of Global Capitalism: Towards a Theory of Uneven Geographical Development*. London: Verso.

Hausman, D.M. (1992) *The Inexact and Separate Science of Economics*. Cambridge: Cambridge University Press.

Henderson, J.V. (ed.) (2005) *New Economic Geography*, Chichester: Edward Elgar.

Hoare, A. (1992) Review of Krugman's *Geography and Trade*. *Regional Studies*, 19: 679.

Hodgson, G.M. (2006) The problem of formalism in economics. In *Economics in the Shadow of Darwin and Marx*. Cheltenham: Edward Elgar. pp. 116–134.

Johnston, R.J. (1992) Review of P. Krugman's *Geography and Trade*, *Environment and Planning*, 24: 1006.

Johnston, R.J., Hepple, L.W., Hoare, A.G., Jones, K., and Plummer, P.S. (2003) Contemporary fiddling in human geography while Rome burns: Has quantitative analysis been largely abandoned – and should it be? *Geoforum*. 34: 157–61.

Kaldor, N. (1972) The irrelevance of equilibrium economics. *Economic Journal*. 82: 1237–55.

Krugman, P. (1991a) *Geography and Trade*. Cambridge, MA: MIT Press.

Krugman, P. (1991b) Increasing returns and economic geography. *Journal of Political Economy*. 99(3): 483–99.

Krugman, P. (1995) *Geography, Economics and Development*. Cambridge, MA: MIT Press.

Krugman, P. (1996) *The Self-Organising Economy*. Oxford: Blackwell.

Krugman. P. (1998) What's new about the new economic geography? *Oxford Review of Economic Policy*. 14(2): 7–17.

Krugman, P. (2000a) Where in the world is the new economic geography? In G.L. Clark, M. Feldman, and M. Gertler (eds) *The Oxford Handbook of Economic Geography*. Oxford: Oxford University Press. pp. 49–60.

Krugman, P. (2000b) How complicated does the model have to be? *Oxford Review of Economic Policy.* 16(4): 33–42.

Lawson, T. (1997) *Economics and Reality.* London: Routledge.

Lawson, T. (2003) *Re-Orienting Economics.* London: Routledge.

Lawton Smith, H. and Bagchi-Sen, S. (eds) (2006) *Economic Geography: Past, Present and Future.* London: Routledge.

Leamer, E. and Storper, M. (2001) The geography of the internet age, *Working Paper 8450.* National Bureau of Economic Research, Cambridge, MA.

Lee, R. and Wills, J. (eds) (1997) *Geographies of Economies.* London: Arnold.

Leyshon, A., Lee, R., and Williams, C.C. (eds) (2003) *Alternative Economic Spaces: Rethinking the Economic in Economic Geography.* London: SAGE.

Maki, U. (1992) On the method of isolation in economics. *Poznan Studies in the Philosophy of the Sciences and Humanities,* 26: 319–54.

Malerba, F., Nelson, R., Orsenigo, L. and Winter, S. (1999) 'History-friendly' models of industry evolution: The computer industry. *Industrial and Corporate Change,* 8: 3–40.

Marchioni, C. (2004) Geographical economics versus economic geography: Towards a clarification of the dispute. *Environment and Planning, A,* 36: 1737–53.

Markusen, A. (1999) Fuzzy concepts, scanty evidence and policy distance: The case for rigour and policy relevance in critical regional studies. *Regional Studies,* 33: 869–84.

Martin, P., (2005) The geography of inequalities in Europe. *Swedish Economic Policy Review.* 12.1: 85–108.

Martin, R.L. (1999a) The new 'geographical turn' in economics: Some critical reflections. *Cambridge Journal of Economics,* 23: 65–91.

Martin, R.L. (1999b) The 'new economic geography': Challenge or irrelevance?, *Transactions of the Institute of British Geographers,* 24: 385–90.

Martin, R.L. (ed.) (2008) *Economy: Critical Essays in Human Geography.* Aldershot: Ashgate

Martin, R.L. and Sunley, P.J. (1996) Paul Krugman's, *Economic Geography,* 33: 148–61.

Martin, R.L. and Sunley, P.J. (2001) Rethinking the 'economic' in economic geography: Broadening our vision or losing our focus. *Antipode,* 33(2): 148–61.

Martin, R.L. and Sunley, P.J. (2006) Path dependence and regional economic evolution. *Journal of Economic Geography,* 6: 395–435.

Martin, R.L and Sunley, P.J. (2007) Complexity thinking and evolutionary economic geography. *Journal of Economic Geography.* 7: 573–602.

Metcalfe, J.S., Foster, J., and Ramlogan, R. (2006) Adaptive economic growth. *Cambridge Journal of Economics,* 30: 7–32.

Monk, A.H.B. and Monk, C.S. (2007) Economic geography: The rising star of the social sciences. *Oxonomics,* 2: 2–7.

Nash, S. (2004) On closure in economics. *Journal of Economic Methodology,* 11: 75–89.

Neary, J.P. (2001) Of hype and hyperbolas: Introducing the new economic geography. *Journal of Economic Literature,* XXXIX: 536–61.

Ottaviano G.I.P. and Puga, D. (1998) Agglomeration in the global economy: A survey of the 'new economic geography'. *World Economy,* 21: 707–31.

Overman, H. (2004) Can we learn anything from economic geography proper? *Journal of Economic Geography,* 4: 501–16.

Perrons, D. (2001) Towards a more holistic framework for economic geography. *Antipode,* 33: 208–15.

Plummer, P. and Sheppard, E. (2001) Must emancipatory economic geography be qualitative? *Antipode,* (33): 194–99.

Pratten, S. (2007) Realism, closed systems and abstraction. *Journal of Economic Methodology,* 14: 473–97.

Puga, D. (2002) European regional policies in the light of recent location theories. *Journal of Economic Geography,* 2: 372–406.

Ramlogan, R. and Metcalfe, S. (2006) Restless capitalism: A complexity perspective on modern capitalism. Chapter 5 in E. Garnsey, and J. McGlade, (eds) *Complexity and Co-Evolution.* Cheltenham: Edward Elgar, pp. 115–46

Robert-Nicoud, F. (2005) The structure of simple 'new economic geography' models (or, on identical twins). *Journal of Economic Geography,* 5: 201–34.

Robinson, J. (1978) History versus equilibrium. Chapter 12 in *Contributions to Modern Economics.* Oxford: Blackwell.

Scott, A.J. (2004) A perspective of economic geography. *Journal of Economic Geography,* 4: 479–99.

Sheppard, E. (2000) Geography or economics? Conceptions of space, interdependency and agency. In G.L. Clark and M. Gertler, (eds) The *Oxford Handbook of Economic Geography.* Oxford: Oxford University Press. pp. 99–119.

Sheppard, E. and Barnes, T.J. (eds) (2000) *A Companion to Economic Geography.* Oxford: Blackwell.

Sjöberg, O. and Sjöholm, F. (2002) Common ground?: Prospects for integrating the economic geography of geographers and economists. *Environment and Planning, A,* 34: 467–86.

Storper, M. and Venables, A. (2004) Buzz: Face-to-face contact and the urban economy. *Journal of Economic Geography*, 4: 351–70.

Sugden, R. (2000) Credible worlds: The status of theoretical models in economics, *Journal of Economic Methodology*, 7: 1–31.

The Economist (1999) Knowing your place. *The Economist*. March 11.

Venables, A.J. (2005) European integration: A view from geographical economics. *Swedish Economic Policy Review*, 12: 143–69.

PART 2

Political Economies of Space I

4

Making Sense of Globalization: Hegemonic and Counter-Hegemonic Geographies

Richard Peet, Ipsita Chatterjee
and Elaine Hartwick

INTRODUCTION: CONCEPTS OF GLOBALIZATION

Capitalism has been international in scope since the Europeans went out and 'discovered the world' 500 years ago. Ideas, capital, labour and resources drawn from societies across the globe made European capitalism possible. As measured by mass movements across global space, such as the migration of people, or the movement of investments, capitalism in the early twenty first century is only as international as it was by the late nineteenth century. Yet, recently in geography, as in many other disciplines, a new sense of internationalism has developed among people who think for a living. An intensification of long-distance interchange, and faster communications linking more people, has resulted in a new global era and, perhaps, a new, more worldly type of human existence – perhaps even a new global personality. Beginning in the 1960s, and continuing through the present, the realization has grown that capitalism is assuming a new, more expansive, yet contradictory spatial form. Various terms including extensification and internationalization have been used to describe this ongoing process – globalization being merely the most prominent.

What is this thing called 'globalization'? Definition of the term is hotly contested. Yet there came to be several, similar uses, with fairly wide acceptance, across a range of related disciplines. The sociologist Roland Robertson (1992: 8) understands globalization to be 'the compression of the world and the intensification of consciousness of the world as a whole'. Anthony Giddens (1990: 64), another sociologist, speaks about 'the intensification of world-wide social relations which link distinct localities in such a way that local happenings are shaped by events occurring many miles away'. And the geographer David Harvey (1989: 240) says that late twentieth century people 'have to learn to cope with an overwhelming sense of *compression* of our spatial and temporal worlds'.

These brief descriptions reveal two consistently related themes: global space is effectively getting smaller ('compressed'), not in physical terms, but in terms of the times taken for people, objects and images to traverse physical distance. As a result, social interactions have rapidly increased across spaces that had once confined economies and cultures. So change seems to have occurred in the scale at which even daily life is led, especially in terms of the interchange of images and information, the more spatially fluid of the many elements that influence opinions, beliefs, tastes and livelihoods. The human experience has globalized as the times separating spaces have collapsed. Putting this a little more realistically, an increasing proportion of people now live a geographically schizophrenic life in which the local inter-cuts with the global. Understood this way, globalization offers opportunities for disparate peoples to know and, perhaps, appreciate each other, by living 'closer' together. A globalized humanity, composed still of somewhat different peoples, at last seems possible. In this sense, globalization should be welcomed, as a potential for the good of a diverse but connected humanity.

However, other, more critical thinkers realize that behind such optimistic statements lurks the possibility that something quite different has been happening. The particular way in which globalization is brought about might destroy its inherently liberating potential. Giddens, for instance, has referred to globalization as 'influence at a distance'. The geographer Neil Smith (2005) outlines an 'American Globalism' brought about by neoconservative and neoliberal means. David Harvey (2005) sees neoliberal globalization dominated by a resurgent capitalist class of CEOs and big shareholders. This raises the question of whose influence? That is, globalization might be accompanied, even caused, by an intensification of concentrated class power.

The 'communications media' that technically annihilate space saturate everyone with the same mesmerizing images, creating a new and less interesting future by homogenizing what necessarily becomes a virtual experience. The multinational corporations that integrate production systems into one global economy simultaneously dominate competing labour forces, and more effectively manipulate a world of consumers buying the same things from the same chain of stores ('wall-to-wall Wall-Marts'). Global governance institutions, such as the World Bank and the International Monetary Fund (IMF), bring entire continents of people under the same pernicious, undemocratic control. And a President of the world's most powerful country threatened, bombed and invaded other countries more or less at will.

Rather than disparate peoples peacefully interacting as space collapses, an alternate idea has grown that one culture dominates the others, one economy or polity controls others, one set of institutions becomes globally hegemonic. As the space of global reach expands, the power of global influence concentrates. The institutions that control economies, project cultural themes, form political ideals that accumulate into larger entities – mega-institutions – and condense into fewer and more similar places – power centres. Putting this more realistically, a tendency can be seen towards the concentration of power accompanying, or even forcing, globalization – and ruining its humanitarian potential.

Still further, even these notions of concentration, homogenization and domination as linked aspects of globalization might themselves be criticized as insufficient or overly simplistic. An understanding of the dialectics of social processes operating over global space suggests that forces expanding from centres of power not only meet resistances originating in spaces of continuing difference, but strengthen, re-invigorate, re-invent and re-direct these resistances. And resistance based in fundamentalism uses the most modern of military means. Thus the geography of globalization becomes a more complex intellectual pursuit as the need for understanding and insight becomes more urgent to guide a new geographical exploration of the world. Here we look at the critical traditions in and around the discipline of geography that begin to make sense of globalization processes under constant re-structuring and re-interpretation.

FROM POLITICAL ECONOMY TO RADICAL GEOGRAPHY

Most critical geographic approaches to globalization derive from the writings of Karl Marx and his collaborator Friedrich Engels. Marx and Engels (1848, 1969) concurred with their intellectual predecessor, G.W.F. Hegel (1807, 1967), that conflicts and oppositions drive societal development – this means looking at societies in terms of relations and contradictions. But the idealist philosopher Hegel saw societies as directed by the quandaries faced by a mystical World Spirit, and global development as the expression of some kind of spiritual essence – an idea that finds resonance in contemporary notions of 'the end of history' or the 'victory of the forces of freedom' (Fukuyama, 1989). The materialist Marx, by contrast, saw societies expressing the expansion of real economic and social systems, with globalization resulting from the expansion specifically of capitalism. Marx, therefore, concentrated on the actual economic and social relations involved in socio-spatial processes, as with oppositions between classes, regional economies, political systems or ethnic groups. And at the heart of social relations, in Marx's analysis, is the process of 'exploitation'. For Marx (1976), societies are exploitative when uncompensated surplus labour, or its products, are taken from the working class by the ruling, or owning, class – exploitation being an arena of struggle, with the dominant class using a combination of economic, political and ideological force, and the dominated class resisting through overt means such as social organization and rebellion, and hidden means, like reluctant compliance.

Globalization is the expansion of the space in which capital directly or indirectly exploits labour. That is, whereas previously national capitalists primarily exploited national and regional labour forces, with the external arena used as source of raw materials or peasant-produced products, now global capitalists survey the world looking for regional labour forces to exploit and manipulate. Whereas previously labour resisted capital locally and nationally, through unionization for instance, now resistance is generalized to include a wider range of social movements scattered over global space. In such a social context, where exploitation is generalized to the world scale, consciousness similarly must take new ideological forms which rationalize and legitimize the new global system, as with notions of globalization bringing 'development for everyone', globalization bringing about 'poverty reduction' or globalization as 'inevitable progress'. As these terms suggest, a globalized economic system requires new versions of the ideologies of universalism. Likewise, whereas previously, exploitative societies had to develop repressive state apparatuses to contain and divert protest, now global capital uses global governance organizations, Such as the World Bank and IMF, to contain the upsurge of protest from a world of angry peoples.

Critical political-economic ideas, such as these, have long proved appealing to people of conscience, concerned about the sorrows and pains of the human condition. Marxist ideas were resurrected when, in the middle 1960s, protest erupted over issues such as inequality, racism, sexism, the environment and the Vietnam War. As part of such protests, radical movements grew in most of the social sciences and in some natural sciences as well. In the discipline of Geography it took time for the connections between nineteenth century theoretical radicalism and twentieth century radical geography to be realized, in part because Marxism had long been repressed, to the extent that Marx's name was virtually unmentioned in geographic education before 1965 (Peet, 1977).

Yet the revolutionary events of the late 1960s, such as the burning of large sections of cities in the western world, student-worker uprisings in Paris in 1968, massive anti-war protests, and the re-formation more generally of a radical culture of incessant protest, made the concerns of the traditional discipline of geography, for all its quantitative update, or its humanistic concern, seem socially and politically irrelevant to radicalized students and faculty members. From the middle 1960s onwards, articles dealing with more 'socially relevant' geographic topics (for example, Morrill, 1969–1970; Albaum, 1973) began to appear in some of the discipline's mainstream journals, and in 1969, *Antipode: A Radical Journal of Geography* was founded at Clark University in Worcester, Massachusetts, specifically to publish the new work.

The late 1960s and the early 1970s were years of political involvement and intellectual excitement unique in the modern history of geography. Looking back from the present, when the gains made then have become commonplace, and even *passe*, it is difficult to realize how dramatic the shift was taking place between the kinds of interests predominating in the geography of the middle 1960s, such as barn types, or the journey to shop, and those already beginning to dominate in the middle 1970s, such as urban and regional poverty, discrimination against women, or Third World underdevelopment. 'Social relevance', a key phrase at the time, was conceived not in a vague way, as 'feeling sorry for one's fellow human being', but as actively taking sides with oppressed people, advocating their causes through research and writing, and pressing for fundamental social change through 'geographic expeditions'. Even so, the development of social theories adequate for these tasks proved difficult for geographers trained in muddy-booted field work, regional description, or quantitative spatial techniques. Theoretically sophisticated ideas tended to form in areas of radical geography with clear connections with more heavily theorized streams of thought outside the discipline. One of the earliest connections, related to globalization, was an interest in 'imperialism'.

IMPERIALISM

There had been previous geographical interest in the Third World and the geopolitics of Western expansionism. This interest was revived when, in the 1950s and 1960s, at first the French, and then the US, waged war on the peasants and workers of Vietnam. Radical opponents interpreted the Vietnam War as a contemporary symptom of an historical process of imperialism. A series of articles drew on the existing stock of sophisticated radical ideas dealing with questions of underdevelopment, centre-periphery relations, and imperialism to provide the theoretical insight necessary for supporting anti-war protests. In the best of this work, James Blaut (1970) argued that the European model of the world took a uni-centric spatial form, with a distinctive geometry: an inner European space originally closed from an outer non-European space, that accumulated knowledge and technology, followed by a later process of conquest from this empowered base.

'The West', Blaut argued, was seen as having some kind of unique historical advantage (race, environment, culture, mind, spirit) which gave it superiority over all other people in all other regions. European civilization was supposedly generated mainly by inner processes – Europe made history – while non-Europeans played little or no crucial role in epochal events (cf. Wolf, 1982). 'The rest of the world' was portrayed as traditional, with non-Europeans characterized as primitive and unprogressive, barbarous and heathen, less intelligent and less virtuous than the Europeans. The expansion of the Europeans was thought of as self-generated, a 'striving outward', with innovation and modernity diffusing and becoming less evident with distance from the global centre so that, whenever non-Europeans showed evidence of progress this was proportional to the European impact on their society. This amounted, said Blaut, to a global diffusion model, with the underlying belief generalized as 'diffusionism' (i.e. the idea that all significant cultural processes flow from the European centre to the non-European periphery. Diffusionism involves a geo-history of waves of progress moving from centre to periphery as 'modernization').

Blaut (1976) compared this with a Third World ethnoscientific model of the world as multi-centric, with centres of incipient or proto-development springing up at strategic points throughout the Old World. In a 'Third Worldist' understanding, Blaut argued, the multi-centred pattern of relatively equal levels of development was disrupted by the European plunder of the New World (the European 'discovery' being due solely to the fact that the Iberian centres of expansion were closest to America), the consequent flood of bullion into Europe, and the resulting commercial, industrial and scientific-technological development. 'Thereafter the dialectic of development and underdevelopment intensified, and the world economy fixed itself in place'. (Blaut, 1976: 1)

The final version of these ideas was published by Blaut (1994) as *The Colonizers's Model of the World*, a work dedicated to undermining the belief that European civilization had some unique historical advantage that made it permanently superior to all other communities. Blaut (1994; see also Blaut 2000) showed that diffusionism remained relatively undisturbed at the heart of most western historical and geographical scholarship. He argued instead that, rather than internal factors, colonialism and imperialism led to the development of Euro-America and the underdevelopment of Asia, Latin America and Africa.

In saying this, Blaut was repeating a more general position established by dependency theory that the geographical development of world capitalism destroyed or transformed earlier social systems, converting them into sources of its own further development.

For Andre Gunder Frank, a leading dependency theorist, the economic, political, social and cultural institutions of the underdeveloped countries resulted from the penetration of capitalism, rather than being original or traditional (Frank, 1969). Drawing on Marxist analyses of the class expropriation of surplus value, especially Paul Baran's (1960) version, which emphasized the potential surplus which could be made available for investment under non-capitalist circumstances, Frank argued that external control resulted in the expropriation (and thus local unavailability) of a significant part of the economic surplus produced in Third World countries that were actively *under*developed (made less developed) by the expropriation of their surplus product. In other words, for theorists such as Blaut and Frank, poverty in the Third World is not endemic, it is produced by exploitation from the First World, by globalization. Third World debts do not result from over-borrowing, but from excessive exploitation. Therefore, poverty reduction and debt relief in contemporary globalization should not stem from moral pity, but from social justice – that is compensating Third World peoples for the labour, resources and money that has long been taken from them.

SPATIAL RELATIONS

During the 1970s, a series of articles, mainly appearing in *Antipode*, drew out the spatial implications of works by Marxist theorists. The idea was to move theoretically from contradictions in the historical dynamic of the accumulation of capital, to manifestations of these contradictions as uneven development in space, and then to move back again, uneven development became an essential aspect of the capital accumulation process. One main component of this position was the build-up of crises within regions expressed outwardly in space. The main theorists elaborating this perspective were David Harvey and his students.

For Harvey (1975), the Marxist theory of growth under capitalism placed capital accumulation at the centre of a dynamic and inevitably expansionary mode of production. This dynamism encountered barriers (in labour, means of production, markets) which precipitated crises (chronic unemployment, realization crises, where production cannot be consumed, etc.) which eventually resulted in a shift in the accumulation process to a higher plane (new social wants, new markets, new sources of labour, etc.). Newly 'rational' locational patterns were inevitable, necessary parts of capital accumulation. But there was a spatial aspect to contradiction that Harvey found to be fundamental: in overcoming spatial barriers and 'annihilating space with time' spatial structures were created which ultimately acted as barriers to further accumulation. This was particularly the case with immobile, fixed capital (i.e. means of production fixed in space) rather than more mobile variable capital (labour). For capital then had to negotiate a path between preserving the value of past investments in the built environment (the urban landscape, for example) and destroying these investments to make new room for accumulation, increasingly in new regions of the globalizing economy. The virtue of Marx's location theory lay in the way space could be integrated into 'fundamental insights into the production of value and the dynamics of accumulation' (Harvey, 1975: 13). And the virtue of Harvey's analysis is that it brings out the contradictions inherent in capitalist globalization.

A series of theorists in the Marxist tradition had connected capitalism's internal contradictions with its external 'solutions', such as the violent penetration of pre-capitalist societies (Lenin, 1975; Luxembourg, 1951) and the production of a centre-periphery spatial organization in the resulting global economy (Baran, 1960; Frank, 1969). For Harvey, imperialism was the main geographical necessity deriving from the expansionary dynamic of accumulation; the specific economic form of imperialism (whether it be a search for markets, cheaper labour, places to invest surplus capital, new sources of raw materials, etc.) varied over time and was a matter for empirical, historical analysis.

In terms of geographic theory this dynamic theory of contradictions contrasted with conventional location theory, with its equilibrium analysis of optimal spatial configurations. Marxist theory 'commences with the dynamics of accumulation and seeks to derive out of this analysis certain necessities with respect to geographical structures. The landscape which capitalism creates is also seen as the locus of contradiction and tension, rather than as an expression of harmonious equilibrium' (Harvey, 1975: 13). Thus the internal and external dimensions of space were linked to each other and with capital accumulation. Revolutions in the productive forces, the increasing scale of production, and the concentration and centralization of capital, were paralleled by urban agglomeration in a widening international capitalist space.

The culminating of this early line of Marxist analysis came with Harvey's *The Limits to Capital* (1982), a reading of Marx's *Capital* organized around three 'cuts' at a general theory of capitalist crisis. The first cut saw crises of over-accumulation – more capital produced than opportunities for using it – resolved through violent episodes of the destruction of value, times when capitalists turned on each other, with workers ending up paying the social costs (Harvey, 1982: 190–203). The second cut examined the expression of productive crises in money and finance, speculative booms and busts which require the intervention of the state. In an internationalized economy, crises take the form of inter-state competition over shifting the effects of devaluation, with national policies to export the effects of crises, and imperialism, neo-colonialism and even war as potential 'solutions' (Harvey, 1982: 324–329). The third and last cut integrated geographically uneven development: devaluations of capital are systematized into the continuous restructuring of space through interregional competition. Harvey focused on what he called 'switching crises' (in the movement of capital from one place to another) and crises in the hierarchy of capitalist institutions, so that problems which originate in the chaos and confusion of local events build upwards into global crises.

For Harvey the basic rhythm involves regional economies, or more broadly regional class alliances, periodically alleviating internal crises through transformations in external relations in a spatial 'fix' which has imperialism as its integral component – hence 'an interpretation of inter-imperialist wars as constitutive moments in the dynamics of accumulation' (Harvey, 1982: 443). What better reason, he asked, could there be for declaring that there is a need for a saner mode of production?

POWER/GEOGRAPHY

Even so, the following years saw a retreat from structural theories of societies and their spaces – for example by paying more attention to agency in 'structuration' theories, paying greater regard to 'localities' or being sceptical of the claims of 'metanarratives' of truth and progress (Peet, 1998). By the 1990s, it had become clear that the broad, structural generalizations made earlier by Marxists and other critical theorists had to be complemented by intermediate, more nuanced, yet still critical modes of analysis dealing with states and organizations. Similar arguments were being made about conventional, 'main stream' economic geography – that it abstracts economic action from its contexts whereas, in reality, economic activity is socially and institutionally situated (Martin, 1994; Scott, 1995; Sunley, 1996; Martin, 2000) (See Chapter 3).

One of many responses takes the form of an 'institutional geography'. A more institutionally attuned economic geography looks at the shaping of global space economies by environments of institutions. For example, one main strand of institutionalist interest focused on social regulation and governance and the effect of policies in shaping global, national, regional and local economies (Amin, 1999). Most simply, 'institution' in arguments like these means an organizational entity, located in a space, with a mission and declared purpose, backed by command over vital resources (ideas, expertise, money, connections). A more productive sense of the term 'institution' is Foucault's (1980) notion of a 'community of experts', an elite group controlling an area of knowledge and expertise, and forming the base for a power regime understood as a discursive formation (Foucault, 1991). In this sense of the term, institutions can be 'mapped' through analysis of the arrangement of institutions within complexes located in space – with 'arrangement' being formative, rather than derivative, of policy power – and examining the power relations between institutional power centres and more dependent peripheries. However, the essential idea, looking from a critical perspective, remains tracing the discourses and imaginaries produced in institutional complexes to underlying class interests.

In other words, mapping institutions as they are clustered in space (in power centres) is a productive approach to the geography of global power (see 4). In advanced modernity governance policies and practices are conceived by experts in institutions concentrated at only a few power centres, global cities that exercise power in world space. This conception, 'global power centre', derives from Sassen's (1991: 4) notion of 'global cities'. These are concentrated command points in the organization of the world economy; key locations for finance and specialized service firms which together constitute the capacity to produce global control. Thus, financial power has accumulated disproportionately in the leading industrial countries, especially the US, but also the United Kingdom, Germany and Japan. Control is centralized in cities of the industrial heartland that move from being company and corporate headquarters into being 'capital markets' or financial centres for global finance capital.

The globalization of the late twentieth century saw an increased concentration of capital at the top of this global hierarchy, especially New York, London, Tokyo and Frankfurt, with one city, New York, consistently presiding over the rest (Poon et al., 2004). The traditional dominance of New York (with London increasingly challenging this position as political and financial crises intercede) comes not only from the amount of capital the city controls and the technological sophistication with which money can be moved from Wall Street to any where in the world (Warf, 2000) but also from the extent to which the city is itself globalized in terms of institutions and transactions. Essentially this kind of global power is exercised by controlling access to the largest capital accumulations in the world and directing flows of capital in various forms – as equities, bonds, derivatives, foreign exchange and direct investment – to uses and places that are approved of by Wall Street banks and investment firms (Peet et al., 2003). Power is exercised too through influences exerted on the formation of global economic policy by institutions of global governance that, at best, are indirectly elected (*through* governments) but are involved in the regulation, management and control of national economic policy and which cluster their headquarters in relatively few places.

The resulting centres of global power are exclusively cities in Western capitalist countries: either the capitals of leading national powers, overwhelmingly New York (for example, the United Nations) and Washington DC (the International Monetary Fund and World Bank), or definitely Western, but officially neutral, political urban spaces, including Geneva, Switzerland (the World Trade Organization and many UN agencies). Policy is legitimated more by science and expert opinion than by elections and democratic consent. This may sound fine – a kind of global Plato's Republic, wisely directed by modern-scientific, rather than classical-philosopher, kings. More critically, scientific, humanitarian governance may be read as a new, kinder-faced version of Western imperialism.

Global governance and expert-designed economic policy have a power/geography in two of the main senses of this originally Foucauldian term. First, the world cities where governance institutions congregate and experts co-mingle display landscapes imbued with the trappings of Western power – locating the headquarters, and much of the bureaucracy, in such centres lends the policies they prescribe the aura of Western authority. Second, this ambient content is released as 'power effects' as policies extend over space and are adopted, under varying conditions of compulsion, in capital cities the world over. The two power/geographies re-enforce one another in a symbiotic embrace.

As a result, the main international financial institutions, the IMF and the World Bank, have become powerful institutions indeed. At any time the economies of 120 nation states, and the livelihoods of 2.5 billion people, might be under their direct supervision, through the 'structural adjustment' that governance institutions impose as a condition for granting loans to countries undergoing crises. Global institutions condition 'aid to the poor' on the adoption by deserving countries of a set of neoliberal policies that insist on an exaggeratedly market-organized and export-oriented economy. This set of policies is said to produce the economic growth that creates jobs and reduces poverty. Yet these are also policies that favour free enterprise and private capital investment. And the only reason for private investment is to make profit. Governance institutions, many argue, therefore act, at least in part, in the interest of global finance capital. The connection between capital, governance and centralized power over the lives of billions of people all over the world lies through the imposition of neoliberal economic policies. We live in an era of neoliberal globalization.

NEOLIBERALISM

Neoliberalism is an entire structure of beliefs founded on right wing, but not conservative, ideas about individual freedom, political democracy, self-regulating markets and entrepreneurship. Neo*liberalism* renews the beliefs of early modern, and especially nineteenth century, British 'classical' liberalism is a critical reaction to twentieth century social democratic Keynesianism. Neoliberal ideals, kept alive during the post-war period by theorists such as Friedrich von Hayek, Milton Friedman, and the Chicago School of Economics, were adopted by the governments of Margaret Thatcher in Britain and Ronald Reagan in the United States, and were adopted or re-emphasized by the IMF and World Bank in the 1980s.

Under the sway of neoliberal beliefs since then, the global institutions governing the development of the world economy have consistently advocated a set of virtually identical economic policies to national governments. These 'Washington Consensus' policies favour an outward-oriented, export economy, organized through markets, with minimal state regulation, along with privatization, trade liberalization and limited (state) budget deficits (Williamson, 1997). They are enforced through powerful means, such as 'structural adjustment' or the refusal of emergency loans or not getting debt relief. Even more importantly, the IMF/World Bank stamp of approval strongly influences the decisions of bond rating firms and investment analysts on whether to commit or withdraw funds from a country. Economic policies stemming from the neoliberal perspective are promoted by global institutions with regard to a model of what policy should look like, regardless of national circumstance, cultural tradition, or social structure, or of previous traditions in the political economy of development, or what the people of a country really need in the way of necessities (Peck and Tickell, 1994, 2002; Tickell, and Peck, 1995; Peet et al., 2003; Harvey, 2005).

Neoliberal policies calling for a decrease in domestic barriers to trade and capital flow increase the porosity of political boundaries, and hence aid 'spaces of flows' (Castells, 2003) or deterritorialization. In the sub-national context, structural adjustment and privatization

brought about by World Bank and IMF policies release land, resources and labour, originally in the formal sectors of nations, into the informal and free market sectors. What is described as a 'post-Fordist flexible production' system then utilizes the newly released land, labour and resources from the informal sectors of economies. The production regime is described as 'flexible' because the production process is no longer bounded within the producing nation, and unrestricted capital can 'fly' beyond national boundaries. Flexible production benefits as the formal sectors in developing nations shrink with state-owned domestic industries being increasingly outcompeted (Harvey, 2003).

Free-flowing capital can now utilize place-culture- and gender-specific cheap labour in the informal sectors of other nations (Wright, 1997). Production is carried out in small batches with outsourced, subcontracted labour in job-specific casual employment. The adoption of such a production regime becomes imperative under increased border porosity and the foreign competition introduced by neoliberal policies. Thus, a neoliberalizing state must move away from welfare and subsidy to assume an entrepreneurial role, privatizing economic activities and expanding informal sectors, which can then be brought under flexible production (Harvey, 1989).

The twin processes of de- and re-territorialization are carried out hand-in-hand by neoliberalization and flexible production. By adopting free-market economic policies, the neoliberalizing state opens up for privatization national/regional/local industrial and commercial spaces and markets previously under state control. Greater penetration of foreign goods in previously indigenous markets and the privatization of previously state-controlled sectors bring about new terms of trade, often out-competing indigenous producers, and laying-off workers. The out-competed and laid-off workforce is pushed into part-time casual jobs in the informal sector and their families are also pushed into the job-market to compensate for the drop in family income (Stiglitz, 2002). The adoption of neoliberal open-market policies therefore causes workers, their families and sometimes whole communities to move from their original jobs, homes, and localities to resettle in places with greater opportunities for casual employment. This migration (reorganization/uprooting) leads to the de-territorialization of communities and forced alterations in livelihood strategies of people previously involved in the older production regime (Starr, 2001). Flexible production manifested in sweatshops and subcontracted work in cities, absorb de-territorialized communities, ethnic groups dispossessed of their original jobs, livelihoods, and often homes (Harvey, 1992). From a critical geographic perspective, neoliberalism has been a disaster visited on the world's poor by centralized, expert power.

THE GEOGRAPHY OF RESISTANCE

Yet for every tendency towards the concentration of control and the intensification of domination, there are counter moves that decentralize power and generate opposition. So we find globalization as westernization contested by diverse counter-tendencies, social movements ranging from sea turtle activists to Al Qaeda terrorists. As we have argued, globalization is usually understood in terms of a shrinking of physical distance, the dissolution of barriers, time-space compression, greater flows and faster communications: essentially greater and faster movement of commodities, people, information, ideas and ideologies (Brown, 2001; Castells, 2001; Ceglowski, 2000; Halliday, 2001; Harvey, 2001; Ohmae, 2000; Strange, 2001). Time and space have indeed been compressed (Harvey, 1989, 1992) due to a speeding-up of communications and transport, creating a world of flows of commodities, culture, foreign direct investment, aid and experts, and resulting in a de-rootedness or de-territorialization that Castells (2003) describes as 'spaces of flows' and Hartwick (1998) as 'chains of connection'.

Some argue that the re-shaping of global space by international flows and connections has not produced increasing social integration (Appadurai, 2001; Smith, 2001; Mann, 2001; Harvey, 1992). Indeed nations, regions and societies at smaller, 'local' scales have stubbornly refused erasure by resisting 'secular waves' of economic and cultural integration (Shupe and Hadden, 1988). Fragmented ideologies of religion and ethnicity have (re)crystallized at the local level, while intra-national and intra-regional social conflicts erupt between ethnic and religious groups. Social conflicts at these more local levels are often explained as resulting from inward-looking and particularistic loyalties present still in local spaces (Hetne, 2001; O'Neill, 2001; Brown, 2001). Shupe and Hadden (1988), for example, account for the resurgence of 'local' social conflicts in the globalizing era by emphasizing that free market globalization is limited in its ability to homogenize. Others, such as Friedman (1989) and Barber (2001), argue that the world is increasingly divided into a 'McWorld' or 'Lexus' of western consumerism and free market competition, and the 'Olive tree' or 'Jihad' of increased local ethnic, religious conflicts. Huntington (2000) takes this a step further, suggesting that the global future will see increased clashes between civilizations along religious fault lines.

This last set of more conventional theorists (Friedman and Huntington especially) make two main, overly-simple, assumptions: they assume that global forces are unidirectional, all-powerful and secularizing, with the local as the romantic 'other', invariably beyond the reach of the global; and social conflicts are assumed to be inevitable, unless local scales like communities, nations and regions assimilate into the larger 'global community'. The global and local are viewed as separate categories and the panacea lies in 'successfully taming' the local. An alternative perspective, after Swyngedow (1997), suggests that the global and local cannot be seen as ontologically given, confrontational scales; rather each should be viewed as mutually constitutive of the other. That is, resistance and social conflicts can be understood by viewing local phenomena as dialectically related to the global.

For Joseph (2002), social conflicts at local scales are not discrete local events – a nostalgic 'outside' to the global – but are complexly connected to global processes of economic and cultural globalization – the local re-inventing itself in symbiosis with the dynamic global. In that context therefore, a resurgence of social conflict in the era of globalization (Melluci, 1988) cannot be discounted as coincidental and uniquely local, completely disconnected from global processes. The de-territorializing aspects of globalization have been well-documented through studies of flows, patterns, migrations (Brenner, 1999; Dicken, 1994). Re-territorialization of the local places through indigenization, reinvention and rejuvenation is also a result of the same globalizing forces and so far has been under-studied. The 'spaces of places' of communities, cultures, nations re-territorializing through rejuvenation of the local, indigenization of the local, requires more attention.

Additionally, much of the existing literature on globalization tends to segregate into discrete economic, socio-cultural and geographical components. Economic analyses deal with production, trade, capital movement, and labour market segmentation (Hirst and Thomson, 2001; Sachs, 2000). Sociological and anthropological analyses emphasize cultural processes, such as identity formation, the spread of consumer culture, and the media and its influence on communities (Appadurai, 2001; Smith, 2001; Huntington, 2000). Geographical analyses deal with socio-cultural phenomena restructured at various scales, like place, locale, region, nations (Herod, 1995; Brenner, 1999; Harvey, 2001; Peck and Tickell, 2002). Relatively few attempts have been made to integrate economic, socio-cultural and geographic explanations in obtaining a comprehensive understanding of social conflicts. An integrated approach would transcend one-sided interpretations from specific disciplines, providing a more nuanced understanding.

CONCLUSION: COUNTER-HEGEMONIC GLOBALISMS

One position, then, is that globalization was produced by the expansion of Western corporate and imperialist domination and is essentially uni-centric, homogeneous, and unchallengeable. The other position is that the very expansion of Western capitalism initiates or re-juvenates cultural (for example, religious), political and economic opposition as people all over the world support political and social movements of resistance. Hence, globally-hegemonic discourses such as neo-liberalism are confronted in the peripheries by alternative conceptions deriving from the experiences of oppressed peoples in re-territorializing spaces – for example, social movements and political parties coming to power in several Latin American countries in the early 2000s. For, as the Marxist cultural theorist Raymond Williams insisted, 'the hegemonic' is neither total nor exclusive. Rather, oppositional cultures continue to exist. For Williams (1977: 125), these alternatives may be 'residual' – based on experiences lived in the cultures of previous social formations – or 'emergent', in the sense of the creation of new meanings and values, new significances and experiences, that are not fully incorporated into the dominant. Even with intensive globalization, different spaces exist in discontinuous time sequences, so that oppositional groups contend with the residues of dominations discarded elsewhere or, more realistically, long integrated into synthetic, new kinds of domination – contention with feudal social formations, for instance.

Continuing exclusion from material benefits is the main experiential base projecting residual resentments into emergent alternatives as fully fledged counter-hegemonies. Intellectuals marked by class, ethnic or gender difference often serve as spokespersons for what otherwise may amount to sullen resistance, or defiance phrased in narrative forms restricted to a local culture. These intellectuals have their own bases in alternative power complexes, situated around social movements or unions, and often represented locally and internationally by non-governmental organizations, alternative powers that are different in that they employ more informal media of thought, discussion and dissemination.

The uneasy contestations and articulations between hegemony and various sub- and counter-hegemonies yield ranges of contradictory locations, hybrids that result in sudden shifts of allegiance as contexts, opportunities and life-choices change. Contestations between the hegemonic and the counter-hegemonic are punctuated by episodes of violence including riots. This is because counter-hegemonic discourses derive their persuasive powers from the collective wills of oppressed peoples, from the experiences of the poor and down-trodden, from pangs of hunger and the cries of sick children, from the loss of respect in the death of a culture. It is on behalf of the dispossessed at the margins of hegemony that acts of spectacular violence penetrate into the heart of hegemony. This is the globalization in torment that the twentieth century bequeaths as a birthday present to the twenty first century.

REFERENCES

Albaum, M. (1973) *Geography and Contemporary Issues*. New York: John Wiley.

Amin, A. (1999) An institutionalist perspective on regional economic development. *International Journal of Urban and Regional Research*. 23: 365–78.

Appadurai, A. (2001) Disjuncture and difference in the global cultural economy. In M. Featherstone (ed.) *Global Culture*. London: SAGE. pp. 295–310.

Baran, P. (1960) *The Political Economy of Growth*. New York: Monthly Review Press.

Barber, B.R. (2001) Jihad vs. Mcworld. In P. O' Meara, H. D. Mehlinger, and M. Krain (eds) *Globalization and the Challenges of a New Century*. Bloomington: Indiana University. pp. 23–33.

Blaut, J. (1970) Geographic models of imperialism. *Antipode*, 2(1): 65–85.

Blaut, J. (1976) Where was capitalism born? *Antipode* 8(2): 1–11.

Blaut, J. (1994) *The Colonizer's Model of the World*. London: Guilford.

Blaut, J.M. (2000) *Eight Eurocentric Historians*. New York: The Guilford Press.

Brenner, N. (1999) Globalization as reterritorialization: The re-scaling of urban governance in the European Union. *Urban Studies*, 36(3): 431–51.

Brown, C. (2001) The idea of world community. In D. Held and A. McGrew (eds) *The Global Transformations Reader*. Cambridge: Polity Press. pp. 453–61.

Castells, M. (2001) The global economy. In D. Held and A. McGrew (eds) *The Global Transformations Reader*. Cambridge: Polity Press. pp. 259–73.

Castells, M. (2003) *The Power of Identity*. Oxford: Blackwell.

Cheglowski, J. (2000) Has globalization created a borderless world? In P. O'Meara, H. D. Mehlinger, and M. Krain (eds) *Globalization and the Challenges of a New Century*. Bloomington: Indiana University Press. pp. 101–11.

Dicken, P. (1994) Global-local tensions: Firms and states in the global space-economy. *Economic Geography*, 70(2):101–28.

Foucault, M. (1980) *Power/Knowledge: Selected Interviews and other Writings, 1972–1977*. New York: Pantheon.

Foucault, M. (1991) Governmentality. In G. Burchall, C. Gordon, and P. Miller (eds) *The Foucault Effect: Studies in Governmentality*. London: Harvester Wheatsheaf. pp. 87–104.

Frank, A.G. (1969) *Capitalism and Underdevelopment in Latin America*. New York: Monthly Review Press.

Friedman, T. L. (1989) *The Lexus and the Olive Tree*. New York: Farrar, Straus and Giroux.

Fukuyama, F. (1989) The end of history? *The National Interest*. 16: 3–18.

Giddens, A. (1990) *The Consequences of Modernity*. Cambridge: Polity.

Halliday, F. (2001) Global governance: Prospects and problems. In D. Held and A. McGrew (eds) *The Global Transformations Reader*. Cambridge: Polity Press. pp. 431–41.

Hartwick, E. (1998) Geographies of consumption: A commodity chain approach *Environment and Planning D: Society and Space*, 16: 423–37.

Harvey, D. (1975) The geography of capitalist accumulation. *Antipode*, 7: 9–21.

Harvey, D. (1982) *The Limits to Capital*. Oxford: Blackwell.

Harvey, D. (1992) The factory of fragmentation. In J. T. Roberts and A. Hite (eds) *From Modernization to Globalization*. Oxford: Blackwell. pp. 292–97.

Harvey, D. (1989) *The Condition of Postmodernity*. Oxford: Blackwell.

Harvey, D. (2001) Time-space compression and the postmodern condition. In D. Held and A McGrew (eds) *The Global Transformations Reader*. Cambridge: Polity Press. pp. 82–91.

Harvey, D. (2003) *The New Imperialism*. New York: Oxford University Press.

Harvey, D. (2005) *A Brief History of Neoliberalism*, Oxford: Oxford University Press.

Hegel, G.W.F. (1807, 1967) *The Phenomenology of Mind*. New York: Harper Publishers.

Herod, A. (1995) The practice of international labor solidarity and the geography of the global economy. *Economic Geography*, 71(4): 341–63.

Hetne, B. (2001) Global market versus regionalism. In D. Held and A. McGrew (eds) *The Global Transformations Reader*. Cambridge: Polity Press. pp. 68–75.

Hirst, P. and Thompson G. (2001) Globalization and the history of the international economy. In D. Held and A. McGrew (eds) *The Global Transformations Reader*. Cambridge: Polity Press. pp. 274–86.

Hudson, R. (2004) Conceptualizing economics and their geographies: Spaces, flows and circuits. *Progress in Human Geography*, 28(4): 447–71.

Huntington, S. P. (2000) The clash of civilizations? In P. O'Meara, H. D. Mehlinger, and M. Krain (eds) *Globalization and the Challenges of a New Century*. Bloomington: Indiana University Press. pp. 3–23.

Joseph, M. (2002) *Against the Romance of Community*. Minneapolis: University of Minnesota Press.

Lefebvre, H. (2000) *The Production of Space*. Malden, MA: Blackwell.

Lenin, V.I. (1975) *Imperialism: The Highest Stage of Capitalism*. Peking: Foreign Languages Press.

Luxembourg, R. (1951) *The Accumulation of Capital*. London: Routledge and Kegan Paul.

Mann, M. (2001) 'Has globalization ended the rise and the rise of the nation-state?' In D. Held and A. McGrew (eds) *The Global Transformations Reader*. Cambridge: Polity Press. pp. 136–47.

Martin, R.L. (1994) Economic theory and human geography. In D. Gregory, R. L. Martin, and G.E. Smith (eds) *Human Geography: Society, Space and Social Science*. Basingstoke: MacMillan. pp. 21–53.

Martin, R. (2000) Institutional approaches in economic geography. In E. Sheppard and T. Barnes (eds) *A Companion to Economic Geography*. Oxford: Blackwell. pp. 77–94.

Marx, K. (1976) *Capital: A Critique of Political Economy*. Harmondsworth: Penguin.

Marx, K. and Engels, F. (1848, 1969) Manifesto of the Communist Party. In Karl Marx and Frederick Engels, *Selected Works*, Vol. 1. Moscow: Progress Publishers. pp. 108–37.

Melucci, A. (1988) Social movements and the democratization of everyday life. In John Deane (ed.) *Civil Society and the State: New European Perspectives*. London: Verso.

Morrill, R. (1969–1970) Geography and the transformation of society *Antipode*, 1(1):6–9 and 2(1): 4–10.

Ohmae, K. (2000) The rise of the region state. In P. O'Meara, H. D. Mehlinger, and M. Krain (eds) *Globalization and the Challenges of a New Century*. Bloomington: Indiana University Press. pp. 93–100.

Peck, J. and Tickell, A. (1994) Jungle law breaks out: Neoliberalism and global-local disorder. *Area* 26: 317–26.

Peck, J. and Tickell, A. (2002) Neoliberalizing space. *Antipode*, 34: 380–404.

Peet, R. (1977). *Radical Geography*. Chicago: Maaroufa Press.

Peet, R. (1998) *Modern Geographical Thought*. Oxford: Blackwell.

Peet, R. with Hartwick, E. (1999) *Theories of Development*. New York: Guilford.

Peet, R. et al. (2003) *Unholy Trinity: The IMF, World Bank and WTO*. London: Zed Books.

Poon, J.P.H., Eldredge, B. and Yeung, D. (2004) Rank size distribution of International Financial Centers. *International Regional Science Review*, 27(4): 411–30.

Robertson, R. (1992) *Globalization*. London: SAGE.

Sachs, J. (2000). International economics: Unlocking the mysteries of globalization. In P. O'Meara, H. D. Mehlinger, and M. Krain (eds) *Globalization and the Challenges of a New Century*. Bloomington: Indiana University Press. pp. 217–26.

Sachs, J. (2005) *The End of Poverty: Economic Possibilities for Our Time*. New York: Penguin Press.

Sassen, S. (1991) *The Global City: New York, London, Tokyo*. Princeton: Princeton University Press

Scott A. (1995) The geographic foundations of industrial performance. *Competition and Change*, 1: 51–66.

Shupe, A. and Hadden, J. (1988) Is there such a thing as global fundamentalism? In J.K. Hadden and A. Shupe (eds) *Secularization and Fundamentalism Reconsidered*. New York: Paragon House. pp. 109–22.

Smith, A.D. (2001) Towards a global culture? In M. Featherstone (ed.) *Global Culture*. London: SAGE. pp. 171–90.

Starr, A. (2001) *Naming the Enemy: Anticorporate Movements Confront Globalization*. London, New York: Zed Books.

Stiglitz, J. E. (2002) Globalism's discontents. *The American Prospects Online*. January 1.

Strange, S. (2001) The declining authority of the states. In D. Held and A. McGrew (eds) *The Global Transformations Reader*. Cambridge: Polity Press. pp. 148–55.

Sunley, P. (1996) Context in economic geography: the relevance of pragmatism. *Progress in Human Geography*, 20: 338–55.

Swyngedow, E. (1997) Neither global nor local: 'Glocalization' and the politics of scale. In K. Cox (ed.) *Spaces of Globalization: Reasserting the Power of the Local*. New York: Guilford. pp. 137–66.

Tickell, A. and Peck, J. (1995) Social regulation after Fordism: Regulation theory, neoliberalism and the global-local nexus. *Economy and Society*, 24: 357–86.

Warf, B. (2000) New York: The Big Apple in the 1990s. *Geoforum*, 31: 487–99.

Williams, R. (1977) *Marxism and Literature*. Oxford: Oxford University Press.

Williamson, J. (1997) The Washington consensus revisited. In Louis Emmerij (ed.) *Economic and Social Development into the XXI Century*. Washington: Inter-American Development Bank.

Wolf, E. (1982). *Europe and the People without History*. Berkeley: University of California Press.

Wright, M. (1997) Crossing the factory frontier: Gender, place and power in the Mexican Maquiladora. *Antipode*, 29(3): 278–302.

Unpacking Globalization: Changing Geographies of the Global Economy

Neil M. Coe

INTRODUCTION

Globalization is literally all around us; not only in terms of the webs of global connections into which we are increasingly tied as we go about our everyday lives, but also as a way of understanding the nature of the world in which we live. Globalization is at once both a multi-faceted concept, and a set of real, material changes in the global system, with the two aspects interacting and reinforcing each other in complex ways. Figure 5.1 provides a useful handle on the rise of globalization as an idea. Using a measure derived from the Arts and Social Science Citation Indexes, it shows how the number of published academic articles with the term globalization in the title mushroomed during the 1990s and since 2000 has averaged over 600 per year. This growth in academic usage has been paralleled by a similarly dramatic expansion in political and media adoption. In the early twenty-first century, globalization has become a ubiquitous term which is

attached to a wide variety of domains such as the economy, socio-cultural dynamics, politics, migration and environmental change. Arguably, the term is now so broadly and loosely used that it has become a rather ill-defined or fuzzy concept that needs to be treated with caution by economic geographers (Markusen, 1999).

A great deal has been written about the rise of globalization as a discourse (or set of ideas), the neoliberal politics that underlie its rise, and the ways in which the discourse has been mobilized to justify policy interventions (or indeed, non-interventions) by 'naturalizing' the global scale of economic activity (see for example, Kelly, 1999; Cameron and Palan, 2004). But globalization has far more than discursive significance, and the task of this chapter is to explore the manifest changes in the global economy that the term is trying to capture. These encompass: the development of new information and communication technologies; the incorporation of large parts of the globe into an integrated world economy;

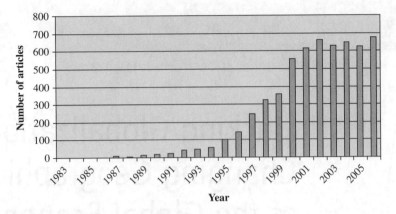

Figure 5.1   The rise of 'globalization' as concept.

Source: Arts and Social Science Citation Indexes (http://wok.mimas.ac.uk/)
Note: Includes both 'globalisation' and 'globalization'.

the rapid growth of the newly industrializing economies (NIEs) including most recently China and India; and, most importantly, the spread of the social relations of capitalism and its inherent dynamics as the norm around which economies function.

Indeed, the general rise in usage depicted in Figure 5.1 serves to conceal a heated debate within, and across, a broad range of social science disciplines as to how globalization should be defined, interpreted and analysed. As we shall see, such differences of opinion are not just semantic; they influence the concept's utility in a number of profound ways. Economic geographers have been an integral part of these debates, although not perhaps as much – or as centrally – as one might expect given the geographical connotations of the word itself and the processes it invokes (see Dicken, 2004, for more on this). The stance that will be developed in this chapter is that globalization is most meaningfully deployed when capturing the 'step-change' in processes of international economic integration that has occurred over the last few decades.

More specifically, this chapter will explore the interrelationships between the changing nature of the global economy and various attempts to conceptualize these changes. In particular, it will position globalization with respect to the changing *international divisions of labour* that have characterized

different phases of world economic history and how these have been interpreted from a *political-economic* perspective. Such a viewpoint seeks to reveal and to offer a critique of the inherent power asymmetries and inequities of the capitalist system and their uneven developmental outcomes. I start the analysis by moving towards a working definition of globalization processes.

THE GLOBALIZATION DEBATE: CHARTING A MEANINGFUL PATH

Following Held et al. (1999), a useful way into the sprawling globalization debate is to identify three broad, but very different, positions on globalization and what it might mean. First, *hyperglobalists* posit that we now live in a fully globalized and borderless world in which national borders no longer matter. Business gurus such as Theodore Levitt (1983) and Kenichi Ohmae (1995), for example, have described a homogenized global marketplace in which money, images, knowledge, technology and products rapidly circulate the globe, untroubled and unimpeded by boundaries or matters of nationality. In this new environment, the ability of the nation state to effect economic growth in its territory is seen to be massively on the wane. Second, globalization *sceptics* suggest that both the novelty and extent of contemporary globalization has been exaggerated. Writers such as Hirst and Thompson (1996), for example, have argued that by some measures (for example, international trade and capital flows) the world economy was actually more open and integrated in the decades leading up to the First World War (1870–1914). Their assessment is that we currently inhabit an international rather than globalized world economy in which the role of the nation state and its policy formulations is still critical.

Neither of these perspectives can take us very far towards a meaningful analysis of globalization, however. Once we look beyond the rhetoric and anecdotal evidence offered up by the hyperglobalists, we see a world riven by huge social and geographic inequalities, and exhibiting widely varying degrees of global interconnection and interdependency. Equally, *contra* the sceptics, the global economy of today is clearly profoundly different from that of the late nineteenth century in terms of the degree and nature of international economic interactions. To progress any further, we need to develop a middle way or *transformationalist* perspective which sees globalization as an ongoing set of processes that are increasing in extensity and intensity, but are not even close to approaching any kind of homogenized end state of universal global interconnection. From this perspective, globalization represents changes in the *nature* of the world economy, rather than an epochal shift to a global mode of organization.

We need, moreover, to have an effective working definition of globalization if it is to have analytical purchase on real world dynamics. As we have already seen, as a term globalization is now so widely and commonly used – often simply to refer to any aspect of human life that has an international component – that in many cases it has been evacuated of any useful meaning. As economic geographers, we need to be clear about the kinds of economic processes to which we are attributing the term. Hence, a key element of developing a transformationalist position is (following Dicken et al., 1997) to distinguish processes

of globalization from those of *internationalization*. Internationalization refers to the simple extension of economic activity across national borders, reflecting a *quantitative* change in the extent of economic activity. Globalization, on the other hand, is best thought of as a relative increase in the *functional integration* or interdependency of economic activity across global space and is therefore reflective of *qualitative* changes in the nature of cross-national economic activities.

Once this distinction has been established, we can see that the contemporary global economy is characterized by a much *deeper* form of integration than that of 1870–1914 (see for example Dicken et al., 1997). Indeed, while until 1950 the world economy could effectively be described as a series of relatively self-contained national economies engaged in arms-length trade, a far more interconnected and integrated global system has subsequently developed through intersecting and overlapping processes of internationalization *and* globalization, the intensity and speed of which have accelerated since the 1970s. These changes are reflected, for example, in growing levels of international trade, foreign direct investment and capital flows, and the growing number of transnational corporations (TNCs), international strategic alliances and international subcontracting networks. While there is not space here to profile and map these dynamics in detail (for such an analysis, see Dicken, 2007), the following statistics give an impression of the magnitude of this change in both the scale and nature of international economic activity. By way of a baseline comparison, total world Gross Domestic Product (GDP) increased fourfold from US$12,000bn to US$48,245bn over the period 1982–2006 (UNCTAD, 2007):

- World trade expanded more than fivefold over the period 1980–2006, with exports of merchandise and commercial services rising from US$2400bn to US$14839bn (www.wto.org);
- Global stocks of foreign direct investment grew twenty-fold over the period 1980–2006, rising from US$616bn to US$12,474bn (UNCTAD, 2007);

- Cross-border mergers and acquisitions have grown substantially: for the year 1987 the total value of such transactions was US$74.5bn, but in 2006 the figure was US$880bn, although it has risen as high as US$1143bn in 2000 (UNCTAD, 2007);
- International strategic alliances now proliferate: just over 42,000 cross-border deals were signed in the period 1989–1999, accounting for 68% of all strategic alliances (Kang and Sakai, 2000);
- In the early 1990s there were some 37,000 TNCs with 170,000 foreign affiliates: by 2006 there were some 78,000 TNCs, with 780,000 overseas affiliates generating US$25,177bn in sales and employing 72.6 million workers (UNCTAD, 2007);
- The average daily turnover of foreign exchange on the world's currency markets was US$2900bn in 2006, as compared to US$590bn in 1989;
- In terms of international migration, in 2005 it was estimated that 190 million people were living outside the country of their birth, a figure which had more than doubled from the 1970 figure of 81 million (and a rise from 2.2 to 3.0 percent of the total global population) (http://esa.un.org/migration/);
- International tourist arrivals have grown from 287 million in 1980 to 846 million by 2006, with associated revenues of US$733bn (www.world-tourism.org).

The global economy is also characterized by the growing geographic complexity of these transnational flows and linkages, with more and more – but by no means all – countries and sectors being brought into their purview. In order to further understand this complexity we next need to explore the notion of *spatial divisions of labour*.

SPATIAL DIVISIONS OF LABOUR

The term division of labour describes the way in which different groups of workers are allocated to different productive tasks. We can think of various kinds of divisions of labour. The social division of labour points to the division of workers into different sectors of activity (for example software workers or steel workers). The technical division of labour speaks to how production processes are divided into different tasks which are in turn allocated to specialized workers (for

example managers, supervisors, administrators, researchers, assembly workers). The gender division of labour recognizes how certain jobs tend to be assigned to men or women within society (for example male merchant bankers or female nurses). What is central to our current discussion, however, is the notion of the spatial division of labour, which refers to the way in which particular sectors and/or elements of the production process are concentrated in particular places. In essence, it is about mapping, and explaining, the geographical nature of the social, technical and gender divisions of labour within society.

The concept of the spatial division of labour was elucidated particularly well in the work of Massey (1984), who explored how these spatial variations are both created and exploited by the ongoing restructuring of capitalist firms in their pursuit of profit (see also Chapters 17 and 25). Although Massey's analysis is nuanced and intricate, following Peck (1996: 156), we can summarize her central argument in five steps:

- Growing global competition is driving corporate restructuring;
- Corporate restructuring is leading to the separation of the control functions performed by managerial workers from the execution functions undertaken by manual workers, as social and technical divisions of labour deepen;
- This functional separation of control from execution is an increasingly geographical process, with the different functions being located in places that offer an appropriate labour supply. Most simply, low-skilled manual tasks are located in peripheral areas, while managerial and R&D tasks are undertaken in core cities and their immediate hinterlands;
- As different processes of corporate restructuring ensue, layers of investment spread across the economic landscape, creating new production geographies and redefining the nature of relationships between places as they gain or lose different kinds of economic activities. In particular, shifting patterns of control functions will alter relations of dependency between different places;
- New spatial divisions of labour are created through the complex interactions between new layers of investment and the pre-existing

economic activities in a particular place. These interactions will take on different forms in different places.

In short, the spatial division of labour is a concept that reveals the reciprocal relations between processes of economic restructuring and the particularities of places.

Different spatial divisions of labour are underlain by different corporate structures. Most simply, we can distinguish between *cloning* and *part-process* structures. In the cloning structure, the production apparatus is simply replicated in different localities, with ultimate control residing in headquarters situated in one particular production branch (usually the initial place of origin of the firm). In the part-process format, there is a technical division of labour between branch plants, with components being made in one location and passed on to another for final assembly. Three points follow from this. First, the different stages of the production process may have different labour requirements, and hence tend towards different kinds of location. Second, these spatial divisions of labour can be constructed through either inter-firm (externalized) or intra-firm (internalized) networks. Third, and most importantly, this part-process format increases the level of interdependency within the system as assembly in one place cannot occur without the supply of components from another. Moreover, it reveals the significance of external control, with potentially vital decisions about operations in a particular place being taken in another locality.

How, though, can these ideas inform the globalization debate? Importantly, spatial divisions of labour can be organized at a range of spatial scales. Massey's theory was grounded in a detailed empirical analysis of intra-national spatial restructuring in the UK economy in the 1960s and 1970s, in which she described the emergence of a new spatial division of labour in manufacturing based upon a separation of skilled and managerial tasks (performed in many cases in London and the Southeast) from unskilled

manufacturing work done in so-called branch plants (located in areas such as Northeast England and Southeast Wales). However, one of the defining characteristics of the global economy over the last two to three decades has been the dramatic increase in the number of firms (i.e. TNCs) organizing their spatial divisions of labour at the international scale.

More specifically, using the work of Dicken (2007), we can delimit at least four different forms of TNC production organization:

- *Globally concentrated production*: products are made in a single place and then exported to foreign markets;
- *Host-market production*: each national market is served by its own production unit, meaning there are no sales across national borders;
- *Product specialization for a regional or global market*: production units specialize in production of one product for sales throughout a regional, or occasionally global, market;
- *Transnational vertical integration*: each unit performs a distinct part of the production process. The units may be aligned in a chain sequence, or one plant may assemble components from a variety of suppliers.

This last category is particularly important: globalization, as defined in this chapter, depicts the emergence of functionally-integrated, part-process spatial divisions of labour at the global scale. With this conceptual apparatus in place, we can now move on to consider the historical emergence and development of these different kinds of divisions of labour in the global economy.

INTERNATIONAL DIVISIONS OF LABOUR

It is helpful to distinguish between three separate attempts to conceptualize international spatial divisions of labour, which broadly coincide with different phases of development of the global economy.

The International Division of Labour (IDL)

First, it is possible to identify the traditional *International Division of Labour* (IDL) that took shape by the nineteenth century and prevailed largely unaltered until the 1950s. The IDL essentially depicted a trading system characterized by shallow integration. The theories of classical economists, and in particular Ricardo's notion of comparative advantage – which stated that countries would specialize in producing goods for which they had a comparative cost advantage, and import those for which they did not – have often been used to explain its emergence. In this system, shaped initially by global trading empires, and later by the rise of the USA as an economic power, the developing world or 'periphery' was largely relegated to providing raw materials and agricultural plantation products (for example, coffee from Brazil, copper from Chile, gold and diamonds from South Africa) for the industrialized economies of the 'core' (Western Europe and the USA). High-value manufactured goods were exchanged between the industrialized countries, and some were exported back to developing countries which therefore performed a dual role as both sources of raw materials and markets for finished products. The economies of scale achieved in the core countries, combined with control over production technologies, allowed them to undercut local production in the colonies of Latin America, Africa, Asia and Oceania.

Writing in the second half of the nineteenth, Karl Marx described the IDL thus: 'one suited to the requirements of the main industrial countries, and it converts one part of the globe into a chiefly agricultural field of production for supplying the other part which remains a pre-eminently industrial field' (1976: 579–580). In essence, this was a *dependent* form of economic development in developing countries: while they often possessed abundant natural resources and large labour pools, their economies became dominated by agricultural and mineral exports to the industrialized countries. In turn, the IDL was underpinned by the financial power of banks in the core which made the profits of the system available for reinvestment. However, *contra* the assumptions of the classical economists, this was not an open trading system in which all parties benefited, rather it was an unequal regime – created, imposed and sustained through the exercise of political power as part of an imperialist project – in which the developing world was dependent on the core for markets, capital and technology. For critical scholars such as Samir Amin (1976) and Andre Gunder Frank (1976), the resultant economic underdevelopment of the developing world was actively produced by an inherently unfair IDL (see Chapter 6).

The New International Division of Labour (NIDL)

From the 1960s onwards, a New International Division of Labour (NIDL) supposedly started to emerge in which certain developing countries took on new roles within the global economy through the investment strategies of TNCs. The NIDL thesis described the establishment by European, North American and Japanese TNCs of a global manufacturing system based on establishing labour-intensive export platforms in so-called 'newly industrializing economies' (NIEs). The NIDL theory, proposed most explicitly by Fröbel et al. (1980), argued that falling rates of profitability in manufacturing production in core countries were combining with market saturation and under-consumption as market growth lagged behind productivity increases. In response, TNCs used their global reach to relocate production from the industrial core to low-cost production sites in the NIEs; the manufactured goods were then in turn exported back to core markets from the offshore branch plants. Crucially, the system depended on new technologies that allowed production fragmentation, thereby creating tasks that could use often young and female, semi-skilled or unskilled workers in the periphery. Two kinds of technology were important: process technologies that allowed the subdivision of the manufacturing process into simple and self-contained tasks, and transportation technologies such as jet aircraft and containerized shipping that allowed the efficient shipment of both components and finished goods. Under the NIDL, world trade increasingly consisted of flows of parts and components between plants of the same company located in different countries.

Fröbel et al.'s analysis was based on detailed empirical analysis of three phenomena: the international relocation of German-owned textile and garment production over the period from 1960–1975 both within Europe, and beyond to North Africa and Asia; similar trends across a broader range of German manufacturing industries; and the emergence of 'free production zones' (which increasingly became known as Export Processing Zones) across countries in Africa, Latin America and Asia. The appearance of these designated zones for export production – often offering a range of tax incentives – from the 1960s onwards as the most obvious physical manifestation of the emerging NIDL. Coming from a neo-Marxist standpoint, the NIDL thesis was in part a critical examination of the consequences of these shifts for workers at both ends of this new spatial division of labour. For the industrial core, it was argued that the result of this new cost-based import competition was deindustrialization and widespread job losses. For the NIEs that received inward investment, a new form of dependent development was created in which the new manufacturing platforms offered low skill employment and were only weakly connected to the local economy (Fröbel et al., 1980).

One of the first attempts to theorize these developments from the TNC perspective can be found in the work of Hymer (1975). He argued that there was nothing inevitable about the course of action chosen by TNCs in the 1960s and 1970s, which could equally have chosen to take their mass produced consumer products to global markets. Instead, they opted to pursue the higher rates of profit

available from broadening the range of products produced for richer markets, and did so more efficiently through establishing a hierarchical division of labour that saw strategic decision making and control functions concentrated in the major cities of developed countries, and day-to-day operations and productive activities widely dispersed across the globe in response to the pull of labour, markets and materials. Hymer (1975: 38) likened this new 'regime of North Atlantic Multinational Corporations' to 'a new Imperial system' which would perpetuate uneven development as only low wage employment was being relocated, the profits from which were in turn being repatriated to the industrialized economies. In short, value being created by TNCs in the NIEs would not necessarily remain there (for more on Hymer, see Chapter 25).

Overall, the NIDL pointed to the growth of production in the global periphery through the very same forces – trade, capital flows, and TNCs – that were seen to block development there in the IDL regime (Fagan and Webber, 1999). The changing geography of the global economy in the 1960s and 1970s seemed to offer support to the NIDL thesis. Between 1953 and 1980, the developed countries' share of world manufacturing output fell from 95% to 82% while the developing countries share expanded from 5% to 18%. Throughout the 1970s and 1980s, the Asian 'tiger' NIEs of Singapore, Hong Kong, South Korea and Taiwan were recording average growth rates of over 10% per year in terms of both manufacturing output and exports, while strong growth rates were also exhibited by India, Brazil and Mexico. As globalization processes have accelerated since the 1980s, however, a number of important limitations with the NIDL thesis have become readily apparent.

Critiquing the NIDL

Since its initial formulation, subsequent developments in the global economy have revealed the NIDL to be a major simplification of a complex and rapidly shifting reality. In effect, the thesis describes a specific form of IDL that has developed in a restricted range of labour-intensive manufacturing activities (for example, garments, electronic components, consumer goods), rather than a new global mode of growth. What Fröbel et al. identified in their work is perhaps best thought of as one element of the TNC-investment driven globalization that has profoundly re-shaped the global economy over the last three decades. For a number of important reasons, therefore, the NIDL has limited utility for describing and explaining contemporary patterns of global economic interaction:

- It underplays the ongoing importance of the 'traditional' IDL in a range of natural resource and agribusiness sectors – such as oil, gold, coffee and cocoa – which continue to be dominated by Western TNCs and markets.
- The range of NIE economies has broadened and deepened considerably. By the 1990s, the first wave NIEs of East Asia and Latin America had been joined by a second wave of economies exhibiting strong growth rates in terms of both output and exports, most notably, India, Malaysia, Thailand, Indonesia, the Philippines, and China. By 2000, the leading 13 NIEs were accounting for 16% of global production and 23% of global merchandise exports.
- The thesis over-emphasizes the role of cheap offshore competition in causing job losses in developed countries, underplaying the role of technological and organizational change within those economies driving redundancies through productivity increases, for example. Put another way, it overstates the significance of cheap labour and absolute notions of surplus value (i.e. that created by increasing the amount of time worked) at the expense of relative notions of surplus value (for example, that created by increasing the intensity and productivity of labour).
- It does not give enough emphasis to the importance of state policies in the NIEs–such as the provision of subsidies and low tax rates, labour market flexibility, low levels of unionization, protection of domestic capital and the use of non-tariff trade barriers – for securing inward investment and driving economic growth. The heavily state-managed form of export-orientated

growth that emerged in the Asian tiger economies has been particularly significant.
- The thesis underplays rising levels of investment by TNCs into the NIEs, for example in the motor vehicle and chemical industries, to access fast growing domestic markets rather than labour pools. China and India, for example, are now attracting huge amounts of market-orientated inward FDI.
- It downplays the importance of local capital in the NIEs within the global economic system, for example in terms of joint ventures with foreign TNCs, and local firms plugged into international systems through subcontracting and franchising relationships. Moreover, levels of outward investment from TNCs based in the NIEs have been growing strongly. While such investments were negligible until the beginning of the 1990s, outward FDI from developing countries accounted for over 13% of the world total stock, and 14% of world flows (US$1600bn and US$175bn respectively) by 2006 (UNCTAD, 2007). The four Asian tigers, along with China, Malaysia and Brazil, account for a huge proportion of these flows, however. While much of this investment has been from 'first wave' NIEs into 'second wave' countries (for example, from Singapore to China), leading TNCs from these countries (for example, South Korea's Samsung and LG) have undertaken significant investments into developed countries.
- It overlooks the continuing high levels of TNC investment between developed countries: in 2006, for example, 66% of inward FDI went to developed economies, with the European Union alone receiving 41% of the global total. Interestingly, this is a reversal of the traditional IDL which saw 65% of global FDI going to developing economies back in 1938 (UNCTAD, 2007).
- Despite the manufacturing focus of the NIDL thesis, international divisions of labour are becoming increasingly apparent in service sectors. The world's inward stock of service FDI grew sevenfold over the period 1990–2005, from an estimated US$869bn to over US$6,111bn, and its share of the world FDI stock rose from 49% to 61% (its was only 25% in the early 1970s) (UNCTAD, 2007). While traditionally these flows have been dominated by trading and financial service TNCs, other service sectors such as electricity, telecommunications, water supply and business services have risen to prominence. Although much of this investment is of the market-orientated 'branch plant' variety, functional

or 'part-process' divisions of labour are also now emerging with respect to call centres, routine or back office functions, IT services and also for certain research and development operations (UNCTAD, 2004, 2005). For example, many Western transnational financial service firms now find it advantageous to conduct routine clerical functions in overseas sites – Ireland, India and the Caribbean are prime examples – with low cost, English-speaking workers.

Putting these various elements together, we can see that the global economy that has developed apace over the last two to three decades is considerably more sectorally and geographically complex than the one being described by Fröbel and colleagues in the 1970s. How, then, might we conceptualize this new global system?

The new global division of labour?

The contemporary global economy is clearly not characterized by one single type of IDL but rather many different forms. Rather than disappearing, the traditional IDL and the NIDL remain important in a range of industries (for example, natural resources and clothing/toys, respectively) and have subsequently been overlain by, and interacted with, newer and more complex international divisions of labour. There have been many attempts to try and conceptualize this system. While Coffey (1996) continued to use the language of core and periphery in his characterization of a 'newer' international division of labour, for many the sectoral and spatial complexity within the world economy has become far more intricate than the simple core-periphery model implicit in the IDL and NIDL approaches. As Held et al. (1999:429) observe, 'the old North-South hierarchy has given way to a more complex geometry of global economic and productive power relations…under conditions of globalization distributional patterns of power and wealth no longer accord with a core and periphery division of the world, as in the early twentieth century, but reflect a new geography of

power and privilege which transcends political borders and regions'.

This complex geometry is captured, in part at least, in the various notions of the 'newest' IDL, the 'global division of labour and power', and the 'new global' division of labour. For Castells (1996: 147, emphasis in original):

> the newest international division of labor is constructed around four different positions in the informational/global economy: the producers of high value, based on informational labor; the producers of high-volume, based on lower-cost labor; the producers of raw materials, based on natural endowments; and the redundant producers, reduced to devalued labor... The critical matter is that these different positions do not coincide with countries. *They are organized in networks and flows, using the technological infrastructure of the informational economy.*

These geographies contribute to what Mittelamn (2000: 41) refers to as the global division of labour and power. This notion stresses less the networked geographies of production than the varied geographies across which globalization takes place and is formed:

> What is new about the contemporary period is the manner of and extent to which domestic political economies are penetrated by global phenomena. There is no single wave of globalization washing over or flattening diverse divisions of labour both in regions and industrial branches... Varied regional divisions of labour are emerging, tethered in different ways to global structures, each one engaged in unequal transactions with world centres of production and finance and presented with distinctive developmental possibilities. Within each region, subglobal hierarchies have formed, with poles of economic growth, managerial and technological centres, and security systems.

For Dicken (2003: 9, emphasis in original):

> [T]hese developments signify the emergence of a *new global division of labour*... the straightforward exchange between core and peripheral areas, based upon a broad division of labour, has been transformed into a highly complex, kaleidoscopic structure involving the *fragmentation* of many production processes and their *geographical relocation* on a global scale in ways that slice

through national boundaries... Both old and new economic activities are involved in this re-sorting of the global jigsaw puzzle in ways that also reflect the development of technologies of transportation and communications, of corporate organization and of the production process itself... Today, the nature and the geography of the global economy are being transformed further by a shift towards an *information*, or *knowledge-driven*, economy...

Taking these three related but different perspectives together, we can discern the following six key characteristics of today's global economic system. First, the complexity of international divisions of labour is continually increasing. In many sectors, increasingly complex 'part-process' structures are developing, enabled by ongoing developments in transport, communication and process technologies. Most profoundly, the combined processing and communication power of personal computers and the Internet allows the close control and monitoring of complicated and spatially-extensive production systems, supported by highly efficient logistics, container and air-freight operations. A personal computer hard disk drive assembled and tested in Singapore, for example, may represent the final stage of a manufacturing process linking together operations in the USA, China, Thailand, Malaysia, Indonesia and the Philippines.

Second, there is a general trend for firms to make more use of *externalized* networks (extra-firm relationships) as compared to *internalized* networks (intra-firm relationships) when constructing international spatial divisions of labour. This dynamic is reflected in the growing levels of international subcontracting and strategic alliances. For Dicken (2003), this necessitates a broadening of the definition of a TNC to reflect the fact that a firm can coordinate and control foreign operations without owning them. Sports gear manufacturers Nike and Reebok, for example, exert very tight control over their webs of suppliers across Asia, but do so through contractual terms and conditions rather than direct ownership. Other sectors such as car and electronics manufacturing are also characterized by extremely complex tiers of subcontractors.

Third, while spatial divisions of labour have always been fluid and shifting, they are arguably becoming more dynamic and liable to rapid change at the international level. This flexibility derives from the use of certain technologies and organizational forms that enable the fast spatial switching of productive capacity. In particular, by using often spatially disparate external networks of suppliers and subcontractors, firms can quickly switch contracts between different firms and places without incurring the costs of moving production themselves. The speed of circulation within the global economy has also dramatically increased, not only in terms of knowledge and products through advanced communication and logistics systems respectively, but also with respect to the vast sums of capital that circulate through the globally-integrated financial system.

Fourth, the global economy is distinctly regionalized, particularly around the three key 'triad' regions of North America, Europe, and East and Southeast Asia which together account for approximately 85% of world manufacturing production, 80% of world merchandise trade, and are the source for 80% of the world's stock of FDI. Regionalization, in this context, refers to the functional integration of economic activities across contiguous groupings of countries rather than at the global scale (Dicken, 2007). These regional systems are created and shaped by the interplay between the regional production strategies of TNCs and the policies of regional economic blocs (such as the EU, NAFTA, APEC and ASEAN) as both seek to reap the benefits of regional economic integration. For TNCs, pursuing functional integration at the regional scale may reflect the limit of economies of scale for certain manufacturing processes, allow greater customization and quick delivery for differentiated markets, and facilitate more effective management and control of subsidiaries (Dicken, 2005). The result is regional economies that are highly internally diverse. Mittelman (2000), for instance, describes a stratified 'Asian regional division of labour' that ranges from the global cities of Hong Kong and Singapore to the intensive manufacturing of China's coastal provinces.

Fifth, as both Castells (1996) and Dicken (2003) make clear, we are witnessing relative increases in the information or knowledge intensity of production systems. In contemporary capitalism, productivity and competitiveness depend heavily on the ability to generate, process and apply different forms of knowledge. This is reflected in the way that many developed country TNCs are outsourcing basic production activities in order to focus more fully on tasks such as research and development, marketing and branding.

Sixth, and finally, it has become clear that the key organizational unit of the global economy is no longer either the national economy, as it was in the IDL, or the TNC and its internalized networks, as it was in the NIDL. Rather, it is perhaps more productive to think of the regionally or globally extensive *chains* or *networks* of connections that are involved in the production of different goods and services. Gereffi and Korceniewicz (1994: 2) propose that we analyse *Global Commodity Chains* (GCCs): 'sets of interorganizational networks clustered around one commodity or product, linking households, enterprises, and states to one another within the world-economy'. Relatedly, Coe et al. (2004: 471) conceptualize the *Global Production Network* (GPN) as 'the globally organized nexus of interconnected functions and operations of firms and non-firm institutions through which goods and services are produced, distributed and consumed'. The key to such approaches is that they explore the fluid intra-, inter- and extra-firm network linkages that constitute contemporary production systems, and consider the developmental implications for the various places they connect.

In combination, these six attributes reveal the rapid intensification of globalization processes over the past two-to-three decades. How though, can we characterize the on-the-ground geographies of this evolving global economy? Clearly, the geographies being created by these complex and over-lapping global divisions of labour are extremely uneven.

Globalization is not spatially homogenizing, but instead depends upon, and contributes to, uneven geographic development at different scales. Different territories are integrated into the global system to greater or lesser extents, and some are currently excluded almost entirely (for example, sub-Saharan Africa). Following Dicken (2007), it is helpful to consider this unevenness at various scales. At the *macro*-scale, as described above, the world economy is dominated by the three triad zones of North America, Europe, and East and Southeast Asia. At the *meso*-scale there is a variety of trans-border clusters and corridors of economic activity that functionally bind together a variety of urban centres. In East Asia, for example, we can think of the intense interconnections and investments between Taiwan, Hong Kong, and the coastal provinces of Southern China. At the *micro*-scale, economic activity is ultimately located in individual places, and most typically in urban areas of all sizes, from small villages and towns to massive capital cities. As we have seen, globalization has meant that these key cities and their hinterlands – 'city-regions' – are increasingly interdependent and interconnected through different kinds of global production networks. Accordingly, the metaphor of *nodes in global networks* is perhaps the most effective way of describing the real-world geographies of the global economy (Amin and Thrift, 1992).

CONCLUSION

'The world is flat' opined the New York Times journalist Thomas Friedman in his 2005 book of the same name. Friedman's (2005: 10) somewhat speculative and anecdotal analysis describes a new era of globalization from the year 2000 onwards that has been 'shrinking the world from a size small to a size tiny and flattening the playing field at the same time' and in which fibre-optic networks and new forms of software allow individuals all over the world – rather than states or companies – to connect to, and compete within, the global economy.

An economic-geographical perspective, however, suggests a rather different reality. The defining characteristic of the global economy is not its evenness, but rather its huge spatial variability. The world is not flat: rather it has massive peaks and troughs in terms of power, wealth, connectivity and control. This contemporary system is far too complex to characterize as one particular kind of international division of labour. The precise form of interconnection and interdependency will vary from place to place, from sector to sector, and ultimately, can be delineated only at the level of a particular global production network. Equally, thinking back to the arguments around the new international division of labour (Fröbel et al., 1980) outlined above, these forms are not shaped either by states or TNCs, but the *interaction* between these two key agents of the global economy. In some cases the state – and the regional and supra-national institutions of which they are a part – may have the upper hand; in others, TNCs will be dominant; and, in some instances, they will work together to promote economic development whilst, in others, they will be rivals.

Dealing with this complexity, and the speed of change in the global economy, poses significant conceptual problems. The current rates of economic development in Central and Eastern Europe, China and India, for example, may necessitate further adjustments to frames of understanding and interpretation. This ongoing interplay between theory and reality is both inevitable, and necessary. One thing remains clear, however: without the benefits of a critical economic-geographical perspective, our understanding of this global system is severely limited.

REFERENCES:

Amin, A. and Thrift, N. (1992) Neo-Marshallian nodes in global networks. *International Journal of Urban and Regional Research*, 16: 571–87.

Amin, S. (1976) *Unequal Development*. New York: Monthly Review Press.

Cameron, A. and Palan, R. (2004) *The Imagined Economies of Globalization*. London: SAGE.

Castells, M. (1996) *The Rise of the Network Society*. Oxford: Blackwell.

Coe, N.M., Hess, M., Yeung, H.W.-C., Dicken, P. and Henderson, J. (2004) Globalizing regional development: A global production networks perspective. *Transactions of the Institute of British Geographers*, 29: 468–84.

Coffey, W.J. (1996) The 'newer' international division of labour. In P.W. Daniels and W.F. Lever (eds) *The Global Economy in Transition*. Harlow: Longman. pp. 40–61.

Dicken, P. (2003) *Global Shift: Reshaping the Global Economic Map in the 21st Century*, (4th edn). London: SAGE.

Dicken, P. (2004) Geographers and 'globalization': (yet) another missed boat? *Transactions of the Institute of British Geographers*, 29: 5–26.

Dicken, P. (2005) Tangled webs: Transnational production networks and regional integration, *SPACES Working Paper 2005–04*, Faculty of Geography, Philipps-University of Marburg, Germany.

Dicken, P. (2007) *Global Shift: Mapping the Changing Contours of the World Economy*, (5th edn). London: SAGE.

Dicken, P., Peck, J. and Tickell, A. (1997) Unpacking the global. In R. Lee and J. Wills (eds) *Geographies of Economies*. London: Arnold. pp. 158–66.

Fagan, R.H. and Webber, M. (1999) *Global Restructuring: The Australian Experience*, (2nd edn). Melbourne: Oxford University Press.

Frank, A.G. (1976) *Capitalism and Uneven Development in Latin America* New York: Monthly Review Press.

Friedman, T.L. (2005) *The World is Flat: A Brief History of the Twenty-first Century*. New York: Farrar, Straus and Giroux.

Fröbel, F., Heinrichs, J. and Kreye, O. (1980) *The New International Division of Labour*. Cambridge: Cambridge University Press.

Gereffi, G. and Korzeniewicz, M. (1994) (eds) *Commodity Chains and Global Capitalism*. Westport: Praeger.

Held, D., McGrew, A., Goldblatt, D. and Perraton, J. (1999) *Global Transformations: Politics, Economics and Culture*. Cambridge: Polity Press.

Hirst, P. and Thompson, G. (1996) *Globalization in Question*. Cambridge: Polity Press.

Hymer, S. (1975) The multinational corporation and the law of uneven development. In H. Radice (ed.) *International Firms and Modern Imperialism: Selected Readings*. Harmondsworth: Penguin.

Kang, N-H. and Sakai, K. (2000) International strategic alliances. *Directorate of Science, Technology and Industry Working Paper 2000/5*. Paris: OECD.

Kelly, P.F. (1999) The geographies and politics of globalization. *Progress in Human Geography*, 23: 379–400.

Levitt, T. (1983) The globalization of markets. *Harvard Business Review*, 61: 92–102.

Markusen, A. (1999) Fuzzy concepts, scanty evidence, policy distance: The case for rigor and policy relevance in critical regional studies. *Regional Studies*, 33: 869–84.

Marx, K. (1976) *Capital Volume 1*. Harmondsworth: Penguin.

Massey, D. (1984) *Spatial Divisions of Labour*. London: Macmillan.

Mittelman, J.H. (2000) *The Globalization Syndrome: Transformation and Resistance*. Princeton, NJ: Princeton University Press.

Ohmae, K. (1995) *The End of the Nation State*. London: HarperCollins.

Peck, J. (1996) *Workplace: The Social Regulation of Labour Markets*. New York: Guilford Press.

UNCTAD (2004) *World Investment Report 2004*. Geneva: UN.

UNCTAD (2005) *World Investment Report 2005*. Geneva: UN.

UNCTAD (2007) *World Investment Report 2007*. Geneva: UN.

6

The Consequences of Economic Globalization

Peter Sunley

INTRODUCTION

The first few years of the twenty-first century witnessed a global economic boom and a dramatic increase in the intensity and extensity of global economic integration. It was no coincidence that this period also saw a wave of highly optimistic, liberal diagnoses of globalization and its consequences. As Bisley (2007:16) remarked 'the supporters of a largely economic version of globalization and those who present it as a positive and universal force are, at present, largely in the ascendancy.' The eminent economist Jeffrey Sachs (2005), for example, recently argued that the latest dramatic round of globalization represents a momentous transition from an era of world economic divergence and North Atlantic dominance that prevailed between 1750 and 1950, to process of convergence. He suggests that the forces of divergence unleashed by the first industrial revolution and reinforced by colonialism have finally been superseded as globalization diffuses ideas and technological capacity. The opening of previously closed economies and the

adoption of liberalization policies in China, Russia and India have roughly doubled the size of labour force in the integrating world economic system (Venables, 2006). On current trends, by 2025 the Chinese economy measured by GDP will be larger than that of the US and by 2050 that of India will also be larger. According to Sachs (2005:187), 'The overwhelming dominance of the West, which lasted half a millennium, is probably *passé*'. In this view, the integration of trade, production, finance and the spread of global treaties and conventions acts to spread economic growth through the diffusion of technologies to those countries that adopt open liberal economic policies. In similar fashion Wolf (2004) celebrated the benign consequences of liberal globalization, which in his view provided a golden opportunity for growth and poverty reduction. While Wolf conceded that global finance was somewhat different from trade, he nevertheless asserted that the liberalization of money flows was also desirable. Finally, in a more populist and extreme version of this liberal optimism, Friedman (2006) identified a historical turning point involving the emergence of a world-wide creative and collaborative network or platform. In a typically brash and hyperbolic phrase he argued, 'This platform now operates without regard to geography, distance time, and, in the near future, even language. Going forward, this platform is going to be at the centre of everything' (ibid., 205).

In the light of the recent turbulence in the world economy, some of the claims of this liberal optimism have quickly been exposed as exaggerations and statements of faith. But what processes generated these ideas, and what remains of this interpretation of the consequences of economic globalization? In some contrast, economic geographers have been far more cautious and ambivalent about the implications of globalization. It may be true that, with some notable exceptions, economic geographers have made only a limited contribution to globalization debates (Dicken, 2004). Nevertheless their lower profile and hesitant evaluation of globalization has better withstood the test of time. By the late 1990s geography came to a something of a consensus regarding the first principles shaping the complex outcomes of globalization (see Coe and Yeung, 2001). This insisted that economic globalization is a profoundly contradictory set of processes that have much more uneven and indeterminate dynamics than an underlying structural trend to convergence would imply. As Dicken et al. (1997) argued, globalization is a complex of inter-related processes which are not free floating but constituted through these economic and institutional contexts. 'As with all processes, globalization is realized unevenly, interacts in unpredictable ways with counter- and co-functioning processes and melds in a complex and contingent fashion with extant (historically and geographically specific) institutional and economic structures' (ibid., 166). Thus the continued importance of place and territory is not a refutation of globalization, as processes at different scales are interactive rather than alternatives (Kelly, 1999).

The aim of this chapter is to argue that, despite the appearance of new and intensified forms of globalization, this geographical interpretation remains a more helpful and convincing starting point for understanding their consequences than versions of the liberal transformation model. Liberal economic accounts of globalization certainly appreciate the immense significance of the geographical changes involved in the growth of China and the other large industrializing economies. However, underlying these ideas is the notion that global market integration must eventually generate some sort of spatial equilibrium in which opportunity, income and prosperity eventually converge. While globalization undoubtedly has both beneficial and detrimental dimensions, this chapter argues that there is little evidence to suggest that recent developments in the forms of economic globalization represent the start of a process of global convergence. The belief that economic globalization means a movement to a flat equilibrium is highly optimistic and over-generalized and underestimates the importance of several key themes in the geographical literature.

The first of these themes is that globalization is a deeply contradictory creature as it acts to erode some geographical differences at the same time as it builds new forms of agglomeration and localization (Bisley, 2007). As Storper (2003) has argued, we should recognize the resolute significance of an economy of territories or places, composed of institutions and connections at local, regional and national scales, as well as the massively increased economy of global flows and networks. Using the example of outsourcing and supply chains, the chapter argues that both types of economy are changing but this does not mean that one is superseding or replacing the other. The second relevant theme in geographical discussions of economic globalization is that the regulatory or governance context, at various scales, exerts a key influence on its outcomes (Harvey, 2006). Despite the growth of non-state and network forms of governance, nation-states, both individually and collectively, continue to be a core component of this context, even as their forms and functions have been changed by globalization and its powerful constituent discourses (Kelly, 1999; Hay, 2008; Yeung, 1998). In this way, the outcomes of globalization are politically negotiated and mediated (Tickell and Peck, 2003).

As a consequence of these fundamental points, recent economic globalization has amplified key instabilities and vulnerabilities which are downplayed in liberal visions of opportunity and convergence. Given capitalism's constant innovation and search for profit, it is well known that its geography is marked by an incessant spatial form of creative destruction in which regional and urban economies rise and fall (Storper and Walker, 1989). However, this tendency has been intensified by the fast motion and connectivity of the contemporary global economy. In the context of a neo-liberal, market-friendly regulatory framework, economic globalization has created and amplified certain engines of instability which produce volatile crises and recessions which cascade across highly interconnected and permeable economies. The third section of the chapter outlines how the expansion of global finance and credit, and its interaction with trade circuits, has created an intensely powerful source of instability. The growth of production networks and new territorial agglomerations has taken place within a particular configuration of trade and financial systems that, ironically, has been termed 'supercapitalism' (Reich, 2008). The tumultuous financial crisis between 2007 and 2009 brought this period to an abrupt and costly halt so that the future geography of globalization will be much more uncertain and complex than a process of global dispersion.

UNBUNDLING AND RE-TERRITORIALIZATION

It is now well known that the last few decades of the twentieth century witnessed a spectacular integration of the global economy through flows of goods, capital, ideas and, to a lesser extent, people. Between 1950 and 2000 world merchandise trade increased almost twenty-fold (Dicken, 2007). Foreign direct investment (FDI) has increased markedly in recent years, with most of this increase taking place via mergers and acquisitions. An estimated 73 million workers were employed in foreign affiliates of MNCs in 2006, nearly three times more than in 1990. In 1982, inflows of FDI totalled $59 billion; by 2006 they had grown to $1,306 billion, the second highest annual total ever recorded, the peak total being $1,411 billion in 2000 (UNCTAD, 2007). Of the total stock of world FDI, just over 70% is located in the developed world. However, FDI inflows to China have increased to over $60 billion during the last few years (Thun, 2008).

These rapid increases in trade and multinational investment were, of course, a product of falling transport and communication costs, as well as the liberalization and opening of many economies. The increasing use of 40 foot shipping containers has been particularly important and by 2005 more than 3,500 cargo ships crossed the seas loaded with 15 million containers (Reich, 2008). At the same time, internet-based communication allows the near instantaneous transmission of complex codified information at very low cost. Together these changes have facilitated the rise of a new form of globalization. Baldwin (2006) describes this as a new industrial revolution, based on the unbundling of factories and offices into finely resolved tasks that can be widely spread across space.

The integration of trade has gone hand in hand with the disintegration of production (Feenstra, 1998). Disintegration produces the growth of outsourcing so that tasks previously performed within firms are now being purchased via a market relationship. This has involved the splitting up or fragmentation of activities and their purchase of goods and services from suppliers rather than their in-house supply or manufacture. Where outsourcing transfers jobs from one country to another it is also frequently labelled 'offshoring' (Grossman and Rossi-Hansberg, 2006). The effect is to break-up the production process so that the many tasks required to manufacture goods or provide services are performed in several different locations. Tasks are separated in time and space so that, in one sense, countries are trading in tasks which constitute a production or value chain rather than the discrete goods or services that are produced through such chains. Trade in parts and components has been growing rapidly and is now reportedly 30% of total manufacturing trade (Venables, 2006). Sturgeon (2002) argues that this has led to a new system of manufacture which he terms modular production networks. In this system, lead firms have cut their costs, increased their flexibility and spread the risks of market volatility by contracting their production to large and capable 'turn-key' suppliers with generic manufacturing capabilities. Friedman (2006) provides the example of a Dell laptop computer which involves sourcing of components by 30 companies involved with about 400 suppliers located in North America, Europe but primarily Asia. Another example is the Apple fifth generation i-pod, which is assembled in China by Taiwanese manufacturers. Three of its 10 most costly components are from Japan, two from the US, three from Taiwan and one from Korea (Linden et al., 2008). While the scale of outsourcing is notoriously difficult to establish, according to some estimates, three million US manufacturing jobs were lost as production migrated abroad between 1977 and 1998 (Harrison and McMillan, 2006 cited in McGrew, 2008).

The latest round of globalization has been distinctive in the way in which it has seen the rise of global production networks or global value chains in which leading firms control networks of suppliers (Gereffi, 2005). This produces a growing functional integration of the global economy (Henderson et al., 2002; Dicken, 2007). It has been closely associated with the growth of manufacturing in some developing countries, as the extension of global production networks has dovetailed

with reforms that have reduced trade barriers and converted economies to a market focus. According to Friedman (2006) the expansion of global supply chains represents one of the key forces behind the appearance of a flat world. He argues that ten forces have "flattened" or shrunk the world in economic terms, including the birth of the internet, the development of workflow software, outsourcing and off-shoring, and advances in communication technologies. Rapid technological advance and the spread of ideas have led to the emergence of economic markets that are contestable across the globe. Companies face less friction in allocating tasks to anywhere in the world. In short, Friedman envisages a new economic model based on an open access platform in which people, irrespective of their location, have an unprecedented opportunity to connect and collaborate.

Even in an age of outsourcing, however, this flat world prediction is both an exaggeration and a misperception. It is beyond doubt that developing countries have become important exporters of manufacturing goods in recent years. However, exports of manufactures are highly concentrated in around a dozen economies which include the Asian tiger economies, China, India, and Mexico. In 1996 the top 10 developing country exporters accounted for 88% of developing country manufactured exports (Lall, 1998). The new global distribution of supply chains is in fact more limited than accounts such as Friedman's suggest (Dicken, 2007). As Storper (2003) argues, two types of forces continue to produce spatial concentration of economic activity in the global economy. The first are 'distance to market' effects and the second are linkages and externalities including both traded and untraded relationships between firms. I address each in turn below.

A wave of strong critical reaction to Friedman has stressed that distance remains stubbornly important to international trade and that distance to market and the costs of overcoming distance are still significant. While the freight costs of shipping goods may be as low as 4% of their import value, the gravity model of trade is remarkably persistent so that most countries continue to trade more with their neighbours. The mean effect of distance on trade is about 0.9 which implies that a 10% increase in distance leads to a 9% reduction in international trade flows. Moreover, statistical reviews provide no evidence that this distance effect has weakened in the second half of the twentieth century (Brakman and van Marrewijk, 2007; Disdier and Head, 2008). Hence, on some measures the regionalization of trade within the triad of North America, Europe and East Asia has been more important than the growth of inter-regional trade (Hay, 2008). Part of the reason for this is that perishability and obsolescence mean that the value of many products declines with the time taken to get them to market. Another reason is that the value of a product, such as a complex instrument or engineering tool, depends on information associated with the product (Leamer and Storper, 2001). If this information is embedded in individual people then the costs of shipping it may actually have increased because of rising airport and traffic congestion. Trade costs are also shaped by the frequency and complexity of exchanges so where many firms are disintegrated and externalized trade costs may actually have risen rather than fallen (McCann, 2008).

The second set of effects that mean that the flat world is an illusion are the upstream linkages and externalities associated with agglomeration. Leamer (2007) argues that contestability has increased in recent decades only in sectors characterized by mundane codifiable work. Routine tasks, whether cognitive or manual, are much more susceptible to off-shoring because they can be well-described in rules and symbols, whereas other types of task cannot be captured in a rules-based logic. In many other economic sectors markets continue to be negotiable and embedded in personal relations between people, therefore, high value added activities in services and manufacturing continue to cluster in high wage, high cost locations (McCann,

2008). Tasks that require codifiable information are easy transferred because the knowledge can be expressed in a symbol system. However, tasks that require tacit knowledge based on complex non-codifiable messages are best communicated in face-to-face interchange where visual contact helps to build and maintain personal relationships (Leamer and Storper, 2001). This tends to suggest that there are limits to outsourcing. While it is dominant in some consumer goods markets, most US studies estimate that only 10–20% of the labour force is currently employed in jobs that could be offshored (Baldwin, 2006). Furthermore, tentative attempts to measure the scale of jobs involved so far report relatively small percentages of total employment (Kirkegard, 2007).

As noted earlier, paradoxically the growth of globalization promotes new forms of place-specific territorial connections and relations, and part of this involves the building of new spaces and clusters of industries. As Scott and Storper (2003) argue cities and urban areas can economize on capital intensive infrastructure and thereby benefit from economies of scale. Second, the backward and forward inter-linkages of firms in cities and regions are important sources of productivity gains. Third, the formation of dense local labour markets around multiple workplaces allows firms to raise their productivity and allows workers to raise their incomes. Partly as a result of these effects, globalization has been closely related to the accelerating pace of urbanization and the expanding size of megacities in many countries (Van der Ploeg and Poelhekke, 2008). By 2015 it is projected that 600 million people will live in approximately 60 cities with populations greater than 5 million (Kraas, 2007). Spatial economic disparities in many economies have risen (Kanbur and Venables, 2007). One of the major forces behind this is that each type of global offshoring and network expansion has been associated with the growth of types of regional agglomeration and re-territorialization.

Initially the fragmentation of production generated the first stage of export-oriented industrialization and the growth of labour-intensive assembly jobs in low wage economies. Such jobs were often located in export-processing zones (EPZs) established to attract foreign direct investment through the provision of infrastructure, tax concessions and streamlined administrative procedures. In 1975 there were close to 80 EPZs in 25 countries but by 2002 there were 3000 in 116 countries. However, China accounts for 70–80% of the total EPZ workforce of 43 million workers (Gereffi, 2005). This expansion of this type of labour intensive production has been controlled by large global buyers. For example, in 2003 Walmart spent $15 billion on Chinese-made products and 80% of the 6000 factories in the firm's network of suppliers were in China (Gereffi, 2005). Nike is another well known example (see Donaghu and Barff, 1990). About 75,000 people are employed in the production of shoes and clothing for Nike in Asia, though only a few hundred of these are employees of the company (Feenstra, 1998).

In the context of uncertain markets and constantly shifting product differentiation dense external transactions allow both suppliers and buyers to compensate for variability and uncertainty by providing access to resources at short notice. The globalization of supply chains has furthered the rise of specialized regional agglomerations of dense networks of interrelated producers in sectors such as clothing and consumer goods. For example, the liberalization of the Chinese economy since its adoption of market-oriented reforms in 1978 involved the rapid growth of clusters of clothing and consumer goods industries in coastal provinces and large cities (Fan and Scott, 2003; Wen, 2004). With preferential development policies, coastal provinces such as Guangdong, Jiangsu and Shandong become the sites of marked localization of foreign-led manufacturing clusters (Wen, 2004). The emergence of Southern China occurred as a result of a massive shift of capital from Hong Kong and Taiwan in order to take advantage of lower production costs on the mainland (Scott, 2006). By 2004

China was by far the largest exporter of clothing with an export value nearly $72 billion or 31% of the global total (Scott, 2006).

A second type of offshore activity emerged in the 1980s as lead firms in capital and technology intensive value chains set up production chains not only to assemble finished goods but also to develop supply bases for key intermediate goods and components in sectors such as electronics computers and automobiles. As these industries globalized, some Asian firms were able to capture significant subcontracting for MNCs (Yeung, 2007). This added further impetus to the growth of Chinese regions which developed from labour intensive assembly into suppliers of electronic and other components. As a result, the rapid economic growth of China has involved the emergence of a remarkable range of specialized industrial clusters and 'supply chain cities' (Gereffi, 2008). To take Just two examples in different types of sector, 80% of the world's metallic shell lighters are made in the city of Wenzhou in Zhejiang province (Thun, 2008; Wei et al., 2007), and the cluster in Datang produced nine billion pairs of socks in 2003 (Gereffi, 2008). In 2002 China displaced the EU and Mexico as the biggest exporters to the USA of computers, consumer electronics and other IT products, though of course many of these exports involved the assembly of components sourced abroad (Glyn, 2006).

One of the key lessons of value chain and production network approaches is that the opportunities for *upgrading* and developing new supply capabilities are shaped by relationships in different types of global value chain, as well as by the institutional agreements that govern regional and global trade (Humphrey and Schmitz, 2002; Bair and Gereffi, 2003). Spaces for full package production and more advanced manufacturing can open up as lead firms outsource more knowledge intensive opportunities and some regions have thereby managed to upgrade their supply capabilities. For example, Saxenian (2006:124) describes how Taiwan has managed to transform itself 'from a poor island specializing in producing toys, umbrellas and footwear into a global center of electronic systems design, manufacturing and logistics'. From the late 1970s, American and Japanese consumer electronics and semiconductor firms began to invest in Taiwan to employ low cost labour. The rising number of Taiwanese producers also entered Original Equipment Manufacturing (OEM) relationships with PC retailers. In OEM or full package production the customer provides detailed technical blueprints and components that allow the contractor to complete integrated production. This is usually distinguished both from simple component assembly operations and from more advanced manufacturing that requires design and marketing capabilities (Gereffi, 2005). Foreign buyers demanded improvements in quality and they became a crucial source of knowledge for new product design and development. Saxenian (2006) explains how the growth of a network form of production involving many small specialist producers in the Taipei-Hsinchu region involved the return migration of a large number of US-trained engineers and computer specialists from Silicon Valley. Entrepreneurship was boosted by such 'brain circulation' and the subsequent collaboration between local firms and those located in Silicon Valley. As a result the increasing capabilities of Taiwanese firms allowed them to move into original design manufacturing. They captured a growing share of global IT manufacturing so that by 2000 Taiwan ranked as the third largest producer of IT hardware. 'By 2001 Taiwan, a country with a population of 22 million people, was producing 27 million desktop PCs per year and dominating the global market for notebook computers' (Saxenian, 2006:171).

The third type of new global supply chain has seen the outsourcing and offshoring of *services*. This has involved the rise of customer service call centres and the development of software and other business services. In India, for example, multinationals have invested in low skill and labour intensive, but increasingly automated, processes such as customer service, call centres, and accounting billing and payment services. The salaries of experienced IT professionals in India are roughly 13–17% of those in the UK and USA (Rüdiger, 2007). From the 1970s some software programming services moved to India and subsequently service provision has moved into more complex work as educational policy has increased skill levels (Altenburg et al., 2008). India's rates of growth of service exports averaged 35% per annum between 2000 and 2005 (Dossani and Kenney, 2007). Much of this growth has been driven by multinational service providers setting up subsidiaries in India, and, in turn, these firms have also outsourced to further cut their costs so that Indian software service providers have grown remarkably. By 2003 General Electric employed over 12,000 people, while HSBC employed in excess of 10,000 people in India in 2005. IBM India had increased its workforce to 60,000, and Covergys, a call centre operator, employed 10,000 in 2005. In total it was estimated that in 2003 the Indian software industry employed about 250,000 people (Arora and Gambardella, 2004).

This growth has again been tied to a dynamic of urban clustering. Most notably, by 2006 Bangalore was home to 1500 IT companies and most firms are headed by individuals who have lived and worked overseas (Basant, 2006). There is a great deal of debate about the employment consequences of this wave of service globalization, as many developed economies are now highly dependent on service jobs. According to Dossani and Kenney (2007:787), 'During the next decade it is likely that globalization will sweep through the ranks of developed country service workers.' However, it is worth noting that while India has developed a large business service export sector (with exports of $18.6 billion in 2002) this remains sixth in global ranking. Again, in contradiction with a flat world prediction the largest exporters of business services continue to be rich industrialized countries led by the US and UK (Amiti and Wei, 2005).

LUMPY DISPERSION?

As a result of the importance of increasing returns effects some economists have qualified liberal dispersal theories and argued that globalization produces a process of *lumpy dispersion*. According to Venables (2006:79), 'much activity will move out of existing centers, but relocation will be lumpy benefiting some regions more than others and recoalescing into new patterns of agglomeration'. Economic growth will occur in sequence, not in parallel, as some countries join the convergence club while others are left behind. At the head of the queue are regions that neighbour existing centres with low transport costs such as coastal regions.

This process of lumpy dispersion clearly has resonance with recent development in East Asia where rising labour costs have resulted in shifts in investment to neighbouring regions. For instance, from the 1990s Taiwanese PC component makers began shifting their labour intensive activities to mainland China to exploit lower labour and land costs. Most of these investments were initially clustered in the city of Dongguan in the Pearl River Delta and by 2000 there were 1,800 PC firms in this city, 80% of them established by Taiwanese firms, while one-third of Taiwan's IT products were manufactured in China. By 2003, approximately 40,000 Taiwanese companies were located in the mainland including 10,000 in the greater Shanghai area (Saxenian, 2006). In the same year, China replaced Taiwan as the third largest IT producer with $92 billion in exports. Foreign firms, mostly Taiwanese, accounted for 85% of these exports, although several large international Chinese electronics firms have also grown in importance and reach. In total, perhaps two-thirds of the inputs for China's processing activities come from Hong Kong, Japan, Korea and Taiwan (Ravenhill, 2006).

But while forms of lumpy dispersion many have been created by East Asian production networks, it is highly uncertain whether such dispersion will continue and, in addition, whether it applies to any significant degree outside these specific regional networks. The evidence that this is a widespread process is rather thin. Simply participating in a global supply chains does not guarantee the conditions for endogenous growth and upgrading as some low cost sectors may not be strongly territorially embedded or anchored and have few local linkages or spillovers (Bair and Peters, 2006). As Yeung (2007) has argued, the growth of East Asian economies has involved complex and hard to replicate triangular couplings between the strategies of Asian firms, global production networks, and the institutional home base (developmental state) advantages of these firms. Their regionalization has been based on distinctive and hybrid Chinese business networks (Sum, 1999; Yeung, 2006). It is also unclear whether future wage increases in China will provoke further relocations of labour intensive industries. Some cities have seen wage increases of up to 50% in three years but because labour still contributes only a small fraction of the total cost of production these increases may not be sufficient to induce relocation as the other competitive advantages of China's industrial clusters will strengthen and deepen (Thun, 2008). A key question will be whether such activities relocate to the enormous labour pools of inland China, or to other countries such as Vietnam and the Philippines (Ravenhill, 2006a). Realizing the opportunities presented by the globalization of technology is highly dependent on policies to increase learning (Archibuigi and Pietrobelli, 2003). To this effect, China has made unprecedented investments in education with the annual number of university graduates doubling between 2000 and 2004 to 3.8 million. Moreover, Saxenian (2006) emphasizes that the personal networks of Chinese engineers, with ties both to Silicon Valley and Hsinschu-Taipei, have been essential to technological upgrading.

More generally, most analyses of world inequality cast radical doubt on the view that globalization has resulted in a widespread dispersion of prosperity and a flattening of the global income distribution. Despite falling numbers living in the extreme absolute poverty, in terms of simple national average incomes, there is no evidence of international income convergence. At the same time international inequality weighted by population shows some decline since 1978 mainly as a result of China's fast growth rate (Milaovic, 2006). Leamer (2007) shows that despite the growth of average incomes in India and China between 1980 and 2000, incomes at the top of the global distribution have grown even faster so the net effect was for China and India to catch up with middle income countries but not with the richest states. Changes in the distribution of world consumption are dominated by the effects of poverty reduction and the growth of a middle class in China and without these trends would look dismal (Wade, 2004). As Edwards (2006: 1681) writes 'Once China is removed from the picture, the rich–poor gap is seen to persist so that the rich get richer while the poor, especially those in the low income and lower-middle income countries get more numerous'. Falling inequality is not a generalized feature of the world economy and absolute income gaps are widening (Wade, 2004). Despite all the methodological complexities surrounding the measurement of global inequality, there is some agreement that the level of inequality is close to its highest historical level. The ratio between the income received by the richest 5% and the poorest 5% of people is 165 to 1 so that the richest earn in about 48 hours what the poorest earn in a year (Milanovic, 2006).

Predictions of continuing dispersion through globalization overlook or down play the fact that positive feedbacks and increasing returns for some yield displacement and deindustrialization for others. The growth of exports from China has intensified competition between low wage labour intensive agglomerations (Scott, 2006; Lowder, 1999). According to Leamer (2007: 110), 'The global competition for these footloose jobs was and is hopelessly intense'. Thus, a wide range of labour intensive clusters in poor and middle income countries struggled to cope with the accession of China to the World Trade Organization (for examples see Scott, 2005; Cling et al., 2005). The reduction of the clothing quotas set by the Multi-Fibre Agreement in January 2005 also led to a dramatic surge in Chinese exports to the USA. In just five months China's textile and clothing imports rose by 64% which eroded the position of many other low income exporters (Seyoum, 2007; Kaplinsky and Morris, 2008). With full deregulation and removal of quotas it is predicted that production will consolidate in the leading exporters, so that producers in Latin America, Africa and the Caribbean are likely to lose market share. Kaplinsky (2006) argues that the export of manufacturing products from China, together with the increasing concentration of global buying in the hands of multinational retailers, has reduced the prices of manufactured products relative to commodities.

China's imports of raw materials have also raised the prices of these commodities creating problems for other importers of these resources. Of course, some of these effects may be countered by growing exports of raw materials and primary products to China (Yueh, 2007), and over time there is little doubt that the growth of China will provide a huge market for labour intensive manufactures (Rowthorn, 2006). But, in turn, this may yield disadvantageous types of specialization in export sectors with lower growth and less scope for learning (Lall et al., 2005). As China's exports have become more technologically sophisticated there is evidence that they have displaced the exports of other Asian exporters (Greenaway et al., 2008). This has been offset by the way in which China has been an engine of growth for neighbouring ASEAN countries as it draws in large volumes of imports and components from, and runs a trade deficit with, these states (Ravenhill, 2006b). However, the consequences for manufacturing elsewhere are more damaging. As Winters and Yusuf (2007: 33) note, the biggest challenges posed by China, and to a lesser degree India, are to middle income countries in Asia and Latin America:

> These are the countries into whose product space China in particular looks set to expand; they are the members of production networks that may be threatened by China's move into component manufacturing; and they are the recipients of FDI designed to create export platforms for the multinational corporations.

For instance, China's success in exporting car parts and electronic components to the US has meant that Mexico, despite NAFTA, has struggled to consolidate its share of these markets (Dauderstadt and Stetten, 2005; Gereffi, 2008).

THE UNSTABLE CONSEQUENCES OF 'SUPERCAPITALISM'

A final set of reasons for doubting liberal convergence interpretations of globalization's consequences is that the growth of outsourcing and the rapid rise of supply clusters took place within the context of a particular phase of globalization. Production networks are driven by the necessity, willingness and ability of consumers to acquire the products and services but, despite this, consumption rarely figures in the scripts on globalization (Dicken, 2007). The recent spread of these networks took place in a period when rapid consumer growth in many parts of the developed world was driven by the expansion of credit, driven by the globalization of finance. Reich (2008) describes this as the emergence of a period of intense competition or 'supercapitalism'. In this account, the transformation of formerly place-dependent corporations into global supply chains has boosted corporate profitability and filled shops with low cost manufactured goods. But while globalization brought advantages to consumers in terms of access to cheap consumer goods, and advantages to investors in terms of higher shareholder returns, it has

also exaggerated income inequality. In the Western world, intensive competition between firms has restrained wage growth among lower skilled groups, whilst generating vast pools of wealth for a few at the top of the income distribution. In 1968 the CEO of General Motors took home in pay and benefits about 66 times the pay of a typical GM worker, in 2005 the CEO of Walmart earned 900 times the pay of his average employee. The ample rewards of top management jobs and large financial investments, in the context of reduced state redistribution, have funded the growth of a transnational elite of superrich individuals (Beaverstock et al., 2004). Income distributions within many countries, not only rich ones but also populous poor and middle income states, have become more unequal in recent decades (Milanovic, 2006). In fact a majority of the world's population live in countries where inequality is rising (Dollar, 2007). While globalization's effects are difficult to pin down and it is clearly not the only cause, it has certainly been one of the major forces behind rising wage inequality and has given huge benefits to the wealthiest groups (Galbraith, 2007).

'Supercapitalism' has been inextricably linked with the deregulation of many key sectors, including the financial services industry. It was driven by a neoliberal regulatory regime which has argued that financial markets are most efficient when left to control themselves. As a result, the institutions and regulatory authorities necessary to sustain global financial integration exist only in rudimentary form (Clark, 2005). This institutional deficit allowed investors to reap huge profits by using computers and complex software to create new classes of financial products and investment vehicles. Simultaneously a short-termist performance culture rewarded traders with astronomical bonuses and encouraged them to take on ever greater risks (Tickell, 2000). Many of the new financial assets were forms of derivatives whose value is derived from the value of other financial assets (ibid.). By the end of 2007 the notional value of global derivatives contracts was $600 trillion, which is eleven times world economic output (*The Economist*, 2008).

As a result, over recent decades the rate of growth of global financial circuits, especially speculative foreign exchange markets and derivatives markets, has been phenomenal. World foreign exchange trading reached $1,900 billion per day in 2004, three times the level of 1989 (Glyn, 2006). The bulk of this expansion was driven by constant hedging, arbitrage and speculative position-taking in international markets (Swyngedouw, 2004). Roughly 90% of these flows were thought to be moving around in search of speculative gain (ibid.). Traditional banking regulations and investor caution were bypassed as financial firms gained more freedom to compete and develop complex and opaque financial instruments (Wade, 2008; Glyn, 2006). The growth of finance has raced ahead of the growth of production or trade and the total value of global financial assets increased from $12,000 billion in 1980 to £200,000 billion in 2007 (Garten, 2008).

This growth of global finance has had several important, and widely discussed, consequences. First of course it generated a highly uneven distribution of financial assets (Sarre, 2007). Many of those working in the control centres of global finance accumulated vast fortunes. At the top of the pile, for example, the average pay of 26 managers of major American hedge funds in 2006 was $363 million (Reich, 2008). Second, however, the explosion of global financial circuits has also produced the rise of new offshore financial centres and emerging markets as investments in liberalized stock markets allowed fast rates of growth in these industrializing economies (see Palan, 1998; Sidaway and Bryson, 2002). These markets have been subject to rapid swings in confidence among investors which has produced sudden switches between large inflows and outflows of financial capital. With periodic losses of confidence and herding behaviour by investors, emerging markets have been subject to frequent crises, including crashes in Argentina, Mexico,

Russia and most dramatically in East Asia in 1997–1998 (see Pauly, 2008). In fact, between during 1973–1995 there were 95 financial crises in emerging markets involving average output losses of over 9% of GDP (Schmuckler, 2004).

For the purpose of this chapter, it is important to note that the expansion of global finance and the expansion of production networks during this period of 'supercapitalist' boom were linked in several ways. 'Supercapitalism' has to a significant degree been funded by credit expansion. Turner (2008) argues that wages in the developed world have been driven down by the movement of jobs offshore in the developed world, the threat of relocation, and by the rising share of national income devoted to corporate profits. In an attempt to maintain disposable incomes and maintain economic growth, developed economy governments, led by the US and UK, pushed the expansion of credit and consumers were encouraged to borrow. The downward pressure on prices of consumer goods resulting from globalization allowed central banks to keep their interest rates very low. At the same time, financial globalization allowed the emergence of a new public and private borrowing that drove a massive expansion of debt. In the UK in 1997 total debt held by individuals stood at £570 billion, just over ten years later it reached £1,512 billion, a leap of over 165% (Turner, 2008). The borrowing binge in the US also meant that household debt had reached 140% of disposable income at the end of 2007 (*The Economist*, 2008).

In this credit-fuelled global economy, the USA experienced an unprecedented housing boom. Between 2000 and 2005 its average house prices grew by 50% and a wide range of financial institutions competed to lend mortgages to poorer social groups on the mistaken assumption that house prices could only go up (Morris, 2008). The surge of credit was facilitated by two key innovations in financial instruments. The first was securitization, in which mortgage lenders first unbundled and the repackaged their loans into collateralized mortgage obligations and sold them to other banks, which in turn sold them to pension funds and other investors (Coakley, 1994; Leyshon and Thrift, 2007). This enabled mortgage lenders to build booming mortgage businesses with relatively small capital reserves. Such mortgage securities are an example of collateralized debt obligations which are financial bundles that group loans or bonds into a single product that can be sold in order to spread risk across financial institutions. The second key innovation was credit default swaps which were types of insurance policies bought by banks to purportedly insure themselves against loan defaults. The market for these swaps is said to total £3,506 billion (Münchau, 2008). Again, these acted to spread and share risks and lull investors, in Morris' words (2008: 61), until it appeared that 'The mathematicians had banished risk'.

This credit-bubble and the growth of housing prices allowed rising consumer expenditure which in turn attracted enormous volumes of imports from industrializing economies. The USA has been running an increasing trade deficit for several decades but by 2006 it had increased to $750 billion. Its consumer boom sucked in huge quantities of consumer goods, particularly from China. In 2003, for example, the US spent $59 billion on imports of high-technology goods from China, including 31 million DVD players, 7.5 million notebook computers and 20 million mobile phones (Branstetter and Lardy, 2006). This consumption was sustained by a huge amount of overseas borrowing (Glyn, 2006). In effect, capital flowed back to the US as manufacturing, oil and other natural resource exporters accumulated large dollar reserves through their export earnings and invested these in American financial assets such as Treasury bonds and mortgage based financial assets (Wade, 2008). Most of this money came from private investors and central banks in Russia, China and the Gulf. By 2005 foreigners owned 50% of the total stock of US Treasury Bonds, enabling the US to maintain lower interest rates

than otherwise possible and to fund its balance of payments deficit (McGrew, 2008). In a cyclical process, low interest rates acted in turn to push up consumption in the US. Thus the investment flows cemented strong complementary relationships between the USA and East Asian exporters (Nordhaus, 2008).

From late 2007 this conjuncture of financial globalization and the expansion of consumer markets quickly disintegrated and the globalization of systemic financial risk has led to the worst global financial crisis since the early twentieth century. The upward spiral of credit and consumption ended with a downturn in the American housing market from 2006 (Sidaway, 2008). Falling house prices meant that recent house buyers could no longer refinance their mortgages at the end of an initial period of lower interest rates, so that mortgage defaults and repossessions accelerated. This triggered a sequence in which investors and banks became aware that the foundations of their huge pyramids of complex debt instruments were non-performing loans that could not be repaid. The devaluation of these loans has destroyed the financial standing of those banks most heavily exposed to mortgage-based lending, such as Lehman Brothers in the US and Northern Rock in the UK. As the Bank of England (2008) notes, in an interconnected global system losses spilled across markets with unexpected virulence and speed, creating an 'adverse spiral' between the draining of confidence and financial losses. The loss of confidence in key financial institutions has now led to a generalized 'credit crunch' as banks have become wary of lending both to each other and to other businesses. Facing a severe contraction in lending and the decimation of banks that are too big to be allowed to fail, governments in the core industrialized economies have been forced to part-nationalize banks and use taxpayers' money to absorb astronomical losses in order to avoid a complete collapse in the global financial system. The crisis caused severe recessions in the major advanced capitalist economies as well as downturns in emerging market economies, and there is even a high risk of a deep and prolonged world-wide economic recession.

Given this global financial crisis, outsourcing networks and their host economies clearly face a much more difficult and problematic economic context. Some commentators suggested optimistically that the industrializing Asian economies have sufficiently strong endogenous growth that they have 'decoupled' from the developed world. The effect of the financial crisis may therefore may well be to speed up the transfer of the locus of economic growth from the West to the emerging Asian giants. In this view, the rising wealth of China's rising middle class may act to cushion its economy from economic vagaries else where (Edwards, 2006). However, China has a high degree of openness (exports and imports represent 70% of its GDP) so that its fate is increasingly and inextricably tied to that of the global economy (Yueh, 2007). Notwithstanding the significant growth of domestic Asian markets, it remains true that industrialization in East Asia has been driven by access to developed country markets, and to the American market in particular. Indeed, around three quarters of world consumption expenditure is accounted for by spending in the West (Dauvergne, 2008), so that a recession there will have severely adverse effects on export sectors and outsourcing networks. For instance, it is telling that in the late 1990s, 58% of Indian software exports went to the USA, 21% to Europe and 6% to Japan (Arora et al., 2001). In addition, those developing economies that have relied heavily on overseas borrowing and foreign capital are already suffering from a withdrawal of credit and the reversal of capital flows. However, whatever the long-term outcomes of the crisis it is clear that the global economy is entering a period of severe political-economic tensions and slower growth. In this context, later entrants to global industries face even greater competition, volatility and trade rivalry, and the argument that their entry will somehow yield a general process of economic convergence looks even more dubious.

CONCLUSIONS

This chapter has offered several critiques of optimistic liberal versions of the dispersion of capitalism and their idea of a shift to an era in which convergence prevails and erodes differences in the global economic landscape. First, they overlooked some of the contradictory geographical dynamics inherent in globalization, the continued significance of centripetal forces and the uneven competitive consequences of re-territorialization. Second, these views also underestimated the way in which the rise of certain emerging economies and the rapid spread of outsourcing depended on the existence of a particular conjuncture of financial, consumption and production processes linked by credit creation. In hindsight the liberal predictions of a new trend to convergence and opportunity were a product of their peculiar time and they mistook contingent geographical outcomes for an inexorable structural and system-wide trend. Finally, and perhaps most importantly they were unbalanced as they recognized new opportunities and routes for economic growth but missed the instability and spirals of vulnerability created by economic globalization in an age of 'supercapitalism'.

There is little doubt that this constellation has now unravelled. Even before the recent collapse of financial globalization, several commentators were arguing that growing signs that the world economy would at some point retreat from globalization. Ferguson (2005) argued that the previous era of globalization (between 1870 and 1914) once seemed as unstoppable as contemporary globalization and had ended disastrously and that another doomsday scenario was plausible for the recent era of globalization. Indeed, several commentators pointed out that the global economy was facing a series of mounting stresses. The rising costs of oil and raw materials and the declining popularity of globalization due to increasing income inequalities have led to growing political support for protectionist measures and undermined enthusiasm for free trade and capital mobility

(Gilpin, 2000). Most significant is the growing realization that credit-fuelled globalization has intensified a set of environmental risks and externalities, especially resource depletion and carbon emissions, and that both nation states and global institutions have so far proved unable and unwilling to deal with these costs (Hirst and Thomson, 2002). What is certain is that globalization is a political construction and its future depends on how states respond to these escalating pressures (McGrew, 2008). These responses will determine whether the global economy either undergoes a retreat from globalization and economic interdependence, or a significant change towards a more carefully regulated and social-democratic form of governance in which markets are better managed. Of course, the growth of some forms of global production and service networks will continue, as will the powerful increasing returns and territorialization processes driving the large emerging economies. The technological improvements that facilitated outsourcing and the fragmentation of production will not cease and, in a recessionary climate, corporations may well intensify their efforts to outsource and seek lower cost production sites for some tasks and, indeed, to increase their access any markets that continue to grow. Yet without the consumption boom driven by global credit, these networks are sure to grow more slowly and selectively. In a new era in which globalization is yet more uneven, limited and contested it will be some time before the liberal ideas of global economic convergence come close to regaining their former ascendancy.

REFERENCES

Altenburg, T., Schmitz, H. and Stamm, A. (2008) Breakthrough? China and India's transition from production to innovation. *World Development*, 36(2): 325–44.

Amiti, M. and Wei, S. (2005) Fear of service outsourcing: Is it justified? *Economic Policy*, 20(42): 308–47.

Archibugi, D. and Pietrobelli, C. (2003) The globalisation of technology an its implications for developing countries: Windows of opportunity or further burden? *Technological Forecasting and Social Change*, 70: 861–83.

Arora, A. and Gambardella, A. (2004) The globalization of the software industry, National Bureau of Economic Research wp 10538, http://www.nber.org/papers/w10538.

Arora, A., Arunachalam, V., Asundi, J., and Fernandes, R. (2001) The Indian software services industry. *Research Policy*, 30: 1267–87.

Bair J. and Gereffi, G. (2003) Upgrading, uneven development and jobs in the North American apparel industry. *Global Networks*, 3(2): 143–69.

Bair, J. and Peters, E.D. (2006) Global commodity chains and endogenous growth: Export dynamism and development in Mexico and Honduras. *World Development* 34(2): 204–21.

Baldwin, R. (2006) *Globalisation: The Great Unbundling(s)*. Prime Minister's Office, Economic Council of Finland.

Bank of England, (2008) *Financial Stability Report*, Issue 24, October. London: Bank of England.

Basant, R. (2006) Bangalore cluster: Evolution, growth and challenges, Indian Institute of Management WP 2006–05–02.

Beaverstock, J., Hubbard, P., and Short, J.R. (2004) Getting away with it? Exposing the geographies of the super-rich. *Geoforum*, 35: 401–07.

Bisley, N. (2007) *Rethinking Globalization*. Basingstoke: Palgrave Macmillan.

Brakman, S. and Van Marrewijk, C. (2008) It's a big world after all: On the economic impact of location and distance. *Cambridge Journal of Regions, Economy and Society* 1(3): 411–38.

Branstetter, L. and Lardy, N. (2006) China's embrace of globalization, National Bureau of Economic Research Working Paper 12373, http://www.nber.org.papers/w12373.

Clark, G.L. (2005) Money flows like mercury: The geography of global finance, *Geografiska Annaler*, 87 B: 99–112.

Cling, J.-P. Razafindrakoto, M., and Roubaud, F. (2005) Export processing zones in Madagascar: A success story under threat. *World Development 33(5): 785–803*.

Coakley, J. (1994) The integration of property and financial markets. *Environment and Planning A*, 26 (5): 697–713.

Coe, N.M. and Yeung, H.W. (2001) Geographical perspectives on mapping globalisation. *Journal of Economic Geography*, 1: 367–80.

Dauvergne, P. (2008) Globalization and the environment, Chapter 14 in J. Ravenhill (ed.) (2nd edn) *Global Political Economy*. pp. 448–77.

Dauderstädt, M. and Stetten, J. (2005) China and globalisation. *Intereconomics*. July/August, pp. 226–34.

Dicken, P. (2007) *Global Shift: Mapping the Contours of the Changing World Economy* (5th edn). London: SAGE.

Dicken, P., Peck, J., and Tickell, A. (1997) Unpacking the global. Chapter 12 in R. Lee and J. Wills (eds) *Geographies of Economies*. London: Arnold, pp. 158–66.

Disdier, A. and Head, K. (2008) The puzzling persistence of the distance effect on bilateral trade. *The Review of Economics and Statistics*, 90: 37–48.

Dollar, D. (2007) Globalization, poverty and inequality since 1980. Chapter 4 in D. Held and A. Kaya (eds.) *Global Inequality*. Cambridge: Polity Press. pp. 73–103.

Doraghu, M. and Barff, R. (1990) Nike just did it: International subcontracting and flexibility in athletic footwear production, *Regional Studies*, 24, 537–52.

Dossani, R. and Kenney, M. (2007) The next wave of globalization: Relocating service provision to India. *World Development*, 35(5): 772–91.

Edwards. P. (2006) Examining inequality: Who really benefits from global growth? *World Development* 34(10): 1667–95.

Fan, C.C. and Scott, A.J. (2003) Industrial agglomeration and development: A survey of spatial economic issues in East Asia and a statistical analysis of Chinese regions. *Economic Geography*, 79(3): 295–319.

Feenstra, R.C. (1998) Integration of trade and disintegration of production in the global economy. *Journal of Economic Perspectives*, 12(4): 31–50.

Ferguson, N. (2005) Sinking globalization. *Foreign Affairs*, December.

Friedman, T.L. (2006) *The World is Flat*. London: Penguin.

Galbraith, J.K. (2007) Global inequality and global macroeconomics. Chapter 7 in D. Held and A. Kaya (eds) *Global Inequality*. Cambridge: Polity Press. pp. 148–75.

Garten, J. (2008) We need a new Global Monetary Authority. *Financial Times*, Friday September 25, page 19.

Gereffi, G. (2005) *The New Offshoring of Jobs and Global Development*. ILO Social Policy Lectures Geneva: International Institute for Labour Studies.

Gereffi, G. (2008) Development models and industrial upgrading in China and Mexico, *European Sociological Review*, 25(1): 37–51.

Gilpin, R. (2000) *The Challenge of Global Capitalism: The World Economy in the Twenty-First Century*, Princeton: Princeton University Press.

Glyn, A. (2006) *Capitalism Unleashed: Finance, Globalization and Welfare*. Oxford: Oxford University Press.

Greenaway, D., Mahabir, A. and Milner, C. (2008) Has China displaced other Asian countries' exports? *China Economic Review*, 19: 152–69.

Grossman G.M. and Rossi-Hansberg, E. (2006) *The Rise of Offshoring: It's Not Wine for Cloth Anymore*. Working Paper Princeton University.

Harvey, D. (2006) *Spaces of Global Capitalism*. London: Verso.

Hay, C. (2008) Globalization's impacts on states. Chapter 10 in J. Ravenhill (ed.) *Global Political Economy* (2nd edn). Oxford: Oxford University Press. pp. 314–45.

Henderson, J., Dicken, P., Hess, M., Coe, N., and Yeung, H.W. (2002) Global production networks and the analysis of economic development. *Review of International Political Economy*, 9(3): 436–64.

Hirst, P. and Thompson, G. (2002) The future of globalization, *Cooperation and Conflict*, 37(3): 247–65.

Humphrey, J. and Schmitz, H. (2002) How does insertion in global value chains affect upgrading in industrial clusters? *Regional Studies* 36 (9): 1017–27.

Kanbur, R. and Venables, A. (2007) Spatial disparities and economic development. Chapter 9 in D. Held and A. Kaya (eds.) *Global Inequality*, Cambridge: Polity Press. pp. 204–15.

Kaplinsky, R. (2006) Revisiting the revisited terms of trade: Will China make a difference? *World Development* 34(6): 981–95.

Kaplinsky, R. and Morris, M. (2008) Do the Asian drivers undermine export-oriented industrialization in SSA? *World Development*, 36(2): 254–73.

Kelly, P. (1999) The geographies and politics of globalization. *Progress in Human Geography* 23(3): 379–400.

Kirkegard, J.F. (2007) *Offshoring, Outsourcing and Production Relocation: Labor Market Effects in the OECD Countries and Developing Asia*. Peterson Institute for International Economics, Working Paper 07–02.

Kraas, F. (2007) Megacities and global change: Key priorities. *The Geographical Journal*, 173(1): 79–82.

Lall, S. (1998) Exports of manufactures by developing countries: Emerging patterns of trade and location. *Oxford Review of Economic Policy*, 14(2): 54–73.

Lall, S., Weiss, J., and Oikawa, H. (2005) China's competitive threat to Latin America: An analysis for 1990–2002. *Oxford Development Studies*, 33(2): 163–94.

Leamer, E. (2007) A flat world, a level playing field, a small world after all, or none of the above? A review of Thomas L. Friedman's *The World is Flat*. *Journal of Economic Literature XLV*: 83–126.

Leamer E. and Storper, M. (2001) The economic geography of the internet age. *Journal of International Business Studies*, 32, (4): 641–65.

Leyshon, A. and Thrift, N. (2007) The capitalization of almost everything: The future of finance and capitalism. *Theory, Culture, and Society*, 24(7–8): 97–115.

Linden, G., Kraemer, K., and Dedrick, J. (2008) Who captures value in a global innovation network? The case of Apple's iPod, *Personal Computing Industry Centre*.

Lowder, S. (1999) Globalisation of the footwear industry: A simple case of labour? *Tijdschrift voor Economische en Sociale Geografie*, 90(1): 47–60.

McCann, P. (2008) Globalization and economic geography: The world is curved not flat. *Cambridge Journal of Regions, Economy and Society*, 1(3): 351–70.

McGrew, A. (2008) The logics of economic globalization. Chapter 9 in J. Ravenhill (ed.) *Global Political Economy* (2nd edn). Oxford: Oxford University Press. pp. 277–313.

Milanovic, B. (2006) Global income inequality: A review. *World Economics* 7(1):131–57.

Morris, C.R. (2008) *The Trillion Dollar Meltdown, Easy Money, High Rollers and the Great Credit Crash*. New York: Public Affairs.

Münchau, W. (2008) How a downturn could turn into a disaster. *Financial Times*, Monday 8 September, p.13.

Nordhaus, K. (2008) The United States and East Asia in an age of financialization. *Critical Asian Studies*, 37(1): 103–16.

Palan, R. (1998) The emergence of an offshore economy. *Futures*, 30(1): 63–73.

Pauly, L.W. (2008) The political economy of global financial crises. Chapter 8 in J. Ravenhill (ed.) *Global Political Economy* (2nd edn). pp. 241–72.

Ravenhill, J. (2006a) Is China an economic threat to Southeast Asia?, Department of International Relations ANU Canberra Working Paper 2006/4.

Ravenhill, J. (2006b) Globalization, poverty and inequality. *New Political Economy* 11(4): pp. 583–87.

Reich, R. (2008) *Supercapitalism: The Battle for Democracy in an Age of Big Business*. London: Icon Books.

Rowthorn, R. (2006) *The Renaissance of China and India: Implications for Advanced Economies*. UNCTAD Discussion paper No. 182.

Rüdiger, K. (2007) *Offshoring, a Threat for the UK's Knowledge Jobs*. Working paper. London: The Work Foundation.

Sachs, J. (2005) *The End of Poverty*. London: Penguin.

Sarre, P. (2007) Understanding the geography of international finance. *Geography Compass* 1(5): 1076–96.

Saxenian, A. (2006) *The New Argonauts*. Harvard: Harvard University Press.

Schmuckler, S. L. (2004) Financial globalization: Gain and pain for developing countries. *Federal Reserve Bank of Atlanta Economic Review*, Second Quarter: 39–66.

Scott, A. (2005) The shoe industry of Marikina city, Phillipines: A developing country cluster in crisis. *Kasarinlan: Phillipine Journal of Third World Studies*, 20(2): 76–99.

Scott, A. J. (2006) The changing global geography of low-technology, labor-intensive industry: Clothing, footwear and furniture, *World Development* 34(9): 1517–36.

Scott, A. J. and Storper, M. (2003) Regions, globalization, development. *Regional Studies*, 37(6–7): 579–93.

Seyoum, B. (2007) Trade liberalization and patterns of strategic adjustment in the US textiles and clothing industry, *International Business Review*, 16: 109–35.

Sidaway, J. (2008) Subprime crisis: American crisis or human crisis?, *Environment and Planning D*, 26(2): 195–98.

Sidaway, J. and Bryson, J. (2002) Constructing knowledges of 'emerging markets': UK-based investment managers and their overseas connections. *Environment and Planning A*, 34: 401–16.

Storper, M. (2003) Globalization, localization and trade. Chapter 8 in G. Clark, M. Feldman and M. Gertler (eds) *A Handbook of Economic Geography*. Oxford: Oxford University Press. pp. 146–65.

Storper, M. and Walker, R. (1989) *The Capitalist Imperative*. Oxford: Basil Blackwell.

Sturgeon, T. (2002) Modular production networks: A new American model of industrial organization. *Industrial and Corporate Change*, 11(3): 451–96.

Swyngedouw, E. (2004) Globalisation or 'glocalisation'? Networks, territories and rescaling. *Cambridge Review of International Affairs*, 17(1): 25–48.

The Economist (2008) When fortune frowned: A special report on the world economy, 11 October 2008.

Thun, E. (2008) The globalization of production. Chapter 11 in J. Ravenhill (ed.) (2nd edn) *Global Political Economy*. Oxford: Oxford University Press. pp. 346–72.

Tickell, A. (2000) Dangerous derivatives: controlling and creating risks in international money. *Geoforum*, 31: 87–99.

Tickell, A. and Peck, J. (2003) Making global rules: Globalization or neoliberalization. In J. Peck and H. Yeung (eds) *Remaking the Global Economy*. London: SAGE. pp. 163–81.

Turner, G. (2008) *The Credit Crunch: Housing Bubbles, Globalisation and the Worldwide Economic Crisis*. London: Pluto Press.

UNCTAD (2007) World Investment Report, 2007, United Nations, http://www.un-ngls.org/site/article.php3?id_article =357

Van der Ploeg , F. and Poelhekke, S. (2008) Globalization and the rise of mega-cities in the developing world. *Cambridge Journal of Regions, Economy and Society*, 1(3): 477–501.

Venables, A.J. (2006) Shifts in economic geography and their causes. *Federal Reserve Bank of Kansas City Economic Review*, Fourth Quarter, 61–85.

Wade, R.H. (2004) Is globalization reducing poverty and inequality? *World Development* 32(4): 567–89.

Wade, R.H. (2008) The first world debt crisis and the desirable policy response. Guest Lecture New Zealand Treasury 31 March, http://www.treasury.govt.nz/publications/media-speeches/guestlectures/wade-apr08

Wei, Y., Li, W., and Wang, C. (2007) Restructuring industrial districts, scaling up regional development: A study of the Wenzhou model, China. *Economic Geography* 83(4): 421–44.

Wen, M. (2004) Relocation and agglomeration of Chinese industry. *Journal of Development Economics*, 73: 329–47.

Winters, L.A. amd Yusuf, S. (2007) Introduction: Dancing with giants. Chapter 1 in L. Winters and S. Yusuf (eds) *Dancing with Giants: China, India and the Global Economy*. Washington: The World Bank and Institute for Policy Studies, Singapore. pp. 1–34.

Wolf, M. (2004) *Why Globalization Works*. London: Yale University Press.

Yeung, H.W. (1998) Capital, state and space: Contesting the borderless world. *Transactions of Institute of British Geographers NS* 23: 291–309.

Yeung, H. W. (2006) *Chinese Capitalism in a Global Era*. London: Routledge.

Yeung, H.W. (2007) From followers to market leaders: Asian electronics firms in the global economy. *Asia Pacific Viewpoint*, 48(1): 1–25.

Yueh, L. (2007) The rise of China. *Irish Studies in International Affairs*, 18: 35–43.

PART 3

Political Economies of Space II

The Local in the Global

Martin Jones

INTRODUCTION

How can we think about the 'local' in the 'global', given that both terms, as Swyngedouw (1997) has suggested, are eminently powerful and heavily loaded in our spatial and political vocabularies? Two possible interpretive roads came to mind when thinking about writing this chapter. The first was notions of 'scale' and second was the 'contours of economic development'. The two, I would argue, are interrelated and economic geographers should have an advantage in explaining this to social and political scientists, economists, and even people in the so-called real world.

At the time of writing, human geographers have been getting very excited about the possibilities and impossibilities of 'scale' (with 'local' being one such scale). For political economists of scale, the state responds to the challenges of globalization by reshuffling the hierarchy of spaces in which economic action and intervention occurs (Brenner, 2004). Varieties of localisms and regionalisms are the spatial outcomes of this: sometimes generating new spaces and sometimes reworking old geographies (Brenner et al., 2003). This view of things has been challenged by network theorists, who take issue with the notion that there are bounded spaces to be enacted and managed. They insist on less hierarchical or 'flatter' interpretations, which are seen to give open-ended possibilities for geographies of the local (Marston et al., 2005). This ongoing debate will probably settle when all this can be empirically demonstrated. As Harvey (1981) argued when commenting on the turn towards behavioural approaches, there is a language of theory and a language of empirical investigation, and hopefully the two will meet in this instance.

My contribution in this chapter cuts across these debates and should thus be read in conjunction with the chapter that follows (Chapter 8). I want to explore the 'local in the global' – that is, the iterative and nuanced dynamic between 'the local' and extra-local forces – although it will become apparent that this in-here/out-there dichotomy is false and any critical understanding of socio-spatiality should see this road as an interrelated two-way flow of traffic. I do this through the lens of economic development and economic restructuring. This gives me a focus for discussion on such a broad and wide-reaching topic and also a way of grounding economic geography. This is perhaps not fashionable nowadays, but it is practical all the same. Economic geographers have always been fascinated by 'economic development', probably because of the visual (industrial landscapes, trading estates, enterprise parks, development agency building) and the political/policy traditions of the broader discipline. By 'economic development' I am referring to two things, which are never mutually exclusive: (1) the evolution of economic landscapes across space over time and the ways in which this is linked to the reshaping of localities within an internationalizing and globalizing word; and (2) the key triggers for this, whether based on particular place-based or endogenous activities or stimulated by state-fostered frameworks of support and investment across the fields of economic policy.

This chapter is divided into three sections. First, I discuss traditional approaches to 'the local' in economic geography that stress the constituents of the (local) economy, linkages and mechanisms of cumulative causation, and outline how this had an applied dimension in economic management in the so-called Fordist epoch. Second, I turn to look at the growing interest in the local during the 1980s and consider the rise of the 'locality debate' in the UK and elsewhere. I also briefly examine the idea of 'global senses of place' (Massey, 1994) constructed through the unbounded intersections of global, local or what Swyngedouw (1997) has called 'glocal' processes. This leads me to a discussion of post-Fordism, the 'new regionalism', and the ways in which 'softer' local economic governances have been emerging over the past twenty years, in an era of more intense globalization. I particularly focus on the ways in which economic geographers have been trying to reposition 'the local' within the contours of state spatial restructuring and then discuss an alternative perspective associated with 'thinking space relationally'. Throughout my discussion, it will become evident that I am interested in process-based (or processual) approaches to the 'local in the global'. I see globalization not as some 'end of geography' scenario and the death of the territorial local (on which, see

Morgan, 2004) but as a qualitative reworking and repositioning of the relationships between local–global, global–local, centre–local, local–centre, etc. (see Jones and Jones, 2004).

GOLDEN AGES: LOCAL TRANSMISSIONS OF GROWTH IMPULSES

Pick up most economic geography textbooks published between the 1950s and 1970s and they will invariably present ideas of local and global as virtually separate and disconnected intellectual terrains. Economic geography was curiously sandwiched at this time between an idiographic concern with areal differentiation (uncovering spatial difference and patterns) and a transition to nomothetic principles (universal law generation). In this section, I want to focus mostly on 'the local', because this is where economic geographers did most of their thinking and conducted their empirical studies, with political geographers experimenting with early ideas of internationalization and globalization through the sub-fields of geopolitics, world economies, and development geographies (see Agnew, 1987). Based mostly within frameworks of neoclassical economics and its emphasis on matters such as isotropic and unbounded landscapes, rational assumptions of behaviour therein, and perfect market knowledge, the goal at this time was to dissect the local (and the local economy primarily) as a series of discrete actors, elements, and interactions that could ultimately be modelled in accordance with ideal-type assumptions of location and behaviour *in space*. This was in many ways a *flat economic geography* – not bothered with uncovering socio-economic and spatial complexities, and certainly not concerned with teasing out those connections that contemporary scholars get excited about (such as scale and networks, for example). Accordingly, Hodder and Lee's text *Economic Geography* made the astute observation that '[n]one of the individual elements is taken to have any meaning outside the context of the economy to which it belongs' (1974: 13).

This localized approach to 'the local' – devoid of many external connections – is evident, obvious and completely deliberate when one considers the topics of discussion outlined in the classic text *Location in Space* by Lloyd and Dicken (1972). Having delimited the economy as box-like relations between production, distribution, circulation, consumption, allocation and regulation, the chapters in the book focus on spatial organization, transport costs, and variations in production costs and demand. It then progresses to analyse how all this can be modelled in different ways to get an understanding of the geographical constitution of the space-economy as a series of spatial clusters (with the economic geographer being concerned with the spatial organization of economic *systems*). Such clusters are seen to result from the formation of groupings of activity, which in turn require attention to processes of agglomeration. Building on the work of Weber and Lösch, 'localized economies of scale' are delimited by drawing attention to key interaction effects among costs, scales of activity, and demand, etc. In turn, local economic landscapes evolve over time and across space through triggers to development (key industries or investment decisions), multiplier effects and cumulative growth regimes, emanating often from resource-based economies and their interconnected industrial activities repeatedly reinforcing each other.

This geographical economics went hand-in-hand, first time around (see Chapter 3), with how state policy-makers and practitioners dealt with economic stimuli and internal growth dynamics, and also began to deal with the limits to endogenous resource-based economic development. This was the golden-age of Atlantic-Fordism and its mode of regulation known as spatial Keynesianism invaliding, state polity based on mass production, sector-spatial specializations of the divisions of labour, mass consumption and modes of socialization all feeding accumulation (see Box 7.1 for a defini-

tion), and an international financial and geopolitical regime that offered the basis for continuity and planning in national economic development. National interests were articulated through a particular spatial-temporal matrix of chosen local areas, deemed to be supportive of this mode of growth. Accumulation developed accordingly and had a distinct local and regional economic geography – ship building and steel in England's North East, coal in South Wales and Yorkshire, the creation of military industrial complexes in South West England and California, and manufacturing in distinct belts across North America and Western Europe (Marshall, 1987). This followed a period of pre-Fordist extensive accumulation, which had a less distinct regional geography. Box 7.1 summarizes some of the academic vocabulary used to convey these ideas.

When this 'regime' of accumulation started to slow-down, due to ongoing internal (relations of production, class and social struggles) and external (internationalization) shocks – comprehensively detailed in stock economic geography literatures – the local as an agglomeration node was promoted first through an acceleration of local state initiatives developed successfully over the years (such as the development of industrial estates, the provision of loans, incentives, etc.) and, secondly, through intensified national state intervention to create the local triggers and transmission belts for accumulation via regional and then urban planning, which provided huge subsidies and, temporarily at least, put on the brakes on the international movement of capital in the form of FDI (Ward, 1994). Economic geographers were well-placed to analyse and critique all this – the discipline had gradually shifted with the convergence of regional and economic geography in the 1970s, which gave some of the tools to switch analysis from the causes of economic location to the consequences of location and local economic restructuring. Early examples of this were Manners et al.'s (1972) *Regional Development in Britain* and the informative text *UK Space* by House (1974). Behavioural and then structural approaches to economic geographies of

---

Box 7.1   Some Neo-Marxist Vocabulary

See, for example, Jessop (1992); Tickell and Peck (1992).

Regime of accumulation

This is used to denote a macro-economically coherent phase of capitalist development. There are connections here with 'long-waves' of economic growth, which emphasize technological phases of development (Marshall, 1987). The regime of accumulation, however, is not reduced to purely techno-economic concerns: it is forged through the 'structural coupling' of accumulation and regulation developed through 'chance discovery', involving trial-and-error experimentation.

Accumulation system

This explores the production-consumption relationship, whereby the individual decisions of capitalists to invest are met by demand for their 'products' through the market place. Convergence between production and its ongoing transformations and the conditions of final consumption can provide the basis for a RoA.

Mode of regulation

At one level this captures the integration of political and social relations, such as state action and legislation, social institutions, behavioural norms and habits, and political practices. For the purposes of undertaking research, modes of regulation can be unpacked as: the wage relation; forms of competition and the enterprise system; money and its regulation; the state and its forms and functions; and the international regime. The effectiveness of these institutional forms and their interrelations varies over time and across space.

   Collectively these three terms allow regulation theorists to analyse the economy in its 'integral' sense, i.e. they are concerned with the social, cultural, and political context in which economic reproduction occurs. The spatial aspects of this are often expressed through:

Mode of societalisation

A term used to discuss the pattern of institutions and social cohesion, or the spatial patterning of regimes of accumulation.

'the local' followed, classed as 'alternative perspectives' in Part Two of Lloyd and Dicken (1972), which reflected an interest in the decisions of economic 'actors' in an increasingly volatile economic climate. The next section focuses on the spatial consequences of economic restructuring through notions of locality.

ECONOMIC RESTRUCTURING: LOCALITIES AND THE LOCALITY DEBATE

Massey's (1984) text *Spatial Divisions of Labour* marked the dawn of a new era for how geographers thought about 'the local' in

an increasingly internationalizing and globalizing world being fuelled by the collapse of Fordist-Keynesian compromises. The economic background was critical, with five trends taking place in manufacturing across local areas in North America and Western Europe: slowing productivity, declining output, trade deficits, collapsing profitability, and reductions in employment (Martin and Rowthorn, 1986). This was happening at the same time as changes in the monetary conditions of exchange from inflationism to anti-inflationism. In addition, Massey emphasized three interrelated mechanisms driving local economic restructuring under advanced capitalism: intensification (increasing labour productivity and obtaining the same output with a reduced workforce), rationalization (cutting capacity in response to intensification and/or relocating capacity elsewhere geographically), and technical change (labour saving methods of production such as mechanization and manufacturing improvement). This, in turn, influenced three spatial structures of production: locationally concentrated and vertically integrated, cloning branch-plants, and part processing systems. The inevitable impact of all this was job-losses, with a geographical anatomy of uneven development and distinctive localities emerging under globalization and economic restructuring, which Massey (1984; see also Lovering, 1989) sought to uncover by way of a 'restructuring approach' based on five principles:

1. Linkages need to be made between local economies and processes operating at regional, national and international scales.
2. Local economic factors and economic changes need to be linked to constellations of social, political, technical and cultural concerns.
3. Critical focus has to be placed on the role of labour (and class relations) in the location imperatives of firms.
4. Analysis of local and regional economic change should begin with broad economic processes and then examine impacts on localities, thereby identifying a two-way relationship between local conditions and broader processes (the specific and the general).
5. Over time, and across space, the links between 'the local' and 'the global' produce different 'rounds of investment', which build up in layers and influence the role 'the local' plays in the next wave of restructuring and investment.

The intellectual goal was to tease out the dialectic between space and place by looking at how localities were being positioned within, and in turn help to reposition, the changing national and international division of labour. For Massey (1991), 'the local in the global' is not simply an area around which one can draw a line; instead, it is defined in terms of sets of social relations or processes under consideration. This highly influential 'new regional concept of locali-

ties' (Jonas, 1988) influenced two government-sponsored research initiatives in the UK, delivered through the Economic and Social Research Council – the Social Change and Economic Life programme and the 'Changing Urban and Regional Systems' (CURS) programme. Both were given substantial funding and charged with remits to uncover the effects of international and global economic restructuring on local areas and to explore why different responses and impacts were reported in different places. Independent of these programmes, locality research was already taking place in Lancaster University (Murgatroyd et al., 1985) and Sussex University (Duncan, 1989) and this fuelled an interest in this important topic. However, as Barnes (1996) highlights, notions of 'locality' differed across all these interventions and a focus on the CURS programme is especially helpful in getting behind the meaning of locality.

In seeking to put 'the local' into 'the global', the CURS initiative set out to undertake theoretically-informed empirical research in seven localities between 1985 and 1987. The goal was to examine the extent to which localities themselves could shape their own transformation and destiny as agents rather than be passive containers for processes passed-down from above. A series of mainly metropolitan 'de-industrial' towns/regions and rural areas undergoing restructuring were selected for analysis – Swindon, Thanet, Cheltenham, Middlesbrough, East Liverpool and South Birmingham were the case-study sites – with the results being published in two edited books (Cooke, 1989a; Harloe et al., 1990). Each book contained detailed chapters on each locality, with research teams uncovering (with varying degrees of success) the impacts of globalization and economic restructuring on 'the local' through different 'rounds of investment' occurring over time and with local politics producing locality interactions.

Worthy of note here was the work of Hudson (1989, 1990) and Beynon et al. (1989), whose research closely followed

Massey's theoretical and interpretative framework. Their account of economic change in England's North East region seemed to demonstrate a 'locality effect' of local particularities in global times, i.e. the different ways in which 'rounds of investment' can be read in the local economic landscape, how local politics played a role in international investment decisions and, in turn, how attempts to cope with de-industrialization either by building a service-based economy or by using state-sponsored local economic initiatives to create employment opportunities, were working themselves out on the ground. The story starts out in the nineteenth century with an account of how 90% of the local employment basis was based in coal, iron and steel, and shipbuilding. This resource-based 'carboniferous capitalism' model, driven by its location in space, developed as successful locality and economic restructuring pressures gradually increased though foreign competition were accommodated with a switch to the production of inorganic chemicals, which grew to a peak in the 1960s.

Further global economic competition encouraged the state to propose a 'technical modernization of the locality' by investing in technical change and under-writing the costs of research and development in order to provide a competitive advantage. This was largely unsuccessful due to the increasing fragmentation of geographies production and the specialization of the North East in the lower-order 'screw-driver jobs' economy. The development of an enterprise culture in the 1980s through Enterprise Zones, Urban Development Corporations, Training and Enterprise Councils, and eventually Development Agencies, brought jobs to the locality, but these were largely part-time and had limited multiplier effects in the local economy. However, the political culture of the North East and the relationship between business and state interests was successful in bringing car manufacturing to the locality in the form of Nissan although, as with most forms of inward-investment, this economic strategy had questionable sustainability due to the volatility of global production regimes (see Hudson, 2000).

As argued by Duncan and Savage (1991), and later reinforced by Barnes (1996), there is a difference between locality research (the CURS findings) and the resulting 'locality debate' across human geography and the social sciences, which was fuelled both by a rethinking of how socio-spatial relations may be theorized across these disciplines (itself bound up with a transition from Marxist to poststructuralist research enquiry), and by shifting research methodologies and practices. With all this in mind, things were inevitably going to be messy and, between 1987 and 1991 the journal *Antipode*, published a series of often-heated exchanges on the significance of localities.

The initial assault came from North America. Smith (1987) bemoaned the perceived shift away from (Marxist) theory to empirics and saw this initiative as nothing more than a 'morass of statistical data':

> Like the blind man with a python in one hand and an elephant's trunk in the other, the researchers are treating all seven localities as the same animal (Smith, 1987: 63).

This was supported, to a differing degree, by Harvey (1987), who saw these projects as refusing to engage in any theoretical or conceptual adventures. In a more balanced manner, the resumé by Duncan (1989) saw locality – in the wrong hands – as a form of 'spatial fetishism'. He asked in what sense can localities act or is it the social forces within these spaces that have this capacity? Duncan then questioned the relationships within a defined territorial unit and also the relationships between spatial scales. Ward (1989) recognized the value of locality for empirical research but also highlighted that the scale of locality changes according to the object of analysis. Cooke (1987, 1989b), the Director of CURS, took a more defensive and ultimately pragmatic line, arguing that CURS was about seeking to make some general claims from multi-site case-study research. The CURS findings were, therefore, empirical and not empiricist.

A special issue of *Environment and Planning A* offered further critique and extension, and suggested that the locality concept was still a valuable one. For Jackson (1991), unsuccessful and at times dangerous attempts were being made to read cultural change and political change from the economy, rather than seeing these as being embedded in each other's presence. Pratt (1991) took a similar line and suggested that it was necessary to look at the discursive construction of localities and their material effects. Paasi (1991) encouraged scholars to take 'geohistory' more seriously and offered the idea of 'generation' to distinguish between the concepts of locality, place and region. Duncan and Savage (1989, 1991) pushed what they saw as the missing agenda of place-formation and class formation and the interconnections of these within and between localities. Cox and Mair (1991) offered an interesting US account of localities as arenas for economic development coalitions and ways of exploring the fixing and scaling of socio-spatial relations. They took debate forward and brought agency to the fore through notions of 'local dependency', the 'scale division of labour' and the 'scale division of the state' – concepts that highlighted the location and mobility of actors at different times. Cox and Mair claimed this avoided 'spatial fetishism' (a criticism levelled by Sayer, 1991) as locality is seen not in physical terms but as a 'localized social structure'. Cox (1991) pushed this further in work on the new urban politics. This claimed that capital was not as hypermobile as globalization theory was arguing at the time. This was due to the territorial organization of the (probably peculiar in relation to capital-labour relations in Ohio) US local state system. However, by claiming that localities could ultimately act, as opposed to the social relations in these strategically-selected spaces acting, this was probably pushing things too far. Finally, Massey's (1991, 1994) intervention offered some sensible qualifiers on what CURS had initially set out to achieve. By focusing on 'localities, reaction and progressiveness' this began to shift the scale of debate from locality to 'senses of place'.

During the mid-1990s economic geographers became preoccupied not so much with localities *per se* but rather with the links between space and place as a way of looking at the 'local in the global'. Reviewing the locality debate and noting the gaps over missing politics, Beynon and Hudson (1993) made some interesting points on our local-global times: 'space' for these authors captures the rather abstract domain of capital, with 'place' being 'meaningful' situations established by labour. 'Meaningful' was never fully defined or demonstrated, apart from reference to historically-contingent economic identities and attachments, and the important point that 'place-based' is not necessarily reducible to notions of 'place-bound'. Commenting on related themes, Massey wrote an extension to the debate in the journal *Marxism Today*, reprinted in her collection *Space, Place and Gender* (1994). Massey's account goes something like this. Globalization is happening but probably not as we know it. Time-space compression (the shrinking-world thesis) is socially and spatially differentiated due to the different mobility potentially of people in place. 'Power geometries', a metaphor for capturing geographies of power, exist and therefore constrain some and enable others. This makes generalizations about the powerlessness of 'the local' in a globalizing world rather unwise (cf. Harvey, 1989): what is needed instead is to understand and see localities through a 'global sense of place' – they are interconnected nodes in spaces of flows, stretching back and forth, ebbing and flowing according to how these are positioned by, and positioning, socio-spatial relations. Two distinctions are then made to understand 'the local in the global'. The first is a 'regressive sense of place', based not on embracing the potentials of globalization but instead having an obsession with heritage and other forms of 'romanticized escapism'. The second is a more 'progressive sense of place', based on harnessing and making the most of difference and diversity through those stretched-out connections. Massey discusses this through her own experiences of living in Kilburn (a cosmopolitan area of North London) and her approach has no truck with locality perspectives that stick to administrative boundaries or tightly-drawn labour market areas. Localities as 'global senses of place' are *relational* in the sense of seeing the local as an unbounded mosaic of different elements always in a process of interaction and of being made. In short, one cannot explain locality or place by only looking inside it, or outside it; the 'out there' and 'in here' matter *together* and are dialectically intertwined.

NEW LOCALITIES: NEW REGIONALISM TO RELATIONAL SPACE

Academic trends, certainly in economic geography, closely mirror political and policy events, and the approach offered by Massey certainly did not go away. Her post-localities interpretation of the 'local in the global' inspired a generation of academics to adopt a relational approach to their geographical enquiries. Before discussing this, I would like to frame 'the local in the global' through a discussion of how economic geographers started to get very excited about what they saw as the re-emergence of regional economies and new spaces of economic governance across the globe – places such as Baden-Württemberg (Germany), Emilia-Romagna (Italy), Silicon Valley, Boston, San Diego (all US), and the Rhône-Alpes (France) (see, also, Chapter 18). These spaces had initially been flagged by writers talking about post-Fordism and the geographies of flexible accumulation. Scott, for instance, in *New Industrial Spaces* (1988), offered a new way of looking at agglomeration and the development of distinct local territorial production complexes or industrial districts. Whereas Fordist accumulation, discussed above, was favoured by and grew in accordance with economies of scale and vertical

integration, economic development after-Fordism was seen to be linked to spatially-specific economies of scope resulting from the vertical disintegration of production and the development, amongst other things, of flexible working practices and shared support mechanisms. The geographical extent of this phenomenon and its reproducibility and sustainability was discussed at length in various edited collections (see Storper and Scott, 1992) and debates shifted through the 1990s to examine the governance of local economies in global contexts through a 'new regionalist' perspective – as part of a broader 'institutional-turn' in economic geography.

By contrast, in economic geography, John Lovering (1999) argued that new regionalist thinking was made up of at least four distinct and quite different perspectives. First, post-Fordist approaches associated the rise of regions with an underlying economic logic, whereby the vertical disintegration of production is pivotal to the formation of agglomeration economies which, in turn, encouraged clusters of industrial districts at a supra-local and sub-national scale. Second, approaches associated with a politically charged discourse of globalization, considered the nation state to be unable to regulate economic interests. In the place of national economic management, which is thought to be increasingly dysfunctional, a 'region state' is presented as the most appropriate site for instilling competitiveness and guaranteeing economic growth (Cooke, 1995). Third, accounts that displayed a concern with connections between production and changing labour markets based on particular high-order skills. The region was presented as the most appropriate scale to govern a 'knowledge-intensive' economy, based on jobs associated with the research and development sector. Fourth, and finally, a more ambitious set of accounts, loosely labelled the 'associational economy' model, sought to explore the connections between production and the governance of economic activity, with its analytic weight placed mainly on the latter. With differing degrees of sophistication at integrating such concerns, these ranged from Amin and Thrift's (1994) 'new institutionalism', to the 'regional world' framework provided by Storper (1997), and an 'innovative, learning regions' approach sponsored by Cooke and Morgan (1998), which I discuss briefly below.

These approaches shared a common interest with 'the local in the global' in the use of theories of conventions – practices, routines, agreements and their associated informal or institutional forms, which bind economic actors together so that mutual behavioural expectations co-ordinate their actions in 'local worlds of production' to ultimately pin-down or hold-down the global (Storper, 1993). In contrast, to inquiry in economic geography that privileged the nation state/ national scale, the new regionalism explored the territory-based foundations of economic life and the so-called 'reflexive' institutions that acted as 'frameworks of action' in governing local economic development in a global context. It was suggested that only at the regional scale could conventions, ranging from political-economic culture to the behaviour of economic agents, be harnessed. For Storper, regions are 'a key, necessary element in the "supply architecture" for learning and innovation' (1997: 22). Following the work of evolutionary economists, such as Dosi and Lundvall, the regional scale was identified as the most appropriate site for nesting territorial and scalar fixes based on a nexus of 'untraded interdependencies'.

Elements of this fourth mode of thinking were pivotal to the writings of Cooke and Morgan (1998) who promoted an 'innovation, learning regions' explanation in economic geography. Their approach is particularly important because, by highlighting structures of governance associated with economic growth occurring in dynamic regions, they suggested that policy blueprints can be constructed to help less favoured regions (such as Wales in their case study) to increase their economic prosperity. A starting point for this argument sees a 'region state' emerging to challenge the break-up of old

uncertainties and established hierarchies associated with the Fordist-Keynesian institutional compromise. This region state is a reflexive set of institutions able to combat economic uncertainty and bring about industrial co-operation through communication structures that monitor and share information. Drawing on developments underway in Italy and Germany, the region state provides a regulatory framework for nurturing the development of robust 'regional innovation systems' which, in turn, helps to raise regional economic prosperity. In intelligent regions such as Baden-Württemberg, for instance, there is a public-private provision of collective services, through institutions such as chambers of commerce and regional development agencies, related to training and technology transfer. These institutional supports provide a means of collectivising the action of economic agents and preventing market failure.

Again, issues of scale are crucial for effective economic governance. For Morgan, the operation of institutional routines and their associated societal conventions – also known as 'social capital' – 'are best developed at the regional level because this is the level at which regular trust-building, can be sustained over time' (1997: 501). Cooke extends this view, arguing that regions represent the only scale in and through which to establish a 'system of collective order' within so-called global disorder. Regions, therefore, represent increasingly important bases of economic coordination at the meso-level. This is conditioned by the globalizing context, closer inter-firm collaboration and, crucially, "the soft infrastructure of enterprise support provided by innovative substate governance institutions ... [I]t is the institutional capacity to attract and animate competitive advantage, often by the promotion of cooperative practices among economic actors, that gives regions a strong conceptual and real identity' (1998: 15).

This orthodoxy has been subjected to academic critique. First, Lovering (1999) sees the new regionalism as yet another academic trend that 'talks up' scale to justify a particular theoretical perspective and policy narrative, and in the process falls foul of institutional functionalism and crude economism. This line of criticism is not new: Lovering (1995) previously attacked the 'new localist' approach to globalization for making claims based on limited empirical evidence and ignoring the non-economic factors (class struggle, the state, social relations, etc.) that help to produce particular geographies of economic development. Extending these concerns, the new regionalism is perceived to have a number of practical and theoretical inadequacies. Philosophically, the new regionalism is deemed guilty of 'bad abstraction' – it ignores the role of multiple and contingent factors (both economic and non-economic) that produce regions. For this reason Lovering argues that the region is becoming a 'chaotic conception'; generalized claims are being made based on selective empirical evidence to support the centrality of this scale for stimulating economic growth. Consequently, he argues, this approach is a theory led by selective empirical developments and recent public policy initiatives. It is 'a set of stories about how *parts* of a regional economy *might* work, placed next to a set of policy ideas which *might* just be useful in *some* cases' (Lovering, 1999: 384, original emphasis).

Second, MacLeod (2001a, b) has offered a more balanced but equally perceptive review, critique, and extension of this approach. This is driven by sensitivity to the different ways in which regions are produced and a search for an analytical framework able to tease out the 'local in the global' connections between economic success, social processes, institutional frameworks, and political context. Additionally, MacLeod highlights the dangers of fast policy transfer; that is, the borrowing of policy ideas by importing them 'out of context', as methods of securing economic growth. This agenda is pursued by suggesting that the new regionalism is guilty of a reliance upon a 'soft institutionalism', an approach which sees institutions as socio-cultural frameworks of support that 'hold down' the global, to explain economic success based on institutions. In other words, the research question becomes: do institutions in fact originate, in a historically contingent manner, from the political-economic and socio-economy institutionalization of the economy over time and across space?

Building on this, the new regionalism is deemed to lack an explanation of the state and state action, which is often the arena in and through which regions are being constructed and politically mobilized. Without an explicit theorization of the state and its scalar manifestations, we are left with a 'thin political economy'. In short, not focusing on these drivers of regional change and development can lead to a 'distorted policy' for those seeking to build appropriate mechanisms for 'the local in the global'. Successful local and regional economic development, however defined, is invariably a path-dependent and geographical specific experience: examples of innovation rarely travel and, if they do, bits often drop-off en-route. Similar arguments have also been made by Hadjimichalis (2006a, b) and is required reading for those seeking to take these ideas forward.

Third, and in a more indirect manner, this thinking has been challenged by relational approaches to space, where – building on the work of Massey (1994) – geographies are made through stretched-out and unbounded relations between hybrid mixtures of global flows and local interactions that are interconnected. No longer is space a container or independent backdrop for existence, nor is there a concern for a distance between points; instead, uncovering networked, nodal, and open place-based relationships is where it is at. This argument has been clearly articulated by Amin and colleagues applying a 'thinking space relationally' approach to regions in geography (Amin, 2004; Amin et al., 2003; also Gibson-Graham, 1994). Similar arguments have been made by those advocating a 'flat ontology' approach to human geography (see Marston et al., 2005). In the 'unbounded' or 'relational region' thesis there is no automatic promise of territorial integrity, which challenges the idea of 'regional worlds', such that:

> spatial configurations and spatial boundaries are no longer necessarily or purposively territorial or scalar, since the social, economic, political and cultural inside and outside are constituted through the topologies of actor networks which are becoming increasingly dynamic and varied in spatial constitution. (Amin 2004: 33)

Radical open-ended politics and economics of *place* are proposed, in opposition to frameworks of so-called bounded economic development, to create spaces of opportunity for localities under globalization. This perspective is evidenced in *Cities: Reimagining the Urban*, a book in which Amin and Thrift (2002) view localities as unbounded, fluid, complex and mixed entities, formed through recurring practices, movements, and experiences. They claim this has implications for developing successful economies, building frameworks of economic governance, nurturing civic participation and delivering radical democracy, and generally doing well out of globalization.

Informed by Massey's progressive sense of place, putting 'the local into the global' has 'far less to do with territorial properties (such as localized linkage, local identity and identification, scalar politics, and governance) than with *the effects of spatial and temporal exposure and connectivity* (such as continual and open-ended change, juxtaposition of difference, overlap of networks of different global connections)' (Amin, 2002: 391, emphasis added). *Cities* accordingly mixes visions of visiting theatre groups, craft fairs, cosmopolitan urban festivals, multicultural floats and street parties – all encompassing the experiential *practice* of democracy (Amin and Thrift, 2002: 152–153; also Amin et al., 2000) – with those significant material gains associated with Scandinavian-style work-sharing and planning arrangements, Dutch time-management schemes (better work-life balances), inclusive examples of using public space, and flagging all these up

as innovative examples of relational socio-economic development in action.

This is interesting stuff that stretches the imagination of economic geography in local-global times. However, those working within state theoretic frameworks and more grounded approaches to economic geography have taken issue with the *realpolitik* of 'the local' grappling with the challenges of globalization. For example, it is important to consider the ways in which cities and regions can be categorized as a 'problem' by the state and those seeking to direct resources to different geographical areas. It is also important not to lose sight of the ways in which 'contentious politics' (Leitner et al., 2008) are being played out across the globe. One instance of this in recent years has seen the distinguishing of territorially-articulated spaces by those campaigning for devolved government and cultural rights. These spaces are not out there waiting to be found, but they are being mobilized and managed in the era of the post-national political constellation. Such spaces become central for conducting territorial political struggles over economic and cultural identities (Jones and MacLeod, 2004). Pushing this further, Tomaney (2007) argues that localities are more than the local articulation of global flows and concerns with territorialized culture need not necessarily be atavistic, archaic, or regressive as Massey and others would have it.

CONCLUSIONS

Debates over the local in the global have shifted ground considerably over the past 50 years. I would argue that they have closely mirrored how geographers have interpreted space in the discipline. Initially, there was a concern with *absolute space*, whereby the local and the global were treated independently. Concerns with *relative space* then lead us to consider the relationship between spaces, places or localities in an increasingly global world of internationalizing processes and patterns. Last, *relational space* is a truly radical attempt to collapse analysis into networked concerns such that there is no global and local to talk about, only unbounded geographies of becoming. Sites become the sources of analysis, but how sites relate to each other is not clear.

In the contemporary era, I would encourage future work in the area of the 'local in the global' to pay particular attention to power relations flowing through localities. Localities are not out there waiting to be found, but they are used by the state as 'territorial shapes' for public policy and are also mobilized by political actors when staking claims for identity and representation. These are concerns easily forgotten but they allow researchers to highlight issues of intra-local and inter-local based enrollments of subjects within state-based governmental projects or to trace civil society-centered mobilizations that emerge from ongoing class, social and political struggles.

Additionally, now that 'city-regions' (Scott, 2001) are being presented as the latest way of 'holding-down' the global and producing successful local economic development, I would follow Beauregard and Pierre (2000) and argue that strengthening local capacities makes more sense than automatically adopting a multitude of international initiatives.

REFERENCES

Agnew, J. (1987) *The United States in the World-Economy: A Regional Geography.* Cambridge: Cambridge University Press.

Amin, A. (2002) Spatialities of globalization. *Environment and Planning A*, 34: 385–99.

Amin, A. (2004) Regions unbound: Towards a new politics of place. *Geografiska Annaler*, 86B: 33–44.

Amin, A. and Thrift, N. (1994) Living in the global. In A. Amin and N. Thrift (eds) *Globalization, Institutions, and Regional Development in Europe.* Oxford: Oxford University Press.

Amin, A. and Thrift, N. (2002) *Cities: Reimagining the Urban.* Cambridge: Polity.

Amin, A., Massey, D. and Thrift, N. (2000) *Cities for the Many Not the Few.* Bristol: Policy Press.

Amin, A., Massey, D. and Thrift, N. (2003) *Decentering the Nation: A Radical Approach to Regional Inequality.* London: Catalyst.

Barnes, T. (1996) *Logics of Dislocation: Models, Metaphors, and Meanings of Economic Space.* New York: Guilford.

Beauregard, R.A. and Peirre, J. (2000) Disputing the global: A sceptical view of locality-based international initiatives. *Policy and Politics*, 28: 465–78.

Beynon, H. and Hudson, R. (1993) Place and space in contemporary Europe: Some lessons and reflections. *Antipode*, 25: 177–90.

Beynon, H., Hudson, R., Lewis, J., Sadler, D., and Townsend, A. (1989) 'It's all falling apart here': Coming to terms with the future in Teesside. In P. Cooke (ed.) *Localities: The Changing Face of Urban Britain.* London: Unwin Hyman.

Brenner, N. (2004) *New State Spaces: Urban Governance and the Rescaling of Statehood.* Oxford: Oxford University Press.

Brenner, N., Jessop, B., Jones, M., and MacLeod, G. (2003) *State/Space: A Reader.* Oxford: Blackwell.

Cooke, P. (1987) Clinical inference and geographical theory. *Antipode.* 19: 69–78.

Cooke, P. (ed.) (1989a) *Localities: The Changing Face of Urban Britain.* London: Unwin Hyman.

Cooke, P. (1989b) Locality-theory and the poverty of 'spatial variation'. *Antipode*, 21: 261–73.

Cooke, P. (1995) Introduction-regions, clusters and innovation networks. In P. Cooke (ed.) *The Rise of the Rustbelt.* London: UCL Press.

Cooke, P. (1998) Introduction: origins of the concept. In H.J. Braczyk, P. Cooke, and M. Heidenreich (eds) *Regional Innovation Systems: The Role of Governances in a Globalized World.* London: UCL Press.

Cooke, P. and Morgan, K. (1998) *The Associational Economy: Firms, Regions, and Innovation.* Oxford: Oxford University Press.

Cox, K. and Mair, A. (1991) From localised social structures to localities as agents. *Environment and Planning A*, 23: 197–213.

Duncan, S. (1989) What is locality. In R. Peet and N. Thrift (eds) *New Models in Geography: Volume Two.* London: Unwin Hyman.

Duncan, S. and Savage, M. (1989) Space, scale and locality. *Antipode.* 21: 179–206.

Duncan, S. and Savage, M. (1991) New perspectives on the locality debate. *Environment and Planning A*, 23: 155–64.

Gibson-Graham, J.K. (1994) Reflections on regions, the White Paper and a new politics of redistribution. *Australian Geographer*, 25: 148–53.

Hadjimichalis, C. (2006a) Non-economic factors in economic geography and in 'new regionalism': A sympathetic critique. *International Journal of Urban and Regional Research*, 30: 690–704.

Hadjimichalis, C. (2006b) The end of Third Italy as we knew it? *Antipode*, 38: 82–106.

Harloe, M., Pickvance, C. and Urry, J. (eds) (1990) *Place, Policy and Politics: Do Localities Matter?* London: Unwin Hyman.

Harvey, D. (1981) Conceptual and measurement problems in the cognitive-behavioural approach to location theory. In K.R. Cox and R.G. Golledge (eds) *Behavioural Problems in Geography Revisited*. London: Methuen.

Harvey, D. (1987) Three myths in search of a reality in urban studies. *Environment and Planning D: Society and Space*, 5: 367–76.

Harvey, D. (1989) *The Condition of Postmodernity: An Enquiry into the Origins of Cultural Change*. Oxford: Blackwell.

Hodder, B.W. and Lee, R. (1974) *Economic Geography*. London: Methuen.

House, J.W. (1974) *The UK Space: Resources, Environment and the Future*. London: Weidenfield & Nicolson.

Hudson, R. (1989) *Wrecking a Region: State Policies, Party Politics and Regional Change in North East England*. London: Pion.

Hudson, R. (1990) Trying to revive infant Hercules: The rise and fall of local authority modernization policies on Teesside. In M. Harloe, C. Pickvance and J. Urry (eds) *Place, Policy and Politics: Do Localities Matter?* London: Unwin Hyman.

Hudson, R. (2000) *Production, Places and Environment: Changing Perspectives in Economic Geography*. London: Prentice Hall.

Jeckson, P. (1991) Mapping meanings: A cultural critique of locality studies. *Environment and Planning* A23, 215–28.

Jessop, B. (1992) Fordism and post-Fordism: A critical formulation. In M. Storper and A. Scott (eds) *Pathways to Industrialization and Regional Development*. Routledge.

Jonas, A. (1988) A new regional concept of localities. *Area*, 20: 101–10.

Jones, M. and Jones, R. (2004) Nation states, ideological power and globalization: Can geographers catch the boat? *Geoforum*, 35: 409–24.

Jones, M. and MacLeod, G. (2004) Regional spaces, spaces of regionalism: Territory, insurgent politics, and the English question. *Transactions of the Institute of British Geographers*, 29: 433–52.

Leitner, H., Sheppard, E. and Sziarto, K.M. (2008) The spatialities of contentious politics. *Transactions of the Institute of British Geographers*, 33: 157–72.

Lloyd, P.E. and Dicken, P. (1972) *Location in Space: A Theoretical Approach to Economic Geography*. London: Harper & Row.

Lovering, J. (1989) The restructuring approach. In R. Peet and N. Thrift (eds) *New Models in Geography: Volume One*. London: Unwin Hyman.

Lovering, J. (1995) Creating discourses rather than jobs: The crisis in the cities and the transition fantasies of intellectuals and policy makers. In P. Healey, S. Cameron, S. Davoudi, S. Graham, and A. Madani-Pour (eds) *Managing Cities: The New Urban Context*. Chichester: Wiley.

Lovering, J. (1999) Theory led by policy: The inadequacies of the 'new regionalism' (illustrated from the case of Wales). *International Journal of Urban and Regional Research*, 23: 379–95.

MacLeod, G. (2001a) Beyond soft institutionalism: Accumulation, regulation, and their geographical fixes. *Environment and Planning A*, 33: 1145–67.

MacLeod, G. (2001b) New regionalism reconsidered: Globalization, regulation, and the recasting of political economic space. *International Journal of Urban and Regional Research*, 25: 804–29.

Manners, G., Keeble, D., Rodgers, B. and Warren, K. (1972) *Regional Development in Britain*. London: Wiley.

Marshall, M. (1987) *Long Waves of Regional Development*. Basingstoke: Macmillan.

Marston, S.A., Jones, J.P. III, and Woodward, K. (2005) Human geography without scale. *Transactions of the Institute of British Geographers*, 30: 416–32.

Marston, S.A., Jones III, J.P., and Woodward, K. (2005) Human geography without scale. *Transactions of the Institute of British Geographers*, 32: 264–76.

Martin, R. and Rowthorn, B. (eds) (1986) *The Geography of De-industrialisation*. Basingstoke: Macmillan.

Massey, D. (1984) *Spatial Divisions of Labour: Social Structures and the Geography of Production*. Basingstoke: Macmillan.

Massey, D. (1991) The political place of locality studies. *Environment and Planning A*, 23: 267–81.

Massey, D. (1994) *Space, Place and Gender*. Cambridge: Polity.

Morgan, K. (1997) The learning region: Institutions, innovation and regional renewal. *Regional Studies*, 31: 491–503.

Morgan, K. (2004) The exaggerated death of geography: Learning, proximity and territorial innovation systems. *Journal of Economic Geography*, 4: 3–21.

Murgatroyd, L., Savage, M., Shapiro, D., Urry, J., Walby, S., Warde, A. and Mark-Lawson, J. (1985) *Localities, Class, and Gender*. London: Pion.

Paasi, A. (1991) Deconstructing regions: Notes on the scales of spatial life. *Environment and Planning A*, 23: 239–56.

Pratt, A.C. (1991) Discourses of locality. *Environment and Planning A*, 23: 257–66.

Sayer, A. (1991) Behind the locality debate: Deconstructing geography's dualisms. *Environment and Planning A*, 23: 283–308.

Scott, A. (1988a) Flexible production systems and regional development: The rise of new industrial spaces in North America and Western Europe. *International Journal of Urban and Regional Research*, 12: 171–85.

Scott, A.J. (1988b) *New Industrial Spaces: Flexible Production Organization and Regional Development in North America and Western Europe*. London: Pion.

Scott, A.J. (2001) Globalization and the rise of city-regions. *European Planning Studies*, 9: 813–26.

Smith, N. (1987) Dangers of the empirical turn: Some comments on the CURS initiative. *Antipode*, 19: 59–68.

Storper, M. (1993) Regional 'worlds' of production: Learning and innovation in the technology districts of France, Italy and the USA. *Regional Studies*, 27: 433–55.

Storper, M. (1997) *The Regional World: Territorial Development in a Global Economy*. New York: Guilford Press.

Storper, M. and Scott, A.J. (eds) (1992) *Pathways to Industrialization and Regional Development*. London: Routledge.

Swyngedouw, E. (1997) Neither global nor local: 'Glocalization' and the politics of scale. In K.R. Cox (ed.) *Spaces of Globalization: Reasserting the Power of the Local*. New York: Guilford.

Tickell and Peck (1992) Accumulation, regulation and the geographies of post-Fordism: Missing links in regulationist research. *Progress in Human Geography*, 16: 190–218.

Tomaney, J. (2007) Keep a beat in the dark: Narratives of regional identity in Basil Bunting's Briggflatts. *Environment and Planning D: Society and Space*, 25: 355–75.

Ward, A. (1989) A recipe for a pudding: A comment on locality. *Antipode*, 21: 274–81.

Ward, S.V. (1994) *Planning and Urban Change*. London: Paul Chapman.

8

Critical Sociospatial Theory and the Geographies of Uneven Spatial Development

Neil Brenner

INTRODUCTION: CAPITALISM AND GEOGRAPHICAL DIFFERENCE

Spaces are different from one another. Think, for instance, of the neighborhoods, cities, regions or countries you have lived in or visited. Upon traveling elsewhere, to an unfamiliar location, differences become readily apparent. You are confronted with landscapes that do not resemble those to which you are accustomed. You may begin to catalogue the differences you experience. And you may struggle to decipher the hidden meanings that lurk behind these perceptions. This may in turn lead you to reflect upon the specificity, perhaps even the arbitrariness, of the spaces with which you are most familiar. Difference is thus no longer equated with the distant, the far-away, the exotic. It is revealed as being embedded within your own immediate surroundings, now understood in relation to multiple possible ways of organizing the spaces of everyday life.

The experience of geographical difference – that is, the recognition that spaces across the world differ from one another – is central to capitalist modernity. Of course, earlier historical social formations were not composed of smooth, homogenous settlement patterns and contained plenty of geographical heterogeneity. Long-distance networks of commerce, cultural exchange and warfare exposed populations to otherness, not only among people, but among places and territories. Geographical difference is thus hardly unique to the modern age. And yet, as Marx and Engels famously argued in the *Communist Manifesto* of 1848, the ability of populations to travel long distances, and thus to encounter otherness, has intensified qualitatively during the modern capitalist epoch, with its intrinsically globalizing dynamics. It continues to be enhanced in the early twenty-first century, as worldwide flows of capital, trade and migration accelerate and intensify.

Some commentators have claimed that geographical differences are today being annihilated, as the forces of 'globalization' homogenize the landscapes of everyday life. Most critical geographers reject such claims. They have argued, to the contrary, that late modern capitalism has been premised upon an intensification of differences among places and territories, even as the mobility of capital, commodities and populations is enhanced

(Cox, 1997; Lee and Wills, 1997). Struggles for a sense of place, for territorial rootedness and for a unique institutional-geographical niche remain as intense as ever (Massey, 1996). Precisely as interconnections among dispersed spaces around the globe are thickened, geographical differences are becoming more rather than less profound. Spatial unevenness thus remains endemic to the contemporary global capitalist (dis)order (Smith, 1997).

Given the centrality of geographical differences to contemporary capitalism, the task of deciphering their basic contours, their origins and their consequences would seem to be of particular urgency. Fortunately, such an inquiry has long been a central concern of human geography, broadly understood as the attempt to analyze the nature, construction and historical evolution of human spatial organization (hereafter, 'sociospatial organization,' or still more simply, 'sociospatiality'). The interdisciplinary field of human geography would thus appear to provide a useful intellectual resource for understanding the current historical moment.

During the last three decades, critical geographical scholarship has confronted the problem of geographical difference in a focused, theoretically reflexive way. The concept of *uneven spatial development* lies at the heart of such analyses. This concept is derived from Marx's foundational account of capital circulation in *Capital* (1976), where the notion of uneven development was used to describe the existence of differential growth rates among various sectors (or 'departments') of the capitalist economy. The latter concept was subsequently reinvented in the early twentieth century by socialist intellectuals such as Lenin, Luxemburg, Bukharin, Trotsky and (decades later) Mandel, who were concerned to understand the global expansion of the capitalist mode of production through imperialism and colonialism (Smith, 1984). The concept of uneven *spatial* development was introduced by radical geographers in the late 1970s and early 1980s, a period of extraordinary

intellectual creativity thanks to the path-breaking contributions of writers such as Lefebvre (1991 [1974]), Harvey (1982), Massey (1985), Smith (1984) and Soja (1985). Through their work on uneven spatial development (hereafter, 'USD'), these scholars and others in their intellectual milieux developed new ways of conceptualizing the production of geographical difference under modern capitalism.

According to this perspective, the existence of geographical difference is not simply an expression of the discrete qualities of particular places or territories. Rather, patterns of USD are produced through the historically specific social relations of capitalism. Just as importantly, these authors have argued that patterns of USD are mediated through large-scale institutional forms (such as the modern state) and diverse social forces (such as capitalist firms, business organizations, trade unions, property owners and place- or territory-based social movements). This means, in turn, that the analysis of geographical difference necessarily entails an inquiry into the 'politics of space' (Lefebvre 2008 [1976]) through which historically specific structures of sociospatial polarization are produced. Finally, critical geographers have argued that, even though certain deep structures of sociospatial inequality have persisted throughout the history of capitalism, USD is necessarily articulated in historically and contextually specific forms. Thus, for example, while global inequality and the urban/rural divide have remained persistent, durable features of capitalism, their precise geographical contours have been significantly reshaped during the course of capitalist development.

Geographical differences, then, are not pregiven or immutable features of the social landscape. Under modern capitalism, they are produced, in the form of USD, through historically specific political-economic processes. It is only through an understanding of such processes that changing historical forms of USD can be deciphered.

PROCESSES OF UNEVEN SPATIAL DEVELOPMENT

For purposes of a critical analysis of geographical difference, four key macrotheoretical claims can be derived from the critical-geographical literature on USD (on which see, most recently, Harvey, 2006):

- Patterns of USD result from an underlying tension within capitalism 'between the rising power to overcome space and the immobile spatial structures required for such a purpose' (Harvey 1985: 150). On the one hand, capital is inherently expansionary, orientated towards the overcoming of all geographical barriers to its expanded accumulation. On the other hand, the impulse to accelerate and expand the circuit of capital is premised upon the production of relatively fixed, immobilized sociospatial configurations. Examples of the latter include urban built environments, regional industrial agglomerations, large-scale transportation networks, information and telecommunications grids, systems of social reproduction and state regulatory institutions (Harvey, 1982). Therefore, as Harvey (1985: 145) notes, 'spatial organization is necessary to overcome space'.
- In developing this argument, Smith (1984: 87–90) points to the twin contradictory tendencies between spatial mobility and fixity and between geographical differentiation and universalization in the uneven development of the production of space under capitalism.

The differentiation of geographical space in the last century or so is a direct result of the need, inherent in capital, to immobilize capital in the landscape. It is all very well that $500 million can be whizzed around the world at the push of a button, but it must come from somewhere and be en route to somewhere. This somewhere is the production process, where in order to produce surplus value it is necessary that vast quantities of productive capital be spatially immobilized for relatively long periods in the form of factories, machinery, transport routes, warehouses and a host of other facilities. The spatial immobilization of capital in this way, or as national capitals delimited by the boundaries of the nation state, is simultaneously the production of a differentiated geographical space. Insofar as this immobilization process is matched by the mobility of capital, these opposing tendencies throw up not a random but a patterned internal differentiation of world space …

… the pattern which results is one of *uneven development*, not in a general sense but as the specific product of the contradictory dynamic guiding the production of space. Uneven development is the concrete mani-festation of the production of space under capitalism.

- The tension between capital's space-annihilating impulsion and its equally endemic dependence upon fixed sociospatial configurations unleashes a dynamic of continual restructuring, or 'creative destruction', under capitalism. Historically specific sociospatial infrastructures enable capital to circulate at accelerating turnover times, and within ever widening geographical parameters, but these infrastructures can provide no more than a temporary resolution to capital's endemic crisis-tendencies (Harvey, 1985). Consequently, when the tension between dispersal (space-annihilation) and concentration (space-dependency) becomes unmanageable, pressures to rework inherited sociospatial arrangements escalate, albeit in contextually specific ways. Thus ensues an often tumultuous process of sociospatial restructuring in which diverse social forces attempt to transform the inherited infrastructures upon which the accumulation process has, quite literally, been grounded. The outcome of such contestations is open-ended, for there is never any guarantee that the contradictions of an inherited sociospatial configuration will be effectively displaced.
- Because, as Harvey (1985: 150) notes, 'capitalist development must negotiate a knife-edge between preserving the values of past commitments made at a particular place and time, or devaluing them to open up fresh room for accumulation', the history of capital is

thoroughly discontinuous, and its geographies are chronically inconstant (Storper and Walker, 1989). It is grounded, fundamentally, upon a process of incessant, crisis-driven self-transformation, but one which is punctuated by periods of temporary stability in which dominant political-economic forces attempt, at least provisionally, to preserve established sociospatial arrangements. Harvey (1985) has famously suggested that such periods entail a form of 'structured coherence' or 'spatial fix' (see also Jessop 2006). Spatial fixes cannot, it must be emphasized, abolish the endemic socio-technological dynamism, institutional volatility and geographical instability of capitalism. Nonetheless, they entail the establishment of a temporarily stabilized, organizationally coherent and relatively durable pattern of sociospatial relations for production, exchange, consumption and everyday life.

The *longue durée* trends of USD under capitalism are direct products of the contradictory processes outlined above. Capital accumulation hinges upon the production of historically specific and internally differentiated sociospatial configurations. At the same time, patterns of USD are periodically disrupted due to capital's impulsion, in the wake of crisis, to 'creatively destroy' established sociospatial infrastructures. As new spatial foundations for capitalist development are provisionally established, inherited forms of USD are rewoven, generally in ways that modify some of their contours while reproducing others. In this sense, USD is not only the *product* of capitalism, but a basic *precondition* for its systemic reproduction. As Soja (1989: 107) explains, 'Capitalism [...] intrinsically builds upon regional or spatial inequalities as a necessary means for its continued survival. The very existence of capitalism presupposes the sustaining presence and vital instrumentality of geographically uneven development'. Accordingly, the analysis of USD must attempt to capture not only the restless dynamism of capitalist sociospatiality, its endemic instability,

volatility and malleability, but also its apparent structured coherence during periods in which relatively stabilized infrastructures for the process of capital circulation have been consolidated.

GEOGRAPHIES OF UNEVEN SPATIAL DEVELOPMENT

'Mille feuille'/A thousand leaves

Up to this point, our discussion has deployed the term 'space' as a generic category for describing geographical difference. We have thus referred to 'spaces', 'sociospatiality', 'spatial differentiation', and, most generally, to 'uneven spatial development', without delineating the specific forms in which they are articulated. At this stage, it is essential to examine more closely the fabric of social space, and specifically, the contours of USD. To this end, Lefebvre's (1991) emphasis on the *polymorphic* character of social space provides a useful starting point. From this point of view, the geographies of any social process – such as urbanization, state power, capital accumulation or uneven development – cannot be understood with reference merely to a singular principle or all-encompassing pattern. Instead, several intertwined yet analytically distinct processes are involved in the production of modern sociospatiality:

- The process of *place-making* entails geographical proximity, the embedding of social relations within particular locations and patterns of areal (horizontal) differentiation (Massey, 1996; Gieryn, 2000; Paasi, 2004).
- The process of *territorialization* entails the enclosure, bordering and parcelization of social relations (Sack, 1986; Taylor, 1994; Newman and Paasi, 1998).
- The process of *scaling* entails the vertical differentiation of social relations among (for instance) global, supranational, national, regional, urban and/or local levels (Smith, 1995; Howitt, 1998; Swyngedouw, 1997).

- The process of *networking* entails the establishment of transversal, topological or 'rhizomatic' interconnections across geographically dispersed locations or organizational units (Whatmore and Thorne, 1997; Leitner, 2004; Sum, 1997; Castells, 1996).

It is thus methodologically imperative to view every social space as a medium and outcome of diverse processes of sociospatial structuration, and consequently, to subject each of the latter to sustained analysis. In his classic work of sociospatial theory, *The Production of Space*, Lefebvre (1991; 85–88 [1974]) develops this point through his thesis of the 'superimposition and interpenetration of social spaces':

> ... the *places* of social space are very different from those of natural space in that they are not simply juxtaposed: they may be intercalated, combined, superimposed [...] Consequently the local [...] does not disappear, for it is never absorbed by the regional, national, or even worldwide level. The national and regional levels take in innumerable 'places'; national space embraces the regions; and world space does not merely subsume national spaces, but even (for the time being at least) precipitates the formation of new national spaces through a remarkable process of fission....

In one vivid formulation, Lefebvre (1991: 88) likens the superimposed dimensions of social space within capitalist modernity to the intricate, asymmetrical layerings within a *mille feuille* pastry – a powdery French dessert that means, literally, 'a thousand leaves'. While Lefebvre's somewhat fanciful culinary metaphor may distract us momentarily from the intricacies of sociospatial theory, it has direct implications for the discussion at hand. For, like the *mille feuille*, formations of USD are composed of complex articulations among multiple patterns, contours, lines, folds, points, clusters and edges. Drawing upon the distinction between place, territory, scale and networks introduced above (see also Brenner et al., 2006; Dicken et al., 2001; Paasi, 2004; Sheppard, 2002), the remainder of this chapter elaborates this contention through a series of macrogeographical generalizations regarding the evolutionary patterning of USD during the *longue durée* history of capitalism.

While I have found it useful in what follows to devote a separate subsection to each of the four dimensions of sociospatiality mentioned above, we shall see that these dimensions are mutually formative and inextricably intertwined. Accordingly, the distinction between place, territory, scale and networks should thus be understood as a purely analytical device designed to decipher the hypercomplex layerings of modern sociospatiality. The discussion begins with a discussion of how place articulates and mediates patterns of USD, but then systematically integrates each of the other dimensions of sociospatiality to create a more geographically nuanced depiction.

Places and uneven spatial development

Capitalism emerged within a differentiated geographical landscape inherited from previous modes of production. Key features of the latter included food production zones, precapitalist urban systems, feudal systems of agricultural production and land tenure, absolutist state structures, and local and long-distance trading networks (Knox and Agnew, 1995). Nonetheless, even in its incipient stages, capitalist expansion entailed profound transformations of places, above all through the establishment of new spatial divisions of labor in which dispersed geographical locations were assigned specific functional roles within the rapidly expanding capitalist world market. Initially, under merchant capitalism (1600–1750), these spatial divisions of labour were articulated closely with circuits of precapitalist trade and the geographies of inherited resource endowments – for instance, the locations of waterways, raw materials, mineral supplies and so forth. However, with the progressive industrialization of capital since the mid-eighteenth century, and the increasing integration of the labour process into circuits of accumulation, specifically capitalist spatial divisions of labour emerged that have been based predominantly upon socially constructed economic assets such as agglomeration economies. Under these circumstances, beginning in the core zones of western Europe and eventually extending throughout the world economy, urbanization processes dramatically accelerated as capital and labour were concentrated within large-scale, specialized production complexes and long-distance trade networks were at once expanded and thickened. On a macrogeographical level, these trends also entailed the consolidation of a worldwide grid of places differentiated according to their functions within the spaces of global accumulation (Läpple, 1978). This differentiated landscape of places and place-making processes has articulated patterns of USD in at least five key ways:

- First, new spatial divisions emerged within expanding centres of capitalist production through residential segregation, the functional differentiation of urban space and the consolidation of new urban infrastructures for production and social reproduction.
- Second, the urban/rural divide was exacerbated as rapid industrialization fuelled large-scale urbanization and an increasing peripheralization or 'underdevelopment' of rural spaces. The division between two distinct *types* of places – capital-rich, industrializing urban centres and capital-poor, predominantly agrarian peripheries – thus became an essential axis of capitalist USD (Myrdal, 1957).
- Third, as places across the global periphery were transformed into sites for the primary extraction, processing and export of raw materials, a worldwide pattern of USD emerged in which core, capital-rich zones of large-scale industrialization were differentiated from peripheral, capital-poor areas of relative underdevelopment (Wallerstein, 1974).
- Fourth, as industrial restructuring has accelerated since the nineteenth century, new forms of inter-place differentiation have rippled across the global system. As Storper and Walker (1989: 5) explain, 'each wave of industrialization brings into existence new growth centres and growth peripheries, stimulates disinvestment in some areas and the radical restructuring of others, and reshuffles spatial production relations and patterns of

territorial income distribution and politics'. Such restructuring processes have unsettled the concrete patterns associated with each of the three previously mentioned forms of place-based USD (intra-urban, urban/rural and global core/periphery).
- Fifth, places may become basing points and arenas for social mobilizations that destabilize broader patterns of USD (Harvey, 1989). This is because, even as capital strives to transform places, place-based commitments persist in the form of everyday routines, regimes of social reproduction, institutionalized political compromises and sociocultural identities. Such place-based commitments are often articulated quite sharply when broader processes of capitalist restructuring destabilize places and patterns of inter-place relations. Consequently, capital's impulse to rework spatial divisions of labour in search of new opportunities for profit-making may encounter stiff resistance from those whose everyday lives, livelihoods and identities are tightly enmeshed within those sociospatial landscapes. The resultant forms of place-based 'revulsion and revolt' may assume reactionary or progressive forms (Harvey, 1989) but, whatever their political valence, the cumulative impact of such mobilizations is to insert an element of friction into capital's process of creative destruction. Places, in other words, cannot be creatively destroyed according to the whim of capital; rather, their evolution is an object and stake of intensive sociopolitical contestation and negotiation (Hudson, 2001).

Territories and uneven spatial development

Capitalism emerged in medieval Europe within a decentralized mosaic of political-economic spaces. This mosaic encompassed, among other spatial forms, small city-state enclaves, inter-urban networks, bishoprics, duchies, principalities and a patchwork of absolutist state structures lacking fixed territorial boundaries (Spruyt, 1994). However, following the Peace of Westphalia of 1648, the principle of territoriality became an increasingly foundational basis for organizing political life. Despite continued institutional and geographical diversity among them, states were now understood to occupy mutually exclusive, nonoverlapping, contiguous and sovereign territorial spaces, and were reflexively monitored as such (Ruggie, 1993). Borders were now seen clearly to separate the 'inside' from the 'outside' of states, and the domestic/foreign divide came to serve as a basic reference point for political-economic activity (Walker, 1993). With the consolidation of mercantile capitalism, this grid of state territories was entrenched as both statesmen and capitalists attempted to expand international trade, to consolidate national markets and, thereby, to increase national wealth (Braudel, 1984). The territorialization of worldwide social space continued during the first industrial revolution through (a) the intensified regulation of inter-state boundaries; (b) the increasing internal parcelization of state space among intergovernmental administrative hierarchies; (c) the development of enhanced infrastructural capacities through which states could attempt to extend their authority within their borders; and (d) the imperialist conquest and territorial division of peripheralized zones of the world economy (Maier, 2000).

These territorializations of political-economic life were maintained during subsequent rounds of capitalist industrialization in the nineteenth and twentieth centuries, even through phases of profound geoeconomic and geopolitical instability. But this is not to suggest that territoriality has remained static within the Westphalian system. On the contrary, its specific roles have evolved significantly. The power and wealth containers of early modern territorial states were superseded, during the last two centuries, by new forms of state developmentalism, nationalism and welfarism that were likewise grounded upon distinctively territorial structures and strategies (Taylor, 1994). Concomitantly, the concrete geographies of interstate borders and intra-state jurisdictional divisions have periodically been modified, whether through warfare, internal

rebellions, legal decisions or social protest. And, as inter-state relations have evolved in relation to the broader dynamic of worldwide capitalist development, new, large-scale territorial institutions (for instance, the European Union, NAFTA, ASEAN and Mercosur) have been introduced that encompass multiple (national) state structures. Nonetheless, the underlying principle of territoriality has been reproduced as a basic dimension of modern political-economic space. Most crucially for our purposes, the evolving landscapes of state territorial organization have mediated forms of USD in at least five central ways:

- First, as the Westphalian interstate system has been consolidated and extended throughout the world, territory has come to serve as a taken-for-granted category for the understanding of sociospatial organization more generally (Häkli, 2001). As a result, patterns of USD have been widely conceptualized in territorial terms, whether in institutionalized forms of data collection (for instance, in national censuses, OECD statistical tables or World Bank development reports), in political discourse (for instance, in debates on spatial inequalities within territorially demarcated areas such as Europe, Britain, the South East of England or London) or in everyday life (for instance, in popular representations of 'Africa' or 'the ghetto').
- Second, even when the concrete geographies of capital are being thoroughly rearranged, the modern interstate system has continued to provide a relatively fixed, stable grid of institutionalized sociospatial divisions – a world of parcelized, bordered spaces – in and through which the process of capital circulation may unfold. Such borders may impose significant constraints upon the capitalist drive to relocate investment activity, and more generally, to engage in creative destruction.
- Third, state territorial borders and internal jurisdictional boundaries have direct, durable implications for the concrete forms in which place-based inequalities are articulated. This is because different types of state territorial structures and regulatory arrangements

organize widely divergent conditions for capital circulation. For instance, the relative costs and availability of labour-power, equipment, land and raw materials, the nature of transportation and communications infrastructures, and the level of taxation and tariffs may diverge among different state territories, as well as among intra-state political jurisdictions. Such inter- and intra-territorial differences are likely to have profound ramifications for the locational geographies of capital and, by implication, larger-scale spatial divisions of labour. In this sense, the geographies of (state) territories not only interpenetrate place-based patterns of USD, but directly shape them.

- Fourth, in significant measure due to their territorially centralized institutional structures, state institutions have the capacity to mobilize political strategies to influence patterns of USD directly both within and beyond their borders (Brenner, 2004). States may pursue this goal through diverse policy instruments, including industrial policies, economic development initiatives, infrastructure investments, spatial planning programmes, labour market policies, regional policies, urban policies, housing policies, international trade agreements and imperialist interventions, all of which have direct or indirect ramifications for intra- and supra-state geographies of production, reproduction and circulation. While the concrete effects of such interventions have varied considerably, and have often been considerably at odds with their declared purpose, this brief catalogue of spatial strategies illustrates the multifarious ways in which states have attempted to influence patterns of USD both within and beyond their jurisdictions.

- Finally, the territorial structures of the state provide various overlapping institutional arenas in which social movements may attempt to modify inherited forms of USD. As indicated previously, insofar as places represent the most immediate geographical terrain on which the disruptive consequences of capitalist creative destruction are experienced, social movements concerned to influence patterns of USD frequently assume a place-based

form. Crucially, however, the 'nested hierarchical structures' of the state (Harvey, 1982: 430) may likewise become an important platform for social forces concerned to confront the dislocations of creative destruction. Insofar as place-based mobilizations attempt to harness the institutional capacities of the state, they assume an at least partially territorial form. At the same time, many mobilizations around the geographies of creative destruction are orientated towards the pursuit of political influence (regarding, for instance, public revenue flows, electoral outcomes, policy agendas or legal arrangements), and thus assume an even more immediately territorial form. Finally, capitalists may adopt territorial strategies of their own, harnessing state institutions in order to preserve, modify or transform the spatial divisions of labour upon which their accumulation strategies depend. In this manner, the territorial structures of the state become a terrain of political contestation in which diverse social forces struggle to influence the geographies of capital accumulation (Cox, 1990).

Scales and uneven spatial development

The preceding discussion of places and territories in the geographies of USD has presupposed a third dimension of sociospatial differentiation that has not yet been made theoretically explicit – that of geographical scale. In addition to the 'horizontal' or areal differentiation of social practices across places and territories (geographical scope), there is also an equally fundamental, 'vertical' differentiation in which social relations are hierarchically articulated among – for instance – global, supranational, national, regional, metropolitan and/ or local scales (Swyngedouw, 1997; Collinge, 1999). The specific labels given to different spatial scales are less important, for present purposes, than the fundamental dimension of sociospatiality to which they refer. Insofar as any social, political or economic process or institutional form is internally differentiated into a vertical hierarchy of relatively discrete spatial units, the problem of its scalar organization arises (Brenner, 2001). Thus understood, like other macrogeographical processes under capitalism, USD is profoundly scale-differentiated (Smith, 1984). Indeed, all of the aspects of USD discussed above are typically articulated in scale-differentiated forms.

The establishment of distinctively capitalist spatial divisions of labour and the territorialization of political power during the course of capitalist industrialization entailed not only the transformation of places, the consolidation of new intra- and inter-place divisions, the territorial extension of capitalism beyond its European heartlands and the territorial segmentation of sociospatial inequality throughout the capitalist space-economy. These developments were closely intertwined with qualitatively new forms of scalar differentiation, including, most centrally:

- The consolidation and entrenchment of the *global* scale, embodied in the world market, as the ultimate geographical horizon for capitalist expansion (Wallerstein, 1974).
- The consolidation and entrenchment of the *national* scale, embodied in the politico-institutional hierarchies of the territorial state, as an institutionalized terrain of mediation within the process of intercapitalist competition (Smith, 1995). This national scaling of USD also involved the modular replication of the territorial state form to create a worldwide system of nationally configured political spaces (Taylor, 1994).
- The institutionalization of the *urban* and *regional* scales, embodied in major metropolitan centres, as key spatial niches for agglomerations of capital and labour (Storper and Walker, 1989). This urban and regional scaling of USD also involved the strategic positioning of cities and city-regions within a broader hierarchy of sociospatial forms stretching from the local to the global scales.
- In close conjunction with the latter trends, processes of USD have been articulated with several additional geographical scales, including: (a) the *neighbourhood* scale, embodied in intra-urban zones of association and political

jurisdiction; and (b) the *supranational* scale, embodied in institutionally demarcated spaces of capital circulation and political regulation that encompass multiple national states but do not extend to the entire globe.

Each of the aforementioned scalings of USD have been tightly intertwined with place-based and territorial inequalities; yet their scalar dimension cannot be adequately understood in terms of, or reduced to, either of the latter axes of sociospatial differentiation.

Because scales are defined relationally, the coherence of those listed above can be grasped only with reference to their distinctive positions within the broader interscalar hierarchies in which they are embedded. Concomitantly, because the functions, institutional expressions and interconnections among these scales have evolved significantly during the long-term history of capitalism, their differentiation should not be treated as an absolute functional requirement for the reproduction of capital. Nonetheless, insofar as the differentiation among the neighbourhood, urban, regional, national, supranational and global scales has been reproduced even as historically specific spatial divisions of labour and territorial arrangements have been creatively destroyed, they must be viewed as deep structures within capitalism's restlessly changing geographical landscape.

However, just as place-based and territorial patterns of USD have been reworked during the geohistory of capitalism, so too have its scalar geographies. The scalar configuration of USD has assumed historically specific forms *within* the capitalist system and, concomitantly, has been periodically junked and rewoven (Swyngedouw, 1992; Brenner, 1998). These successive waves of 'rescaling' represent an essential medium and expression of USD under capitalism.

- Mercantile and early industrial capitalism involved a generalized condition of 'scale relativization' (Collinge, 1996) in which no single scale served as the dominant level of political-economic organization. Patterns of USD were articulated at multiple spatial scales, from the urban (within and among towns, cities and city-states) and the national (within and among emergent absolutist state forms) to the imperial (within and among long-distance trading systems, inter-urban leagues and imperial networks) and the global (within and beyond the emergent capitalist world economy). Spatial scales thus provided a relatively malleable scaffolding in and through which USD could be differentiated among diverse types of places, territories and zones of exchange.

- This situation was rearticulated during the period of territorial state consolidation that began in the eighteenth century and continued through successive waves of capitalist industrialization and restructuring well into the twentieth century. From this broad period until the termination of national-developmentalist capitalism (early 1970s), the national scale gradually became predominant as at once a crystallization point for USD and an institutional locus for political strategies to manage the latter. To be sure, patterns of USD were articulated powerfully at all other spatial scales as well, from the global to the local, but the increasing territorialization of political-economic life during this epoch was inextricably linked to a generalized nationalization of sociospatial inequality (Maier, 2000).

- The most recent round of worldwide capitalist restructuring of the post-1970s period has decentred the nationalized 'scalar fix' (Smith, 1995) that underpinned previous rounds of capitalist industrialization and engendered a renewed turn towards scale relativization. The expansion in the roles of transnational corporations and global finance capital, coupled with the consolidation of a new international division of labour, the emergence of postfordist forms of industrial agglomeration, the intensification of international diasporic flows, and the growing importance of new information technologies in mediating worldwide

economic transactions, are among the most significant indicators of this systemic realignment (Agnew and Corbridge, 1994).

- Some scholars have characterized these trends with reference to the purported ascendancy of a single spatial scale – as, for instance, in accounts of the 'new globalism', 'triadization', 'Europeanization', the 'new regionalism', the 'new localism' or the 'local-global nexus' (for a useful overview, see Lee and Wills, 1997). By contrast, the argument proposed here is that the scalar architecture of capitalism as a whole – and, specifically, of USD – is being contested and reworked (Brenner, 1998; Swyngedouw, 1997). This line of interpretation builds upon the important observation that previously nodal, subordinate or marginal spatial scales – from the global and the supranational to the regional and the local – have acquired a renewed significance in contemporary political-economic processes and struggles.

- The claim is not that the national scale is being superseded, or that any other scale has now acquired a dominance akin to that of the national during previous periods of capitalist geohistory. Rather, the significance of the national is now ever more tightly linked to other, supra- and sub-national scales of political-economic organization than was previously the case. Concomitantly, patterns of USD are no longer configured coherently around a single, predominant scale of political-economic organization. These developments arguably represent the *differentia specifica* of contemporary forms of scale relativization. Indeed, for Jessop (2000: 2179):

[T]here is no new privileged scale around which other levels are now being organized to ensure structured coherence within and across scales. Instead there are continuing struggles over which spatial scale should become primary and how scales should be articulated and this is reflected in a more complex nesting and interweaving of different scales as they become rearticulated [...] The new political economy of scale does not involve a pregiven set of places, spaces or scales that are merely being reordered. Instead, new places are emerging, new spaces are being created, new scales of organization are being developed and new horizons of action are being imagined ...

However, the contemporary relativization of scales must not be misconstrued as a transcendence or alleviation of USD. For, as Smith (1997: 183) pointedly argues, 'The global restructuring of the 1980s and 1990s embodies not so much an evening out of social and economic development levels across the globe as a deepening and reorganization of existing patterns of uneven geographical development'. Deciphering the interplay between contemporary scale relativization and these newly emergent forms of USD represents one of the most urgent analytical tasks in contemporary studies of rescaling processes.

In sum, this discussion suggests several key ways in which scaling processes may influence, and in turn be shaped by, processes of USD.

- The *differentiation of scales* under capitalism generates a hierarchical but often tangled scaffolding of sociospatial forms in and through which processes of USD may be organized.
- Scalar configurations are themselves internally differentiated insofar as they contain divisions of labour among their constitutive tiers (*scalar divisions of labour*).
- *Scalar fixes* may emerge insofar as interscalar relations are provisionally stabilized around a relatively coherent, durable scalar division of labour.
- As scalar fixes are destabilized and interscalar relations are unsettled, *rescaling processes* ensue in which reconfigured interscalar hierarchies and, on occasion, new scales of political-economic organization, are produced.
- As interscalar arrangements are contested, a *politics of scale* emerges in which diverse social forces struggle to reorganize the functions, organizational embodiments and/or interconnections among spatial scales (Smith, 1995).

Networks and the futures of uneven spatial development

These considerations bring us to one final dimension of USD that has attracted considerable attention in recent years – namely, the role of networks as the basis for a mode of sociospatial organization based upon 'points of connection and lines of flow, as opposed to [...] fixed surfaces and boundaries" (Whatmore and Thorne, 1997: 289). For Whatmore and Thorne (1997: 295), networks represent a 'mode of ordering of connectivity' in which diverse social spaces are linked together transversally across places, territories and scales. In closely analogous terms, Leitner (2004: 248) suggests that networks 'span space' by establishing horizontal, capillary-like, topological interlinkages among geographically dispersed nodal points (Leitner, 2004: 248). Consequently, 'the spatial surface spanned by networks is [...] fluid and unstable' insofar as (a) the degree of connectivity among network nodes may fluctuate; (b) patterns of network membership may fluctuate; and (c) multiple networks may overlap, interpenetrate and crosscut one another (Leitner, 2004: 248–49).

Network geographies have long figured centrally in the geohistory of capitalism, and they have been enmeshed with the uneven geographies of places, territories and scales in nearly all of their concrete forms. Indeed, inter-firm networks, diasporic networks, inter-city networks, infrastructural networks, inter-state networks and network-based social movements have thoroughly interpenetrated the place-based, territorial and scalar geographies of mercantile, industrial, Fordist – Keynesian and globalizing capitalism surveyed above. Three brief examples illustrate the influence of networks upon patterns of USD.

- Capital accumulation has long hinged upon networked relationships among firms. Although capitalist firms within the same sector compete for profit shares, others engage in cooperative relations through subcontracting, information sharing and diverse 'untraded interdependencies' (Storper, 1996). Such interfirm linkages have intensified patterns of urban-regional agglomeration, and by implication, the broader geographies of USD.

- The globalization of the interstate system has entailed networked relationships both within and among national state apparatuses. Through international organizations, international treaties, international agreements and other types of informal regulatory and judicial agreements, networks have played an important mediating role in governing the global interstate system (Rosenau and Czempiel, 1992). Networks have also long figured centrally in intergovernmental relations within each national state, where they have served to coordinate activities among diverse agencies, branches and tiers of government. Insofar as such networks influence the geographies of capital investment, public expenditure and sociopolitical struggle, they also impact patterns of USD.
- While social movements frequently assume place, territory- and scale-based forms, they have also deployed networked modes of organization. From the international socialist movement to ACT UP and the global justice movement, the activities of social movements have long depended upon networked interspatial ties as a basis for communication, organization and mobilization across places, scales and territories. Insofar as networking strategies impact the ability of social movements to influence processes of sociospatial change under capitalism, they also impact historically specific formations of USD.

In sum, whether they are produced by capitalist firms, state institutions, social movements or any other organized social forces, networks may impact patterns of USD in at least two central ways.

- First, networks generally crosscut place-based, territorial and scalar patterns of USD. In so doing, network formations may reinforce, interrupt or destabilize intra-place divisions, spatial divisions of labour, territorial borders, inter-territorial relations or scalar hierarchies. Concomitantly, networks may also reinforce rather than alleviate extant geographies of sociospatial inequality (Sheppard, 2002).
- Second, and contrary to popular representations of networks as nonhierarchical and democratic, many actually existing networks are internally stratified and externally exclusionary. They generally contain power hierarchies that marginalize some social forces at the expense of others, both within and beyond the network (Leitner and Sheppard, 2002). These may be manifested through the differential abilities of participants to influence network operations; through the establishment of divisions of labour that differentially allocate resources, tasks and burdens; or through the establishment of rules of closure that limit participation to particular individuals, groups or organizational entities. While these network-based power relations may be expressed in variegated socio-organizational forms, they may be closely intertwined with USD to the extent that they impact patterns of sociospatial organization (see for example, Dicken et al., 2001).

The question of how network geographies are impacting contemporary patterns of USD is a matter of considerable scholarly contention. Some globalization researchers have suggested that networks are today superseding the geographies of place, territory and scale upon which so much of the geohistory of capitalism has been grounded. Alongside predictions that territoriality is being dissolved due to processes of deterritorialization (see, for instance, O'Brien, 1990), this position has recently been articulated through several influential interventions, including Castells' (1996) notion of the 'space of flows,' Amin's (2002) arguments for a 'nonscalar and topological' interpretation of globalization and Marston et al.'s (2005) recent plea for a 'flat ontology'. Of course, these authors' diverse concerns cannot be reduced to the theme of USD, but they do imply that inherited formations of sociospatial inequality – whether organized within and among places, territories or scales – are now being transcended through a radically new form of sociospatiality, based upon an ontology of networks.

It is not possible here to settle the question of how inherited patterns of USD are being remolded. Nonetheless, the arguments developed in this chapter provide grounds for skepticism regarding any approach that privileges a singular dimension of sociospatiality. The observation that networked forms of sociospatial organization have acquired renewed significance under contemporary capitalism is of considerable significance. However, this does not logically translate into the claim that places, territories and scales no longer exist, or no longer serve to mediate processes of USD. To proceed otherwise is to reduce the *mille feuille* of modern sociospatiality into a singular, totalized image, that of the network. From the point of view developed in this chapter, it is more plausible to envision a scenario in which networked geographies are being *rearticulated* with inherited patterns of place-making, territorialization and scaling through an uneven, contested process of creative destruction.

CODA

The investigation of USD has long been central to the agenda of critical sociospatial theory. Against this background, this chapter has explored the sources of USD under capitalism and, on the basis of an analytical distinction among four key dimensions of sociospatiality, investigated its polymorphic sociospatial expressions.

But this analysis leaves open the question of whether, and if so how, contemporary forms of sociospatial polarization might be alleviated or transcended. This is, in fact, a central concern for critical sociospatial theorists, whose studies of USD have been intended to unmask some of the underlying mechanisms of domination, marginalization and exclusion upon which contemporary political-economic geographies are grounded. This is in turn viewed as a crucial precondition for the mobilization of alternative visions of sociospatiality in which progressive or radical principles, such as social justice, grassroots democracy, cultural diversity and environmental

sustainability, would supersede the capitalist imperative of endless accumulation (Harvey, 2006). Thus conceived, the theory of USD provides a key intellectual basis on which to connect the lived experience of geographical difference – our starting point in this chapter – to a broader analysis and critique of sociospatial inequality under capitalism.

REFERENCES

Agnew, J. and Corbridge, S. (1994) *Mastering Space*. New York: Routledge.

Amin, A. (2002) Spatialities of globalization. *Environment and Planning A*, 34: 385–99.

Braudel, F. (1984) *The Perspective of the World*. Berkeley: University of California Press.

Brenner, N. (1998) Between fixity and motion: Accumulation, territorial organization and the historical geography of spatial scales. *Environment and Planning D: Society and Space*, 16: 459–81.

Brenner, N. (2001) The limits to scale? Methodological reflections on scalar structuration. *Progress in Human Geography*, 15(4): 525–48.

Brenner, N. (2004) *New State Spaces*. New York: Oxford University Press.

Brenner, N., Jessop, B., Jones, M., and MacLeod, G. (2006) *State/Space and the Political Economy of Capitalism*. Lecture at NIRSA, National University of Ireland, Maynooth, 15 May.

Castells, M. (1996) *The Rise of the Network Society*. Cambridge, MA: Blackwell.

Collinge, C. (1999) 'Spatial Articulation of the State: Reworking Social Relations and Social Regulation Theory', unpublished paper. Centre for Urban and Regional Studies, University of Birmingham.

Collinge, C. (1999) Self-organization of society by scale. *Environment and Planning D: Society and Space*, 17: 557–74.

Cox, K. (1990) Territorial structures of the state. *Tijdschrift voor Economische en Sociale Geografie*, 81(4): 251–66.

Cox, K. (ed.) (1997) *Spaces of Globalization*. New York: Guilford.

Dicken, P., Kelly, P., Olds, K., and Yeung, H.W. (2001) Chains and networks, territories and scales. *Global Networks*, 1(2): 89–112.

Gieryn, T. (2000) A space for place in sociology. *Annual Review of Sociology*, 26: 463–96.

Häkli, J. (2001) In the territory of knowledge: State-centered discourses and the construction of society. *Progress in Human Geography*, 25(3): 403–22.

Harvey, D. (1982) *The Limits to Capital*. Chicago: University of Chicago Press.

Harvey, D. (1985) The geopolitics of capitalism. In D. Gregory and J. Urry (eds) *Social Relations and Spatial Structures*. London: Macmillan. pp. 128–63.

Harvey, D. (1989) *The Urban Experience*. Baltimore: Johns Hopkins Press.

Harvey, D. (2006) *Spaces of Global Capitalism*. London: Verso.

Howitt, R. (1998) Scale as relation. *Area*, 30(1): 49–58.

Hudson, R. (2001) *Producing Places*. New York: Guilford Publishers.

Jessop, B. (2000) The crisis of the national spatio-temporal fix and the ecological dominance of globalizing capitalism. *International Journal of Urban and Regional Research*, 24(2): 323–60.

Jessop, B. (2006) Spatial fixes, temporal fixes and spatio-temporal fixes. In D. Gregory and N. Castree (eds) *David Harvey: A Critical Reader*. Malden, MA: Blackwell.

Knox, P. and Agnew, J. (1995) *The Geography of the World Economy* (2nd edn). London: Edward Arnold.

Läpple, D. (1978) Gesellschaftlicher Reproduktionsprozeß und Stadtstrukturen. In M. Mayer, R. Roth and V. Brandes (eds), *Stadtkrise und soziale Bewegungen*. Frankfurt am Main: Europäische Verlagsanstalt. pp. 23–54.

Lee, R. and Wills, J. (eds) (1997) *Geographies of Economies*. London: Arnold.

Lefebvre, H. (1991 [1974]) *The Production of Space*. Cambridge, MA: Blackwell.

Lefebvre, H. (2008 [1976]) Reflections on the politics of space. In N. Brenner and S. Elden (eds) *Henri Lefebvre: State, Space, World*. Minneapolis, MN: University of Minnesota Press [forthcoming].

Leitner, H. (2004) The politics of scale and networks of spatial connectivity. In E. Sheppard and R. McMaster (eds) *Scale and Geographic Inquiry*. Oxford: Blackwell. pp. 236–55.

Leitner, H. and Sheppard, E. (2002) 'The city is dead, long live the net': Harnessing European interurban networks for a neoliberal agenda. In N. Brenner and N. Theodore (eds) *Spaces of Neoliberalism*. Oxford: Blackwell. pp. 148–71.

Maier, C. (2000) Consigning the twentieth century to history. *American Historical Review*, 105(3): 807–31.

Marston, S., Jones, J.P., and Woodward, K. (2005) Human geography without scale. *Transactions, Institute of British Geographers*, 30: 416–32.

Marx, K. (1976 [1867]) *Capital* (*Translated by Ben Fowkes*). New York: Penguin.

Massey, D. (1985) *Spatial Divisions of Labour*. London: Macmillan.

Massey, D. (1996) *Space, Place and Gender*. Minneapolis, MN.: University of Minnesota Press.

Myrdal, G. (1957) *Rich Lands and Poor*. New York: Harper & Brothers.

Newman, D. and Paasi, A. (1998) Fences and neighbours in the postmodern world. *Progress in Human Geography*, 22(2): 186–207.

O'Brien, R. (1990) *Global Financial Integration*. London: Pinter.

Paasi, A. (2004) Place and region: Looking through the prism of scale. *Progress in Human Geography*, 28(4): 536–46.

Rosenau, J. and Czempiel, E.-N. (eds) (1992) *Governance without Government*. Cambridge: Cambridge University Press.

Ruggie, J. (1993) Territoriality and beyond: Problematizing modernity in international relations. *International Organization*, 47(1): 139–74.

Sack, R. (1986) *Human Territoriality*. New York: Cambridge University Press.

Sheppard, E. (2002) The spaces and times of globalization. *Economic Geography*, 78(3): 307–30.

Smith, N. (1984) *Uneven Development*. Cambridge, MA: Blackwell.

Smith, N. (1995) Remaking scale. In H. Eskelinen and F. Snickars (eds) *Competitive European Peripheries*. Berlin: Springer Verlag. pp. 59–74.

Smith, N. (1997) The Satanic geographies of globalization. *Public Culture*, 10(1): 169–92.

Soja, E. (1985) Regions in context. *Environment and Planning D: Society and Space*, 3: 175–90.

Soja, E. (1989) *Postmodern Geographies*. New York: Verso.

Spruyt, H. (1994) *The Sovereign State and its Competitors*. Princeton, NJ: Princeton University Press.

Storper, M. (1996) *The Regional World*. New York: Guilford.

Storper, M. and Walker, R. (1989) *The Capitalist Imperative*. Cambridge, MA: Blackwell.

Sum, N.-L. (1997) Time-space embeddedness and geo-governance of cross-border regional modes of growth. In A. Amin and J. Hausner (eds) *Beyond Market and Hierarchy*. Cheltenham, UK: Edward Elgar. pp. 159–95.

Swyngedouw, E. (1992) The Mammon quest: 'Glocalisation', interspatial competition and the monetary order. In M. Dunford and G. Kafkalas (eds) *Cities and Regions in the New Europe*. London: Belhaven Press. pp. 39–68.

Swyngedouw, E. (1997) Neither global nor local: 'Glocalization' and the politics of scale. In K. Cox (ed.) *Spaces of Globalization*. New York: Guilford Press. pp. 137–66.

Taylor, P.J. (1994) The state as container. *Progress in Human Geography*, 18(2): 151–62.

Walker, R.B.J. (1993) *Inside/Outside*. New York: Cambridge University Press.

Wallerstein, I. (1974) *The Modern World-System I*. New York: Academic Publishers.

Whatmore, S. and Thorne, L. (1997) Nourishing networks. In D. Goodman and M. Watts (eds) *Globalising Food*. London: Routledge. pp. 287–304.

9

Space, Place and Labour

Philip Kelly

INTRODUCTION

When the DVD of the final Star Wars movie was released in October 2005, it contained a second disk featuring a fascinating behind-the-scenes look at the making of the movie. The initial conception of the project had occurred in director/producer George Lucas' Skywalker Ranch in California, but filming was done in Sydney, Australia, and post production editing and animation in London and Los Angeles. A staggering 7,000 people had been directly involved in the making of the movie – from actors and accountants, to wardrobe designers and winch operators. Their efforts were appreciated by the movie-going public. Having cost US$113 million to produce, the film's worldwide box office receipts amounted to US$848 million. Even after distribution companies and cinema chains had taken their share, this left a handsome profit for George Lucas and his privately owned production company.

But how were the thousands of individuals that contributed to the film along the way rewarded for their efforts? To be sure, many were paid well, but clearly they collectively generated value that far exceeded what they were paid. In other words, they created a surplus, and this was retained by those who had employed them to do their work. This is, fundamentally, the essence of capitalist production – the commodification of labour power and its sale to an employer who, in turn, reaps the benefits of the surplus value that is generated from the sale of the final product. The same process is at work whether we are talking about a blockbuster movie or a cup of coffee.

Capitalism is not, however, the only system through which labour is deployed and work is done. Indeed, work done under a capitalist labour process may be only the tip of the iceberg when we examine more closely the efforts that many of us exert in our daily lives (see, for example, Chapters 22 and 23). Broadly speaking, we can identify two other kinds of work. First, much is achieved through alternative, non-capitalist, labour processes, which may be as benign as volunteer work for community organizations or a cooperative, or as malignant as slave or feudal labour in which work is performed as an obligation without wages being paid. These forms of labour process are more extensive than is often acknowledged and it would be wrong to assume that capitalist labour processes, in which work is bought as a commodity, is the only way in which things get produced. Even within a 'capitalist' enterprise – selling its products or services in a market economy and driven by the imperative to make a profit – not all labour may be supplied through a capitalist labour process. For example, the publisher of this book might occasionally take on unpaid student interns interested in learning more about the publishing industry, its books might be evaluated before publication by reviewers who expect no compensation, and its paid employees might perform unpaid overtime work.

Second, work of all kinds requires that workers be sustained and reproduced and so 'reproductive' labour is an essential pre-requisite for everything else. Some of this may actually be done through a capitalist labour process, for example by employing a cook, cleaner, driver, laundry service, or babysitter. But in reality, for most people in most of the world, the vast majority of the work done to keep themselves and their families fed, clothed, housed, etc. is done within the family and on the basis of a labour process that is non-capitalist in nature. Without this labour, there simply wouldn't be a workforce for other kinds of production. Nevertheless, this work, which often has distinctively gendered divisions of labour, is often neglected and seldom included in formal economic accounting systems.

We can, therefore, identify three broad forms of labour process – capitalist, alternative, and reproductive. In each case, work is being done and value is being created. This value might be as visible and direct as the transformation of cloth and thread into an item of clothing that will ultimately be sold in retail stores. It might be as indirect as sleepless nights feeding a newborn baby who will ultimately be a creator of value herself. The critical questions that arise, regardless of the labour process involved, concern who, and where, gets to keep the value that is generated. This contestation lies at the heart of many political struggles – from large trade union organizations, to fair trade and living wage campaigns, to domestic disputes over who will do the laundry. The question of 'where' value is generated and circulated means that these struggles are fundamentally geographical ones. The spatiality of economic processes leads us to question the characteristics of the places where labour is done, the relationships between such places, and the circulation of value across space. It is such geographies that we will explore in this chapter.

The first section of the chapter explores the meaning and the role of *place* in empowering and disempowering workers in their claims for a greater share of the value they create. Here we take place to mean the geographical rootedness of workers and workplaces. But place also implies a unique (but open-ended and dynamic) intersection of flows and processes across *space*, interacting with a distinctive local historical landscape and society. In the second section we therefore explore the broader spatialities of the labour process as they affect contestations over the allocation of value. These spatialities occur at multiple scales – the local, regional, national and so on, but scale represents more than simply a system for the typologizing or categorizing of space. In the third section we will examine the production and construction of *scale* in relation to the labour process. Scale is produced in the sense that when workers, employers or others act to assert their claim on a share of the value generated in the labour process, they often do so at multiple scales – for example when a workplace dispute is escalated to a national level strike. In such cases, workers are producing a scale at which to prosecute their claims. Scale is also constructed, however, in the sense that our understanding of labour processes may be shaped by representations. For example, a classic contemporary construction of scale involves the representation of the global scale of competition in order to justify limits on wages and benefits – the global is being constructed as the scale of reality at which a particular labour process negotiation has to be understood.

THE IMPORTANCE OF PLACE FOR LABOUR

In the production of goods and services, labour is essential. It is not the only thing needed – land, infrastructure, capital, equipment, raw materials, etc. are also usually required – but labour is the one ingredient in whose absence nothing will happen. Labour is, however, a curious thing. In a capitalist system it is traded and exchanged in the same way as land, commodities, etc., but it has other characteristics as well – most importantly, it is *us*. Labour comprises real people in all of our diversity and complexity, living cultural, social and political lives in particular places. Furthermore, labour is a commodity that is organized, disciplined, regulated, housed, socialized, acculturated, educated, and trained. In each of these processes, place is fundamentally important.

At the most fundamental level, we all live local lives. We are all embedded in particular countries, regions, cities, and neighbourhoods, and it is with these places that we develop associations, affinities and identities. Even among the most mobile and transnational individuals, with multiple homes and citizenships, research has shown that people still become embroiled in their localities. In Vancouver, Canada, for example, many immigrants have arrived from Hong Kong under a programme that seeks to attract entrepreneurs and investors. A significant number have subsequently divided their time between homes in Vancouver and Hong Kong, where they continue to have employment or business interests. Families separated in this way have come to be known as 'astronaut' families, because of the amount of time husbands, in particular, who are working in Hong Kong, are spending in the air (Waters, 2003).

Astronaut family arrangements are an interesting starting point because they highlight several dimensions of mobile capital and labour in a globalizing world. Two features are particularly relevant here. The first is that despite the transnational and mobile nature of their working lives, there is evidence that they and their families develop a rootedness in Vancouver – this might be through schools, neighbourhoods, social networks, or just everyday places like shopping malls. Thus, even with great mobility, there is still a strong sense of attachment to place. This is an important

phenomenon, and not just for those with transnational lifestyles. Being rooted in a place, and feeling an affinity for that place (for cultural, social, political, historical, or perhaps religious reasons) is a fundamental feature of workers (and essential for the re-creation, or reproduction, of new generations of workers). These feelings are significant because they explain, in part, why workers are not necessarily ultra-mobile and willing to move to wherever there is work. Instead, they are very often attached to particular places. This relative immobility can be an important drawback in the contestation between workers and employers, especially when the latter can credibly threaten to leave a locality unless workers grant concessions.

It is also in particular places that workers develop ties with each other, and these ties can grow into collective forms of representation such as trade unions. Thus a strong sense of camaraderie and solidarity can emerge based on collective, place-based experiences and cultures. This is perhaps most evident historically in the steelmaking, shipbuilding, mining, logging and manufacturing towns of Europe and North America where trade union traditions first emerged and remain the strongest. It is primarily where certain kinds of low-paid and low-status occupations have concentrated in a particular place that class consciousness has emerged. In such places, it is the attachment to a place as a lived environment for reproductive labour – based on schools, daycares, shops, community organizations, etc. – that creates loyalties. Often, these place-based (as much as class-based) loyalties are the most powerful motivations in struggles to protect local jobs.

Recently, trade unions have also discovered the importance of developing ties with other social movements in the places where they operate. This process of 'community unionism' has created alliances to mobilize around issues that are important locally, especially where broad local interests coincide with union bargaining objectives. In the Canadian context, for example, the

International Ladies' Garment Workers Union (ILGWU) collaborated with immigrant community organizations, religious groups and women's rights activists in order to reach home workers who had little collective organization or protection (Tufts, 1998; for UK examples see Wills, 2001). It is also usually attachment to a place that fosters at least the benign forms of alternate work that were discussed earlier. Voluntary work and community involvement is usually an outcome not just of commitment to a particular issue (for example, environmental protection, heritage preservation, poverty alleviation, etc.) but also a commitment to a particular place (which in turn creates the *meaning* of that place).

The second aspect of astronaut families that is of interest here is that while astronaut spouses (in nearly all cases male) work in Hong Kong, the reproductive labour of their households is carried out by their wives in Vancouver using funds remitted by their husbands. This is a rather dramatic separation of roles – and is a product of many in the Hong Kong business community seeking a potential bolt-hole outside China following the UK's 1984 agreement to return the colony to the People's Republic in 1997 – but it highlights the other forms of work that are being done to raise children and maintain a home, and in this case it is labour that has become entirely the responsibility of the wife. It also highlights the importance of the reproductive and consumption sides of life in fostering the emotional attachments to a particular place noted above.

The unusual aspect of the 'astronaut' family is that the family migrates while the husband stays where they all used to be. In most other cases of migration, of course, it is the waged worker who migrates and sends money back to his or her family. The reproductive labour (cooking, cleaning, etc.) of the astronaut spouse in Hong Kong, for example, is most likely being done by a domestic worker, who has probably come from the Philippines. In this case it is the migrant worker who is likely to be sending money home to her family. In the case of such a

worker, rootedness in Hong Kong as a place may be much less important – she is likely to see herself as enduring painful separation from her family in order to support them economically. In her case, however, a different dimension of place is likely to be important – one that relates to the place of the home as a place of work. For migrant domestic workers around the world (for example in Singapore, Canada, Saudi Arabia, as well as Hong Kong) somebody else's home becomes their workplace and the features of that place become very important in the conditions of their labour (see Pratt, 2004). For example, the amount of free time that they are allocated by their employer, the private space to which they have access, and even the food that they can eat, are all determined through a negotiation with the employer in whose home they are living. The nature of their work*place* as a home is therefore fundamental both to their labour process and to their non-working lives.

In other kinds of places, different kinds of resolutions will be reached in the relationship between employer and employee. Retail sales clerks, factory workers, home garment workers, tourist guides, construction labourers, call centre operators, etc., all experience places of work that are configured very differently and result in quite varied negotiations of the labour process. Reproductive labour in the home presents even greater contrasts, as there is no formal contract defining the duties or rewards for such work. Instead, it is often the result of a gendered and generational division of labour between household members (see England, 1996; Mitchell et al., 2004).

So far we have seen several examples of the ways in which place is of central importance to working lives – by creating rootedness in particular locations, by fostering solidarity, and by constituting the nature of the relationship with an employer (or a spouse). Places are, however, important to employers and managers as well. There is a popular notion that global capitalism now involves footloose and mobile businesses that can relocate without difficulty, but this is actually a rather misleading idea. While it is true that a competitive capitalist market can lead to the rapid growth or decline of firms in particular places, and large firms may be able to play one location off against each other, the actual relocation of firms from one place to another is much less common. We need, therefore, to distinguish between firms as individual capitalist enterprises and the capitalist system as a whole. Many firms have a great deal invested in the places where they are located – investments that cannot be recovered if the funds cease operation at these locations. These are sometimes known as 'sunk costs' (Clark and Wrigley, 1995). In the service industry (for example retailing, healthcare), customers and markets are local, and so relocation would usually make no sense. For the tourism industry, the place itself is usually the 'product'. Even manufacturers who produce goods for a much larger, even global, market have invested in production facilities, trained workers, established logistics networks, and become acquainted with government regulations, all of which tie them to a particular place. And, of course, managers or owners of businesses are themselves workers who have developed affinities with the places where they live.

The most specialized high-technology firm may, surprisingly, be attached to a particular place because of the highly skilled workforce that it needs. Such workers may only be found in certain places where clusters of firms exist, and so there is little choice for employers other than to locate there. The classic case is Silicon Valley, in California's Santa Clara County. The technological dynamism and innovation of electronics firms located there is dependent upon highly skilled engineers and computer scientists. The pool of talented workers is so concentrated in the region that firms in many parts of the electronics industry *need* to be there. But the availability of talent is only one dimension. A further feature of Silicon Valley is the rapid turnover of employees at all levels, from production line operators to CEOs. The result is

that ideas and information diffuse and circulate very rapidly, creating a 'milieu' where innovation is fostered. An individual firm thus benefits from a collective set of ideas and experiences in a way that would be difficult outside the cluster (Angel, 2000; for a different example see Henry and Pinch (2000) on the British motor sport sector, and Chapter 18). In other creative industries, such as graphic design, computer animation, and film editing, a similar process of talent clustering happens, such that particular places become necessary locations for those activities – hence the specific places around the world used for the production of the Star Wars movie noted earlier.

Firms do not, however, just locate in particular places for concentrations of highly skilled and well-paid workers. For those industries that are mobile and are seeking low production costs, the presence of a socially marginalized group of potential workers requiring only very low wages, might be an attractive feature. People in particular places may be marginalized because they are members of minority ethnic groups, they are migrants, and/or because they are women. In her classic study of industrial restructuring in the 1980s, for example, Doreen Massey (1984) showed how new investment in UK manufacturing was locating in declining regions, such as the coal mining towns of South Wales. It was doing so because a pool of female workers was available that needed to work in order to support families after mine closures (see Chapter 17). Without the same tradition of working class mobilization as male miners, local women were an attractive workforce. In a similarly declining region of older industrialization, Hanson and Pratt (1995) showed that firms in Worcester, Massachusetts, located in suburban areas in order to tap into a supply of female workers who needed to stay close to home so that they could combine work with domestic responsibilities – hence we see the ways in which reproductive work gets integrated with capitalist labour processes.

The tendency to locate economic activities in particular places with devalued workers is, of course, also evident internationally. In the *maquiladora* factories located near the Mexico–US border, numerous manufacturing firms take advantage of workers marginalized on the basis of gender and ethnic/national difference (Wright, 1999). Similar processes of marginalization exist in sites of low cost manufacturing around the world – the feature that all have in common is that the subordination of a particular class of workers coincides with other, local, forms of subordination, for example around gender and ethnic identities.

Place, then, is a fundamental component of the contestation over who does what kinds of work and how they are rewarded. Its effects are, however, complicated and contradictory. The rootedness of workers, largely on account of the reproductive sides of their lives, leaves them vulnerable to an employer's 'threat to exit'. The attraction of investment in places with weak and marginalized populations highlights capitalism's ability to take advantage of such de-valuation. But at the same time, it is embeddedness in a local community that can be a source of class consciousness and solidarity in the struggle for value. And employers too become rooted in place. They may, for example, be dependent on past investments or sunk costs, localized sources of workers with the characteristics they need, or, less tangibly, their own place-based commitments.

SPACE, LABOUR CONTROL AND WORKER AGENCY

So far, we have emphasized the importance of place for both workers and firms. But essentially we have treated places as unique 'containers' for life, work, and the creation of value. A place is, however, far more than a bounded container. It is also a unique intersection of multiple flows and processes occurring across space (see Chapters 4 to 6, and 8). Thus to understand working lives in particular

places, we also need to comprehend the role of relationships across space. Here we will consider three ways in which space is important in the experience of workers: first, as a basis for a capitalist system of economic development; second, as a mechanism of labour control under capitalism, and; third as the outcome of labour activism and agency.

Exerting discipline and control over labour is a perennial problem for employers. A competitive and growth-orientated capitalist system creates an imperative to squeeze ever more out of a workforce – longer working hours, less pay, greater responsibilities, fewer fringe benefits, shorter breaks, fewer holidays, all adding up to greater productivity. At the same time, employers are competing for workers and so they cannot take any of these trends to their ultimate conclusion. Instead, they must temper the imperative to get more out of labour with the need to attract and retain workers. They are also subject to the regulatory control of governments, which mediate relationships between employers and workers. Furthermore, waged workers are, collectively, the customers for the products or services that they are making, and so at the level of the capitalist system as a whole, there is a contradiction between the tendency to pay workers as little as possible while at the same time needing an ever-increasing market demand.

These tensions and contradictions within the capitalist system are never entirely reconciled, but workable solutions are established in particular places and at particular times. Space is a fundamental tool in the creation of such resolutions. One form of resolution, noted above, is the creation of local forms of regulation that mediate labour processes. A wide range of state programmes, from specific controls such as minimum wages and workplace safety, to more general structures such as welfare, education and healthcare provision, all mediate the relationship between employers and their workers. These forms of regulation often take on localized forms so there is a specific geography to labour market regulation (Peck, 1996).

At a more abstract and systemic level, however, we can also consider the role played by space in the dynamics of capitalism – as a way of 'fixing', at least temporarily, some of the contradictions that are inherent in the system. Where the tensions identified above lead to falling profits for capitalist enterprises in a particular place (due to high costs of production, or low market demand), then one way of resolving the problem is to find new 'spatial fixes' (see Chapter 8). One spatial fix in the manufacturing sector might be to access new sources of raw materials that are less expensive, or even to find entirely new raw materials that are only available in distant locations. For example, in colonial Southeast Asia, rubber plantations were established to supply the industries of Western Europe in the nineteenth century, just as timber plantations are now being developed in the same region to supply furniture manufacturers, such as IKEA, which can no longer source materials in their home countries. Another spatial fix might be to move jobs from places with higher wages to those with lower ones. Hence in the 1980s and 1990s, many Japanese and Korean firms making components for cars and electronics devices moved their production facilities to Southeast Asia or China. Similarly, many North American insurance companies and banks have moved routine paper-processing facilities and call centres to the Caribbean or India in order to cut labour costs and maintain profitability (Bryson, 2007). When viewed across the whole global economy, we can see these kinds of shifts as mechanisms through which capitalism, as a system, utilizes space in order to stay profitable. The result is an uneven pattern of development in which growth and decline across space are integral to the capitalist system. In fact, we could go even further and suggest that capitalism *needs* space in order to reconcile its contradictions (Harvey, 1982).

Within spaces of production, however, the problem of labour control remains. A workforce needs to be disciplined in order to match the requirements of a given labour process. In a clothing store, such discipline

might relate to demeanour, dress, and customer interaction, as well as more basic matters such as punctuality and placing a limit on wages. In a factory, the latter considerations will clearly be relevant, along with the speed and quality with which tasks are performed on a production line. Whatever the setting, space is frequently an important element of a labour disciplining system. First, at a micro-scale the location and movement of employees is often carefully defined and monitored – time spent away from a work station, or movement around a retail store, is often the subject of careful planning and close surveillance. Mobility outside the workplace might also be closely monitored – in many new industrial estates in the developing world, employees are housed in dormitories adjacent to their workplaces and their movement outside these spaces is carefully controlled (Kelly, 2002).

Second, workplaces may be constructed as exclusionary spaces, in which access is closely regulated. In such instances, again quite common in the export processing zones of the global South, barbed wire, high walls and armed guards at gatehouses serve to keep out political agitators or union organizers. In a different way, but with the same effect, the use of home-based work in the garment sector serves as a mechanism for dispersing workers across space so that organizing is far more difficult. While we have so far examined only capitalist labour processes, we could also expand this point to include reproductive labour. The home is socially, and legally, constructed as a *private* space and therefore the gendered and generational divisions of labour within it are construed as beyond the scope of *public* institutions – and thus beyond the normal legal restrictions on working conditions and hours. This particular way of defining the space of the home is what allows the frequent neglect, as an economic process, of reproductive work that goes on there. It also means that struggles over domestic divisions of labour are seen as matters for feminist politics rather than labour politics.

Third, the widespread use of migrant labour forces serves as a space-based disciplining mechanism. In Malaysia, for example, production line work in the electronics industry is now often carried out by internal migrants from other parts of the country, or international migrants from Indonesia or Bangladesh. The result is that workers are often tied to a specific employer by a contract and risk deportation if they press for further rights or benefits. Meanwhile, their family members back home are dependent on the money they send, thereby increasing their acquiescence to factory discipline. The same scenario also exists for the Filipino domestic workers in Hong Kong mentioned earlier, and their compatriots around the world. In many wealthier societies, the vulnerabilities of illegal migrants are especially exploited as they live and work outside normal legal protections that are defined within national spaces of citizenship.

While space is evidently significant in the process of labour control, it is also important to recognize the opposite possibility – that people may play a part in shaping the spatial configuration of their working lives. Andrew Herod (2001) provides an example of this in the case of dockers in seaports on the East coast of the United States. Faced with the threat of job losses due to containerization in the 1950s and 1960s, the dockers' union fought political and legal struggles to ensure that certain types of containers continued to be packed or unpacked at the waterfront, rather than at inland sites staffed by non-union personnel. In this way, the spatial arrangement of an economic activity was pro-actively shaped not by economic logic but through contestation on the part of workers. Another example is found in the auto sector in Canada, where collective agreements between the Canadian Auto Workers and the major manufacturers (Ford, General Motors and Daimler-Chrysler) regularly include clauses that commit employers to investment in particular plants, thereby shaping the geography of the industry (Holmes, 2004).

PRODUCING AND CONSTRUCTING SCALE

Implicit in much of our discussion so far has been the notion of scale. In its common usage, scale simply refers to a spatial level at which processes happen. Thus, we talk about the urban scale, the national scale or the global scale. In that sense, scale is being used to imply a container – for example, labour markets might operate at an urban scale, a public healthcare system might be national, while certain parts of the financial sector might be global in scale.

In recent years, however, geographical conceptions of scale have gone well beyond this sense of scale-as-container (see Chapters 7, 8 and 10). Instead, scale is now seen not just as an *outcome of* economic and political processes but also as a fundamental *component of* them. Andrew Herod (2001: 38–39), who has extensively applied such an approach to the issue of labour processes, explains this shift in thinking:

> … industrial regions, metropolitan areas, national boundaries, and the global scale of contemporary capitalist production are historically and geographically created human constructions, subject to reformulation as economic and political conditions change. There is, in other words, nothing inherent about scale, and there are no 'natural' scales by which to order and organize human geographies. Rather, scales are historically and geographically negotiated. For example, the scale of the 'home' is dependent upon notions of the family (nuclear or extended) and the lines of demarcation between public and private spaces – is the home a private space and refuge from the public sphere (and, if so, for whom?), or may these enclaves of the 'private' be transcended and made public by the intervention of the state, which may seek to regulate to a greater or lesser degree certain activities conducted within the 'privacy' of one's own home? Likewise, the 'national' scale certainly became more important with the transition from feudalism to industrial capitalism and the growth of imperial rivalries, though, in the contemporary period it may well be declining in some aspects under the dual assault of devolution and supranationalism. Given such realities, the questions geographers (and others) should therefore ask, perhaps, are not how scale orders social processes but, rather, how social actors create geographic scales through their activities.

The outcome of research by Herod and others is that we now understand scale not simply as a way of *describing* what is happening in labour struggles, but as a *constitutive part* of those struggles. Just as we saw space in the last section as more than simply the area or location in which labour processes take place but rather as a tool used in the contestation between workers and employers, the same can be said about scale. The constitution of economic processes at certain geographical scales is a political process and one that is fundamental to the contestation over how the value created by labour is shared. There are two senses in which scale is significant in this way and we will label them the *production* of scale and the *construction* of scale.

The production of scale involves the ways in which the geographical scope of economic processes is, at a given point in time, settled at a particular scale. There is nothing natural about this. Rather, it is the outcome of the needs of the capitalist system and the negotiation between employers and workers. The path-breaking articulation of this idea was provided by Neil Smith (1984) who conceived of scales as the spatial resolution of contradictory tendencies within capitalism. These contradictions, noted earlier, involve the tensions between an imperative for employers to be mobile and restless in their search for profit but at the same time the need to immobilize themselves by investing in particular locations. The ways in which this tension is resolved at any point in time gives rise to coherent scales of economic activity. At the urban scale, there is a coherent space of commuting patterns whereby individuals' working lives are united with their daily lives of reproduction and consumption. At the regional scale, divisions of labour exist such that regions may become identified with particular roles and sectors – for example, the electronics industry in California and agriculture in the mid-West of the United States. At the national scale, the state is involved in regulating the relationship

between employers and labour. At the global scale, the expansionary tendencies of capitalism are played out with the imperative to develop global markets and global production networks.

The important point, however, is that none of these scales are permanently fixed. They are reflections of particular moments in time and are liable to be recast as the dynamics of capitalism move on. In the case of the urban scale, for example, the notion that labour markets are constituted by journey-to-work areas is rendered increasingly out-dated by the growing use of migrant labour in major cities from San Francisco, to Singapore, to Sydney. The result is that labour markets, for both highly paid executives and low paid service workers alike, are being re-produced at a global scale – a process driven by increasing competition and the capitalist imperative for profitability. In the case of the national scale, the regulation of labour relations is, in some contexts, being passed on to supra-national scales of governance. In the European Union, for example, state functions that would once have been the jurisdiction of national governments are being unified at a continental scale in the name of creating larger, more efficient, and more profitable, markets. An example of this process is the harmonization of educational, trade, and professional qualifications in order to facilitate an enlarged labour market.

We can, however, also see cases where smaller, rather than larger, scales are produced for the negotiation of labour relations. It is, for instance, often in the economic interests of employers to ensure that the negotiation of wages and working conditions happens at the smallest scale possible. In Japan, and increasingly elsewhere, very few national-level trade unions exist and wages are instead negotiated at the scale of individual enterprises. Where Japanese firms have moved overseas, this scale of labour relations has been replicated through factory-level 'labour-management councils' or 'enterprise unions'.

It is worth noting, however, that the production of scale is not always exclusively in the hands of employers. There are also examples of workers themselves actively producing scales at which labour–management relations should be negotiated. In particular, organized labour has sometimes sought to negotiate its relationship at the scale at which employers are operating. Andrew Herod's research on US dockworkers in the 1950s, noted earlier, has provided a particularly striking example. Herod (2001) shows how dockers' unions successfully fought to negotiate the terms of their employment on a regional scale (along the full length of the US East coast) rather than on a port-by-port basis, as preferred by their employers. Highlighting a more recent example, Jane Wills (1998) has argued that globalization (i.e. the *production* of the global as a scale for capitalism) offers similar opportunities for workers to operate on a transnational scale. In particular, Wills points to the example of European Works Councils, which are a product of the 1993 Maastricht Treaty that saw closer economic integration in Europe. The treaty required that employers with workforces in more than one European country must finance an annual meeting of employees' representatives from across Europe. The result was the first ever legal requirement obliging multinational corporations to bridge different national scale relationships with their employees. Alongside other examples of international trade union bodies (such as the International Confederation of Free Trade Unions and the World Federation of Trade Unions), this illustrates the possibilities for workers to produce their own scales of operation, and to operate at multiple scales simultaneously.

While scales have been *produced* by employers, workers and states in various ways, it is important to note that scale is also *constructed*. Here, we are drawing a distinction between the political and economic processes that produce scales and the ways in which such scales are understood, imagined or represented – and thereby constructed. This

separation of the 'material' and the 'discursive' should not, however, lead us to underestimate the material power of discursive representations. Often, it is precisely the discursive construction of scale that assists in mystifying the production of scales noted above, thereby concealing the political implications of scale production for labour relations.

Perhaps the clearest example of scalar construction is in the discourse of globalization that has been so rampant in the last decade. While technological, competitive and institutional processes have indeed been *producing* a global scale, the global has also been actively *constructed*. This has been particularly evident in the language used by national governments to represent the economic policy options that are open to them. Across every continent, governments have proclaimed globalization as an external force that is irresistible. Thus workers and their relations with employers are construed as needing to respond to the requirements of global competition, global standards, and global trends. Within a very short space of time, the global has become represented as the scale at which economic processes *have* to be understood and calibrated (Kelly, 1999; Cameron and Palan, 2004).

To take a very different example, the scale of the home is also the object of discursive construction. While *produced* by social and legal processes, as noted earlier, the home is also *constructed* in discourses of privacy, identity and gender. A particularly important construction of the home is as a feminine space in which responsibilities for reproductive work rest primarily with women. In their study of Worcester, Massachusetts, mentioned earlier in this chapter, Susan Hanson and Geraldine Pratt (1995) have shown how such gendered constructions of the domestic scale also affect the working lives of women in waged employment. The expectation that they should also attend to domestic chores and child care responsibilities meant that women generally had to find jobs within a shorter commuting distance than their male counterparts in order to coordinate their waged work with the reproductive work. Again, therefore, we see how the construction of scale can have material implications for working lives.

CONCLUSION

We started this chapter by noting the multiple forms of work that co-exist in modern societies. Although much of the subsequent discussion focused on waged work under capitalist labour processes, it was also clear that these are inseparable from reproductive labour in particular. Taking place, space and scale in turn, we then outlined the profoundly spatial nature of struggles over the valuation of work. It is worth noting, however, that is impossible to discuss any one of these three concepts (place, space, scale) without invoking the other two and so the separation here is an artificial one.

The rootedness of workers in particular places creates vulnerability, but at the same time raises the possibility of a collective class consciousness and place-based solidarity. We also noted that places matter for employers too, and they may be more dependent upon, and attached to, particular places than we imagine. At a smaller scale the nature of the work-place itself is often very important in shaping labour relations – nowhere is this more so than when the home is a place of work.

Space too is more than simply a container for labour processes. It is instead an element that shapes the labour relation, not just as a territorial container, but also as the configuration or geographical arrangement of economic relations. The internal contradictions of a capitalist system are temporarily settled either by localized regulation or by the spatial fix of geographical shifts across space. At a less abstract level, space is also important in the disciplining of labour, either through the control of employees' mobility, the creation of exclusive spaces of productive or

reproductive work, or through the use of migrant workers. Occasionally, however, it is workers who shape the spaces of an economic activity.

Finally, we tackled the notion of scale, noting that the concept has come to be recognized as much more than a simple container for economic processes. Instead, scale is produced by economic processes and the scales that are pertinent at any given time reflect the outcome of political contestation. The idea that scale is not a natural 'thing' but rather a historically and contingent outcome of struggle is rather counter-intuitive. But as we saw from specific examples, the production of scales at which labour's value will be determined is quite central to this contest – whether the upper hand is with workers, or, more commonly, employers. The naturalization of this state of affairs is an important effect of the construction of scale.

REFERENCES

Angel, D. (2000) High technology agglomeration and the labor market: The case of Silicon Valley. In M. Kenney (ed.) *Understanding Silicon Valley: The Anatomy of an Entrepreneurial Region*. Stanford University Press.

Bryson, J. (2007) The 'second' global shift: The offshoring or global sourcing of corporate services and the rise of distanciated emotional labour. *Geografiska Annaler*, Series 89B: 31–43.

Cameron, A. and Palan, R. (2004) *The Imagined Economies of Globalization*. London: SAGE.

Clark, G. and Wrigley, N. (1995) Sunk costs: A framework for economic geography. *Transactions of the Institute of British Geographers*, 20(2): 204–23.

England, K. (ed.) (1996) *Who Will Mind the Baby? Geographies of Child-Care and Working Mothers*. London and New York: Routledge.

Hanson, S. and Pratt, G. (1995) *Gender, Work and Space*. New York: Routledge.

Harvey, D. (1982) *Limits to Capital*. Oxford: Blackwell.

Henry, N., and Pinch, S. (2000) Spatialising knowledge: Placing the knowledge community of Motor Sport Valley. *Geoforum*, 31(2): 191–208.

Herod, A. (2001) *Labor Geographies: Workers and the Landscapes of Capitalism*. New York: Guilford Press.

Holmes, J. (2004) Re-scaling collective bargaining: Union responses to restructuring in the North American auto industry. *Geoforum*, 35(1): 9–21.

Kelly, P.F. (1999) The geographies and politics of globalization. *Progress in Human Geography*. 23(3): 379–400.

Kelly, P.F. (2002) Spaces of labour control: Comparative perspectives from Southeast Asia. *Transactions of the Institute of British Geographers*, 27(4): 395–411.

Massey, D. (1984) *Spatial Divisions of Labour: Social Structures and the Geography of Production*. London: Macmillan.

Mitchell, K., Marston, S.A. and Katz, C. (eds) (2004). *Life's Work: Geographies of Social Reproduction*. Oxford: Blackwell.

Peck, J. (1996) *Workplace: The Social Regulation of Labour Markets*. New York: Guilford.

Pratt, G. (2004) *Working Feminism*. Minneapolis: University of Minnesota Press.

Smith, N. (1984) *Uneven Development: Nature, Capital, and the Production of Space*. New York, NY: Blackwell.

Tufts, S. (1998) Community unionism in Canada and labor's (re)organization of space. *Antipode*, 30(3): 227.

Waters, J. (2003) Flexible citizens? Transnationalism and citizenship amongst economic immigrants in Vancouver. *The Canadian Geographer/Le Geographe canadien*, 47(3): 219–34.

Wills, J. (1998) Taking on the cosmocorps: Experiments in trans-national labor organization. *Economic Geography*, 74: 111–30.

Wills, J. (2001) Community unionism and trade union renewal in the UK: Moving beyond the fragments at last? *Transactions of the Institute of British Geographers*, 26: 465–83.

Wright, M. (1999) The politics of relocation: Gender, nationality and value in the maquiladoras. *Environment and Planning A*, 1601–17.

PART 4

Political Economies of Space III

10

The Geographies of Capitalism

Susan Christopherson

INTRODUCTION

One of the most valuable intellectual developments to emerge from the globalization debates has been intensified interest in the geographies of capitalism and in questions of spatial scale, networks and hierarchies, and uneven development. The undermining of taken-for-granted ideas about a world economy organized in a stable set of state 'containers' or territories has stimulated theoretical and empirical work based on alternative conceptions of global space. Geographers and other spatially oriented social scientists have been quick to applaud the move away from 'the iron grip of the state on the sociological imagination' (Taylor, 1996: 1923). Rather than marking the end of geography, the discourse of globalization has led to a resurgence of thinking and writing about space and time (Agnew, 1994). New ideas about the flows and connections that transcend national boundaries and about the role of sub-national regions have enriched our grasp of the processes shaping a 'global' economy, including processes of exclusion. By contrast with these more expansive transnational perspectives, the analysis of politically-bounded territories appears not only old-fashioned but singularly limited as a way to understand the emerging world economy.

In this chapter, I examine how new ways of analyzing and interpreting the geographies of capitalism have emerged in the wake of critiques of territorially-based understandings of the world capitalist economy. I also argue that the nation state as political territory remains important to the enterprise of understanding the emerging geographies of capitalism. Concepts of scale and networks as well as cognitive relational geographies have enriched our understanding of the geographies of capitalism. What we can learn from a more sophisticated understanding of connections and scalar relationships, however, needs to be held in tension with – and to complement rather than supplant – knowledge of 'global' processes emanating from bounded political territories. To make this argument I first discuss accounts that have been influential in shaping public perceptions of 'globalization' and the particular geographies associated with those accounts. I then examine the parallel discussions that emerged among geographers about scale, networks, and particularly, the dynamic processes constructing the contemporary spaces of capitalism. Finally, I suggest how the new geographic discourse continues to illuminate the role of the state in the contemporary geography of capitalism.

THE END OF THE NATION STATE (AND GEOGRAPHY): THE GLOBAL ECONOMY AS A BORDERLESS WORLD

The idea that the global expansion and integration of capitalist markets (or what is popularly known as globalization) is associated with demise of the nation state and thus of the taken-for-granted geography of the world, has been taken up in both scholarly and popular literature and from dramatically different perspectives. The most widely known arguments regarding the decline of the nation state emerged in the context of what John Gray (2006) refers to as business-utopian models, such as those of Friedman (2005). The models posit that a combination of universal market forces, rooted in competitive individualism, and the time-space compression made possible by new technologies, make national economies irrelevant or, at best, only capable of adaptation. These accounts are interesting as ideology but also because they represent a project to disassociate the political territories that were critical to the emergence of capitalism from the processes constructing contemporary capitalist economies, that is, to normalize and de-politicize capitalism.

These depictions of the emerging geography of capitalism portray it as the product of a relentless, systemic, rational process rarely specifying how, why or under what auspice change is occurring. To the extent a cause is identified, it is technological change. Friedman, for example, likens the changes occurring in the contemporary world with those that emerged with Gutenberg's introduction of the printing press or with the industrial revolution. They are the products of individual actions and, ultimately, uncontrollable.

This conception of an exogenous set of processes that results in a global market free

of institutional barriers is consonant with ideas of rational capitalism as a system that overrides territorially-defined political economies because of its appeal to universal motivations of self-interest and individual wealth generation. At the heart of the borderless world is the unimpeded flow of capital, information, and labour across national borders and the development of consumption patterns that are disassociated from national and regional cultures but instead express 'global' tastes (Ohmae, 1995). Ohmae's understanding of the role of the nation state in capitalism underpins his argument concerning its irrelevance in the global economy. The state functions, through state policy, as an intermediary and arbiter of economic activities; the ability of transnational firms to escape these functions spells the state's demise as an institution (Yeung, 1998).

This narrow understanding of the role of the state underpins a particular interpretation of the direction and end point of global market integration, the 'convergence' model. As Berger (2006: 37) describes: 'The breakdown or the negotiated surrender of national controls over the flows of capital, goods and services across borders means that producers everywhere find themselves in competition.' With the inevitable state 'surrender' via deregulation, market convergence 'shrinks the resources under national control for shaping economic and social outcomes and the legitimacy of national cultures and institutions' (ibid.).

Not surprisingly, the convergence model of capitalist development is particularly dominant in the United States for, despite all the fear of decline and out-sourcing it engenders, convergence is understood as moving toward a US 'world' of Walmart, Big Macs, blue jeans, commercial entertainment television, and Microsoft Windows. In the convergence model, the US is closest to a pure market economy. Deregulation and the undermining of state legitimacy will, thus, inevitably result in US-style production and distribution systems. Global financial markets, as well as culture, will be fundamentally American.

Even in the convergence model, however, geography does not wholly disappear. Remaining in this account of the geography of global capitalism are three types of space. First, there is the 'global' as an abstract space, a game space, a space of production functions, nodes and flows. This is a 'Wikipedia World', without authorities or power relations. It is a world where the standards that govern work and commerce are set and controlled by transnational corporations, such as Microsoft, which are assumed to be autonomous, competitive actors. This version of global space resonates with the business utopian model laid out by Ohmae, Friedman and others. It exists in the minds of TNC leaders as a perfect world, one in which they are able to exist outside political territorial constraints and yet use the resources associated with citizenship. Barnet and Muller (1974: 16) captured this utopian contradiction in their interview with the chairman of Dow Chemical:

'I have long dreamed to buy an island owned by no nation . . . and of establishing the World Headquarters of the Dow Company on the truly neutral ground of such an island, beholden to no nation or society. If we were located on such truly neutral ground we could then really operate in the United States as US citizens, in Japan as Japanese citizens, and in Brazil as Brazilians rather than being governed in prime by the laws of the United States. . . .'

Second, there is geography as a barrier – a new version of environmental determinism used to explain the exclusion of places from what (theoretically) are universal markets. In this exclusionary geography, distance from the sea or the presence of a tropical climate explain why a place is 'off the network' (Gallup et al., 1999). Finally, there is the natural economic zone – the industrial district or region, which emerges with the decline of nation state authority. In this geographic conception, the nation state becomes a fly-over zone, insignificant except as a space you need to traverse in order to reach '*the* region': such as Tuscany, Baden-Wurttemberg or Silicon Valley, for example. This version of capitalist territory is not to be confused with the 'obsolescent' idea of politically-governed places, including nation states. It is closer to the concept of the city-state, within which a form of proto-capitalism emerged in the sixteenth and seventeenth centuries. City-state authority and legitimacy support space transcending capitalist networks much like Italian City states hosted merchant networks in the early phases of mercantile capitalism (Arrighi, 1994).

The attempt to ignore power and politics in the expansion and integration of global markets does have its critics, however. Those scholars who recognize the links between territorial authority and capitalist development have continued to emphasize the ways in which the emergent geography of global capitalism is a political as well as an economic construction (Strange, 1996; Agnew, 1994). In particular, the legitimacy of territorially-based authority at national and regional scales provides for enforcement of regulatory conditions critical to capital accumulation, such as property rights. It also marshals and subsidizes key inputs to capitalist development, including skills and infrastructure.

These critiques have, at their core, a historical understanding of the inextricable relationship between state power, authority and legitimacy and the development of capitalism. It is this understanding that provides a theoretical basis for arguments to counter the ideology and geography of 'stateless' global capitalism.

A COUNTER-OFFENSIVE TO THE BORDERLESS WORLD

One valuable commentary on the concept of the borderless world has emerged under the rubric of 'varieties of capitalism' (Hall and Soskice, 2001; Thelen, 1999). The 'varieties of capitalism' school has focused attention on the political institutions that underlie market governance regimes. Because these political institutions differ among national territories, with strong input from labor in some regimes, such as Germany, and almost none in others, such as the US, they construct different incentive structures for the firms that operate within them (Peck and Theodore, 2007). These incentive structures affect firm choices in a range of spheres, including labor deployment, commodity chain organization, and location decisions. They also create different types of competitive advantages (Christopherson and Clark, 2007). From a 'globalization' perspective, they influence how firms emerging in (and benefiting from) different national incentive structures perceive and attempt to structure global market governance. The battle over the rules that will govern global trade thus has its origins in nationally constituted power relations.

This commentary, however, is also limited, in the sense that it focuses on the set of national territorial states that are most developed and coherent, primarily those represented in the Organization for Economic Cooperation and Development (OECD). Within these territorial states, the ability of capitalists to transcend national political territories has proved to be limited, in part because of sophisticated and complex political apparati at the national scale, which have developed over time both to support capital accumulation and to ameliorate its negative consequences. These accounts create a counterpoint to the conception of a single rational capitalism transcending territories. Ultimately, they reach back to Polanyi's conceptions of the economy as an instituted process and Max Weber's analysis of the relationships between society and economy. They also build on a literature that examines the highly differentiated ideas of economy and economics that emerged among proto-capitalists, shaping the kinds of national economic governance structures that eventually emerged.

Historical analysis has illuminated how the idea of an 'economy' that is conceived of as separate from society gradually emerged.

This 'economy' was organized around the calculable, predictable accumulation of wealth and the institution of such practices as double-entry bookkeeping (Poovey, 1998). An interdisciplinary conversation about space, time, and process also recognized work on the historical networks (religious, trade, political, and social) that created the connections among territorial spaces, including those operating long before the emergence of capitalist markets and the nation state (Wolf, 1982). Historical accounts provide both depth and continuity to our understanding of the strategies of those who would be modern global capitalists. Braudel, for example, in describing the motivations of sixteenth century merchant capitalist, notes their selectivity with respect to markets and spheres of action:

> While capitalism was most at home in the sphere of commerce, it did not occupy the whole of this sector, but elected residence only on routes and in places where trade was most lively. In everyday, traditional exchange or the very local market economy, capitalism took little interest. Even in the developed regions, there were some tasks it willingly handled, others it shared, and others again which it would not accept, leaving them firmly alone . . . Capitalism was thus invariably borne along by a general context greater than itself, on whose shoulders it was carried upward and onward. (1982: 374)

The selectivity of capitalism, in which significant dimensions of life, including some types of markets, lie outside the interests of capitalists, has been emphasized by feminist geographers analyzing local production and reproduction systems not integrated into capitalist markets (Katz, 2001; Gibson-Graham, 1996). Their analyses are critical to understanding the processes constructing the geographies of contemporary capitalism as selective and partial, as exclusive rather than universal.

The critics of the narrative of globalization as convergence also draw from studies of the historical development of 'national capitalisms' such as that of Berk (1994) and Perrow (2002) whose analyses of the emergence of the corporation in the United States demonstrate how a distinctive form of national capitalism evolved, rooted in the power of merchant land speculators and the relative weakness of manufacturers and craft labor and, not coincidentally, intense competition among city regions. This form of capitalism relied on particular ideas about economy, society, and space, and was constructed by politically powerful actors. These actors used the apparatus of the state to change the definition of the corporation from a state-chartered entity to that of an individual. This redefinition sheltered the corporation from a wide range of risks and gave corporate owners and managers the prerogative to influence regulation of the economy. Certain institutions, such as the courts in the US case, became key arbiters in disputes over questions about the operation of a capitalist economy, such as those involving the distribution of risk and the allocation of property rights.

The analysis of how US capitalism developed in conjunction with the exercise of political power is important because of the comparative institutional analysis it enables but also because US capitalism has been considered synonymous with a 'universal' prototypical model of rational capitalism. Unfortunately, only a handful of scholars treat the US as the distinctive, idiosyncratic political construction that it actually is (Agnew, 1987; Skowronek, 1982; Perrow, 2002).

At the same time that the idea of a borderless world, a world without geography, was being debunked because of its neglect of the intrinsic connection of the state and capitalism, however, a parallel discussion also emerged. It developed in concert with a fundamental skepticism concerning the state as a political-economic container and the use of 'containerization' as the basis for interpreting international relations, whether cooperative or competitive. This discussion did not reject the territorial 'nation state' out of hand but recognized it as a spatial construction that has precluded analysis of a wide variety of dynamics shaping the global economy, such as inter-ethnic relations migration flows and

not incidentally, the expansion and integration of capitalist markets. Contributing to this critique of the nation state as the basis for explaining the emerging geography of global capitalism is a rich literature on the 'partialness' of nation state legitimacy and authority (Ruggie, 1993).

A key dimension of this work is its intense interest in dynamic processes. As Agnew (1994) noted, state-based conceptions of social relations have been problematic not simply because they place social relations in an arbitrary box but because they are static. In general, dynamic approaches reject a conception of space as fixed in favor of one in which space is conceived of in conjunction with time and in a process of continuous transformation (Arrighi, 1994; Massey, 1994, 2006; Brenner, 2004). Finally, the conception of the state as a container of social relations became problematic for two reasons: (i) a theoretical critique raised issues about the fixity of territorial boundaries and the partialness of the territorial state project, and; (ii) empirical evidence illustrated transformative processes whose boundaries are not congruent with those of nation states or only partially controlled by them. The idea of 'failed states' reflects the limits of the nation state concept as does the reemergence of independent ethno-regions.

Thus, in this emerging work, there is a dual concern: what processes underlie the exclusion of spaces or de-territorialization? And; how are new spaces, places, and territories of capitalism being created? The key question then becomes how political-economic space is being re-created in a way more useful to a capitalist firm attempting to produce and distribute products in markets no longer defined by national boundaries.

More open substantive questions about spatial forms and processes took geographers down a variety of different paths and made it possible to conceptualize new ways of thinking about the geographies of capitalism. Studies of scale and networks, in particular, have evoked their own counter-critiques enriching the continuing dialog.

EMERGING PERSPECTIVES ON THE GEOGRAPHIES OF CAPITALISM

Scale as hierarchy and cognitive construction

Despite the prevalence of idealized 'spaceless' models, the description and analysis of globalization and the geography of contemporary capitalism is inherently spatial. Still, in the popular and much of the academic literature, spatial concepts lack a sense of time and dynamism. They also neglect the question of who is constructing or reconstructing space and to what end. Questions of scale, for example, are intrinsic to the discussion of the emergence of global capitalism (see Chapter 9). The most popular phrase invoking action in response to global capitalism, 'think globally, act locally', describes a world reduced to two scales of action and influence. Rarely, if ever, is a question raised about whether the two scales accurately represent options for thinking or action.

At a higher level of sophistication, theorists of scale focus on its inherent verticality, inquiring how action at one scale produces both anticipated and unanticipated consequences at another scale. For example, trade liberalization, although undertaken at the national scale, has consequences for regions and localities depending upon their economic composition. Privatization of rail systems, for example, has differential consequences for regions depending on whether the density of traffic can be generated to support the profit imperatives of a privately run corporation. While usually informative, this approach frequently takes the composition of scale for granted as fixed and static.

A more radical departure from conventional notions is a conception of scale as constructed under particular political and economic conditions (Smith, 1992, 1996; Porter and Sheppard, 1998). This dynamic notion of scale looks at processes rather than simply at places, and at territories as scales of action. For example, the ascension of suburban political power presents an opportunity to reconstruct urban space in the interest of suburbanites and to diminish the role of the city and its residents and their access to needed public resources. Here the process of change and shifts in relative power provide a key to understanding the redesigning and redefining of territories.

In another innovative conceptualization, feminist theorizing has introduced an ideological dimension to the understanding of scale which, given its inherent verticality, becomes associated with ideas about hierarchies of theoretical significance and social power. So, feminists reject the understanding of the local as contained within, and in a vertical hierarchical relationship with, the global, particularly given the association of the local with the household and women and the global with high order male abstraction (Nagar et al., 2002). Feminists advocate a relational approach as an antidote to the hierarchical limitations of scale and the conceptions of significance it imputes. This non-geometric conception makes it possible to understand how the bond trader in the City of London may feel more 'proximate' to Wall Street in New York than he does to many neighborhoods in London simply because these neighborhoods and their residents are not relevant to his daily activities. These mental maps of the geography of capitalism are also in constant dynamic flux as one set of relationships is brought into cognitive proximity and others recede.

The concept of cognitive proximity is valuable in interpreting how spaces of resistance to processes of economic and political transformation are fore grounded, as in the demonstrations in Seattle and Washington against the World Trade Association. It also helps explain why persistent poverty, such as that in the Mississippi Delta in the US, can become visible, that is more proximate, because of media attention. A sense of proximity can also recede as other more distant places (such as Darfur) are brought into focus and public attention. For feminist geographers, the relational approach also raises questions about the divide drawn between theories of 'the global' and those theories that probe households and communities. Although divided in academic discourse, both are integral to dynamic change and spatial transformation.

Networks and the questions of power and position

Networks constitute the other commonly accepted way of describing the geography of global capitalism, most usually in combination with scalar analysis. In a well-known formulation, clusters of firms at the local scale combine with networks of territories across transnational space to construct what Castells (1996) referred to as a global network society, paralleling Arrighi's (1994) analysis of the relationship between capitalist accumulation and state formation. Theories of who is connected and in what ways are rooted in assumptions about how technology-driven process and product innovations transcend space, creating universal access to commodities and ideas. These assumptions encompass both the potential of universal 'connectivity' (as in the internet) and the continuation of hierarchy (as in global cities) based in established networks and first mover advantages.

Networks have an ambiguous relationship with territories; that is, with politically-defined and bounded units. At the intra-regional scale, networks of firms that provide agglomeration economies are explained as a developmental form that can enable the region to escape from the exigencies of global capitalism – particularly the cost-based competition that results from trade liberalization and open 'deregulated' markets. Regions are not created as equals in this global game, however. Endogenous regionalists argue that regions succeed or fail in the global economy because of characteristics internal to the region, including the quality of human resources and investment in research and development (Romer, 1994). Most regions, particularly those located outside the largest urban centers, however, simply don't have what it takes to innovate and thus, to produce

economic dynamism (Duranton and Puga, 2000; Rodriguez-Pose and Storper, 2006). This formulation results in a 'spiky' or mountainous economic world in opposition to Friedman's flat variety.

Explanations of regional success or failure (and thus, of inequality) based in endogenous regional characteristics, such as the presence of effective governance or an entrepreneurial spirit, are limited by their neglect of how power relations construct regional capacity. Empirical research indicates that regions are neither autonomous nor isolated from extra-regional political decisions. These decisions, such as those to deregulate key transport industries and foster a trade regime favouring transnational firms, have profound consequences for the spatial location of economic activities at the regional scale. The impetus for investments – in university systems, national defense, agricultural commodity price supports, or in return for campaign contributions by corporate actors – is rarely explicable at the intra-regional scale. These decisions, however, can and do alter the incentive structure that governs firm decisions to invest in one region or another.

In the narrative of globalization as regional firm-networks linked across transnational space, however, regional dependence on political action and multi-scalar state policy is almost completely obscured. Transnational networks are depicted as fundamentally anti-territorial because they abstract the network from 'the logic and meaning (of places)' (Castells, p. 412; cited in Sheppard, 2002). The concept of networks is used, in fact, to reinforce the irrelevance of territory. From this anti-territorial perspective, network-based conceptions of the geography of contemporary capitalism actively confront the utility of scale as a descriptive mode, emphasizing the space extensive, horizontal and connective role of networks especially in the creation of extra-regional formations (Dicken et al., 2001).

As with conceptions of scale, skeptical perspectives on networks have begun to emerge. Skeptics question the de-territorialized, de-politicized conceptions that dominate some depictions of networks and the way in which they limit our understanding of the geography of capitalism, how it is emerging and what forms it is assuming. In particular, they question the silence on power relations within the network. These critiques point out that networks provide a way of eluding basic questions of agency and structure. According to Sheppard (2002: 317) 'Networks are represented as self-organizing, collaborative, non-hierarchical, and flexible, with a distinctive topological spatiality'. Critiques from a variety of perspectives and empirical research on actually existing networks have reintroduced the question of power and inequality into network theory, with important implications for how we conceive of the networks that are being constructed in global space (Graham, 1998; Zook and Brunn, 2006) and within regions (Grimshaw and Rubery, 2005). As Sheppard (2002: 318) cautions,

> more attention needs to be paid . . . to the internal spatial structure of and power hierarchies within networks and to their considerable resilience and path dependence. . . . For those interested in the emerging geographies of capitalism this implies more attention to power and analysis of how actors with particular interests are using networks to create and obliterate boundaries, and re-shaping territories to serve political and economic goals.

The new awareness spawned by both the intense interest in networks and scale and the critiques that have emerged in economic geography is perhaps best exemplified in a literature that questions the emphasis on successful regions and global cities to make a case for understanding the positioning of places that are cognitively 'off the map' of global capitalism. These places are constituted as irrelevant or obsolescent by virtue of their (constructed) status as 'failed states' or lagging regions (Lee and Yeoh, 2004; Robinson, 2002). The analysis of places outside the geography of global capitalism requires not only a sense of how these places and territories are positioned, but also why. Awareness of these excluded places, in fact, returns us to questions of hierarchy and structure but with the added perspective of positionality and

power (Gibson-Graham, 2002; Sheppard, 2002; Zook and Brunn, 2006).

The emerging critiques of scale and networks as ways to depict and analyze the emerging geography of capitalism have both noted the need to reintroduce the idea of power as central to explaining the processes through which the contemporary geography of capitalism takes shape. They have also emphasized the need to understand the cognitive geographies through which people interpret what they see in the spaces and places of the world. In both these cases, the national territory reenters the theoretical arena for it is within national territories and their regulatory regimes that the power to participate in and influence the character of global networks is formed. And, it is still within national territories that popular discourses about globalization, about the meanings of networks and hierarchies in global space take shape, with important implications for political legitimacy, authority, and the exercise of power.

It is not coincidental that 'the language we are trying to use has a political lexicon derived through and molded by state-centred politics' (Taylor, 1994: 2). An idealist view that the terms of discussion are inadequate to the subject does not mean that those terms have not actually defined the terms of the debates and shaped understanding of what is 'the subject'. We can see this influence by looking more closely at differences among national narratives telling us what globalization is and how it works.

NATIONALLY-CONSTITUTED NARRATIVES ON 'GLOBALIZATION'

A flyer for a conference in a near-by city recently landed in my mailbox that effectively captures how context matters in constructing people's understanding of the emerging geography of capitalism. The conference brochure attests: 'By attending this conference you will learn how in a flat world *globalization* is a powerful driver of relentless change' (emphasis added). Globalization is undefined but it certainly excludes notions of politics or citizenship. This flat world definition of globalization takes its form within a national context in which citizens have been redefined as consumers and in which citizenship has few entitlements. It emphasizes the absence of government not its presence. It is about relentless competition among places and firms, wherever they are located. And, it is missing any awareness of nationally constituted advantages awarded to US transnational corporations operating in the 'global economy.' It is globalization without politics and without citizens.

The particular narrative about globalization that has arisen in the United States resonates with deeply held ideas about society, including an idealization of the market and the association of the market with the capacity for individual choice. The normative value placed on market choice is such that an expression in favor of the hindrance of market forces is perceived as anti-social behavior (Konzelmann et al., 2005). Again, ideas are important. Friedman's (2005) *Flat World* is interesting not for what it tells us about the actual processes of global distribution and production but because of what it tells us about how norms, attitudes and values constructed in place and territory – region and nation state – influence interpretations and responses to the forces put in play by capitalists. Friedman's is a distinctively US centric view of globalization, what it means, and what is important or trivial. His narrative tells us more about what Lefebvre (1991) describes as the representation of space than about the actual processes that are connecting places and people in a global economy. It suggests, however, that narratives of globalization are still constructed in place. Friedman's worldview is that of an American looking out at the world and constructing a story of globalization that fits US values, prejudices, and fears.

The popular US interpretation of global capitalism is only one among many. What this cognitive perspective suggests is that there are multiple narratives about the emerging

geographies of capitalism and about 'globalization', where it comes from, what forms it takes, who it is affecting and how.

INTERPRETING THE GEOGRAPHIES OF CAPITALISM: THE NEED FOR ANALYTICAL TENSION

So, how do we move toward more critical interpretations of the contemporary geography of capitalism? Certainly the recent contributions to thinking about scale and networks as well as a developing sense of perceived and relational space have added to the repertoire of those who study the emerging geographies of capitalism. There are two interrelated strands of research that together lay the foundation for a paradigm in economic geography which could better illuminate the dynamics of spatial transformation beyond the regional 'spatial fix' (Harvey, 1982). The first of these strands documents and interrogates increasing spatial inequality, particularly increasing intra-national disparities (Rodriguez-Pose and Gill, 2004). The depth and extent of inequality raises questions about the ability of endogenous regional characteristics to explain the dynamics of spatial transformation. The second strand expresses renewed interest in the role that power plays in enabling particular actors in the process of spatial transformation (Allen, 2003; Sheppard, 2002; Christopherson and Clark, 2007). As considerations of power begin to appear in empirical work, they can influence how we think about networks, the state, and the construction of scale. The consideration of power, scale and the state has taken shape in work on the neo-liberal state and devolution (Hackworth, 2007; Brenner, 2004) but needs to be extended to a broader understanding of political-economic processes.

In this chapter, I have argued that these new perspectives don't supplant older perspectives as much as they enrich and temper them. However difficult, we need to maintain an analytical tension among territorial, relational, and scalar ways of understanding the dynamic processes constructing the contemporary geographies of capitalism (Harvey, 2006). To understand the geographies of capitalism we have to stretch our analytical capacities. Rather than relying on vague references to 'globalization', we need to delineate the on-the-ground processes constructing markets, production chains, actor networks and regulatory regimes. These processes are being carried out by real actors with power to effect change. We need to understand the motivations and interests of the actors in order to understand the kind of capitalism they are making. In understanding and interpreting how capitalists are making and re-making space, we need to use all the analytical concepts at our disposal – concepts of network, scale and dynamic process.

In addition, we need a lively imagination. There are imaginary geographies that help us see and interpret what kinds of capitalism and by extension, what kind of globalization is taking shape. To the extent we can't imagine, or that our categories limit what we perceive or what we bring to understanding, we may miss or misrepresent what is happening. The recent focus on successful regions rather than on the sources of uneven development in contemporary capitalism is a telling example of such myopia (see Chapters 17 and 18).

In the project of spatial transformation, the nation state remains central, if not as a territory then as a set of regulatory institutions with a claim to legitimacy and authority. As was noted earlier, these institutions are vehicles for actors constructing transnational networks and transnational regulatory regimes. They also retain a hold on people's imaginations and thus affect their capacity for political action and social change.

Despite its permutations and capacity to transcend territories, capitalist accumulation depends on the authority and legitimacy of the state. The national political economy, its governance regime and embedded institutions provide would-be global capitalists with capacities *vis-à-vis* their international as well as their intra-national activities. These capacities affect the ways in which firms distribute the risks associated with capitalist enterprise as well as investor expectations regarding returns on their investments. They shape firm strategies *vis-à-vis* emerging world markets, including those aimed at constructing global market governance rules in their own interests. Capitalists may act in transnational markets and through transnational networks but their actions remain motivated and constrained by institutions that emanate from national governance regimes. These institutions include, for example, those that define private property rights and construct employers' relations with those who work for them. In addition, the nation state is central to the ways in which the discourses of 'globalization' are being structured and given social meaning. Although societies and cultures are not concomitant with national territories, political actors can selectively use national myths and ways of thinking about the world to influence how so-called global processes are defined and understood. These understandings, these nationally-constituted ideas, legitimize action by both capitalists and their political supporters. This consonance of interest is manifested in concepts such as that of the 'national champion'.

Finally, there is the positive potential of the state. The national territory is a potential context, via citizenship, of action to construct what becomes the global economy. The question of citizenship is brought to the fore in discussions of the welfare state, illuminating reasons behind different responses to the challenges posed by global markets. It also resides in increasingly contentious debates over immigration. These debates highlight the conflict between the notion of the global as a space in which labor moves freely in response to market forces, and the persistence of the polity as a bounded territory that controls labor flows. As Turner (2006: 146) argues in a critique of cosmopolitanism:

> Citizenship can only function in the nation-state, because it is based on contributions and a reciprocal

relationship between duty and rights, unlike human rights for which there are as yet no explicit duties. To employ the notion of citizenship outside the confines of the nation state is to distort the meaning of the term and to render it meaningless . . . There are limits to the idea of 'sociology beyond societies' because some concepts are not inherently mobile, but necessarily fixed and specific. It does not follow that they are useless; it merely signifies that some institutions cannot become global. . . .

Thus far, the implications of displacing (if only rhetorically) the nation state as a context for the exercise of political power have received insufficient attention. For example, the role of the nation state as a venue within which to organize military strength in order to restructure political-economic space contradicts the new conventional wisdom of decreasing state efficacy and power. The new conventional wisdom of 'the disappearing state' also undermines political-economic critiques of the withdrawal of nation state institutions from responsibility or accountability for social welfare and rationalizes decentralization of these governmental functions to the region. Finally, the negation of the nation state has implications for the exercise of political power by citizens. These questions suggest that the rhetoric and discourse around the negation of the state may be as important as any real process that results in the diminution of state efficacy.

National 'capitalisms' remain an important object of analysis because they constitute places for struggle over governance of capitalism. They are a critical element in the emerging geographies of capitalism, which are being forged from the deconstruction of the taken-for-granted spatial categories of national, regional and local. It is the focus on struggle, contestation, and power over the constitution and governance of spaces that holds the most promise for interpreting the geographies of capitalism. These, perhaps residual, but still critical, roles make the idea that the nation state is 'over' politically problematic, because it is being replaced by the idea that a vaguely defined 'globalization' is driving the creation of new spaces of governance. The negation of state power has worked ultimately against a dynamic and politicized understanding of how the evolving geographies of capitalism are being constructed and interpreted.

REFERENCES

Agnew, J. (1987) The United States in the world-economy: A regional geography. Cambridge: Cambridge University Press.

Agnew, J. (1994) The territorial trap: The geographical assumptions of international relations theory. *Review of International Political Economy*, 1: 53–80.

Allen, J. (2003) *Lost Geographies of Power*. Oxford: Blackwell Publishing.

Arrighi, G. (1994) *The Long Twentieth Century*. London: Verso.

Barnet, R.J. and Muller, R. E. (1974) *Global Reach: The Power of the Multinational Corporation*. New York: Simon and Schuster.

Berger, S. (2005) *How We Compete*. New York: Currency Doubleday.

Berk, G. (1994). *Alternative Tracks: The Constitution of American Industrial Order, 1865–1917*. Baltimore, MD: Johns Hopkins University Press.

Braudel, F. (1982) *The Wheels of Commerce (Translated by S. Reynolds)*. New York: Harper and Row.

Brenner, N. (2004) *New State Spaces: Urban Governance and the Rescaling of Statehood*. Oxford University Press.

Castells, M. (1996) *The Rise of the Network Society*. Cambridge, MA: Blackwell.

Christopherson, S. and Clark, J. (2007) *Re-making the Region: Labor, Power and Firm Strategies in the Knowledge Economy*. New York: Routledge.

Dicken, P., Kelly, P., Olds, K. and Yeung, H. (2001) Chains and networks, territory and scales: Towards an analytical framework for the global economy. *Global Networks*, 1(2): 89–112.

Duranton, G. and Puga, D. (2000) From sectoral to functional urban specialization. *Journal of Urban Economics*, 57: 343–70.

Friedman, T.L. (2005) *The World is Flat: A Brief History of the Twenty-First Century*. New York: Farrar, Straus and Giroux.

Gallup, J.L., Sachs, J.D., and Mellinger, A.D. (1999) Geography and economic development. *International Regional Science Review*, 22(2): 179–232.

Gibson-Graham, J.K. (1996) *The End of Capitalism (As We Knew It): A Feminist Critique of Political Economy*. Oxford: Blackwell.

Gibson-Graham, J.K. (2002) Beyond global vs local: Economics politics outside the binary frame, in A. Herod and M.W. Wright (eds), *Geographies of Power: Placing Scale*. Oxford: Blackwell. pp. 25–60.

Graham, S. (1998) The end of geography or the explosion of place?: Conceptualizing space, place and information technology. *Progress in Human Geography*, 22: 165–85.

Gray, J. (2006) Global delusions. *The New York Review of Books*, 27, April 2006: 20–23.

Grimshaw, D. and Rubery, J. (2005) Inter-capital relations and the network organisation: Redefining the work and employment nexus. *The Cambridge Journal of Economics*.

Hackworth, J. (2007) The neoliberal city: Governance, ideology, and development in American urbanism. Ithaca: Cornell University Press.

Hall, P. and Soskice, D. (2001) *The Varieties of Capitalism*. Oxford: Oxford University Press.

Harvey, D. (1982) *The Limits to Capital*. Chicago: University of Chicago Press.

Harvey, D. (2006) *Spaces of Global Capitalism: Towards a Theory of Uneven Geographical Development*. New York: Verso Press.

Katz, C. (2001) On the grounds of globalization: A topography for feminist political engagement. *Signs*, 26: 1213–34.

Konzelmann, S., Wilkinson, F., Craypo, C. and Aridi, R. (2005) *The Export of National Varieties of Capitalism: The Cases Of Wal-Mart and Ikea*. Working Paper No. 314, Center for Business Research, University of Cambridge. Available at: http://www.cbr.cam.ac.uk/pdf/WP314.pdf

Lee, Y. and Yeoh, B. (2004) Introduction: Globalization and the politics of forgetting. *Urban Studies* 41(12): 2295–2301.

Lefebvre, H. (1991) *The Production of Space*, published 1974, translated by D. Nicholson-Smith. Oxford: Blackwell.

Massey, D., (1994) *Space, Place and Gender*. Minneapolis: University of Minnesota Press.

Nagar, R., Lawson, V., McDowell, L. and Hanson, S. (2002) Locating globalization: Feminist rereadings of the subjects and spaces of globalization. *Economic Geography*, 78: 257–85.

Ohmae, K. (1995) *The End of the Nation State—The Rise of Regional Economies*. London: Harpercollins.

Peck, J. and Theodore, N. (2007) Variegated Capitalism. *Progress in Human Geography*, 31(6): 731–72.

Perrow, C. (2002) *Organizing America: Wealth, Power, and the Origins of Corporate Capitalism*. Princeton: Princeton University Press.

Poovey, M. (1998) *A History of the Modern Fact. Problems of Knowledge in the Sciences of Wealth and Society*. Chicago: University of Chicago Press.

Porter, P. and Sheppard, E.S. (1998) *A World of Difference: Society, Nature, Development*. New York: Guilford.

Robinson, J. (2002) Global and world cities: A view from off the map. *International Journal of Urban and Regional Research*. 26.3 September: 531–54.

Rodriguez-Pose, A. and Gill. (2004) Is there a global link between regional disparities and devolution? *Environment and Planning A*, 36(12): 2097–2117.

Rodriguez-Pose, A. and Storper, M. (2006) Better rule or stronger communities?: On the social foundations of institutional change and its economic effects. *Economic Geography*, 82(1): 1–25.

Romer, P.M. (1994) The origins of endogeneous growth. *The Journal of Economic Perspectives*: 8(1): 3–22.

Ruggie, John G. (1993) Territoriality and beyond: Problematizing modernity in international relations. *International Organization*, 47: 139–74.

Sheppard, E. (2002) The spaces and times of globalization: Places, scale, networks, and positionality. *Economic Geography*, 78 (3): 307–30.

Skowronek, S. (1982) *Buildng a New American State: Expansion of National Administrative Capacities, 1877–1920*. New York: Cambridge University Press.

Smith, N. (1992) Contours of a spatialized politics: Homeless vehicles and the production of geographical scale. *Social Text*, 33: 54–81.

Smith, N. (1966) *The New Urban Frontier: Gentrification and the Revanchivist City*. London: Routledge.

Strange, S. (1996) *The Retreat of the State: The Diffusion of Power in the World Economy*. New York: Cambridge University Press.

Taylor, P. J. (1994) The state as container: Territoriality in the modern world-system. *Progress in Human Geography*, 18: 151–62.

Taylor, P. J. (1996) Embedded statism and the social sciences: Opening up to new spaces. *Environment and Planning A*, 28: 1917–28.

Thelen, K. (1999) Historical institutionalism in comparative politics. *Annual Review of Political Science*, 2: 369–404.

Turner, B. (2006) Classical sociology and cosmopolitanism: A critical defence of the social. *The British Journal of Sociology*, 57, (1): 133–51.

Wolf, E. (1982) *Europe and the People Without History*. Berkeley: University of California Press.

Yeung, H. W.-C. (1998) Capital, state and space: Contesting the borderless world. *Transactions of the Institute of British Geographers*, NS 23: 291–309.

Zook, M. and Brunn, S. (2006) From podes to antipodes: Positionalities and global airline geographies. *Annals of the Association of American Geographers*. 96(3): 471–90.

11

Capitalism and Social Justice

Paul Routledge

INTRODUCTION: MAKING POVERTY PERMANENT

On 2 July 2005, approximately 250,000 people from a broad variety of organizations and groups from civil societies across the world, converged on Edinburgh, Scotland, to demonstrate against the meeting of the G8 (Group of Eight Nations). The G8 – consisting of the US, Canada, Japan, Britain, Germany, France, Italy and Russia – was due to hold an annual summit at nearby Gleneagles from 6th to 8th July where top government officials would discuss issues of macroeconomic management (i.e. running the neoliberal global economy), international trade, terrorism, energy, arms control, etc. The demonstration in Edinburgh made the demand to 'Make Poverty History' both at home and abroad, and was a prelude to the global days of action that had been planned against the G8 throughout the following week. A primary apprehension of the demonstrators in Edinburgh was that the rhetoric of economic concern being articulated by the G8 politicians prior to their meeting – regarding, in particular, the problems of debt confronted by many countries in the majority world – was

contradicted by the realities of neoliberal capitalism to which the G8 politicians subscribed. These realities, discussed later in this chapter, were more likely to make poverty *permanent* than to make it history. As a result, this demonstration represented a recent example of growing international resistances against the perpetrators and practices of capitalism – struggles which articulate demands for social, economic and environmental justice.

This chapter will consider the interrelations between capitalism and social justice, firstly considering the workings of capitalism before discussing the analytical critiques of capitalism articulated by the discipline of political economy, which has been a highly significant theme in the development of the sub-discipline of economic geography. The chapter will then discuss the contemporary capitalist processes of neoliberal globalization and follow this by considering geographical research into these processes, in particular research on contemporary struggles for social justice. The chapter will conclude with a consideration of contemporary political economic approaches to the issue of capitalism and social justice.

CAPITALISM

Capitalism refers to a set of economic and legal institutions that together make the production of things for private profit the normal course of economic organization. It arose in Western Europe between four and six centuries ago, as a system marked by: (i) private property in the means of production, whether land, tools, machines, or ideas; (ii) a legal framework entitling the owner of those means to the profits they generate subject only to non-arbitrary taxation; (iii) a frame-work of contracts within which sales and purchases relevant to the production activity can be carried out, especially the right to hire and fire workers; and (iv) the legal right of the owner to dispose of the profits as well as the property generating those profits in any way he or she chooses, subject to well-specified and justifiable limits. The use of money and the existence of markets become ubiquitous as capitalism spreads, limited only by what individuals may hold property rights in (Desai, 1993).

For its sustained growth capitalism requires investment on a continuing basis, either out of profits previously earned or from credit provided by financial intermediaries. But money, markets, and investment are necessary only inasmuch as they are instrumental to generating profits. The necessary conditions are profits in a system of private property with contractual rights (Desai, 1993). Although markets have existed alongside all manner of different economic regimes and different forms of ownership, capitalism serves a particular kind of market, namely that for labour – the capitalist economic relation in which some people buy other people's labour power. The capitalist market concerns the accumulation of capital through the exploitation of all available means for the increasing of production, whilst at the same time diminishing costs. Capitalism is in its own self-image a Darwinian struggle, a struggle with few winners and many losers (Tormey, 2004).

Factory production with large concentrations of workers in one place, the growth of rapid transport and of communications on a global scale, the growth of cities and the desertion of villages, and the break-down of the household as a major centre of production of consumables all gave capitalism a dynamism and a facility for "creative destruction" of that which was old or even merely recent. Until the eighteenth century capitalism existed side by side with feudal structures. In its preindustrial phase Western European capitalism had already spread its trade network to all parts of the globe, and colonial empires had been established in America, Africa, and Asia. At the outset these empires were sources for the plunder of gold, silver and slaves. But after the Industrial Revolution the network of formal and informal empires established through trade and credit offered ready markets for the industrial products of Western European capitalism. In return these peripheral regions became suppliers of (non-slave but still relatively un-free) labour and raw materials. As informal trade links gave way to territorial conquest across Africa and Southeast and South Asia during the late nineteenth century, capitalism began to be widely identified with imperialism (Desai, 1993).

For the past 200 years, the economy has come to be dominated by a capitalist mode of production in which the pursuit of profit has been the key driving force behind development. This has also led to the emergence of a single world economy as capitalist social relations have spread geographically from their origins in Western Europe across the globe to embrace and in many cases annihilate more 'primitive' societies and systems. Although capitalism as a system has been through periodic crises and even serious challenges from alternative social systems such as forms of Communism in the Soviet Union and China during the twentieth century, it has proved remarkably durable and adaptable in finding solutions to its internal problems (Cumbers and MacKinnon, 2006).

POLITICAL ECONOMY

The discipline termed political economy examines the relationship of individuals to society, the economy, and the state, and is thus an important tool for analysing the dynamics of capitalism. The concept emerged in the eighteenth century and referred to government policy. The English classical economists Adam Smith (1723–1790), and David Ricardo (1772–1823), redefined political economy in terms of two theoretical emphases: first, the production and accumulation of wealth; and second, the distribution of the 'surplus' so produced. The interest in the distribution of the surplus among social classes necessarily expanded inquiry beyond the purely economic and into social and political spheres (Barnes, 2000).

Neoclassical and contemporary mainstream economics assume that economic inequalities in time and space are eradicated by the operation of market forces. There is an in-built assumption that market forces, if left to their own devices, will produce the optimum solution for all, ensuring that economic wealth is evenly distributed. Adam Smith referred to these forces as the 'invisible hand' and subsequently, mainstream economics has held the view that the economy is governed by self-regulating markets where the forces of demand and supply work to eradicate inequalities in time and space (Cumbers and MacKinnon, 2006).

In the mid-nineteenth century Karl Marx (1818–1883) was the first to recognize the centrality of labour and the importance of the labour process to the operation of capitalism. Marx recognized that human labour is fundamentally different to other commodities as the source of surplus value or profit, which in turn drives the process of economic development (referred to as capital accumulation)

Box 11.1

In their analysis of capitalist relations in the nineteenth century, Karl Marx and Frederick Engels prefigure the political economy of neoliberal globalization.

The history of all hitherto existing society is the history of class struggles … The modern bourgeois society that has sprouted from the ruins of feudal society, has not done away with class antagonisms. It has but established new classes, new conditions of oppression, new forms of struggle in place of the old ones … Constant revolutionizing of production, uninterrupted disturbance of all social conditions, everlasting uncertainty and agitation distinguish the bourgeois epoch from all earlier ones. All fixed, fast-frozen relations, with their train of ancient and venerable prejudices and opinions, are swept away, all new formed ones become antiquated before they can ossify. All that is solid melts into air, all that is holy is profaned, and man is at least compelled to face with sober senses his real conditions of life and his relations with his kind. The need of a constantly expanding market for its products chases the bourgeoisie over the surface of the globe. It must nestle everywhere, settle everywhere, establish connections everywhere. The bourgeoisie has through its exploitation of the world market given a cosmopolitan character to production and consumption in every country … All old established industries have been destroyed or are daily being destroyed. They are dislodged by new industries, whose introduction becomes a life and death question for all civilized nations, by industries that no longer work up indigenous raw material, but raw material drawn from the remotest zones; industries whose products are consumed, not only at home, but in every quarter of the globe. In place of the old wants, satisfied by the production of the country, we find new wants, requiring for their satisfaction the products of distant lands and climes.

Source: Marx, K. and Engels, F. (1985 [1848]) *The Communist Manifesto*. New York: International Publishers. pp. 9–12.

under capitalism. His key observation was that the profits accruing to the holders of capital from the manufacture and sale of products and services (whom Marx termed the bourgeoisie) were based upon the exploitation of labour. Profit, or surplus value as Marx describes it, is not therefore the 'just' return to entrepreneurs for risk taking, but instead the result of a fundamentally unequal exchange in the labour market (Cumbers and MacKinnon 2006). Marx's analysis of how capitalism works anticipates many of the processes associated with contemporary globalization (see Box 11.1, and discussion below).

Marxism assumes that the basic actors in the social system are classes defined by their relationship to the means of production and that, internationally, the interests of classes are manifest in the policies of states and other actors. The explanatory argument for Marxism delineates the way in which capitalism generates inherent contradictions – a declining rate of profit, under-consumption, and a growing tension between the socialization of labour and the continued private concentration of ownership and political power – and the efforts of capitalist states to overcome these contradictions (Cumbers and MacKinnon, 2006). For foreign policy this implies that capitalist states must be imperialistic because they need to maximize the opportunities for foreign investment, access to new sources of raw materials, and the use of cheap foreign labour. Thus, capitalism is inherently a system of exploitation and, in the international system, this implies that the wealthy capitalist core will exploit the 'majority world' periphery (Krasner, 1993).

In contrast to neoclassical approaches, Marxist political economy is concerned with questions of the access and control over resources, and the dynamics of differing forms of, and conflicts over, accumulation, property rights, and disposition/distribution of surplus (Peet and Watts, 2004). It articulates a moral case for economic, political, and social justice and transformation that could only be brought about by revolutionary action. Strongly influenced by Marxist political economy, the first articulate opposition to capitalism arose in the form of socialism and anarchism, which, despite important differences, both argued for the collective ownership over the means of production.

Alongside these developments arose trade unions, which, while not always socialist, were interested in regulating the growth of capitalism in ways that would enhance the workers' share in the total surplus. The collectivism of trade unions was adaptable to mass politics, and these led to the emergence of political parties who supposedly represented worker's interests, such as the Labour Party in the UK. In the course of the first half of the twentieth century, as such political parties won national elections, the state came to play a major role in the spheres of the economy involved with the welfare of the labour force (e.g. pensions, social security, and other social provisions (Desai, 1993). The twin pillars of the political economy tradition have been both analysis and action (theory and practice), articulating the myriad interconnections and interdependencies between culture, social structures and institutions, and the economy, the latter's regulation and the political conflicts it generates (e.g. see Wills, 2002). Outcomes are never predetermined but are shaped by relations between key actors (in particular capital, labour and the state). Critically, the nature of these relations will vary over time and space and will also be shaped by non-economic social and cultural influences reflecting the dominant traditions, values and habits that dominate society at any point in time (Hudson, 2001).

Analysing the outcomes of the interaction and interconnection between key actors in the capitalist economy has lead to ongoing policy debates in political economy concerning the attainment of goals other than growth, profits and efficiency. Arguments are made on behalf of equality of income, opportunity, and participation in public life; over notions of social justice, health, housing, social security; over the role of leisure, culture, and individual fulfilment; over gender, ethnicity, race, and other elements of social relationships; over environmental quality and the preservation of resources (Gourevitch, 1993).

The political economy tradition approaches these questions with a set of distinctive tools. It asks cost-benefit questions and considers incentives, markets, self-interest, and institutions. It proposes solutions that take account of collective action problems, monitoring, 'agency', and the delegation of authority. It examines values, culture, and community in the context of institutions and interests. Debates over the role of the state spill over into debates about managing a market economy. Disputes within countries over state-society relations concerning the economy spill over into the international arena and into national policies toward the world economy. Arguments over effective state policy blur into discussions about foreign economic policy and the international economy, which in turn blur into disagreements about the micro-organization of firms, which blur into arguments about culture and state policy, or back to the beginning of the chain (Gourevitch, 1993).

In human geography, interest in political economy first emerged in the late 1960s, in response to the putatively 'value-free' orientation of geographical research at that time. Many geographers believed that this masked complicity with the social forces at the root of inequality, racism, and the alienation that marked modern life (see, e.g. Morrill, 1969; Peet, 1969) (see Chapter 4). In reaction, many geographers turned toward radical theories and politics rooted in anarchism and Marxism. As a result various efforts were undertaken to better facilitate direct involvement by geographers in the solving of social problems (see, e.g., Berry, 1972; Harvey, 1972, 1974).

The advent of radical geography and subsequently Marxist geography coincided with an era of civil unrest, environmental protests, the emergence of the women's movement, student riots, anti-war campaigns and anti-colonial struggles in and against the US, France, Britain and other countries (especially in the Global South). It was the perceived disjuncture between academic geography and contemporary socio-economic problems and struggles that inspired early radical geographers to call for the 'relevancy' of geographical work (Peet, 1977: 11) and the establishment of a people's geography in which research was focused on politically charged questions and solutions and geographers actively involved themselves with the peoples and communities that they studied. Moreover, it also precipitated dramatic changes in the traditional idea of the 'field' and the geographer's relationship to those who lived there, exemplified by William Bunge's 'Geographical Expeditions' in Detroit between 1969 and 1970, where attempts were made to unite both community concerns and mobilization with academic expertise and research (Bunge, 1977).

The political economy approach within geography was particularly associated with Harvey's (1973, 1982) writings on urbanism and later his close, geographical reading and theoretical interpretation of Marx's texts. Geographers analysed the spatial dimensions of capitalism arguing that it produced strong tendencies towards geographically uneven development (Smith, 1990) and a spatial division of labour (Massey, 1984). Initially, the focus was on urban and regional issues, but since the early 1980s political economy has become both more diffuse and more pervasive (Barnes, 2000; Swyngedouw, 2000).

GLOBALIZATION AND THE NEOLIBERAL ECONOMY

Since the Second World War capital has become increasingly mobile, increasingly 'liquid', meaning that capitalists have been able to invest wherever they see the greatest possible return on their investment. They have been able to take advantage of ever-diminishing costs in terms of air freight, communications infra-structure and information technology capabilities to 'outsource' production to hitherto far-flung parts of the world. Contemporary capitalism is marked by the rise to pre-eminence of transnational corporations which, in terms of their size and power, are able to take advantage of whatever opportunities exist to lower the costs of production, typically by shifting production from wealthier to relatively poorer countries, or through consolidation, merger or takeovers. This development, ongoing since the 1960s in lower technology sectors such as clothing and textiles but now spreading to more advanced manufacturing and even some service sectors, has been termed the *New International Division of Labour* (Frobel et al., 1980).

One of the characteristics of contemporary capitalism is that it takes place within a legal and political framework that is now, reflecting the internationalization of trade itself, 'global' in scope. Various agencies and institutions were set up by the most powerful states after the Second World War to oversee the development of international trade. These institutions include the International Monetary Fund (IMF), the World Bank, the G8, and the Organisation for Economic Cooperation and Development (OECD). In addition, various agencies of the United Nations are involved in economic or socio-economic regulation, particularly the United Nations Conference on Trade and Development (UNCTAD). The World Trade Organisation (WTO), set up in 1995, provides a permanent institutional focus for the General Agreement on Trade and Tariff (GATT) discussions (Tormey, 2004).

The rationale of these institutions is to facilitate the ability of capital to move freely, to compete on a 'level playing field', through currency reform, through 'opening up' markets to 'free' competition and ensuring the necessary 'flexibility' of the labour market. This is all in the name of enhancing, promoting and facilitating the ability of capitalists to make profits. Hence, the doctrine of neoliberalism articulates an overarching commitment to 'free market' principles of unfettered trade, flexible labour, and active individualism. It privileges privatization and

deregulation (e.g. of state-financed welfare, education, and health services and environmental protection), and aggressive intervention by governments around issues such as crime, policing, welfare reform, and urban surveillance with the purpose of disciplining and containing those marginalized or dispossessed by neoliberal policies. Alternative development models based upon social redistribution, economic rights, or public investment tend to be undermined or foreclosed (Peck and Tickell, 2002). However, certain alternatives continue to be articulated including alternative market systems (e.g. bartering, local trading systems, 'fair trade' markets, and alternative currencies); alternative capitalist systems (e.g. state enterprise, green capitalist, non-profit and socially responsible firms); and noncapitalist systems (e.g. communal, and independently run enterprises) (e.g. see Gibson-Graham, 1996, 2006).

Although the effects of neoliberalism have been uneven in different countries, global trends are instructive. One billion people live on less than US$1 a day, and the disparities between rich and poor continue to grow: by 1997 the richest 20% of the world's population received 90% of global income (an increase from 70% in 1960), while the poorest 20% received 1% (a decrease from 2.3% in 1960). The combined annual revenues of the largest 200 TNCs are greater than those of 182 countries that contain 80% of the world's population (Ellwood, 2001). According to the World Bank, in 1998, the income of the richest 1% of the world's population equalled that of the poorest 57% (Callinicos, 2003).

Overall, neoliberal policies have tended to regard the whole of life as a resource for corporate profit. In recent years, genetic patenting has illustrated the inexorable nature of this logic as companies vie to patent the very genetic building blocks of life. From a neoliberal perspective, the global 'commons' – i.e. land, forest, seed, and water resources, etc. that have been traditionally collectively-owned and communally managed to restrain over-use and ensure equitable access for direct uncommodified use by communities – are deemed inefficient and contrary to the principles of free market individualism. Rather, all resources are potentially liable to be commodified, privatized and exploited for profit by TNCs or national governments. Hence, there is no outside of the 'commodity' and thus no reason why the genetic code for rice, wheat or bananas could not be bought and sold (Tormey, 2004). As the interests of corporate profit are privileged over those of working people, so neoliberalism has resulted in the pauperization and marginalization of indigenous peoples, women, peasant farmers, and industrial workers, and a reduction in labour, social, and environmental conditions on a global basis. Moreover, neoliberalism has been associated with the 'death of politics', as it ceases to have any meaning beyond terms prescribed by the market. Hence, 'capital and the market alone determine the restructuring of economic, political and cultural life, making all other alternative values or institutions increasingly redundant' (Gills, 1997: 12).

GEOGRAPHICAL RESEARCH INTO GLOBALIZATION

In response to both the emergence of neoliberal globalization as the dominant economic paradigm worldwide, and its deleterious effects, there has been a renewed interest in Marxian political-economy amongst geographers (e.g. Castree, 1999; Smith, 1998), and a renewed concern about the political relevancy of the sub-discipline of economic geography, in terms of wider policy agendas (Martin, 2001; Peck, 1999). Moreover, geographers have begun to research the complexities and politics of globalization (Swyngedouw, 1997, 2000), the continued importance of place (Cox, 1997), the reconfiguration of political practice and the continued role of the nation-state (Samers, 1997), the diverse

forms of welfare state restructuring (Pinch, 1997), the cultures and practices of corporations (Schoenberger, 1997), the new opportunities for resistance (Kelly, 1997), and uneven development of capitalism (Herod, 1998). Geographical perspectives highlight the ways in which 'the economy' is rooted in, and shaped by, particular social practices, cultural mores and institutional frameworks – all of which vary across space whilst being reshaped in different ways in different locations (Amin and Thrift, 1997).

Historically, the state played an important role in the provision of social infrastructure such as education and training systems, public housing and welfare payments to workers who are temporarily unemployed. However, under neoliberal gobalization, the onus is on people to make themselves employable rather than the state or corporations to provide support or employment for those who are not able to work, as Peck (1998) outlines in his analysis of the development of workfare in the USA. Such drastic measures reflect the 'hollowing out' of the state as governments – and their supporters in the electorate – pull back from social commitments, and the economy and market relations are now expected to provide the solution to poverty and unemployment. However, the successful implementation of welfare policies depends on the ability of local economies to generate jobs and on local employers to end discrimination in their employment decisions (Gilbert, 1998).

In breaking this link between macro-economic processes and social exclusion, contemporary welfare policies end up blaming the victims of poverty for their plight. However, challenging the assertion that globalization necessarily involves the end of state intervention, Martin and Sunley (1997) suggest that national legislation remains crucial in moulding the socioinstitutional framework within which firms are located. States remain important actors, not least in prosecuting the interests of their own multinationals in overseas markets and in international trade forums such as the WTO.

SOCIAL JUSTICE AND RESISTANCE

Reflecting a renewed concern about the role of academics in effecting social change, a number of geographers have urged a return to scholarship that provides a framework and focus for political organization and/or strategic intervention (e.g. Harvey, 2000). Alternatives might involve tackling gender inequalities (Perrons, 1998) or promoting employee ownership (see Wills, 1998) that may secure more balanced and long-term economic stability in local life. Of course, the geographical obstacles to building a counterbalance to the neoliberal agenda at a global dimension are immense. As Baddeley et al. (1998) show in the case of Europe, current political-economic developments – despite social policies – tend to be widening spatial disparities and social exclusions rather than narrowing them.

The economic growth attributed to the free market itself is actually due to increased social control over workers and trade-union organizations (Brenner, 1998). Geographers have highlighted the connections between economic change and the political challenges and opportunities it affords workers and their organizations in different locations (e.g., Castree, 2000; Herod, 2000; Radcliffe, 1999). However, Walker (1999) has argued that, in the absence of strong political intervention from trade unions in the workplace, the capitalist class has been able to take the low road to accumulation and further cement the ongoing decline in wages and quality of employment for the majority. Moreover, Moody (1997) questions the extent to which real empowerment can ever take place in the context of globalization, long-term unemployment, falling rates of unionization, new forms of flexible working and the fear of capital relocation. However, in North America workers have successfully organized in urban areas to secure improvements in pay. In Baltimore, e.g., a coalition of civil rights groups, church leaders and labour unions has successfully forged a strategy to advance a minimum wage in the city (see Harvey, 1998). This achievement is part of a wider shift in working-class organization both in the USA and elsewhere (see, e.g. Herod, 1998; Meiksins-Wood et al., 1998).

However, trade unions are by no means the only, nor always the most powerful, opponents of global capitalism. An immense diversity of social movements comprising peasants, indigenous people, the urban unemployed, and autonomous groups have been engaged in resistance to neoliberal globalization in Latin America and Asia in particular, and also in Europe (see Notes from Nowhere, 2003; Starr, 2005). Recent global days of action against neoliberal globalization, organized by networks of such groups (and including trade unions) by way of international protests against the WTO (Seattle, 1999), the World Bank and IMF (Prague, 2000) and the G7 (Genoa, 2001) have renewed interest amongst geographers and other social scientists in internationalism, collective action, coalition building and networking (Featherstone, 2003; Routledge, 2003; Routledge and Cumbers, 2009).

Inspired by the Zapatista rebellion in Chiapas, Mexico, and global days of action, new forms of political solidarity and consciousness have begun to emerge, as social movements, trade unions, NGOs and other organizations increase their spatial reach by constructing networks of support and solidarity for their particular struggles, and by participating with other movements in broad networks to resist neoliberal globalization. These formations inhabit a political space outside of formal national politics (political parties, elections), and address a range of institutions across a variety of geographic scales (local, national, international). Through such networks, different place-based movements are becoming linked up to much more spatially extensive coalitions of interest. At the beginning of the Zapatista rebellion, in Chiapas, Mexico, spokesperson Subcommandante Marcos, sketched out the economic geography of exploitation in the state that had contributed to the emergence of the resistance:

Chiapas is bled through thousands of veins: through oil ducts and gas ducts, over electric wires, by railroad cars, through bank accounts, by trucks and vans, by ships and planes, over clandestine paths, third rate roads, and mountain passes. Billions of tons of natural resources go through Mexican ports, railway stations, airports, and road systems to various destinations: the United States, Canada, Holland, Germany, Italy, Japan – but all with the same destiny: to feed the empire. A handful of businesses, among them the Mexican State, take the wealth of Chiapas and in exchange leave their mark of death and disease ... Chiapas also bleeds coffee. 87,000 Chiapans work in the coffee industry; 35% of Mexico's coffee production comes from this region ... Fifty-five percent of the nation's hydroelectric power comes from this state, as well as twenty percent of all the electric energy of Mexico. Nevertheless, only a third of all Chiapan houses have electricity (Subcommandante Marcos, 1994:1–5).

The forging of new alliances is creating what Esteva and Prakash (1998) consider a pluriverse of interests; that is, the creation of solidarity between a diversity of social movements operating in a variety of socio-political and geographical contexts. They articulate: different ideological (e.g. Marxist, Feminist, Socialist, Anarchist) and post-ideological (e.g. autonomist) positionalities; reformist and radical political agendas, and; different types of activism (Tormey, 2004). They represent a 'movement of movements' (Mertes, 2004; Tormey, 2004). Underpinning such developments is a conceptualization of protest and struggle that respects difference, rather than attempting to develop universalistic and centralizing solutions that deny the diversity of interests and identities that are confronted with neoliberal globalization processes. As such, it is argued that such alliances represent a participatory way of practising effective politics, articulating the ability of different movements to be able to work together without any single organization or ideology controlling a particular network.

Moreover, participation in a network has become an essential component of the collective identities of those involved, with networking forming part of their common repertoire of action and recruitment (Castells, 1997). However, the forging of alliances between increasingly diverse interests, and across social and spatial divides, implies alliances that might become ever more contradictory and problematic (Chin and Mittelman, 1997; Waterman and Wills, 2001). Such concerns are tied up with considerations of place and the ability to act politically in coalitions across diverse geographical scales (see Routledge, 2003; Routledge and Cumbers, 2009).

Nevertheless, at least two important network initiatives have developed: People's Global Action (PGA), a network of coordination, information sharing and solidarity between grassroots social movements from around the world (see Routledge, 2003); and the World Social Forum, a convergence of a huge diversity of social movements, non-government organizations (NGOs), trade unions and other political forces to protest the World Economic Forum (an annual meeting in Davos, Switzerland where political, business, and financial elites meet to determine global economic strategies), and to exchange experiences and pose alternatives to neoliberal capitalism (see Fisher and Ponniah, 2003; Leite, 2005).

In such networks, different groups articulate a variety of potentially conflicting goals (concerning the forms of social change), ideologies (e.g. concerning gender, class, and ethnicity), and strategies (e.g. violent and non-violent forms of protest). As a result, a diversity of place-specific solutions to economic and ecological problems are articulated. However, certain key areas of agreement have emerged, such as (i) the cancellation of the foreign debt in the developing world (which amounted to US \$3,000 billion in 1999); (ii) the introduction of a tax on international currency transactions, and controls on capital flows; (iii) the reduction in people's working hours and an end to child labour; (iv) the defence of public services; (v) the progressive taxation to finance public services and redistribute wealth and income; (vi) the international adoption of enforceable targets for greenhouse emissions and large scale investment in renewable energy; (vii) policies which ensure land, water and food sovereignty for peasant and indigenous people; and (viii) the defence of civil liberties (Callinicos, 2003; Fisher and Ponniah, 2003; Leite, 2005).

CONTEMPORARY POLITICAL ECONOMY

Responding to the emergence of the 'movement of movements' and the issues of diversity and solidarity that it raises, a number of social theorists and geographers have been grappling with the ways in which points of unity or commonality can be found in the context of difference and particularity, in order to unite struggles over cultural difference with those around economic injustice (see Harvey, 1996; Smith, 2000; McDowell, 2000). Transformatory politics depends on bringing together different interest groups to find common cause and cement alliances, without masking the differences between them, uniting the struggle for identity with that for economic justice.

Labour practices are embedded in, and shaped by, social, political and cultural relationships, including family and community relations. Other forms of power relations persist such as patriarchal, caste, feudal relations or even slavery, which crosscut class relations, and are often drawn upon by as part of exploitative strategies by capital, especially in the majority world (Watts, 1993). The more economistic view of labour and class in many Marxist analyses has been critiqued by feminist writers for prioritizing relations in production over other forms of social relation, such as patriarchal domination through which men have traditionally attempted to exclude women from better paid and more prestigious work (Gibson-Graham, 1996).

As Nagar et al. (2002: 279) observe, a feminist analysis recognizes the inseparability of formal and informal economic activities, productive and re-productive spheres; insists on the importance of cultural and political meanings (e.g. of femininity, masculinity, work, justice, activism); entails an

engagement with power and the complex ways power works at multiple geographic scales (e.g. body, household, etc.); and engages with human creativity in people's resistance (and empowerment) to neoliberal globalization. Hence, new forms of 'social-movement trade unionism' at global dimensions (see Waterman, 1998) need to recognize that trade unions have tended to focus their energies on very narrow workplace concerns (wages, conditions, grievances and discipline). Attempts to forge links across borders and across sectors, will require that (at least some) trade unions undergo fundamental transformation in their aims, objectives, structures and strategies.

Capitalism must be analysed as a set of social relations that are mediated through the simultaneous operation of gendered, sexualized, and racialized hierarchies. This will require a political economic approach that is sensitive to place-specificity and the differential impact of capitalist processes and social relations. Hence a political economy of globalization must be from the perspectives of both the majority world and the minority world – a reconceptualization of globalization which pays close attention to the role of place and local knowledges (Escobar, 2001); and on the connections between production and the institutions of employment and reproduction, bodies, households, and communities (Nagar et al., 2002: 278–79). A feminist approach which articulates both an analysis of, and political engagement with, neoliberal globalization across scales has been recently articulated by Cindi Katz (2001: 1222–25):

> To do a topography is to carry out a detailed examination of some part of the material world, defined at any scale from the body to the global, in order to understand its salient features and their mutual and broader relationships ... [P]roducing a critical topography makes it possible to excavate the layers of process that produce particular places and to see their intersections with material social practices at other scales of analysis ... The material social practices associated with globalization work in interconnection, such as when capital, labor, or cultural products move from one place to another,

but they work iteratively as well: the effects of capitalism's globalizing imperative are experienced commonly across very different locales, and understanding these connections is crucial if they are to be challenged effectively ... Accomplishing such a move involves the construction of a countertopography. I want to imagine a politics that maintains the distinctness of a place while recognizing that it is connected analytically to other places along contour lines that represent not elevation but particular relations to a process (e.g. globalizing capitalist relations of production) ... By constructing precise topographies at a range of scales from the local to the regional and beyond, we can analyze a particular issue – say deskilling – in and across place, mapping sites connected along this line. The larger intent is to produce countertopographies that link different places analytically and thereby enhance struggles in the name of common interests. In many ways this builds an oppositional politics on the basis of situated knowledges ... If situated knowledges suggest local particularities of the relations of production and reproduction, their conscious apprehension in a globalized and multiply differentiated world offers fertile political connections across space and scale that have the fluidity to match and confront the deft global mobility of capitalist investment and disinvestments successfully ... Not only does this kind of analysis reveal the simultaneity of different kinds of descriptions but, making good on John Berger's brilliant insight that it is now 'space not time that hides consequences from us' it also reveals the intertwined consequences of globalizing capitalist production in ways that demand a different kind of politics ... any effective politics challenging a capitalist-inspired globalization must have similar globalizing sensitivities, even as its grounds are necessarily local.

Contemporary political economy must also engage with environmental issues. The approach termed political ecology combines the traditional concerns of political economy with an understanding of both the forms and geography of environmental disturbance and degradation and the prospects for green and sustainable alternatives (Peet and Watts, 2004). Political economic and ecological dimensions of life are mutually reinforcing – the pressure of production on resources, transmitted through social relations, impose excessive demands on the environment (Blaikie and Brookfield, 1987; Watts, 1983). Hence political ecology has investigated the causal connections between logics and dynamics of capitalist growth and specific environmental outcomes (O'Connor, 1988); political action over resource access and control (MacKenzie, 1998); the environmentalism of the poor and community struggles over environment and health (Gadgil and Guha, 1995; Pulido, 1996); environmental movements and NGOs (Escobar, 1995); the discursive construction of environmental risks and resource problems (Beck, 1994); gender practices, knowledges and roles (Peluso, 1992); and the geopolitics of the environment (Dalby, 2002; Peluso and Watts, 2001).

In a globalizing world, the struggles for social justice require our understanding of the ways in which the intersections of politics, economics, culture and ecology unfold on the ground and shape our lives and those of our fellow human beings. Moreover, such struggles will require more sophisticated theorizations of political agency, which incorporate economy and culture, class and identity. A political economy approach needs to be collaborative (see Nagar et al., 2002; Cumbers and Routledge, 2004), engaging with resisting others (workers, peasants, indigenous peoples, the unemployed) and their different and multiple interpretations of what constitutes neoliberal globalization and how to resist it and create socially just and ecologically sustainable alternatives. As Appadurai (2000) argues, marginalized people articulate diverse readings and social mobilizations regarding globalization, what he terms grassroots globalization, (e.g. see Starr, 2005; Notes from Nowhere, 2003). An internationalization of political-economic research is necessary, recognizing different (non-Western) theorizations of capitalism, as is the critical engagement of comfortable minority world scholars in the struggles of distant and not so distant others.

REFERENCES

Amin, A. and Thrift, N. (1997) Globalization, socio-economics, territoriality. In R. Lee, and J. Wills (eds.) *Geographies of Economies*. London: Arnold. pp. 147–57.

Appadurai, A. (2000) Grassroots globalization and the research imagination. *Public Culture,* 12(1): 1–19.

Baddeley, M., Martin, R. and Tyler, P. (1998) European regional unemployment disparities: Convergence or persistence? *European Urban and Regional Studies,* 5: 195–215.

Barnes, T. (2000) Political economy. In R.J. Johnston, D., Gregory, G. Pratt, and M. Watts (eds) *The Dictionary of Human Geography.* Oxford: Blackwell, pp. 593–94.

Beck, U. (1994) *Risk and Modernization.* Boulder: Westview.

Berry, B. (1972) More on relevance and policy analysis. *Area,* 4: 77–80.

Blaikie, P. and Brookfield, H. (1987): *Land Degradation and Society.* London: Methuen.

Brenner, N. (1998) Global cities, global states: Global city formation and state territorial restructuring in contemporary Europe. *Review of International Political Economy,* 5: 1–37.

Bunge, W. (1977) The first years of the Detroit Geographical Expedition: A personal report. In R. Peet (ed.) *Radical Geography.* London: Methuen. pp. 31–39.

Callinicos, A. (2003) *An Anti-Capitalist Manifesto.* Cambridge: Polity Press.

Castells, M. (1997) *The Power of Identity.* Oxford: Blackwell.

Castree, N. (1999) Envisioning capitalism: Geography and the renewal of Marxian political economy. *Transactions, Institute of British Geographers,* 24: 137–58.

Castree, N. (2000) Geographic scale and grassroots internationalism: The Liverpool dock dispute 1995–1998. *Economic Geography,* 76: 272–92.

Chin, C. and Mittelman, J. (1997) Conceptualising resistance to globalization. *New Political Economy* 2(1): 25–37.

Cox, K. (ed.) (1997) *Spaces of Globalization: Reasserting the Power of the Local.* New York and London: Guilford Press.

Cumbers, A. and MacKinnon, D. (2006) *An Introduction to Economic Geography: Uneven Development, Globalization and Place.* London: Pearson.

Cumbers, A. and Routledge, P. (2004) Alternative geographical imaginations: Introduction. *Antipode,* 36(5): 818–28.

Dalby, S. (2002) *Environmental Security.* London: Routledge.

Desai, M. (1993) Capitalism. In J. Krieger (ed.) *The Oxford Companion to Politics of the World.* Oxford: Oxford University Press. pp. 112–14.

Ellwood, W. (2001) *The No-Nonsense Guide to Globalization.* London: Verso.

Escobar, A. (1995) *Encountering Development.* Princeton: Princeton University Press.

Escobar, A. (2001) Culture sits in places: Reflections on globalizm and subaltern strategies of localization. *Political Geography,* 20: 139–74.

Esteva, G. and Prakash, M.S. (1998) *Grassroots Postmodernism.* London: Zed Books.

Featherstone, D. (2003) Spatialities of transnational resistance to globalization: The maps of grievance of the Inter-Continental Caravan. *Transactions of the Institute of British Geographers,* 28(4): 404–21.

Fisher, W.F. and Ponniah, T. (eds) (2003) *Another World is Possible.* London: Zed Books.

Frobel, F., Heinrichs, J. and Kreye, O. (1980) *The New International Division of Labour.* Cambridge: Cambridge University Press.

Gadgil, M. and Guha, R. (1995) *Ecology and Equity.* New Delhi: Oxford University Press.

Gibson-Graham, J.K. (1996) *The End of Capitalism (As We Knew It). A Feminist Critique of Political Economy.* Oxford: Blackwell.

Gibson-Graham, J.K. (2006) *Postcapitalist Politics.* London: Minnesota Press.

Gilbert, M. (1998) 'Race', space, and power: The survival strategies of working poor women. *Annals of the Association of American Geographers,* 88: 595–621.

Gills, B. (1997) Editorial: 'Globalization' and the 'politics of resistance'. *New Political Economy,* 2: 11–16.

Gourevitch, P. (1993) Political economy. In J. Krieger, (ed.) *The Oxford Companion to Politics of the World.* Oxford: Oxford University Press. pp. 715–19.

Harvey, D. (1972) Revolutionary and counter-revolutionary theory in geography and the problem of ghetto formation. *Antipode,* 4: 1–2.

Harvey, D. (1973) *Social Justice and the City.* London: Edward Arnold.

Harvey, D. (1974) 'What kind of geography for what kind of public policy?' *Transactions of the Institute of British Geographers,* 63: 18–24.

Harvey, D. (1982) *The Limits to Capital.* Chicago: Chicago University Press.

Harvey, D. (1996) *Justice, Nature and the Geography of Difference.* Oxford: Blackwell.

Harvey, D. (1998) The body as an accumulation strategy. *Environment and Planning D: Society and Space,* 16: 401–21.

Harvey, D. (2000) *Spaces of Hope.* Edinburgh: Edinburgh University Press.

Herod, A. (ed.) (1998) *Organising the Landscape.* Minneapolis: University of Minnesota Press.

Herod, A. (2000) Workers and workplaces in a neoliberal global economy. *Environment and Planning A*, 32: 1781–90.

Hudson, A. (2001) *Producing Places*. New York: Guilford Press.

Katz, C. (2001) On the grounds of globalization: A topography for feminist political engagement. *Signs*, 26(4): 1213–27.

Kelly, P. (1997) Globalization, power and the politics of scale in the Philippines. *Geoforum*, 28: 151–71.

Krasner, S. (1993) International political economy. In J. Krieger (ed.) *The Oxford Companion to Politics of the World*. Oxford: Oxford University Press, pp. 453–55.

Leite, J.C. (2005) *The World Social Forum: Strategies of Resistance*. Chicago: Haymarket Books.

McDowell, L. (2000) Economy, culture, difference and justice. In I. Cook, D. Crouch, S. Naylor, and J.R. Ryan (eds.) *Cultural Turns/Geographical Turns: Perspectives on Cultural Geography*. Harlow: Prentice Hall, pp. 182–95.

MacKenzie, F. (1998) *Land, Ecology and Resistance in Kenya*. London: IAI.

Martin, R. (2001) Geography and public policy: The case of the missing agenda. *Progress in Human Geography*. 25: 189–210.

Martin, R. and Sunley, P. (1997) The post-Keynesian state and the space economy. In R. Lee, and J. Wills (eds.) *Geographies of Economies*, London: Arnold, 278–89.

Marx, K. and Engels, F. (1985 [1848]) *The Communist Manifesto*. New York: International Publishers.

Massey, D. (1984) *Spatial Divisions of Labour*. Basingstoke: Macmillan.

Meiksins-Wood, E., Meiksins, P. and Yates, M. (eds) (1998) *Rising from the Ashes? Labor in the Age of 'Global Capitalism'*. New York: Monthly Review Press.

Mertes, T. (2004) *The Movement of Movements*. London: Verso.

Moody, K. (1997) *Workers in a Lean World*. London: Verso.

Morrill, R. (1969) Geography and the transformation of society. *Antipode*, 1: 6–9.

Nagar, R., Lawson, V., McDowell, L. and Hanson, S. (2002) Locating globalization: Feminist (re)readings of the subjects and spaces of globalization. *Economic Geography*, 78(3): 257–84.

Notes from Nowhere (2003) *We are Everywhere*. London: Verso.

O'Connor, J. (1988) Capitalism, nature, socialism: A theoretical introduction. *Capitalism, Nature, Socialism*, 1: 11–38.

Peck, J. (1998) Workfare: A geopolitical etymology. *Environment and Planning D: Society and Space*, 16, 133–61.

Peck, J. (1999) Editorial: Grey geography? *Transactions of the Institute of British Geographers* NS 24: 131–35.

Peck, J. and Tickell, A. (2002) Neoliberalizing Space. *Antipode*, 34(3): 380–404.

Peet, J.R. (1969) *A New Left Geography. Antipode*, 1: 3–5.

Peet, R. (1977) *Radical Geography*. London: Methuen.

Peet, R. and Watts, M. (2004) *Liberation Ecologies*. London: Routledge.

Peluso, N. (1992) *Rich Forests, Poor People*. Berkeley: University of California Press.

Peluso, N. and Watts, M. (2001) *Violent Environments*. Ithaca: Cornell Univeristy Press.

Perrons, D. (1998) Maps of meaning: Gender inequality in the regions of western Europe. *European Urban and Regional Studies*, 5: 13–25.

Pinch, S. (1997) *Worlds of Welfare: Understanding the Changing Geographies of Social Welfare Provision*. London: Routledge.

Pulido L. (1996) *Environmentalism and Economic Justice*. Tuscon: University of Arizona Press.

Radcliffe, S. (1999) Latina labour: Restructuring of work and renegotiations of gender relations in contemporary Latin America. *Environment and Planning A*, 31: 196–208.

Routledge, P. (2003) Convergence space: Process geographies of grassroots globalization networks. *Transactions of the Institute of British Geographers*, 28(3): 333–49.

Routledge, P. and Cumbers (2009) *Global Justice Networks: Geographies of Transnational Solidarity*. Manchester: Manchester University Press.

Samers, M. (1997) Maghrebin immigration, France, and the political economy of the 'spatial vent'. In A. Herod, G.Ó.Tuathail, and S.M. Roberts (eds) *An Unruly World? Globalization, Governance and Geography*. London and New York: Routledge. pp. 196–218.

Schoenberger, E. (1997) *The Cultural Crisis of the Firm*. Oxford: Blackwell.

Smith, D. (2000) *Moral Geographies: Ethics in a World of Difference*. Edinburgh: Edinburgh University Press.

Smith, N. (1990) *Uneven Development*. Oxford: Blackwell.

Smith, N. (1998) El Niño capitalism. *Progress in Human Geography*, 22: 159–63.

Starr, A. (2005) *Global Revolt*. London: Zed Books.

Subcommandante Marcos (1994) Chiapas: The southeast in two winds, a storm and a prophecy. In *Anderson Valley Advertizer*, 42(31): 1–5.

Swyngedouw, E. (1997) Neither global nor local: Glocalization and the politics of scale. In K. Cox (ed) *Spaces of Globalization: Reasserting the Power of the Local*. New York and London: Guilford Press. pp.137–66.

Swyngedouw, E. (2000) The Marxian alternative: Historical-geographical materialism and the political economy of capitalism. In E. Sheppard, and T.J. Barnes (eds) *A Companion to Economic Geography*. Oxford: Blackwell. pp. 40–59.

Tormey, S. (2004) *Anti-Capitalism: A Beginner's Guide*. Oxford: Oneworld.

Walker, R. (1999) Putting capital in its place: Globalization and the prospects for labour. *Geoforum*, 30: 263–84.

Waterman, P. (1998) *From Labour Internationalism to Global Solidarity*. London: Cassell.

Waterman, P. and Wills, J. (2001) *Place, Space and the New Labour Internationalisms*. Oxford: Blackwell.

Watts, M. (1983) *Silent Violence: Food, Famine and Peasantry in Northern Nigeria*. Berkeley: University of California Press.

Wills, J. (1998) A stake in place? The geography of employee ownership and its implications for a stake-holding society. *Transactions, Institute of British Geographers*, 23: 79–94.

Wills, J. (2002) Political economy 111: Neoliberal chickens, Seattle and geography. *Progress in Human Geography*, 26(1): 90–100.

12

Globalization and the City

Jonathan V. Beaverstock,
James R. Faulconbridge and Michael Hoyler

INTRODUCTION

Cities are civilization. (LeGates, 2003: 18)

Cities are central to neoliberal globalization. (Massey, 2007: 9)

The city is the central tenet and motor of world capitalist development. Today about three billion people are city-dwellers, of which one in three live in slums or conditions of homelessness (UN-Habitat, 2006). By 2030, almost five billion people will be living in cities, again with significant numbers of these urban inhabitants being the poor and needy (UNFPA, 2007). Given that cities are where most people work, live, spend their money or just simply try to survive and make a living, the city is the global fulcrum for production, exchange and consumption on the one hand, and the underworld of abject poverty on the other. Or to put it another way, 'the city is a geographical plexus, acting as a focus for exchanges of all different kinds ... a way of life, a social drama that plays out differently for different people' (Pile, 1996: 19). The city, like no other place on earth, is *the* global site for economic development and power, and stark socio-economic division.

It is not surprising then, that the city, whether 'world', 'mega' or 'ordinary', has become the subject of numerous studies in the discipline of Human Geography and beyond (see respectively: Sassen, 2006; Davis, 2006; Robinson, 2006). In this chapter we examine the city as a key spatial manifestation of capitalism, with the lens fixed on the prefix of the 'world' city. We adopt a political economy perspective, but by no means discuss every theoretical issue or address each critical intervention.

The rest of this chapter is divided into four main sections. First, we discuss the genesis of the world city discourse and briefly chart the development of the relational approach to understanding cities in contemporary globalization. This new conceptualization of world cities as nodes in networks rather than basing points for global capital in urban hierarchies pioneered the development of relational economic geography from the late 1990s onwards. We then discuss how the city has been considered in urban theory, from the Marxist perspectives of writers like Harvey (1973) and Castells (1977) to the ideas of the 'cultural turn' and 'new urbanism' (Amin and Thrift, 2002). Third, our attention turns to a discussion of the 'divided' city, where we outline some of the polarized contradictions and uneven life experiences of living and working in the city, such as social polarization and gentrification. Before we reach a number of conclusions, the final substantive section of the chapter illustrates the contradictions of capitalism in a number of case study world cities – a 'financial city' (Frankfurt), a 'political city' (Washington DC), a 'creative city' (Montréal), a 'consumption city' (Las Vegas) and a 'globalizing city' (Mumbai).

THE GLOBAL NETWORK OF WORLD CITIES

In the late twentieth century, world city research has emerged as an influential strand in urban-economic studies (Brenner and Keil, 2006). The rise of a transnational urban perspective has been closely linked to fundamental changes in the world economy from the 1970s. Prior to the latest onset of economic globalization, cities had been viewed predominantly within (and subordinate to) the framework of the nation-state (Taylor, 2004), despite pioneering attempts to draw attention to a number of 'world cities' as major national centres with a disproportionate share of the world's 'most important business' (Hall, 1966). The restructuring of global capitalism in the form of a 'new international division of labour' (Fröbel et al., 1980) and a worldwide spatial reorganization of pro (see chapter 5), was accompanied by an increased concentration of corporate power in major cities. Friedmann and Wolff (1982; Friedmann, 1986) famously linked both phenomena in their studies on world city formation, in which they discussed 'world cities' as 'basing points' and control centres of capital flows in the world economy. Friedmann's (1986) 'world city hierarchy' was based on a broad range of attribute criteria such as the presence of headquarters for transnational corporations and international institution. It had a

profound influence on world city research in the following decades, not least because of his initial mapping of a global urban system that identified primary and secondary cities in the core and semi-periphery of the world economy.

A major advancement in transnational urban research was Sassen's (1991) concept of the 'global city'. Sassen (1991: 3–4) identified the global city as, 'a new type of city' that functions as, 'command point[s] in the organization of the world economy; … key location for specialized service firms … site[s] of production, including the production of innovations … [and] market[s] for the products and innovations produced'. The emphasis in Sassen's global city approach moved from Friedmann's focus on formal command power, enshrined in corporate headquarters, to advanced producer service firms, engaged in servicing and enabling the internationalization of production. These highly specialized corporate services were identified as key actors in global city formation, given their tendency to cluster in knowledge-rich central city locations of major urban areas. Sassen's (1991) concept of the global city identified London, New York and Tokyo as *the* strategic sites in the world economy.

Arguably the most comprehensive attempt to map and analyse the emergence of a global network of cities has come from a range of studies undertaken by the Globalization and World Cities Research Network (www.lboro. ac.uk/gawc/). This research has shifted the focus of study from the comparative analyses of individual cities at the apex of a global urban hierarchy, to the analyses of inter-city *relations* and their socio-spatial meaning for globalization. Starting from an initial identification of an 'evidential crisis' in much of the world city literature (Taylor, 1999), a first relational empirical roster was developed which identified 55 'world cities', classified as alpha, beta and gamma in terms of their provision of corporate services (in accountancy, advertising, banking and law) (Beaverstock et al., 1999). Problematizing the common conflating of city rankings based on attribute data with urban hierarchies, Beaverstock et al. (2000, 2002) argued for the centrality of a network approach to the study of world cities and developed a first initial analysis of world city networks. Theoretically, this approach adopted Sassen's (1991) focus on advanced producer services as key agents in contemporary global city formation, and combined this with Castells' (1996) idea of cities as nodes and hubs in a 'space of flows' that has come to characterize many of today's social practices.

More recently, Taylor (2001, 2004) has taken forward the concept of a 'world city network' that can be modelled and empirically investigated. Key agents in the process of world city network formation are not the cities themselves, but those who use cities through the creation of intra-city clusters and inter-city relations in their everyday practices. Many leading advanced producer service firms, for example, have created office networks across a number of cities worldwide to provide a 'seamless' service for their corporate clients. Each office network is interpreted as the outcome of a firm's locational strategy that 'interlocks' the cities in its network through a myriad of flows (of information, ideas, people, etc.) between offices. The resulting major analysis of the locational strategies of 100 leading global service firms across 315 cities allows the identification of the most connected nodes in the world economy and forms the basis for more detailed investigations of inter-city relations under conditions of contemporary globalization. For example, the simple notion of 'command power' in earlier studies of a 'world city hierarchy' is replaced by a more nuanced consideration of power differentials in the network (Taylor et al., 2002). What emerges is the notion of 'cities in globalization' (Taylor et al., 2007), the contention that all cities today are affected by globalization processes and hence show some degree of world *cityness*, although they are always embedded in much wider flows that constitute cities at different scales.

The early 'relational approach' (Beaverstock et al., 1999) and specifically Taylor's (2001, 2004) empirical analyses of world city networks, have not gone uncontested (Alderson and Beckfield, 2004; Nordlund, 2004). One conceptual critique comes from a poststructuralist perspective and argues for a more sustained engagement with actor-network theory and non-representational theory in conceptualizing inter-city relations (Smith, 2003). Writing from a postcolonial perspective, Robinson (2006) identifies a failure of transnational urban theory to adequately represent cities of the global South, which she sees as potentially damaging for poorer cities 'off the map'. Robinson (2006) proposes a conceptual reorientation that argues for a consideration of all cities as 'ordinary cities', that are 'diverse, creative, modern and distinctive with the possibility to imagine [...] their own futures and distinctive forms of cityness' (110, 114). Rather than focusing on a narrow economic sector – advanced producer services – Robinson argues for a much broader approach to economic connections and flows that shape the fortunes of cities.

URBAN THEORY: CITIES AS SITES OF SOCIAL DIVISION AND ECONOMIC POWER

Theorizing the city has long been a preoccupation of geographers and it is impossible to do full credit to the array of debates, past and present, in the field of urban theory. Hubbard (2006) does, however, provide a useful route through some of the main discussions and can help us begin to identify two main streams of research from the 1970s. Marxist approaches to the city (Castells, 1977; Harvey, 1973) and their focus upon production, consumption, distribution and exchange relations and the power structures, identified the way the city sustains economic production by, amongst other things, supporting the consumption of the workforce. In addition, the city as a built environment is also recognized as central to capitalist production because of the way property can absorb the profit and loss of economic activities. Hubbard (2006) argues that, although influential, such Marxist-inflected approaches have been extensively criticized for their neglect of issues such as gender, and are based upon totalizing grand narratives that are westernized, blind to post-colonial concerns and, perhaps most significantly, pay little attention to the multiple communities and cultures of any one city (Bridge and Watson, 2000; Soja, 1989; Dear and Flusty, 1998).

Nevertheless, together these two dominant schools of thought offer us a powerful way of examining how cities act as sites of control and regulation for production and consumption. At one level, the presence of the headquarters and offices of leading transnational corporations makes these cities sites for the production of goods (usually services in the post-industrial city) that increasingly have worldwide appeal. The city acts as a site through which both the workforce and its reproduction and the profit and losses of activities can be managed. Hence we see the clustering of financial and real estate services that are the drivers and reproducers of the economies of many cities today (Sassen, 2006).

In addition though, it is also now recognized that it is not only the relations of production and exchange that underlie this process but also a number of other regulating forces. Debates about the changing relationships between states and political authorities and the market, which now has most control over production regimes are important here (Short and Kim, 1999). This has been extensively covered elsewhere (Held et al., 1999) and few would argue against the importance of recognizing the varying degrees of influence each actor has in different situations and places. Perhaps most significant for debates about the city is a recognition of the cultural conditioning of economic production and the way the city is intertwined with the socio-cultural regulation of the economy (Amin and Thrift, 2007)

The socio-cultural fabric of the city regulates production in a range of ways. At one level, the 'institutional thickness' (Amin and Thrift, 1995) and the socially constructed business cultures of the city can be seen as critical to the success of business services and, in particular, finance (see Leyshon and Thrift, 1997). At another level, as Amin and Thrift (2007) show, the city is also an important site for the production of cultural goods (for example, arts and the theatre) that workers want to consume and seek easy access to when choosing their place of work. And at a third and related level, the city is also shown to be a hybrid cultural entity itself, produced by interactions between peoples, their activities and place. This is exemplified by the activities of the *flâneurs* and the inspiration they gain by 'absorbing' the city through their walks (see Hubbard, 2006). Indeed, this third level is said to act as a spur for the production of cultural goods such as furniture and art because of the inspiration designers glean from everyday experience and consumption of the city (Zukin, 1988). It is this latter perspective that is perhaps of most interest here.

The post-modern city and its multiple cultures, ethnicities and resultant consumption cultures is said to produce a new and powerful cosmopolitanism (Short and Kim, 1999). This in itself demonstrates the intricate linkages between the cultural and the economic and the vital role of the city in such production processes. Industries, from advertising (Grabher, 2001) to apparel manufacture (Rantisi, 2002), develop a presence in the city to absorb the influences of these cultures and build products based upon their influences. Consequently, as cultures reproduce themselves differently both between cities and within the diverse and often fragmented districts of a city, a powerful centripetal force develops that sustains cities as important sites of production because of their attractiveness both to workers (because of the accessibility provided to cultural industries) and firms (because of the benefits that 'being there' bring to the innovation process in cultural industries).

Amidst all of this, analyses of the way cities coordinate production and consumption should not be overly territorial. Through the transnational command networks of the firms in these cities (Sassen, 2006; Taylor, 2004), supranational non-governmental organizations (Short and Kim, 1999), the mobility of individuals as workers and tourists (Hannerz, 1996) and even the magazines and television stations emerging from leading world cities (Knox, 2002), the influence of any one city stretches beyond territorially defined boundaries. As Amin and Thrift (2002) have argued, cities should be conceptualized as fluid networks and not as bounded entities. Cities produce, and are produced by, global connections and flows, acting as nodes in an increasingly networked society (Castells, 1996).

THE DIVIDED CITY?

The notion of the 'divided' city is not a new phenomenon. All cities are rife with inequality and difference, and have been so since the dawn of industrial capitalism and before (Engels, 1987; Marcuse, 1989). A re-reading of the urban models of Burgess and Hoyt, for example, shows marked spatial segregations of wealth and living conditions in the city (see Knox and Pinch, 2000). In recent times, numerous studies have illustrated the polarized inequities of life in the post-industrial city (see Davis, 1990; Fainstein et al., 1992; Mollenkopf and Castells, 1991) where, if they are fortunate enough to live in housing and not on the streets, poorer inhabitants live in close proximity to the burgeoning and increasingly affluent middle classes. Marcuse's (1993: 355–56) reading of social division in the post-industrial city suggests that it can be carved into distinctive quarters:

- the luxury city, segregated in enclaves of specific, isolated buildings in the city occupied by the economic, social and political elite;

- the gentrified city, occupied by the professional, managerial and technical social groups;
- the suburban city, apartments near the city centre or outer city housing, occupied by 'mid-range' professionals and civil servants;
- the tenement city, often occupied by 'blue and white collar' workers in the rented sector, and which includes social (public) housing;
- the abandoned city, 'the end result of trickle down, left for the poor, the unemployed, the excluded'.

For Marcuse (1993: 356), these different spatial quarters of the city are reproduced by parallel processes of economic restructuring within the city. For example, the 'big' decision-making, corporate economy of command in the city reproduces the luxury city; the 'city of advanced services' fuels the desire for the gentrified city; the manufacturing, service and public service sector of the city equates to the making of the suburban city; and, the unskilled worker in the formal or informal sectors of the city may reproduce the tenement and, or abandoned city.

One contested argument focusing on the explanation of social inequality and division in the global city is Sassen's (1991) 'social polarization thesis'. Sassen suggested that the concentration of command and control in global cities like London and New York, particularly in advanced producer services and international finance, combined with the shrinking and downgrading of the manufacturing sector, and the process of informalization in all industrial activities fuelled by immigration, has had significant effects on the structure of local labour markets and the distribution of earnings and income. Sassen argues that these processes have created labour market conditions in which there is significant growth in highly-skilled, highly-paid jobs in advanced producer services; low-skilled or unskilled, low-waged jobs in the downgraded manufacturing sector or in those services which are generated by highly-skilled and highly paid workers (for example, cleaners, hotel staff); and the informalization of work in both manufacturing and services. The consequence of this restructuring in labour market demand has been the emergence of polarization in occupational, earnings and income distribution with expanding groups of highly-paid, highly-skilled workers, who live in affluent and gentrified neighbourhoods of the city, and low-paid workers who live elsewhere, which reproduces residential (and ethnic) segregation and 'ghettoization' in the city.

Sassen's (1991) 'social polarization thesis' has generated much debate, particularly by those examining its relevance beyond cities like Los Angeles, Chicago, Boston and the US city system more generally. Hamnett's (1994) work has been very influential in questioning the theoretical and empirical validity of the 'social polarization thesis'. He identifies three major weaknesses. First, there is ambiguity in its conceptual meaning (does social polarization refer to occupational structure or income distribution?) and measurement (relative or absolute?) when translated outside the US context. Second, the thesis is not adequately contextualized in wider meta-narratives which explain social and occupational change in society like, for example, the process of professionalization and growth of the 'new middle class'. Third, the process of informalization (linked to significant legal and alien immigration, and ethnic segregation) is too specific to US-American cities, especially New York and Los Angeles, and does not necessarily apply to Tokyo, London or other European cities.

Putting the 'social polarization' thesis aside, and fast-forwarding to today, casual observation of the cityscape and empirical scrutiny of available urban statistics (for example, on GDP, economic indicators, employment, earnings) continue to show that the city, whether 'world', 'mega' or 'ordinary' remains divided, both socio-economically and spatially, between the 'haves and the have nots' (Beaverstock et al., 2004; Cox and Watts, 2002), with large proportions of the 'have nots' living in the mega-cities of the developing world (UN-Habitat, 2006). The city's burgeoning mass affluent corporate, executive class, whether employed in government, inter-national finance, business services or science and technology will continue to demand selected residential property in particular neighbourhoods (for example the Upper West and East Sides of Manhattan, New York; Chelsea and Kensington, London; Passy-Auteuil, Paris), or act as a global super-gentrifying 'class' (Bridge, 2007; Smith, 2002).

Following analyses of gentrification in the city (see: Butler, 1997; Smith, 1996) there has emerged a rich vein of empirical work which has posited a, 'third-wave of gentrification', so called, 'supergentrification' (Lees, 2003: 2490). Super-gentrification is a process whereby the wealthy, often transnational, cosmopolitan professionals engage in the re-gentrification of selected, already prosperous areas in world cities like London and New York, thus making them highly exclusive and super-expensive neighbourhoods (Lees, 2003). Commentators suggest that these 'supergentrifiers', the super-rich or the 'finan-cifiers' (Lees, 2003: 2487) who work in global finance or the higher echelons of the corporate economy, are an important constituent of a global gentrifying 'class', who are responsible for reinvestment in selected global city neighbourhoods throughout the world (Aktinson and Bridge, 2005). Lees (2003) and Butler and Lees (2006) present case studies of this new phenomenon of super-gentrification in Brooklyn Heights, New York City and Barnsbury, London respectively.

CAPITALISM IN THE CITY

We now discuss a number of case study cities which illustrate how capitalist development and latterly globalization have (re)produced distinctive world city geographies of functionality, unevenness, polarization, inequality and wealth in contemporary society.

Frankfurt: a financial city

Frankfurt's ascendancy to major international city of finance had been preceded by a long history as an important German centre for fairs and banking since the Middle Ages (Holtfrerich, 1999). However, it was only after the Second World War, when Berlin lost its pre-war role as national financial centre in the wake of the division of the city and its spatial isolation from West Germany, that Frankfurt gradually acquired predominance over a number of competing financial centres in Germany (Schamp, 1999). Of prime importance for the subsequent rise of Frankfurt was the decision of the Allied military government to locate the German Central Bank there in 1948. This initiated a path-dependent process that saw the rise of Frankfurt as the new national and increasingly international financial centre (Grote, 2008) as headquarters of major domestic banks relocated to the city from Düsseldorf, Hamburg and other German cities, and foreign banks chose it as the key location for their presence in the country.

Closely linked to its consolidating role as banking and transportation hub, Frankfurt and the wider metropolitan Rhine-Main region have developed into Germany's leading centre for knowledge-intensive services, with major clusters of professional service firms in law, advertising, accountancy, management consultancy and related business activities (Hoyler et al., 2008). This locally contested process (Keil and Ronneberger, 2000) has transformed Frankfurt into Germany's internationally most visible 'global' city, a gateway for international firms and capital that seek entry to the German market. By 1999, many had come to believe that the location of the European Central Bank in the city would lead to another scalar leap and bestow Frankfurt with a major global role in finance. However, little actually happened and rather than gaining at the expense of London, Frankfurt saw no substantive change in its fortune as an international financial centre (Beaverstock et al., 2005). On the contrary, Frankfurt's share of foreign banks has decreased significantly over recent years (Grote, 2008), reflecting a tendency of major transnational firms to concentrate advanced business in truly global centres such as London (Faulconbridge et al., 2007).

Washington DC: a political city

As Sassen (2006) reiterates, capital cities and political cities are not necessarily world cities. There are, of course, important examples of cities that are political, capital and world cities (for example, London) but there are also plenty of examples that counter this trend (for example, Canberra, which is merely a political city). Washington, DC, as the capital city of the USA, is an interesting example of a political city that has gone global. Conspicuously understudied (except Abbott, 1996, 1999), Washington has developed globalizing tendencies. These have arisen both because of the political influence of actors in the city (the US federal government as well as the various non-governmental organizations with operations in the city including the International Monetary Fund and the World Bank) and because of the economic activities that have developed in association with such political actors and activities over the past thirty years. For example, Beaverstock et al. (1999) classify Washington DC as a gamma (third-level) world city, mainly because of its importance as an accountancy and legal service centre, activities that have spun-off from the city's political status.

Because it is not the territorial assets of a city that define its global significance but, rather, its articulations in the world city network, the globalness of Washington, DC is, then, a result of the way domestic political functions have produced transnational connections (Abbott, 1996). This, of course, cannot be disconnected from US foreign policy and the significance of the USA as a donor to the World Bank, something that underlies the cluster of lobby groups and campaign organizations that now exist around Capitol Hill (Gerhard, 2003). Moreover, because of the power of key actors in Washington DC to control the regulatory environment influencing business, many TNCs locate in the city to participate in intensive forms of lobbying that can determine future policy directions. This brings with it the associated transnational service firms that have lifted the city's status as a world city (Beaverstock et al., 1999).

Montréal: a creative city

Creativity and the city is now one of the most contested topics of urban academic and policy debates (Florida, 2002). Montréal has long been recognized as a creative city with 450,000 workers employed in 'creative' industries (Stolarick and Florida, 2006). Rantisi and Leslie (2006) note how service sector activity and employment also reinforce the success of the city, supporting artists with an essential network of boutique retailers specializing in selling one-off and design-heavy products. Being a creative city has now caught the imagination not only of the residents of Montréal, but also the city's politicians. Through the city's Commissioner of Design, Montréal embarked on a neo-liberal branding strategy aimed at making the city globally competitive as a design centre. *Commercial Design Montréal*, as the plan was known, aimed not only at improving infrastructures, but also at the marketing of the city to both businesses and tourists (Rantisi and Leslie, 2006), and at developing transnational dimensions through cooperation established with St Etienne in France, a city with similar aspirations to be known as a design capital.

One of the spin-offs from all of this is the gentrification often associated with the rise of cultural industries and the disposable capital they produce. As Ley (2003) notes, artists attract a range of other gentrifying professionals to a city and create new challenges for places such as Montréal. But, as Peck (2005) reminds us, this is to be expected when a Richard Florida-style entrepreneurial recipe is followed for the development of a creative city. Not everyone in the city can be part of the gentrifying creative class. Nevertheless, with the growing valorization of cultural economies, cities such as Montréal have the potential to exploit their status as a so-called 'creative' city and tap into a growing global industry where design is recognized as a form of value-added in products.

Las Vegas: a consumption city

Las Vegas has come a long way from an 'oasis' on the road to California in the 1830s to the tourist mecca that it is today, attracting 44 million visitors in 2007 (City of Las Vegas, 2008). In 1935 it was already attracting 300,000 visitors (Roske, 1986), but it was the 1950s that cemented the city's reputation as an entertainment resort *par excellence*, with the transformation of little clubs into spacious casinos and hotel entertainment complexes (Moehring, 1989). New household name hotel 'resorts', like the Flamingo, Stardust, Sahara, Caesars (stet) Palace and the Golden Nuggett, became magnets for gambling, entertainment and leisure, and international stars like Frank Sinatra, Dean Martin and Jerry Lewis among others (Findlay, 1986). Las Vegas continued to boom during the 1960s and 1970s, with multi-million dollar investment in the entertainment industry and, by 1969, it was regularly attracting over 2 million visitors per year (Moehring, 1989). Global superstars like Elvis Presley and Tom Jones played the major hotels and casino gambling became part of a multi-faceted entertainment complex comprising theme parks, a thriving wedding, divorce and sex worker industry, as well as extensive shopping malls (Hannigan, 1998) which firmly cemented its global tag as either 'Sin City' or 'Lost Wages' (Amis, 2006; Gottdiener et al., 1999).

However, during the 1980s, increased competition from Atlantic City and other forms of legalized gambling encouraged Las Vegas' developers to become more elaborate with their themed resorts and fantasy attractions (Gottdiener et al., 1999). In 1989, The

Mirage became the first 'megaresort' with its Volcano and Polynesian theme, costing $700 million, followed by other famed examples such as: Excalibur, an Arthurian Camelot legend theme (costing $290 million); and, MGM Grand, a 5,000 room hotel, health spa, 15,200 seat arena for sporting events, night-club and 33 acre theme park (Gottdiener et al., 1999). By July 2006, the city reached a population of 0.6 million, had almost 30% of its workforce employed in leisure and hospi-tality, and generated revenues of $9.4billion from an estimated 28.9 million visitors (City of Las Vegas, 2008). *Viva Las Vegas!*

Mumbai: a globalizing city

Mumbai, formally known as Bombay before 1995, has the reputation of being India's most cosmopolitan, creative and commercial city (Patel, 2007). It is the home of Bollywood and India's premier financial centre (Harris, 1995). Bombay's early growth was overseen by British interests as a port and archetypal colonial city, which had developed into a manufacturing city post-Independence (Pacione, 2006), and a 'most modern city' (Patel, 2007: 64) by the end of the twentieth century. The city-region is home to about 17 million people, which makes it one of the largest and most densely populated mega-cities on earth (Pacione, 2006). It is estimated that the city will soon have 27 million inhab-itants (Bombay First, 2008). Mumbai is a divided city. About six million (50–60% of the population) are slum dwellers, living in overcrowded conditions with basic or no clean water, sanitation and access to health, education and formal employment, and a further three million living on the sidewalks or in derelict buildings (McKinsey, 2003; Patel, 2007; UNDP, 2002). Moreover, as the manufacturing sector faltered sharply from the 1980s, affecting labour-intensive indus-tries like textiles (which shrank from 27% of the share of city jobs in 1976 to 12.5% by 1991), the rise in unemployment has shifted considerable volumes of labour into the

informal sector, thus reproducing the cycle of poverty (Harris, 1995; Patel, 2007).

In contrast, the city's service sector has flourished under conditions of globalization and enhanced the fortunes of Mumbai's middle classes (Nijman, 2007). Employment in financial and business services has increased by over 40% since the 1970s, and the city's globally successful creative cluster, Bollywood, has generated significant job growth, with an estimated 140 film releases per annum (Patel, 2007). Related to proc-esses of globalization, Mumbai has been a major beneficiary of corporation offshoring and outsourcing (in IT-enable services, back office functions, call centres, software devel-opment). For example, in the software indus-try, 85 foreign firms had set up new plants in Maharashtra, while 76 local firms had bene-fited from expanded relationships with for-eign companies by 2002/03 (UNCTC, 2004). Mumbai based firms have been able to diver-sify their activities with foreign companies as investments have deepened over time. Mumbai has also benefited from foreign company investment in higher value-added financial and producer services. Grant and Nijman's (2002) survey of the locational preferences and functionality of domestic and foreign companies in Mumbai high-lighted the emergence of a 'global' Central Business District (CBD) at Nariman Point, which emerged specifically from the interna-tional financial and producer service econ-omy. In the context of other international financial centres, Mumbai is ranked as 41st (from 50) in the Global Financial Centres Index (Z/Yan, 2007).

Looking towards the future, local business interests under the auspices of Bombay First (www.bombayfirst.org/), with the support of local government, engaged McKinsey & Co. (2003) to produce a 'Blueprint' for Mumbai to turn itself into a 'world class' city by 2013, which would rank alongside Shanghai or Singapore (Katakam, 2003). This plan recom-mends a $40billion investment in the city's economy, transportation, low-income hous-ing, infrastructure (water supply, sanitation, education), healthcare, finance and governance, to deliver economic growth and improvements in the quality of life of its population. But, many are already questioning the availability of such investment finances, the unrealistic time-scale of the plan, its overall political objectives and its disengagement with wider environmental issues (Katakam, 2003; Pacione, 2006).

CONCLUDING REMARKS

In this chapter we have discussed some aspects of capitalist development and the city, especially those associated with so-called 'world' cities. The city and its place in a relational network of other cities, whether 'world' or 'ordinary', has been the key spatial manifestation of the unequal forces of capitalism. World cities display complex geometries of strategic control (Sassen, 2006) and power relations (Allen, 2003) be they represented as static urban hierarchies or relational economic geographies of connectivity (Friedmann, 1986; Taylor, 2004). But, as Robinson (2006) reminds us, just because a city is not connected in the circuit of advanced services, does not mean that it is not a world city in other dimensions of capital accumulation.

All cities are world cities in one way or another but they may be embedded in different circuits of globalization. Beyond the world city discourse, it is important to remember that theorizing the city has a long lineage in human geography and other cognate social sciences, with perspectives drawn from structuralists and post-structural approaches, from writers such as Harvey (1973) and Soja (1989). These together, then, in combination with the writings on new urbanism (Amin and Thrift, 2002) makes theorizing the contemporary city and its coordinating role in economic production and consumption a complex affair that must take into account more than simply the economic, but also the socio-cultural and political manifestations of life in the city, something that often has implications well beyond national boundaries.

We have also discussed the city as a place of uneven opportunities and social relations for its inhabitants, reproduced by wider processes of economic restructuring and urban change. The contested concept of the 'divided' city, broadly distinguishing between the rich and middle-classes and the low-paid and underclass, exposes the geographies of the 'haves and the have nots' in urban living. In juxtaposition to the city being the crux of command and control, wealth generation and the playground of the mass affluent, the notion of the *unequal* city is omnipresent (Hamnett, 2003), whether in terms of income distribution, employment opportunities, ethnic segregation, housing, homelessness, and opportunities for existing and new immigrant communities (Buck et al., 2002). Our brief vignette of Mumbai illustrates an enormous cleavage in social justice where millions of people live in abject poverty alongside a growing privileged new middle class, in a rapidly globalizing world city. Cities will continue to be sites of control and coordination for the capitalist system through uneven processes of the material and the immaterial in the production and reproduction of everyday life.

REFERENCES

Abbott, C. (1996) The internationalization of Washington D.C. *Urban Affairs Review*. 31: 571–94.

Abbott, C. (1999) *Political Terrain*. Chapel Hill: University of North Carolina Press.

Alderson, A.S. and Beckfield, J. (2004) Power and position in the world city system. *American Journal of Sociology*, 109: 811–51.

Allen, J. (2003) *Lost Geographies of Power*. Oxford: Blackwell.

Amin, A. and Thrift, N. (2007) Cultural-economy and cities. *Progress in Human Geography*, 31: 143–61.

Amin, A. and Thrift, N. (2002) *Cities*. Cambridge: Polity.

Amin, A. and Thrift, N. (1995) Globalisation, institutional thickness and the local economy. In P. Healey, S. Cameron, S. Davoudi, S. Graham, and Madani-Pour (eds) *Managing Cities*. Chichester: Wiley. pp. 91–108.

Amis, M. (2006) Poker, panic and a pair of sevens. *The Sunday Times Magazine*, 17th September.

Atkinson, R. and Bridge, G. (eds) (2005) *Gentrification in a Global Context*. Oxford: Routledge.

Beaverstock, J.V., Smith, R.G., and Taylor, P.J. (1999) A roster of world cities. *Cities*, 16: 445–58.

Beaverstock, J.V., Smith, R.G., and Taylor, P.J. (2000) World-city network: A new metageography? *Annals of the Association of American Geographers*, 90: 123–34.

Beaverstock, J.V., Doel, M.A., Hubbard, P.J., and Taylor, P.J. (2002) Attending to the world: Competition, cooperation and connectivity in the world city network. *Global Networks*, 2: 111–32.

Beaverstock, J.V., Hubbard, P., and Short, J.R. (2004) Getting away with it?: The changing geographies of the global super rich. *Geoforum*, 35: 401–07.

Beaverstock, J.V., Hoyler, M., Pain, K., and Taylor, P.J. (2005) Demystifying the euro in European financial centre relations: London and Frankfurt, 2000–2001. *Journal of Contemporary European Studies*, 13: 143–57.

Bombay First, www.bombayfirst.org (accessed 03/03/2008).

Brenner, N. and Keil, R. (eds) (2006) *The Global Cities Reader*. London: Routledge.

Bridge, G. (2007) A global gentrifier class? *Environment and Planning A*, 39: 32–46.

Bridge, G. and Watson, S. (2000) City economies. In G. Bridge and S. Watson (eds) *A Companion to the City*. Oxford: Blackwell. pp. 101–14.

Buck, N., Gordon, I., Hall, P., Harloe, M., and Kleinman, M. (2002) *Working Capital*. London: Routledge.

Butler, T. (1997) *Gentrification and the Middle Classes*. Aldershot: Ashgate.

Butler, T. and Lees, L. (2006) Super-gentrification in Barnsbury, London. Globalization and gentrifying global elites at the neighbourhood level. *Transactions of the Institute of British Geographers*, 31: 467–87.

Castells, M. (1997) *The Urban Question*. London: Arnold.

Castells, M. (1996) *The Rise of the Network Society*. Oxford: Blackwell.

City of Las Vegas (2008) *Las Vegas 2007* (available from www.lasvegasnevada.gov/Government/7480.htm).

Cox, R. and Watts, P. (2002) Globalization, polarization and the informal sector: The case of paid domestic workers. *Area*, 34: 39–57.

Davis, M. (1990) *City of Quartz*. London: Verso.

Davis, M. (2006) *Planet of Slums*. London: Verso.

Dear, M. and Flusty, S. (1998) Postmodern urbanism. *Annals of the Association of American Geographers*, 88: 50–72.

Engels, F. (1987) *The Condition of the Working Class in England*. Rickmansworth: Penguin.

Fainstein, S.S., Gordon, I. and Harloe, M. (eds) (1992) *Divided Cities*. Oxford: Blackwell.

Findlay, J. (1986) *People of Chance*. Oxford: Oxford University Press.

Faulconbridge, J., Engelen, E., Hoyler, M., and Beaverstock, J.V. (2007) Analysing the changing landscape of European financial centres: The role of financial products and the case of Amsterdam. *Growth and Change*, 38: 279–303.

Florida, R. (2002) *The Rise of the Creative Class*. New York: Basic Books.

Friedmann, J. (1986) The world city hypothesis. *Development and Change*, 17: 69–83.

Friedmann, J. and Wolff, G. (1982) World city formation: An agenda for research and action. *International Journal for Urban and Regional Research*. 6: 309–44.

Fröbel, F., Heinrichs, J. and Kreye, O. (1980) *The New International Division of Labour*. Cambridge: Cambridge University Press.

Gerhard, U. (2003) Local activity patterns in a global city-analysing the political sector in Washington, DC. *GaWC Research Bulletin* 99. http://www.lboro.ac.uk/gawc/rb/rb99.html

Gottdiener, M., Collins, C.C. and Dickens, D.R. (1999) *Las Vegas*, Oxford: Blackwell.

Grabher, G. (2001) Ecologies of creativity: The village, the group and the heterarchic organisation of the British advertising industry. *Environment and Planning A*, 33: 351–74.

Grant, R. and Nijman, J. (2002) Globalization and the corporate geography of cities in the less developed world. *Annals of the Association of American Geographers*, 92: 320–40.

Grote, M.H. (2008) Foreign banks attraction to the financial centre Frankfurt: An inverted 'U'-shaped relationship. *Journal of Economic Geography*, 8: 239–58.

Hall, P. (1966) *The World Cities*. London: Weidenfeld & Nicolson.

Hamnett, C. (1994) Social polarisation in global cities: Theory and evidence. *Urban Studies*, 31: 401–24.

Hamnett, C. (2003) *Unequal City*. London: Routledge.

Hannerz, U. (1996) *Transnational Connections*. London: Routledge.

Hannigan, J. (1998) *Fantasy City*. London: Routledge.

Harris, N. (1995) Bombay in a global economy. *Cities*, 12: 175–84.

Harvey, D. (1973) *Social Justice and the City*. London: Arnold.

Held, D., McGrew, A., Goldblatt, D. and Perraton, J. (1999) *Global Transformations*. Cambridge: Blackwell.

Holtfrerich, C.-L. (1999) *Frankfurt as a Financial Centre*. München: Beck.

Hoyler, M., Freytag, T. and Mager, C. (2008) Connecting Rhine-Main: The production of multi-scalar polycentricities through knowledge-intensive business services. *Regional Studies*, 42: 1095–1111.

Hubbard, P. (2006) *City*. London: Routledge.

Katakam, A (2003) A blueprint for Mumbai. *Frontline*, 20: Nov. 22nd–Dec. 5th.

Keil, R. and Ronneberger, K. (2000) The globalization of Frankfurt am Main: Core, periphery and social conflict. In P. Marcuse and R. van Kempen (eds) *Globalizing Cities: A New Spatial Order?* Oxford: Blackwell. pp. 228–48.

Knox, P.L. (2002) World cities and the organization of global space. In R.J. Johnston, P.J. Taylor, and M.J. Watts, (eds) *Geographies of Global Change*. Oxford: Blackwell. pp. 232–47.

Knox, P. and Pinch, S. (2000) *Urban Social Geography*. London: Prentice Hall.

Lees, L. (2003) Super-gentrification: The case of Brooklyn Heights, New York City. *Urban Studies*, 40: 2487–2509.

LeGates, R.T. (2003) How to study cities. In R.T. LeGates and F. Stout (eds). *The City Reader*. London: Routledge. pp. 9–18.

Ley, D. (2003) Artists, aestheticisation and the field of gentrification. *Urban Studies*, 40: 2527–44.

Leyshon, A. and Thrift, N. (1997) *MoneySpace*. London: Routledge.

Marcuse, P. (1989) 'Dual City': A muddy metaphor for a quartered city. *International Journal of Urban and Regional Research*, 14: 697–708.

Marcuse, P. (1993) What's so new about divided cities? *International Journal of Urban and Regional Research*, 18: 355–65.

Massey, D. (2007) *World City*. Cambridge: Polity.

McKinsey & Co. (2003) *Vision Mumbai*. McKinsey Report, Mumbai.

Moehring, E. (1989) *Resort City in the Sunbelt*. Las Vegas: University of Navada Press.

Mollenkopf, J.H. and Castells, M. (eds). (1991) *Dual City*. New York: Russell Sage Foundation.

Nijman, J. (2007) Mumbai's mysterious middle class. *International Journal of Urban and Regional Research*, 30: 291–95.

Nordlund, C. (2004) A critical comment on the Taylor approach for measuring world city interlock linkages. *Geographical Analysis*, 36: 290–96.

Pacione, M. (2006) Mumbai. *Cities*, 23: 229–38.

Patel, S. (2007) Mumbai: The mega-city of a poor country. In K. Segbers (ed.) *The Making of Global City Regions*. Baltimore: John Hopkins University Press. pp. 64–84.

Peck, J. (2005) Struggling with the creative class. *International Journal of Urban and Regional Research*, 29: 740–70.

Pile, S. (1996) What is a city? In D. Massey, J. Allen and S. Pile (eds) *City Worlds*. London: Routledge. pp. 3–52.

Rantisi, N. (2002) The local innovation system as source of variety: Openness and adaptability in New York City's garment district. *Environment and Planning D*, 36: 587–602.

Rantisi, N. and Leslie, D. (2006) Branding the design metropole: The case of Montréal, Canada. *Area*, 38: 364–76.

Robinson, J. (2006) *Ordinary Cities*. London: Routledge.

Roske, R. (1986) *Las Vegas*. Tulsa: Continental Heritage Press.

Sassen, S. (1991) *The Global City*. Princeton: Princeton University Press.

Sassen, S. (2006) *Cities in a World Economy*. London: SAGE.

Schamp, E.W. (1999) The system of German financial centres at the crossroads. From national to European scale. In E. Wever (ed.) *Cities in Perspective*. Assen: Van Gorcum. pp. 83–98.

Short, J.R. and Kim, Y.-H. (1999) *Globalization and the City*. Harlow: Prentice Hall.

Smith, N. (1996) *New Urban Frontier*. New York: Routledge.

Smith, N. (2002) New urbanism: Gentrification as global urban strategy. *Antipode*, 34: 427–50.

Smith, R.G. (2003) World city actor-networks. *Progress in Human Geography*, 27: 5–44.

Soja, E. (1989) *Postmodern Geographies*. London: Verso.

Stolarick, K. and Florida, R. (2006) Creativity, connections and innovation: A study of linkages in the Montréal region. *Environment and Planning A*, 38: 1799–1817.

Taylor, P.J. (1999) So-called world cities: The evidential structure within a literature. *Environment and Planning A*, 31: 1901–04.

Taylor, P.J. (2001) Specification of the world city network. *Geographical Analysis*, 33: 181–94.

Taylor, P J. (2004) *World City Network*. London: Routledge.

Taylor, P.J., Walker, D.R.F., Catalano, G. and Hoyler, M. (2002) Diversity and power in the world city network. *Cities*, 19: 231–41.

Taylor, P.J., Derudder, B., Saey, P. and Witlox, F. (eds) (2007) *Cities in Globalization*. London: Routledge.

UNCTC (2004) *The Shift towards Services*. New York: UNCTC.

UNDP (2002) *Human Development Report 2002 Maharashtra*. New York: UNDP.

UNFPA (2007) *State of World Population 2007*. New York: United Nations.

UN-Habitat (2006) *State of the World's Cities 2006/07*. New York: United Nations.

Zukin, S. (1988) *Loft Living*. London: Radius.

Z/Yan (2007) *The Global Financial Centre Index 2007*. London: Z/Yan.

13

Towards a Critical Economic Geography of Workfare

Michael Samers

INTRODUCTION

What *is* workfare (or 'activation' as it is commonly called in the Anglophone literature on continental European countries)? As Jamie Peck (2001) points out, it is a 'vague umbrella term' that refers to a broad array of 'welfare-to-work policies, job training and employability programs, and active-benefit systems' (p. 1). More specifically, Peck (2001: 12) defines workfare as having three dimensions: first, individualization (in other words, individuals *must* participate in workfare programs together with behavioural training – such as how to dress for job interviews, etc.; second, systemic organization (workfare is system-wide, meaning that welfare benefits are tied to finding employment); and third an active functionality (that is, workfare functions to push the poor into work – it is active, rather than passive labour market policy). An additional dimension of workfare (especially in the UK) that is not included in Peck's three points is that compulsory training is required in order to receive benefits, what Jones (1995, 1996) labels 'trainingfare'.

Perhaps there are two other less tangible facets of workfare that deserve our attention: the increasing assumption that individuals should be financially responsible for themselves, rather than buoyed by welfare policies; and that workfare is designed as a policy with the 'supply' of workers in mind, not the supply of jobs. The distinctiveness of workfare can be understood in a comparison with welfare. As Peck explains:

> Where welfare stands for the principle of needs-based entitlement and universality, workfare stands for compulsion and selectivity. Where welfare stands for passive income support, workfare stands for active labor market inclusion. Where welfare constructs its subjects as claimants, workfare reconstitutes them as jobseekers: the status of being *on* welfare is replaced by the transitory experience of being processed (back) into work *through* workfare. (p. 12)

With this understanding of workfare in mind, my purpose in this chapter is not to offer a sustained criticism of workfare (there are hundreds of books, reports, and papers, that have achieved this very aim already, and I am largely sympathetic to both their

moral outrage at workfare and their scepti-
cism of policy 'success' (see, for example,
Schragge, 1997; Evans, 2007; McDonald
and Marston, 2005). Instead, my intention is
three-fold; first, to excavate briefly the
rather short history of research on workfare
by *Anglophone* economic geographers
working on Europe and the United States
(acknowledging that other traditions of economic geography may have produced different narratives of workfare). Second, to
ask whether we can identify some sort of
uniquely *economic geographical* approach
to the different manifestations of workfare,
and if so, to discern what such putative
'economic geographies of workfare' can
add to the vast writings of political scientists and sociologists on the subject? Third,
I ask what implications 'economic geographies of workfare' have for the study of
economic geography broadly-speaking, and
for (what has come to be called) 'labour
geographies' (and their gendered and racialized dimensions) more specifically.

TOWARDS GEOGRAPHIES OF WORKFARE

People who work sitting down get paid more than
people who work standing up.

Ogden Nash (date unknown)

Ogden Nash's quip captures something of the
nature of workfare-type jobs in what might be
called post-Fordist/neo-liberalized labour
markets. Although I will not discuss the character of these jobs, below I explore briefly
how economic geographers engaged with
workfare's ascendance. Since the 1970s,
labour issues – especially those that involve
less-skilled labour – have remained at the
heart of many economic geographers' concerns, either because they remained sympathetic to the struggles of the world's less
fortunate, or because economic geographers
wished to understand labour's role in uneven
capitalist development. Such sympathies or

analytical desires also explained much of the
engagement with political economic critiques
of capitalism more generally, in the form notably of (neo-) Marxism, Regulation Theory, or
socialist-feminism. By the 1990s, these interests together had intertwined to produce what
is now referred to as 'labour geography' (or
'labour geographies'), a corpus of writings
that has placed workers at the centre of analyses of capitalism, and connected their lives to
changes in the nature of labour markets and
global political economy more broadly (for
example, Benner, 2002; Castree et al., 2003;
Herod, 1997, 2001; McDowell, 2001, 2004;
Peck, 1996; Wills, 1998). These economic,
political, and social changes, which many
economic geographers (and certainly others)
would associate with the rise of 'post-Fordism'
and 'neo-liberalism' during the 1980s, are
argued to encompass a movement away from
the structures of welfare typical of the second
half of the twentieth century and towards
workfare strategies across Europe and North
America – a movement that political scientists
and sociologists began to document in the US
in the 1980s. Yet during this period, many
policy-makers in the UK still regarded the
'concept' of workfare as a distinctly American
practice (despite that its origins seem to be
diffuse and unclear). And perhaps it was not
until Bob Jessop published his now widely-
cited paper on the rise of the 'Schumpeterian
workfare state' (1993) that scholars in the UK
and the rest of Europe began to notice changes
in the regulation of the 'less-skilled' end of the
labour market. Jessop (a sociologist) argued
that a transition from a Keynesian Welfare
State (KWS) to a Schumpeterian Workfare
State (SWS) had begun sometime in the
1980s. In other words, capitalist states increasingly sought to encourage and foster technological innovation, national or regional
economic competitiveness, and labour market
(and other) 'flexibilities', in and through
changes in economic and social policy.

During the mid-1990s, Jessop's argument
set an agenda for research among a small
number of economic geographers interested in
changing labour markets including the analysis

of Training and Enterprise Councils in the UK (Peck and Jones, 1995; see also Jones, 1995, 1996, 1998), and trade union involvement and local boards for training in Canada and elsewhere (Rutherford, 1996, 1998). In general, economic geographers interested in labour markets had now drawn a relationship between fundamental changes in state practices and labour market governance. Yet as workfare became increasingly inscribed into the institutional reality of Europe and North America, the focus shifted from explicitly assessing the reality of the emergent Schumpeterian Workfare State, to gauging the precise contours of the evolution of workfare.

This involved two substantial research projects: one by Jamie Peck, in which he sought to investigate the development of workfare in Canada, the UK, and the US, and another by Peter Sunley (see Chapter 6), Ron

Martin (see Chapter 3), and Corinne Nativel on the UK. Jamie Peck, in his now landmark *Workfare States* (2001), elaborated on the studies that he undertook with colleagues both within and outside geography as well as drawing upon the work of numerous other political scientists and sociologists involved in tracking the development of workfare in the US since the 1980s. Without conducting a comprehensive review of Peck's work, it is worth rehearsing some of the arguments in *Workfare States* that are relevant to our discussion in this chapter.

Peck set out to 'map' what he called the 'workfare offensive' of the second half of the 1990s. As he put it, *Workfare States* presented a 'political-economic critique of the recent origins, current form, and future prospects of the workfare offensive' (p. 21). (see Box 13.1.)

Box 13.1   Discourses of the 'workfare offensive' in the UK and the US: similarities across the UK Labour Party, and Democrats and Republicans in the US

Former UK Prime Minister Tony Blair (Labour Party)

'… the principles guiding reform and our vision of the future welfare state are clear. We want to rebuild the system around work and security. Work for those who can, security for those who cannot.' DSS (1998: I), cited in Heron and Dwyer (1999: 92).

Former US President Bill Clinton (Democrat)

'… This legislation [the Personal Responsibility and Reform and Work Opportunity Reconciliation Act, 1996 or PRWORA] provides an historic opportunity to end welfare as we know it and transform our broken welfare system by promoting the fundamental values of work, responsibility, and family.' At the signing of the enactment of PRWORA, on 22 August, 1996.

President George W. Bush (Republican)

'I've described myself as a compassionate conservative, because I am convinced a conservative philosophy is a compassionate philosophy that frees individuals to achieve their highest potential. It is conservative to cut taxes and compassionate to give people more money to spend. It is conservative to insist upon local control of schools and high standards and results; it is compassionate to make sure every child learns to read and no one is left behind. *It is conservative to reform the welfare system by insisting on work; it's compassionate to free people from dependency on government.* It is conservative to reform the juvenile justice code to insist on consequences for bad behavior; it is compassionate to recognize that discipline and love go hand in hand.' [emphasis in italics added] From his speech announcing his consideration of the Republican nomination for the presidency of the United States, 7 March, 1999.

More precisely, Peck wished to assess whether workfare represented a new 'regulatory fix' that tied such an 'offensive' to the rise of contingent labour markets (that is low-paid, unstable, temporary work) in 'neo-liberalized countries' (p. 6). He attempted to identify a structural logic to workfare (that is, some logic that propelled states towards adopting workfare strategies), as well as paying attention to the diversity of local outcomes. In his empirical analysis, Peck focused on the experience of the United States, but he also sought to show how workfare discourses and policies were transferred abroad, and thus complemented his analysis of the US with an exploration of the rise of workfare in Canada (especially Ontario) and the UK.

Peck articulated a number of significant arguments concerning the development of workfare. First, and at a very basic level, Peck argued that workfare was about

creating workers for jobs that nobody wants. In a Foucauldian sense, it is seeking to make 'docile bodies' for the new economy: flexible, self-reliant, and self-disciplining (p. 6)

(though it is useful here to add that 'economic migrants' – especially low paid/low-skilled migrants also serve this purpose). Second, he demonstrated that national governments (and individual states or provinces) had 'downloaded' programmes to the local level. Or as he put it '… nationally constituted welfare regimes … [have been] … giving way to locally constituted workfare regimes' (p. 11). Third, Peck showed how local experiments into workfare (especially in the town of Riverside, California, in New York State, and in the state of Wisconsin) were deemed successful by the varied proponents of workfare, and as a consequence central to 'translocal fast-policy transfers' (p. 15). However, the 'success' of such experiments, Peck warns, would have had little credibility if general unemployment levels had not been falling in these economies, and if there had been a lack of 'contingent' jobs (that is jobs which are temporary and/or part-time, have few health or other social

benefits attached to them, and do not pay a 'living wage') during the second half of the 1990s. Nonetheless, Peck argues that these experiments had resonance outside the United States through *transnational* fast-policy transfer' (that is the rapid transfer of workfare discourse and policy *from* mainly the US *to* Canada and the UK). Fourth and more generally, Peck claimed that while a certain 'workfare logic' is identifiable (p. 23), the diversity of national and local workfare outcomes could not be denied either (in other words, there were 'many workfare states'). This did not mean, however, that workfare states were simply the symmetrical opposite of welfare regimes – that is a 'hollowed out' post-Fordist version of welfare states, but rather represent what Peck calls its 'regulatory antonym' (p. 16). Fifth, following the work of Piven and Cloward (1971), Peck maintained that workfare-type strategies are probably cyclical, that is they are enforced when jobs are abundant, and slackened when they are scarce. However, Peck argued that their introduction and enforcement in the 1990s occurred at the very time that jobs were increasingly low-paid, temporary, and included few benefits. He pushed this argument yet further, claiming that workfare did not simply involve matching potential employees with low wage jobs, but that workfare itself lowered the 'wage floor' (that is the prevailing lower limit of wages) which in turn might be *creating* contingent work. In other words, the supply of available workers facilitated the development of extremely low-wage, temporary jobs with few benefits.

Although Peck's book clearly had antecedents in economic geography, he succeeded in placing workfare firmly on its agenda, and *Workfare States* continues to provide a benchmark volume for future research. Yet if Peck's book proved to be impressive in terms of its scope and the breadth of its analysis, it also drew some criticism. Michael Webber (2002), for example, attacked Peck's book on the grounds that it focused on 'big men, and their discourses'. Indeed, he lamented:

It says almost nothing about oppositional politics, whether formally at the centre or more informally on the local grounds. It says nothing about the lives of ordinary men and women who are subject to this new regime: there are no longitudinal studies of their experiences of workfare or of their lives after a job placement. (p. 1322)

I will need to say something more about Webber's point concerning the neglect of oppositional politics, particularly with respect to economic geography, but for the moment let us focus on Webber's latter reservations which were shared by other reviewers (for example, De Verteuil, 2003; Reimer, 2002). There seemed to be two related criticisms: one methodological and one empirical. From a methodological perspective, most reviewers of the book regretted Peck's focus on institutional actors (those involved in policy implementation, etc.) rather than more engagement with those on the receiving end of workfare – that is the workers themselves. From an empirical perspective, Webber also argued that 'we need longitudinal evidence of the failings of workfare' (p. 1322).

In fact, at around the same time, Sunley et al. (2001) (see also Sunley et al., 2006), rigorously addressed this longitudinal question by interrogating the policy effects of workfare in the UK, and more specifically the performance of the UK's 'New Deal for Young People' (NDYP) – a workfare/activation programme aimed at those between 18 and 24 years. In their thorough empirical investigation based mainly on quantitative data, they address Webber's concern for 'longitudinal evidence', and echo many of Peck's dismal conclusions. Sunley et al. argue principally that positive assessments of the NDYP largely ignore considerable local and regional variation. They note that participants in the largest cities and 'depressed industrial' labour markets of (mainly) northern England fared the worst, particularly in relation to rural areas. There was considerable evidence of 'churning' and 'recycling' in such labour markets from unemployment into subsidized jobs and vice versa, as many of the jobs had limited duration. This implied that the characteristics of local labour

markets were central to the (effective) functioning of workfare. The precise findings of their analysis aside, what is particularly useful here is their convincing discussion of how an explicitly spatial lens on the performance of workfare-type programmes can have crucial policy implications. In this case, they argue for improving the individual 'employability' of participants, and improving the local labour market conditions of certain areas. In other words, there is a need to address both the supply *and* the demand side of labour markets. And I would add that this dual focus might also benefit from using qualitative evidence from the perspective of workers, and not simply the largely government-based quantitative data that Sunley et al. (2001) mobilize in their study.

WHAT CAN GEOGRAPHIES OF WORKFARE DO FOR THE STUDY OF WORKFARE BY OTHER SOCIAL SCIENTISTS?

The significance of 'place', 'space', territory (or scale) should be viewed, I maintain, as geographers' key contribution to the study of workfare. Even though Webber (2002) argues that in *Workfare States*, 'The geography of labour markets (inner cities – suburbs; centralized – federal states) is highly stylized and unimaginative' (p. 1322), and leaving aside the notion of, and critique of scale altogether (see Marston et al., 2005), then Peck and Sunley et al. have addressed the salience of these geographic concepts explicitly in ways which political scientists and sociologists, for example, have not (although for exceptions, see Herd et al., 2005 on localization in Ontario's workfare programme, or McDonald and Marston, 2005 on workfare in Australia). However, in the discussion below my aim is not to defend disciplinarity; rather to gauge how economic geographers – if 'space' is indeed 'their thing' – might legitimately contribute to the critical analysis of workfare.

To begin with, the importance that is attached to geographical analysis (by this I mean an analytics of place, space, territory or scale) may be in part related to political stances on workfare and to the aims of any given study. That is, on the one hand, for those critical of workfare *on philosophical/moral/ethical grounds* (for example, those who object to forced work in an unequal capitalist system, or at least work for poverty-level wages), a spatial lens on the matter may be unnecessary (for example, White, 2004). What is crucial rather for these scholars, or commentators, journalists, and activists is to show how political discourses and policies have served to steamroller workfare across different national state spaces (in this respect, the national state space is assumed to be the inevitable location of policy). Nevertheless, others (such as Peck, 2001, 2002) insist on an explicit spatial (or, to be more precise, 'scalar') lens in order to show how the geographical construction of workfare serves itself to constitute a more 'regressive' political economy – in short, 'neo-liberalism'. In this case, an outright critical stance and an analytics based around the geographical concepts above are not necessarily mutually exclusive.

On the other hand, for those such as Sunley et al. (2001, 2006) there is less reservation about workfare as a social idea and more about its actual implementation, including its neglect of the demand side of the labour market. In fact, they suggest that the NDYP is appropriate where local job surpluses exist and upward job mobility a possibility (though what 'local' entails and how that may affect job matching is another question altogether). In this sense then, quite clearly a spatial scrutiny of workfare policy matters, or to put it differently, space, place, and scale become elements of policy evaluation.

WORKFARE AND ECONOMIC GEOGRAPHY: IMPLICATIONS AND WAYS FORWARD

In the shadow of global security concerns, sustainable (economic) development, and climate change, the disturbing novelty of workfare may have waned as a topic for analysis, but workfare continues to evolve, and its implications for economic geographers are manifold. Let me outline 10 such implications, and suggest some ways forward for the study of workfare for geographers and related social scientists.

The past was no picnic

There is a need here to develop a more critical historical geography of work(fare) and welfare that does not romanticize the Keynesian welfare state. That is, if workfare might be viewed as a form of working poverty (albeit through coercion) then such a phenomenon is certainly not new to the United States, for example. In the US during the 1950s (the apparent heyday of the Keynesian welfare state), the majority of African-Americans were working but poor, and prominent liberal discourse in the US during these years consisted of much of the same moralizing attitudes towards the poor that were associated with the rise of neo-conservatism/neo-liberalism and so forth during the 1980s (for example, Mittelstadt, 2005). True, such omnipresent moralizing discourses may have been absent from most social democratic governments in Europe during the post-war years, but they never fell far from view, especially amongst European social conservatives.

In the more recent past, during the 1990s, it may be worth recalling that the implementation of workfare in UK and US policy was as much a product of the supposedly more left-leaning Labour and Democratic parties as it was of the more right-leaning Conservative and Republican parties in the United States. For example, consider the following report on conditions at a New York hospital in the mid 1990s:

> Some recipients working at Bellevue Hospital [a large mental hospital in New York City], transporting patients or changing beds, say there are so many workfare workers now at the hospital that they are 'falling over each other', with virtually none obtaining

full-time jobs. 'Why should they actually hire anyone?' asked Pat Simmons, a 49-year-old woman who said she had worked 26 hours a week at Bellevue for nearly two years without gaining a real job. 'We all but work for free'. Excerpt from 'Discontented workfare laborers murmer "union"'. (*New York Times*, 27 September 1996)

Workfare and the contradictory ways that geographers perceive workers

It might be argued from a 'post-structuralist' perspective that studies of the geographies of workfare may serve inadvertently to disempower workers, since typically little is said – to reiterate Webber's point – about oppositional movements and the possibilities of other forms of worker in – favourable economic development. In contrast to Herod's (1997) argument that those who analyse capitalism should focus on the way in which workers *constitute* the geography of capitalism, or Gray's (2004) insistence that low-paid service work is not inherently low-paid, but the result of an 'institutional vacuum', and that workers *do* organize in unions to raise the aggregate level of wages, the literature on geographies of workfare ignores this oppositional dimension. In overlooking this dimension, existing studies of workfare may be argued to 'perform' a certain kind of economy. Put differently, in the literature on the economic geography of workfare so far, workers are viewed as the *victims* of workfare, and neo-liberalism more broadly. In short, there seems to be a split in the way in which workers are conceptualized by (most) economic geographers and the role they play in shaping the geography of capitalism in the twenty-first century.

Is work on workfare unusual?

Indicative of a similar epistemological, political, and substantive chasm, what is most striking about research on workfare is how dissonant it is with respect to other emerging themes in economic geography (such as the

alternative economies/diverse economies literature) (Cameron and Gibson-Graham, 2003; Gibson-Graham, 2003; Leyshon, 2005; Leyshon et al., 2003). In other words, while the literature on workfare acknowledges the way in which policy is discursively constructed through convincing economic 'success stories', most of the discussions of workfare assume some sort of structural logic associated with the political economy of capitalism, which is very much at odds with other recent writings that seek to dispense with what Said (1993) called the 'dispiriting inevitability' of Marxist arguments about capitalism, or even the notion of an 'economy' itself (see Chapter 24), in order to highlight the economy/capitalism's performative/ 'virtual' constitution, and to valorize noncapitalist forms of activity (Miller, 1998; Gibson-Graham, 1996; Mitchell, 2002).

Workfare and the question of political economy

Without subscribing to the view of Gibson-Graham or Mitchell that there is no singular economy 'out there' (a proposition that would probably alarm many economic geographers), there may be a need to bring fresh insights to the relationship between workfare and political economy. Such insights may draw out a concept beyond the Schumpeterian Workfare State, such as Jessop's own revision in the form of a Schumpeterian Workfare *Postnational Regime* (Jessop, 2002), or a similar tendency to emphasize the contradictory and unstable character of neo-liberalism and its innumerable varieties (for example, England and Ward, 2007; Peck and Tickell, 2002; Herod and Aguiar, 2006; Leitner et al., 2006). Yet, despite the appeal of (a qualified) neo-liberalism as a concept to describe the workfare offensive, it remains flawed and inadequate. For one, the Gramscian, neo-Marxist/regulationist-inspired notion of neo-liberalism neglects the political economy of racism and sexism which serves to shape labour market policies in the advanced economies (Bezuidenhout and Fakier, 2006). For example, that African-Americans, many of them women, constitute a significant proportion of workfare participants in the US may not be simply the product of a 'war' against the 'working classes', but of a combination of a system of white racial hegemony (for example, Omi and Winant, 1986) and gender oppression. Some even go as far as to dismiss the concept of 'neo-liberalism' altogether because it is either an umbrella term (which ignores a new moralism about work and family) or because of the limitations and inadequacies of combining Marxist and poststructuralist theory to conceptualize social and political-economic change (Barnett, 2005; McDowell, 2004). In the same vein, Barnett (2005) argues that the concept of neo-liberalism is 'consoling' because it shows how people are 'got at' by some centre, which they then can presumably blame or hate. Instead, he argues, one might return rather to certain 'classical' aims of social theory (p. 11). Unfortunately, Barnett's explanation of such 'classical' aims remains unclear, but it does behove us to undertake the difficult work of understanding social action and social forces in ways that may be obscured by the constant refrain of 'neo-liberalism'. In terms of workfare, this might imply a tighter, less ambitious naming and conceptualization of the workfare offensive, such as 'administrative recommodification' (Holden, 2003); it might entail an emphasis on a more 'agentic' (in other words, typically a focus on individual or a group's actions) and 'embodied' construction of workfare's divergent moral assumptions and policy contours. Such an approach might involve a sustained exploration of relationships between workfare participants and caseload managers across different national spaces (and other 'scales' or territories) in ways which are occluded by the expansive concept of neo-liberalism (for example, Cope, 2001; Daguerre, 2004; McDonald and Marston, 2005, and indeed Peck, 2001). Despite the criticisms above of neoliberalism (or other umbrella-like political economic concepts), it would be incorrect

to deny the commonly oppressive policies which now operate to one degree or another across the globe (see Herod and Aguiar, 2006).

The importance of the evolution of workfare for understanding the geographies of capital accumulation

Whatever reservations some scholars held with regard to *Workfare States*, a clear strength of the book is Peck's reluctance to develop the sort of relatively rigid typologies of welfare systems associated with Esping-Andersen's now classic *The Three Worlds of Welfare Capitalism* (1990). In other words, Peck refused the temptations of classifying Canada, the UK, and the United States into particular types of workfare states, and instead concentrates on the *process* of constructing workfare as a 'regulatory project'. This in turn can provide further fodder for understanding the *process* of economic development, by showing how states rely on contingent labour markets to fuel capital accumulation, particularly, but not exclusively, among cities in the advanced economies. To provide one example, the absorption of the unemployed or the intermittently employed into workfare-type jobs where unionization is unlikely (or even forbidden), may serve to further impede the development of already weakened trade unions. This too has implications for the economic geographies of capital accumulation.

Workfare is not simply a UK – North American phenomenon

One might be forgiven for thinking that workfare is simply a feature of the apparently more 'flexible' labour markets of Anglophone countries (for example, Bradley et al., 2000), but in fact workfare has also emerged in socalled social neo-corporatist economies (for example, Germany), neo-statist economies (for example, France), or even countries of the 'global south', albeit with different kinds and levels of coercion or compulsion (see Clasen and Clegg, 2003; Daguerre, 2004; Handler, 2003; Lodomel and Trickey, 2000). In fact, one might distinguish between 'work-first' programmes in countries such as the UK and the US, and 'human capital'/activation programmes in France and some Scandinavian countries, for example. Yet few, if any, Anglophone geographers have examined workfare issues beyond Canada, the UK, and the US (but see Etherington and Jones, 2004 on a comparative discussion involving Denmark).

The need for dialogue between economic and social geographers

The preoccupation with the political economy of workfare or its generalized outcomes has meant a neglect of the intersection between the concerns of economic geographers and those of other social/economic geographers, particularly feminist geographers. In this respect one might explore the *social* geographies of cities through an ethnography of workfare participants, which may or may not reinforce the goals of elucidating a 'big picture' political economy (Haylett, 2003b, c; McDowell, 2004). But there are further possibilities for this *rapprochement*, that might include a nexus of the political economy of workfare and the feminist literature (see below), a critical re-reading of 'class' and classed subjects (Haylett, 2003c) and the so-called 'underclass debate', and a dialogue with the literature on those with 'multiple needs' and work – life balance problems (Dean, 2003). As Dean puts it, we do not need 'work first', we need 'life first'. In any case, the meeting of economic geographers and social geographers might also involve an engagement with the literature on 'social exclusion' (Byrne, 1999; Cameron, 2006; Levitas, 1996; Room, 1995; Samers, 1998). After all, it was the 'third way' social theorists and 'policy gurus' such as Anthony Giddens (1998) in the UK who argued that welfare actually *contributed to* 'social exclusion'.

The need to bring in gender in particular into the study of workfare

In particular, the connection with social geographers should involve a sustained attention to the question of gender in workfare-oriented labour markets. It is true that most economic geographers have nodded at its significance, but at the same time do not adopt a theoretical approach which has gender (alongside ethnicity, 'race', or class) at its centre. As a number of authors have stressed (see Boyer, 2003; Haylett, 2003c; Lewis, 2001; Macleavy, 2007; McDowell, 2001; and Reimer, 2002), this is crucial since women – especially poorer women – are at the forefront of the workfare offensive. Such a perspective would not necessarily dismiss a neo-Marxist perspective entirely, but rather emphasize the differential impact (and indeed) burden that workfare places on women. What is needed then is a sustained engagement between the study of workfare and a political-economic geography that does not ignore an *explicit* theorization and empirical analysis of 'race', ethnicity, or gender (see, for example, McDowell, 2001, 2004; Reimer, 2002).

What is the relationship between workfare participants and migrant labour?

While Peck (2001) suggests that work training programmes provide labour which competes with unsubsidized labour insofar as sub-minimum wages are paid, to my knowledge, there is no discussion of some of the changing relationships between immigration and citizens at the bottom end of the labour market. There is a substantial economics literature on the possible effects of low-skilled/low-paid immigrants on citizen workers, but we know very little about the dynamics of the availability of workfare jobs and their duration in the context of – *perhaps* – increased job competition for the most menial of positions, not simply because of prevailing macro-economic conditions as suggested by Peck (2001) and Sunley et al. (2006), but also because of employers' ostensible propensity to hire (informally employed) undocumented migrants instead of citizens involved in workfare programmes.

From scholarship to policy?

Debates about either the objective status or performative character of the (global) political economy aside, the interventions by Peck and Sunley et al. suggest the ways in which geographers – economic geographers in particular – may become more involved in what Peck (1999) calls 'grey geographies'; that is, the geographies of public policy (Martin, 2001). There is enormous scope for building on the extant literature on the economic geography of workfare, extending such analyses to other countries from a comparative perspective, and providing policy proposals to the various levels of government involved. In part this can be accomplished, not simply by contesting the 'rolling back of welfare' and the 'rolling forward of workfare' (which may be vital, yet predictable), but in offering policy proposals for new forms of socially-useful work that involve social and economic relationships dissimilar to those which so many are now currently subjected. This combination of critical analysis and 'progressive' policy proposals in this regard may be economic geography's greatest challenge.

CONCLUSIONS

When a man [*sic*] tells you that he got rich through hard work, ask him: 'Whose?'

Don Marquis (date unknown)

Workfare is one of the more insidious elements of what many now call 'neo-liberalism'. There is a wide spectrum of measures used to coerce people into training and/or workfare-type labour markets across different national and sub-national state spaces. It would appear then, that we are returning to 1834, when Prime Minister Earl Grey established the

Poor Laws in England, and predicated 'help' only on the basis of work in the workhouses. Today, unemployment has become not only an economic condition, but it has once again evolved into a morally unacceptable one. It is, as so many have argued, about disciplining the poor.

But workfare is also condensed in Don Marquis' biting adage that at the foundations of capitalist accumulation lies the tedious, intermittent, and low-paid toil of those who are viewed as a potential burden on states and societies. That is, workfare is not just about social control, but also about generating profits for employers ever in search of low-paid, flexible labour. Economic geographers would do well to tease out this relationship between uneven development and this 'pool' of contingent labour. Yet as I stated at the outset, my aim has not been to provide a sustained critique of the 'workfare offensive' – a task prolifically accomplished across the social sciences, nor has it been to launch an empirical assessment of workfare policy and its failings. Rather, I have been mostly concerned to gauge the contribution which economic geography might make to a critical discussion of the subject; to assess the implications of workfare for the study of economic geography, and to point to some ways forward for future research.

In this respect, while political scientists and sociologists have endlessly documented the rise of workfare and its policy limitations, the contributions of economic geographers have been visibly sparser. Even in the US, where one might expect extensive research by economic geographers – or any geographers for that matter – there are actually very few contributions beyond Peck's work. Cope (2001), Cope and Gilbert (2001), Haylett (2003a, b), and Johnson-Webb (2002) provide exceptions. The dearth of studies here is unfortunate since the analysis of space/place and scale is vital to understanding both the construction of the 'workfare offensive' but also in evaluating the outcomes of policies for those caught in its labour markets. In this context, while the extant analysis of workfare throws up a number of implications for the future exploration of workfare and for 'labour geographies' more broadly, there is insufficient space here to reiterate these implications. In outlining them, however, I sought no more than to provide a non-exhaustive agenda for how economic geographers might engage with the development of workfare. In particular, there is a need to continually document and explain the deleterious and differential affects that workfare has on the livelihoods of workers whose lives are often marked by the intersection of class, racial, ethnic, and gender oppression. This does *not* have to involve a particular kind of methodology (such as ethnography) nor necessarily more locally-oriented analyses; it could very well involve quantitative analysis at a spatially wider level of resolution. Yet whatever methodology or the 'scale' or territoriality of such analyses, economic geographers need to think carefully about how space matters to the causes and consequences of the continual development of workfare.

For those who are committed to understanding this evolution of workfare policies, but at the same time are less than enamoured by them, there are limited, if encouraging signs (especially in the US) that the most disenfranchised workers are protesting against the worst consequences of workfare, and this gives us a little bit more hope that new forms of economic life might be forged.

ACKNOWLEDGEMENTS

Thanks to Linda McDowell, Kevin Ward, and Andrew Leyshon for comments on previous versions of this chapter.

REFERENCES

Barnett, C. (2005) Consolations of 'neo-liberalism'. *Geoforum*, 36: 7–12.

Benner, C. (2002) *Work in the New Economy*. Oxford: Basil Blackwell.

Bezuidenhout, A. and Fakier, K. (2006) Maria's burden: Contract cleaning and the crisis of social reproduction in post-apartheid South Africa. *Antipode*, 38(3): 462–85.

Boyer, K. (2003) At work, at home? New geographies of work and care-giving under welfare reform. *Space and Polity*, 7(1): 75–86.

Bradley, H., Erikson, M., Stephenson, C., and Williams, S. (2000) *Myths at Work*. Cambridge: Polity Press.

Byrne, D. (1999) *Social Exclusion*. Open University Press.

Cameron, A. (2006) Geographies of welfare and exclusion: Social inclusion and exception. *Progress in Human Geography*, 30(3): 396–404.

Cameron, J. and Gibson-Graham, J.K. (2003) Feminising the economy: Metaphors, strategies, politics. *Gender, Place and Culture*, 10(2): 145–57.

Castree, N., Coe, N., Ward, K., and Samers, M. (2003) *Spaces of Work: Global Capitalism and Geographies of Labour*. London: SAGE.

Clasen, J. and Clegg, D. (2003) Unemployment protection and labour market reform in France and Great Britain in the 1990s: Solidarity versus activation. *Journal of Social Policy*, 32(3): 361–81.

Cope, M. (2001) Between welfare and work: The roles of social service organizations in the social regulation of labor markets and the regulation of the poor. *Urban Geography*, 22(5): 391–406.

Cope, M. and Gilbert, M. (2001) Special issue: Geographies of welfare reform-Introduction. *Urban Geography*, 22(5): 385–90.

Daguerre, A. (2004) Importing workfare: Policy transfer of social and labour market policies from the USA to Britain under New Labour. *Social Policy and Administration*, 38(1): 41–56.

Dean, H. (2003) Re-conceptualising welfare-to-work for people with multiple problems and needs. *Journal of Social Policy*, 32(3): 441–59.

De Verteuil, G. (2003) Review of *Workfare States*, by Jamie Peck, *Economic Geography*, 79(1): 95–106.

England, K. and Ward, K. (eds) (2007) *Neoliberalization: States, Networks, Peoples*. Oxford: Blackwell.

Etherington, D. and Jones, M. (2004) Beyond contradictions of the workfare state? Denmark, welfare-through-work, and the promise of job rotation. *Environment and Planning C-Government and Policy*, 22(1): 129–48.

Evans, P.M. (2007) (Not) taking into account of precarious employment: Workfare policies and lone mothers in Ontario and the UK. *Social Policy and Administration*, 41(1): 29–49.

Gibson-Graham, J.K. (1996) *The End of Capitalism (As We Knew It)*. Oxford: Basil Blackwell.

Gibson-Graham, J.K. (2003) Enabling ethical economies: Cooperativism and class. *Critical Sociology*, 29(2): 123–61.

Giddens, A. (1998) *The Third Way*. Cambridge: Polity Press.

Gray, M. (2004) The social construction of the service sector: Institutional structures and labour market outcomes. *Geoforum*, 35(1): 23–34.

Handler, J. (2003) Social citizenship and workfare in the US and Western Europe: From status to contract. *Journal of European Social Policy*, 13(3): 229–43.

Haylett, C. (2003a) Remaking labour imaginaries: The internationalising project of welfare reform. *Political Geography*, 22(7): 765–88.

Haylett, C. (2003b) Care, class and welfare reform: Reading meanings, talking feelings. *Environment and Planning A*: Special Issue on Geographies of Care. 35(5): 799–814.

Haylett, C. (2003c) Culture, class and urban policy: Reconsidering equality. *Antipode: a Journal of Radical Geography*, 35(1): 33–55.

Herd, D., Mitchell, A., and Lightman, E. (2005) Rituals of degradation: Administration as policy in the Ontario Works Programme. *Social Policy and Administration*, 39(1): 65–79.

Herod, A. (1997) From a geography of labor to a labor geography: Labor's spatial fix and the geography of capitalism. *Antipode*, 29(1).

Herod, A. (2001) *Labor Geographies: Workers and the Landscapes of Capitalism*. New York: Guilford Press.

Herod, A. and Aguiar, L.M. (2006) Introduction: Cleaners and the dirty work of neo-liberalism. *Antipode*, 38(3): 425–34.

Heron, E. and Dwyer, P. (1999) Doing the right thing: Labour's attempt to forge a new deal between the individual and the state. *Social Policy and Administration*, 33(1): 91–104.

Holden, C. (2003) Decommodification and the workfare state. *Political Studies Review*, 1: 303–16.

Jessop, B. (1993) Towards a Schumpeterian workfare state? Preliminary remarks on post-Fordist political economy. *Studies in Political Economy*, 40: 7–39.

Jessop, B. (2002) Liberalism, neoliberalism, and urban governance: A state-theoretical perspective. *Antipode*, 452–72.

Johnson-Webb, K.D. (2002) 'Workfare' in the triangle: Local context and employer biases against welfare recipients. *Southeastern Geographer*, 42: 1–19.

Jones, M. (1995) Training and enterprise councils: A continued search for local flexibility. *Regional Studies*, 29: 577–80.

Jones, M. (1996) Full steam ahead to a workfare state? Analysing the UK Employment Department's abolition. *Policy and Politics*, 24(2): 137–57.

Jones, M. (1998) Restructuring the local state: Economic governance or social regulation? *Political Geography*, 17(8): 959–88.

Leitner, H., Peck, J., and Sheppard, E. (eds) (2006) *Contesting Neo-liberalism: Urban Frontiers*. New York: Guilford Press.

Levitas, R. (1996) The concept of social exclusion and the new Durkheimian hegemony. *Critical Social Policy*, 16(1): 5–20.

Lewis, J. (2001) British Prime Minister Tony Blair's workfare policy and how it affects women. *Esprit*, 3–4: 174–86.

Leyshon, A. (2005) Introduction: Diverse economies. *Antipode*, 37(5): 856–62.

Leyshon, A., Lee, R., and Williams, A. (2003) *Alternative Economic Spaces*. London: SAGE.

Lodomel, I. and Trickey, H. (eds) (2000) *'An Offer You Can't Refuse': Workfare in International Perspective*. Bristol: Policy Press.

Macleavy, J. (2007) Engendering New Labour's workfarist regime: Exploring the intersection of welfare state restructuring and labour market policies in the UK. *Gender Place and Culture*, 14(6): 721–43.

Marston, S.A., Jones III, J.P, and Woodward, K. (2005) Human Geography without scale. *Transactions of the Institute of British Geographers*. 30(4): 416–32.

Martin, R. (2001) Geography and public policy: The case of the missing agenda. *Progress in Human Geography*, 25(2): 189–210.

McDonald, C. and Marston, G. (2005) Workfare as welfare: Governing unemployment in the advanced liberal state. *Critical Social Policy*. 25(3): 374–401.

McDowell, L. (2001) Father and Ford revisited: Gender, class and employment change in the new millennium. *Transactions of the Institute of British Geographers*, 26(4): 448–64.

McDowell, L. (2004) Work, workfare, work/life balance and an ethic of care. *Progress in Human Geography*, 28(2): 145–63.

Miller, D. (1998) Conclusion: A theory of virtualism. In J. Carrier, and D. Miller (eds) *Virtualism: A New Political Economy*. Oxford: Berg Press.

Mitchell, T. (2002) *Rule of Experts: Egypt, Techno-politics, Modernity*. Berkeley and Los Angeles: University of California Press.

Mittelstadt, J. (2005) *From Welfare to Workfare: The Unintended Consequences of Liberal Reform, 1945–1965*. Chapel Hill: University of North Carolina Press.

Omi, M. and Winant, H. (1986) *Racial Formation in the United States: From the 1960s to the 1980s*. New York: Routledge,

Peck, J. (1996) *Workplace: The Social Regulation of Labor Markets*. New York: Guilford Press.

Peck, J. (1999) Editorial: Grey geography? *Transactions of the Institute of British Geographers*, 24(2): 131–35.

Peck, J. (2001) *Workfare States*. New York: Guilford Press.

Peck, J. (2002) Political economies of scale: Fast policy, interscalar relations, and neo-liberal workfare. *Economic Geography*, 78(3): 331–60.

Peck, J. and Jones, M. (1995) Training and Enterprise Councils: Schumpeterian workfare state, or what? *Environment and Planning A*, 27: 1361–96.

Peck, J. and Tickell, A. (2002) *Antipode*, 34(3): 380–404.

Piven, F.F. and Cloward (1971) *Regulating the Poor*. New York: Random House.

Reimer, S. (2002) Review of *Workfare States*, by Jamie Peck, *Annals of the Association of American Geographers*, 92(2): 341–83.

Room, G. (ed.) (1995) *Beyond the Threshold: The Measurement and Analysis of Social Exclusion*. Bristol: The Policy Press.

Rutherford, T. (1996) The local solution? The Schumpeterian workfare state, labour market governance and local boards for training in Kitchener, Ontario. *Regional Studies*, 30: 413–28.

Rutherford, T. (1998) 'Still in training?' Labor unions and the restructuring of Canadian labor market policy. *Economic Geography*, 74(2): 131–49.

Said, E. (1993) *Culture and Imperialism*. London: Vintage.

Samers, M. (1998) Immigration, 'ethnic minorities', and social exclusion in the European Union: A critical perspective. *Geoforum*, 29(2): 123–44.

Schragge, E. (ed.) (1997) *Workfare: Ideology for a New Underclass*. Toronto: Garamond Press.

Sunley, P., Martin, R., and Nativel, C. (2001) Mapping the new deal: The local disparities in the performance of welfare-to-work. *Transactions of the Institute of British Geographers*, 26: 484–512.

Sunley, P., Martin, R., and Nativel, C. (2006) *Putting Workfare in its Place*. Oxford: Basil Blackwell.

Webber, M. (2002) Review of *Workfare States*, by Jamie Peck, *Environment and Planning A*, 34(7): 1320–22.

White, S. (2004) What's wrong with workfare? *Journal of Applied Philosophy*, 21(3): 271–84.

Wills, J. (1998) Taking on the CosmoCorps? Experiments in transnational labor organization. *Economic Geography*, 74(2): 111–30.

PART 5

Political Economies
of Nature

The Economy of Nature: From Political Ecology to the Social Construction of Nature

Gavin Bridge

INTRODUCTION: ENCOUNTERS WITH NATURE

Living, writes Philip Roth (1998) in his prize-winning novel *American Pastoral*, is a profoundly social experience in which we consistently fail to understand those whom we encounter: we 'get people wrong, and then get them wrong all over again' and, as a consequence, we 'mangle with our ignorance every day.' Viewed from the vantage point of the present, economic geography's encounters with nature over the past fifty years look very similar: in its attempts to understand the relationship between economic activity and the non-human world, economic geography first got nature wrong, and then proceeded to get it wrong again and again. Worked over, re-worked, and now worked out as a singular category, nature has been truly 'mangled' over the last few decades. But through these encounters, economic geography has acquired vocabularies and philosophies for engaging things non-human, and for thinking about the categories

of modern science that make it possible to speak of 'nature' and 'economy' as if they are separate realms. Getting nature 'wrong,' then, is a symptom of a broader struggle within human geography to come to terms with the non-human. And, for economic geography, there has been much to come to terms with since it was the marginalization of nature that helped to define modern economic geography as a field.

This chapter is divided into four sections. The first section reviews modern economic geography's 'default position' on nature: as an unproblematic object, a stage upon which the real business of economy takes place, requiring little in the way of explanation. By highlighting the consistency of this reductive approach across some of the most well-worn divides in post-war economic geography, the first section establishes a context for appreciating the wholesale problematization of nature which has characterized economic geography since the late 1980s. The second, third and fourth sections examine how contemporary economic geography, by absorbing influences from Marxism, feminism, science studies, and post-colonial studies, has come to recognize nature not as an organic substrate but as a social product, a terrain that is at least as historical as it is ecological, that is cultural and political before it is physical. By insisting that the biophysical world – and the categories we use to describe it as such – are constituted socially rather than given, research on 'nature' profoundly unsettles notions of external constraint and natural order that are frequently associated with popular discussions of scarcity, resources, or environment.

The second section charts the beginnings of economic geography's problematization of nature. It examines an influential argument – the 'production of nature' – which radically overhauls technocratic and romantic notions of nature as an 'other world' outside society. The third section explores the influence on economic geography of a large and diverse literature on the social construction of nature. This work highlights the constitutive role of culture and knowledge in the making of nature and is, in part, a critical reproach to what is perceived to be the unwarrantedly narrow and 'productivist' orientation of the 'production of nature.' The literature is internally divided, however, and adopting a 'strong' or 'weak' version of constructionism implies quite different intellectual objectives for engaging nature within economic geography. The fourth section focuses on recent efforts to compensate for the overly-socialized accounts of constructionists by recovering a role for the generative and productive capacities of the non-human world. Collectively this work makes the point that the social production of nature must engage with diverse biophysical processes and, as a consequence, nature's production is never completely social.

Before we proceed, however, two points of caution. First, divisions of the field for didactic purposes are necessarily artificial, and the four-way sectioning of research described above is no exception. That said, economic geography has been characterized by an evolution in thinking on nature since the 1980s, and the chapter's four sections map the broad outlines of this chronological transition. The impetus for these developments has been primarily theoretical: the dynamic of critique and counter-critique is a hallmark of contemporary economic geography, an internal churning that calls to the mind the 'mangle of ignorance' through which nature consistently exceeds the categories and vocabularies we devise to describe it. But any transition in thinking has also been informed by events in the worlds of science and human experience. Recognition of anthropogenically-driven environmental change at unprecedented rates and scales has become widespread: to borrow a phrase from environmental historian J.R. McNeill (2001), it is abundantly clear that we are living in 'prodigal and peculiar' times. Socionatural phenomena like Hurricane Katrina, invasive species, BSE and bird/swine flu also demonstrate that we can often 'get nature wrong' in the practical arts of natural resource and environmental management (see Scott, 1999).

The second caveat is that contemporary Anglo-American economic geography is a broad-backed beast (as this volume attests) and it is only a comparatively small section of this wide field that has engaged in the process of rethinking economy–nature relationships described here. Although one now finds nature discussed in work by economic geographers on international trade, foreign direct investment, rural restructuring, commodity chains, international development, and neoliberalism, it still is possible to study economic geography without encountering nature. In itself this is not necessarily a bad thing. The broader point which this chapter makes, however, is that the encounter with nature is remaking economic geography in some significant ways. Even if one is not particularly interested in the fleshy and gritty worlds it opens up, the engagement with nature will be widely felt.

NATURE LOST AND FOUND

Open an Anglo-American book on economic geography from the pre-Second World War period and you will find its pages studded with references to climate, soils, energy resources, minerals, water, and topography. With roots in the commercial geographies of the late nineteenth century, these regional economic geographies invoke the natural world as a 'foundational layer' which is alternately a storehouse of possibilities or a constraint on human endeavor. Either way, the non-human world is regarded as a significant influence on the form and pattern of subsequent economic phenomena, giving rise to a 'naturalistic geography of primary production' (McNee, 1959: 193). Today we may critique such accounts for their utilitarian and ahistorical construction of nature as 'resources' and their undialectical approach to the links between physical geography and socio-economic form. Yet pre-war economic geography demonstrates an engagement by economic geography with the gloriously variable 'stuff' of nature, and presents a stark contrast to the sanitized, de-natured accounts produced by economic geography in the period between the late 1940s and the early 1980s.

At what point, then, did economic geography come to 'lose' nature? The marginalization of nature within economic geography constitutes a key moment in the 'great divorce' between the 'economic' and the 'cultural' that took place within post-war Anglo-American human geography (Hanson, 1999). In seizing spatial relations for its territory, economic geography sought to abstract 'the spatial' from its environmental context: equated with the idiographic and the unique, nature was an irrelevant context impeding abstraction and generalization (see Chapters 1 and 2). Nature was not excluded entirely from spatial science, but was presented in ways that decreased its analytical significance. For example, in seeking to overcome what they saw as economics' historical neglect of space at the expense of time, spatial economists such as Losch (1954) and Isard (1956) relied on a concept of space – the isotropic plain – that would enable it to be incorporated within the substitution analysis framework of economics. By reducing space and nature to a single dimension – distance – the effect of 'geography' could be compared with other factor costs. Not all spatial science

assumed an isotropic plain, but the treatment of nature as an economic substrate was remarkably consistent. Nature also assumes a marginalized presence in spatial science via a frequent resort to naturalistic metaphors, particularly those drawn from physics (Barnes, 1996). Gravity models, for example, attempted to explain social and economic flow patterns via an analogy with Newton's equation for gravitational force. Such work sought universal laws governing social interaction, the '*lex parsimoniae* which pervades nature and has its counterparts in the economic and social order' (Warntz, 1957: 7). Although nature appears to be central – in the form of 'natural laws' – this is a remarkably reductive conceptualization: all socio-historical and biophysical context is stripped away, leaving nature as little more than the equations of physics.

It was against such pauperized conceptions of social and economic life that neo-Marxian and other radical approaches to economic geography directed their creative energies in the late 1960s. While thoroughly reconceptualizing the social and exposing the fallacy of spatial (as opposed to socio-spatial) processes, the innervating winds of Marxism initially were far less revolutionary in their conceptualization of nature. Conventional histories of economic geography point to a deep rupture in the 1970s as spatial science conceded ground to Marxism. However, viewed through the alternate lens of nature rather than space, economic geography illustrates more continuity than rupture at this point. Both neo-classical economic geography (associated with spatial science) and the political-economic approach to economic geography (which emerged as a reaction to spatial science in the 1970s) relegated nature as both empirical focus and theoretical objective. Indeed, both paradigms – while differing widely in their epistemologies, methodologies, and vision of praxis – were united in their reduction of nature to a utilitarian factor of production with neither agency nor causality. Post-war economic geography, then, did not so much overlook nature as be actively complicit in its abstraction and marginalization. The blunt fact is that economic geography had very little to say on resource or environmental issues at a time when the linkages between economic growth, development and the environment were acquiring huge social and political significance.

In the last 30 years economic geography has begun to engage the relationship between socio-economic organization and the natural world. Such epic questions are at the heart of western thought: they find contemporary expression, for example, in discussions over how technological and social innovation (higher resource productivity, better environmental planning) might free people from resource shortages or oppressive pollution burdens); or in critical appraisals of how 'saving nature' or 'protecting resources' increases the control exerted by some people (usually the rich) over the lives of other people (usually the poor), a 'domination of nature' which is, at the same time, a domination by those with social power of those without. Initial contributions to these questions within economic geography came from a handful of researchers who, energized by developments in radical geography in the 1970s, weighed in on the 'matter of nature' by drawing on historical materialism (Fitzsimmons, 1989). The most thoroughly worked out contribution within geography came from Neil Smith (1984) in his book *Uneven Development*. Smith rejected the philosophical and political limitations of the prevailing approach to nature on the political left – the 'domination of nature' thesis – and, in its place, he offered a theory of 'the production of nature':

The idea of the production of nature is indeed paradoxical . . . if judged by the superficial appearance of nature even in capitalist society. Nature is generally seen as precisely that which cannot be produced; it is the antithesis of human productive activity . . . But with the progress of capital accumulation and the expansion of economic development, this material substratum is more and more the product of social production, and the dominant axes of differentiation are increasingly societal in origin. In short, when this immediate appearance of nature is placed in historical context, the development of the material landscape presents itself as a process of the production of nature. The differentiated results of this production of nature are the material symptoms of uneven development. At the most abstract level, therefore, it is in the production of nature that use – value and exchange – value, and space and society, are fused together . . . So completely do human societies now produce nature, that a cessation of productive labour would render enormous changes in nature, including the extinction of human nature. (Smith, 1984: 33–35)

The provocative juxtaposition of production (an explicitly human activity, variant in its form over time and space) with nature (popularly understood as that-which-is-not-human, timeless and universal) serves as a deliberate jolt to consciousness. Smith's central point is that we have our metaphors and our ontology wrong: in making a living (i.e. the economy) societies do not 'impact', 'transform' or 'dominate' nature – since these presuppose nature and society to be separate realms. Rather, what we conventionally call nature (fields, forests, oceans, even the ecologies of urban landscapes) are outcomes of economic processes. Consider rivers, for example. We commonly recognize how river systems are dammed, channeled, drained, and diverted (and even made to flow backwards, as William Cronon (1991) shows for Chicago in his book *Nature's Metropolis*) in the service of particular social interests. The specific point of the claim to being 'produced' is not that the environment is changed in some way by human action, but that the natures we see around us (from landscapes, to assemblages of species, to animal bodies) have been configured in ways that serve the interests of those with economic power. Richard White makes this point in *The Organic Machine* (1995), which documents the remaking of social and ecological relationships around the Columbia River (in the northwestern United States). During the twentieth century the river came increasingly to be valued for its capacity to produce electrical energy. White argues that the large dams and diversions constructed on the river since the 1930s have not 'killed' or 'destroyed' the Columbia (as many environmentalists claim) but have produced alternative river ecologies: 'the architects of the new river . . . wanted the river and its watershed to say electricity, lumber, cattle and fruit and together these have translated into carp, shad and squawfish instead of salmon'. It is these alternate ecologies that underpinned the development of the Pacific North West around irrigated agriculture and low-cost electricity. It was through the production of such 'new natures', then, that large-scale users of water and electricity (irrigation, aluminum smelting) consolidated their power.

Naming the 'economy' as capitalist is central to Smith's argument, although at first brush it may seem an obvious, even banal observation. Economies in the twenty-first century are capitalist? Who knew?! The point of this naming, however, is to be specific about the relationships that produce nature and space, and to profoundly disturb the naturalism so often associated with discussions of economic relations that involve the physical environment. In *The Conquest of Bread*, for example, Richard Walker (2004) avoids the homage to alluvial soils, diverse ecosystems and favorable climate that ordinarily passes for explanation of the jaw-dropping fecundity of Californian agriculture. He argues instead that the profusion of crops are an expression of the *capitalist* nature of agriculture: in the State's olive and avocado groves, vineyards and poultry houses, wheat ranches and canneries, Walker reveals the hand of capital 'in making the land yield up its gifts, the plants perform miracles, the animals stagger under their own weight, and the waters flow uphill'. The diverse natures of California agriculture, then, are the product of an 'economic logic that has run full throttle . . . for 150 years' (p. 302).

Smith was not the first to argue that diverse 'natures' – geographies of agriculture, hazards, wilderness or famine, for example – should be read as expressions of social relations (see, for example, Harvey, 1974). At the time Smith was writing *Uneven Development* a more empirical set of research interests were crystallizing around forests, grazing commons,

rice paddies, and habitat conservation areas in the developing world. Collectively – and often retrospectively – known as political ecology, this eclectic body of work traces twin roots to peasant studies, and to the radical hazards literature of the late 1970s (Susman et al., 1983; Watts, 1983). In contrast to Smith's theorization of labour as the historical relation to nature, political ecology is characterized by a focus on the concrete practices of making a living from the land, and by attention to how these practices are structured by social institutions (state policies, development initiatives, market access) operating at a range of geographical scales. Political ecology shares the revelatory ambition of the 'production of nature' thesis: of showing how apparently 'natural' phenomena – soil erosion, famine, scarcity, population pressure – are, at least in part, social in origin. Blakie and Brookfield's (1987) opening claim that soil erosion is a 'social problem' refers not to how land degradation has social and economic consequences for farmers, but to how such phenomena emerge from the way society is organized. As they put it, 'land managers may find themselves responding to changes in their social, political and economic circumstances quite independently of changes in the intrinsic properties of the land which they employ' (p. 3).

In summary, then, the 'production of nature' thesis has bequeathed to economic geography a way of thinking about the social relation to nature that:

- understands all manner of 'natures' – seeds, scarcity, flood risk, famine – as outcomes of economic and political processes, rather than events or objects outside political economy (and therefore immune from political–economic analysis and social critique);
- conceptualizes ecological 'limits' as relative to existing socio-economic organizational forms and not as unchanging external constraints;
- emphasizes the historical reworking of nature, rather than positing a pristine or 'edenic' state into which economy intrudes;
- fixes on work/labour as the primary means by which natures are produced;

- identifies the dominant institutions shaping contemporary natures as 'capitalist' and stresses the systemic character of capitalism;
- recognizes the 'creative-destructive' potentiality of capitalism and gives weight to its generative and emergent moments;
- has as its guiding questions 'how we produce nature and who controls this production of nature' (Smith, 1984: 63).

Since *Uneven Development*, then, economic geographers have largely accepted the argument put forward by Smith that nature and economy are 'inner-related', that they constitute an historical unity (what Swyngedouw (1999) chooses to term 'socionature') rather than a dichotomy and that, accordingly, designations like 'capitalist natures' reveal more than they obscure. In the last 10 years, however, work has sought to disaggregate 'production' into specific processes. This finer-grained approach finds expression in work on the enclosure of the global environmental commons, the commodification of bodies and life, the marketization of environmental goods and services, the normalization of 'environmental' rationalities, and the proliferation of different forms of environmental governance. This profusion of research has been driven by the desire to understand the historical specificity of the contemporary neoliberal period, to understand the distinctive ways in which socionatures are produced under neoliberalism, and to ascertain the extent to which neoliberalism necessarily – rather than contingently – rests on re-working existing relations with the natural world.

One of the most vigorous recent contributions to economic geography comes from ecological modernization (Mol, 1995; Gouldson and Murphy, 1997; Angel and Rock, 2000). Ecological modernization is a convenient shorthand for a bundle of different ideas that originated in Europe in the late 1980s, and which concern the institutional reflexivity of capitalism in face of ecological crisis. As empirical research, ecological modernization identifies how environmental criteria have moved from the margin to the centre of decision-making in many environmentally-intensive sectors (chemicals,

mining, paper, forestry), and how a combination of technological innovation and carefully-crafted environmental policy can improve the environmental performance of firms and the economy as a whole. As a theoretical agenda, ecological modernization addresses the moment at which modernity appears to turn in on itself, a process of reflexive modernization in which phenomena that were regarded as 'external' to the economy (environment, pollution, risk) become the focus of strategy and the basis for economic growth and renewal (as expressed, for example, in the work of Ulrich Beck and Anthony Giddens). An 'eco-mod' perspective shares with the 'production of nature' thesis an acknowledgement of the creativity and internal dynamism of capitalism, and an emphasis on the relentless incorporation and reformulation of the 'outside' as an 'inside' as capitalism expands. It also accepts the basic premise of Smith's thesis – that nature does not exist outside economy but is its product – although it interprets this not as a transhistorical condition (as Smith does) but as an historical moment marking the maturation of contemporary capitalism. Ultimately, then, ecological modernization captures something of the production of nature thesis but ends up rearticulating the nature – society dualism that is so central to the ideas and practices of modernity, the very dualism that Smith's thesis sets out to dissolve.

Smith's thesis now seems stunningly prescient: we live in world in which technological practices like cloning, genetic modification, and genetic testing and selection can produce plant and animal species that are made-to-order. Yet these developments also mean that the 'production of nature' is now an unremarkable claim, and the thesis itself seems ill-suited for teasing apart differences in the way biological natures (self-generating plant and animal species, for example) and geophysical natures (oil, copper, water, for example) are enrolled in capitalism, or for identifying the distinctiveness of 'neoliberal natures' compared to those of other eras of capitalism. Indeed, the 'production of nature' now seems a rather blunt analytical instrument for assessing the complex entanglements of economies and ecologies. Recent work offers two distinctive critiques of the production of nature thesis: (1) nature is not produced solely via the economy, as a whole host of non-economic processes (that may be only weakly linked to capitalism) play a role too; and (2) the production of nature is often an incomplete and partial process that must contend with the material properties and generative capacities of physical and biological processes. These two critiques have provided starting points for renewed efforts to rethink nature within economic geography, and they are discussed in the third and fourth sections below.

Production or construction? Both metaphors emphasize processes of social assembly rather than essences that are innate and fixed. But whereas Smith's thesis points to how nature is an outcome of the social relations surrounding production (specifically *capitalist* production), research on the social construction of nature embraces a full range of social relations that exceed those of 'economy'. Social construction, therefore, un-tethers the assembly process from practices of work/labour and attaches it instead to a diversity of human activities – science and knowing, consumption and solidarity, governance and rule – that do not easily fit within the category 'industry' or 'metabolism'. Work on nature's social construction questions what counts as nature, 'refute(s) taken-for-granted beliefs about the essential nature of things' (Demeritt, 2001) and demonstrates how meaningful social differences are produced and sustained via 'cultures of nature' – the knowledge claims, categories, and discourses we use to describe the biophysical world. This is by no means a singular literature, however, as constructionism is a broad body of work that draws on several different philosophical traditions (see Demeritt, 2002).

Resource geography – economic geography's often neglected cousin – has long recognized that nature is a cultural category. In one of the outstanding economic geography text books of its time, Zimmerman (1933) argued that natural resources were cultural appraisals of 'neutral stuff': because the social norms and demands that determine what counts as a resource vary over time and space, he wrote, 'resources are not; they become'. Philosopher Ian Hacking (1999) terms this an 'historical constructionist' position, since it shows how the morphology, meaning and even existence of contemporary 'spaces of nature' have been shaped in significant ways by cultural and political processes operating over time. Recent work within economic and resource geography, however, takes a significantly stronger constructionist position to argue that claims about nature can sanction social injustice. This position is described by Hacking as an 'unmasking constructionist' because constructions – like wilderness, competition, or sustainability – are shown to be particular rather than universal, and because the objective of research is to reveal how ideas about nature can 'do political work' for dominant social groups. Some of the clearest demonstrations of how politics are built into constructions 'at the upstream end' (Demeritt, 2001) can be found in work documenting the different imaginaries and epistemologies through which indigenous and other groups understand and contest natural resource development (Braun, 1998; Howitt, 2001). Anna Tsing's (2005) *Friction*, for example, draws attention to how 'coal' is not an uncontested concept. Coal resources must be 'coaxed or coerced' from the ground, and the meaning of coal – and hence its existence as an economic commodity – is inherently unstable all the way along the commodity chain. Thus within economic geography work on the social construction of nature is closely linked with a 'critical human geography' – one that seeks to contest and challenge received categories and produce forms of knowledge that challenge rather than affirm existing power relations.

Everyone knows a commodity: It is the material good of capitalist production and the object of consumers' desire. Commodities seem so familiar that we imagine them ready made for us throughout every stage of production and distribution, as they pass from hand to hand until they arrive at the consumer. Yet the closer we look at the commodity chain, the more every step – even transportation – can be seen as an arena of cultural production . . . A lump of coal travels from a mine in Kalimantan to a power plant in India. Before it achieves an existence as a lump of coal, it is part of the landscape under a village field. Somehow it must be coaxed or coerced out of this landscape. Once mined, it still must travel to a warehouse and from there to a port city, where the coal ships can dock. It must be sorted and graded, and managers will have to make sure no one mixes the poor-quality coal with the good. It must meet specifications. If it sits too long in the warehouse, or in the ship at harbor, it will lose all its value to storage and docking costs. At the other end of its journey, it must convince the power plant managers that the contract has been met . . . In these shifts the lump of coal rubs up against other participants in the chain: unhappy villagers, conveyor belts, contracts. In its shape, its cost, and its composition, coal is made in the friction of the commodity chain . . . The managers who facilitate this process can tell us: To produce a commodity is the work of the translator, the diplomat, and the power-crazed magician. (Tsing, 2005: 51–52)

Outside the physical sciences, the assertion that nature is a social construct now scarcely raises an eyebrow. Within economic geography this idea shows up in three distinctive areas of inquiry. The first is research which shows how turning raw nature into primary commodities (fruit, flowers, fish, or gemstones, for example) rests on an array of cultural practices. This work questions the conventional understanding of commodities as free-standing, economic things and is illustrative of the broader research effort within economic geography – the so-called 'cultural turn' – to demonstrate how non-economic phenomena play a significant role in constituting the economic. Commodities may be the 'economic cell form of capitalism' (Watts, 1999) but they do not just spring forth through economic laws of supply and demand: they are, as Tsing points out (above), 'an arena of cultural production'. For example, Becky Mansfield (2003) in an analysis of the Pacific seafood industry shows how cultural norms regarding quality – which can revolve around quite specific understandings

of texture and taste – are key to understanding the peculiarly stretched geographies of this industry. Similarly, work on the uprooting of genetically modified crops in the UK shows how ideas about purity and pollution are integral to the way these crops enter the food supply chain (Boal, 2001). At its simplest, then, this work argues that nature-based commodities are in part culturally – and not just economically – produced.

A second application in economic geography is in research on the cultural politics of nature. Categories, concepts, and metrics drawn from culturally-specific readings of nature play active roles in producing social and political distinctions (about the 'naturalness' of a gendered division of labour, for example) that are integral to the functioning of contemporary economies. The strong separation of humans from (other) animals, for example, rests on a host of cultural concepts: a first-order categorization (built around notions of communicative capacity and perception) that allows us to separate ourselves from other mammals, and a set of second-order categorizations (centred on ideas about emotion, sentience, and capacity for pain) by which we sanction certain behaviours – co-habitation, slaughter, conservation, experimentation – for some species but not others. These categorizations are immensely significant as they underwrite the striking (and often deeply troubling) 'animal geographies' of urban pets, pharmaceutical laboratories, cattle feedlots and factory farms (Philo, 2000).

Taking seriously the cultural content of nature means engaging with the scientific and vernacular practices of knowledge production through which the world is disclosed. Grounded in specific geographical and historical contexts, knowledge is a richly cultural enterprise but also one that has clear economic and political value. As it has become more attuned to the contextual nature of knowledge, so economic geography has begun to recognize how environmental discourses create objects of analysis (climate change, or genetic code for example), establish political subjectivities, or privilege particular geographical scales for policy intervention (the global environment).

Although not always self-identifying as 'economic geography', much of this work addresses the means by which people make a living and/or focuses on issues that have significant economic implications. Leach and Mearns' *Misreading the African Landscape* (1996), for example, illustrates how ecosystem science constructs objects of inquiry that diverge strikingly from the 'local' knowledge and understanding of landscape users. Understood by western science as a degraded forest ecosystem, the savanna-forest assemblage of western Africa has been subject to policies that restrict forest use by local people. Yet to those who live and work this landscape, savanna-forest is an actively enhanced forest: tree cover has expanded along with human settlement rather than being degraded by it. The authors reflect on how science came to produce its truth statements about 'savannization' and how, first in the colonial period and then after independence, these remarkably stable discourses effectively obscured alternative readings of the landscape.

A *third* area of research examines the role that ideas about nature play in the formation of political subjects and subjectivities. The emphasis here is on how, given the endless possibilities for constructing the world in particular ways and the profound plurality of knowledge, certain constructions become widely socialized. Although the Marxian lens of 'ideologies of nature' offered by Smith provides one way to view this cultural component, economic geographers have, in the main, turned to alternative social theorists to understand the association between culture, knowledge and power. In Gramsci's concept of hegemony, for example, economic geography finds a way to understand the role cultural institutions play in achieving the consent of non-ruling classes; while Foucault's concepts of regimes of truth, biopower and govermentality provide a way to describe a diffuse, self-regulatory form of power that works through biological categories. The passage by Anna Tsing (cited previously) is from a larger work exploring the ways in which Indonesia has come to be understood as a frontier of globalization. Tsing argues against this view of the 'global economy' as a structure assembled kit-like over time, and proposes instead that the economy appears as a structure because it is performed that way. Like the export commodities (coal, timber, gold) which define Indonesia's global role as a resource periphery, the identity of people living on Kalimantan, Sumatra or Sulawesi is neither singular nor stable and so their status as subjects of globalization is constantly being negotiated. Fernando Coronil (1997) is equally fascinated with the 'unremarkably natural' way in which primary commodities can come to define the identity of neocolonial states. In *The Magical State* – an account of the historical evolution of the Venezuelan petro-state – he explains how oil first became a 'potent form of hallucination' in Venezuela in the 1930s. Coronil works back and forth between what he calls Venezuela's 'two bodies' – the political body (the citizenry) and the biophysical body (rich subsoil). He shows how, through the centralization of state control over natural resources, the Venezuelan state has consistently used oil wealth – and, more importantly, the *idea* of oil wealth – to bolster its modernizing authority to forge the imaginary community of the Venezuelan nation.

Both Coronil and Tsing are intrigued by the spectacular and dramaturgical dimensions of encounters with nature. Although heirs to social construction, Coronil and Tsing deploy theatrical metaphors – performance, spectacle, prestidigitation, magic – in preference to those of discursive assembly. Development projects – coal mines, oil wells, large dams, forestry programmes – are interpreted as 'performances', moments of active intervention and bodily presentation through which are created the distinctions and identities we ordinarily use to describe the world. By concentrating on the *practices* that produce meaningful difference, recent work in economic geography questions the distinction between representation and reality that underpins earlier work on the social construction of nature. In *The Rule of Experts* – on the modernization of Egypt and the rise of 'the economy' as an arena of state management – Tim Mitchell (2002) refuses the metaphor of (the social) construction (of the economy) precisely because it fails to problematize adequately the relationship between representation and 'the real'. Rather than start with the economy as separate realm that then comes to be represented in a particular way, Mitchell is interested in reading 'the economy' as a separation (from nature, history, society) achieved via practices of science, mapping, and law. Mitchell shows how, by producing 'the economy' as an apparently separate realm, these practices 'stage the world' in ways that give tremendous power and authority to those who profess to manage the economy.

Some of the most interesting engagements with social construction, then, have been on the fringes of economic geography in disciplines such as anthropology and development studies. Nonetheless, economic geography has been receptive to this work, which shows how:

- the production, circulation and reformulation of ideas about nature are deeply imbricated within the geographies of economic life;
- what counts as 'nature' is a product of claims that are made about and for nature; knowledge, narrative and discourse, therefore, are among the primary means through which natures (forests, genes, wetlands) are given their form and meaning;
- constructions of nature are particular rather than universal because they emerge from – and reproduce – prevailing political-economic relations; there is, then, a cultural politics of nature;
- although deeply discursive, nature does not magically sublimate from words into material form; rather, natures are 'enacted' and performed through the actions of institutions and individuals;
- the idea of 'the economy' as an autonomous realm rests on practices of separation which isolate 'economy' from society, nature and history; part of what research on 'nature and economy' is about, therefore, is drawing attention to the practices that produced the effect of separation in the first place.

If firm distinctions between production and construction ever were possible, they have certainly become blurred with time. Indeed, recent research is less interested in illustrating nature's debt to cultural or political economy, than in showing how the materiality of nature may be a source of unpredictability, unruliness and resistance to human intention (Bakker and Bridge, 2006). The point this literature makes is that nature may indeed be produced and/or constructed, but the materials and processes that comprise the biophysical world are not infinitely malleable: nature possesses lively and generative capacities, and sometimes behaves in ways that confound efforts to produce it in particular ways and/or defies properties that are attributed to it. Scott Prudham's (2003) work on tree improvement, for example, exemplifies this attention to how biophysical systems can present obstacles or surprises to capital accumulation. Prudham's argument is that the biotic qualities of trees – how they reproduce over long time scales, how genetic stock varies over space, how large areas of land are needed to grow trees in ways that achieve economies of scale – present barriers to capital and help to explain why forestry in the Pacific North West has taken a distinctive organizational form: extensive co-operation between private firms and public agencies with research on tree improvement being socialized (via state agencies and academics) rather than undertaken proprietarily:

> With a commercial rotation age along the Pacific coast of roughly sixty to eighty years, Douglas fir [cultivation] is particularly problematic, making socially produced Douglas fir a distinct form of fixed capital. The significance of such long growing times is exacerbated by uncertainties regarding returns on investment in tree improvement, not least because of the sheer novelty of the undertaking ... Yet time is also an issue and of the essence in breeding. Delays are introduced in waiting for seedlings to grow large enough to provide a basis for their evaluation, while retained varieties must be allowed to reach sexual maturity before they can be crossed with other selected varieties to produce improved seed: Douglas fir, under normal conditions, take twelve to fifteen years to produce flowers ... [and] has proven difficult to propagate from cuttings and shoots. Yet mass production is absolutely essential to justify greater investments in tree improvement ... To ensure that like breeds with like, tree improvement makes use of distinct seed-source zones [which

restrict] ... the area from which genotypes may be selected and crossed while at the same time typically spanning multiple land ownerships. To achieve the greatest possible gains within each zone, different landowners ... must share genetic resources ... [and] firms in the Pacific Slope region have tended to co-operate extensively ... including sharing genetic resources as common property. (Prudham, 2003: 641–42)

This work illustrates what Braun (2006) terms the 'friction of nature' – the way that biological and physical systems 'make a difference' to the functioning of economy. Karen Bakker's research on the privatization of water in the UK, for example, argues that it is water's material properties that make its commercialization inherently difficult. Water is a weighty substance that is expensive to transport relative to its value, and it requires large-scale infrastructural investments that act as a barrier to entry for new firms. These conditions produce the classic 'market failures' of supply monopoly and environmental externalities (in the form of pollution). In addition, the complex social entanglements of water – the fact that water is a physiological necessity and has historically been regarded as a public good – render it a particularly 'uncooperative commodity' (Bakker, 2003). The materiality of nature, however, is not simply an obstacle to capital. By taking circulation rather than production as his entry point, Henderson (1998) shows how the biotic character of Californian agriculture – the temporal rhythms of planting and harvesting, and the state's great ecological diversity – created opportunities for banking interests. The long growing periods between planting and harvesting and the chaotic geographies of soil and climate may have impeded the rationalization of farming, but the growth and geographical expansion of California banking in the early twentieth century was based on using these impediments as a way of appropriating value. Although clearly rooted in the political economy tradition, work based on the primary sector (forests, minerals, fish, agriculture) recasts the production of nature as a form of 'co-production', a

'conjoined materiality' in which humans and non-humans participate in the production of socionature.

There are multiple origins to this work which have yet to be fully synthesized. One strand grows out of research on the 'metabolism of production' (by researchers working under the banner of ecological Marxism) that focuses on the distinctive character of labour in biologically-based industries like agriculture and forestry. Research in agro-food studies has focused on the disjuncture in agriculture between production time (which is reliant on the biophysical processes of germination and crop growth) and labour time (the comparatively shorter period of planting and harvesting) and uses this to explain the incomplete entry of capitalist social relations (the wage relation) into farming – epitomized in the present day by the survival of the family farm. In this work, then, the emphasis has clearly shifted from how capital produces nature to the ways in which nature shapes dynamics of accumulation or, as Leff (1995) and Prudham (above) neatly put it, to an interest in 'how ecological processes are inscribed in the dynamics of capital'.

A second strand draws on economic historian Karl Polanyi, whose arguments about the socially-embedded character of economic relations in *The Great Transformation* (1944) have been a source of inspiration elsewhere in economic geography (Hess, 2004; Gertler, 2003). It is Polanyi's approach to the rampant commodification of land and life associated with liberal or *laissez-faire* capitalism that has interested nature-focused economic geographers. Polanyi observed that although land, labour and money underpin commodity production, they are unlike most other commodities because they are not produced exclusively for sale. Commodification, therefore, works differently for 'fictitious commodities' like nature and labour: their irrevocable ties to systems of life, livelihood and social reproduction (which are only partially capitalist) present a barrier to their complete commodification. Turning nature into commodities, therefore, is far from smooth as the 'social "production of nature" is never completely social' (Prudham, 2003).

Collectively engagements with nature's effectivity – the difference that nature makes to economic processes – raise the question of how we understand the materiality of nature. There is a tension here that centres on an epistemological distinction between a (critical realist) position that regards nature as a material force, and a (post-structural) position that sees nature as a cultural artifact (i.e. as an effect of ways of thinking that we typically classify as 'science'). The objective of the former is to explain how the structures and internal processes of the natural world function; while in the latter the objective is to identify the practices through which nature and/or its various structures and processes are able to acquire their social status as material properties. Morgan Robertson (2004) productively works this tension in his research on wetland banking in the United States. He accepts the broad argument of the production of nature – that ecological relations do political work, and that 'remaking nature' is a means to sustain accumulation – and shows how this is far from a smooth and uncomplicated process. However, rather than arguing that these obstacles stem from the biophysical properties of wetlands, he proposes instead that they are *effects* of the ecosystem science through which wetland systems are known and narrated to the market. His point is that ecosystem science has struggled to produce the standardized and place-less (i.e., geographically generalizable) measures of wetland services that are necessary for trading in wetland services to take place. Here, then, we find a recognition of how nature often presents challenges to accumulation but an insistence on the constructivist critique: that because nature is *always* narrated and constructed, analysis must remain open to the way the 'qualities' of nature are achieved via the practices of science.

In summary, work on the 'friction of nature' introduces to economic geography a recognition of how:

- the social production of nature is never fully social, since it must contend with biological and physical systems that operate over spatial and temporal scales that do not match those of economy;
- commodification (and other processes through which nature is rendered fit for economy) is often only partially achieved because it must confront processes that can be resistive to commodification;
- labour, time and space work differently in nature-based industries, and present distinctive challenges as well as opportunities;
- relations to nature can become politicized in many different ways, and these can emerge as significant tensions that require co-ordination and regulation if they are not to impede accumulation.

FROM THE MIDDLE OF A LIVELY FIELD: A TENTATIVE CONCLUSION

To what do these varied encounters between economic geography and nature amount? Several axioms have emerged from the 25-year process of engagement and critique that began with the 'production of nature'. These largely uncontested understandings form a shared core for most researchers working on issues of nature within economic geography. Around this common core, however, is a contested penumbra, a grey area in which there is no uniformity of perspective. Among the core axioms are, first, that 'nature' is not a singular entity; and second, that it is necessary to distinguish between Nature (as ideology) and the richly diverse material natures within which corporate and personal economies are immersed. A third is that nature is demonstrably historical: from milk cows to climate change, a weight of evidence now strongly suggests that the common-place notion of nature as a realm external to society simply will not do. And a fourth is that the material artifacts we take to be nature are best described as 'socionatures' since they are products of processes which are neither wholly social nor wholly biophysical.

Modern economic geography successfully defined itself as a field largely by relegating nature to something that did not need explaining. The awakening of the field to nature, therefore, is something of a paradoxical project since it was nature's marginalization that defined the realm of possibility for economic geography for so long. Admitting nature is, therefore, more than a simple process of 'spoon in and stir' since it changes the ground on which economic geography stands. It leads, for example, to thinking about production as a process of materials transformation in which environmental change (i.e. the production of nature) is integral rather than incidental to economic activity (see Hudson, 2001); to enlarging the circle of relevant 'economic' actors from states and firms to the institutions of civil society; and to considering how some of the basic categories used by economic geographers (such as 'economy,' 'society' or 'culture') do not exist outside of the practices which oppose them to nature. Thinking about nature in economy, then, becomes a way to reveal the boundaries, categories, and dualisms that sustain modern geography (Whatmore, 2002).

So, getting nature wrong has been no bad thing for economic geography. The capacity to critique and reformulate is, of course, a tribute to the capacity for critical reflection which is a hallmark of contemporary human geography. Economic geography can, therefore, be rightly proud of its encounters with nature to date: after all, as Roth points out in *American Pastoral* 'getting people right is not what living is all about anyway. It's getting them wrong that is living, getting them wrong and wrong and wrong and then, on careful reconsideration, getting them wrong again. That's how we know we are alive: we're wrong'.

REFERENCES

Angel, D. and Rock, M. (2000) *Asia's Clean Revolution: Industry, Growth and the Environment*. Sheffield, UK: Greenleaf Publishing.

Bakker, K. (2003). *An Uncooperative Commodity: Privatizing Water in England and Wales*. Oxford University Press.

Bakker, K. and Bridge, G. (2006). Material worlds? Resource geographies and the 'matter of nature'. *Progress in Human Geography*, 30(1): 1–23.

Barnes, T. (1996) *The Logics of Dislocation: Models, Metaphors and Meanings of Economic Space*. New York: Guilford Press.

Blakie, P. and Brookfield, H. (1987) *Land Degradation and Society*. Routledge.

Boal, I. (2001) Damaging crops: Sabotage, social memory, and the new genetic enclosure. In N. Peluso, and M. Watts (eds) *Violent Environments*. Ithaca: Cornell University Press. pp. 146–54.

Braun, B. (1997) Buried epistemologies: The politics of nature in (post) colonial British Columbia. *Annals of the Association of American Geographers*. 87(1): 3–31.

Braun, B. (2006) Environmental issues: Global natures in the space of assemblage. *Progress in Human Geography*, 30: 644–54.

Coronil, F. (1997) *The Magical State: Nature, Money, and Modernity in Venezuela*. Chicago: University of Chicago Press.

Cronon, W. (1991) *Nature's Metropolis: Chicago and the Great West*. New York: W.W. Norton.

Demeritt, D. (2001) The construction of global warming and the politics of science. *Annals of the Association of American Geographers*, 91(2): 307–37.

Demeritt, D. (2002) What is the social construction of nature? A typology and sympathetic critique. *Progress in Human Geography*, 26(6): 767–90.

Fitzsimmons, M. (1989) The matter of nature. *Antipode*, 21(2): 106–20.

Gertler, M. (2003) Tacit knowledge and the economic geography of context, or The undefinable tacitness of being (there). *Journal of Economic Geography*, 3(1): 75–99.

Gouldson, A., and Murphy, J. (1997) Ecological modernization: Economic restructuring and the environment. *The Political Quarterly*, 68(5): 74–86.

Hacking, I. (1999) *The Social Construction of What?* Cambridge, MA. and London: Harvard University Press.

Hanson, S. (1999) Isms and schisms: Healing the rift between the nature-society and space-society traditions in human geography. *Annals of the Association of American Geographers*, 89(1): 133–43.

Harvey, D. (1974) Population, resources, and the ideology of science. *Economic Geography*, 50(3): 256–77.

Henderson, G. (1998). *California and the Fictions of Capital*. Philadelphia: Temple University Press.

Hess, M. (2004) 'Spatial' relationships? Reconceptualising embeddedness. *Progress in Human Geography*, 28 (2): 165–86.

Howitt, R. (2001) *Rethinking Resource Management: Justice, Sustainability and Indigenous Peoples*. London and New York: Routledge.

Hudson, R. (2001) *Producing Places*. Guilford Press.

Isard, W. (1956) *Location and Space-economy: A General Theory Relating to Industrial Location, Market Areas, Land Use, Trade, and Urban Structure*. Cambridge: MIT Press and Wiley.

Leach, M. and Mearns, J. (1996) *Misreading the African Landscape*. Cambridge University.

Leff, E. (1995) *Green Production: Toward an Environmental Rationality*. New York: Guilford Press.

Losch, A. (1954) *The Economics of Location*. New Haven: Yale University Press.

Mansfield, B. (2003) Spatializing globalization: A geography of quality in the seafood industry. *Economic Geography*, 79(1): 1–16.

McNee, R. (1959) The changing relationships of economics and economic geography. *Economic Geography*, 35(3): 189–98.

McNeill, J. (2001) *Something New Under the Sun: An Environmental History of the Twentieth Century World*. New York: W.W. Norton.

Mitchell, T. (2002) *Rule of Experts: Egypt, Techno-politics, Modernity*. Berkeley: University of California Press.

Mol, A. (1995) *The Refinement of Production: Ecological Modernization Theory and the Chemical Industry*. Utrecht: Van Arkel.

Philo, C. (2000) *Animal Spaces, Beastly Places: New Geographies of Human-Animal Relations*. London and New York: Routledge.

Polanyi, K. (1944) *The Great Transformation*. New York: Farrar and Rinehart.

Prudham, S. (2003) Taming trees: Capital, science and nature in Pacific slope tree improvement. *Annals of the Association of American Geographers*, 93(3): 636–56.

Robertson, M. (2004) The neoliberalization of ecosystem services: Wetland mitigation banking and problems in environmental governance. *Geoforum*, 35: 361–73.

Roth, P. (1998) *American Pastoral*. New York: Random House.

Scott, J. (1999) *Seeing Like a State: How Certain Schemes to Improve the Human Condition Have Failed*. New Haven: Yale University Press.

Smith, N. (1984) *Uneven Development*. Oxford: Basil Blackwell.

Susman, P., O'Keefe, P., and Wisner, B. (1983) Global disasters, a radical interpretation. In K. Hewitt (ed.) *Interpretations of Calamity*. Boston, London, and Sydney: Allen and Unwin. pp. 263–83.

Swyngedouw, E. (1999) Modernity and hybridity: Nature, regeneracionismo, and the production of the Spanish waterscape, 1890–1930. *Annals of the Association of American Geographers*, 89(3): 443–65.

Tsing, A. (2005) *Friction: An Ethnography of Global Connection*. Princeton and Oxford: Princeton University Press.

Walker, R. (2004) *The Conquest of Bread*. The New Press.

Warntz, W. (1957) Transportation, social physics and the law of refraction. *Professional Geographer*, 9(4): 2–7.

Watts, M. (1983) On the poverty of theory: Natural hazards research in context. *Interpretations of Calamity: From the Viewpoint of Human Ecology*. London: Allen and Unwin. pp. 231–62.

Watts, M. (1999) Commodities. In P. Cloke, P. Crang, and M. Goodwin (eds) *Introducing Human Geographies*. London: Arnold.

Whatmore, S. (2002) *Hybrid Geographies: Natures, Cultures, Spaces*. London: SAGE.

White, R. (1995) *The Organic Machine: The Remaking of the Columbia River*. Hill and Wang.

Zimmerman, E.W. (1933) *World Resources and Industries: A Functional Appraisal of the Availability of Agricultural and Industrial Resources*. New York and London: Harper and Brothers.

15

The Antonymies of Sustainable Development: Sustaining What, How, and For Whom

David Demeritt

INTRODUCTION

At first glance, it seems difficult to find fault with the idea of 'sustainable development'. Coined in the early 1980s, the term was popularized by the United Nation's World Commission on Environment and Development (WCED) in its 1987 report called *Our Common Future*, but more commonly known as the 'Brundtland Report', after the chair of the Commission, Gro Harlem Bruntland, former Prime Minister of Norway. The Bruntland Report famously defined sustainable development as 'development that meets the needs of the present without compromising the ability of future generations to meet their own needs' (WCED, 1987: 54). With this ideal of sustainable development, the WCED sought to reconcile the seemingly opposing goals of economic growth and environmental protection while giving due regard to questions of justice and the aspirations of the poor in the global south.

Partly as a result of the internal tensions among these objectives, there is more than a little vagueness about exactly what is being sustained, how, and for whom. Some critics complain that sustainable development is focused too narrowly on human needs and on sustaining those bits of the environment used by or valuable to humans. Such 'shallow sustainability' is sometimes contrasted with a second sort of 'deep sustainability' that recognizes the fundamental rights and existence value of non-humans. The first, 'shallow' strand of sustainable development thinking reflects its origins in natural resource management and in the ideas and concepts that sustained it. Forestry and fisheries science were avowedly instrumental and anthropocentric. Their initial focus was on developing techniques to maximize the sustainable yield of economically valuable resources. In recent decades, however, natural resource managers have come to embrace a much broader and more holistic conception of the environments and associated values they are trying to sustain. Sustaining the health of whole ecosystems, rather than just the commodities they produce, is increasingly now the formal goal of environmental management schemes. As we will see in the first part of this chapter, that expansion of the aims and objects of environmental sustainability reflects the hard won lesson that timber yields and fish stocks cannot be maintained, at least not for long, if they are managed in isolation from the wider ecosystems in which they exist.

But this first deepening of the environmental dimensions of sustainability also reflects a second and simultaneous set of challenges to any narrow focus on environmental sustainability and nature preservation alone. Developing countries have often reacted sceptically to demands from northern governments and environmental groups that they desist from exploiting their natural resources in the interests of protecting the global environment. In a famous statement at the UN Stockholm Environment Conference in 1972, the Brazilian Minister of the Environment is reported to have said, 'If it is a choice between pollution and industry, or no pollution and no industry, give us your pollution' (quoted in Cohen et al., 1998). Likewise people have often resisted the efforts of state organizations to lock up natural resources in state owned or managed reserves. With the rise of co-management schemes, they have become increasingly successful in insisting upon their right to participate in and benefit from the use and management of environmental resources.

This chapter explores these countervailing tensions over the meaning and practice of sustainability. It begins by using the specific case of forest resources to trace the history of sustainable development and the expansion of resource management ideas of maximum sustained yield to encompass wider environmental considerations. Then, it turns to the simultaneous process of opening up the concept of sustainability to encompass ideas of social and economic development. Finally, it uses the example of climate change to explore the problems but arguably also the necessity

of using economic valuation techniques of cost-benefit analysis to inform decisions over how best to resolve tradeoffs between competing sustainability imperatives.

FROM MAXIMUM SUSTAINED YIELD TO ENVIRONMENTAL SUSTAINABILITY

Though the specific terms 'shallow' and 'deep' sustainability may be new, the tension between these alternative conceptions of environmental sustainability is a long-standing one. Scientific conservation emerged during the nineteenth century against the backdrop of growing concern about the depletion of forests and other natural resources. For romantics, the heartlessness with which forests were exploited was symptomatic of a deeper spiritual malaise in which people were alienated from themselves and from each other as much as from the natural world around them. 'Pine', intoned the American transcendentalist Henry David Thoreau (1972: 121), 'is no more lumber than man is, and to be made into boards . . . no more its true and highest use than the truest use of a man is to be cut down and made into manure'. At the same time, of course, forests also provided essential resources in what was still largely a wooden world: timber for shipbuilding and construction, fuel for heating and cooking, and land which farmers could clear to feed growing urban populations.

Richard Grove (1995) has argued that the experience of colonizing tropical island 'Edens' – small islands such as Mauritius where ecosystems were fragile and natural resource stocks easily depleted – was crucial in triggering awareness of the environmental limits to growth. Furthermore, insofar as it was colonial states that took the first active steps to conserve and manage scarce natural resources as part of their wider programmeme of ruling over colonial territories, scholars such as Grove look to colonialism for the origins of scientific forestry and of state-sanctioned environmental conservation more generally.

British imperial experience in India was an important model for the scientific conservation movement in the late nineteenth century United States. Modelled after the colonial Indian Forest Department, the US Forestry Division (later renamed the Forest Service in 1905) was created in 1880 to study the problem of forest depletion and potential solutions to it. Soon after, in 1891, Congress created the first national forest reserve, reversing a century of public land policy in the United States by specifically setting aside federal lands from pre-emption by or sale to settlers.

Scientific forest conservation was about much more than simply setting forest lands aside for the future; it also meant using them more rationally and efficiently. The first steps in this practical programme of what US President Theodore Roosevelt (1905) called 'perpetuation . . . by use' were to protect forests from fire and ensure their future growth. Conservationists complained that too often forests were treated like a non-replenishable mine, to be cut-over once and then abandoned to fire and waste, rather than being managed rationally as renewable resources, like crops, or alternatively, as a sort of bank account yielding an annual dividend of arboreal growth. The comparison of forests to an accumulating fund of capital was more than a way of winning over a sceptical forest industry. Its implications were deeply practical and political. Non-merchantable species, long ignored by loggers, were suddenly reconstituted as weeds and ecological competitors. Scientific foresters experimented with herbicides and other techniques to favour the growth of merchantable species over their competitors.

To manage and maximize forest yields scientific experts drew on the silvicultural model of the normal forest, first developed in Germany to inform forest harvesting, growth, and management (Figure 15.1). This silvicultural system guaranteed a sustainable yield by rotating the harvest around a larger 'working circle' so that the harvest in any year equalled the annual growth over the area of the entire working circle. In its idealized plantation form, it produced a landscape of equal sized blocks of even-aged, single-species stands

with a normal distribution of age classes, varying from the youngest to mature and merchantable timber. However, few forests in the United States corresponded to scientific foresters' picture of such a normal or regulated forest. The first problem was institutional. The normal forest model of silviculture presumed a consolidation of forest land ownership and centralization of management that was incompatible with the often fractured nature of land tenure in the United States. The second problem was environmental. Instead of the normal distribution of age classes presumed by the model, many areas of North America were dominated by old growth forest, which boasted large volumes per acre but relatively little net annual growth. As a consequence, professional foresters termed such forests 'overmature' and argued that, as *ab*normal forests, they had to be liquidated so that they could be replaced by younger faster growing trees needed to achieve the idealized maximum sustainable yield that scientific forestry and its normal forest model made it possible to project with apparent precision (Demeritt, 2001).

The analogy of forests to natural capital provided a basis for protecting future forest supplies, but it was harder to justify the protection of non-market public goods derived from forests in terms of sustaining crop yields or natural capital. Consider flood abatement, which was one of the benefits of federal forest reserves widely touted to otherwise sceptical western farmers and US Senators. Flood abatement is what economists call an externality. Since lumbermen do not capture the benefits of it, flood abatement is not something that strict profit-maximizers have any incentive to consider. If it happens at all, it is only as an unanticipated by-product of forest management focused solely on maximizing the economic value of timber. Likewise, the scenic and recreational value of forests are also unpriced public goods, whose social value the market, and thus the idea of conserving natural capital, does not account for. Concerted campaigning by environmentalists succeeded in changing the 1976 National Forest Management Act so

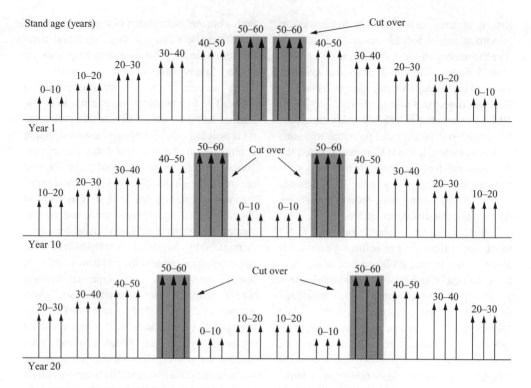

Figure 15.1   The normal forest model of silviculture. Demeritt (2001).

that the US Forest Service would be formally charged with taking non-economic forest values into account in preparing its management plans.

Scientific foresters have come to question the wisdom of a science focused on lumber production without regard to the wider ecological effects of this management strategy. The idea of managing the forest as if it were natural capital and the confidence in science that it reflected encouraged foresters to treat the forest as an assemblage of individual objects that can be managed more or less in isolation from one another. The environmental historian Nancy Langston (1995) has described how well-meaning but misguided forest management in the Blue Mountain forests of eastern Oregon, led to a dizzying series of unexpected effects and unintended consequences.

> For example, fire protection and insect control involved efforts to control natural disasters by eliminating the unpleasantness and engineering it out of existence. Fire managers tried to prevent catastrophic fires by suppressing all small fires. Insect managers tried to control insect damage by killing insects as soon as they appeared, or by simplifying individual stands so insects could not survive. In spite of these effects, attempts at fire and insect control led to only worse devastation. Suppressing fires led to fuel accumulations, slowed the growth of many forests and made future fires more intense. Changing old growth stands to even aged stands in order to control insects only eliminated insect predators, and contributed to the catastrophic insect damage now apparent in the Blues. A refusal to tolerate low intensity fires made moderate fires behave more erratically, just as a refusal to tolerate low intensity insect damage made future damage worse. (Langston, 1995: 296)

Such problems have led to recent calls for the development of a 'new forestry', focused 'on the maintenance of complex ecosystems and not just the regeneration of trees' (Franklin, 1989: 38). Ecosystem management, designed to sustain the 'health' of forest ecosystems, has recently been adopted as the official policy objective of the US Forest Service (1992). This new conception of forest conservation is undoubtedly a response by the Forest Service to outside pressure from environmentalists, but it is also a product of some of the different ways in which the forest is now being framed as an object of knowledge in ecology and environmental geography more generally. The aims and objects of so-called new forestry depend fundamentally upon scientific ideas and techniques, first developed by ecologists but now widespread in other scientific disciplines as well, that set up the forest as a coherent ecosystem whose inter-related parts are connected by flows of matter and energy (Hagen, 1992). These practices make it possible to imagine the forest as an ecosystem whose health might be monitored and managed, rather than, as in more traditional silviculture, as a disparate collection of age classes.

FROM ENVIRONMENTAL TO SOCIAL SUSTAINABILITY

Running in parallel to this first deepening of natural resource management into environmental sustainability was a second process that helped to open up the idea of sustainability (and the environmental movement with which it was associated) to broader concerns with social justice and economic development. During the 1970s and 1980s, a rising tide of concern about desertification, soil erosion, and famine as well as, somewhat later, biodiversity loss, deforestation, and climate change, focused international attention on the relationships between development and the environment. In the first instance many of these environmental problems were blamed on human population pressure. Environmental NGOs, international development organizations, and multi-lateral lending agencies pressured developing countries to take more active measures to protect endangered species and their habitats from over-exploitation by local populations.

One of the most popular ways of doing this was by creating national parks and reserves. Following the US model of parks as wilderness areas in which human activity was severely restricted, Tanzania created Arusha National Park and wild life reserve on the slopes of Mount Meru. At a stroke local pastoralists found longstanding hunting and grazing practices officially reclassified as poaching and trespassing. Refusing to recognize the legitimacy of these new restrictions on their land use or lacking economically viable alternatives, local residents widely ignored them, leading to persistent low level conflict between them and the state officials responsible for overseeing the park. This kind of conservation strategy had strong colonial overtones. The newly independent state of Tanzania set up a park in the very same area previously reserved for big game hunting by the British colonial government. In both cases, conservation policy provided an opportunity for a comparatively weak state to try to extend its sovereignty over distant lands and peoples who in turn often resisted its control (Neumann, 1998).

Very similar stories of conflict over parks can be told in many other developing countries. During the 1980s, the World Bank made loans to developing countries contingent upon their establishing such protected areas. Under its influence the land area held within protected areas increased rapidly, reaching more than 10% of the earth's surface by 2000 (West et al., 2006). The rationale for this policy was the belief that the root of wildlife depletion lay in poaching and habitat encroachment by irresponsible local residents. Thus in Tanzania, the World Wide Fund for Nature lobbied the government vigorously to strengthen the prohibitions on grazing and poaching in Arusha National Park, which it sees as key to wider international strategies for conserving endangered populations of elephant and black rhino. In turn, however, this coercive style of conservation has often sparked bitter resentment from local residents deprived access to resources they regarded as legitimately their own. In the absence of local consent, the effectiveness of these 'fortress conservation' schemes depends upon the ability of often weak states to exercise police powers and stamp out resistance from local residents and others.

Such struggles between the state and local residents over control and access to environmental goods have become commonplace in many developing countries and a key empirical concern for the academic field of political ecology. Emerging in geography and anthropology during the 1980s and early 1990s, this interdisciplinary research field challenged simplistic Malthusian explanations of environmental problems as caused by over-population. Political ecologists emphasize how environmental problems are often rooted in underlying economic and political struggles. For instance in her study of Indonesia, Peluso (1992) showed how efforts to create national forest reserves were exploited by vested political interests within Indonesia for their own private benefit. Local people were deprived of their customary rights to forest resources and in many cases forcibly evicted from areas that were then turned over to logging contractors well connected to the military junta. Rather than conserving tropical rainforests, creating state forest reserves has, in the context of endemic corruption and grinding poverty, often served instead to accelerate the impoverishment both of the forest and the people living in it.

In response to such failures, environmentalists now increasingly emphasize the importance of poverty reduction and economic development as necessary parts of environmental conservation efforts. This dual concern received its first widespread international attention through the IUCN's (1980) World Conservation Strategy Report, which first coined the term 'sustainable development' to describe this new approach. This broadening of traditional concerns with environmental sustainability to encompass concerns with human development and social and economic sustainability was driven by two distinct, but complementary arguments. First, there was the moral argument that as a matter of principle, sustainability must meet human needs. This argument had long been advanced in international treaty negotiations by India,

Brazil, and other developing countries jealous of their sovereign right to exploit their own natural resources for the benefit of their populations. However, it did not gain much traction in international environmental policy deliberations until the 1980s when it was conjoined to a second more practical and instrumental argument that since human poverty causes environmental degradation, poverty reduction must be addressed as a necessary part of any solution to environmental problems such as resource depletion, biodiversity conservation, and pollution control. For example, two of the leading causes of decline in the endangered tiger population in India are habitat encroachment and poaching. Poverty is at the root of both these problems, and so any plan to sustain the tigers must also meet the development needs and aspirations of local residents. The one cannot be sustained without the other, at least not for long. Accordingly, management plans now seek ways of ensuring that local residents benefit economically – and are seen to benefit – from environmental conservation through eco-tourism or other forms of economic activity such as the exploitation of non-timber forest products whose use is compatible with habitat conservation (Adams, 2001).

With the Bruntland report, this idea that environmental sustainability can and should be made compatible with economic growth and human development has become mainstream. For instance, the *Report of the World Summit on Sustainable Development* (2002: 1) refers to three 'interdependent and mutually reinforcing pillars of sustainable development – economic development, social development and environmental protection'. This is sometimes called the triple bottom line, and it has become central to the rhetoric of corporate social responsibility and to the policy discourse of ecological modernization (Hajer, 1995). Proponents of ecological modernization insist that redesigning the industrial ecology of economic production processes to make them more environmentally efficient will also make them economically efficient and profitable. For example, combined heat and power systems (often called CHP) capture the heat produced in generating electricity and use it for domestic heating, enabling them to be much more efficient and cost effective than stand alone power plants that waste heat by merely venting the steam produced by electricity generation. In terms of policy measures, ecological modernization is often associated with various eco-taxes and other economic instruments, such as tradeable pollution permits, designed to encourage this kind of technical innovation by making the price of a commodity reflect, or in technical terms *internalize,* the full environmental costs of its production, use, and disposal.

Another common strategy for ensuring that environmental conservation meets the needs of local people is by involving them in local management decisions. As with sustainable development itself, the idea of participation is fraught with tension between the principle that participation is a right in and of itself and the instrumental argument that it is simply a means to more efficient and locally acceptable environmental conservation. Participation was a mainstay of the Agenda 21 that emerged from the 1992 UN Conference on Environment and Development. Its attractions are several. First, recent research has refuted simplistic ideas that customary common property regimes lead inevitably to a tragedy of the commons. Instead, economic geographers studying common pool resources as diverse as fish, grazing, and forests have emphasized the potential effectiveness of informal systems of community-based resource management in sustaining those resources (for example, McCay and Acheson, 1987). Second, devolving responsibility for management to local communities also promises to reduce the direct costs to the state of environmental management while at the same time increasing levels of compliance among local actors who are repositioned as partners in the resulting regime. However, as Agrawal (2005) emphasizes, encouraging participation in environmental governance involves much more than simply redistributing existing powers from the state to civil society groups and individuals. It is productive, in the

Foucaultian sense of creating new forms of identity and norms of conduct. Through their participation in environmental governance schemes, individuals are invited to become self-regulating 'environmental subjects . . . for whom the environment constitutes a critical domain of thought and action' (Agrawal, 2005: 17). Agrawal calls this process 'environmentality' and argues that its success depends on the simultaneous implementation of three strategies: the creation of governmentalized localities that can undertake regulation in specified domains, the opening of territorial and administrative spaces in which new regulatory communities can function and the production of environmental subjects whose thoughts and actions bear some reference to the environment (Agrawal, 2005: 14).

One of the most common ways in which this kind of awareness and environmental subjectivity is now being inculcated is through product labelling and certification schemes (Goodman, 2004). In addition to the information that consumer products are legally required to provide, such as nutritional information on food, there is also a wide variety of voluntary certification schemes, whose logos and labels signify various things about the social and environmental conditions of their production and trade. In tracing those relationships up and down the supply chain, certification schemes follow in the wake of a now well established body of work by economic geographers focused on the long chain of relations of production and consumption embodied in particular commodities (for example, Hartwick, 1998). Different certification schemes are concerned with different issues. Whereas the blue and green FAIRTRADE mark indicates that the product in question meets certain 'developmental criteria and objectives for social, economic and environmental sustainability', in particular providing a 'minimum price considered as fair to producers' (Fairtrade Labelling Organizations International, 2008), the ISO 14000 icon demonstrates that a product or producer meets a series of international environmental management standards first devised for the 1992 Earth Summit.

Despite the potential for confusion created by the wide range of different product certification schemes, and the different standards certified by, for instance, the US Department of Commerce's 'Dolphin Friendly' logo and the blue fish logo of the Marine Stewardship Council, the proliferation of eco-labels has had important normalizing effects on the conduct of producers and consumers alike. Consumers are not simply 'empowered' to take account of the wider social and environmental implications of their consumption practices; they are also, in some sense compelled to become greener consumers. The very ubiquity of such information is making ethical deliberation a normal part of consumption, in the double sense that such considerations are becoming both ordinary and expected. In turn, producers know that they are being watched and so must consider how their own performance measures up and how consumers are likely to respond to it.

PUTTING SUSTAINABLE DEVELOPMENT INTO PRACTICE: THE ECONOMICS OF CLIMATE CHANGE

Notwithstanding the obvious tensions it embodies, the notion of sustainable development has succeeded beyond the wildest dreams of the UN WCED chair, Gro Bruntland, whose report did so much to popularize the idea that environmental sustainability can and should be made compatible with economic growth and human development. The follow-up United Nation's Conference on Environment and Development, held at Rio in 1992, was attended by more Heads of State than any previous international conference. It led directly to the signing of the UN Framework Convention on Climate Change designed to 'prevent dangerous anthropogenic interference with Earth's climate system' (UNFCCC, 1992: article 2).

But the example of climate change also starkly illustrates the difficulties of putting sustainable development into practice. For many environmentalists climate change represents the most tangible evidence of unsustainable development. The former UK Chief Science Advisor, Sir David King (2004: 176) has argued that 'climate change is the most severe problem that we are facing today – more serious even than the threat of terrorism'. Against that view, a number of critics, particularly from developing countries, charge that this concern with *global* environmental problems, like climate change, is an essentially 'Northern' one (for example, Middleton et al., 1993; Redclift and Sage, 1998). From this perspective, the environment is not self-evidently or exclusively global in scale. Rather, for developing nations and poor people in them, the long-term threat of global climate change holds little meaning, and, if not dismissed altogether as a mere social construction, is not regarded as a matter of immediate concern as compared to the more basic and immediate needs of sanitation, health, and hunger.

The tension between these two views is reflected in the text of the UNFCCC itself. Its first principle states: 'The Parties should protect the climate system for the benefit of present and future generations of humankind, on the basis of equity and in accordance with their common but differentiated responsibilities and respective capabilities' (UNFCC, 1992: Article 3, para 1). However, as the controversies over the Kyoto Protocol and a successor to it have clearly demonstrated, there is no international consensus about what those common but differentiated responsibilities are and thus on who should do what and when. The United States has refused to sign up to binding greenhouse gas emissions reductions that do not also encompass India and China, whereas those countries insist that although their emissions are also increasing very rapidly – by some estimates China is already the world's leading emitter – their per capita emissions are low, less than 15% of per capita emissions from USA in 2000 (Baumert et al., 2005: 22).

To resolve these political differences over the relative importance of climate change, scientists have tried to quantify the costs and benefits it will entail. Lomborg (2004) asked a group of Nobel Prize winning economists to rate 32 different proposals for addressing the major development challenges of our time. Although they did not deny the existence of global warming, they argued that immediate and large scale reductions in greenhouse gas emissions were not cost-effective, relative to the long term benefits they would produce, and that addressing AIDS, malnutrition, malaria, and water borne disease would yield much higher levels of net benefits for the same cost. By contrast, the recent Stern Review (2006: iv) of the economics of climate change argues 'the benefits of strong and early action far outweigh the economic costs of not acting'.

As UK prime minister, Tony Blair (2006) joined environmentalists in hailing the Stern Review for 'demolish[ing] the last remaining argument for inaction in the face of climate change', but he and they ignored the value laden judgements built into these ostensibly scientific estimates of the costs of climate change (cf. Demeritt and Rothman, 1999):

One of the most contentious issues is the practice of discounting. Discount rates are a mechanism used by economists to estimate the present value of future costs and benefits. Estimates of the net present value of future climate change impacts and mitigation are extremely sensitive to this analytical choice. For example, with a 7% discount rate, as would be commonly used in short-horizon project analysis, the net present value of damages of £1 billion 50 years hence is £33.9 million while the same damages 200 years hence are worth only £1,300 today. Discounting makes it extremely difficult to justify, on economic grounds at least, any immediate action to deal with global climate change.

At its heart, the practice of discounting presumes a single, impatient agent for whom a dollar today is worth more than a dollar tomorrow. This, of course, is the time-preference principle upon which interest charges on bank loans and deposits are based. Insofar as spending money now on climate change mitigation to help future generations means that the same money cannot be simultaneously invested in AIDS prevention or poverty alleviation, mainstream economists argue that discounting is necessary to evaluate the trade-offs involved in those different policy choices. However, the long time horizons and potential for irreversible changes with global warming raise fundamental issues of inter-generation equity. Many environmentalists have argued that in this context discounting is unfair to future generations. Accordingly, Stern's analysis of the present value of immediate emission reductions and future climate change impacts uses a discount rate of 2–3%. This is much lower than would normally be used in project level cost-benefit analyses. Lomborg (2006) complains that Stern's use of such an 'extreme and unrealistically low' discount rate, conceals the true scale of the trade-offs involved in spending money now to address climate change as against other environmental problems:

> [S]pending just 1% of GDP or $450 billion each year to cut carbon emissions seems on the surface like a sound investment. In fact, it is one of the least attractive options. Spending just a fraction of this figure – $75 billion – the UN estimates that we could solve all the world's major basic problems. We could give everyone clean drinking water, sanitation, basic health care and education right now. Is that not better?

Lomborg's analysis is itself highly controversial. Critics have challenged both the methods he has used to estimate the costs and benefits of different policy options and the underlying assumption that this kind of economic analysis is the only rational way to choose between them. There is an important tension in the application of such economic appraisal methods between the need to open up discussion of the merits of different policy options and the tendency to use the inevitably contestable results of such analyses to close down policy choice around the option favored by the powerful.

CONCLUSION

What is sustainable development? This chapter has traced the history of the idea and shown how an initially narrow concern with maximizing the yield of economic resources has become steadily broader and more multi-dimensional. It might be charged that the notion of sustainable development is little more than a fudge that skirts over all of the difficult political and economic conflicts entailed by those questions about sustaining what, how, and for whom. But conceptual elasticity can also be a strength too, insofar as it provides the discursive space to draw together and thereby align otherwise antagonistic interests and concerns. For instance, at the first Earth Summit in 1992, more than 170 states signed up to the ideal of sustainable development and pledged to address the problem of anthropogenic climate change, which is arguably the greatest exemplar of global unsustainability. And yet, as the example of climate change shows all too well, it is easier to agree on the broad principles of sustainability than on how they should be applied in any particular case. Although the UNFCCC is committed to the principle of avoiding 'dangerous' climate change, it is not clear what that might mean: dangerous for whom? How, and by whom, is this to be decided? And even if there were some agreement on what degree of climate change were dangerous and on the atmospheric concentration of greenhouse gases likely to bring on that dangerous state, there would still be debate about the timing and distribution of emission reductions (or other measures) required to put the planet on such a sustainable pathway. Ultimately these are political questions, and while science may

help clarify the trade-offs involved in particular courses of action, it can never be sufficient for deciding where to go or how best to get there.

REFERENCES

Adams, W.M. (2001) *Green Development: Environment and Sustainability in the Third World*. London: Routledge.

Agrawal, A. (2005) *Environmentality: Technologies of Government and the Making of Subjects*. Durham: Duke University Press.

Baumert, K.A., Herzog, T., and Pershing, J. (2005) *Navigating the Numbers: Greenhouse Gas Data and International Climate Policy*. Washington: World Resources Institute. Last accessed 21 February 2008 from http://archive.wri.org/publication_detail.cfm?pubid=4093#1

Blair, Rt. Hon. T. (2006) PM's comments at launch of Stern Review. Last accessed 21 February 2008 from http://www.number10.gov.uk/output/Page10300.asp

Cohen, S.J., Demeritt, D., Robinson, J., and Rothman, D. (1998) Climate change and sustainable development: Towards dialogue. *Global Environmental Change*, 8: 341–71.

Demeritt, D. (2001) The statistical enframing of nature's limits: Forest conservation in the progressive-era United States. *Environment and Planning D: Society and Space*, 19: 431–59.

Demeritt, D. and Rothman, D. (1999) Figuring the costs of climate change: An assessment and critique. *Environment and Planning A*, 31: 389–408.

Fairtrade Labelling Organizations International (2008) *Generic Standards*. Last accessed 21 February 2008 from http://www.fairtrade.net/generic_standards.html

Franklin, J. (1989) Toward a new forestry. *American Forests*, 95 (November-December): 37–44.

Goodman, M.K. (2004) Reading fair trade: Political ecological imaginary and the moral economy of fair trade foods. *Political Geography*, 23: 891–915.

Grove, R. (1995) *Green Imperialism: Colonial Expansion, Tropical Island Edens, and the Origins of Environmentalism, 1600–1860*. New York: Cambridge University Press.

Hagen, J.B. (1992) *An Entangled Bank: The Origins of Ecosystem Ecology*. New Brunswick: Rutgers University Press.

Hajer, M.A. (1995) *The Politics of Environmental Discourse: Ecological Modernization and the Policy Process*. Oxford, UK: Oxford University Press.

Hartwick, E. (1998) Geographies of consumption: A commodity-chain approach. *Environment and Planning D-Society & Space*, 16: 423–37.

IUCN (1980) *The World Conservation Strategy*. Geneva: International Union for the Conservation of Nature and Natural Resources.

King, D. (2004) Climate change science: Adapt, mitigate, or ignore? *Science*, 303: 176–77.

Langston, N. (1995) *Forest Dreams, Forest Nightmares: The Paradox of Old Growth in the Inland West*. Seattle: University of Washington Press.

Lomborg, B. (ed.) (2004) *Global Crises, Global Solutions*. New York: Cambridge University Press.

Lomborg, B. (2006) Stern Review: The dodgy numbers behind the latest warming scare. *Wall Street Journal*, 2 November. Last accessed 21 February 2008 from http://opinionjournal.com/extra/?id=110009182

McCay, B. and Acheson, J. (eds) (1987) *The Question of the Commons*. Tucson: University of Arizona Press.

Middleton, N., O'Keefe, P. and Moyo, S. (1993) *Tears of the Crocodile: From Rio to Reality in the Developing World*. London: Pluto.

Neumann, R.P. (1998) *Imposing Wilderness: Struggles over Livelihood and Nature Preservation in Africa*. Berkeley: University of California Press.

Peluso, N.L. (1992) *Rich Forests, Poor People: Forest Access and Control in Java*. Berkeley: University of California Press.

Redclift, M.R. and Sage, C. (1998) Global environmental change and global inequality: North/south perspectives. *International Sociology*, 13: 499–516.

Roosevelt, T. (1905) Forestry and foresters. *Proceedings of the Society of American Foresters*, 1: 3–9.

Stern, N. (ed.) (2006) *The Economics of Climate Change: The Stern Review*. Cambridge: Cambridge University Press. Last accessed 21 February 2008 from http://www.hmtreasury.gov.uk/independent_reviews/stern_review_economics_climate_change/stern_review_report.cfm

Thoreau, H.D. (1972) In J.J. Moldenhauer (ed.), *The Maine Woods*. Princeton: Princeton University Press.

UNFCCC (1992) United Nations Framework Convention on Climate Change, FCCC/INFORMAL/84 GE.05–62220 (E) 200705. Last accessed 21 February 2008 from http://unfccc.int/resource/docs/convkp/conveng.pdf

US Forest Service (1992) *Ecosystem Management of the National Forests and Grasslands*, policy letter 1220–1, 4 June. Washington DC: Government Printing Office.

WCED [World Commission on Environment and Development] (1987) *Our Common Future*. Oxford: Oxford University Press.

West, P., Igoe, J., and Brockington, D. (2006) Parks and people: The social impacts of protected areas. *Annual Review of Anthropology*, 35: 251–77.

16

Towards Visceral Entanglements: Knowing and Growing the Economic Geographies of Food

Michael K. Goodman

INTRODUCTION[1]

As I sit down to write this chapter, I have just finished my breakfast: two cups of organic Fair Trade coffee and a bowl of organic cereal sprinkled with blueberries (of course, *also* organic *and* a good source of anti-oxidants!). Letting my mind wander and my stomach do its thing, I decide that, instead of immediately starting to work, I would first trawl the day's morning news on the Web. I quickly spot the following rather troubling headline: 'Profiteers Squeeze Billions Out of Growing Global Food Crisis' (Lean, 2008). Continuing on, I come upon a related yet even more troubling headline: 'Let them eat dirt: Multinationals reap benefits of commodity crisis' (Silverstein, 2008). My attention fully grabbed, I stop for a quick read:

The soaring price of [food] commodities worldwide has been a disaster for the poor, with reports coming out of Haiti that some people don't have enough money to pay for food and are reduced to eating dirt. But these are happy times for multinational food and grain giants. Patricia Woertz, chairman and CEO of Archer Daniel Midlands (ADM), 'the world leader in bio-energy', said last month that 'Volatility in commodity markets presented unprecedented opportunities. Once again, our team leveraged our financial flexibility and global asset base to capture those opportunities to deliver shareholder value'. Meanwhile, Cargill profits were [up] 86% last quarter. Greg Page, Cargill chairman and CEO, has said: 'Prices are setting new highs and markets are extraordinarily volatile. In this environment, Cargill's team has done an exceptional job measuring and assessing price risk, and managing the large volume of grains, oilseeds and other commodities moving through our supply chains for customers globally'.

Food, glorious, food indeed – for some at least. So, while in the midst of what might be called the growing global food 'crisis',[2] I tank up on 'quality' Fair Trade and organic foods and various food multinationals such as ADM and Cargill[3] tank up on profits. Yet others, as the opening lines suggest, are forced to close their eyes and *imagine* eating – or, apparently if lucky, eat dirt. And, while relatively quiet as of yet, food prices are, as one report puts it, 'rocketing' in much of the Global North – and in Europe in particular – to cause a so-called 'bombshell in the shopping basket' (Blair, 2008).

What this opening points to, among other things, is the important and almost inescapable need to understand the contemporary global and daily shifting *economic geographies of food*, and, in particular, their *inequalities*. And, specifically, in this chapter, I want to submit that any attempt fully to explore food's inherently uneven economic geographies must involve not only understanding the processes and politics of food production but also the very processes and politics of its *consumption*. Indeed, the political economies of nature necessary for food production are inextricably and – in Roger Lee's words (2006; see also Chapter 24; Hudson, 2005) – ordinarily *entangled* with the political *and* cultural economies of food consumption (see also Chapter 20). In other words, knowing how to 'know' food as eaters (and academics) is just as imperative as knowing how we grow the stuff (Goodman and DuPuis, 2002) in order to more fully understand and appreciate the relationships between food and society. Yet, there is also an essential *extra-ordinariness* to food that must also be considered. Thus, in order to capture the *normal* ordinariness *and* extra-ordinariness in food, there is a need to think on and engage with the deeply *visceral* entanglements embedded in food that set it apart from other commodities and 'resources' as considered in economic geography (see Chapter 14 and Bakker and Bridge, 2006).

Stated more schematically, this chapter attempts to make two interrelated arguments that work towards a more coherent, specific and dedicated consideration of the economic geographies of food. First, the study of food necessitates, at the least, a consideration of the processes, politics and, indeed, economic geographies of consumption in order more fully to understand the 'place' of food in our livelihoods, lifestyles and economic geographies. Building on important but disparate writing in the sub-discipline (for example, Coe et al., 2007, Chapter 4 and 10; Cook et al.,

2006; Crang, 2008; Crewe, 2000; Goss, 1999; Hartwick, 1998, 2000; Jackson, 1993), I explore several ways that we might more systematically consider the 'work' that consumption and consumer cultures (Jackson, 1999) do in *constructing* and *being constructed* by food geographies. Consumption cannot remain merely a 'bolt on' consideration as the end of the processes of production as has sometimes been the case; this is especially true in light of the important role that consumption plays in our everyday lives and its growing ties to our identities, politics and forms of citizenship in much of the global North (see also Chapter 20; Bevir and Trentmann, 2007; Seyfang, 2005).

More specifically, I want this chapter to focus in part on the possibilities but also the limitations of consumption politics in making more ethical and 'alternative' economic geographies (Leyshon et al., 2003a) in, for example, the movements and markets as Fair Trade and organic foods. As recent research details, ethical forms of food consumption are 'serving to rework the boundaries between the functions of the market, state and civil society' (Hughes et al., 2008) by inserting notions of responsibility into the governance regimes of supermarkets in the US and UK. At the same time, though, these very same governance regimes can re-inscribe older forms of 'imperial' power relations between the global North and South, with supermarkets – even in ethical food networks – dictating labour practices and contract relations with respect to small-scale vegetable producers in Africa (Friedberg, 2003, 2004, 2007). Others, such as Julie Guthman (2007a), have christened consumer choice-based forms of politics as simply 'anaemic' and just one more feather in the cap of neo-liberal environmental and social governance that, while perhaps tasting good for some of us, does not fundamentally transform the relations of inequality within contemporary food systems. Understanding the inequalities in the quality as well as the quantity of food consumption at a range of scales – the fact that I am able to munch on healthy organic blueberries while Haitians turn to dirt – is the imperative of any economic geography of food worth its salt.

My second argument relates to how the economic geographies of food might be framed. Here, drawing on Elspeth Probyn (2000), I suggest that the complex and situated visceral nature of food – food as profound and deeply *felt* in the gut, yet also quite ordinarily instinctive, elemental and 'everyday' in the biological sense – needs to inform considerations of its economic geographies. This viscerality of food, then, is about the powerful role that food plays in constructing and re-constructing our lives, identities, families, communities and cultures and the uneven economic geographies these create and in which they are enmeshed. Yet, I also want to argue that it is just as important to consider how food is viscerally and materially entangled in the landscapes of contemporary capitalistic political economies. This chapter is, then, about the powerful role that uneven economic geographies – and also uneven environmental, social and political geographies – play in shaping and reshaping food and how these political economies construct and reconstruct our lives, identities, families, communities and cultures.

The remainder of the chapter is organized as follows. First, I develop several ways of taking food consumption more fully into account in order to understand its economic geographies. Second, I use Fair Trade and other 'alternative food geographies' (Maye et al., 2007) as examples of how the processes and politics of consumption can be complicit in the creation of novel economies, and especially, those defined by relationships of care and responsibility (Lawson, 2007). Here, I also consider the established but growing *transgressions* between the alternative economic geographies of foods and those of more conventional political economies; such transgressions are is best exemplified in the expanding sale of alternative foods like organic and Fair Trade through mainstream retailers such as large, multinational supermarkets. At this stage, however, I want to make several very brief claims about food's 'otherness' as an entry point for developing the chapter's arguments.

THE DIFFERENCE THAT FOOD (CONSUMPTION) MAKES

Very much more than just the usual buffet of concerns that inhabit economic geography and more mainstream economics, I submit that food is different[4] from other commodities and thus needs to be considered differently. Think here across the following three points – in and amongst many others – by way of an argument.

First, ask yourself a question: when was the last time you went without eating at least *something* during the day? Indeed, if you are living in a well-off region of the world as I am (United Kingdom), you probably ate *too much* based on the recommended daily intake of calories as stated by groups like the Food and Agricultural Organisation. The point here is that, similar perhaps to water (for example, Bakker, 2007) but different from other commodities (for example, clothing, cars, houses, etc.), food – in one form or another – is a biological imperative that is non-substitutable for human existence as we know it. For me, this is at the core of food's difference.

Second, not only is food key to material and physical reproduction, it is also key to the production and reproduction of cultures, societies, and people's identities. Indeed, in an effort to 'fit in' as a transplant in the UK, I have now officially adopted beans on (buttered) toast as one of my staples, something quite unimaginable to the typical North American. In a way then, food is central to the making of culture(s) and, as in mine, many food cultures are quite hybrid these days thanks to globalization. But food's difference is not contained only in the ordinary food 'events' such as one's daily breakfast; rather, the cultural and highly social character of food often scales up to the extraordinary events of, for example, festive meals and the specific family food traditions that go along with these. Moreover, food is invested with all sorts of meanings, from those of particular memories (for example, that special dish made each Christmas), to emotion, care and responsibility (for example, Kneafsey et al., 2008; Probyn, 2000, Valentine, 1999). For me, 'bringing home the bacon' (sometimes literally) for my family is deeply imbued with relations of responsibility and care as it is tied directly to my 'performance' as a university lecturer. Further, even the micro-scale act of cooking the evening meal, preparing that 'special' dish for someone – or bringing food in so that it appears that *no one* has to cook – can comprise an act of care, laden with the emotions of love and conviviality yet, at the same time, deeply entangled with the materialities involved in producing, transporting and consuming food. Clearly, negative feelings surrounding food abound as well, from the quotidian nature of the 'guilty pleasure' of eating chocolate to the anorexic's crushing guilt of eating anything at all. In short, food is entangled literally, figuratively and most intimately in and through the ways in which we make ourselves, our societies *and* our economic geographies.

Third, as Friedberg (2003b) astutely observes, food is now more than ever sold with a story. Thus, a new and performing 'knowledge economy' has sprung up attached to commodities like organic and Fair Trade foods telling tales of where and how they have been produced. But for many foods, it is much more than just the simple provisioning of the geographic origins of an item or ingredient. Indeed, the geographic concept of 'place' is now very much the provenance of organic but also other, so-called 'quality' foods (see Goodman, 2003; Goodman and Goodman, 2008).

For example, the Pipers 'Sea Salt and Somerset Cider Vinegar' Crisps I bought at my local farmshop are 'Made by Farmers' but also, as the back of the (empty) bag states, '. . . made in Lincolnshire': We only use the best and freshest potatoes. They are washed, sliced, and cooked in sunflower oil to bring you a delicious, crunchy hand produced crisp . . . At Pipers Crisps, we go to great lengths to find small, individual suppliers who make an exceptional product. Our Cider Vinegar is made by Burrow Hill Cider in Somerset. The Cider is pressed from traditional cider apples, over 40 varieties are grown in some 150 acres of orchards. Selected apples are pressed and fermented in oak vats to mature. The result is a superior vintage quality cider. The connections to farmers and landscapes do not end here and indeed, they are extended in the virtual spaces of the Web; this is quite easy to see from the images and texts from the Pipers Crisps website below.

Figure 16.1   Landscapes of food production.

Yet, this is only half of the story of how foods are now being sold in relation to food 'place' (Feagan, 2007; Morgan et al., 2006). In these new geographies of quality foods, it is not just the story of where and how foods are produced, but also the very 'place' of their purchase. The idea – through farmers' markets, farmshops, and food delivery schemes – is to reduce the social, economic and literal distance between the fork and field. The goal then is that, through these provisioned knowledge regimes of food's place and its novel places of purchase, there is the (re) embedding and (re)-placement of food in the (re)connected networks of production and consumption (see Goodman, 2002; Hinrichs, 2000; Holloway and Kneafsey, 2004).[5] And, most recently, another geographical idea – that of the 'local' – has made itself known as concept, practice and politics in much of the food-scapes of Europe and the US (Goodman and Goodman, 2007). These (re)connections of food consumption to its production – theoretically in academic work (Goodman, 2002) and practically in novel provisioning economies and geographies (Kirwan, 2006; Johnston and Baker, 2005) – and the politics evinced by these (re)connections (Allen, 2004; Guthman, 2004, 2007a, b), has been a key element in the broad range of work on *alternative food networks* (Goodman and Goodman, 2008). All of this points to the important and, I would argue, unique ways that food – in the particular form of alternatives – is unevenly remaking and rescaling economic geographies through the specific processes of the performativity of food stories, the consumption of 'quality' foods (by those who can afford them) and the growing drive to (re)localization.

With that said – and while I make myself another cup of coffee – let's now turn to some ways that might help us 'work-up' consumption in the economic geographies of food.

CONSUMING ECONOMIC GEOGRAPHIES: LET'S FEAST!

Writing in *Remaking Nature* (Braun and Castree, 1998), Allen Pred (1998: 151) states something profound yet slippery:

... the nature of consumption at this precarious moment needs to be re-cognized – seen again and thought anew – in such a manner that its inseparability from nature becomes every bit as explicit as its deep entanglements with politics, the economy and culture.

But how might we take this re-cognition forward in a more concrete way? What I want to do – with Pred's statement as a kind of loadstone – is to collate and sketch out a few consumption-related themes in recent work on agro-food studies, alternative food networks, and elsewhere in Geography; some of these link up either explicitly or implicitly with the chapters in this volume but from often different angles. These themes – and the questions that arise in their context – are limited in scope and detail, but suggest some potentially fruitful avenues for thinking around the economic geographies of food and the contemporary shifting economic geographies of consumption.

Embedded food economies

Drawing in part on the work of Mark Granovetter (1985; see also Krippner, 2001), notions of the *embeddedness* of economic activities – that they are enmeshed in culture, politics, networks, territories and spaces – have formed a particular axis of research and writing in economic geography (for example, Hess, 2004; Coe et al., 2008). The concept of embeddedness has also been taken up to some fruitful ends in agro-food studies as a way of conceptualizing the growing importance of indicating production place and ecological concerns in quality foods and, most specifically, in the 'closer' provisioning networks and social relationships between farmers and consumers. David Goodman (2003:1) has been one to lead this charge suggesting that

[e]mbeddedness, trust, place and their variants [are valuable] conceptual touchstones but in the service of empirically grounded analyses of alternative food practices, institutional mechanisms of rural governance and policy, and the potential of [alternative agro-food networks] as engines of rural economic dynamism.

He has been cautious however, in deploying this notion, as embeddedness has the potential to overplay the 'niceties' of capitalism and leave the issues of exploitation and hardcore political economic 'profit-at-any-and-all-cost' imperatives too neatly to the side (Sayer, 1997, 2001). Sonnino and Marsden (2006) go a little further to problematize but also situate embeddedness directly at the centre of their suggested research agenda on alternative food networks in Europe. They are interested in a more 'holistic' approach to embeddedness in food by understanding the '. . . political, institutional, and regulatory context in which alternative food networks operate' and 'the local/regional context in which they take shape' (Sonnino and Marsden, 2006: 189). Yet, while interested in how these new foods (re)embed the connections (social, economic, ecological) between production and consumption, consumption *itself* – as process, as practice, as politics – gets little sustained play here. As Pred suggests, these relations are always and already embedded in consumption but also embedded *as* and *through* consumption processes, practices, and politics. And lest we forget, consumption itself is networked and indeed embedded in the relations and subjectivities of class, gender and race, as well as in one's identity as, say, an 'ethical' consumer (Barnett et al., 2005).

Food knowledge and knowledgeable foods

Discussions of knowledge around commodities have figured greatly in accounts of food in Geography (for example Cook and Crang, 1996). As Hughes et al. (2008: 351) argue, the concern in this work is with the *circulation* of the knowledge of commodity biographies '. . . that shape consumers' understandings of the journeys taken by goods through production and distribution networks'. Indeed, plugging this 'knowledge deficit' within consumers' understanding of the environmental and social impact of the goods they purchase is proving to be one of

the cornerstones of sustainable consumption movements and policies in the UK. Providing this knowledge about origins and the social and ecological conditions under which goods are produced has become the hallmark of 'quality' foods such as organic and Fair Trade (Goodman, 2004). Yet, even without knowing where our food comes from, we are intimately and inextricably *materially* connected to those places, be they to the pig farms that produce our bacon and/or those idyllic 'natural' farms that grow our organic lettuce mix (Goodman, 1999).

But how do consumers actually engage with and alter their practices and thus potentially open up – but also close down – such economic geographies? This is a particularly pertinent question given the ways in which social and environmental concerns have entered mainstream debates through Corporate Social Responsibility schemes that are the standard operating procedure for just about every 'big business' player concerned with their brand value. Recent work by Sally Eden and colleagues (Eden et al., 2008a, b) is beginning to address these issues by looking into consumers' engagements with commodities in the form of food-labelling 'assurance' schemes made up of 'local', organic and ethical foods. They are finding that there is a problem with this 'knowledge-fix': providing consumers with information in the form of labels and logos is not as straightforward as many make it out to be. Neither is it an uncomplicated way more sustainably to 'fix' the food system. What is at issue is:

> . . . how people weigh up seemingly contradictory or competing information from multiple sources in order to make sophisticated judgements about that most basic necessity: food. (Eden et al., 2008a)

Thus, the 'hows' and 'whys' of consumers' engagement with commodity knowledge(s) and the effects (or not) that these (non)-engagements have on 'alternative' economic geographies represent one possible yet important avenue work engaging with food's contemporary economic geographies.

The consuming power of food

Power in the food system, and in particular the power of corporations and agribusiness to *control* the food system, has played well in agro-food studies for sometime now (for example, Hendrickson and Hefferenan, 2002; Magdoff et al., 2000; McMichael, 2000; Whatmore, 1995). Indeed, what Morgan et al. (2006) call 'looking into the eyes of the hog' has generously slopped over into more popular media with the likes of *Fast Food Nation* (Schlosser, 2001), Morgan Spurlock's (2004) paean to McDonald's in *Super Size Me*, and Michael Pollan's *Omnivore's Dilemma* (2006). Here, in some accounts, consumerist-driven – or at least consumer-dependent, alternative and quality foods – are positioned as forms of resistance in opposition to the State-enabled, corporate-controlled global food sector. And, no matter how anaemic, problematic or contradictory consumption choice-led pathways to change might be (for example, Guthman, 2007a, b; Freidberg, 2003a, b), there is no denying the power these politics have had in capturing collective and economic imaginations. From the corporate-connected (RED)™ campaign, developed through Bono's concern with African development,[6] to Australia's Banrock Station winery (see Figure 16.2) which gives consumers licence to 'help the Earth one glass at a time', consumer choice has quickly become *the* way of doing business.

However, there are critical limits to such tactics. The description and images of the 'Good Earth Fine Wine' conservation campaign of Banrock Station says nothing about the environmental consequences of shipping Australian wine to the UK to be consumed by 'conservation wine' connoisseurs.

Thus, in recent work on alternative food networks, more critical research and writing has started to look into the nitty-gritty practices of these networks, their governance regimes and their potentially awkward relationships of power. First, 'quality' in food and other commodities is slippery at the best

Figure 16.2   Does it get any better than this? Saving the Earth by drinking wine.

of times; it is subjective and very often subject not only to tastes but to the market. Because of this – how and by whom it is defined and deployed – quality acts as a 'boundary-making' governance tool (Bryant et al., forthcoming) in that it often becomes the arbiter of who is included with in particular networks and who is left out. Erecting boundaries has been one result of the mainstreaming of the Fair Trade market, where some of the poorest producing cooperatives and farmers are left at the wayside because the quality of the goods they grow are not up to snuff (Lockie and Goodman, 2006; Renard, 2005). Second, the development and deployment of production and certification standards, as in Fair Trade and organic markets, also involve the development and deployment of new governance regimes that denote the exercise of power by (historically Northern) standards institutions. Thus, international regulatory regimes in alternative food networks dictate how commodities are, and can be, produced to impact on the livelihoods of people in positive but sometimes complex and unintended ways (see, for example, Moberg, 2005; Lyon, 2006; Getz and Schreck, 2006; Mutersbaugh, 2002). Thus, given their neo-liberal, market-orientated characteristics, ethical and alternative consumption networks are not quite as innocent as they have been characterized and might seem to be on the surface.

Yet, in the rush to find and lionize food alternatives, the larger and more complex questions of power in the food system – who gets to eat what, how much and why – have receded into the background. In particular, a compelling case is being constructed to make the exploitation of labour much less 'invisible' as one of the cornerstones of research on conventional and alternative food networks (for example, Harrison, 2008; Harrison and Wolf, 2008; Guthman, 2004). In addition to this work, it is vital to continue looking into questions of (the lack of) food consumption, especially in a continuingly unequal world where many – even in the overconsuming North – do not have

enough to eat and/or suffer various forms of food deprivation, a situation that even many farmworkers find themselves in. At the same time but without ducking these wider questions of power, research and writing on alternative and quality food networks might open up novel and 'hopeful spaces' of thinking the economy 'differently' (Gibson-Graham, 2006; Leyshon et al., 2003b; Lawson, 2007); here these alternatives might serve as forms of critique that may then act to hold States and corporations responsible for the inequalities of consumption in which they are complicit. The not-so-easy trick, however, is to work out how to turn hope and critique into practice and politics in order to make these alternative forms of praxis 'sticky' in the fickle worlds of the consumer choice and taste.

VISCERAL GRUB: FOOD AS ORDINARILY AND EXTRA-ORDINARILY FELT

In returning to think more about food's difference in relation to its consumption, it is well worth considering Probyn's (2000: 32) argument:

> [e]ating refracts who we are. . . . [It] recalls with force the elemental nature of class, gender, sexuality, nation. But beyond these monumental categories, eating . . . extends our understanding and appreciation of the rich complexity of living in the present. . . . For some, this means wearing one's stomach on one's sleeve: thinking about where food comes from, or how core identities are now ingested in multicultural ways of being in the world. As such, these alimentary identities are ways of reworking the categories that once defined us. Now, beyond a model of inside and out, we are alimentary assemblages, bodies that eat with vigorous class, ethnic and gendered appetites, mouth machines that ingest and regurgitate, articulating what we are, what we eat and what eats us.

Probyn's point is that the viscerality of food is in its connections – inside, outside, gender, sexuality, etc – but also how food contains the emotional, the inexpressible, and the biological and how these are all inseparable and entangled in complex, complementary and ambiguous ways. So not only does my breakfast make me through the biological metabolization of organic cereal and Fair Trade coffee, but it is also about me making myself and who I am as a middle-class (relatively) 'conscious' consumer who now feels he is connected to poor coffee producers in Nicaragua and organic farms in Britain.[7] In short, food is ordinary in its characteristic as simply the 'fuel' that keeps us going, but also in the meals that make us who and what we are. We often eat without thinking as it becomes so much a part of our daily routines and engagements with others. Yet, at the very same time, food is also extra-ordinary in its characteristics as a biologically-necessary 'fuel' and also in the meals that make human (and non-human) beings who and what they are. It is sometimes necessary to think quite hard about where the next meal might come from – especially in times of poor access and extreme hunger – or during those special occasions (for example, holidays and celebrations) when food takes on particularly important meanings. You are what you eat – literally – but also how, when, where and why you eat.

And yet, while suggesting these more cultural interpretations of food's (and consumption's) place in more than just economic geographies, it is imperative not to lose sight of the material connections between bodies and ecologies, but also the historical, continuing and equally inseparable *visceral* connections that food has with the contemporary processes of global capitalism. This point resonates with my arguments above about the circulations of power *of* and *in* food networks. As one readily available example, for most of the post-war era, coffee has been the second most valuable globally-traded commodity after oil and the coffee commodity chain touches and, indeed, determines the lives of tens of millions throughout the world. Yet, 50% of this trade is controlled by just four companies,

with only 10% of the value produced trickling back down to the farmers who actually planted, cultivated and harvested the coffee (Daviron and Ponte, 2005).

And, even more insidiously, as markets shift around biofuels and changing global food demands, increasing profits for agrofood multinationals such as ADM and Cargill equate with growing misery for many of the world's poor whose 'effective demand' is simply below that of the recent Northern penchant for 'environmentally friendly' petrol. Other work on retail-scapes points to the local, national and now international (Wrigley et al., 2005; Blythman, 2004; see also Chapter 20) power of food retailers to determine what it is and how most eat but also what and how food is produced. In 2007, Tesco had 31% of the UK market for groceries,[8] and – what might be shocking for some but exciting for others – a growing proportion of the market for organic foods.

In sum, these ideas about the visceralities of food – along with the theme of food's embeddedness, the knowledge economy, and the specific questions of power and inequality – contain important avenues for thinking more broadly across the powerful and undeniable role that food consumption has in creating not only economic and political geographies, but, indeed, the very lifeworlds that construct these geographies. I turn now to consider the growing relations of care being invested in novel food geographies and their transgressive properties.

TRANSGRESSIVE FOODS: BUILDING ECONOMIC GEOGRAPHIES OF CARE THROUGH CONSUMPTION

With the mainstreaming of environmental concerns in much of the global North, consumption has begun to take on green but also a newer 'ethical' hue (Harrison et al., 2005). From rapidly growing organic food markets, through hybrid cars, to British Petroleum re-branding itself as 'Beyond Petroleum', these growing concerns have shifted economic geographies in practice and/or at least in greenwashed principle. Some of the more 'hearty' versions of ethical consumption include those provisioning networks mobilized around the relations and ethics of care: care of and for Others, care of and for Nature, care of and for doing and thinking economies 'otherwise' (Gibson-Graham, 2006). This is often about care 'at a distance' which spans spatial and other (socio-cultural, economic, political, material) divides (Barnett et al., 2005; Goodman, 2004; Smith, 2000; Whatmore and Thorne, 1997). The massive and rapid growth of the Fair Trade market, in particular, is a substantial infiltration of an ethics of care and responsibility into commodity-based 'nourishing networks' (Whatmore and Thorne, 1997; see also Raynolds et al., 2007). Yet both Fair Trade and organic foods, in some ways, are about the care of 'Other' places – Fair Trade in looking after the conditions of peasant farmers; and the organic in its concern for nature – in the provisioning of what Whatmore and Clark (2006) refer to as 'good food'. But these relations are present even in quality foods more generally. Take, for example, Pipers crisps (see above). The descriptions on the bag and the website are very much about developing relations of care among consumers, the food and the conditions of production. Thus, the knowledge-fix provided by information about the farmers growing the various ingredients and the specific landscapes they come from is not just about providing the knowledge itself, but providing this knowledge so it can work at getting people to care about where and from whom the food comes.

These relations are also about the 'care of the self' in eating something not only tasty and 'care-fully' made, but something more 'authentic' – *vis a vis* more conventional networks – in the greater closeness to landscapes, nature and farmers exhibited in Pipers' production networks. And, especially for organic food networks, care of the self involves the deliberate avoidance of pesticide residues and industrially-produced foods (Guthman, 2003).

Recent work by Kneafsey et al. (2008, 157–158) has begun more seriously and extensively to investigate these relations of care; they start from the following question: 'to what extent and how do we value food, its production, its distribution and its consumption?'. To answer this, they investigate several "alternatives" to predominant food supply arrangements, examin[ing] the identities, motives and practices of people actively involved in trying to produce and consume food in ways which allow them to address a variety of societal and individual concerns about food. The key for them is how this ethics of care is conceptualized and practised by consumers. Consumers involved in five different alternative food schemes were found to be:

> . . . knowledgeable, thoughtful and caring on many levels. They are far from the model of the alienated, economic rationalizer searching out cheap, convenient food and knowing little of the implications. Rather they are rational on their own terms, participating in practices that have an emotional, or moral, logic as well as an economic one. 'Reconnection' with the production of their food has had wide ranging implications for most of these consumers. Involvement in these schemes went beyond relationships with individuals and, for some participants, encompassed much broader notions of community, education and support for a way of life they believed in. Participation in the 'alternative' food sector allowed for and encouraged practices that embraced caring at many levels.

As they conclude about the wider implications and, indeed, politics of this ethics of care in reconnection:

> [p]articipation in 'alternative' food schemes might not save the world, at least not in the short term, but it might help to build the knowledge, and positive relationships that create the capacity for change . . . [and support] all those who want to build more equitable, more sustainable, and more closely connected relationships between consumers and the producers of their food.

Yet, one of the most interesting contemporary characteristics of alternative food networks is how they are now thoroughly *transgressed* – i.e. invaded, crossed-over, mixed-up and colonized – into, by and with conventional food economic geographies.[9] No longer is Fair Trade only available at dusty charity shops or through mail-order, nor is organic food defined by dirty, wilted, holey lettuce sold to and by 'beards and sandals' types. Rather, both fairly traded and organic food has become thoroughly mainstream and, as quality has increased and been accentuated over time, prominently displayed and sold in almost every supermarket chain. This is particularly the case in the UK as many have worked to improve their green and 'local-farmer-friendly' credentials to consumers. Both Fair Trade and organic products are now very much the provenance of middle- and upper-class consumers concerned with food quality and food's qualities. Yet, as Wal-Mart/Asda[10] begins to expand its own-label brand of organic products as well as its product lines for Fair Trade goods, price conscious consumers might very well become the new 'growth' segments for these markets.

How do we better account for and theorize these continuing and growing transgressions of the alternative and mainstream (for example, Kneafsey et al., 2008; Holloway et al., 2007)? Specifically, how do we account for the novel 'power geometries' (Massey, 1993) in alternative foods and their governance and how will this begin to change over time as they get even more deeply entrenched in conventional and unequally powerful networks? What is the scope for, and possibilities of, even newer 'alternatives' – perhaps organic farmer cooperatives, consumer-led organic cooperatives (Little et al., 2010), or even the expansion of alternative provisioning networks such as food boxes and farmers' markets – to form in response to further supermarket 'capture' of organic and Fair Trade markets? More generally, what scope is there in economic geography to talk about these processes of transgression? This issue has been raised in *Alternative Economic Spaces* (Leyshon et al., 2003a), but little has focused specifically on consumption and consuming processes (but cf.

Hughes et al., 2008; see also Chapter 20) related to these transgressions or the role of consumers as thinking, feeling and doing agents. Thus, building on the arguments in the chapter, what are the ways in which alternative food consumption is shifting some of the economic geographies of food?

One way that this might be seen to be happening in interesting ways involves the development of new modes of governance in Fair Trade networks. But these new modes are not just in relation to more conventional networks but also with respect to 'normal' and historically-constituted Fair Trade commodity chains. Here, portions of two companies – Divine Chocolate initially (see Doherty and Meehan, 2006; Doherty and Tranchell, 2005; Tiffen, 2002), but now also OKé USA Bananas[11] – are actually *owned* by the farming cooperatives from which the cacao and bananas are respectively sourced. This is what the 'OKé difference' means:

An OKé banana and a Not OKé banana are two different things.

For starters, OKé growers own 50% of the company – this ensures they receive an OKé wage, along with OKé living and working conditions. These guys don't ride in the back of stretch limos but they do get to enjoy the fruits of their labors, and rightly so. But . . . you ask, what's inside that ripened OKé banana skin for me? Well, the answer is the knowledge you've got yourself a banana that shows some respect for the person who produces it and the environment it's produced in – and that will make it taste better than any other banana you've ever tasted. Believe me. (OKé USA, 2008)

This shift in ownership and Fair Trade governance is promising in that ownership of at least one portion of the means of production – in the form of the company buying, shipping and selling the Fair Trade bananas – might have lasting transformative and powerful political potential. How far these governance regimes might spread and/or consolidate market power remains to be seen, but at least they define a novel space of hope in the typically very unequal regimes of economic power and ownership between North and South.

WATCH THIS (FOOD) SPACE: TOWARDS VISCERAL ECONOMIC GEOGRAPHIES OF FOOD

As David Harvey (1990) laments in one of his most famous writings, the grapes sitting on your store shelves are silent and so cannot speak to you about where, who and by whom – and especially for Harvey – through what processes of social and environmental exploitation they were produced. In the two decades since he wrote about these 'silent grapes', academics, journalists and others have taken up this charge and started to speak for various commodities, especially food, through various forms of innovative analyses. Indeed, now many of the commodities – and especially quality foods – have started to tell these stories about themselves as a selling point and in response to consumers' growing and continuing unease about where their foods come from.

In the round, though, in economic geography, these engagements with commodities – and I would argue in economic geography as a field more generally – have focused on the processes and networks of production. The grapes are beginning to speak, but they are telling only a part of the story; in short, the politics and process of the economic geographies of consumption have remained relatively over-shadowed and under-examined. And yet, as I have argued here, for analytical as well as political reasons considerations of consumption and consumers should be up-front and centre – stage. And this is especially the case in the study of food. At the very least, it may be possible to explore how the shifting concerns of consumers to more 'ethical' consumption via Fair Trade and organic products, for example, are constructing, transgressing and politicizing novel and existing economic geographies, whilst, at the same time, these concerns are partial, limited and limiting in their bids to make food networks more sustainable.

In food studies, some inspiring and interesting work along these lines has begun (for example, Cook et al., 2004; Cook and Harrison, 2003). Yet much more theoretical and empirical work remains to be done, especially on transgressive spaces of food where the 'alternative' is thoroughly mixed up with more conventional and powerful networks. Indeed, going into a Wal-Mart/Asda store to buy organic carrots and/or Fair Trade coffee thoroughly problematizes what might stand as food politics in contemporary societies and suggests that these politics might be much 'dirtier' than many (for example, Guthman, 2007a, b) would like. In addition, it is my hope that the embeddedness, knowledge and networks of power in, and the visceralities of, food might inform work on the economic geographies of, food, and 'transgress' into research and writing on other commodities, economic geography more generally.

There is one line of work, however, that is a 'must': uncovering and understanding the continuing and now accentuated inequalities of who eats what, how much, why and where. If I had to eat dirt for breakfast, I would want to know first of all, why, but then what the hell to do about it. And, here, we must not let those working on and in alternative food networks off the hook: uncovering inequalities in food consumption is not just a question about quantity, but also about the inequalities inherent in food quality and qualities and the structures that work to construct these inequalities. Thus, exploring the limits to but also the spaces opened up by alternative food networks and economic geographies – I have to hope – can serve only to make more hopeful food geographies in a continuingly unequal world.

Now, let's see . . . what's for lunch?

NOTES

1 Many thanks to David Goodman, Ian Cook, Mike Raco, Clare Herrick, Rob Imrie, and Catherine Dolan for their critical and encouraging comments on this chapter. Thanks also to Roger Lee and Andrew Leyshon for their support and patience in crafting these rather messy thoughts into something resembling coherence.

2 In rather simplistic terms, this contemporary 'crisis' – unlike those food 'crises' in the past which were crises of food production (i.e. too little) and access resulting in the Green Revolution – is one generated specifically by the unequal geographies of food consumption, and particularly the new Northern demands of 'environmentally friendly' bio-fuels and grains to the expanding middle-classes of India and China. Clearly, rises in oil prices are also to blame.

3 ADM and Cargill are large multinational, agro-food corporations, each controlling substantial portions of the global trade in all sorts of food-stuffs from basic grains to ingredients to 'finished' foods; for more on these two corporations, see Hendrickson and Heffernan (2002). For an account of the corporate control of the food system, see the excellent *End of Food* (Roberts, 2008).

4 This is one of the key contributions that Robert's *The End of Food* (2008) also attempts to make; to gain access to the author speaking about this point, see The Commonwealth Club (2008).

5 These reconnections are most often designed for some combination of environmental and/or socio-economic friendliness in the provisioning of organic foods or in foods that are marketed and sold directly to consumers (for example, farmers' markets) to allow farmers to capture more of the value of their products. For work directly related to the connections made in Fair Trade networks, see Goodman (2004).

6 The campaign has partnered with some of 'the world's most iconic brands' such as American Express, Dell Computers, Microsoft, Apple and Gap so that a portion of the (RED)-sanctioned purchases of particular products by 'responsible' consumers go to promote AIDS campaigns and development in Africa. As some of the promotional material states 'The Result? You have a new iPod and you helped save a person's life' (see http://www.joinred.com/red/); now, what could be wrong with that?!

7 For more on thinking about these complex corporeal metabolisms that haunt food, see Fitz Simmons and Goodman (1998).

8 Four firms – Asda (16%), Morrisons (11%), Sainsbury's (16%), and Tesco (31%) – have a dominant 75% of the UK market for all grocery sales (Cabinet Office, 2008).

9 Indeed, the fate of the organic market is very much attached to the cost of conventional food and that of oil. As the price of 'regular' food and petrol rises, there is less income available for consumers to buy quality foods and so these markets suffer (Naughton, 2008). In a way, then, organic food markets and their 'health' have been very much tied to the 'cheap' food and fuel policies of much of the North.

10 Asda is wholly owned and operated by US multinational retailer Wal-Mart.

11 See http://www.okeusa.com/

REFERENCES

Allen, P. (2004) *Together at the Table: Sustainability and Sustenance in the American Agrifood System*. University Park: Pennsylvania State University.

Bakker, K. (2007) The 'commons' versus the 'commodity': Alter-globalization, anti-privatization and the human right to water in the global south. *Antipode*, 39: 430–55.

Bakker, K. and Bridge, G. (2006) Material worlds?: Resource geographies and the 'matter of nature'. *Progress in Human Geography*, 30(1): 5–27.

Barnett, C., Cloke, P., Clarke, N., and Malpass, A. (2005) Consuming ethics: Articulating the subjects and spaces of ethical consumption. *Antipode*, 37: 23–45.

Bevir, M. and Trentmann, F. (eds) (2007) *Governance, consumers and Citizens: Agency and Resistance in Contemporary Politics*. Basingstoke: Plagrave Macmillan.

Blair, D. (2008) Food prices are rocketing all over Europe. Telegraph, 31 May. Accessed: http://www.telegraph.co.uk/news/uknews/20055502/All-over-Europe-food-prices-stay-high-A-bombshell-in-the-shopping-basket.html

Blythman, J. (2004) *Shopped: The Shocking Power of British Supermarkets*. London: Fourth Estate.

Braun, B. and Castree, N. (eds) (1998) *Remaking Reality: Nature at the End of the Millennium*. London: Routledge.

Cabinet Office. (2008) Food: An analysis of the issues. Available: http://www.cabinetoffice.gov.uk/strategy/work_areas/food_policy.aspx

Coe, N., Kelley, P., and Yeung, H. (2007) *Economic Geography: A Contemporary Introduction*. London: Blackwell.

Coe, N., Dicken, P. and Hess, M. (2008) Introduction: Global production networks—debates and challenges. *Journal of Economic Geography*, 8: 267–69.

Commonwealth Club (2008) The end of food (Paul Poberts), June 18, Available: http://www.commonwealthclub.org/archive/08/08–06roberts-audio.html and http://wordforword. publicradio.org/programs/2008/06/27/

Cook et al. (2004) Follow the thing: Papaya. *Antipode* 36, 642–64.

Cook et al. (2006) Geographies of food 1: Following, *Progress in Human Geography*, 30(5): 655–66.

Cook, I. and Crang, P. (1996) The world on a plate: Culinary culture, displacement, and geographical knowledges. *Journal of Material Culture*, 1: 131–53.

Cook, I. and Harrison, M. (2003) Cross over food: Re-materializing postcolonial geographies. *Transactions of the Institute of British Geographers* 28, 296–317.

Crang, P. (2008) Consumption and its geographies. In P. Daniels, M. Bradshaw, D. Shaw and J. Sidaway (eds) *An Introduction to Human Geography: Issues for the 21st Century*, pp. 376–98. Harlow: Pearson.

Crewe, L. (2000) Geographies of retailing and consumption. *Progress in Human Geography*, 24(2): 275–90.

Daviron, B. and Ponte, S. (2005) *The Coffee Paradox: Global Markets, Community Trade and the Elusive Promise of Development*. London: Zed Books and CTA.

Doherty, B. and Meehan, J. (2006) Competing on social resources: The case of the day chocolate company in the UK confectionery sector. *Journal of Strategic Marketing*, 14: 299–313.

Doherty, B. and Tranchell, S. (2005) New thinking in international trade?: A case study of the day chocolate company. *Sustainable Development*, 13: 166–76.

Eden, S., Bear, C. and Walker, G. (2008a) Mucky carrots and other proxies: Problematising the knowledge-fix for sustainable and ethical consumption. *Geoforum*, 39: 1044–57.

Eden, S., Bear, C. and Walker, G. (2008b) Understanding and (dis)trusting food assurance schemes: Consumer confidence and the 'knowledge fix'. *Journal of Rural Studies*, 24: 1–14.

Feagan, R. (2007) The place of food: Mapping out the 'local' in local food systems. *Progress in Human Geography*, 31(1): 23–42.

FitzSimmons, M. and Goodman, D. (1998) Incorporating nature: Environmental narratives and the reproduction of food. In B. Braun and N. Castree (eds) *Remaking Reality: Nature at the Millennium*. London: Routledge. pp. 194–220.

Freidberg, S. (2003a) Cleaning up down South: Supermarkets, ethical trade and African horticulture. *Social and Cultural Geography*, 4(1): 27–43.

Freidberg, S. (2003b) Not all sweetness and light: New cultural geographies of food. *Social and Cultural Geography*, 4(1): 3–6.

Freidberg, S. (2004a) *French Beans and Food Scares: Culture and Commerce in an Anxious Age*. Oxford: Oxford University Press.

Freidberg, S. (2007) Supermarkets and imperial knowledge. *Cultural Geographies*, 14(3): 321–42.

Getz, C. and Shreck, A. (2006) What organic and fair trade labels do not tell us: Towards a place-based understanding of certification. *International Journal of Consumer Studies*, 30(5): 490–501.

Gibson-Graham, J.K. (2006) *A Post-capitalist Politics*. Minneapolis: University of Minnesota Press.

Goodman, D. (1999) Agro-food studies in the 'age of ecology': Nature, corporeality, bio-politics. *Sociologia Ruralis*, 39: 17–38.

Goodman, D. (2002) Rethinking food production-consumption: Integrative perspectives. *Sociologia Ruralis*, 42(4): 271–77.

Goodman, D. (2003) The quality 'turn' and alternative food practices: Reflections and agenda. *Journal of Rural Studies*, 19: 1–7.

Goodman, D. and DuPuis, M. (2002) Knowing and growing food: Beyond the production-consumption debate in the sociology of agriculture. *Sociologia Ruralis*, 42(1): 6–23.

Goodman, D. and Goodman, M. (2007). Localism, livelihoods and the 'post-organic': Changing perspectives on alternative food networks in the United States. In D. Maye, L. Holloway and M. Kneafsey (eds) *Constructing Alternative Food Geographies: Representation and Practice*, pp. 23–38. Oxford: Elsevier.

Goodman, D. and Goodman, M. (2008). Alternative food networks. In R. Kitchin and N. Thrift (eds) *International Encyclopedia of Human Geography*. Oxford: Elsevier.

Goodman, M. (2004) Reading fair trade: Political ecological imaginary and the moral economy of fair trade foods. *Political Geography*, 23(7): 891–915.

Goss, J. (1999). Consumption. In P. Cloke, P. Crang and M. Goodwin (eds) *Introducing Human Geographies*, pp. 114–22. London: Arnold.

Granovetter, M. (1985) Economic action and social structure: The problem of embeddedness, *American Journal of Sociology*, 91(3): 481–510.

Guthman, J. (2003) Eating risk: The politics of labeling transgenic food. In R. Schurman and D. Kelso (eds) *Engineering Trouble: Biotechnology and its Discontents*, pp. 130–51. Berkeley: University of California.

Guthman, J. (2004) *Agrarian Dreams?: The Paradox of Organic Farming in California*. Berkeley: University of California Press.

Guthman, J. (2007a) Commentary on teaching food: Why I am fed up with Pollan et al. *Agriculture and Human Values*, 24: 261–64.

Guthman, J. (2007b) The polyanyian way?: Voluntary food labels and neoliberal governance. *Antipode*, 39: 456–78.

Harrison, J. (2008) Confronting invisibility: Reconstructing scale in california's pesticide drift conflict. In M. Goodman, M. Boykoff and K. Evered (eds) *Contentious Geographies: Environment, Meaning, Scale*. Aldershot: Ashgate. pp. 115–30.

Harrison, J. and Wolf, S. (2008) Introduction to symposium-charting fault lines in US agrifood systems: What can we contribute? *Agriculture and Human Values*, 25: 147–49.

Harrison, R., Newholm, T., and Shaw, D. (eds) (2005) *The Ethical Consumer*. London: SAGE.

Hartwick, E. (1998) Geographies of consumption: A commodity chain approach. *Environment and Planning D: Society and Space*, 16: 423–37.

Hartwick, E. (2000) Towards a geographical politics of consumption. *Environment and Planning A*, 32(7): 1177–92.

Harvey, D. (1990) Between space and time: Reflections on the geographical imagination. *Annals of the Association of American Geographers*, 80: 418–34.

Hendrickson, M. and Heffernan, W. (2002) Opening spaces through relocalization: Locating potential resistance in the weaknesses of the global food system. *Sociologia Ruralis*, 42(4): 347–69.

Hess, M. (2004) 'Spatial' relationships?: Towards a reconceptualization of embeddedness. *Progress in Human Geography*, 28(2): 165–86.

Hinrichs, C. (2000) Embeddedness and local food systems: Notes on two types of direct agricultural markets. *Journal of Rural Studies*, 16: 295–303.

Holloway, L. and Kneafsey, M. (2004) Producing-consuming food: Closeness, connectedness and rurality in four 'alternative' food networks. In L. Holloway and M. Kneafsey (eds) *Geographies of Rural Cultures and Societies*. Aldershot: Ashgate. pp. 262–82.

Holloway, L., Kneafsey, M., Cox, R., Venn, L., Dowler, E. and Tuomainen, H. (2007). Beyond the 'alternative'–'conventional' divide?: Thinking differently about food production-consumption relationships. In D. Maye, L. Holloway and M. Kneafsey (eds) *Alternative Food Geographies: Representation and Practice*, Oxford: Elsevier. pp. 77–93.

Hudson, R. (2005) *Economic Geographies: Circuits, Flows and Spaces*. London: SAGE.

Hughes, A., Wrigley, N. and Buttle, M. (2008) Global production networks, ethical campaigning and the embeddedness of responsible governance. *Journal of Economic Geography*, 8: 345–67.

Jackson, P. (1993) Towards a cultural politics of consumption. In J. Bird, B. Curtis, T. Putnam, G. Robertson and L. Tickner (eds) *Mapping the Futures: Local Cultures, Global Change*. London: Routledge. pp. 207–28.

Jackson, P. (1999) Commodity cultures: The traffic in things. *Transactions of the Institute of British Geographers 24*, 95–108.

Johnston, J. and Baker, L. (2005) Eating outside the box: Foodshare's good food box and the challenge of scale. *Agriculture and Human Values*, 22: 313–25.

Kirwan, J. (2006) The interpersonal world of direct marketing: Examining quality at UK farmers' markets. *Journal of Rural Studies*, 22: 301–12.

Kneafsey, M., Holloway, L., Cox, R., Dowler, E., Venn, L., and Tuomainen, H. (2008) *Reconnecting Consumers,*

Producers and Food: Exploring Alternatives. Oxford: Berg.

Krippner, G. (2001) The elusive market: Embeddedness and the paradigm of economic sociology. *Theory and Society*, 30: 775–810.

Lawson, V. (2007) Geographies of care and responsibility. *Annals of the Association of American Geographers*, 97(1): 1–11.

Lean, G. (2008) Profiteers squeeze billions out of growing global food crisis. *The Independent UK*, 5 May. Available: http://www.alternet.org/workplace/84382/

Lee, R. (2006) The ordinary economy: Tangled up in values and geography. *Transactions of the Institute of British Geographers*, 31(4): 413–32.

Leyshon, A., Lee, R. and Williams, C. (eds) (2003a) *Alternative Economic Spaces*. London: SAGE.

Leyshon, A., Lee, R. and Williams, C. (2003b) Introduction: Alternative economic spaces. In A. Leyshon, R. Lee, and C. Williams (eds) *Alternative Economic Spaces*. London: SAGE. pp. 1–26.

Little, R., Maye, D. and Illbery, B. (2010) Collective purchase: Moving local and organic foods beyond the niche market. *Environment and Planning A*, 42: 1797–813.

Lockie, S. and Goodman, M. (2006) Neoliberalism and the problem of space: Competing rationalities of governance in fair trade and mainstream agri-environmental networks. In T. Marsden and J. Murdoch (eds) *Between the Local and the Global: Confronting Complexity in the Contemporary Agri-food Sector*. Oxford: Elsevier. pp. 95–120.

Lyon, S. (2006) Evaluating fair trade consumption: Politics, defetishization and producer participation. *International Journal of Consumer Studies*, 30(5): 452–64.

Magdoff, F., Foster, J. and Buttel, F. (2000) *Hungry for Profit: The Agribusiness Threat to Farmers, Food and the Environment*. New York: Monthly Review Press.

Massey, D. (1993) Power-geometry and a progressive sense of place. In J. Bird, B. Curtis, T. Putnam, G. Robertson and L. Tickner (eds) *Mapping the Futures: Local Cultures, Global Change*. London: Routledge. pp. 59–69.

Maye, D., Holloway, L. and Kneafsey, M. (eds) (2007) *Alternative Food Geographies: Representation and Practice*. Oxford: Elsevier.

McMichael, P. (2000) The power of food. *Agriculture and Human Values*, 17: 21–33.

Moberg, M. (2005) Fair trade and eastern Caribbean banana farmers: Rhetoric and reality in the anti-globalization movement. *Human Organization*, 64(1): pp. 4–15.

Morgan, K., Marsden, T. and Murdoch, J. (2006) *Worlds of Food: Place, Power, and Provenance in the Food Chain*. Oxford: Oxford University Press.

Mutersbaugh, T. (2002) The number is the beast: A political economy of organic-coffee certification and producer unionism. *Environment and Planning A*, 34: 1165–84.

Naughton, K. (2008) Natural response: As prices of organic foods rise, plain old fruits and vegetables suddenly look better. *Newsweek*, 12 May. Available: http://www.newsweek.com/id/135377

OKé USA. (2008) The OKé difference. Available: http://www.okeusa.com/profile_unauth.php?des=Sales

Pollan, M. (2006) *The Omnivore's Dilemma*. New York: Random House.

Pred, A. (1998) The nature of denaturalized consumption and everyday life. In B. Braun and N. Castree (eds) *Remaking Reality: Nature at the End of the Millennium*. London: Routledge. pp. 150–68.

Probyn, E. (2000) *Carnal Appetites: Food, Sex, Identities*. London: Routledge.

Raynolds, L., Murray, D. and Wilkinson, J. (eds) (2007) *Fair trade: The Challenges of Transforming Globalization* London: Routledge.

Renard, M. (2005) Quality certification, regulation and power in fair trade. *Journal of Rural Studies*, 21: 419–31.

Roberts, P. (2008) *The End of Food*. Boston: Houghton Mifflin.

Sayer, A. (1997). The dialectics of culture and economy. In R. Lee and J. Wills (eds) *Geographies of Economies*. London: Arnold. pp. 16–26.

Sayer, A. (2001) For a critical cultural political economy. *Antipode*, 33: 687–708.

Schlosser, E. (2001) *Fast Food Nation: The Dark Side of the All-American Meal*. Boston: Houghton Mifflin.

Seyfang, G. (2005) Shopping for sustainability: Can sustainable consumption promote ecological citizenship? *Environmental Politics*, 14(2): 290–306.

Silverstein, K. (2008) Let them eat dirt: Multinationals reap benefits of commodity crisis. *Harper's Magazine*, 21 May. Available: http://harpers.org/archive/2008/05/hbc-90002975

Smith, D. (2000) *Moral Geographies: Ethics in a World of Difference*. Edinburgh: Edinburgh University Press.

Sonnino, R. and Marsden, T. (2006) Beyond the divide: Rethinking relationships between alternative and conventional food networks in Europe. *Journal of Economic Geography*, 6: 181–99.

Spurlock, M. (2004) *Super Size Me*. Showtime Networks Inc.

Tiffen, P. (2002) A chocolate-coated case for alternative international business models, *Development in Practice*, 12(3 & 4): 383–97.

Valentine, G. (1999) A corporeal geography of consumption. *Environment and Planning D: Society and Space*. 17: 329–51.

Whatmore, S. (1995) From farming to agribusiness: The global agro-food system. In R. Johnston, P. Taylor, and M. Watts (eds) *Geographies of Global Change: Remapping the World in the Late Twentieth Century*. Oxford: Blackwell. pp. 36–49.

Whatmore, S. and Clark, N. (2006) Good food: Ethical consumption and global change. In N. Clark, D. Massey, and P. Sarre (eds) *A World in the Making*. Milton Keynes: The Open University. pp. 363–412.

Whatmore, S. and Thorne, L. (1997) Nourishing networks: Alternative geographies of food. In D. Goodman and M. Watts (eds) *Globalising Food: Agrarian Questions and Global Restructuring*. London: Routledge. pp. 287–304.

Wrigley, N., Coe, N., and Currah, A. (2005) Globalizing retail: Conceptualizing the distribution-based transnational corporation (TNC). *Progress in Human Geography*, 29(4): 437–57.

Uneven Development: Geographies of Economic Growth and Decline

17

Geographies of Economic Decline

Ray Hudson

INTRODUCTION

In this chapter I want to focus upon the ways in which economic geographers – and others – sought to come to terms with uneven development, geographies of economic decline and the de-industrialization that blighted both national and, more specifically, many regional economies from the later 1960s and to review the sorts of explanations that they constructed in the 1970s and 1980s. Such changes were integrally linked to changes in geographies of production and the emergence of new spatial divisions of labour, at varying spatial scales (see Chapter 5). Thus the empirical context for the chapter is the industrial decline in many of the former 'workshops of the world' of industrial capitalism – such as the 'old' industrial regions and city-regions/conurbations (for convenience, referred to as 'regions' in what follows) of the mid-West and north east of the USA, north east England, south Wales and central Scotland in the UK, Nord-Pas de Calais in France, the Ruhr in Germany, Wallonia in Belgium and so on – the list is a long one – as one facet of changing international and intra-national divisions of labour.

Such changes in the economic well-being of regions posed two sorts of problems. First, they posed challenges for policy makers, charged with responsibilities to regenerate these regions and secure their economic future. Such policy makers struggled to find solutions to the problems posed by industrial decline, not least because of a failure to understand the reasons for rapid shifts in the economic health of regions and the processes underlying these changes. Second, economic geographers concerned to understand the changing geography of regional economic growth and decline quickly realized the inadequacies of much of the theoretical developments of the 1950s and 1960s (such as neo-classically inspired location theories that assumed away the problems of uneven development and the need to account for them – for a contemporary summary, see Hamilton, 1967; see also Chapters 1–3) in providing a basis for understanding such changes. On the other hand, engagement by some economic geographers (such as Keeble, 1967) with the work of economists like Hirschman (1958) and Myrdal (1957) concerned with disequilibrium and core-periphery relations provided a much more promising entry point to considerations of uneven development, growth and decline. This raised questions as to how to construct more powerful explanations of uneven development – not least for those who sought to advise policy makers seeking to address the problems of decline. It is these explanatory and theoretical questions that are the main focus of concern in this chapter (see also Chapter 8).

EXPLAINING DE-INDUSTRIALIZATION AT THE NATIONAL SCALE, TACKLING DE-INDUSTRIALIZATION AT THE REGIONAL SCALE

As the UK had emerged as the first major capitalist industrial economy, it was perhaps no surprise that it was the first major national economy to experience significant de-industrialization, beginning in the 1960s but accelerating in the 1970s. It is worth noting that de-industrialization can be defined in various ways, with differing implications as to the social distribution of resultant gains and losses in terms, for example, of falling shares of manufacturing employment or output, or absolute declines in manufacturing employment or output. For the moment, however, these definitional differences will be ignored, drawing on the evidence of absolute decline in manufacturing employment and (from 1973) manufacturing output. This led initially to three differing accounts that sought to explain national de-industrialization (see Rowthorn, 1986) which, by implication, would also be relevant to other industrialized countries in the fullness of time.

The first of these was the Maturity Thesis, which located manufacturing decline within the framework of a general theory of historical development and structural change. This envisaged the UK as the first country to reach the state in development known as 'maturity', in which the share of manufacturing in total employment begins to fall. This in itself was taken to explain why the decline in manufacturing employment began earlier in the UK than in other major capitalist economies, and why it was more pronounced there. The second was the Trade Specialisation Thesis, which suggested that manufacturing

decline in the UK was simply a consequence of the UK's changing position in the international division of labour as a consequence of the growing importance of non-industrial trade since the early 1950s. The third can be termed the Failure Thesis, seeing manufacturing decline as a symptom of economic failure, of a growing failure of industrial production in the UK to compete internationally or to produce the output required for a prosperous and fully-employed economy. One consequence of the absolute decline in manufacturing employment was that demand for services was depressed, so that service activities grew more slowly than they might otherwise.

There are several points that can be made about these three differing explanations. First, they are cast at the level of the national economy and, while there are undoubted differences at the national scale in patterns of economic growth and decline, the pattern of de-industrialization was strongly regionally differentiated. Second, they refer specifically to manufacturing rather than industrial employment more generally – and the effect of including the decline of activities such as coal mining is sharply to reinforce the regionally-differentiated pattern of de-industrialization. If only by implication, the service sector (recognizing that this is a rather imprecise concept) is seen as of little import. Third, there is at best a weak and implicit consideration of the interplay of corporate strategies and state policies in explaining the sectorally and regionally differentiated pattern of de-industrialization, of understanding the relationships between disinvestment and the decline of some industries and fresh investment in industries new to these places. In short, any consideration and conceptualization of causal process is at best weak and thin.

One implication of these national level accounts is that regional de-industrialization could be seen as a consequence of changes in the international division of labour, albeit mediated by central government policies, such as those towards the public sector and nationalized industries (such as coal, steel and shipbuilding: for example, see Beynon et al., 1991; Hudson, 1989) and key sectors of private sector manufacturing (such as chemicals and engineering: for example, see Beynon et al., 1994). While there are undoubted links between changes at international and intra-national scales, to regard the latter as simply a consequence of the former is too simplistic (a point elaborated below). Nonetheless, as a result of the perceived connection between international and intra-national changes, some academics and policy makers initially saw the changing international division of labour that gave rise to regional economic problems as also offering a potential solution to the problems of regional de-industrialization by offering possibilities for new forms of regional re-industrialization. Thus, the initial policy response to the decline of 'old' industries was to seek to attract branch plant investment in 'new' industries to address regional problems (see Chapter 25). There was a belief that this would provide long-term – if not permanent-solutions to the problem of regional de-industrialization via re-industrializing in this way.

Such policies were not particularly new, however, since there was a long history of seeking to promote inter-regional and indeed international re-location of industry, initially within the UK and subsequently in most advanced capitalist economies. Moreover, they had had, at best, limited success in the past in alleviating regional problems. What was new was the increasingly heavy emphasis upon attracting branch plant investment by multi-national companies (MNCs) located outside the UK, informed by a belief that the national state could shape the economic development trajectories of peripheral and problematic regions for the better via the financial incentives of regional policies. This turned out to be a not wholly unproblematic solution, however, since it meant that key functions in the capitalist division of labour (such as high level decision making and control, R&D and advertising and marketing) were absent from these regions. The consequence was the creation of externally-controlled branch plant economies, characterized by a diversity of industries but a homogeneity of routine stages of production, global outposts vulnerable to closure in times of economic decline or simply when they reached the end of their economically useful lives to the parent company. In short, by the early 1980s it was becoming clear that the 'solution' was in fact simply a new form of the problem as capital flight accelerated, with MNCs now cast as the new villain of the piece. This suggested that policy makers needed to be informed by much more sophisticated understandings of regionally-concentrated economic decline and that economic geographers needed to develop more powerful theoretical accounts, which might inform practice and, possibly, provide a basis to underpin more effective policies.

CAPITALISM AND UNEVEN DEVELOPMENT, I: THE RE-DISCOVERY OF MARXIAN POLITICAL ECONOMY

What these changes were making increasingly clear was the need for a more sophisticated understanding of the dynamics of industrial (dis)investment and the relationships between corporate strategies and priorities and regional development strategies and priorities and, more generally, patterns and processes of geographical uneven development. There was a visible tension between corporate and regionally-based and defined interests – no longer could it be assumed that what was good for corporate interests was necessarily appropriate as the basis for regional development policies. More specifically and immediately, it was evident that there was a need to get beyond descriptions of MNC behaviour and moralistic critiques of 'bad' MNCs to a deeper understanding of the processes giving rise to regionally uneven growth and decline.

After some exploration of using ideas from dependency theory and theories of underdevelopment at a national scale to understand intra-national uneven development (for example, see Carney et al., 1976), economic geographers increasingly focused on Marxian analyses of the inner dynamics of the capitalist mode of production (that is, the particular combination of social relations and technologies that defined capitalist economies *as* capitalist) and the structural context, specific imperatives and constraints of the political-economy of capitalist development. This was part of a more general re-discovery of the Marxian tradition in the social sciences from the 1960s. Economic geographers interested in issues of uneven development, of the growth of some regions juxtaposed alongside the decline of others, thus began to explore the ways in which Marxian approaches could deepen understanding of these issues, seeing uneven development as genetically-encoded within capitalist social relations. It is also worth noting that other social scientists were also paying increasing attention to issues of spatially uneven development as part of this re-invigoration of Marxian scholarship (for example, see Poulantzas, 1978, especially pp. 92–120). Indeed, some specifically identified the centrality of intra-national uneven development and the production of 'regional problems' to the accumulation process. For example, Ernest Mandel (1968: vol.1, p. 373) argued that 'unevenness of development as between different parts of a single country' is an essential pre-condition for capital accumulation and that its significance had been greatly under-estimated in previous Marxian analyses. This cross-disciplinary and cross-national interest was important in enriching the debate within geography, not least as Marxian analysis was generally more powerfully developed outside the Anglo-American speaking world.

Without doubt, the outstanding figure in this exploration of Marxian approaches to uneven development within geography was David Harvey; indeed, his magisterial *The Limits to Capital* (1982) was less of an exploration and more of a reconstruction of an historical-geographical materialism that developed Marxian approaches in significant ways (for a re-consideration of this book,

which confirms its lasting value to economic geographers, see Castree et al., 2004). In the course of this, Harvey located the issue of regional uneven development and geographies of economic growth and decline squarely in the context of a Marxian political-economic analysis of capitalist economies and more specifically in relation to his 'third cut' at crisis theory and the integration of uneven development into the theory of crisis. Uneven development was no longer seen as an unfortunate by-product of capitalist development, but as integral to the crisis-prone process of capitalist development. As he explained:

> Our task is to construct a 'third cut' at crisis formation which specifically acknowledges the material qualities of social space as defined under capitalist relations of production and exchange. The first cut theory of crisis . . . dealt with the underlying source of capitalism's internal contradictions. The 'second-cut' theory examined temporal dynamics as these are shaped and mediated through financial and monetary arrangements. The 'third-cut' theory . . . has to integrate the geography of uneven development into the theory of crisis. The task is not easy. We have to deal somehow with multiple, simultaneous and joint determinations. . . . This lack of unique determinations makes theorization difficult. (Harvey, 1982; 425)

In short, capitalist development was conceptualized as necessarily and unavoidably uneven, simultaneously encompassing regions of growth alongside those of decline, with former regions of growth becoming regions of decline and vice-versa. This insistence that capitalist development was dynamic, with an open-ended trajectory rather than a known equilibrium end-point, with some regions flipping between trajectories of growth and decline, and with the result that there could never be even development, had some momentous implications. First, it came as a major theoretical challenge to much of economic geography (and indeed mainstream economics), premised on assumptions of static equilibrium. Second, it came as a major challenge to policy makers who believed that problems of spatially concentrated economic decline could be solved via an appropriate policy mix. Third, and perhaps most significantly, politically it emphasized that capitalist economies and societies were unavoidably characterized by inequality, socially as well as spatially, raising questions as to how such chronically unequal economies and societies could be reproduced. But this is to anticipate.

Within a Marxian framework, production of profits through the production of commodities results from a company bringing together fixed, constant and variable capital (more concretely, machinery in factories, raw materials of various sorts and other manufactured inputs to production, and workers) in a specific location. For capital, the point of production is to produce profits via organizing work in such a way that the commodities produced have a greater value than the inputs needed to produce them. As the only source of new value creation is the living labour of workers (since the value embodied in constant and fixed capital is simply transferred to the new commodities in the course of production), this requires that work and the labour process be organized in particular ways. This is necessary so that surplus-value – that is, the difference between the value of inputs and outputs and the basis of profits – is produced in sufficient quantity in specific workplaces.

Production is always, in this sense, place-specific – so that the cessation of production and the devalorization of capital always has place-specific effects as companies become bankrupt or shift production between locations in search of profits and survival. Perhaps Harvey's key insight, therefore, in the context of understanding geographies of economic decline was to recognize that the devalorization of capital is central to the coercive processes of capitalist competition and capital accumulation, and that devalorization is always, necessarily, place-specific. 'Devalorization' in this context may refer to the physical destruction of factories, machinery and the means of production but more often refers to the fact that companies simply cease to produce in a particular location as they shift production – and capital – to a more profitable location. The physical assets of plant and machinery remain as material artefacts but

they no longer function as fixed capital, while the company no longer lays out constant capital (on raw materials or manufactured components, for example) or variable capital (to purchase labour-power via hiring workers on the labour market). Thus, as a result of a company closing production in a particular region, people lose their jobs from its factories, other companies that supplied that company lose markets and maybe also shed labour, local service companies that provided goods and services to those employed in these factories experience falling sales and so they too may shed labour . . . and so on in a locationally-concentrated spiral of decline.

However, Harvey emphasized that companies do not simply face a choice between locations in seeking greater profits but also a choice between locational and technological change. As he puts it (1982: 390): 'Capitalists can individually hope to acquire relative surplus value for themselves – excess profits – by adopting superior technologies or seeking out superior locations. A direct trade-off exists, therefore, between changing technology or location in the competitive search for excess profits'. Changes in the technology of production may be a strategy for maintaining production in a particular place whilst changing location may be a strategy for maintaining the viability of a particular production technology. However, it could equally well be a strategy to enable a new and radically different production technology and associated labour process to be introduced by moving to a location in which people lack experience of such work (such people are often referred to as 'green labour', lacking either experience of industrial work in general or of work in a particular industry). Put another way, while the introduction of new technologies (with or without change in location) is always informed by a strategy of relative surplus-value production, re-locating an existing technology to a cheaper production cost location centres on the production of absolute surplus-value. In these ways, processes of uneven development are reproduced whilst geographies of production are altered, often radically.

In summary then, Harvey emphasized that both the place-specific establishment and ending of production are central to the economic geographies of capitalist growth and decline. He emphasizes that 'the production of spatial configurations is necessarily an active moment in the dynamics of accumulation' (ibid., 440). As he was very well aware, understanding just why production takes place where it does within the social relations of capital is a non-trivial issue, so that (1982: 388), '[t]he location of production under capitalism is a very intricate affair subject to multiple determinations'. However, it is only fair to point out that Harvey himself tended to emphasize a trade-off between locational and technological choices and did not go far beyond this in seeking to elaborate why particular forms of production were established in particular places. In this sense, his exploration of the 'multiple determinations' was deliberately limited as he tended to develop his argument via making 'some drastic simplifying assumptions' (ibid., 425) in recognition of the complexity of these multiple determinations – for example, in terms of the dichotomy between location and technology. In addition, and relatedly, while recognizing that the production of spatial configurations is an active moment in the accumulation process, he pays limited attention to the particular characteristics of particular places as formative elements in these shifting economic geographies of uneven development.

CAPITALISM AND UNEVEN DEVELOPMENT, II: SOCIAL RELATIONS OF PRODUCTION AND SPATIAL DIVISIONS OF LABOUR

While Harvey's work was an unrivalled intellectual achievement, and enormously increased understanding of processes of uneven development within capitalist relations of production, it centred on an analysis of capitalist development and uneven development at quite a high level of abstraction – necessarily and

unavoidably so, since he wished to locate this in terms of Marxian political-economy and its value-theoretic approach. As such, it incorporated a strong sense of regionally differentiated growth and decline, of why some regions grew whilst others declined and why some that had once been centres of the accumulation process were now peripheral to it. However, he had less to say about precisely how these processes unfolded in particular places, and indeed upon how the socially-produced character of these places itself helped shape that unfolding.

One of the first attempts to specify in more detail particular corporate strategies and mechanisms of place-specific job destruction was that by Doreen Massey and Richard Meegan (1982), who identified three analytically-separate forms of production re-organization that led to employment decline in manufacturing firms: intensification; rationalization; and technical change. Different forms of re-organization were characteristically found in different sectors. Intensification refers to changes designed to increase the productivity of labour but without major new investment or substantial reorganization of production techniques: in short, it involves workers working harder and longer to increase productivity and output. Rationalization involves a simple reduction in total capacity – with companies making choices as to where to cut capacity, for example on the basis of relative productivities between plants. Technical change refers to job loss as a result of significant investment, often related to changes in production techniques – that is, job shedding investment. The first strategy prioritizes the production of absolute surplus-value, the second seeks to raise profitability by devalorization of fixed capital without altering production technologies (although the threat of closure typically enables companies to increase absolute surplus-value production), while the third focuses on the production of relative surplus-value. In practice, a company could well be deploying all three strategies simultaneously.

Massey was subsequently to elaborate upon these insights in her major work *Spatial Divisions of Labour: Social Structures and the Geography of Production* (1984). In this, as the title suggests, her prime concern was understanding the ways in which the social relations of capitalist production and of different functions within that process were distributed over space – indeed, in being allocated between locations, these functions actually defined social space – and how this led to differential regional growth and decline.

> The overall argument of this book is that behind major shifts between dominant spatial divisions of labour within a country lie changes in the spatial organization of capitalist relations of production, the development and reorganization of what we shall call spatial structures of production. Such shifts in spatial structures are a response to class relations, economic and political, national and international. Their development is a social and conflictual process; the geography of industry is an object of struggle. The world is not simply the product of capital's requirements. Partly for that reason, and for others – technical and organisational characteristics of an industry, for instance – the range of spatial structures is wide. Together they produce a particular form of spatial patterning of society – an overall spatial division of labour. . . . [N]ew spatial divisions of labour represent whole new sets of relations between activities in different places, new spatial patterns of social organisation, new dimensions of inequality and new relations of dominance and dependence. Each new spatial division of labour represents a real, and thorough, spatial restructuring. There is more than one kind of 'regional problem'. (Massey, 1984:7–8)

It is important to acknowledge that Massey emphasizes the conflictual character of the processes through which the spatiality of the economy is established and, thereby, the significance of power relations, agency and practice – collective and not just individual – in the construction of economic geographies. As she puts it (ibid., 85) '[s]patial structures are established, reinforced, combated and changed through political and economic strategies and battles on the part of managers, workers and political representatives'. Nor are such struggles confined to the boundaries of national territories. While she was mainly concerned with the distribution of activities within the territory of the national state, this was clearly understood as part of a broader international geography of capitalist production, exchange and trade (for example, see Fröbel et al., 1980). Moreover, Massey emphasized that uneven development was not simply a product of social processes and an active moment in the dynamics of accumulation but that the character of place had a formative influence upon those same processes. As such, spatial divisions of labour were both a product of capitalist development but also simultaneously helped shape the form of that development and the dynamics of the accumulation process.

Consequently, Massey sought to link two sets of issues – one concerned with production and social class (drawing heavily, but not exclusively, on the work of Wright, 1978), the other with spatial organization, seeking to extend much of the existing literature on geographies of employment by relating the spatial distribution of jobs to the geographical organization of relations of production. She emphasized that the social structure of the economy and the social relations of production necessarily develop spatially 'and in a variety of forms' (Massey, 1984: 68) and that spatial structures and organisational forms are co-determining. She argues strongly that '[I]t is important to stress that there *is* a whole variety of ways in which capitalist production can be organized geographically and great variety in the way in which the relations of production can be structured over space' (ibid., 68). This insistence upon a variety of spatial forms is crucial (and links back to Harvey's point about multiple determinations and the lack of a unique determination). In many ways, Massey's work can be understood as an attempt to throw light upon this complexity, further to unravel these multiple determinations and better to understand precisely why some activities and functions were located in some places but not in others, why some places experienced economic growth and others decline as a result of corporate decisions about capital (dis)investment.

Given this potentially enormous variety of spatial forms, Massey (like Harvey in focusing upon the trade-offs between location and technology) sets out a number of exemplary simplified structures. She focused upon three of these: locationally concentrated spatial structures, with no intra-firm hierarchies and all stages of the production process in the same location; cloning branch plant spatial structures; and part-process spatial structures. The latter two are both characterized by intra-firm hierarchies, by the location of different functions and activities within the firm in different places. However, whereas the second has cloned branch plants in a variety of locations, the third is characterized by different production functions (for example component production and the assembly of components into final products) in different places. These intra-firm hierarchies have two distinct components. The first is the spatial organization of the technical division of labour in terms of elements of the process of production, with a spatial separation of mental and manual labour and of work with different levels of skill and knowledge (for example, R&D in some regions, skilled manual work in others and unskilled or deskilled work in yet others). The second is the spatial organization of relations of ownership, possession and control. Massey makes the important point that differences between locations may well have influenced both the need for such hierarchies as well as the form that they have taken and have been a stimulus to the development of particular technical divisions of labour in such a way as to be able (literally) to exploit these locational differences (ibid.,74).

Importantly, she stresses that these three examples are 'fairly simple cases' and that these 'clear forms' are unlikely to be found very often in 'the real world'; furthermore, she is at pains to emphasize that 'the intention is not to set off a search for them' (ibid.,76) – a stricture that others subsequently have not always heeded (see Chapter 25). However, Massey's work also indicated the ways in which particular types of region might become the location of particular industries and/or particular stages in production processes, and that many would be vulnerable as a result of bankruptcy, corporate decisions to close capacity, or to switch the location of routine production functions on the basis of production cost differentials. Thus regional economic decline could reflect a variety of processes, depending on the types of industry and function found in a region. Once again, the place-specificity of devalorization, in conjunction with the specifics of particular corporate strategies, becomes of central importance.

Regions characterized by industries in which all the functions of firms were co-located could suffer decline in output and employment due to the bankruptcy of those firms – or employment loss as a result of these firms switching activities with a low skill content to cheaper production locations while keeping higher order functions in the 'home' region. Some regions in which cloned branch plants were located could suffer loss of output and employment due to intra-firm competition between regions – some 'win' as others 'lose'. Such cloned branch plants are particularly vulnerable to closure when firms are faced with over-capacity and seek to bring productive capacity more in line with market demand. Similarly regions that were the location of component production or assembly within corporate organizational structures of part-processing could experience loss of employment and output as some existing plants were kept open while others were closed – or all existing plants making a particular component close as production is moved to a new region. In contrast to cloned branch plants, however, closure of a plant in a part-process structure will have knock-on implications for other plants – both those that supply it and those that form markets for its products. These examples by no means exhaust the variety of possible reasons for regional economic decline as a result of changing corporate locational preferences but they do indicate the variety of reasons and processes that may underlie observed decline in regional economies.

Massey was particularly anxious to clarify issues relating to branch plants, regional dependence and regional economic decline, illustrating the point by drawing distinctions between regions with cloned branch plants and those that were part of part-process organizational structures. She emphasizes that there are significant differences *between* these two spatial structures. In both, branch plants are subject to external ownership and control, 'but in the part-process structure, where there is both a managerial hierarchy and geographical separation of stages of production, regions 'lower down' the hierarchy will be subject to both external ownership and production dependence, and the effects of these two forms of subordination are very different' (ibid., 101). Again, the point is that this difference is only one example of the ways in which corporate organizational structure and regional vulnerability to different forms of economic decline may interact. Regional economic fortunes are thus subject to corporate (dis)investment strategies that are subject to the strongly disciplining effects – if not quite iron laws – of market competition.

Finally, it is worth pointing out that at around the same time as Massey was developing her ideas about geographical structures of production and spatial divisions of labour, Alain Lipietz was coming to essentially similar conclusions on the basis of analyses of the spatial structure of the French economy (for example, see Lipietz, 1977) and indeed Massey acknowledges his work. Recognizing that the former distinction between Paris and 'the French desert' was no longer adequate for understanding the emergent spatial structures of the French economy, Lipietz arrived at a three-fold classification of regions within part-processing structures that reflected the differential distribution of functions and activities within the capitalist division of labour – R&D in the Paris region, skilled manufacturing in others and unskilled manufacturing in different regions. Lipietz (1978) also extended his analysis to spatial structures within service activities, the first analysis to do so. His work

again made it abundantly clear why some regions would be prone to economic decline whilst others (in the French case, especially Paris) would continue to prosper (albeit on the basis of intra-regional uneven development). However, it was not until Lipietz's work began to be translated into English (see Lipietz, 1980) that it began to have a wider influence, an influence that burgeoned as he expanded his concerns to the international as well as intra-national divisions of labour (for example, see Lipietz, 1987) – an instructive example of issues of translation and the situations in which ideas will 'travel'.

REFLECTIONS AND CONCLUSIONS

Certainly the path-breaking contributions of Harvey and Massey (and indeed Lipietz) deepened understanding of processes of uneven development within capitalism, and specifically of processes of regional economic decline, in significant ways. Although their starting points are rather different, Harvey and Massey essentially come to similar conclusions about regional uneven development and regional economic decline. Companies use and create regional uneven development as an integral part of their competitive strategies. Seeking to lower production costs by introducing new technologies of production and radically new ways of working in existing industrial regions typically leads to job loss there. Productive capacity remains but at the price of employment decline. Alternatively, a company may seek to lower production costs by switching location. In this case, both capacity and jobs disappear. Such spatial switches in the location of production can constitute a 'weak' form of competitive strategy (that is, one that focuses on lowering the cost of production of mature commodities), designed to maintain 'old' ways of producing by moving them to lower cost base locations – and as a result often abandoning the 'old' industrial regions in which they had formerly been located. However, spatial switches can also be linked to the introduction of new technologies and a search for new locations with more attractive labour market conditions in which radical changes in ways of working can be more easily introduced (for example, because they have less unionized and/or militant workers unused to industrial work). For some time, the search for new locations has been global rather than intra-national, resulting in an endless scouring of the globe for cheaper production cost locations and/or shifting investment to emerging markets (for example, see Dicken, 2004). The net result is 'capital flight' from 'old' industrial regions in former core areas of capitalist production. At the same time, these regions are unsuitable as locations for 'strong' competitive strategies – that is, investment in innovative new products for which competition is based on aspects such as quality and originality rather than simply cost – for this sort of strategy is one that is typically present in core rather than in peripheral regions, which lack appropriate 'hard' and 'soft' infrastructures. Although regional policy makers seek to make these regions attractive to new 'knowledge-based' activities via a range of inducements, their efforts meet with, at best, limited success (Hudson, 2010). In this way, processes of uneven development are reproduced and the economic composition and functions of regions qualitatively differentiated, whilst geographies of production are altered, often radically.

While there were – and still are – very considerable strengths in the approaches set out by Harvey and Massey in the 1980s, both also have their limitations. These were in part self-imposed as they were seeking to set out ways of thinking about and understanding capitalist economic geographies, and as a result emphasized certain aspects while ignoring others in developing their theoretical perspectives. They were not seeking to give a comprehensive account of contemporary capitalist economic geographies but rather to specify the conceptual basis of and tools for such accounts to be developed. Harvey's analysis was developed at a high

level of abstraction as he sought to delineate 'the limits to capital' and establish that uneven development was, as it were, genetically encoded in capitalist relations of production. As he made clear in a brief 'Afterword' many issues to do with the role of the state, forms of organization of capital, institutions and culture, for example, were left under-developed as a result. Massey was more concerned to explore the relationships between the variety of socio-spatial forms that capital could adopt and the constitutive and formative role of spatial difference in these processes. However, she too had surprisingly little theoretically to say about the state, especially given her emphasis upon the significance of the national territory and the national state as the prime political regulator of that space. While there are, for example, references to Bob Jessop's work, his important theoretical contribution (1982) on the capitalist state finds no mention. Furthermore, Massey paid comparatively little attention to issues such as out-sourcing and sub-contracting, mergers and acquisitions or strategic alliances and joint ventures and their implications for uneven regional growth and decline. Even so, let there be no doubt that their contributions remain of great value to contemporary economic geographers seeking to understand issues of uneven development and geographies of economic decline.

The last two or so decades since the appearance of these canonical works by Harvey and Massey have witnessed considerable change in economic geography. Not least, both have continued to develop their own work in innovative ways (for example, see Harvey, 1989, 1996: Massey, 1994, 2005; Allen et al., 1998). In addition, other economic geographers have led the way in the exploration of a variety of approaches including evolutionary economics, institutional approaches to the social sciences, regulationist accounts and the (so-called) 'cultural turn' (which are discussed elsewhere in this handbook – see especially Chapters 3 and 8 – and so are not discussed further here, although see Hudson, 2001, 2004, 2005). In many ways these can be seen as responses to the approaches advocated by Harvey and Massey. In some cases this has involved attempts to elaborate and build on their work by more fine-grained analyses of uneven development and the socio-spatial organization of the economy, in others to put forward alternative and competing approaches.

There has been much work that has sought to understand the ways in which regions are produced as socio-spatial ensembles, with particular (unique) characteristics and the ways in which these relate to regions being incorporated into, and expelled from, circuits of capital and the accumulation process. Others have emphasized the role of knowledge and learning as the basis for regional economic success and the revival of depressed regional economies (see Chapter 18). There has also been increasing emphasis upon understanding the variety of corporate strategies, in exploring the rich variety of process, product and organizational innovations through which firms seek competitive advantage through strategies of 'weak' and 'strong' competition, of the ways in which firms both sub-contract production and form a variety of joint ventures or strategic alliances with other firms as part of organizational strategies, and the way in which companies seek to produce and use spatial difference in the production of profits (for a fuller discussion, see Hudson, 2001). As a result, there is now a more comprehensive knowledge of the 'how', 'what' and 'where' of production and a deeper understanding of the relations between corporate policies, regional development strategies and regional economic decline.

However, much of the work in economic geography in the last 15–20 years on both firms and regions has come to focus upon particular firms, industries or regions, giving 'thick descriptions' and often more powerful understanding of the specificities of particular cases. In the course of this, however, they have frequently lost meaningful connection with the broader political-economy in which these firms and regions are located and lack the sort of systemic perspective which the pioneering work of Harvey and Massey brilliantly opened up and elaborated. In short, while having much to say about the 'how', 'what' and 'where', typically this is at best loosely connected to the 'why' of capitalist production – an issue that was central to work of Harvey and Massey (and that of Lipietz) and a proper understanding of the evolving geographies of capitalist economies.

There is, therefore, much to be gained and learned from returning to this work and the systemic perspectives that it provides on issues of uneven development and economic decline. Failure to acknowledge the broader political-economic perspective that such work puts forward can lead to a serious underestimation in development strategies of the difficulties of regions escaping from marginalization and re-positioning themselves *vis a vis* the main circuits of capital in the global economy. Crucially, there are grave dangers in ignoring the sort of perspective developed by Harvey, Massey and Lipietz that sees the process of capitalist development as combined *and* uneven through time and over space. For this can lead to a dangerous idealism that suggests that economic decline can be reversed by simply transferring the experiences and institutional and organizational forms characteristic of (temporarily) economically successful regions to economically less successful 'problem regions' so that all regions can be successful in a 'win win' world. This way of thinking is both theoretically inadequate and politically dangerous and as such something that should be avoided at all costs.

REFERENCES

Allen, J., Cochrane, A. and Massey, D. (1998) *Re-thinking the Region*. London: Routledge.

Beynon, H., Hudson, R., and Sadler, D. (1991) *A Tale of Two Industries*. Milton Keynes: Open University Press.

Beynon, H. Hudson, R., and Sadler, D. (1994) *A Place Called Teesside*. Edinburgh: Edinburgh: University Press.

Carney, J.G., Hudson, R., Ive, G., and Lewis, J., (1976) Regional underdevelopment in late capitalism: A study of North East England. In I. Masser (ed.) Theory and practice in regional science. *London Papers in Regional Science*, No. 6, Pion, London. pp. 11–29.

Castree, N., Essletzbichler, J. and Brenner, N. (Convenors) (2004) Symposium: David Harvey's *The Limits to Capital*: Two decades on. *Antipode*, 36: 401–549.

Dicken, P. (2004) *Global Shift* (4th edn). London: SAGE.

Fröbel, F., Heinrichs, J. and Kreye, O., (1980) *The New International Division of Labour*. Cambridge: Cambridge University Press.

Hamilton, I. (1967) 'Models of industrial location.' In R.J. Chorley, and P. Haggett (eds). *Models in Geography*. London: Methuen. pp. 361–424.

Harvey, D. (1982) *The Limits to Capital*. Oxford: Blackwell.

Harvey, D. (1989) *The Condition of Post-modernity*, Oxford: Blackwell.

Harvey, D. (1996) *Justice, Nature and the Geography of Difference*. Oxford: Blackwell.

Hirschman, A. (1958) *The Strategy of Economic Development*. New Haven.

Hudson, R. (1989) *Wrecking a Region*. London: Pion.

Hudson, R. (2001) *Producing Places*. New York: Guilford Press.

Hudson, R. (2004) Conceptualizing economies and their geographies: Spaces, flows and circuits. *Progress in Human Geography*. 2: 447–470.

Hudson, R. (2005) *Economic Geographies*. London: SAGE.

Hudson, R. (2010) From knowledge-based economy to . . . knowledge-based economy? Reflections on changes in the economy and development policies in the North East of England. *Regional Studies*. 44, (in press).

Jessop, B. (1982) *The Capitalist State*. Oxford: Martin Robertson.

Keeble, D. (1967) 'Models of economic development.' In R.J. Chorley and P. Haggett (eds), *Models in Geography*. London: Methuen. pp. 243–302.

Lipietz, A. (1977) *Le Capital et Son Espace*. Paris: Maspero.

Lipietz, A. (1978) La Dimension Régionale du development du Tertiaire. *CEPREMAP Report Number 7801*, Paris.

Lipietz, A., (1980) The structuration of space, the problem of land, and spatial policy. In Carney, J., Hudson, R. and Lewis, J. (eds) *Regions in Crisis*. Croom Helm. Beckenham. pp. 60–75.

Lipietz, A. (1987) *Mirages and Miracles*. London: Verso.

Mandel, E. (1968) *Marxist Economic Theory*, vol. 1. London: Merlin.

Massey, D. (1984) *Spatial Divisions of Labour: Social Structures and Spatial Divisions of Labour*. London: Macmillan.

Massey, D. (1994) *Space, Place and Gender*. Cambridge: Polity.

Massey, D. (2005) *For Space*. London: SAGE.

Massey, D. and Meegan, R. (1982) *The Anatomy of Job Loss*. London: Methuen.

Myrdal, G. (1957) *Economic Theory and Underdeveloped Regions*. London: Methuen.

Poulantzas, N. (1978) *State, Power, Socialism*. London: New Left Books.

Rowthorn, B. (1986) De-industrialisation in Britain. In R. Martin and B. Rowthorn (eds) *The Geography of De-industrialisation*. London: Macmillan. 1–30.

Wright, E.O. (1978) *Class, Crisis, State*. London: New Left Books.

18

Geographies of Economic Growth I: Industrial and Technology Regions

Nick Henry and Stuart Dawley

INTRODUCTION

For a period of some two decades beginning around the 1970s, the leading nations and regions of the world economy experienced dramatic economic upheaval as the 'golden age of Fordist capitalism' faltered. In turn, the world map of economic geography was re-made as the industrial heartlands of, principally, the USA and Western Europe experienced sustained and dramatic job loss and their associated (industrial) conurbations were decimated as people and jobs left the cities. As cities hollowed out, and suburbs expanded, the characteristic urban pattern of Burgess's concentric rings was transformed: the increasingly dilapidated CBD (Central Business District) was surrounded by swathes of now redundant and derelict factory buildings (or 'brownfield sites') and the 'zones of transition' exploded (literally in rioting) as the 'inner city problem' was born.

And yet, by the first decade of the twenty-first century, it was hard to imagine (or even see) this picture of the Western industrial city at the heart of the industrial region. The inner city, or at least pockets of it, still remained but was increasingly hidden away amongst the shopping malls, clubbing zones of the night time economy, waterside developments and prestige apartment blocks of regenerated and revitalized cities. 'City living' was back (for those able to choose in the first place) and city breaks were in.

To a great extent, the city living architecture of re-fashioned warehouse apartments and skyscrapers was driven not by the making of physical goods but by the economic dynamics of the service sector; for example, the financial and business services and the act of consumption in its many retail and leisure guises. For some, the rise to dominance of these sectors has led to arguments for the post-industrial city, but it is still the case that wealth creation is being driven also by a new set of high value-added manufacturing activities (for example, biotechnology, software, performance engineering, specialist consumer goods, etc.) and many of the city living occupants are the flexible, knowledge workers of these new sectors of growth. And it is these industrial and technology sectors, and their distinctive geographies of districts, clusters and regions, which is the subject of this chapter. Or put another way, just as economic geographers were coming to terms theoretically with the geography of decline, so a new geography of economic growth was in the making before their very eyes – once again setting new challenges to geographers in identifying and understanding the form and function of the economy.

In this chapter we review some of the explanations for the new industrial regions (or spaces) and their characteristic geographies. The chapter begins by identifying those socio-economic processes (such as technological change) which were commonly argued to be driving a new era of capitalism (the knowledge-driven economy) and, with this, the formation of a new global economic geography. The bulk of the chapter reviews the range of theories put forward to explain a new geography of districts and clusters – a geography of access to specialist knowledge and learning rather than access to raw materials, land and energy. Moreover, what this chapter also seeks to stress is that these theories were the product of trained (groups of) individuals – theorists and researchers – creating stories about the economic change that unfolds before our eyes. Following a review of the more dominant theories or stories of economic geography, the chapter ends by drawing attention to the continued diversity of new economic geography and its theories.

UNDERSTANDING GEOGRAPHIES OF ECONOMIC GROWTH

In trying to understand the new geography of economic growth, a range of analytical descriptions has been put forward by economic geographers across the world (for example, post-industrial, post-Fordist, industrial divides, techno-economic paradigms, flexible accumulation, etc.). These descriptions reflect at least two aspects:

- that theory-making, especially in times of newness or uncertainty, and within certain standards of methodological rigour, is a process of competitive trial, error and perspective across a (cross) disciplinary community of scholars, commentators and policymakers; and
- that each alternative and often overlapping description represents an attempt to capture and combine those economic processes (or drivers or factors) that best explain why the economy, and its geography, is developing as it is.

On the first point of theory-making, the process can be described as the creation of 'stories' about what is taking place (but by those trained in the art of story making – for example, researchers – and using certain key tools of the trade – for example, concepts and evidence). Moreover, it is important that the 'place' of these theorists is recognized. For example, this chapter opened by describing the 1970s decline of Western cities and regions. Yet much of this decline was driven by the first stirrings of contemporary economic globalization – when the creation of the New International Division of Labour saw large tranches of manufacturing from Western Europe moving to the Newly Industrializing Countries (NICs) such as Taiwan, Thailand and the Philippines. For theorists in the West this was the geography of decline; for those focusing on the NICs this was a story of new geographies of growth (and one which has continued with the continued expansion of what has been termed the Newer International Division of Labour and the arrival of a new set of NICs such as Indonesia and Bangladesh). Indeed, and highlighting the historical specificity of much theory making or storytelling, the current story of growth revolves around the so-called BRIC economies (Brazil, Russia, India and China).

On the second point of competing analytical descriptions (or stories), what can be highlighted is that most stories of the contemporary economy in what was previously labelled the developed world have drawn upon a common set of drivers of economic growth, including:

- *Globalization:* the integration of more and more parts of the globe in to capitalist production and markets and the increasing speed, ease and normality of economic flows (money, labour, materials, information, etc.) across national borders;

- *Technological change:* the rise of information and communication technologies (ICTs) and their transformational power – particularly the compression of time/space – across economic and social processes;
- *New patterns of market demand and consumption:* characterized by differentiation (customized, segmented, niche, lifestyle) and speed of change (for example, ever shortening product life cycles);
- *Knowledge and innovation:* the capacity to generate new ideas, products and services in the face of global competition, technological change and fast-moving, differentiated markets; and
- *The resurgence of agglomeration and the re-emergence of the region:* the uneven process of globalization leading to the concentration of economic activity (spatial agglomeration) in particular spaces across the globe variously described as districts, clusters and learning regions.

Furthermore, and the subject of the next part of this chapter, what has also unified many of the recent theorizations of economic change is *how* they have sought to explain how these processes of economic change have created, and are creating, new geographies of the economy. In essence, a pluralistic body of economic geographical thought has been defined drawing on an eclectic range of theories and concepts of social and economic change – from science and technology studies through the range of social sciences (including the new discipline of business and management) to issues of culture, language and text drawn from the humanities.

THE NEW GEOGRAPHIES OF ECONOMIC GROWTH: INDUSTRIAL DISTRICTS, KNOWLEDGE CLUSTERS AND GLOBAL NETWORKS

Drawing, then, on a widespread recognition of common processes of change, a range of theories/stories have been put forward over the last 15 years or so to both describe, and

explain, the new global economic geography. Those outlined here focus in the main on the geographic transformations which have occurred in (Western) Europe and North America and which have been identified as emblematic of the leading edge of capitalist economic development.

New industrial spaces

In 1988, Allen Scott outlined probably the first comprehensive description of the emergent geographies of economic growth – what he described as the New Industrial Spaces. Scott (1988) identified three types of space:

- *New Industrial Districts:* dense agglomerations of, normally, small and medium-sized firms specializing in the high-quality production of a particular good or service (such as shoes, textiles, ceramics, furniture, etc.). The archetypal example of the time was the set of Italian industrial districts known as the Third Italy;
- *High Technology (sunbelt) Areas:* a diverse range of technopoles, corridors and innovative complexes, often in previously unindustrialized areas, growing through their 'capture' of the 'sunrise' high technology industries (for example, biotechnology, computers, R&D). The most famous example is Silicon Valley but virtually every country in the world has subsequently 'found' its sunbelt area – including the UK's Western Crescent/M4 Corridor; the Golden Banana of Spain/Italy; Ile de France Sud; Taedok Valley, Korea; and Medicon Valley, Scandinavia (see Box 18.1);
- *Flexible Production Enclaves within Old Industrial Regions:* a diverse set of examples of hotspots of economic development in the regions and cities at the centre of the previous geographies of economic decline; for example, the film industry of Los Angeles (Hollywood) or the fashion industry in Paris.

Importantly, Scott highlighted how these three types of areas were all outcomes of a common process of change – the re-agglomeration of production – and he went on to theorize how this re-agglomeration was happening. Scott argued that the changing nature of the economy (globalization, speed-up,

Box 18.1   Medicon Valley, Öresund Region, Scandinavia

The Öresund Region, comprising Skane in Sweden and Zealand, Lolland, Falster and Bornholm (including Copenhagen) in Denmark, has a population of 3.5 million – one-third of this population is on the Swedish side and two-thirds on the Danish. The region is connected by the Oresund railway and motorway bridge completed in 2000. Comprising employment of some 41,000 in life sciences, including 5,000 researchers across a range of specialisms, Medicon Valley is one of the top three European destinations for life-science investment projects.

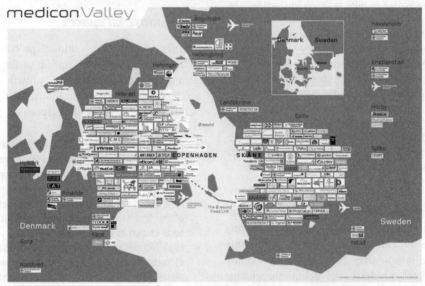

Source: http://www.mediconvalley.com/images/MV-map2007_Msjaelland_FINAL_LOW.jpg

flexibility, customization, etc.) was driving geographical concentration and the rise of districts and high-tech areas. The key mechanism of this was what he called the 'transaction costs thesis'. Simply put, to meet the competitive demands of producing high value goods in the twenty-first century requires producers to continually improve products, processes, skills, technology, etc. – and to do so quickly and flexibly. This has led to a greater tendency of firms to meet these demands through working together rather than trying to do everything 'in-house'. Firms have expanded their input-output activities and this implies more external linkages and transactions (meetings, supplies, ideas, etc.) with a shifting array of partners. Each of these transactions have a cost which increases over distance – so the answer is to locate close to the array of potential partners and suppliers, i.e. agglomeration. As Scott (1988:177) explained:

> The greater the spatial dispersion of producers, the more onerous these costs will be. The immediate consequence is that selected sets of producers with particularly elevated intragroup interaction costs will tend to converge around their own geographical centre of gravity and thus to engender definite nodes of economic activity on the landscape . . . Hence, via the play of centripetal locational adjustment, external economies of scale (a non-spatial phenomenon) are eventually transmuted into and consumed in the specifically spatial form of agglomeration economies.

The result is the array of New Industrial Spaces – economic nodes of production – within a globalized production system.

New Industrial Districts (NIDs)

During the 1980s and 1990s, as the major industrial regions of Europe went through the substantial pain of deindustrialization and decline, analysis of economic growth rates across the regions of Europe highlighted the remarkable and sustained growth of the North Eastern and Central part of Italy. Previously not known for its industrial capacity – in comparison to the declining regional manufacturing heartland of Northern Italy and the lagging region and branch plant economy of the South ('the Mezzogiorno') – explaining the growth of what became known as the Third Italy became the centre of attention for theorists of regional development (Becattini, 1987; Camagni, 1991; Amin and Robins, 1990). In particular, it became the centre of attention for Italian economists and geographers who outlined how a series of small towns and districts had become the centres of international production for a range of specialized and high quality goods such as ceramics, leather goods, clothing, and specialist machinery. Moreover, this industrial phenomenon was based on dense networks of small and medium-sized enterprises, a size of enterprise which had been increasingly labelled as 'economic history' in the face of the global march of the mass production, and extremely large, multi-national corporation during the previous Fordist era.

Of particular theoretical significance was these theorists' return to the work of the economist Alfred Marshall on explaining why spatial agglomeration occurs. Originally writing in the late nineteenth and early twentieth centuries to explain British industrial districts such as the Sheffield steel industry, Marshall provided a set of key factors driving agglomeration. He highlighted how groups of small, locally owned firms drew on the collective resources of their district for their industrial competitiveness. Substantial trade across the supply chain of these districts occurred and drove further specialization of supply inputs delivered locally. Similarly, a skilled and local labour pool of workers geared to the industry developed and, more broadly, the local infrastructure (transport, property, services, education, training, etc.) became attuned to, and supportive of, the particular needs of the local industry. Taken

together, Marshall argued how these processes developed an industrial atmosphere in which 'the industry is in the air'; that is, exists in such a way that local life understood, revolved around and supported the particular requirements of the local industrial specialism. Agglomeration economies – in terms of cost advantages – were gained by individual firms in the location both because of this specialist supportive environment for the industry (localization economies) and, potentially, where districts were identified in larger urban areas through the economic concentration of different industries together (urbanization economies).

The New Industrial Districts of the Third Italy exemplified these processes in operation once again in contemporary times and, indeed, the detailed work on the Italianate (range of Italian) industrial districts expanded and 'updated' the basic theoretical concepts of Marshall. In particular, this work showed the active development of district resources through co-operation amongst industrialists, unions, local and regional policymakers, etc., such as shared technical centres, training activity and supportive regulatory regimes. In some senses, then, this work identified the active construction of 'industry in the air' by local institutions and governance regimes and, in turn, contributed to a new strand of explanation in economic geography. Known as the institutionalist perspective (Amin, 1999; Martin, 2000), this work encapsulates a broader explanatory recognition of the social embeddedness of economic activity (Granovetter, 1985). Overall, the NIDs served to exemplify the rediscovery of the impact of agglomeration economies and a form of industrial structure – dense networks of small and medium-sized companies – that had been viewed as a historical and theoretical backwater in terms of understanding the contemporary economy.

Yet, just as geographers of the West could have been accused of sidelining the growth of the Newly Industrializing Countries (or, indeed the economic transformations of post-socialist Eastern Europe), so some of the stringent claims for the SME (small and medium sized) enterprise networks of the Italian industrial districts as *the* new industrial archetype were shown to be somewhat exaggerated. However, their theoretical insights around what was causing localized concentrations of production in an avowedly global world were used more broadly to understand the 'stickiness' of a range of places which were experiencing sustained economic growth, including through multinational investment, branch plants and satellites (Markusen, 1996).

Untraded interdependencies: the pathway to innovative and learning regions

In 1995 Michael Storper articulated how geographers' interest in the re-agglomeration of production and the 'resurgence of the region' was being mirrored across the social sciences through a general recognition of the significance of the region to the organization of economic life. This resurgence was compared to the previous weight given to the 'national' scale of the economy (debates still rage about the relative weight of influence of different spatial scales including, for example, the global, macroregional and the local and the multi-scalar nature of the organization of economic life, see Peck, 2002).

Storper reviewed much of the work of economic geographers and social scientists (such as that on new industrial spaces and industrial districts). Drawing on this review, he proposed a further development in understanding the re-agglomeration of production or, more broadly, and as he termed it, the territorial economy. In this he meant, quite simply, the continual challenge to explain the ever present issue of why firms and economic activity choose to locate in certain places (or territories) as against others – and, invariably, at certain times in history in similar types of regions.

Previous work had showed how in an economic era where fast and flexible responses to market demands are required, networks of small firms could continually re-combine their input-output structures to deliver. This generated increased transaction costs and agglomeration could help reduce these costs and, therefore, increase cost competitiveness. Storper accepted this argument but argued it was only part of the explanation. Cost reduction through traded relationships is important but, and in line with a growing body of parallel literature, to compete in the global world of value-added and knowledge-driven capitalism requires innovation and learning in order to produce new innovative products, to identify and respond to new consumption trends, deliver creative and aesthetic solutions, etc. Or put another way, if Fordism was about mass production for mass consumption – the exact same car produced as cheaply as possible so that everyone can have one -knowledge capitalism is about the hundreds of variations of cars you can buy, the myriad additional pieces of technology that are bundled within them (from electronic windows to heated seats to collision avoidance systems), the 'identity' you portray through your consumption choice of brand (shall it be Ford, Ferrari, Skoda, Honda, BMW, etc.?) and the almost continuous launch of new choices within these brands funded by complex financial products. For Storper, the issue was how firms create the capacity to identify, respond to, ride, and even set these trends – for without this capacity they will struggle and survive only by seeking the low cost labour locations of ever far flung places (and with it an inevitable move to low value products). Moreover, how do they deal with the uncertainty and unknowability of trying to read the next technological trend – such as PDAs or 3G Phones – and the next consumer trend – 'my phone is too complicated . . . but, hey, this colour is cool!'.

Storper's answer was '*untraded* interdependencies'; just as we started this chapter talking about theory as 'story-telling by trained story tellers' so it is in business. Which technology? How will it develop? Where can you apply it? Will people buy it?

What will make them buy it? Will it harm the environment? Will it offend people? Will something else take its place? How cost effectively can we make it? What skills will we need? etc., etc. – all these are questions that have to be asked and answered, and in a 'fast moving world' these decisions are a continuous process and once one is made it rebounds on the others. Storper's argument was that we have specialist story tellers in all these spheres – scientists, marketing managers, production engineers, human resources, financiers – and that through them and the firms, universities, trade magazines, professional networks, the social clubs that they make up, they develop conventions, rules, practices, etc. to create 'worlds of production' – essentially, a best guess framework for making decisions about what next product and how to make it in different sectors and parts of the economy.

His point was that just as we talked about 'industry in the air' earlier, so untraded interdependencies and worlds of production were an extension of this – specialist knowledge about the industry looking forwards, gathered from all sorts of channels inside and outside the firm, generally not formally traded or bought (i.e. untraded) and *territorialized*. In other words, certain places are known to create and provide this knowledge; they are local worlds of production. Moreover, if they are leading edge, they may define the world of production for the industry elsewhere. So, think film production, think Hollywood (or perhaps Bollywood); think computer software, think Silicon Valley; think perfume, think Paris; think fashion, think Milan; think finance, think City of London or Wall Street.

Essentially, Storper's work on untraded interdependencies argued that 'localized learning' was as, if not more, important than transaction costs – it is no use making a cheap product if it is old-fashioned, the wrong technology and no-one wants to buy it – especially in a knowledge-driven economy. And in doing so, Storper reflected the beginnings of a major new theoretical pathway in economic

geography; namely, that innovation and learning is the key to regional competitiveness, such economic processes are inherently social and cultural, and that spatial proximity (agglomeration) enhances learning and innovation. In turn, this pathway has led to characteristic descriptions of the new regions of growth as innovative milieux (Camagni, 1995), regional innovation systems (Cooke and Morgan, 1998), learning regions (Florida, 1995) and, ultimately, to knowledge-based theories of spatial agglomeration (Malmberg and Maskell, 2002). According to Florida (1995: 257), for example:

> Regions are becoming focal points for knowledge creation and learning in the new age of global, knowledge-intensive capitalism, as they in effect become *learning regions*. These learning regions function as collectors and repositories of knowledge and ideas, and provide the underlying environment or infrastructure which facilitates the flow of knowledge, ideas and learning. In fact, despite continued predictions for the end of geography, regions are becoming more important nodes of economic and technological organization on a global scale.

In effect, knowledge-based theories of economic location focus on the importance of gaining and using types of knowledge (scientific, craft, aesthetic, organizational, creative, etc.) in production to keep learning, innovating and ahead of your competitors. Within this broader context, a critical distinction is made between codified (or explicit) knowledge and tacit knowledge. Codified knowledge refers to formal systematic knowledge that can be imparted relatively easily – through, for example, operating manuals. Tacit knowledge, in contrast, refers to direct experience, expertise and practical know-how. Using a mobile phone, you might read the manual or just experiment, or ask a friend to show you; you can either read-up on how to ride a bike or just get on it and see what happens!

In terms of geography, the critical distinction which has been made is that codified knowledge is easily transferred – you can access the manual from anywhere through the web – whereas tacit knowledge is much more local, and place-based (such as your friend showing you how). And so, the argument goes, districts and local worlds of production are centres of knowledge production – by universities, by firms, by networks of people, by technical colleges, etc. – and it is the dense interaction of these factors that creates unique combinations of local knowledge that firms can tap in to and use to drive forward innovation, learning and competitiveness. There remains much debate over types of knowledge and their 'fixity' in space and place (with arguments against the crude 'tacit equals local' and 'codified equals global' dichotomy) but, overall, the focus has remained on knowledge, innovation and learning as critical location factors for explaining the spatial configuration of the new economic geographies.

Business clusters

Cluster theory is one of the newest theorizations of the re-agglomeration of production in contemporary economic geography and has, undoubtedly, been one of the most influential. Indeed, its success in international and policy circles has led to claims that this has been a story or theory driven by policymakers with the traditional theorists (that is academics) running to catch up and offer explanations and evidence to policymakers keen to implement this new model of regional development (see, for example, Lovering, 1999). The concept's power is partly attributable to it being associated with the work of one man in particular, Michael Porter of Harvard Business School, and his global consultancy activity. Porter (1998) defines clusters as:

> geographical concentrations of interconnected companies, specialized suppliers, service providers, firms in related industries, and associated institutions (for example, universities, standards agencies and trade associations) that compete but also co-operate. (Porter, 1998: 197)

In many senses, clusters theory is an amalgam of the various concepts and explanations reviewed above. Once defined, Porter argues that clusters drive economic growth based on processes which he encapsulates within the concept of the 'competitive diamond'. The diamond is comprised of four sets of factors:

- *Demand conditions*: generally, successful clusters will supply global markets and at the cutting edge of demand. Put another way, their customers will be highly demanding – wanting and expecting the best – and this demand continually challenges the cluster and its firms to improve;
- *Related and supporting industries*: this is the mass of interconnected firms that make up the geographic concentration (cluster), providing specialist inputs of goods, knowledge and learning through their dense interaction;
- *Factor conditions*: these are the factors of production (land, labour, capital, knowledge, energy, etc) that are brought together within the firm to produce a good. The argument is that these are brought together in a specialist and unique manner conducive to the competitiveness of the cluster. Examples would be specialist labour or the availability of venture capital attuned to the type of industry;
- *Context for firm strategy and rivalry*: the cluster is a dynamic and churning system of firms who compete and collaborate in shifting production networks with, for example, firm births, deaths and takeovers. Being 'in the mix' of this critical mass allows monitoring of rivals, access to industry know-how and, generally, enhanced understanding of the competitive environment. In Storper's terms (see above), you are part of the world of production.

Cluster theory has, literally, been applied all over the world – in developed and developing countries, at international, national, regional and local levels, and across pretty much all sectors imaginable. Indeed, this (mis?)use of the concept to explain virtually any 'concentration of firms in a sector' has led to a questioning of a concept which is seemingly able to explain economic geography *anywhere* (Martin and Sunley, 2003). Nevertheless, the concept has been successfully used to explain a number of new industrial spaces, districts or regions and the theory continues to be developed (see Box 18.2).

Box 18.2   The UK's Motorsport Valley cluster

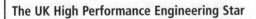

In 1999, it was estimated that 75% of single-seat racing cars used in more than 80 countries across the world emanated from Motorsport Valley. In Formula 1, 7 of the 11 F1 Teams were based in the UK, as was the supply of a third of their engines and three World Rally Championship teams (Henry et al., 2003). Over the decade from 1990 to 2000, the top 50 UK motorsport engineering firms had experienced an (unadjusted) average turnover growth rate of some 523%.

In 2005, the UK motorsport industry was estimated to be worth some £6bn (12% of the global market) and employ over 40,000 employees. Of the four global motorsport championships – F1, A1GP, World Rally Championship (WRC) and World Touring Car Championship (WTCC) – 50% of the constructors/teams continued to be based in Motorsport Valley (Henry et al., 2007).

The cluster continues to evolve through the application of its unique skills to a range of *performance engineering* challenges – whether in satellites, marine engineering, defence or medical instruments (the UK high performance engineering star).

The UK High Performance Engineering Star

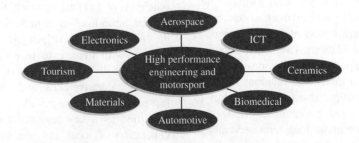

Global networks: knowledge circulation and production

Arguably, the preceding theories we have reviewed coalesce around the importance of the local, on knowledge as a key factor of production and on the socio-economic basis of knowledge production. In turn, in the ongoing process of theory production, recent work within new economic geography has increasingly focused on the 'socio-economic mechanisms' of knowledge production (for example, its production within the firm, between firms or within new forms of firm relationships such as strategic alliances and projects, and production in unison with other economic actors such as universities, unions, trade associations and local political structures). As this work has expanded, it has been argued that work on the geography of economic knowledges has moved beyond the confines of localized learning processes to reflect a more open and diverse understanding of the spatialities and forms of knowledge, learning and innovation (Bryson et al., 2000; Amin and Cohendet, 2004; Hughes, 2007). In particular, three themes have come to the fore: the non- or extra-local dimensions of knowledge production; the array of organizational forms being created in order to achieve new knowledge production; and, the role of key individuals and (mobile) sets of knowledge workers in driving economic development.

Regarding non-local contributions to cluster and district development, for example, authors such as Bathelt et al. (2004) have questioned the extent to which empirical evidence demonstrates that local forms of networking should be deemed more advantageous for the competitiveness of firms and regions than non-local relations. They use the concept of 'global pipelines' to demonstrate how firms establish trans-local relations (transactions, partnerships, research links, etc.) to access 'less familiar bodies of knowledge that could be important for long-term survival and growth. . .(and as a) source of novel ideas and expert insights useful for innovation processes'

(Maskell et al., 2006: 998). These global pipelines have the potential to complement and enrich the cluster's own territorially embedded learning processes and knowledge repositories – termed 'local buzz' – which encompass information flows, gossip, face-to-face contacts, co-locations, etc. As demonstrated in Figure 18.1, the buzz and pipeline perspective take the relations of a cluster beyond the regional scale and emphasise a more open and diverse spatial perspective of knowledge flow. In sum, the value of plugging-in to both local-buzz and global-pipelines is deemed mutually enforcing – local interpretive communities become integrated and enriched with knowledges such as new technological and market related information 'pumped in' from elsewhere.

In parallel, other sets of studies have sought to create a more nuanced understanding of the diversity (and geography) of organizational forms through which knowledge is created, embedded and transferred. Here, studies range from knowledge formation within 'communities of practice' (Wenger, 1998), to the creation of 'temporary firms' around large multinational project networks (for example, see Grabher's (2004) work on global advertising) to the role of international trade fairs and conventions acting as 'temporary clusters' (Maskell et al., 2006).

Moreover, in the move to more network-based forms of production and the bringing together of specialist knowledges to deliver new products and processes, the critical scale of the 'individual' – and the embodied knowledge and talent of people – has been emphasized. Whether acting as the 'animateur' (or lynchpin) of a cluster network, the 'entrepreneurial academic' of a university spin-out, the 'far-sighted Mayor', or the 'serial entrepreneur with finance to invest', the highly geographically mobile cadre of 'knowledge workers', 'creative class' and, ultimately, the fast emerging 'global middle class' has been identified as a key resource for the future generation of local and regional economic growth in the knowledge-driven economy (Pike et al., 2006).

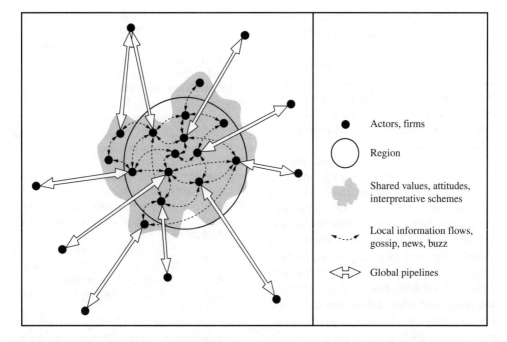

Figure 18.1   Local buzz and global pipelines.

Source: Bathelt et al., 2004: p 46.

DIVERSIFYING GEOGRAPHIES OF ECONOMIC GROWTH?

Having read the preceding sections, you may not believe it, but what has gone before is a highly stylized and simplified gallop through at least two decades of work that is seeking to come to terms with the global economic geography of the industrial and technology regions of today. Our focus has been on the 'new regions' of the so-called advanced economies including their new technologies, sectors and industrial forms. It is argued that these are the driving forces of the new economy, the signifiers of all that is new and what is to come, but these activities are by no means the majority of the economy, and its diverse spaces.

As it stands, what we have told is a story of districts and clusters and millieux and local production complexes, etc. and to a lesser extent of their global connectivity to other parts of the world and other spaces of knowledge. What these economic spaces represent is just part of what is known as the global mosaic of contemporary economic geographies – which is an attempt at a concept to recognize and capture the complexity of economic spaces that now comprise the global economic geography of today and which is reflected across the pages of this book. And what they represent, also, is the high profile end of the spectrum – the success stories of economic growth that policy makers want to emulate, business journalists want to write about, consultants want to peddle and many academics want to visit. What we have provided above is an attempt to chart some pathways through the rich array of material that comprises this caucus of work on the new economic geographies.

Our point here is not to argue that these stories should not be created and told – indeed, at their best they highlight stunning products, meaningful work and high quality lifestyles – but it is to argue that they are just one aspect of the global mosaic. For example, the rise of the local in economic life has also been the story of micro-firms, social enterprises, local economic trading systems and community economies (see, for example, Gibson-Graham, 2005). And, similarly, the expansion of capitalist production into new parts of the globe and the restructuring of multinational production has seen the rapid insertion of new regions and places into global production networks on a scale never previously witnessed (see Dicken, 2007).

This leads us to our second point, that the economy is made both empirically and figuratively. Or in other words, the economy is going-on 'out there' but it is us who choose how to describe it and write about it – what to look at, what to ignore, and whether, for example, the story is of a glass half-full or half empty. Which means, also, that the story of theory development we have just written is both partial and driven by our particular theoretical predilections (indeed, it would be surprising if the editors didn't choose us to write this chapter because we are known for these predilections). It is important – both in terms of a level of arrogance and in not being 'blinded' to new development – that these predilections are recognized. It is important, also, to understand that others have encouraged us, funded us, and provided material for us to tell these stories. There are, in other words, reasons why some stories get told and circulated and others do not – there is a political economy to theory-making and story telling.

REFERENCES

Amin, A. (1999) An institutionalist perspective on regional economic development. *International Journal of Urban and Regional Research*, 23: 365–78.

Amin, A. and Cohendet, P. (2004) *Architectures of Knowledge: Firms, Capabilities and Communities*. Oxford: Oxford University Press.

Amin, A. and Robins, K. (1990) Industrial districts and regional development: Limits and possibilities. In F. Pyke, G. Becattini, and W. Sengenberger (eds) *Industrial Districts and Inter-Firm Cooperation in Italy*. Geneva: International Institute for Labour Studies. pp. 185–219.

Bathelt, H., Malmberg, A. and Maskell, P. (2004) Clusters and knowledge: Local buzz, global pipelines and the process of knowledge creation. *Progress in Human Geography*, 28: 31–56.

Becattini, G. (1987) Introduzione: Il distretto industriale marshalliano cronaca di un ritrovamento. In G. Becattini (ed.) *Mercato e Forze Locali: Il Distretto Industriale*. Bologna: Il Mulino. pp. 7–34

Bryson, J., Daniels, P., Henry, N., and Pollard, J. (eds) (2000) *Knowledge, Space, Economy*. London: Routledge.

Camagni, R. (ed.) (1991) *Innovation Networks: Spatial Perspectives*. London: Belhaven-Pinter.

Camagni, R. (1995) The concept of innovative milieu and its relevance for public policies in European lagging regions. *Papers in Regional Science*, 74: 317–40.

Cooke, P. and Morgan, K. (1998) *The Associational Economy: Firms, Regions and Innovation*. Oxford: Oxford University Press.

Dicken, P. (2007) *Global Shift: Mapping the Changing Contours of the World Economy* (5th edn). London: SAGE; New York: Guilford Press. p. 599.

Florida, R. (1995) Toward the learning region. *Futures*, 27: 527–35.

Gibson-Graham, J.K. (2005) Surplus possibilities: Postdevelopment and community economies. *Singapore Journal of Tropical Geography*, 26(1): 4–26.

Grabher, G. (2004) Learning in projects, remembering in networks? Communality, sociality, and connectivity in project ecologies. *European Urban and Regional Studies*, 11: 103–23.

Granovetter, M. (1985) Economic action and social structure: The problem of embeddedness. *American Journal of Sociology*. 91: 481–510.

Henry, N., Angus, T., and Jenkins, M. (2003) *A Study into the UK Motorsport and Performance Engineering Cluster*. London: DTI.

Henry, N., Angus, T., Aylett, C., and Jenkins, M. (2007) *Motorsport Going Global: The Challenges Facing the World's Motorsport Industry*. Basingstoke: Palgrave MacMillan.

Hughes A. (2007) Geographies of exchange and circulation: Flows and networks of knowledgeable capitalism. *Progress in Human Geography*, 31(4): 527–35.

Lovering, J. (1999) Theory led by policy? The inadequacies of the 'new regionalism' (illustrated from the case of Wales). *International Journal of Urban and Regional Research*. 23: 379–95.

Malmberg, A. and Maskell, P. (2002) The elusive concept of localization economies: Towards a knowledge-based theory of spatial clustering. *Environment and Planning A*, 34: 429–49.

Markusen, A. (1996) Sticky places in slippery space: A typology of industrial districts. *Economic Geography*, 72(3): 293–313.

Martin, R. (2000) Institutional approaches in economic geography. In T. Barnes, and E. Sheppard (eds) *Companion to Economic Geography*. Oxford: Blackwell. pp. 77–94.

Martin, R. and Sunley, P. (2003) Deconstructing clusters: Chaotic concept or policy panacea? *Journal of Economic Geography*, 3: 5–35.

Maskell, P., Bathelt, H. and Malmberg, A. (2006) Building global knowledge pipelines: The role of temporary clusters. *European Planning Studies*, 14: 997–1013.

Peck, J. (2002) Political economies of scale: Fast policy, interscalar relations, and neoliberal workfare. *Economic Geography*, 78(3): 331–60.

Pike, A., Rodriguez-Pose, A., and Tomaney, J. (2006) *Local and Regional Development*. London: Routledge.

Porter, M. (1998) *On Competition*. Boston, MA: Harvard Business Review Press.

Scott, A.J. (1988) *New Industrial Spaces: Flexible Production Organisation and Regional Development in North America and Western Europe*. London: Pion.

Storper, M. (1995) The resurgence of regional economies, ten years later: The region as a nexus of untraded inter-dependencies. *European Urban and Regional Studies*, 2: 191–221.

Wenger, E. (1998) *Communities of Practice: Learning, Meaning and Identity*. Cambridge: Cambridge University Press.

19

Geographies of Economic Growth II: Money and Finance

Michael Pryke

INTRODUCTION

'Oi you, shut your mouth and look at my wad! Loadsamoney!' Crude, yes, but in many ways these words sum up the culture of money that spread selectively through Britain from the mid-1980s, and beyond. Out of the manufacturing wasteland that was much of the UK throughout the 1970s and the recession-beaten early 1980s, the excesses of finance and money became more and more apparent as the 1980s, the decade of 'serious money', progressed. The map shaped by serious money was, however, seriously selective and represented extreme social and economic geographies that were the outcome of significant political economic change, not just within Britain but globally as the enabling project of neoliberalism gained dominance throughout the decade to the present. It was not however going to be 'loadsamoney' forever. The euphoria of the 1980s ended in national and international financial crises.

Yet, lest it be forgotten, '*Financial crises are nothing new*'. The words, which seem to convey a sense of world-weariness, are taken from the opening page of an influential Report written in 1999 by the Independent Task Force, a group sponsored by the US Council on Foreign Affairs. To underscore their point, the Report's authors continue:

> In the past 20 years alone, more than 125 countries have experienced at least one serious bout of banking problems. In more than half of these episodes, a developing country's entire banking system essentially became insolvent. And *in more than a dozen cases, the cost of resolving the crisis was at least a tenth – and sometimes much more – of the crisis country's annual total income.* (Peterson et al., 1999: 1–2; original emphasis)

Nothing new maybe, but as this last point indicates financial crises take a human toll; they are both geographically widespread and socially and politically far-reaching. Over recent decades financial extremes have ranged from: the USA's 'savings and loan crisis' of late 1980s; Europe's ERM devaluation in the early 1990s; the mid 1990s Mexican currency crisis; the Latin American debt crisis of the 1980s; and, the Asian crisis of 1997 that spread quickly to cover a geography that stretched from Estonia, Russia, to

Brazil, Argentina and New Zealand. Capitalism's geo-economic history tells of many such crises, all of which share as their cause the malfunctioning of financial markets. Just to take one example, Wade and Veneroso (1998: 3–4) explain the unexpected repercussions of the 1997 Asian crash:

> How could the widely acknowledge real estate problems of Thailand's banks in 1996 and 1997 have triggered such a far-reaching debt-and-development crisis? The devaluation of the Thai baht in July 1997 was followed by currency crises or financial instability in Indonesia, Malaysia, the Philippines, Taiwan, Hong Kong, Korea, Estonia, Russia, Brazil, Australia and New Zealand. Commodity producers around the world have suffered. Yet there were few signs of impending crisis, such as rising interest rates in the G-7 countries or a sudden suspension of capital flows to developing countries after the baht devaluation. On the contrary, bank lending to Asia actually rose to a record level in the third quarter of 1997. The Japanese government's de facto credit rating agency, the Japan Center for International Finance, gave Korea one of its highest credit ratings for any developing country in June 1997. The IMF and the World Bank lavished praise upon the governments of the region through 1997, including on the Korean authorities as recently as September 1997.
>
> What began as a debt crisis has become a fully fledged development crisis. Throughout this most successful of developing regions living standards are falling as unemployment rises and the effects of huge devaluations work through into higher import prices. Many millions of poor people are at risk, and many millions of people who were confident of middle-class status feel robbed of their lifetime savings and security. It is not a humanitarian tragedy on the scale of North Korea, but the loss of security and productivity is a tragedy nonetheless, almost as cruel as war.

Against such a background of volatility and instability it is unsurprising that 1980s was also the moment when geographers, led by the likes of David Harvey, Nigel Thrift and Andrew Leyshon, began to turn their critical attention towards the processes generating remarkably uneven life chances that result from economies run on and for the needs of high octane finance.

As financial markets generally began to undergo some much needed repair in the 1990s, the nature of geographical inquiry

changed, too, as this chapter suggests. The intellectual shift reflected both the impact of financial collapse and the geographies that emerged and how these should be understood, *and* the influence on investigations into geographies of finance and money that resulted from conceptual dialogue struck with neighbouring disciplines. Both elements of this shift are mirrored well in a book edited by leading geographers that appeared in the mid 1990s. In their introduction to *Money, Power and Space*, the editors flagged the need to recognise 'the importance of money in the restructuring of contemporary capitalism' (Corbridge and Thrift, 1994: 3). The 'comparative neglect' of money by geographers may be difficult to fathom, as the editors remarked, but work that has been undertaken by economic geographers over the past few decades has certainly addressed the earlier omission and would seem to point to the inseparability of money, finance and space. In focusing geographical understandings of 'economic' processes on studies of money, finance and financial markets, not only have place, space and spatiality been moved centre stage, this has been achieved in ways that make aspatial accounts of the workings of finance and the financial system look distinctly shaky. In the performance, 'Money and Finance' space is no longer a bit part – it is a headline act. As Roger Lee argues 'Money is the most geographical of economic phenomena' (1999: 207; see also Martin, 1999a; Leyshon, 1995, 1997, 1998). Money gains this position arguably because of the nature of the market economy:

> The very essence of a market economy is that it operates by a generalized process of exchange. All means of production and all goods and services produced can be, and are, bought and sold, including the services of labour. Economic life is driven by individual and corporate calculation of profit and loss. The market economy fosters a complex division of labour, in which each individual's well being is linked by a myriad of sales and purchases to thousands of individuals throughout the world. In such an economy money is a necessity. Without money the organization of this multidimensional interactive system

would be impossible . . . In a market economy, flows of money determine the flows of inputs and outputs. Possession of money defines power in the market place. Accordingly, with the development of the market system the monetary system that supports it has become ever more elaborate. Money doesn't simply facilitate exchange, it sets the wheels of commerce in motion. (Eatwell and Taylor, 2000: 9–10).

As this suggests, we should remember that 'money is a social relation'; it is a medium that depends on authority and through which authority and power may be exercised (Ingham, 2004). Thus, given the centrality of money and finance to the market economy, and because 'money is politics' (Kirshner, 2003), it is helpful to provide an outline of the wider social, political, technical and cultural context for the key developments noted in the remainder of the chapter. These developments gain their significance because they help to frame the flows and to shape the territories of money and finance; to money and finance, culture and technology, for example, lend a potential spatial reach and affect the geographical impact of the modern money economy. The effect of the set of rules and regulations governing the movement of private finance over the post-war period, is the first of these developments. These rules, commonly referred to as a financial architecture, moved from being a tightly state orchestrated system, known as the Bretton Woods Agreement, to a new financial architecture that began to emerge following the collapse of the Agreement in the early 1970s (Leyshon and Tickell, 1994). The significance of this point lies in the way the collapse signalled the (largely US inspired) growing influence of the private sector in the design, implementation and organization of the financial architecture felt to be best suited for international financial markets and flows. The shift is also significant as it is central to neoliberalism, a political and economic set of ideas that promotes 'free markets' and central to which is the goal of achieving global scope for private finance (Strange, 1994; Panic, 1985; Leyshon, 1996; Martin, 1994; Harvey, 2005).

The consolidation of the political power of neoliberalism from the 1980s onwards, and its effect on the thinking of nation states and international institutions, such as the IMF and the World Bank, are relevant both to the quantitative and geographical expansion of private finance and to the manner in which economic geographers have reappraised their theoretical approaches to the subject of finance, and the generation of research agendas.

Second, and integral to this ideological refurbishment, is the regulatory change that accompanied the post-Bretton Woods world. Key here is the impact of the reregulation of both capital markets – markets in finance that bring together large investment banks, international financial organizations, quoted companies and the like – and retail financial markets. In the UK, which perhaps has the most developed consumer credit markets in western Europe, the latter group takes the form of high street banks and building societies that sell mortgages, loans, credit cards, and the like, and which in Britain nowadays include retailers such as supermarkets offering 'special offer' mortgages at the checkout. The combined reregulation of these interrelated markets – high street banks accessing capital markets to be able to offer financial products such as fixed rate mortgages, for example – were to have significant spatial effects from the 1980s onwards. Indeed, the latter development, was driven by mortgage-backed securitization imported from the US. Capital market reregulation for instance was to impact the spatial configuration of financial centres (as the following section highlights), while the new set of rules for competition amongst providers of high street finance was to have long-term consequences on who was to gain access to private sector finance and at what price (as research covered in the section third makes clear).

Lastly, the accompanying technological advances are contextually important because in many ways they determine the technical feasibility of change within financial markets and their consequent geographical reach.

The growth of screen based trading in Forex (foreign exchange) markets and the instantaneous settlement of financial transfers potentially across the globe, are two obvious examples. Yet behind developments in ICT and their application to financial markets, is an all-important shift in the 'attitude of people to money and to the monetary process' (Schumpeter, in Swedberg, 1991: 341). The so-called 'democratization of finance' (Frank, 2000: 92; Erturk et al., 2005) that gathered pace in 1990s America, for instance, and which changed 'American thinking about money and business', or the 'loadsamoney' mindset that swilled around Britain in the 1980s, are two contemporary illustrations of such attitudinal about-turns. Here the suggestion is to understand the application of technology to money and finance less in terms of any simple technological determinism, and more as the translation through the medium of the latest ICT of a 'new money imaginary' and 'culture of money'. The outcome of this fusion is the making of real financial geographies. These geographies are at times quite an intricate and paradoxical interplay between flows and territories, as the next section highlights.

The remainder of the chapter makes use of this context to explore work that has investigated first the lingering importance of specific financial territories, such as Wall Street and 'the City', to the orchestration and making sense of myriad, increasingly entangled, flows of financial instruments. The power or influence of the growing volumes of financial flows shaped and traded in such financial centres is the subject of the following section. Before concluding the chapter with several theoretical reflections on the expanding field of geographies of money and finance, the penultimate section keeps with the theme of financial power but directs attention to more everyday finance – the financing of personal loans and mortgages, access to banking services and so on – and relates work undertaken on life as it were underneath the dominant rhythms of a re-regulated, neoliberal, financial regime.

THE RELEVANCE OF FINANCIAL TERRITORIES IN A SPACE OF FLOWS

Finance and financial markets are central to the operation of the system of market exchange; moreover, they have become concentrated in a few particular places. Within global financial market places, such as the City of London and New York's Wall Street, financiers, bankers and a host of other financial market traders and dealers make markets in a growing range of increasingly sophisticated forms of global finance. Global financial markets deal with flows of financial assets and financial information that cross the territorial borders of nation states. Financial markets then are sophisticated combinations of technologies and human organizations located in specific territories.

Sparked by the types of change noted earlier – such as reregulation and technological advances – the 1980s onwards saw a rash of claims about the shift towards a space of flows, as one of the leading proponents of this thesis phrased it (Castells, 1996) and the 'end of geography' (O'Brien, 1992). There was an accompanying invitation to think that international or global finance in particular is really something quite new – its movements are swift, it is all about speed and its romps around the world do indeed seem aptly described as global. In short, to think (mistakenly, as Thrift, 2002 notes) that nowadays all is new in the world of finance, that all is 'hyperactive'. For while the latest technological developments may have played havoc with space, place and the significance of locations, have not been wholly undermined (Martin, 1994: 263). On the contrary, it would appear that financial markets are continually dreaming up categories of territories – such as so-called offshore financial centres (Palan, 2003),[1] and the relatively new investment category 'emerging markets'[2] – which in turn become integral to operation of financial flows. This correction to the 'everything is flows' thesis is particularly apposite in the case of financial centres. As economic geographers have shown, certain territories, such as the financial markets to be found in London, collectively known as 'the City' or Wall Street in New York, matter enormously.

Research carried out in the 1980s and 1990s, much of it focused on the City of London, provided a timely reminder that first neither technological developments nor the reregulation of financial markets spell the end of financial centres, as more recent research (Sassen, 1991, 2004) and official data (BIS, 2005) demonstrate. Second, that technology in itself does not fabricate financial products; it facilitates their fabrication. For it is easy to forget that finance – no matter how abstract or digitized it may seem – involves production; financial flows have to be made to flow; work goes into giving movement to finance. This work involves an array of human qualities such as trust and emotions (Pixley, 1999, 2002, 2004), not easily displaced by the latest piece of software. This early work explored the paradox that lies at the heart of global financial markets and financial flows: the more ethereal finance appears to become, the greater the need for specific territories dedicated to making sense of abstract flows; that is engaging at an individual and organizational level in trying to judge for example where market sentiment lies or figuring which way markets are likely to move. The work of economic geographers filled the considerable gaps in 'economic' explanations (such as transaction costs and information economies) that aimed to account for the persistence of financial centres. Just what makes the economies of agglomeration work? Do economies of scale simply happen in thin air? Taking their cue from developments within the social sciences more broadly, geographers insisted on the social and cultural production of agglomeration economies. The 'economies of scale and agglomeration' 'are themselves dynamic social and cultural practices' (Pryke and Lee, 1995: 331). Technological developments, no matter how fast moving their introduction may make the world, become entangled in their implementation in dense social, cultural and historical geographies that mark out the territories of financial centres. 'As geographically distinct sets of social and cultural relationships, external economies reflect both the particular place in which – and distinctive social and cultural practices through which – their realization occurs' (ibid.).

Yet while these points are important, just as it is relevant to note that Wall Street, the City, Frankfurt, Tokyo, and so on, are still very much information centres, just as was Amsterdam, Europe's first financial centre, in the seventeenth century (Smith,1984: 999–1004). Neither set of answers tells us fully how such financial centres manage to negotiate their way through a series of regulatory, competitive and technological change, noted at the outset of the chapter, that have undone so many other territories.

To tackle this issue, the City of London serves as an example. Pryke (1991) attempted to capture the social and spatial transition that took place in the City of London in the build up to the reregulation of the City's financial markets, the so-called 'Big bang', which took place in 1986. The reading of this change clearly emphasizes the numerous spatialities involved in what might otherwise be viewed as a straightforward technical and regulatory matter; the move, in other words, from on the so-called floor exchanges to screen-based trading. The City was to work its way through time in the manner that gave spatial expression to its rules and regulations. The City was thus able to hold down financial innovation within very specific territories. Paying close attention to the production of space (Allen and Pryke, 1994) enabled geographers to say more about the 'rules of play' that held together the City's financial community, exemplified best perhaps in ways employed by one of the City's leading institutions, the Bank of England, in its supervision of incoming foreign banks. The Bank employed an almost ceremonial surveillance of space in order to impress upon new arrivals the importance of place and in so doing acted as a financial synchromesh, slowing down the pace of change in international financial markets to the more acceptable rhythm of the City's old spatial matrix (Pryke, 1991). In a similar fashion, the City's other financial markets were able to innovate their way through time by ensuring the 'perpetuation of business mannerisms uniquely identifiable with the markets of the City core' (Pryke, 1991: 202). Such cultural and social practices helped the City to agglomerate: orchestrated through the regulatory channels such as the Bank of England, the defining qualities of an 'imagined' Englishness, such as good manners, high morality and tolerance, become the cultural tools for spatially monitoring the City's communities (ibid.). Informal regulation worked. Annual reports and accounts, for instance, and written regulations were not central to this style of spatial policing. Personal contact, spatial propinquity, conversations about who were 'really the right people to be about' in the City were key to this spatial rule and the territorial shaping of the City as a financial centre (ibid., 207–8). Amin and Thrift (1992) made similar points when they drew attention to financial centres as 'neo-marshallian nodes'. These authors offered a socially and culturally inflexed interpretation of financial centres that reflected economic geographers, demand that the economics of economics, as it were, be opened-up for questioning. Just as there were calls for the strictly 'economic' explanation of agglomeration economies to be extended to include the social and the cultural, so this work reflected a wider social science concern to embrace the cultural, to question the usefulness of what is termed dualistic thinking that keeps apart economy and culture. Thrift (1994) argues exactly this in an influential paper the essence of which captures the issue in the article's title: 'the social and cultural determinants of international financial centres'.

Pryke and Lee (1995) drew attention to the still present need – even in the world of abstract global flows – to have somewhere to 'place your bets'. This work also drew attention to three important interrelated factors that not only highlight the importance of territory in a world of flows, but begin to unsettle a belief in the usefulness of a hard edged conceptualization to the 'economic'. Agglomeration economies, external economies of scale, and similar – in other words, the conceptual mainstay of a strictly economic approach to the role and persistence of financial centres – all need to be asked to justify their explanatory status. Turn attention instead, they suggest, both to the organizational make-up of financial firms located in financial centres and to the practices required in order for these firms to make profits. Firms in financial centres need to cooperate in order to compete; there is a need to know something of the character of person who is going to be at the end of a 'phone transaction'. Deals have to be 'talked up', particularly if a new product is being designed, and talked through, and transactions, involving lengthy discussions, such as syndicated loans or mergers and acquisitions, are often concluded with a handshake (Laulajainen, 2003: 332). In 'global' financial markets, trust remains crucial and it is formed locally. This point applies to Wall Street, just as it does to offshore financial centres such as the Cayman Islands (Hudson, 1999).

Financial centres thus involve the purposeful production of service space (Allen and Pryke, 1994) – a process that is not gender blind. Financial centres such as the City and Wall Street are remarkably testosterone-packed spaces. Geographers' understanding of the production of space helped to point to how the character of somewhere like the City, a collection of spaces which were for such a long time the home of England's 'financial aristocracy' (Checkland, 1957; Cassis, 1987), produced a form of masculinity, the lingering scent and effects of which can easily be detected today (McDowell, 2001; McDowell and Court, 1994a–c; see also Zaloom, 2003), as recent industrial tribunals in the UK indicate. According to research by the GMB Union into official pay statistics, the pay gap between the sexes is wider in the City of London than anywhere else in the country. Women working full-time in the City of London earn 58% of the average

City man's salary – creating a gap far wider than the national average (Turner, 2005).

Indeed, in arguing for the 'repoliticization of financial risk', de Goede argues that 'high finance' remains gendered. The commercialization of risk in finance she says is 'a profitable cultural process that rests upon gendered constructs of danger and security'; the use of sophisticated mathematical models to assess risk is part of the 'glamorous masculinity' associated with global finance (2004: 207; see also 2005: 21–46).

Locations such as the City of London, and New York's Wall Street, are specific territories that exhibit most strongly the culture of global finance. The term 'culture' refers to the intermingling of information, values, expertise and contacts found there. The experts and market players form themselves into social networks which work on the basis of trust, interpretive schemes – that is, strategies to make sense of what is going on – and, of course, more information (Thrift, 1994). All these features of current financial flows and financial centres call for more, not less, face-to-face meetings; people active in the market and the organizations they work for, together with the institutions regulating their activities, need a physical, material, presence to work through endless, complex financial flows (Knorr-Cetina and Bruegger, 2002; Zaloom, 2003). The more dematerialized and digitized finance becomes – that is the more able it is to flow – the greater the need for territories, but territories of a specific kind (Sassen, 2004: 245). The territories of global finance that we call 'financial centres' act functionally; financial markets require making; they require 'socio-technology' as Buenza and Stark (2002) term it, that is, a mix of people, organizations such as investment banks and brokers, technologies and buildings. All of this – materials and people – is required to cope with an 'identifying characteristic of financial markets': their incompleteness means that they are always on the verge of 'mutating' if not 'exploding into something else' (Knorr-Cetina, 2003; Knorr-Cetina and Bruegger, 2000a, 2000b: 170).

Financial centres have a symbolic role too. To be a player of note in the game of global finance still requires the right address, membership of a specific territory. Moreover, territories such as the City of London and Wall Street, symbolise the authority and influence of private finance.

INFLUENTIAL FLOWS

An inseparable part the concentration of financial organizations and institutions in financial centres is the power or influence that financial markets may exert on other economic agents, be they corporations, such as the large public companies listed on the UK's FTSE 100, or governments of developed or (so-called) developing countries (Hardie, 2005). Such influence is another way of conceptualizing the effective spatial reach of such centres. If the triumph of the market in the 1980s, signalled by the rise of neoliberalism, saw the solidification of the 'finance conception' of the firm (Fligstein and Markowitz, 1993), the 1990s witnessed the effects of 'financialization' on corporate thinking (Feng et al., 2001). The 'culture of money' and the ideology of shareholder value were further to influence the discourse – the sets of meanings about what is involved in 'meeting City expectations', the accepted language for talking about the running of a successful corporation, and so on – that runs between firms and financial markets. As Karel Williams remarks:

> Financialization reworks the hierarchy of management objectives as it reorients the firm: if firms have to organize process and please consumers in the product market, they must also now satisfy professional fund managers and meet the expectations of the capital market. The result is a new form of (financial) competition of all against all whereby every quoted firm must compete as an investment to meet the same standard of financial performance. (Williams, 2000: 6; see also Froud et al., 2000)

Unsurprisingly, there has been an accompanying rise in the number of channels through which the influence of private finance and financial markets work. The influential workings of private finance markets may now take a variety of forms, two of which have attracted the attention of economic geographers and are the focus of this section. First, there is the influence of so-called *rating agencies*. Second is the influential power of market or sector *analysts*, those individuals within financial organizations such as investment banks that make recommendations to 'buy' or 'sell' a firm's stock or shares, decisions that may make or break corporations.

Rating agencies

The two most powerful rating organizations, S&P and Moodys, are headquartered in New York, one of the world's most powerful and influential financial territories. This territorial concentration of financial and finance related power, holds the potential for channelling the influence of private sector financial flows into far broader geographies (Pryke, 1999; Clark and Wojicik, 2003). In concluding his study of rating agencies, Timothy Sinclair suggests something of the making of these geographies and the consequences. Rating agencies 'are changing the norms and practices of commercial and public life around the world, along manifestly [North] American lines . . . the judgements of the agencies reflect a particular view of the world – the mental framework of rating orthodoxy' (2005: 46). Paraded as facts, opinion as much as hard, and thus supposedly objective, analysis of ratios, inform the agencies' judgements. The rating process is thus a social phenomenon – and it is a cultural one, too, it could be added.

The significance of noting New York as the home territory of both S&P and Moody's, and the gradual adoption of the practices of rating established by the two dominant agencies by the 'global' financial community, is to note how geographies of influence may work their way through the flows of global finance. All in all, it is tempting to agree with

Sinclair when he states fairly unequivocally that, 'The rules that govern important dimensions of the world are being transformed by the work of the agencies, affecting work life and democracy in places touched by financial globalization' (2005: 174).

Sinclair (2005) uses the term 'second superpowers' to describe the world's major bond rating agencies, the likes of Moody's (Moody's Investor Service) and S&P (Standard and Poor's). 'Their arsenal' he writes 'is an occult one, largely invisible to all but a few most of the time' (1–2). As he argues, what is interesting about these authors is the authority accorded to what they author – a system of rating from 'top quality' investment worth to highly risky capital market adventures:

> market and government actors take account of rating agencies not because the agencies are right but because they are thought to be an authoritative source of judgements, thereby making the agencies key organizations controlling access to capital market. (Sinclair, 2005: 2)

The influence, the authority, of rating agencies has increased with the liberalization of financial markets.

The explosion of financial innovation from the 1980s onwards (Henwood, 1998, 51) together with the complexity of financial markets and the emerging new financial architecture, have combined to alter the form of financial regulation. Regulation nowadays is 'more codified, institutionalized, and juridified. Rules are more elaborate and formal, with fewer tacit understandings' (Sinclair, 2005: 46). Moreover, regulation devolves from the state to the private sector in ways approved by state authorities. The retreat of the state does not mean that there is no need for 'rules and protocol'; financial markets still require some sort of architecture if chaos is not to ensue. The:

> international financial system has invented these itself. Perhaps the most prominent and powerful example of this invention of private sector institutions of governance by the international financial system is the credit rating agency. (Thrift, 1999: 281)

The rating agencies now view themselves as 'socially sanctioned judges of prudent economic and financial behaviour' (ibid.) not just at a national scale, but globally. This development has quite considerable implications for the numerous influences that financial flows contain and convey, and the geographies that result.

Sector analysts

Economic geographers have argued that the influence of private finance works through another set of financial agents: analysts who monitor the performance of quoted companies, those companies to be found in the pages of the FT, for example, under the heading FTSE 100. The analysts act as mediators between corporations and financial markets. They produce a potentially highly influential form of financial knowledge (Wrigley et al., 2003). To appreciate their role it is helpful to recognize a few simple but essential points. Firms need funds in order to do what they do, be this making cars or selling mobile phones. There are two funding sources available to them: debt and equity. The combination of these forms of finance shape the financial structure of any corporation. Agents such as analysts, assess the viability of a firm through the 'imagery' of capital structure (Fligstein, 2002: 151). The imagery of capital structure builds on the bedrock of financial economics, and together they inform how a firm's finances should be assessed in terms of its ability to 'optimise returns' – 'is the firm capable of showing a return on capital employed (ROCE) of "x" per cent?', to employ the thinking of financialization (Williams, 2000). Both financial economics and imagery such as capital structure, and the general financial discourse of which they form a part, shape the 'calculative frame' established by analysts (Beunza and Garud, 2004). This is one way of understanding how the financial knowledge circulated by analysts to financial market participants is made. Financial centres then may be seen as places where financial power and influence are shaped, where a financial discourse is promoted and made to circulate through a firm's thinking, with potentially wide reaching geographical effects. The influence of the City, of so-called City opinion, knows no geographical limits. Financial influence works 'at a distance' through the authoritative discourse and 'calculative practices' (Miller, 2001) of sector analysts (as well as through rating agencies) and the whole institutional structure of corporate finance (Wrigley, 1999).

Debt may take a variety of forms but essentially is a specific loan for a particular project and is sourced from capital markets. Equity, the raising of finance through share issues, means that a firm is under obligation to show a return on the money advanced in the form of shares bought and sold through official exchanges. Both means of raising finance expose a firm to different groups of financial organization and open them to varying forms of scrutiny characteristic of each group. It is through such channels that the influence of finance may work. Finance thus affects 'corporate geographies' and the geographical structure of the economic landscape (Clark and Wrigley, 1997; Clarke et al., 2004).

Firm strategies must then chime with accounting principles such as earnings per share, as well as the commonly understood demand to 'show profits'. This again points to what is involved in meeting 'City/Wall Street expectations', and in 'keeping on the right side of 'City/Wall Street opinion'. This is a specific financial discourse. Like all discourses, it relies on language and materials for the effective communication of meaning: it involves the specialist vocabularies of financial markets, of reports and accounts, their circulation amongst analysts and investors, presentations by a firm's financial directors to banks and institutional investors. This discourse is in itself *spatial*, both in how it gains its power and how this power achieves its reach. Financial power is dependent on the symbolism of particular spaces – the splendid offices of financial institutions in the City, for

example – for its authority. The spatial effectiveness of this power is achievable through
the paraphernalia that makes-up this discourse. The annual reports and accounts, the
headlines in the *FT* when a firm declares its
interim or end-of-year figures, the analysts,
reports based on these results and passed to
the institutional investors and translated into
'buy, sell or hold' recommendations for
equity traders, the telephone calls, the face-
to-face meetings in City offices and bars . . .
all have the potential to spread the influence
of financial markets over company actions
across the UK.

More recently, there have been calls for
economic geographers to 'engage with, and
understand, the world of financial analysis,
not least as the regulation of that world
undergoes profound change' (Wrigley et al.,
2003: 382). There has been other work on
the role of analysts in relation to pension
funds (Clark, 2000, 2003) and emerging
markets (Sidaway and Bryson, 2002). This
work, and that of Yeung (2003), looks at the
value of analysts to the production of knowledge about particular sectors and areas of
financial markets. Theses actors help to produce what Phil O'Neill (2001) calls 'financial narratives'. Over simply, analysts'
reports piece together stories that tell institutional clients and fund managers 'what's hot,
and what's not'. Whether the analysts unearth
startling material is open to question.
Analysts, akin into the 'lounge singers' of
capitalism's 'casinos', either tend towards
consensus in their reports and forecasts to
avoid possible embarrassment if things go
wrong, or else seek out the 'most attention
with the most daring forecast' (Henwood,
1998, 101). In the USA, for instance, the
implementation of shareholder value as a
way of conceptualizing the corporation
meant that firms were financially reorgan-
ized, 'downsized' (to use the language of
shareholder discourse) to demonstrate to
investors that the right action was being
taken to raise share prices (Zuchermann,
1999; Fligstein and Shin, 2004; see also
Zorn et al., 2005).

Whatever the personal motives of the
authors, the consequences of action taken
based on these reports and forecasts make
geographies. Depending on the recommendations, there is either a rush to invest in
certain sectors, or a panic to get out and to
high tail it into territories now deemed to
offer richer pickings. Left in the wake of
these decisions are potentially highly uneven
geographies of 'social exclusion' and 'economic redundancy', as well of course territories of fabulous and seemingly unending
wealth, such as Silicon Valley, in California.
Both outcomes, although extreme, give a
flavour for first the interrelationship between
the formulations of knowledge in the continuous making of financial markets *and*
second how the exercise of this knowledge
translates into financial power. Combined
both sets of processes have potential geographical consequences (Clark and Wojcik,
2003).

THE SPATIALITIES OF RE-REGULATION

The political shift that took place in the
1980s and which affected so dramatically the
workings of wholesale capital markets did
not leave untouched the world of so-called
retail finance; that is the everyday finance of
banks accounts, credit cards, personal loans,
mortgages and so on. This signalled what
Thomas Frank calls the 'democratization of
finance' – a term that for him signalled a
'vast sea change in American thinking about
money' (2000: 92). By the mid-1990s in the
USA, the multiplication of money through
the stock market had become an everyday
expectation of the middle class. According to
Frank, 'The [stock] market had become an
integral facet of their lives' (*op. cit.*, 134).
Reminiscent of Zelizer's (1994) earmarking
of money, Frank observed that the stock
market 'held money for their children's college tuition, money to get them through an
emergency, money for the great vacation they

were saving for, money for retirement' (2000: 134). This effortless enrichment achieved on behalf of middle class America by financial alchemists along Wall Street obscured the political shift that lay behind the general adoration of 'the market'. As Frank remarks, 'It is not a coincidence that each of these necessities – pensions, shelter, education – were things Americans had once sought to ensure through union activity or government intervention. Things that Americans once believed were theirs simply by virtue of being citizens, things that could and should be available to everyone in a democratic society' (ibid., 135). Many poor Americans, many of them Black Americans, caught up in the hurricane that hit New Orleans, might nod their approval.

As the opening section noted, information is key to the workings of international finance. Information and communications technologies are just as central to the retail financial sector. Information flows and electronically aided assessment of risk and credit worthiness are just as central to the decisions made by a high street building society to provide a £5k unsecured loan, as they are to the decision making of a syndicate of global investment banks to lend to a multinational corporation. The outcomes of such assessment describe geographies, too, geographies that may be highly uneven.

In the UK, two pieces of 1986 legislation – the Financial Services Act and the Building Societies Act – triggered reregulation within retail financial services markets. The Act's aim was 'shake-up' the supply side; to establish a competitive free-for-all with ultimate aim being to establish a 'free market' in personal finance and to encourage citizens, particularly those on moderate incomes and above, to both become financially literate and to build their own financial portfolios. The ideal was financial self-sufficiency at a time when the state was to move away from being responsible for many areas of life previously associated with the welfare state, such as health cover and pensions (Martin, 1999a, 1999b; Pollard, 1999). Financial

markets, from the capital market through to high street retail finance providers, were to be the new 'common sense' and were to stoke the rise of 'pension fund capitalism' (Clark, 1999). In the years before the stock market crash of 1990 when house prices, as well as stock prices, were soaring, such ideas were relatively easy for many people to make sense of and to feel included. While retail banks and building societies were busy rethinking the customer as 'client', fashioning financial products to see people through life from the cradle to the grave, rethinking trust and the strategies to brand successfully their growing range of products, the day seemed to have won conclusively by the 'loadsamoney' culture. As Thomas Frank observed as he reflected (rather optimistically) on the unfolding of a very similar process in the USA 'While the world of finance had once been a stronghold of WASP [White Anglo Saxon Protestant] privilege, an engine of elite enrichment,[3] journalist and PR man alike agreed that it had now been transformed utterly, being opened to all. This bull market was the Gotterdammerung of the ruling class, the final victory of the common people over their overlords' (Frank, 2000: 92). In competitive and open personal financial markets, money's endless 'malleability' and the idea of 'effortless enrichment' (Simmel, 1990; see also Dodd, 1994) seemed anything but an ideological illusion.

The processes of regulatory change and competition in the UK and the USA (Tickell, 2001) contained new geographies of delivery of financial services that began to emerge only some years post re-regulation. The flows of financial products may have broadened and grown – just take a look for example, at the finance or 'cash' supplements that fall out of the weekend newspapers, the leaflets at supermarket checkouts offering 'special offers' on loans and mortgages – but the re-regulated world of personal finance was to describe altered territories. The process known as 'financial exclusion' (Leyshon and Thrift, 1997) was to mark this new financial landscape. Financial exclusion works in a number of ways. For instance, exclusion may result from a bank deciding to close branches in non-profitable areas, such as inner city locations where there is a lack of 'high net worth' individuals serves as justification for the organization's decision to close branches. The decision to close is often the result of the data profiling of such areas using the organization's own customer database, as well as complementary data bought from businesses specializing in reworking other data sources, including the census, detailing anything from income to credit card ownership, central to which is 'credit scoring' (Leyshon and Thrift, 1999). Data analysis may reveal an area devoid of say 'high net worth' individuals and thus unprofitable to the bank.

Once again, ICT, flows of data and finance seem inseparable. The same developments in ICT that have altered significantly the ways in which global financial markets operate, are employed by organizations involved in retail or everyday credit as they compete for customers. Financial exclusion works electronically: the world of personal finance now harnesses and applies technological developments to mark people out for exclusion. In the creation of new monetary spaces through retail finance, the application of ICT is hardly passive; 'it is political' (Ingham, 2004: 182). Information is again central to flows and shapes the territories of personal finance. What Leyshon et al. (1997) suggest is that this is part of a shift from interpersonal relations – the days, that is, when the local bank manager knew your name – to today when financial organizations employ ICT to establish trust in other, more impersonal ways. Nowadays, they argue, 'trust in customers is being forged through technologically mediated means of information collection functioning "at a distance" so that financial services producers are coming to "read" consumers as "texts", through the medium of databases'. Yet again, databases and electronic flows describe very real geographies.

Those excluded from the financial system are doubly handicapped as they live in both a financial and an information shadow. Such individuals are likely to pay an increasingly heavy price for their exclusion, particularly given the collapse of universal welfare provision and the allied growth of private welfare-related financial products. (ibid.)

More recently Andrew Leyshon and colleagues (2004) pursued this central idea of financial exclusion by addressing both 'ecologies and networks' of privilege and poverty to be found in middle class suburbs and poor inner city areas, as well as peripheral local authority housing estates. Unsurprisingly, their work points to markedly different sets of experiences, very different 'financial ecologies' in both areas. The territories that result from processes of financial exclusion in the poorer areas are notable in that they have become colonized by a 'distinctive set of financial institutions' including notorious door-to-door credit agencies (see also Jones, 2005). In an effort to combat these agencies, the 1980s saw a resurgence in 'local moneys' (something that had last been seen in the UK and USA in the 1920s and 1930s). Putting to one side the question of whether these media are really money (Ingham, 2004: 183–88), LETS (local exchange trading schemes), 'authentic local currencies' such as time dollars in the USA, and credit unions in the UK (Jones, 2005) appeared in areas of social deprivation in particular in an effort to combat financial exclusion. They also served as a local political challenge to neoliberal globalization. Economic geographers have used these developments to flag the ways in which local monies have the potential to help create 'alternative economic geographies'. As Roger Lee notes:

LETS and other forms of local currencies may be part of larger strategy to rebuild and assume a measure of self-determination in local and regional economies, of finding ways in which wealth generated in an area can be kept within it, and of providing an informally and locally determined space within which personal self-confidence may be re-established. (1999: 222; see also Lee, 1996; Thorne, 1996)

Put in such terms, LETS is just one counter move to the neoliberal financial architecture that has given relatively free rein to the 'savage money' (Gregory, 1997) that escaped the regulation of the Bretton Woods era at the beginning of the 1970s. In this respect, the aims of LETs and other forms of local money chime with internationally widespread calls for a more socially responsible financial architecture (Akyüz, 1995, 2004). All such moves recognize that money is a social relation and thus is a form of politics by other means. In their different ways, what they are all saying is that the geographies made through the authority of official money and finance are open to challenge, no matter how daunting the task may seem. Neither official, state money, nor private finance, whether channelled through capital markets or relayed through high street banks and supermarkets, are neutral; politics and class inequality are 'integral to the workings of both forms of money and finance' (Ingham, 2000, 2004).

THEORETICAL CONCLUSIONS

This chapter began by noting the relatively recent arrival of the 'sub-discipline' geographies of money and finance. In the sections that followed it became clear how money and finance have now moved from the fringes towards the centre of interest in economic geography. This move has been so complete that a leading economic geographer now claims that if economic geography is to understand the economic landscape of twenty first century capitalism, then this should be done through an analysis of global financial institutions, their social formation and institutional practices (Clark, 2005a, b). Thus welcomed in from the cold, this does not mean however that the research agenda for research on money and finance is settled. Indeed, far from this being the case, debates and controversies are sure to surround the issue of how economic geographers should approach 'money and finance'. After all, the issues – ranging from the political and social responsibilities that attach to the movement of financial flows, the geopolitics of financial

architecture, the relationships between corporations and financial markets, the blending of financial instruments and the climate, the nature of and working of power exercised through financial flows and markets, and much more – are manifold. What we can be surer about is the need for openness to the range of theoretical and methodological influences that geographers can usefully bring to bear to study such an important subject and the range of inherently geographical issues contained therein. Work on finance and money by economic geographers over recent years shows that to head down Culture Avenue or Economic Alley leads ultimately to a *cul-de-sac* (Barnes, 2001, 2005; Hudson, 2005; Thrift, 1999). Disentangling just what it is that gives the City of London such a long lease of life, to take just one example from the above, demonstrates that clean edged 'economic' analysis leads to a poorer rather than a richer explanation. What economic geographers working in the area of finance have shown is that effort spent exploring the hybridities enrolled in the making of money and finance *and* the hybrid spatialities that result (see Gilbert, 2005), reaps imaginative and fuller geographical understandings of money and finance. The conceptual triptych of 'Money, power, space' remains an important focus for research by economic geographers as they engage in work that might cover a wide spectrum of important issues from imagining new financial architectures, alternative geographies of finance, Islamic finance . . . to the international policy turn to financial markets in an attempt to deal with the effects of climate change – the malleability of money and finance is limitless, it seems!

STOP PRESS

Between the times of submitting this chapter to the editors and writing this addendum one or two things have happened to the world's financial system, as the reader will be all too aware. To try and cram the financial history of the past few years into a couple of paragraphs would be nonsensical. I'll limit myself instead to a couple of comments, one in a sense looking back, the other looking ahead.

Looking backwards . . . it's now clear that the money culture and the financial excesses celebrated in the 1980s and which gave ideological direction to the ensuing couple of decades (a few mishaps along route notwithstanding) proved in the end to be unsustainable; 'serious money' metamorphosed into the most serious financial crisis since the 1930s; the crises in between, it's tempting to say, were minor by comparison (although of course for those who experienced their effects in form of redundancy or homelessness for example, they were anything but trivial). With the financial crash that broke through the surface in 2007[4] almost overnight 'loadsamoney' for the few was transformed into 'loadsadebt' for the many, to be paid for in the form of cut backs in public services and the like for the foreseeable future. The frantic efforts made by governments on both sides of the Atlantic to prop up key institutions, to get 'liquidity' into the system and return 'trust' to the international banking community, involved mind boggling sums of public money. Careful calculations suggest that the total cost of the US financial credit bailout – that is the various measures such as the provision of credit and lending facilities to organizations and markets central to Western finance – stood at \$4.6165 trillion by mid-2009. Loadsadebt doesn't do such a figure justice. The author of this estimate provides a way to make sense of such a number: 'The \$4.6165 trillion committed so far is about a trillion dollars (\$979 billion dollars) greater than the entire cost of World War II borne by the United States: \$3.6 trillion, adjusted for inflation (original cost was \$288 billion)'. Such staggering debt won't disappear quickly and its consequences will be at the centre of the politics of economic growth in the West and beyond for some time to come.

Looking ahead . . . at the time of writing it would seem that every effort is being made by western governments, international institutions

and others sharing their interests to repair and make good the damage done to the aims and objectives of a highly financialized capitalism wrought by the crisis. The nature of the crisis and the wider context would suggest that geographies of economic growth based on the 'business as usual' model will be harder to maintain than this labouring suggests. Why? Well, to use unfettered finance as the fuel to fire-up economic growth simply won't have the desired results: the wood's too wet, as it were, and the belief in finance and its magic has been brought into question by many, not least those in developing countries, who now see the ideological pomp of the Western financialized capitalist model somewhat deflated. Moreover, there's the host of influential issues related to the significant and ongoing shift in the wider global economic context, all of which would seem set to contain the ambitions of the old model of finance fuelled Western growth. Chiefly the continued rise and influence of countries such as Brazil, India and China – the latter in particular is set to maintain its meteoric growth and with that (notably through the accumulation of \$US) to have a significant say in setting the rules for the game of global economics to be played out over the next decade – would suggest anything other than business continuing unproblematically according to Western criteria.

Following the 2007–2009 financial crisis, money, finance, power and space are all alive and well, as it were, albeit reconfigured and reconfiguring as the above suggests; they are clearly central to how the contemporary world works and why it doesn't. To echo the sentiments of Lee et al. (2009) now, more than ever it would seem, is the time for geographers of finance to make significant contributions to research and policy agendas, in some cases already recognized but the importance of which has been magnified as the crisis unfolds (the social and economic inequalities of financialization, the conduct of politics through finance, and so on) while in other cases agendas need to be drafted so as to blend for instance geographies of finance,

economic growth and climate change. All of
these issues and more work through and continue to produce intriguing spatialities. More
the shame, then, if human geography, not just
economic geography, reverted to its own version of business as usual; the model which
failed to recognize the significance of the
analysis of both money and finance to understanding contemporary societies, how they
operate, and how the social relations of
finance and money simultaneously produce
and promote highly uneven life chances.

ACKNOWLEDGEMENTS

Many thanks to Andrew Leyshon and Peter
Sunley for very helpful comments on an earlier
draft of this chapter.

NOTES

1 On the use of offshore financial centres as 'tax
havens' see http://www.taxjustice.net
2 For a financial market commentary on emerging markets see http://www.emergingmarkets.org
3 But the same system produces a class and geographical select elite. The whole *World Wealth Report*
(2003) arguably serves as a useful reminder of the
skewed nature of the present financial system.
4 See http://news.bbc.co.uk/1/hi/7521250.stm for
a helpful timeline of key events.

REFERENCES

Akyüz, Y. (1995) Taming international finance. In
J. Michie, and J. Grieve Smith (1995) *Managing
the Global Economy*. New York: Oxford University
Press. p. 55.

Barnes, T. (2005) Culture: Economy. In P. Cloke, and R.
Johnston (eds) *Spaces of Geographical Thought:
Deconstructing Human Geography's Binaries*. London/
Thousand Oaks/New Delhi: SAGE.

Barnes, T.J. (2001) 'Retheorizing economic geography:
From the quantitative revolution to the 'cultural turn'.
Annals of the Association of American Geographers,
91(3): 546–65.

Beunza, D. and Garud, R. (2004) Security analysts as
frame-makers. *MIMCO*.

Knorr-Cetina, K. and Bruegger, U. (2000) The market as
an object of attachment: Exploring postsocial relations in financial markets. *Canadian Journal of
Sociology*, 25(2): 141–68.

Knorr-Cetina, K. and Bruegger, U. (2002a) Traders'
engagement with markets: A postsocial relationship.
Theory Culture and Society, 19(5/6): 161–85.

Knorr-Cetina, K. and Bruegger, U. (2006) Global micro-
structures: The virtual societies of financial markets.
AJS, 107(4): 905–50.

Clark, G.L. (1999) The retreat of the state and the rise
of pension fund capitalism. In R. Martin, (ed.) *Money
and the Space Economy*. Chichester: John Wiley and
Sons. p. 241.

Clark, G.L. (2005b) Setting the agenda: The geography of global finance WPG 05.03. Oxford: School
of Geography and Environment, University of
Oxford.

Clark, G.L. (2005a) Money flows like mercury: The
geography of global finance. *Geografiska Annaler*,
87B: 2.

Clark, G.L. and Wojcik, D. (2001) The city of London in
the Asian crisis. *Journal of Economic Geography*, 1 (1):
107–30.

Clark, G.L. and Wojcik, D. (2003) An economic geography of global finance: Ownership concentration and
stock-price volatility in German firms and regions.
Annals of the Association of American Geographers,
93(4): 909–24.

Clark, G.L. and Wrigley, N. (July 1997) The spatial configuration of the firm and the management of sunk
costs. *Economic Geography*, 73(3): 285–304.

Clark, G.L., and Thrift, N. and Tickell, A. (2004)
Performing finance: The industry, the media and its
image. *Review of International Political Economy*, 11
(2): 289–310.

Corbridge, S. (1994) Plausible worlds: Friedman, Keynes
and the geography of inflation. In S. Corbridge,
N., Thrift, and R. Martin (eds) *Money, Power and
Space*. Oxford: Blackwell. p. 63.

De Goede, M. (2004) Repoliticizing financial risk.
Economy and Society, 33(2): 197–217.

De Goede, M. (2005) *Virtue, Fortune, and Faith*.
Minneapolis: University of Minnesota Press.

Dodd, N. (1994) *The Sociology of Money: Economics,
Reason and Contemporary Society*. Cambridge:
Polity Press.

Eatwell, J. and Taylor, L. (2000) *Global Finance at Risk*.
Cambridge: Polity Press.

Erturk, I., Froud, J., Johal, S., Leaver, A., and Williams, K.
(2005) The democratisation of finance? Promises,

outcomes and conditions. *CRESC Working Paper Series*, Working Paper no. 9.

Feng, H., Froud, J., Haslam, C., Johal, S., and Williams K. (2001) A new business model? The capital market and the new economy. *Economy and Society*, 30(4): 467.

Fligstein, N. (2002) *The Architecture of Markets: An Economic Sociology of Twenty-First-Century Capitalist Societies*. Princeton and Oxford: Princeton University Press.

Frank, T. (2000) *One Market Under God: Extreme Capitalism, Market Populism, and the End of the Economic Democracy*. London: Secker and Walburg.

Gilbert, E. (2005) Common cents: Situating money in time and place. *Economy and Society*, 34(3): 357–88.

Harvey, D. (2005) *A Brief History of Neoliberalism*. Oxford: OUP.

Henwood, D. (1998) *Wall Street: How it Works and for Whom*. London/New York: Verso.

Hudson, Alan C. (1999) Off-shores on-shore: New regulatory spaces and real historical places in the landscape of global money. In R. Martin (ed.) *Money and the Space Economy*. Chichester: John Wiley and Sons. p.139.

Ingham, G. (1994) States and markets in the production of world money: Sterling and the dollar. In S. Corbridge, N. Thrift, and R. Martin (eds) *Money, Power and Space*. Oxford: Blackwell. p. 29.

Ingham, G. (2004) *The Nature of Money*. Cambridge: Polity Press.

Jones, P. (2005) Creating wealth in the West Midlands through sustainable credit unions: An action research project. *Executive Summary*. Manchester: Association of British Credit Unions.

Laulajainen, R. (2003) *Financial Geography: A Banker's View*. London and New York: Routledge.

Lee, R. (1999) Local money geographies of autonomy and resistance? In R. Martin (ed.). (1999) *Money and the Space Economy*. Chichester: John Wiley and Sons. p. 207.

Leyshon, A. and Thrift, N. (1997) *Money/Space: Geographies of Monetary Transformation*. London and New York: Routledge.

Leyshon, A., Thrift, N., and Pratt, J. (1997) Reading financial services: Texts, consumers, and financial literacy. *Environment and Planning D: Society and Space*, 16: 29–55.

Leyshon, A., Burton, D., Knights, D., Alferoff, C., and Signoretta, P. (2004) Ecologies of retail financial services: Understanding the persistence of door-to-door credit and insurance providers. *Environment and Planning A*, 36: 625–45.

Martin, R. (1994) Stateless monies, global financial integration and national economic autonomy: The end of geography? In S. Corbridge, N. Thrift, and R. Martin (eds) *Money, Power and Space*. Oxford: Blackwell. pp. 253–78.

Martin, R. (1999a) Selling off the state: Privatisation, the equity market and the geographies of shareholder capitalism. In R. Martin (ed.). (1999) *Money and the Space Economy*. Chichester: John Wiley and Sons. p. 261.

Martin, R. (1999b) The new economic geography of money. In R. Martin (ed.) *Money and the Space Economy*. Chichester: John Wiley and Sons. p. 3.

Miller, P. (2001) Governing by numbers: Why calculative practices matter. *Social Research*, 68(2).

Palan, R. (2003) *The Offshore World*. Ithaca and London: Cornell University Press.

Panić, M. (1995) The Bretton Woods system: Concept and practice. In J. Michie and J. Grieve Smith, (1995) *Managing the Global Economy*. New York: Oxford University Press. p. 37.

Pixley J.F. (1999) Beyond twin deficits: Emotions of the future in the organizations of money. *American Journal of Economics & Sociology*, 58(4): 1091.

Pixley, J. (2002) Expectations, emotions and money: Finance organizations and futures. In S.R. Clegg (ed.) *Management and Organization Paradoxes*. Amsterdam/Philadelphia: John Benjamins Publishing Company.

Pixley, J. (2004) *Emotions in Finance: Distrust and Uncertainty in Global Markets*. Cambridge University Press.

Pollard, J. (1999) Globalisation, regulation and the changing organisation of retail banking in the United States and Britain. In R. Martin (ed.) (1999) *Money and the Space Economy*. Chichester: John Wiley and Sons. p. 49.

Pryke, M. (1991) An international city going 'global': Spatial change in the city of London. *Environment and Planning D: Society and Space*, 9: 197–222.

Pryke, M. (1999) City rhythms: Neo-liberalism and the developing world. In J. Allen, D. Massey, and M. Pryke (eds) *Unsettling Cities: Movement/Settlement*. London and New York: Routledge in Association with The Open University. p. 229.

Pryke, M. and Lee, R. (1995) Place your bets: Towards an understanding of globalisation, socio-financial engineering and competition within a financial centre. *Urban Studies*, 32(2): 329–44.

Sinclair, T.J. (2005) *The New Masters of Capital: American Bond Rating Agencies and the Politics of Creditworthiness*, Ithaca and London: Cornell University Press.

Smith, W.D. (1984) The function of commercial centers in the modernization of european capitalism: Amsterdam as an information exchange in the seventeenth century. *Journal of Economic History*, XLIV: 4.

Strange, S. (1994) From Bretton Woods to the casino economy. In S. Corbridge, N. Thrift, and R. Martin (eds) *Money, Power and Space*. Oxford: Blackwell. p. 49.

Swedburg, R. (1991) *Joseph A. Schumpeter: The Economies on Sociology of Capitalism*. Princeton: Princeton University Press.

Thrift, N. (1999) Cities and economic change: Global governance. In J. Allen, D. Massey, and M. Pryke (eds) *Unsettling Cities: Movement/Settlement*. London and New York: Routledge in Association with The Open University. p. 276.

Thrift, N. (1994) On the social and cultural determinants of international financial centres: The case of the city of London. In S. Corbridge, N. Thrift, and R. Martin (eds) *Money, Power and Space*. Oxford: Blackwell. p. 327.

Thrift, N. (2002) A hyperactive world. In R.J. Johnston, P.J. Taylor, and M. Watts (eds) (2002) *Geographies of Global Change* (2nd edn). Oxford: Blackwell.

Turner, D. (2005) National News Business and Economy: Pay gap widest in City, says GMB. *The Financial Times*, 6 May 2005.

Williams, K. (2000) From shareholder value to present-day capitalism. *Economy and Society,* 29(1): 1–12.

Wrigley, N. (1999) Corporate finance. leveraged restructuring and the economic landscape: The LBO wave in US food retailing. In R. Martin (ed.) *Money, and the Space Economy*. Chichester: John Wiley and Sons. p.185.

Zaloom, Caitlin (2003) Ambiguous numbers. *American Ethnologist*, 30: 258–72.

PART 7

Geographies of Consumption and Economic Spectacle

20

Geographies of Retailing and Consumption: The Shopping List Compendium

Louise Crewe

INTRODUCTION: SHOPPING LIST GEOGRAPHY

Shopping is boring. (Koolhaas, 2002)

This chapter aims to uncover why shopping matters geographically and why geographers might be interested in it. Having spent large parts of a 20 year career studying fashion retailing and consumption, it still puzzles me why it is only relatively recently that I haven't had to preface my work with a pre-amble about why fashion is a worthwhile subject for geographical study. It has always seemed that to engage in research on shopping – and particularly for clothes – is to somehow place oneself at the fringe of academic respectability. Consumption studies seem tinged with a sense of moral panic, stigmatized; their subjects of study deemed mildly hysterical or out of control. Fashion consumption in particular has so often been imagined as either superficial (and therefore not worthy of serious attention), or it has been seen as a ghostly presence – appearing immaterial by academics' lack of engagement with its physicality.

Of course such neglect may say rather more about the positionality of the producers of academic geographical knowledge than it does about the state of the fashion industry. Geographers, it has to be said, are notorious for their lack of fashion sense. More meteorology than metrosexual, more grykes than Gucci, the Geography teacher is seldom seen as a style icon. But regardless of academic geographers and their sartorial slip-ups, clothing and its geographies are theoretically important and are rarely trivial or simply about surface display and superficiality. And yet I have always been struck by how badly Economic Geography has treated retailing and consumption and recall heated debates with my PhD supervisors who continually tried to steer me towards a modelling and store location approach to retailing.

But this was never where my interests lay. I have never really understood why retail geography, potentially one of the most interesting parts of the sub-discipline, has been studied in such a way as to make it one of the most boring. Nick Blomley's early comments about retail geography being a blinkered, introverted and under-theorized segment of economic geography rang true for me. Blomley argued that retail geography was oblivious and seemingly indifferent to developments outside its self-contained, applied and largely descriptive or predictive loop (Blomley, 1996: 238). Geography drew heavily on neo-classical Economics which was notionally granted the accolade of the discipline with the most authority and legitimacy in speaking about markets. The theory assumes that a simple and single-minded calculus of pleasure (spending money) and pain (earning it) is enough to grind out consumption, essentially understood as equivalent to market demand. Much early retail geography followed the economists' lead and was dominated by orthodox quantitative approaches in the spatial science tradition: location theory and spatial modelling shaped the early evolution of retail geography.

I drift into a reverie of recollection of my years at school and university studying retail geography . . . the mind-numbing dullness of practical classes spent plotting Christaller's $k = 3$ higher order centres into a hexagonal landscape, shading in catchment area choropleths, calculating drive-time distances to shopping centres, staring blankly at gravity models and spatial interaction equations, and standing on bleak suburban high streets with a clip board and consumer questionnaire. But if shopping as practice and pedagogy was so boring, how, some 25 years on, has retail geography become such a central component within economic geography and beyond? Identified as lying at the very heart of a reconstructed economic geography (Crang, 1997), retail geography has had a make-over. And whilst markets continue to lead a shadowy existence in economics, geographers have made significant progress in understanding the cultural and social dimensions of markets and in framing markets theoretically.

Retailing and consumption are increasingly creative components in the making of economy. The production, exchange and consumption of commodities is identified as the 'beating heart of capitalism' (Thrift, 2005: 5). Consumer spaces are at once material sites for commodity exchange and symbolic and metaphoric territories. It is suggested that understanding the secret life of things may reveal profound insights into the society, economy, culture and polity of commodity-producing systems (Boyd and Watts, 2005). Retailing has made a major contribution to the contemporary proliferation of material culture and of ways of narrating self and identity. How have Geographers conceptually grasped these connections between commodities, consumers and their spatial and temporal worlds? I will need to look further than school geography lessons in order to understand how and why such a radical re-framing of the sub-discipline emerged.

Thus I turn my attention to more conventional academic sources: the plethora of Handbooks, Companions and Guides to Economic Geography (*Reading Economic Geography* (2003), *A Companion to Economic Geography* (2000), *The Oxford Handbook of Economic Geography* (2000), *The Routledge Studies in Economic Geography* (2006)). Inspired by such a wealth of material I stagger back from the library, buckling under the weight of books. I scour their pages for state-of-the-art insights into retail geography. In the first volume, there is nothing on retailing. How strange. In the second, again, nothing. In all, I manage to find only one chapter on retailing, appearing in the *Oxford Handbook of Economic Geography*, written by Neil Wrigley and beginning with a lament for the profound absence of any consideration of retailing within recent and highly respected volumes on globalization and the transformation of economy (2000: 292–94). In terms of its profile in academic texts on economic geography, retailing and consumption appears as an intellectual post-script if not an apologia, quietly shunted to the end of a volume (if it appears at all).

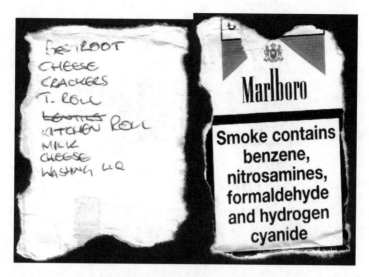

Figure 20.1 Light lunch and fags (no lentils). (*Source: Keaggy, 2007*)

Deflated, defeated, and increasingly panicked, I resort to type. I bash 'compendium' and 'shopping' into a search engine. It is here that I find my inspiration for this chapter. The first search result provides me with all I need to understand the 'new' retail geography. It is an archive of abandoned shopping lists that an avid individual has collected, ordered, annotated and posted on the internet for others to peruse (Keaggy, 2007). Encapsulated within the tatty remains of these discarded shopping lists are insights into the ways in which particular forms of exchange are represented, encoded, translated, practised and institutionalized by people in particular places at particular times.[1] The shopping list above (Figure 20.1), for example, written on the back of a packet of Marlboro cigarettes, tells us more than we might imagine about systems of commodity provision, markets, branding, exchange, consumption and value.

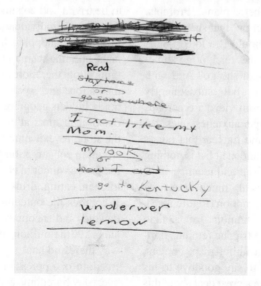

Figure 20.2 Lemons, underwear, go to Kentucky. (*Source: Keaggy, 2007*)

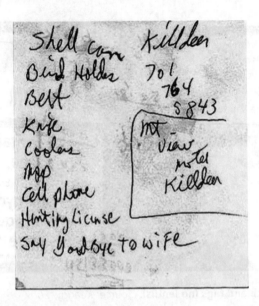

Figure 20.3   Kill deer, say goodbye to the wife. (*Source: Keaggy, 2007*)

Similarly, the shopping list shown in Figure 20.2 shows us a glimpse into a young person's world. A whole set of options are suggested here, all crossed out apart from 'go to Kentucky, read and shop'. (It is only much later that I wonder whether 'go to Kentucky' means the place or the take-away.) Written and then lightly scribbled out yet still legible are a whole number of other thoughts and musings – about family, appearance, social life, bodily display and performance. Prompts, perhaps, things to reflect on (that she acts like her mom? And how should she look? What should she do – stay home, read, or go somewhere? But where should she go? And with whom?). Also etched but subsequently scratched out, erased from view, are perhaps yet greater worries, deeper anxieties, ones that can't be left lying around for fear that others may find them. This abandoned list is nothing less than a narration of self and identity.

A third list also reveals much about the social relations of consumption (Figure 20.3). Presumably an aide memoir for a man embarking on a hunting trip, he reminds himself to buy, or pack, a knife, map, coolers, cell phone and, lastly, to say goodbye to his wife. One could surmise a great deal about this person, his desires, passions and motivations,

from such random scribblings. Presumably the note to 'kill deer' refers to place not practice, but one does wonder.

This self-indulgent polemic by way of an introduction is, I confess, a tactical manoeuvre on my part, employed in order to make a more conceptual set of interventions in the following discussion, to reveal something of the scale and reach of this chapter's subject: retailing and consumption. What may appear to be trivial and ephemeral (a random collection by one individual of an equally random set of used shopping lists) – discarded 'rubbish' one might imagine – can tell us something altogether more profound about markets, mediation and space. The abandoned list holds hidden geographies of acquisition and disposal, it hints at consumers' lives beyond the store, reveals much about choice and constraint in consumption and invites us to imagine the consumer in context – in the home, the kitchen, eating, drinking, alone, with friends. It codifies the outcomes of 'the routines and dawdles and encounters and desires and decisions . . . the millions of conversations on the way there and back . . . imagining the store as freedom or oppression or just as a place of everyday boredoms and pleasures and annoyances' (Bowlby, 1997: 95).

It is via this prompt, the shopping list, that I hope to bring into view the mutually constitutive relations between retailing, consumption, possession and space. Together these may help us on our journey to understanding why shopping matters. I focus on three particular ways of framing the field in order to draw out a set of broader reflections: space, passion and possession. Together I hope they might begin to show how consumption is produced discursively, materially, relationally, interactively. They reveal too the importance of consumers' connections to their objects – their abandoned shopping lists, their till receipts, the rubbish in their bins, the clothes in their charity bag donations, wardrobes or closets, all holding consumption stories untold, perhaps soon to be lost. Or perhaps revealed. Consumer culture cannot be reduced just to commodities, or to shops, or to consumers, but must be understood in terms of relationality; as a recursive loop. In exploring this I am attempting to show how the most mundane, ordinary, invisible and seemingly uninteresting things can be as significant and revealing as the most dramatic.

SPACE

Casting your eye over our skylines is akin to flicking through a glossy magazine such as Vogue. (Sudjic, 1990)

Orthodox accounts of retail geography emphasized the importance of location, but only in as much as this informed attempts to determine and map least cost locations, the spatial margins of profitability and distributions of market potential according to distance and transport costs (Berry and Parr, 1988). More recent accounts have focused on the globalization of retail capital (Wrigley, 2000), the strategic behaviour of large retail corporations and their spatial effects (Wrigley et al., 2005). Supermarkets have come to assume a position of unprecedented importance in contemporary economy, colonizing urban space and driving commodity chains.

The largest global retailers such as Wal-Mart and Carrefour are amongst the top 15 'global' TNCs (Wrigley, 2000: 294) and recent work is addressing the strategic potential for more ethical systems of provision (Hughes, 2007; Hughes et al., 2007, 2008).

More recently, in part as a critique of the undue affordance devoted to capital within retail geography, and more broadly as part of an emergent agenda of emotional geography, a range of work has begun to consider consumers in context and explores shopping as spatial and sensory practice (Crewe, 2010). Challenging the abstract conception of the shop as a functional, smooth, opaque economic surface (Goh, 2002: 6), such work is focusing on shopping-as-practice and in its relation to space (Gregson et al., 2002a, b; Goh, 2002). Retail spaces and architectures are increasingly designed in order to generate positive affective responses in consumers. Of course this is nothing new. In a wonderfully constructed series of timelines, Chung et al. (2001) reveal the long and rich spatial history of the retail form, beginning with the foundation of the city of Catalhoyuk for the trade in commodities in 7000 BC, and ending with Wal-Mart, the largest retailer in the world in 2000. They also explore the ways in which key developments shaped the evolution of retail formats, tracing a number of dimensions through time (money, glass, movement, lighting, communications, nature). In a potent series of images, Chung et al. juxtapose pictures of trading spaces in Rome (110), Isfahan (1585), Paris (1815), London (1851), Milan (1865), Moscow (1893), Houston (1971), Xian, (1994) and Las Vegas (2000). What is startling about this montage is the striking degree of architectural, structural and spatial conformity across the disparate sites and through time. The historical contiguity of retail formats and shopping practices across time and space is quite extraordinary.

And so we see how one of the earliest means through which retail organizations attempted to push brand value was in fact through the creation of new and spectacular worlds into which commodities were inserted – performative spaces under any definition. Walter Benjamin's classic works on the Parisian Arcades explored the then revolutionary visual qualities of the arcades where goods were displayed both for purchase and perusal (Buck-Morss, 1999). Benjamin was perhaps the first consumption theorist whose work aimed to bridge the divide between everyday experience and more conventional academic concerns. His focus on the relations between space, consumption, practice and aesthetics was particularly incisive.

The department stores of nineteenth century Paris were also early exemplars of a new spatial organization of consumption, fantastic dream-worlds where commodities were emplaced in dazzling emporia, their spaces affording a glitter of distraction around the commodity. In what I still regard as perhaps the most brilliant piece of writing on retail space and subjectivity, Nick Blomley's (1996), passionate and powerful reading of Zola's novel, *Au Bonheur des Dames*, reveals how (female) consumers were 'tempted, captured and seduced by the new commodities, artfully displayed' (p. 252). And yet the seductive act of consumption was, like seduction itself, double edged, 'Mouret's seductions are oppressive and politicized. The masculine space of the store is at once a cathedral to femininity, and a prison' (p. 252). The department store, it is argued, was in part about the making of willing female consumers (Bowlby, 1985: 11) – fascinated, seduced, hungry, awe-struck, but also objectified, reduced to relational instruments in discourses of masculine conquest, commerciality and sexuality.

The latest academic iteration of shop-as-spectacular space draws on notions of theatre and performance. Arguably drawing on Pine and Gilmore's early work on the experience economy (1999), the roles of consumer agency, performativity and event-space are informing a number of developments within the architecture of fashion stores. People rarely consume in a blind, passive and gullible fashion but, rather, they 'actively perform their presence. . . . The parameters of agency have been changed' (Amin and Thrift, 2002:124; de Nora, 2000). Retail capital has responded in a number of ways to the affective, performative and emotional requirements of consumers who appeared to tire of the mass middle market offer that characterized UK and US urban spaces during the 1980s and 1990s (Hughes, 2000; Reinach, 2005).

Prada's epicentre stores are one of the clearest contemporary attempts of how retail architecture can be fabricated as part of a strategy to re-envision brand identity and shopping as practice. Located in some of the world's key fashion districts, Prada worked with the Dutch architect Rem Koolhaas to create a number of 'epicentre' stores that would act as monuments to the brand whilst at the same time redefining both what Prada is, does and can become. The difficulty of course is how to maintain and enhance value whilst pursuing a relentless globalization strategy. Koolhaas discusses the danger of repetition that results from indefinite expansion, and underscores the tensions between commerce and culture, between organization and agency, between global branding and (de)-valorization. All too often the corporate drive for commercial return translates spatially into megaloma that eliminates the elements of surprise and mystery that cling to the brand, imprisoning it in a definitive identity. Each additional Prada store potentially reduces aura, contributes to a sense of familiarity and ultimately threatens the viability of the brand as a creative enterprise (Koolhaas, 2002). In spite of this contradiction, Koolhaas' 'solution' to the flagship syndrome was to develop 'bigness' as a theoretical concept. He wrote that, 'in a landscape of disarray, disassembly, dissociation, disclamation, the attraction of Bigness is its potential to reconstruct the whole, resurrect the Real, reinvent the collective' (in Foster, 2002: 51). Koolhaas' original task in designing global Prada stores was to avoid the flagship syndrome under conditions where, he argued architecture is subservient to the market and its terms. The market has supplanted ideology. Architecture has turned into a spectacle (Koolhaas, 2006).

But his solution was arguably to reproduce precisely what he was trying to avoid. He created a limited number of epicentre stores, spectacular spaces of surprise and transgression that he argued could act as devices to renew the brand by counteracting and destabilizing existing notions of 'Prada' as label, logo or shopping space. The epicentre store was intended to act as a conceptual window, a means of capturing and transmitting future directions for the brand. The defining feature of the New York store, for example, is the wave, a curving floor that swoops from street level to basement. The store incorporates a series of aluminium mesh cages suspended from the ceiling that are movable and imitate the up-side down skyline of a hanging city. The space is transformative, unfixed – by day it is used as an area for display and sale, but it is then transformed into a performance space with retractable stage. The fitting rooms are entered through doors with privalite glass that switches from transparent to opaque on entry. Once inside the light is customer-controlled and the rooms are fitted with a series of cameras and plasma screens to record customers trying on their garments; they can then watch themselves again from all angles in instant replay. The images are stored and available for use by the customer in-store or on-line. Screens are used as a key device for looking and seeing throughout the stores and the aim is to overlay commercial functionality with a series of experiential typologies that expand the imaginative potential of shopping.

Quite how successful such spectacular places will be in either commercial or cultural terms remains to be seen, and there are many who see the 'starchitect' model of urban design as little more than the ongoing commodification and commercialization of cityscapes, spectacular structures pompously pedalled by big name architects who have themselves become brands (Foster, 2002; Frampton, 2005; La Cecla, 2008; Sorkin, 2005). Rem Koolhaas, in something of a dialectical twist, appears more recently tacitly to reject 'bigness' and the grand architectural schemes that he once appeared to pioneer and it has been argued that he surfs the dialectic between artistic belief and commercial reality better than most (Foster, 2002: 60). His critics, on the other hand, may find his intellectual credentials altogether more ambiguous: he vehemently critiques contemporary shopping and yet serves as the house architect of Prada; he opposed the spectacular architecture solution of the sort promoted by institutions such as the Guggenheim and yet designed a Guggenheim gallery in that most spectacular, hyper-real city, Las Vegas see Chapter 12; Foster, 2002: 61). The archistar system, critics suggest, has killed creativity, sociality, fashion and architecture by proposing a model of intervention that is theoretically fake, doped with money and based on duplicity and trickery. The model encourages consumers to see flagship stores as models for progressive urban design and development when in fact they are little more than containers without content (La Cecla, 2008). The very victory of the megastore, it is argued, spells its eventual defeat, for like its products, it is almost always obsolete (Foster, 2002: 56). Contemporary retailing, some would thus argue, signals massification, homogenization, cultural meltdown.

So if the marriage between archistars and retail capital is failing to convince many that spectacular experiential retail spaces offer a convincing means of recreating the brand and valorizing the shopping experience, what might the alternatives be? One possibility is a more modest retail format that rejects 'bigness' in favour of more subtle spaces that explicitly question consumption as cultural and political process. One early example of this is the designer-duo Vexed Generation who developed a number of concept stores in London's Soho in the mid-late 1990s that played with ideas of form, function and meaning in consumption. Instead of participating in the spectacular but momentary performance of the bi-annual international fashion weeks as product design showcases, or constructing grand global shops, Vexed mobilized the fabric of their garments and their concept stores and used these as the architectural backcloth to question broader social and political issues. Through their store spaces, Vexed created countercultures of resistance against the urban condition and exposed the injustices inherent in free market economics. Many of their garments are capable of giving 'voice to an inner self that is often imprisoned in everyday life' and subsequently encourages freedom of physicality and perception within cities (Destefani, 2006: 17). Since the company's inception in 1994, their London-inspired street wear has symbolized social, historical and political urban struggles and encouraged clientele to break out of the 'plastic-cage of mass consumerism' (Mansvelt, 2008: 108). Through a range of hoods, collars, zips, concealing masks and parka coats, their weather-proof garments cover most of the body. They therefore render social surveillance redundant, allowing wearers to re-attain social anonymity and provide protection. However, such apparel paradoxically allows wearers to reveal more of themselves, granting them a unique urban identity and increased social and political agency.

The first store, The White Shop on Newburgh Street opened in 1995 and reflected Vexed's concerns about escalating urban surveillance. It comprised a glass box, similar to an incubator. Small slits were cut into the walls surrounding the incubator display unit so customers could peep in, reach in and feel the clothes, but not remove them. The outside of the space was left under decades of grime and the only visible area was a small slice in the otherwise dirty window. A CCTV monitor mounted outside the store monitored the internal goings on. By placing the shop under the surveillance of passers-by, Vexed inverted conventional surveillance tactics. Their second shop on Berwick Street in London's Soho had breathing garments linked to an air compressor. The garments were inflated and deflated as if they were breathing and fast-growing plants such as ivy were threaded through the clothes and sprouted from arm and neck holes to create a living installation and prod the consumer

into thinking about wider environmental issues and questions of garment production and wear. Such retail spaces are far removed conceptually and physically from epicentre-style global flagship stores. Rather, they are explicitly envisaged as critical, questioning places for consumer agency, dissident design and subversion of conventional corporate mores.

A second example is the guerrilla store concept pioneered by Rei Kawakubo of Comme des Garcons. The first in the 'series' was located in a redundant book shop in Berlin. The store captured the rhythm of local culture, used old water pipes to hang a rapidly changing stock and advertised solely through underground advertising on the internet and via grainy black and white posters (Mores, 2006: 149). These temporary stores look to find the cracks in the wall of corporate culture sell garments with no price tags, change their stock every few weeks and disregard any notions of spectacle. They are constructed either from disused or derelict buildings, or from materials that are easily collapsible meaning that these deconstructive spaces emerge and then disappear as quickly as the clothes they display. This strategy takes advantage of the impulses and instincts of the consumer. The guerrilla stores decentralize and deterritorialize conventional fashion spaces and in a broader sense form part of a wider theoretical questioning of the tendencies towards endless nomadism versus desires for more sedentary styles of being, living and rootedness. The architectural reconstruction of decayed urban space forms part of Comme's broader philosophy that 'thinks forward by looking backwards, recycling old things to make them new' (Evans, 2003: 296). This offers a very different vision of future retail based not on the spectacular but on notions of temporality, pace and underground knowledge.

Again we can trace a long genealogy to such framings of retail space – Bakhtin's (1968) evocative descriptions of the vitality and grotesqueness of the market depicted in Rabelais' world is perhaps the most obvious example, although a range of more recent work has explored issues of sociality, tactility, embodiment and the sensory dimensions of a number of spaces of exchange, including car boot sales and second hand shops (Baker, 2000; Gregson and Crewe, 2003; Gregson et al., 2001), and focusing on the walking, touching, scenting, hearing and feeling dimensions of consumption (fun, fear, embarrassment, revulsion).

The significance of this work to a broader reframing of retail geography is the emphasis on shopping space as far more than retinal stimulation. We *feel* retail spaces; they have the capacity to hit all of our sensory registers. Stores are alive, they have agentive capacities – the shock of warm skin hitting cold metal, the creak of the wooden floor, the cramped sweaty bodies in the changing room, the revulsion at one's image reflected back in endless mirrors. Increasingly, the meaning enshrined within retail spaces lies less in surface characteristics and materials (metal, stone, wood, colour) than in consumer's sensory connections to space. Consumption is founded on both hedonistic, bodily, sensory fulfillment and more rational and restrained imagined pleasures; it is both corporeal and cerebral at the same time. 'The relationship between reason and emotion in consumption, as elsewhere, is not simply oppositional, or even that tensionful, but one which is both constituted and consummated in more or less continuous ways' (Boden and Williams, 2002: 499). Actions are intertwined with people's everyday practices and the structure of cultural communities in complex ways. Retail stores are one of a suite of performative economic spaces and processes that are increasingly omnisensory, 'they reach across the senses, using not just vision but also touch, smell, taste, hearing and kinaesthetic (movement) senses in order to produce strong bodily reactions'.

And so we see so clearly how shopping spaces are constituted not simply by the dictates of retail capital and its investment decisions, but are produced, reproduced and made sense of by consumers themselves through their shopping practices and discourses.

Retail architecture in its built, virtual and imagined forms acts not simply as the contextual backcloth against which consumption takes place, but is constituent of commodity value and embodied consumer practice. Different ways of looking, engaging and seeing commodities in and of themselves shape value and meaning. The screen, the store, the catalogue, the billboard, the advert – these are not simply different distribution channels; they are constituent of commodity meaning. Consumers' constitution of in-store geographies connect to the shop's own narrative productions and stories which are themselves in a constant process of flux, of becoming. The shop here 'assumes the role of author and storyteller in relation to the customer-as-reader' (Goh, 2002: 8), although not in any narrow cause and effect sense. Rather, reading and writing the shop sit in mutual and relational constitution.

The importance of this work to a reconstituted retail geography is that it opens up a space for consumer agency and for the challenging or contestation of corporate control over consumption. This more relational approach sees consumption as an emotionally charged process, a sensory experience, in which certain types of products, places and shops are imbued with desire or disgust, love or loathing (Gregson Crewe and Brooks, 2001, 2002;) and where the thermal, acoustic, luminary and olfactory qualities of the space are fully recognized. This may be one means of reanimating the geographer's consumptional imagination, of breathing new emotional life into the classically rational bones of retail geographers who understood capital very well, but were much less convincing in their theorization of consumption.[2] Until we understand how consumers' knowledges and readings of shop space intersect with the multiple and intertextual modes of writing the shop, our understandings of consumption as practised in space will be partial or static. And what this in turn implies is that we must see consumers in context, as entangled within the domain of the shop, not separated from it.

PASSION

I'm through with what fashion has become. For the first time in my life I've cut the ****ing cord ... If I see that you bothered to spend £500 that you didn't have on this season's Balenciaga handbag, I feel sorry for you. (Peter Saville, *Confessions of an Art Director*, Artwork Audley, 2006)

If the first framing of retailing focused on corporate capital and its spatial outcomes, the second framing device positions the consumer as a far more active agent in the determination of retailing and consumption. If we reflect on the consumer more explicitly it is possible to develop an understanding of consumption practice that is far less structurally determined. Consumers are no longer the atomized or isolated economic actors that stalked the pages of classical Geography textbooks. Consumers are increasingly taking cues from one another rather than from conventional channels such as large corporations or printed media outlets, catalysed in part via electronic means of communication such as peer-to-peer networks, sophisticated comparison internet sites, mobile messaging and electronic social networks (Shirky, 2008). The solidarity made possible by the internet provides shared experience; validation is both sought and found. Forrester Research, for example, estimates that 60% of online Europeans now connect with others in mutual interest or support groups. Electronic tribes structured around consumer interests are proliferating (Kozinets, 1999), and accelerating levels of consumer connectedness via electronic means are combining to link always-on consumers who may be always-on-the-move in new and potent ways. This ability to engage with others without co-presence is powerful. The collective absence/presence of co-consumers adds up to significant systems of member-generated value, and online consumer communities are materializing as new spaces for the creation of social identities.

One explanation for the apparent emergence of new forms of consumption tribalism is that it reflects in part a search for identity and a sense of self and social belonging under conditions of risk, fragmentation and uncertainty (Giddens, 1991; Lash, 1993; Warde, 1994). As certitude fragments, identity-creation through consumption becomes a risky business. One response, it has been argued, is the losing of the self into a collaborative subject, connected to others who confirm and endorse our consumption-identities through shared allegiances and passions, enabled in part by the internet. The community validates our choices, our taste. Such groupings appear as shared collectivities, affective assemblages or neo-tribes searching for shared sentiments, or at least approval of their assumed narrations of self (Bauman, 1992; Maffesoli, 1996). Labels, or groupings, become organizing factors in the lives of members, who seek support and affirmation by bonding with others of a similar kind. Quite why consumer groups commit considerable emotional investments to the objects, subjects and texts that they follow is the focus at much debate (Pimental and Reynolds, 2004; Sandvoss, 2005), but the passion, hunger and enthusiasm that these consumers feel for their object of desire is undeniable. They love their things, worship them, cherish them.

The passion and power felt by certain consumers towards their commodities was captured by the photography exhibition Happy Victims in London by Tsuzuki who photographed 30 Japanese individuals who have turned the act of shopping into an obsession, lying somewhere between artistic expression and an unusual kind of fetishism. Worshipping one individual designer, these men and women consume religiously their chosen labels – Jean Paul Gaultier, Anna Sui, Vivienne Westwood – often at the expense of life's other necessities. They turn what are typically tiny apartments into living temples to their fashion gods, resulting in interiors which range from the breathtakingly cluttered to the manically ordered. The 'Happy Victims' sit in minute rooms, lovingly surrounded by pristine garments from the designer of their choice.

The focus of the photographs is not on the individual, who is often blurred, but on the clothing that it is felt defines them. A Buddhist monk is shown in his Tokyo retreat surrounded by his Comme des Garcons collection. Once a month he leaves his temple to visit Tokyo for 'shopping and fun'. In the temple he may wear a robe, but in Tokyo he wears nothing but Comme. He sees the designs as having a religious quality. This fetishistic worship of a brand is echoed again by a photograph of a young Japanese man who describes himself as being so devoted to Hermes that he carries his 500,000 yen Hermes briefcase to work in a (Hermes) towel to protect it from his own sweat. A third image reveals a teacher at Bunka Fashion College and is described as 'Maestro Margiela'. He treasures his collection of Maison Margiela clothes so much that he prefers to eat out than risk infusing his clothes with cooking smells. He keeps only ear drops in his fridge. Tsuzuki produces some quite startling images that reveal the power of certain brands to seduce consumers whose frenetic investment in their chosen subject becomes a way of life. They fall into the deep end of fandom. Their passion becomes transformative, their knowledges finely honed. Significantly Tsuzuki, like the shopping lists above, reveals both the peculiar elements of daily life and the power of consumers as creators.

What is particularly significant about passionate consumption under current conditions is the powerful network effects made possible by electronically-mediated systems of commodity knowledge, circulation and exchange. The internet has enabled consumers to reach out into commodity worlds faster, further and deeper than ever before. Shifts in technology have enabled access to vast amounts of commodity knowledge and information that was hitherto out of reach. This brings with it a whole suite of transformative possibilities that require us to re-conceptualize how, where and why we 'do' consumption. Two particular outcomes appear to be emerging as particularly significant.

First, passionate and informed consumer alliances are enabling the disintermediation (or at least reconfiguration) of 'trusted' intermediaries and knowledge providers. Consumers are relying less on the authority of conventional branding and advertising campaigns for their consumption knowledges and consumption is increasingly determined by consumer-based opinions, reviews and recommendations. This ability for consumers to short-circuit, or see through, the hitherto concealed suite of corporate sales and marketing tactics is enabling new levels of transparency where there is less scope for hype, spin and con. This may significantly empower consumers and offers the possibility at least for new forms of agency and self-determination. At the very least the new technological means of acquiring commodity knowledge and doing consumption are resulting in a new blurring between firms, consumers and the creative process to produce what might be described as a hybrid 'mash culture' (Wilkinson, 2005).

The power of organizing without organizations (Shirky, 2008) via enthusiastic collectivities of consumers require that we re-think our theorizations of agency and power. Producers and retailers are acutely aware of the commodity knowledges residing and circulating amongst groups of consumer subjects and are increasingly and desperately seeking out new mechanisms to harness this and to sustain and refresh our enthusiasm to consume. The result is an accelerating 'connective mutation' (Thrift, 2005) of cycles of production, consumption and reproduction as consumers break into formerly closed systems and processes, and as producers seek means through which to harness such exterior knowledges and draw them back into the corporate realm. Together such processes have the potential to transform how commodity encounters are shaped and practised by the consumer.

At the very least electronically-mediated passionate consumption raise some very serious challenges to corporate systems of consumer management. It is fine for big capital to look to the consumer in search of clues and cues. But if corporations want to play on the street and use its signs, symbols and codes as leverage, they need to be very clear about the rules. Gestural marketing politics simply won't do and there are some real corporate dangers in ceding creative control to unpredictable consumers. The case of the Presto space in Toronto's Kensington Market is one example of this (Fraser, 2002). Presented as hybrid gallery and music venue, the space was located in an ethnically diverse and bohemian, eclectic area. But the seemingly benign building was under constant scrutiny from the outset by private security guards. Upon closer scrutiny it became clear that the space was not in fact a place for fledgling artists or musicians, but was a promotional vehicle for Nike's latest line of footwear (Fraser, 2000). Once the connection to the infamous multinational was exposed any plans Presto had to align itself with a creative, independent scene was thwarted. Residents were vigilant against big businesses trying to inscribe their products with bohemian chic and saw Presto as an imposter. The faux-graffiti façade of the building seemed about as authentic and convincing as a pair of new distressed worn-in jeans. Local protest began apace: the building was vandalized, garbage was left on its doorstep each morning and the venue ceased operation after only a few weeks. Fake authenticity is rarely convincing.

And so whilst superficially organizations may generate the kudos of creative buzz or noise that they so desperately desire, they may also find their brand message and integrity slipping dangerously off-message.[3] The openness of distribution channels in turn makes it far easier and speedier for adversarial or accusatory brand messages to circulate amongst disaffected and self determining community groups. Consumer collectivities may be passionate and enthusiastic. They can also be fractious, unruly and dissonant. Whilst enthusiastic consumers might seem like ideal customers, fans can all too easily fall out of love with their objects of affection which can lead not just to indifference or apathy, but to outright hostility and antipathy. Passion can be dangerous.

Second, there may equally be some less optimistic outcomes for consumers too. The vastness of available information about consumption can create chaos, confusion and contradiction. Insatiable demands for information coupled with raised expectations about the quality of that information can have troubling implications as consumers are finding their way quickly and move deeply into increasingly obscure and potentially unreliable sources of information. As new customer-producers are able continuously to add content in the form of text, audio, video and so on, a public-authoring streaming ethos emerges which can be disorientating and frustrating. Information retrieved from user-generated open systems can be highly variable in its quality and reliability. There are some very clear limits to consumption knowledges and their reliability under such open source models. Where does one find reliable information? Who does one trust? Clearly there is an increasing need for systems of curation and validation with respect to publicly authored consumption sources, but this in turn raises sets of questions about authorship, censorship, control, power and trust.

POSSESSION

Worn cloth testifies to the way in which things become materially, in their consumption as much as their production. (Hauser, 2004: 293)

If the developments outlined above suggest new spatial architectures of retailing, new theorizations of agency and new means of doing consumption, what they lack is a serious exploration of the material culture of things and of the ways in which subject-object entanglements shape commodity value. The objects of retailing and consumption have been followed to their points of origin (but rarely beyond the point of sale). Quite why conventional retailing and consumption geographies have paid such scant regard to processes and practices beyond the point of purchase is curious, and is all the more surprising given the recent intellectual attention afforded to issues of performance, affect and embodiment (Thrift, 2004). For as a number of accounts from outside geography's disciplinary boundaries have revealed so potently, the biographical histories and geographies of things, and their connections to people and places, really do matter (Miller, 1998). And so in this final section I reflect on how retail geography has theorized, or might more fully theorize, commodity value.

Historically, and drawing on neo-classical accounts of the market, value (or more often price) was assumed to be the outcome of variations in supply and demand. As I have argued before, I take issue here with such conceptualizations and suggest that the key to unlocking the secret of value may lie less in the realm of supply and demand curves, nor even in commodity or retail design, but in the auto-topographical potential of goods. Focusing on questions of design, display, wearing, authorship, signature and patina, the value of a commodity may lie ultimately in its social history and geography, in the traces of wear and use embedded within it (Gregson and Crewe, 2003; Gregson et al., 2007; Hauser, 2004). Our objects have memories, that are stored, layered, deposited within them, and it is through the excavation of memory and use that value may emerge. The theoretical question then becomes how we might capture the different mediations through which the subject experiences the object and vice versa (Miller, 1998).

I again draw on the potent example of clothing in order to develop this particular line of argument. Whilst it has long been recognized that things are forever engaged in the process of becoming (Koptyoff, 1986), clothes are in many ways a particularly acute exemplar of this, a unique category of good. For the very act of their wearing is in itself transformative. We wear clothes, clothes wear, they are and become worn. There is beauty in use and worn-in value, and wear

can itself create value – a baby's first sleep-suit, the lover's jumper, stains and rips as signs of enrichment not derision (Schutte, 1998: 7). Fashion travels. Used clothes simultaneously hit a whole number of sensory registers – touch, smell, sight. Revealing the richness of wear requires that we free-up our notions of authorship, authenticity and creation and think hard about who takes credit for a garment's presence and form in the world. For when a garment is purchased it begins to record its own individual story. Whilst the brand, label, signature or author may be the defining feature at the outset and may have informed the initial purchase decision, cycles of use and wear transform the garment and its meaning. The initial brand function is inter-woven and overwritten by new sets of meanings and processes of de- or re-valorization. This layering of meaning and memory is in turn evidence of occurrence – the cigarette burn from a drunken night out, the rip from a fall, the ink from a child's pen. Clothes tell stories. They are repositories of accumulated biographies, their stories caught between the warp and the weft, fused into the thread, layered, accumulated.

Two particular examples are drawn on in order to explore further the ways in which second-hand clothing acts as a memory-bank, as a spatial representation of identity, as a repository of value (see too Gregson and Crewe (2003) and Gregson et al., (2001) on retro and vintage clothing). Both, in rather different ways, emphasize the importance of clothing as social practice and highlight that fashion value is always mobile and contingent. Object value is always a process rather than a revelation or a moment.

The first example is an ongoing project by Martin Mairinger looking at shifts in value and meaning as second hand clothes circulate amongst different owners. Selected items of clothing have been donated, tagged, recorded and a short biography of use has been written by the original owner. When the item is sold on at a dedicated second-hand shop, the buyer can access ownership information online and find out about the garment's past. The project explores the ways in which the second-hand interface yields biographical hookups. The project's long-term concept envisions the establishment of a community of registered users who take advantage of the second-hand shop's offerings not only to acquire clothing but also to establish social contacts within the network of people connected to the shop. The project extends the function of clothes as a storage medium by adding a virtual component: in these second-hand shops each article is provided with a RFID tag via which new owners can store and read digital information on the individual garment.

A virtual library of clothing is thus developed into which owners can add arbitrary information, thus building up and layering each item's unique history of use, wear and re-use. Clothing can be seen here to act as a prototype for open source branding (Mairinger, 2001) whose outcome is the creation of new forms of user-generated brand identity. Crucially, the surplus value encoded within the garment adds up step-by-step with the number of (previous) owners – a classic example of the network effect. Clothes trap and transport information about their owners and these second hand garments use this effect to exaggerate this identity-transmitting component and to turn in-use traces and captured memories into a key component in determining garment value.

The second example is that of the 'Traces' installation by London fashion company Oki-ni.com and contemporary British artist Gavin Turk. The project asked a number of 'key' individuals (contemporary artists, musicians, photographers and designers) to submit their favourite item of (used, worn, old, cherished, loved) clothing to Oki-ni on the promise that they would be returned. The donors were asked to write a short statement about why the garment was so special to them. The artist Gavin Turk then created a unique signature for the project, and a label bearing this signature was stitched into each of the garments, thereby altering, reconfiguring and re-creating value and brand. The collection was then photographed, catalogued and displayed at the flagship Oki-ni store on Savile Row, London. A selection of the collection is to be faithfully reproduced via a collaboration between Gavin Turk, Oki-ni, the original designer of the garment and the owner/wearer. Damage, wear and tear, history and stains were all reproduced in the collection, which were manufactured in very limited numbers for sale via Oki-ni.

The project charted the history and biography of the chosen garments, questioning how their value shifts through time, forming a deep palimpsest, a multi-textured layering through time onto which people, places, practices and processes are inter-woven. Why was the garment special in the first place (Its brand? The original designer? Its cost? Memories of use and wearing? Was it a gift? Given by a special person?). And what does the stitching of a new label by a British artist do to its value and meaning? (Is it now more special? More valuable? Or less, because it is transformed, disfigured, marked, blighted?). Bringing a range of participants and objects together in an unfamiliar assemblage that is simultaneously here and there; material and virtual; a process and a performance; momentary and long-term, the project explores the means by which value is imbued in clothes. We inhabit our clothes, we live in and through them, they reflect and refract our corporeality, they have symbolic resonance and act as markers of identity. As such clothes are potent objects in self-identification. Their value is rarely purely economically determined but rather depends on how a person sees value and meaning, how a garment can be re-enchanted, re-seen, loved anew. Clothes store and reveal corporeal traces of presence and intimacy. The wearer and the cloth are combined, reciprocal, entwined.

REFLECTIONS

So what does this discussion of space, passion and possession all add up to, and more importantly in this context, how does it connect to broader intellectual concerns within economic geography? The easy answer to this is that retail geography matters because it is at once about the prosaic realities of markets, profits and regulation, and at the very same time about uniqueness, rarity, authorship, belonging and meaning. But that is perhaps too easy a solution. A number of other interpretations are possible. The first is both unremarkable and depressing – retail architecture and its spatial tactics, passionate consumption, co-production and an emphasis on possession and biography may be little more than capital's latest attempts to extract surplus value. Key business functions have long been outsourced to low wage economies, particularly in the case of fashion. Attempts to fabricate retail space in order to enhance consumption are scarcely new. Is commodity co-production and the de-centring of innovation and simply the latest stage in the outsourcing process? Possibly.

But I hold onto the interpretation that the tendencies outlined above offer at least the potential for new and exciting ways of making and understanding markets. This reading of contemporary developments offers consumers a range of new ways both to engage with and to be critical of commodification and their objects of desire. Some consumers–the passionate, committed ones–want to build and drive the communities into which they are hooked and are orbiting around in tighter circuits and at faster speeds; the deep end of fandom. Recent technological developments have enabled them to do this more fully and reveal the power of innovatory consumer communities to construct cultures of creativity around their enthusiasms. And in so doing, such collectivities of consumers may have found a means through which to emancipate themselves from market- imposed intelligence streams by creating communities of consumption practice. Whilst it may be an exaggeration to suggest that this enables the market to be circumvented, it certainly suggests a less malleable, stable and predictable market, and one where value determination may lie beyond the

reach of capital narrowly defined. Whatever the case, it seems certain that the tendencies outlined above up-turn, invert, scramble and mash conventional organizational models of innovation and non-imitability, and reveal the very real likelihood that creation and innovation can lie outside the organization. Taken together, this entire suite of processes empowers consumers, allowing them much more range and influence on markets than they (or we) could previously have foreseen, and pulling them into the process of value creation itself. It may in turn engender a significant re-think about the critical capacity of the market constantly to renew itself under conditions where biographies, geographies and histories of use and re-use may hold the key to value.

I suspect that current developments will make for a very powerful reframing of the cultural economy of consumption that will generate significant new understandings of what constitutes the producer and the consumer grouped around the idea of human – object encounters, the social lives of things and the role of use, display and wear in creation. This requires no less than a disentangling of the assumed connections between creation, sale and use; a decoupling of production from consumption in the creation of value. It is archaeology backwards; valorization through a future history of use.

NOTES

1 It would be equally instructive to frame this discussion around till receipts, offering insights into worlds of purchase, payment, credit, audit and traceability. Given ongoing concerns about credit card fraud and identity theft and calls to shred all confidential information, receipts and credit card statements would offer a fascinating insight into consumption that may soon become increasingly rare as a cultural artefact.

2 This phrase is adapted from Boden and Williams (2002: 500).

3 The Burberry 'football hooligan and chav' story is a good illustration of how undesirable consumer groups can usurp and transform brand image in unanticipated and unwanted ways.

REFERENCES

Amin, A. and Thrift, N. (2002) Cities: *Reimagining the Urban*. Cambridge: Polity.

Baker, A. (2000) *Serious Shopping London*. London: Free Association Books.

Bakhtin, M. (1968) *Rabelais and his World*. Cambridge: MIT Press.

Barnes, T., Peck, J., Sheppard, E., and Tickell, A. (2004) *Reading Economic Geography*. Oxford: Blackwell.

Bauman, Z. (1992) *Intimations of Postmodernity*. London: Routledge.

Berry, W. and Parr, J. (1988) *Market Centres and Location*. Englewood Cliffs NJ: Prentice-Hall.

Blomley, N. (1996) I'd like to dress her all over: Masculinity, power and retail capital. In N. Wrigley and M. Lowe (eds) *Retailing, Consumption and Capital: Towards the New Retail Geography*. Harlow: Longman. pp. 238–56.

Boden, S. and Williams, S. (2002) Consumption and emotion: The romantic ethic revisited. *Sociology*, 36(3): 493–512.

Bowlby, R. (1985) *Just Looking: Consumer Culture in Dreiser, Gissing and Zola*. New York: Methuen.

Bowlby, R. (1997) Supermarket futures. In P. Falk, and C. Campbell (eds) *The Shopping Experience*. London: SAGE. pp. 92–110.

Boyd, W. and Watts, M. (1997) Agro-industrial just-in-time: The chicken industry and postwar American capitalism. Chapter 8 in D. Goodman, and M. Watts (eds) *Globalising Food: Agrarian Questions and Global Restructuring*. London: Routledge.

Buck-Morss (1999) *The Dialectics of Seeing: Walter Benjamin and the Arcades Project*. Cambridge: MIT Press.

Chung, C., Inaba, J., Koolhaas, R. and Leong, S. (2001) *The Harvard Design School Guide to Shopping*. Koln: Taschen.

Cook, I. (2006) Geographies of food: Following. *Progress in Human Geography*, 30: 655.

Crang, P. (1997) Cultural turns and the (re)constitution of Economic Geography. Introduction in R. Lee, and J. Wills (eds) *Geographies of Economies*, 3–15.

Crewe, L. (2010) Wear: Where? The convergent geographies of architecture and fashion in *Environment and Planning A*. 42: 2093–108.

De Nora, T. (2000) *Music in Everyday Life*. Cambridge: Cambridge University Press.

Destefani, F. (2006) The Soul Outside. In A. Guerriero (ed.) *Dressing Ourselves*. Milano: Edizioni Charta.

Evans, C. (2003) *Fashion at the Edge: Spectacle, Modernity and Deathliness*. New Haven, CT: Yale University Press.

Fraser (2000) Expressive culture, locality and big business: The case of Presto in Kensington Market, www.culturalstudies.ca

Foster, H. (2002) *Design and Crime*, London: Verso.

Giddens, A. (1991) *Modernity and Self-identity: Self and Society in the Late Modern Age*. Cambridge: Polity.

Goh, R. (2002) Shop soiled worlds: Retailing narratives, typologies and commodity culture. *Social Semiotics*, 12(1): 5–25.

Gregson, N. and Crewe, L. (2003) *Second-hand Cultures*. Berg: Oxford.

Gregson, N., Crewe, L. and Brooks, K. (2001) Bjorn again? Rethinking '70s revivalism through the reappropriation of '70s clothing. *Fashion Theory: The Journal of Body, Dress and Culture*, 5(1): 3–28.

Gregson, N., Crewe, L. and Brooks, K. (2002a) Narratives of the body in the space of the charity shop. In P. Jackson, M. Lowe, D. Miller, and F. Mort (eds) *Commercial Cultures*. Oxford: Berg. pp. 101–21.

Hauser, K. (2004) A garment in the dock: Or, how the FBI illuminated the prehistory of a pair of denim jeans. *Journal of Material Culture*, 9: 293–313.

Hughes, A. (2000) Retailers, knowledges and changing commodity networks: The case of the cut flower trade. *Geoforum*, 31: 175–90.

Hughes, A. Buttle, M., and Wrigley, N. (2007) Organisational geographies of corporate responsibility: A UK–US comparison of retailers' ethical trading initiatives. *Journal of Economic Geography*, 7(4): 491–513.

Hughes, A., Wrigley, N., and Buttle, M. (2008) Global production networks, ethical campaigning, and the embeddedness of responsible governance. *Journal of Economic Geography*, 8(3): 345–67.

Keaggy, B. (2007) www.grocerylists.org

Koolhaas, R. (2002) *Projects for Prada*. Prada Fondazione.

Kopytoff, I. (1986) The cultural biography of things: Commodification as a process. In A. Appadurai (ed.) *The Social Life of Things*. Cambridge: Cambridge University Press. pp 64–94.

Kozinets, R. (1999) E-tribalized marketing?: The strategic implications of virtual communities of consumption. *European Management Journal*, 17(3): 252–64.

Lash, S. (1993) Reflexive modernization: The aesthetic dimension. *Theory Culture and Society*, 10: 1–23.

Maffesoli, M. (1992) *The Times of the Tribes*. London: SAGE.

Mairinger, M. (2001) RFID artproject at www.used.co.at/

Mansvelt, J. (2008) Geographies of consumption: Citizenship, space and practice. *Progress in Human Geography*, 32(1): 105–17.

Miller, D. (1998) *A Theory of Shopping. Cambridge*: Polity.

Pimental, R. and Reynolds, K. (2004) A model for consumer devotion: Affective commitment. *Academy of Marketing Sciences Review*, 5(5): 1–45.

Pine, B. J. and Gilmore, J., (1999) *Experience Economy: Work is Theatre and Every Business a Stage*. Cambridge, MA: Harvard Business School Press.

Reinach, S.S. (2005) China and Italy: Fast fashion versus prêt a porter: Towards a new culture of fashion. *Fashion Theory*, 9: 43–56.

Saville, P. (2006) *Confessions of an Art Dealer*.

Schutte, A. (1993) Patina: Layering a history-of-use on digital objects. MSc Thesis. Massachusetts: MIT.

Shirky (2008) *Here Comes Everything: How Digital Networks Transform our Ability to Gather and Co-operate*. New York: Penguin.

Sudjic, D. (2001) Editorial. *Domus*, n. 838, June.

Thrift, N. (2005) *Knowing Capitalism*. London: SAGE.

Warde, A. (1994) Consumption, identity formation and uncertainty. *Sociology*, 28(4): 877–98.

Wilkinson, M. (2005) 'The Chinese Chav': Dissonant teens and mash culture. *Future Laboratory Trend Briefing*. Spring/Summer.

Wrigley, N. (2000) The globalization of retail capital: Themes for economic geography. In G. Clark, M. Feldman, and M. Gertler (eds) *The Oxford Handbook of Economic Geography*. Oxford: OUP. pp. 292–313.

Wrigley, N,. Coe, M. and Currah, A. (2005) Globalizing retail: Conceptualizing the distribution-based transnational corporation. *Progress in Human Geography*, 29: 437–57.

21

An Economic Geography of the Cultural Industries

Andy C. Pratt

INTRODUCING THE CULTURAL INDUSTRIES

For the purposes of this chapter the cultural industries are: film, television, publishing, music, new media, computer games and animation, advertising, visual arts, architecture and design, the performing arts, and libraries and museums. As I will discuss below, such a definition is controversial. The study of the cultural industries is a relatively new one to social scientists. The field has been explored by researchers in Media and Communications Studies, and to a lesser extent Cultural Studies and Cultural Policy (Cunningham, 2003; Hartley, 2005). Work from these disciplines has traditionally focused on the performance and reception of the cultural industries. The sub-field of Cultural Economics has sought to frame analyses within a more traditional economic discourse paying particular attention to the notion of merit goods (Throsby, 2001). More recently another body of work, mainly based in the disciplines of Geography, Sociology, Management and Organizational Studies, has explored how cultural production

is organized and located (O'Connor and Wynne, 1998; Caves, 2000; Scott, 2000; Hesmondhalgh, 2002). This dizzying array of perspectives is now interweaving, making this research field genuinely inter-disciplinary. Nevertheless, there is considerable value in an economic geographical perspective.

As I will point out in the next section, it is important to clarify and delimit the boundaries of new topics and fields of interest so that everyone is clear about what is, and what is not, being investigated. We often take definitions for granted. Take the example of the economic geography of the motor vehicle industry which, at first sight, seems self-evident in definitional terms: the nature of the product is well-known and it is not too problematic to explore the whole production process. First, it is a recognized and legitimate area of study; second, it has been studied for a long time; finally, statistical and qualitative analyses are readily available. However, the boundaries of industries constantly shift (see for example recent analyses of the car industry (Froud et al., 1998, 2002), and, entirely new industries appear. The cultural industries, as a new object of analysis, present two further problems. First, they do not appear in conventional industrial taxonomies, in effect they are invisible to data collection (see, for example, Table 21.1). Second, conceptually, they have been associated with consumption and thus researchers have not been inclined to look for them in the sphere of production. These problems have shaped the recognition and analysis of, and policies for, the cultural industries, as will be discussed later in this chapter,

Readers will be familiar with the potential role of technology in economic change (see, for example, Pratt, 1996; see also Chapter 18). However, it will also be appreciated that technologies may not simply improve efficiency, but actually transform, or produce entirely new, activities. The cultural industries illustrate this argument well. They are 'new' industries that are developing and changing very quickly (which is itself a challenge to any definition). Take one example: music downloading (Leyshon, 2001). The music industry previously organized the process of selecting, recording and distributing an artist's output, and a proportion of the sales from records were returned to artists via royalty payments. With digital recording, artists can potentially bypass the record companies and deal directly with consumers. Also, it is possible to bypass payment via pirated downloads of MP3 files: the classic example being Napster. This new form of production and distribution has the potential to transform music making, its sale and distribution, and the final location of profits. As in the case of the music industry, such development has destabilized the current organizational norms.

Another even more dramatic example is computer games (Johns, 2006). Games are, in part, dependent on the development of computer technology. Initially developed for arcade slot machines, they were quickly transformed for the home computer market. But without this platform they could not have existed. Computer games have been developed in ever more complex and compelling ways – at first on proprietary platforms, and then cross platform. Games have multiple genres: shoot-em-up, role play, strategy, etc. In recent years games have been further enhanced through crossovers with films and books. Such crossovers may not only provide a narrative structure, but also the character and 'look and feel' of the film/game. Computer games represent the emergence of something from nothing. By contrast, music downloading, for example, built on music in different formats (CD, cassette, vinyl, or even sheet music). In their 20 year or so lifespan, computer games have travelled the road from something that individuals could compile in their bedroom and sell to friends in return for a little spending money to a major industry. In the US, the computer games industry now grosses more than the film industry and represents one of that country's major export earners. Few industries can boast such a meteoric, and relatively unacknowledged, growth.

As will be appreciated, because of this growth, the cultural industries are having an impact on the economy more generally (DCMS, 2001; Siwek, 2002; Pratt, 2004b). Furthermore, they have a particular interest for geographers as they have a distinctive spatial distribution: tending to cluster in parts of cities and to concentrate in a small number of cities in the world. This chapter outlines in four sections the recent development of the study of the cultural industries, their conceptual content and their definition; the challenges that have shaped them; and the consequences of their growth and development. We begin by positioning the cultural industries within academic debates and discuss how they have been conceptualized. The second section is concerned with the problems of defining the cultural industries. In the third section we examine the range of secondary impacts, and in the fourth section we consider the primary impacts of the cultural industries under five headings: production process, the speed of circulation, intermediation, project based firms, and spatial clustering.

THE CONCEPTUAL LOCATION OF THE CULTURAL INDUSTRIES

The study of the cultural industries has, for the most part, been overlooked by the social sciences, and economic geography is no exception in this regard. This is an irony as one of the key themes in recent debates has been the intersection of the social/cultural and the economic, the so-called cultural turn in economic geography (Barnes, 2001). The cultural turn has led to more attention being paid to a range of non-economic theorizing, mainly adapted from social theory. Additionally, it has tended to shift the focus of analyses away from production to consumption (Pratt, 2004c, d and see Chapter 20). Within such a shift one might have expected the cultural industries to be a paradigmatic empirical focus for analyses. The challenge for the analysis of the cultural industries is to 'locate' them within debates in social science, including economic geography. Perhaps because of their novelty they have commonly been positioned merely as 'add-ons' to existing discussions. However, as I will argue, they are worthy of study in their own right. In fact, I would argue that the study of the cultural industries – as an exemplar – might shed more light on these major debates. In the remainder of this section I will outline four narratives based on key binaries that have been commonly used to examine the cultural industries. Before this I want to begin by sketching in the background and context of the study of the cultural industries.

The cultural industries: the back story

The notion of the cultural industries is a contested one involving a number of debates about policy and politics, and about concepts and theories. To take the latter first, there are three main lines of thought. The term *culture industries* was coined by German writers Adorno and Horkheimer (1977) in the 1930s. Associated with the Frankfurt School of critical theory, they sought to react to a mass society in which they felt culture was becoming banal. For them, culture (and meaning) played an essential role as an emancipatory force in the enlightenment. The culture industries, they argued, removed this emancipatory potential. They also reacted against the culture industries extending the capitalist realm into leisure time. In the 1980s French writers, especially Miège (1987, 1989), began to discuss the cultural industries. They pluralized them as, unlike Adorno and Horkheimer, they saw the cultural industries as diverse and different from one another; moreover, they viewed them as contradictory but not all bad. In the late 1990s there were two major inflections of the Miège line of thought. On one hand, there is work that prioritizes the production of texts and how meaning is shaped by ownership and production (Hesmondhalgh, 2002). On the other hand, some analyses view the cultural industries *as* industries and seek to explore the particularities of their organization across production, distribution and consumption (Pratt, 1997, 2004a).

Policy debates about the cultural industries can be linked to the work of UNESCO on communications inequalities. Out of this came an influential report by Girard (1982) that sought to create a framework of measurement. This approach influenced both the Canadian and Australian governments to measure cultural industries. Borrowing on Miège's work, Garnham (1987, 2005) was influential in adapting notions of the cultural industries to industrial policy making in London, a notion that was also explored in other 'Old Labour' run metropolitan areas of the UK. Here the cultural industries were used in part as a form of political mobilization of the youth and, in part, as a contribution to job creation in the de-industrialized cities. With the election of a centrist 'New Labour' government in the UK in 1997 the cultural industries were elevated as a national policy. However, due to their associations with 'Old Labour' they were re-branded as the 'creative industries' thereby linking them to the 'knowledge economy' (Garnham, 2005; Pratt,

2005). The first UK 'mapping' document that sought to measure the economic impact of the 'creative industries' was significant in spawning a number of similar reports around the world (DCMS, 1998).

Despite the popularity of counting employment and output, it is debatable whether any depth of understanding of the creative/cultural industries has been achieved. There remain a number of problematic relationships that are not fully understood: public and private, formal and informal, production and consumption, arts and cultural industries; as well as the differences between the individual industries. Nevertheless, the policy juggernaut carries on, the latest concern being with 'cultural clusters' (Mommaas, 2004; Pratt, 2004a). As commentators have noted, these are often sites of cultural consumption rather than production. Moreover, the objectives of these and other cultural initiatives are instrumental: they seek to achieve social cohesion or urban regeneration rather than cultural excellence. In the following part of this section I explore the four binaries that have been used to examine the cultural industries.

Economization – culturalization

The first debate hinges on the cultural-economy couplet. Authors have argued variously that producers have responded to falling levels of consumption by encouraging either multiple purchases of the same (but differently styled) item, or an interest in designer goods (Lash and Urry, 1993; Scott, 2000). Some authors have argued that this trend has become so pervasive that much economic production, along with its associated transactions, is 'culturalized' in this way. Culture, or culture markers and symbols, are used as a means of product differentiation which may also add to (exchange) value. Thus, we might prefer not just to buy a plain tee-shirt but one that is styled or, one that is linked in to a cultural product such as a band or a film. In

many markets producers may compete as much through a product's design as its function.

On the other hand, there are those commentators who start from the other point of view and argue that culture has become more and more a means of economic transaction. As such, cultural values are usurped by economic values. Thus, predominantly, cultural production is not a craft or artisanal activity, but one that has been transformed into a major industry whose market is dominated by monetary value, or sales, rather than intrinsic value (Caves, 2000; Vogel, 2001). An example of these processes is the ways in which the consumption of music, films or books is structured by 'charts' that are now syndicated in daily newspapers and on television shows.

Art and culture

The economization – culturalization argument is one that runs parallel to the views of the Frankfurt School (Adorno and Horkheimer, 1977; Adorno, 1991). From this point of view the cultural experience – 'the aura' – is one gained through contact and interaction with an original. Mass production separated such contact and so led to weaker and degraded forms of cultural communication. Thus, a strong negative cultural value applied to the 'culture industries'.

This debate has strong resonances with those who pit art against the cultural industries echoing the 'high – low' culture couplet. There is an easy elision here between commercial activities and low culture. The fact that 'low' culture sells, and that 'high' culture generally does not has caused governments to seek to support 'high' culture and 'the arts' (here 'high art' is thought to be intrinsically good). The arguments used to justify such support, are based either on the notion that, without such support, they would collapse under market failure or on the claim of elite idealism (sometimes universalized as humanism). In both cases, 'good' art must be subsidized for the enlightened public good (and is sometimes referred to as a 'merit good' (Baumol and Bowen, 1966; Throsby, 2001)). This is further exacerbated when historically the arts have been supported by the state. Implicitly this constructs that cultural industries as self-sustaining and intrinsically not worthy of support or guidance, or as having cultural value. Thus, historically there is less awareness of the need for, and a lesser competence in, managing the cultural industries.

Cultural and creative

Recently, a challenge to the cultural industries has emerged from a second flank, that of creativity. Increasingly, developed economies have been enamoured by the potential of the 'knowledge economy' to boost productivity (Garnham, 2005). The argument is that developed nations, with high educational investment, have a competitive advantage in knowledge assets (as opposed to manual labour). Moreover, knowledge industries offer a new way of innovating and developing new products. It is claimed that 'creativity' is, more generally, a quality that can transform existing practices and products. Further, it is a quality that has not been traditionally valued in the educational system. So, creativity has become a 'must have' quality (Pratt, 2008). The so-called creative industries are those that deploy a concentration of such skills. For the most part these are what were formerly known as the cultural industries (Pratt, 2005). However, the weakness of the term 'creative industry' is that all industries are creative. Empirically, some writers have sought to identify certain occupations as 'creative'. However, this also ignores the fact that creativity requires application. On its own, a creative spark is just that. A sustainable creative flame requires a broader alliance of producers. The term cultural industry, as used in this chapter, has a more specific focus on the product and process as with other industries that have been traditionally analysed.

Production and consumption

The culturalization of production has led many to conceive of culture as an add-on, or an advertising spin, on the initial product. Commonly, this is viewed as occurring at the site of retailing and in the consumption experience (see Chapter 20). As such this draws upon a cultural studies concern with meaning and interpretation, and a concern with users and consumers (as opposed to producers). In part this broader debate has been positioned against an earlier political economic analysis of cultural production. This is itself deeply embedded in a political debate that the Birmingham Centre for Contemporary Cultural Studies (CCCS) dominated in the 1970s and 1980s. CCCS effectively created 'cultural studies' and were very influential in the character of political engagement with culture and in the perceived failure of sociology at that time to engage with cultural policy or economic issues (McRobbie, 1993). This deep legacy has shaped the way that sociology and cultural studies, and cultural geography, has engaged with culture. Recently, there have been attempts not only to register consumption but to re-engage with analyses of production and, at the same time, to seek to avoid the over-determination of the economic (Crewe, 1996; Jackson, 2002; Miller, 2003; Pratt, 2004c, d; see Chapter 20).

DEFINITIONS

The analysis of any social object is only as good as the definition of it. Thus, it is worth paying some attention to the definition of cultural industries. As suggested above, older or more mature technologies and practices are more adequately captured in analytical frameworks. Accordingly, it is easy to pass over such definitional issues more quickly than is neccessary or desirable with the cultural industries. The analytical problem concerns both the decision about which empirical events should be included in the definition (the 'breadth'), as well as the 'depth', or extent of related process and thus the conceptualization of causality. For example, audio-visual activities and performance may be seen as part of the cultural industries. But is gambling, or sport? In terms of depth, actors and playwrights may be included but should lighting engineers, theatre lighting producers or front of house staff? In practical terms, the cultural industries have been a problematic category both in their conceptualization and empirical measurement. These problems are associated with their newness and the lack of knowledge relative of them. Put simply, if they cannot properly be defined they cannot properly be measured (quantitatively or qualitatively). To all intents and purposes, they are analytically invisible.

One starting point is to conceptualize these activities as the processes that are required to produce products that are used primarily as cultural products. This definition avoids the pitfalls of the culturalization thesis that might define everything as cultural/symbolic. Analytically, a more useful position is that cars, for example, may have a cultural/symbolic dimension, but that they are primarily used for transport and, as such, motor vehicles may be defined accordingly. In practice researchers and policy makers have favoured the notion of a production chain to capture the process of cultural production (see Figure 21.1). The 'chain' analogy is not meant to suggest a linear, or mono-causal process and so, in this sense, a web might be a better notion.

Stage I refers to the various processes by which creative material and intellectual assets are originated and produced. This stage encom-

passes arguably the most visible activities of the sector – the creative fields of authoring (in all its forms from books to dance); design (from buildings to fashion); image-creation (from digital art, to photography and painting); music composition; and digital content origination such as multimedia titles, software packages and electronic games. It also covers activities such as the commissioning of content, the aggregation and packaging of content (for example, by broadcasters), and the commercialization of Intellectual Property Rights (IPR) by, for instance, record labels and book publishers.

Stage II of the production chain concerns the making of 'one offs', or prototypes, which may be reproduced later. It also relates to the production of specialist goods, materials and infrastructure used within the creative industries, such as artists' materials (paints, canvasses, brushes, etc.), film cameras, or the manufacture of musical instruments.

Stage III refers to the activities associated with channelling creative products and services into end-user markets. This relates primarily to the physical processes associated with reproduction and mass distribution (for example, printing, CD replication, shipping and wholesaling, etc.), but also to newer digital and analogue forms of distribution (from broadcast to digital delivery systems). Commonly, these two modes are integrated.

Stage IV refers to the exhibition function embodied both in venue-based activities such as concert halls, theatres and cinemas, as well as the retailing of certain creative products such as books, CDs and videos. In between these lie the informal sites of consumption and display that are important in the creative

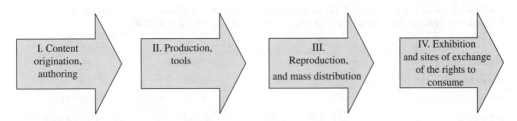

Figure 21.1   Creative industries: a simple, generalized, production chain.

Source: Adapted from Pratt, 1997

Table 21.1   Employment in the Major Industrial Classes in London and South East England, 2000

Industrial class	London	South East
1 Agriculture and fishing	4,622	40,688
2 Energy and water	13,915	19,163
3 Manufacturing	285,840	432,596
4 Construction	130,584	156,292
5 Distribution, hotels and restaurants	887,840	944,068
6 Transport and communications	317,924	242,630
7 Banking, finance and insurance, etc	1,360,242	836,251
8 Public administration, education & health	798,585	810,846
9 Other services	261,110	180,951

Source: Annual Business Enquiry (ONS 2003) Crown Copyright

production system ('the street', for example) i.e. certain places where novel cultural consumption is visible; (Pratt and Naylor, 2003).

Examples of the kind of data that may (or may not, for example, Figure 21.1) be produced on the cultural industries may be seen in Tables 21.2 and 21.3. However, despite the attention grabbing nature of such measures they are only a starting point in understanding the cultural industries and their geographies (see below).

SECONDARY IMPACTS

Analyses of the secondary impacts of culture derive from a traditional economic frame of reference founded upon the assumption that one cannot value arts or culture, but one can

evaluate a proxy: the activity generated around them. Thus, a commonly used technique is to calculate an economic multiplier, where the impact of generated secondary activities such as shopping, transport, and rented hotel rooms are measured (Myerscough, 1988).

Such a viewpoint does give culture a value, but does not equate cultural value with economic value directly. Nevertheless, it actually overlooks, and may even undermine, the contribution of the cultural economy. This form of analysis can very easily lead to an instrumental conception of culture where the 'real value' is merely economic. New consumption spaces may be valued for the generation of outputs even though they might have precious little 'culture'. Whilst economic activity is indirectly generated by culture, the impact is claimed to be derived demand from the 'real' activity

Table 21.2   Employment in the Cultural Industries (broken down cultural industries production system function: I–IV), London, South East and England, 2000

CIPS	London	South East	England
I Content origination	432,150	277,003	1,294,514
II Manufacturing Inputs	16,569	37,961	178,301
III Reproductive activities	41,290	28,292	188,053
IV Exchange	215,770	215,387	1,209,468
All CIPS	705,779	558,643	2,870,345

Source: Annual Business Enquiry (ONS 2003) Crown Copyright

Table 21.3 Employment Change (percent) in the Cultural Industries (broken down by cultural industries production system function: I–IV), London, South East and England, 1995–2000

CIPS	London	South East	England
I Content origination	42.4	46.5	34.1
II Manufacturing inputs	18.1	13.4	6.8
III Reproductive activities	1.9	−3.4	−3.3
IV Exchange	13.9	29.7	46.2
All CIPS	28.9	33.7	22.3

Sources: Annual Business Enquiry; Census of Employment (ONS 2003) Crown Copyright

of the economic base. This argument is a little harsh as it assumes that production is the source of all value and that consumption is the 'icing on the cake'. Yet cities are changing. Manufacturing, and even retailing, have re-located leaving a 'hollowed out' city centre. Thus cities now struggle to justify themselves on the basis of their cultural offerings; arguably culture is the new economic base.

In a broader context, it has been argued that cities have increasingly used cultural activities to sustain shopping centres, theme parks and museums (Harvey, 1989; Zukin, 1995; Hannigan, 1998). Cultural activities have been used as the 'draw'. Redeveloped downtown and waterfront sites have been placed in competition both with other cities and with 'bland and faceless' out of town shopping centres. Of course, changes in retailing have meant that it is commonly the same outlets that dominate both inner and out-of-town sites. Thus, culturally themed shopping and master planned urban environments have been used to place cities in competition for consumers. In this sphere, cities have sought to compete with one another, not simply for retail customers but for mobile investment in manufacture and services and especially high-value, head office functions. The notion here is that if cities are attractive to decision makers and staff that need to re-locate, then the relocation will be popular. Thus, urban competition for foreign direct investment has frequently relied upon investments in iconic developments by international architects (the more controversial, the better). World cities have sustained a 'beauty pageant' based upon a range of primarily building-based high culture offerings (Hall and Hubbard, 1998; Short and Kim, 1998).

A recent version of the secondary, and consumption based, use of culture can be found in the notion of the 'creative class', developed by Richard Florida (Florida, 2002). This is a much heralded notion suggesting that cities can be ranked by their 'pull' on this key group of workers. A more informal but consumption based 'boho/creative' buzz is argued to attract software workers which then attract hi-tech companies. 'Hi-tech' companies are believed to be high growth and high skill employers adding disproportionately to economic growth. And, as the competitive edge of such firms is based upon specific skills, they increasingly need to locate where labour is. This brings us full circle to a 'creative themed' retail environment that will attract workers who will trail high growth employers behind them. In this sense the 'creative/cultural' effect is simply a 'theme-ing' of consumption. This time, it is based upon a further differentiation between types of cultural experience (Pine and Gilmore, 1999). Florida's work in effect broadens the notion of cultural experience from one of high culture to lifestyle. Thus, instead of building executive homes and opera houses, cities have sought to present their support for ethnic and sexual diversity and to develop funky lofts, bars and nightclubs.

A less well-publicized instrumental role for culture has been in the amelioration of social problems (Bennett, 1998). This strategy pre-dates the focus on consumption and looks instead to a humanist notion of art and culture as 'improving'. It is the justification for the establishment of the cultural as a handmaiden of social reform via education and particularly museums, galleries and libraries. The builders of the 'industrial city' used such institutions repeatedly. A good example is that of Victorian England where culture was used to divert the working classes from drinking and social disorder. So, again, a building-based strategy came with a (more explicit) social institutional order.

More recently, culture has been used directly and explicitly as a social tool to improve the life of the poorest members of cities; in this case the aim has been community building rather than transcendence (Matarasso, 1997; Landry, 2000). The UK pioneered such approaches in the late 1990s as part of a core initiative on social inclusion (DCMS, 1999). Evidence exists attesting to the social and health benefits for cultural participation, effects that may also have economic consequences. Good examples are drama workshops that help to build confidence and improve candidates' self-esteem and their chances of getting a job. The central point here is that the objective is not to produce great art, but to build strong communities.

Without doubt, cultural activities can play a role in leveraging other investment into cities and regions. In this context demand is derived from other activities (the high-tech activities attracted), and thus the notion that the cultural has an intrinsic value (economic and cultural) is overlooked. As writers such as Logan and Molotch (1987) have emphasized (albeit in the case of retail, although one could substitute the example of culture), cities may develop powerful governance regimes to favour, sustain and attract such development. Of course, all of this targeted investment provides cultural facilities for a minority that is paid for by taxation of the whole population. In this sense, the investment is socially regressive: it hits the poor disproportionately as they are likely to benefit less from it (through access or preference). We can add that, as well as being derived demand, such investment usually results in a zero-sum game. A gain of tourists, shoppers, or investment in one place represents a loss in another.

Finally, we should point to the wider uses of culture in reinforcing or creating national identity. Anderson's (1991) seminal text argues that imagined communities play a significant role in legitimating the nation state; imagined communities are communities of interest and shared values (Hobsbawm and Ranger, 1992). National museums may help to legitimate colonial or imperial endeavours (Bennett, 1998). Nation states have clearly used the broadcast media to sustain such activities, be it conveying the 'American way' or French culture through filmmaking for example, which may in turn be refracted back on major cities as the locations of 'national' cultural collections. Thus it was argued by some that the establishment of the Tate Modern gallery in London helped to cement the Blairite New Labour vision for the UK in the late 1990s: young, cosmopolitan and modern (Leonard, 1997). These versions of 'heritage' and 'identity' have been used literally to brand cities and to position them in an international tourist market. Policy makers now seek to attract 'cultural tourists' who seek out heritage and cultural experience (Richards, 1996; Pratt, 2000). The key advantage of targeting this group is that they are generally rich.

PRIMARY IMPACTS

It is clear from the above that the uses of art and culture are manifold, but that the lay notion of 'culture as ornament' is dominant, albeit justified by its potential instrumental value. A logical gap exists: the consideration of art and culture in its own right. Arguably, the challenge to a proper consideration of art and culture has been an exclusive concern with their end products, or with artists, rather than the processes of their creation. As noted above, the common stance has been, to invert and paraphrase J.F. Kennedy's Berlin speech in 1963: 'ask not what you can do for culture, but what culture can do for you'.

A novel response to this problem has been developed in relation to the commercial cultural industries; that is to look at them as one would any other industry (Pratt, 1997). Such an approach requires us to confront the idealist notion of 'creativity' and 'art' and explore them as ordinary activities. In this light, sociologists of art and culture, and some economists, have explored the social and economic conditions of production and consumption (Peterson, 1976; Becker, 1984; Scott, 2000; Pratt, 2004d). The broad notion shaping such studies is that of the cultural field, or, the cultural production chain. This is simply a metaphor for the processes that are necessary to transform an idea into a cultural product. Interestingly, empirical analysis shows that the conceptual polarization of economic – cultural, or public – private, is eroded in practice.

PROCESS

Such analyses will be necessarily quantitative *and* qualitative in character if they are to address issues of process and causality. However, the initial focus on measurement of the cultural industries is a pragmatic response to the reality of bargaining in the public policy sphere (Hesmondhalgh and Pratt, 2005). In simple terms, an argument for resource allocation may be deployed when faced with competition in terms of quantitative demands from other departments of government (such as health or education). In such a situation a claim for more resources on the basis that culture is 'good' is unlikely to hold sway. However, it would be unfortunate if *real politik* set the academic research agenda, which should ideally be underpinned by explanation and the identification of causality. Whilst it might be recognized that the cultural industries have an important economic

dimension (as well as a social and a cultural), the mode of analysis that reduces everything to simple economic measures is necessarily partial. It is clear that the complex nature and situatedness of the cultural industries are crucial to their understanding. To approach such an objective it is necessary to go beyond the practices of mapping and explore processes.

At a macro-scale is the fact that most cultural industries have a bifurcated structure: they tend towards the very big and the very small (Pratt, 2004a). So, in the music industry we have, on one hand, the 'majors' such as Sony; and on the other, individual bands. The whole music industry is dominated by just five companies. The multitude of 'labels' that we see on CDs are for the most part simply sub-divisions of the holding company. The majors also have ownership of other forms, print, video, television and film.

There are two immediate implications here: first, the power of ownership and control of the majors as a result of their oligopolistic position. There are issues of 'censorship' or limitations of output against the norms of the market; moreover, there is the question of the power of contract whereby majors can impose favourable conditions on new entrants. Second, the possibility of 're-purposing' intellectual property from one form to another (Howkins, 2001); a possibility that can be further enhanced by cross-marketing (for example, promoting a song through a film). In extremis, like the classic trans-national company stereotype, companies can control almost every aspect of music making from production, through distribution to consumption, as well as the context in which it takes place (for example, television shows, charts and newspapers that are constructed to favour particular norms and forms). It is clear that an informed and subtle eye is needed to observe the interplay of cultural and organizational forms that constitute music production and consumption. Control is not total, alternatives are possible; and, at times new technologies can de-stabilize existing structures (for example, with the initial introduction of MP3 file sharing). However, the well developed tendency for the majors to let smaller players innovate and then cherry-pick successful performers, may limit such resistance and destabilization.

Risk, and the speed of circulation

A further structural characteristic of the cultural industries is one found in all production, that of fashion. In the cultural industries it is marked by a matter of degree. As many writers have pointed out, the 'value' of cultural products extends beyond a functional towards a symbolic level. Within an economic context this meshes with the desire of companies to increase profits: commonly this is achieved via selling 'new products' to a defined market. Cultural goods allow one not only constantly to produce 'new' products, but also to sell multiple versions of what is essentially the same to the same market. In the former case a music CD may be taken as as emblematic of innovation (although, of course, as will be clear there is also huge amount or work involved in sustaining the social and economic institutions that continue to constitute the 'album', or 'single', as a product form.) In the latter case it is possible to see why design has become so important: to create parallel markets for the 'same' product. One may buy another mobile phone because it looks good rather than for its functional qualities; or one may have a phone for different occasions. Put crudely, the phone manufacturer has been able to sell two or more products instead of one.

More generally, this is why fashion (the changing nature of aesthetic supply and demand) is so important to cultural goods markets (in both their economic and non-economic forms). Moreover, as analysts of production have long pointed out, the fashion-effect enables the rate of circulation of goods to be increased. In clothes fashion, seasons now last only a matter of weeks rather than months. By shrinking the temporal window of opportunity during which a product can make the market place, a consequence of this trend is that it reflects back on processes of production and retailing (see Chapter 20).

Moreover, markets tend to have a 'winner-takes-all' form. Here the music chart analogy helps. If a record is released at the breaking wave of a trend, it may have a good chance of success if the emergent market norm has been anticipated. As I have already noted, this window of opportunity is temporally short and very precise in relation to product. Add the fact that cultural products have a significant development lead-time and the level of risk rises. An example from the computer games market illustrates this point.

A game may cost £5m and two years to develop, involving a team of 30–50 people and lots of very expensive equipment. The target release date (usually pre-Christmas) must be hit. Moreover, on the one hand, due to the market and distribution structure, if the game is not a hit (that is, does not enter the charts) within 15 days, it does not secure a place on the retailers' shelf, it will not be distributed and thus it will not sell and so it is unlikely to recoup its investment (Pratt, 2004a). This is a vicious circle that stresses the power of advertising and marketing in making a 'hit' or a 'miss'. On the other hand, if it is a success the initial investment may be repaid many times over.

Under such conditions the nature of the look, feel and experience of products must be fine-tuned. Commonly this relates not only to 'creating markets' (via advertising, advertorials and general market information) but also to subtle learning from users. For example, clothing, shoe, and mobile telephone, designers (amongst others) now regularly employ social anthropologists as 'cool hunters' to 'learn from the street'. In other industries producers and designers seek (physically) to position themselves in the market so that they are party to this information.

Intermediation

It is not only the music industry that has the bifurcated form outlined above; one can point to television, to film, to computer games, architecture, and advertising for other examples. I am not suggesting that all of these forms are the same, nor that they share common institutional structures, or are equally distributed internationally, nationally, or even regionally. There is considerable variation both within and between categories. Accordingly, whilst there are broad similarities, there are also differences. New research is beginning to elaborate the nature and significance of these variations; however, much more work still needs to be done.

A critical consequence of the bifurcated organizational structure is that co-ordination, or intermediation, is important (Bourdieu, 1993; O'Connor, 1998). A common form is the agent, the matchmaker or broker, located between large and small organizations. It is common to refer to intermediaries in the context of the relations between production and consumption which is suggestive of a linear, uni-directional process. This is, I think, a causal mis-identification. I would argue that production and consumption are a unified process involving mediation. Thus a better metaphor would be a web-like set of relations (Pratt, 2004a).

However, in causal terms the mode of mediation between organizational and ownership forms is more critical. These intermediaries have considerable potential to configure and re-configure relations within and across industries. And intermediation should not be reduced to the economic; it is also constituted through the legal and regulatory forms that are in place. Commonly, this will involve the law of copyright and contract, and the collecting societies established to collect and distribute royalties.

Project form

At a smaller scale, many researchers have pointed to the nature of work flow and micro-organization that is commonly found in the cultural industries (and other industries). The project form is commonly discussed as an internal organizational strategy where work is organized in project specific teams, with the project defined by its limited life and eventual termination. There is much discussion of why projects exist in terms of their efficiency or flexibility and of their consequences for labour markets and learning (Grabher, 2001, 2002a). A less commonly remarked upon articulation of the project form is that which occurs outside of the 'large firm'.

This is perhaps best exemplified by the film industry where a nominal production company (maybe just a producer and a director) pitches for funding and distribution for a proposed film. On approval they 'grow' the company to many tens of persons; once the film is complete the company 'evaporates'. Such a form has more extreme consequences for those who work on projects (some may be 'extras', others very highly skilled cinematographers). The labour market for these workers has often been termed the 'boundaryless career' (Jones, 1996). Looked at from the social perspective it can be very difficult to survive in such a market. First, social insurance and banking services are less commonly geared to freelancers; second, work tends to go to those that are already working (based upon reputation). Career breaks, or simply not socializing through networks, can be damaging – or fatal – to a career. Moreover, the rich social embeddedness of project work tends to traditional patterns of discrimination on lines of age, class, gender, and race (Blair et al., 2001).

Grabher (2002b), has pointed to the great sensitivity to place of such labour markets. More specifically, they are socially embedded and networked. In large and small companies there is a significant turnover of staff. In fact many have pointed to the innovative and learning benefits (tacit and theoretical) of such movement for both firms and individuals (see Chapter 18). Such movement is possible only if home location is relatively stable; this leads to the large metropolitan labour pool as the dominant form. The rapid turnover and throughput of employees leads to a latent knowledge resource of being in the 'network' (as opposed to being in an individual firm). As Pratt (2006) has shown, such networks are not simply networks of skills.

They involve subtle market and design intelligence, reinforced through navigating spaces of production and consumption, as well as work and leisure. It is these 'doubly-liminal' spaces that constitute 'cultural quarters' in some cities.

Clustering

It is hardly surprising that, with the research focus on embeddedness, intermediation and tacit knowledge, the question of 'creative clusters' has arisen. There is a popular policy stress on the creation of (consumption) cultural quarters that it is hoped may generate income from tourism, and attract investment (Mommaas, 2004). A second interpretation of creative clusters is a production-based one. Researchers have noted the tendency for cultural producers to co-locate, and for there to be a range of social and cultural, as well as economic interactions between them. The cultural industries are not evenly distributed, but concentrated in a few cities.

The broadly institutional framework that many economic geographers, and those influenced by their work on the cultural industries, have adopted clashes with that of neo-classical analyses that more commonly underpins policy making. Thus, there is a long running debate about the causes and processes of co-location, old and new industrial districts, and cost-minimization, and interaction. For neo-classical economists, the same rule applies to all industries, so what goes for the car industry should apply to cultural production. As noted above, the shortcoming of this is where industrial practices diverge from those expected in theory, as in the case of the cultural industries.

Whilst still rooted in a neo-classical tradition the work of Michael Porter (Porter, 1995, 1998) – who writes from the disciplinary position of business studies – has pointed to the value of clustering in terms of control and efficient management of the value chain (see Chapter 18). However, his analysis has a number of limitations. First, Porter looks at the incremental benefits of stages in the value chain, but not at its strategic control. Thus, his analysis is weak on power and the structuring of industries. Secondly, his abstract model uses the term 'cluster' to refer to scales from the size of a city block all the way up to the size of a nation-state. Accordingly, his model is unable to specify non-traded relations affected by scale and embeddedness. Critically, the application of Porter's work uses employment 'mass' and co-location as a proxy for clustering. Given that clusters are about interaction, this approach considerably weakens the argument.

Nevertheless, Porter's 'cluster solution' to competitive advantage has been popular with national and city governments around the world. Thus, politicians are looking for a 'Porter cluster', and academics are offering insights into non-(pure) economic interaction. In short, this is another example of the barrier that a cultural-economy dualism creates. Given the dominance of Porter's influence, it is not surprising that policy makers have looked to setting aside buildings, or quarters, of cities for the cultural industries with the implicit notion that co-location will lead to interaction, and growth. However, institutional policies, that are unique to the cultural industries, or sub-industries, are now beginning to be examined as a basis of policy making.

CONCLUSIONS

The aim of this chapter has been to outline an economic geography of the cultural industries. A stumbling block in the way of such an aspiration concerns the definition of the cultural industries. The early development of research was undermined by competing definitions, in no small part limited by information availability, and compounded by the rapid transformation of the cultural industries themselves. If nothing else, this should remind researchers that definitions and concepts cannot be taken for granted. Often, we assume the world to be stable when, in fact, it is in flux in both the empirical and conceptual realms. It also points up the common problem of the pragmatic trade off of available information, or data, and conceptual probity. In the end, solutions must be temporary and constantly revised.

Empirically, the cultural industries form a 'new' sector that has achieved some economic importance in some developed countries and has become an aspiration in others. Moreover, cultural industries are not evenly distributed. They have a distinct spatiality concentrated in a few cities, with (some parts of the production chain) grouped in 'clusters'. Their social and cultural impact is clearly increasing, as is the consumption that generates it. The research reported here highlights the blurring of the boundaries of production and consumption.

The study of the cultural industries may in some ways seem esoteric. However, it may have a number of wider resonances. First, the cultural industries provide ready made and pertinent empirical case studies through which to explore the contemporary articulation of the cultural and the economic. Research findings point in the direction of hybridity, of thinking beyond dualisms, and, to paraphrase Latour and Wedgar (1986), of following practices and actions without fear or favour. Such iteration between empirical research and theoretical reflection should represent best practice for all economic geographers. Second, research on the cultural industries should cause readers to question where the social/cultural ends and the economic begins (and vice versa). Economic geography is ideally positioned to forge new insights here as the practices of social and economic life are embedded in time and space, and embodied through practices. Third, whilst a case has been made to privilege the cultural industries as exceptional, they are internally differentiated. This is not to suggest that every instance is different; but that there are a number of structuring practices, represented in research as organizations, institutions, networks and practices. Fundamentally, the cultural industries raise the question of whether 'general' theories of 'the economy', or 'industry', are tenable. And/or, it might be asked whether this social-cultural embeddedness is unique to the 'touchy-feely' cultural sector or, if a search is made elsewhere, it might be found there too.

REFERENCES

Adorno, T. and Horkheimer, M. (1977) The culture industry: Enlightenment as mass deception. In J. Curran, M.M. Gurevitch and J. Woollacott (eds) *Mass Communications and Society*. London: Arnold. pp. 349–83.

Adorno, T. W. (1991) The schema of mass culture. In J.M. Bernstein (ed.) *The Culture Industry: Selected Essays on Mass Culture*. London: Routledge. pp. 61–97.

Anderson, B. (1991) *Imagined Communities: Reflections on the Origins and Spread of Nationalism*. London: Verso.

Barnes, T. (2001) Retheorizing economic geography: From the quantitative revolution to the cultural turn. *Annals of the Association of American Geographers*, 91: 546–65.

Baumol, W.J., and Bowen, W.G., (1966) *Performing Arts – The Economic Dilemma: A Study of Problems Common to Theater, Opera, Music and Dance*. New York: Twentieth Century Fund.

Becker, H.S. (1984) *Art Worlds*. London: University of California Press, Berkeley.

Bennett, T. (1998) *Culture: A Reformer's Science*. London: SAGE.

Blair, H., Grey, S. and Randle, K. (2001) Working in film – Employment in a project based industry. *Personnel Review*, 30: 170–185.

Bourdieu, P. (1993) The field of cultural production, or: The economic worlds reversed. In R. Johnson (ed.) *The Field of Cultural Production: Essays on Art and Literature*. Cambridge: Polity Press. pp. 29–72.

Caves, R.E. (2000) *Creative Industries: Contracts between Art and Commerce*. Harvard: Harvard University Press.

Crewe, L. (1996) Material culture: Embedded firms, organizational networks and the local economic development of a fashion quarter. *Regional Studies*, 30: 257–72.

Cunningham, S. (2003) Cultural studies from the viewpoint of cultural policy. In J. Lewis and T. Miller (eds) *Critical Cultural Policy Studies: A Reader*. Oxford: Blackwell. pp. 13–22.

DCMS (1998) *Creative Industries Mapping Document*. London: Department of Culture, Media and Sport, UK.

DCMS (1999) *A Report for Policy Action Team 10: Arts and Sport National Strategy for Neighbourhood Renewal*. London: Department of Culture, Media and Sport/Social Exclusion Unit, UK.

DCMS (2001) *Creative Industries Mapping Document* London: Department of Culture, Media and Sport, UK.

Florida, R. L. (2002) *The Rise of the Creative Class: And How it's Transforming Work, Leisure, Community and Everyday Life*. New York, NY: Basic Books, pp. 753–54.

Froud, J., Haslam, C., Johal, S., and Williams, K. (1998) Breaking the chains?: A sector matrix for motoring. *Competition & Change*, 3(3): 293–334.

Froud, J., Johal, S., and Williams, K. (2002) New agendas for auto research: Financialisation, motoring and present day capitalism. *Competition & Change* 6(1): 1–11.

Garnham, N. (1987) Concepts of culture–public policy and the cultural industries. *Cultural Studies* 1.

Garnham, N. (2005) From cultural to creative industries: An analysis of the implications of the 'creative industries' approach to arts and media policy making in the United Kingdom. *International Journal of Cultural Policy*. 11: 15–30.

Girard, A. (1982) Cultural industries: A handicap or a new opportunity for cultural development. In A. Girard (ed.) *Cultural Industries: A Challange for the Future*. Paris: UNESCO.

Grabher, G. (2001) Locating economic action: Projects, networks, localities, institutions. *Environment and Planning A*, 33: 1329–31.

Grabher, G. (2002a) Cool projects, boring institutions: Temporary collaboration in social context. *Regional Studies*, 36: 205–14.

Grabher, G. (2002b) The project ecology of advertising: Tasks, talents and teams. *Regional Studies*, 36: 245–62.

Hall, T. and Hubbard, P. (1998) *The Entrepreneurial City: Geographies of Politics, Regime, and Representation*. New York: Wiley.

Hannigan, J. (1998) *Fantasy City: Pleasure and Profit in the Postmodern Metropolis*. London: Routledge.

Hartley, J. (ed.) (2005) *Creative Industries*. Oxford: Blackwell.

Harvey, D. (1989) Flexible accumulation through urbanization: Reflections on 'Post-Modernism' in the American city. In D. Harvey (ed.) *The Urban Experience*. Oxford: Blackwell. pp. 256–78.

Hesmondhalgh, D. (2002) *The Cultural Industries* London: SAGE.

Hesmondhalgh, D. and Pratt, A.C. (2005) Cultural industries and cultural policy. *International Journal of Cultural Policy*, 11: 1–14.

Hobsbawm, E. and Ranger, T. (eds) (1992) *The Invention of Tradition*. Cambridge: Cambridge University Press.

Howkins, J. (2001) *The Creative Economy: How People Make Money from Ideas*. Harmondsworth: Penguin.

Jackson, P. (2002) Commercial cultures: Transcending the cultural and the economic. *Progress in Human Geography*, 26: 3–18.

Johns, J. (2006) Video games production networks: Value capture, power relations and embeddedness. *Journal of Economic Geography*, 6: 151–80.

Jones, C. (1996) Careers in project networks: The case of the film industry. In M.B. Arthur and D.M. Rousseau (eds) *The Boundaryless Career*. New York: Oxford University Press.

Landry, C. (2000) *The Creative City: A Toolkit for Urban Innovators*. London: Comedia: Earthscan.

Lash, S. and Urry, J. (1993) *Economies of Signs and Space*. London: SAGE.

Latour, B. and Woolgar, S. (1986) *Laboratory Life: The Construction of Scientific Facts*. Princeton, NJ: Princeton University Press.

Leonard, M. (1997) *Britain TM: Renewing our Identity*. London: Demos.

Leyshon, A. (2001) Time-space (and digital) compression: Software formats, musical networks, and the reorganisation of the music industry. *Environment and Planning A*, 33: 9–77.

Logan, J. R. and Molotch, H. L. (1987) *Urban Fortunes: The Political Economy of Place*. Berkeley, CA: University of California Press.

Matarasso, F. (1997) *Use or Ornament?: The Social Impact of Participation in the Arts*. Stroud: Comedia.

McRobbie, A. (1993) Cultural studies for the 1990s. *Innovation in Social Science Research*, 6: 269–77.

Miege, B. (1987) The logics at work in the new cultural industries. *Media Culture Society*, 9: 273–89.

Miege, B. (1989) *The Capitalization of Cultural Production*. New York: International General.

Miller, D. (2003) Advertising, production and consumption as cultural economy. In T. D. Malefyt, and B. Morean (eds) *Advertising Cultures*. Oxford: Berg. pp. 75–89.

Mommaas, H. (2004) Cultural clusters and the post-industrial city: Towards the remapping of urban cultural policy. *Urban Studies*, 41: 507–32.

Myerscough, J. (1988) *The Economic Importance of the Arts in Britain*. London: Policy Studies Institute.

O'Connor, J. (1998) New cultural intermediaries and the entrepreneurial city. In T. Hall, and P. Hubbard (eds) *The Entrepreneurial City: Geographies of Politics,*

Regime and Represention. Chichester: John Wiley. pp. 225–40.

O'Connor, J. and Wynne, D. (1998) Consumption and the post-modern city. *Urban Studies*, 35: 841–64.

Peterson, R. A. (ed.) (1976) *The Production of Culture*. London: SAGE.

Pine II, J. P., and Gilmore, J. H. (1999) *The Experience Economy: Work Is Theatre and Every Business a Stage*. Harvard: Harvard Business School.

Porter, M. (1995) The competitive advantages of the inner city. *Harvard Business Review*, 53–71.

Porter, M.E. (1998) *The Competitive Advantage of Nations*. London: Collier Macmillan.

Pratt, A.C. (1996) The emerging shape and form of innovation networks and institutions. In J. Simmie (ed.) *Innovation, Networks and Learning Regions* London: Jessica Kingsley. pp. 124–36.

Pratt, A.C. (1997) The cultural industries production system: A case study of employment change in Britain, 1984–1991. *Environment and Planning A*, 29: 1953–74.

Pratt, A.C. (2000) Cultural tourism as an urban cultural industry: A critical appraisal. In Interarts (ed.) *Cultural Tourism*. Barcelona: Turisme de Catalunya, Diputació de Barcelona. pp. 33–45.

Pratt, A.C. (2004a) Creative clusters: Towards the governance of the creative industries production system? *Media International Australia*, 50–66.

Pratt, A. C. (2004b) Mapping the cultural industries: Regionalization; the example of South East England. In D. Power and A. J. Scott (eds) *Cultural Industries and the Production of Culture*. London: Routledge. pp.19–36.

Pratt, A.C. (2004c) Retail therapy. *Geoforum*, 35: 519–21.

Pratt, A. C. (2004d) The cultural economy: A call for spatialized 'production of culture' perspectives. *International Journal of Cultural Studies*, 7: 117–28.

Pratt, A. C. (2005) Cultural industries and public policy: An oxymoron? *International Journal of Cultural Policy*, 11: 31–44.

Pratt, A. C. (2006) Advertising and creativity, a governance approach: A case study of creative agencies in London. *Environment and Planning A*, 38: 1883–99.

Pratt, A. C. (2008) Creativity, innovation and the city. In P. Hubbard, and J. Short (eds) *Urban Compendium*. London: Routledge.

Richards, G. (1996) *Cultural Tourism in Europe*. Wallingford, UK: CAB International.

Scott, A.J. (2000) *The Cultural Economy of Cities: Essays on the Geography of Image-producing Industries*. London: SAGE.

Short, J.R. and Kim, Y.K. (1998) Urban crises/urban representations: Selling the city in difficult times. In P. Hall and P. Hubbard (eds) *The Entrepreneurial City: Geographies of Politics, Regime and Representation*. London: John Wiley and Sons. pp. 55–75.

Siwek, S. (2002) *Copyright Industries in the U.S. Economy: The 2002 Report*. Washington: The International Intellectual Property Alliance.

Throsby, D. (2001) *Economics and Culture*. Cambridge: Cambridge University Press.

Vogel, H. L. (2001) *Entertainment Industry Economics: A Guide for Financial Analysis*. Cambridge: Cambridge University Press.

Zukin, S. (1995) *The Cultures of Cities*. Cambridge, MA: Blackwell.

22

Doing Gender, Performing Work

Linda McDowell

INTRODUCTION

In this chapter I explore the relationship between gender relations and the service-based economy, focusing on the ways in which men and women perform and embody the social relations of both employment and gender in their daily lives in the labour market. I note the ways in which labour markets are being transformed in early twenty-first century capitalist societies as ever-wider groups in society enter waged labour and as ever more servicing and caring functions are commodified. In service-dominated economies, where employment increasingly is based on the exchange of care and other forms of personal interactions/services, the embodiment of both provider and purchaser has become a central element of the analysis of social relations in the labour market. Thus, new questions about pleasure, desire and discipline have become significant for economic geography.

In service jobs and occupations, a personal interaction between the suppliers and purchasers of services is a typical part of the commodity exchange. The social attributes and sexed bodies of employees have moved centre-stage, as growing numbers of employers demand, and customers expect to interact with, aesthetically-pleasing bodies, especially in high status or high value exchanges. Even at the bottom end of the job market, an aesthetic performance is a common requirement. Jobs at this end of the occupational hierarchy have been termed 'high touch', to distinguish them from the apparently more rational and cerebral 'high tech' work of science and industry (Brush, 1999). But, as I shall show, in both forms of work, the question of embodiment is central. Attributes of sexualized gender identities – sex itself, including questions about sexual harassment, as well as skin colour, age, weight, and accent – are mapped onto different forms of work designated as appropriate for differently sexed and gendered workers.

At the same time as the service sector is expanding, there is also something of a moment of reconsideration, a juncture when established notions of gender are being destabilized and recast, as hegemonic notions of acceptable masculinity(ies) and femininity(ies) and their association with socially valued forms of employment are changing (Adkins and Lury, 2000; Butler, 2004; McDowell, 2001). Here I build on the groundwork laid in Louise Johnson's chapter (Chapter 23). Whether new ways of doing gender are possible in the transformation of work is an open question. A more pessimistic reading of contemporary changes in the labour market sees in this transformation both the re-establishment and deepening of older gender divisions of labour and new, more inequitable interconnections between class and gender (Adkins, 2004).

The argument of the chapter proceeds in three sections. First, the basic features of service dominated labour markets are explored. Second, I explore the significance of concepts such as identity, performance, embodiment, and sexuality in new theories of employment change and then third, empirical examples of the variety of ways in which gender is part of the performance of a range of service jobs are provided. In these post-industrial service economies, other social divisions are also being transformed. Jobs and occupations are becoming increasingly polarized, both in terms of the conditions and patterns of work and in rewards and security of employment. A new social division is opening up between: i) typically masculinized 'self-programmable' labour, where workers (of both sexes) with high level skills and credentials in career positions enjoy the prospect of prosperity, and; ii) a low skilled, often uncredentialized 'generic labour' where workers of both sexes labour under 'feminized' conditions, with low levels of security and poor pay (Castells, 2000). This division is reflected in growing income inequality between individuals and households, as well as widening class and status inequalities. Thus the relations between gender, class, ethnicity, status and skill are being recast in service economies.

THE RISE OF SERVICE SECTOR WORK

As Johnson shows in Chapter 23, work in the widest sense is more than waged employment. It includes all those activities that are central to material existence. Work provides sustenance, goods for exchange and, for some, income and it includes a wide range of activities. Work also takes place in a variety of locations under different conditions and sometimes, although not always, it is rewarded by payment, in cash or in kind (see Chapter 13). Different types of work also confer varying degrees of status and respect and, as feminist theorists have argued the gender of workers is associated both with financial reward and with perceived social status, as well as with the actual definition of the tasks involved in particular occupations. One of the consequences of defining work as waged labour is that for many years it resulted in the exclusion of work undertaken in the home for 'love' from the remit of economic geography. Millions of (usually) women labour within their homes to ensure the social reproduction of their household. Increasingly, in advanced industrial societies, many of these goods and services have become commoditized, available for purchase in markets. After their transfer to the labour market, however, the provision of these services tends to remain feminized. The majority of workers in these jobs are women and, in common with other female-dominated sectors of the economy – clerical work, primary school teaching, nursing, for example – these jobs are low status and typically poorly paid but are also growing in numerical significance.

In the contemporary economy, more than two thirds of all workers, over half of them women, are employed in the service economy and women's participation has risen from one third to half of all waged workers over the second half of the twentieth century. Now, 60% of men and 82% of women in employment work in the service sector. And, as Goos and Manning (2003) showed in their assessment of the UK labour market in the last decade of the twentieth century, the fastest rate of growth has been in 'bottom end' jobs which increased from 1.2 to 1.9 million (and remember this figure undoubtedly excludes a lot of poorly paid, often illegal, 'off the books' work). The jobs that expanded most quickly included sales assistants, checkout operators, cooks, waiters, bar staff, youth workers, telephone sales, security guards as well as some growth in the numbers of nurses, hospital ward assistants and care assistants. Many of these jobs involve serving the needs of customers or caring for their bodily needs and they tend to be dominated by women workers.

Service sector work almost always involves a direct relationship with a client, a customer or a consumer. It is work in which employees 'sell' themselves as part of the transaction (Hochschild, 1983). In other words, the bodily presentation and performance of employees is of crucial significance in the transactions involved in what Robin Leidner (1993), a US sociologist, has termed interactive service work or the British sociologist Carol Wolkowitz (2002) called 'body work'. The jobs and occupations that are currently expanding demand a focus on the body, not only on the bodily performance undertaken by the workers themselves but increasingly, as Wolkowitz (2002) noted, they also involve work on the bodies of others in the 'care, adornment, pleasure, discipline and cure of others' bodies' (p. 497). In both aspects of body work – the care and performance of the workers' own body and the care of other's bodies – social relations based on sexuality, pleasure, desire and fantasy play an increasingly significant part in the employment relation: in hiring and firing, in accepted workplace performances, in interactions between worker and customer or client and in the ways in which gendered attributes are accorded to different types of work and so are differentially rewarded. Work, in other words, has become a performance and the clothes, appearance, weight, facial gestures and general bodily presentation of self have

grown in significance as an essential attribute of an acceptable service sector worker. In the second section I explore this argument in more detail, and define some key terms. In the third section, I provide some case studies of embodied work practices and the ways in which they intersect with socially constructed attributes of acceptable gendered identities.

GENDER, SEXUALITY, PERFORMANCES AND ORGANIZATIONS

For many years, geographers interested in labour market change and economic transformation ignored the personal attributes of workers. Employees *en masse* were seen as labour power which possessed variable levels of skills and which, for geographers at least, varied by region. As individuals they were theorized as rational economic 'men' seeking work that was as well-remunerated as possible. Workplaces or organizations clearly differed in the terms and conditions of employment that they offered but, like their employees, it was assumed that they too were rationally organized to make maximum profits. Perhaps the first challenge to the notion of rational bureaucratic organizations and disembodied non-sexual (and by default masculine) workers that dominated economic geography, sociology and other associated disciplines came in studies that might be grouped under the heading of 'gender and organizations'. Joan Acker's (1990) now-classic paper challenged the notion that organizations consist of profit-maximizing institutions that, through the employment of hierarchies of employees without dependants, achieve market-defined ends. Acker argued instead that organizations are seldom rational or objective but that their structures, cultures and everyday practices are riven with essentialist and non-essentialist assumptions about gender and sexuality in ways which consistently benefit certain workers, typically white heterosexual men. The disadvantaged include that cast of 'Others': women, people of colour, less physically-able workers and people with alternative sexual identities. These Others may be excluded or constructed as less suitable workers, restricted to a narrow range of jobs and occupations that are congruent with their gendered and sexualized identities. In consequence, the division of labour *per se* and organizations and their practices are deeply gendered, maintained by both conscious and unconscious practices.

Acker's work and the organizational case-studies that followed it built on earlier analyses such as Kanter's (1977) work documenting men's dominance of high status occupations and positions. She showed how this dominance was based on women's support services in the workplace and in the home. As well as Acker's work, there are now numerous studies of the ways in which the discursive construction of organizational practices produce and maintain patterns of gendered and sexualized behaviour. This work has added to, even replaced, explanations of gender segregation based on ideas about human capital and/or on socialist-feminist claims about the necessity of domestic labour for capitalist production based on the patriarchal exploitation of women. Not only are gendered assumptions built into definitions of jobs and who does them but organizations also gender and sexualize their workers, in associations of cerebral rationality with men and high tech jobs and, sexy 'service-with-a-smile' in many feminized lower status jobs (Ferree et al., 1999; Hochschild, 1983).

Rosemary Pringle's (1988) analysis of secretarial work was one of the earliest and best of the early studies that documented the importance of sexuality in establishing workplace hierarchies. She showed how workplace-based social relations are based on discourses of desire and pleasure. Gendered sexualized identities are both constructed and challenged through workplace practices in official and unofficial arenas and practices saturated by notions about gender and sexuality that are themselves embedded within wider social structures and attitudes and assumptions about gender and sexuality. Pringle showed how women working as secretaries, for example, drew on different discourses, including the office 'mistress' and the office 'wife', to construct particular sets of power relations between them and their male bosses. Flirting and having fun was a common script for male boss/female secretary interaction, as well as the extension of office duties into 'homemaker' tasks (making coffee, arranging food at meeting, buying flowers for the office or gifts for the boss's household for example). Between women bosses and women secretaries the social relations were more straightforward and less deferential, typically confined to office-based and work-related activities, but in some cases also more conflictual.

Studies building on Pringle's path-breaking work typically have drawn on two connected sets of theoretical arguments. The first is Foucault's (1978) insistence that the body is less a 'natural' biological feature than an inscripted surface on which temporally – and culturally – specific sets of ideas, images, institutional structures, practices and regulations about bodily practices are written. Through the operation of a wide range of forms of social regulation, including self-discipline, 'conforming' or 'docile' bodies are produced and reproduced through everyday social practices. These bodies typically conform to conventional social notions of acceptable versions of masculinity and femininity. The second set of arguments are based on the work of Judith Butler (1990, 1993) who draws on psychoanalytic, feminist and post-structuralist theories in her theorization of identity. She insists on the provisional status of identity, constructed within language and discourse, arguing that gender is a 'regulatory fiction' constructed within discourses that normalize heterosexuality. Her notion that gender is 'performative' has been crucial to studies of labour market behaviour but it is important to recognize that her term defines not an individualized, voluntary performance but rather identities that are constructed through pre-existing discursive structures (see Salih, 2002).

What these arguments do is to link sexuality to Leidner and Wolkowitz's arguments about the body. In embodied, sexualized performances the attributes of a desirable and desiring body become significant and play a part in the interactions in service economies, whether employees are selling burgers, financial advice, a toy for a child or a ride at Disneyland. Some organizations make the requirement of an idealized, typically white, clean, slim, young, and often sexualized body an explicit part of the recruitment process. The sexualized bodily performances of both men, but especially women, air stewards is notorious, illustrated, for example, in a campaign Cathay Air ran in the 1980s which included the slogan: 'I'm Cindi, fly me'. US employment theorist Airlie Hochschild termed this presentation of self (Goffman, 1969) at work the 'management of emotions', captured in the title of her book *The Managed Heart* in which she looked at a range of service sector jobs including air stewarding. US philosopher Iris Marion Young (1990) took these ideas a step further in her book *Justice and the Politics of Difference* where she redefined inequality, suggesting that it is more than a question about the distribution of income. Instead she argued that contemporary structures of inequality are composed of 'five faces of oppression', one of which is the body or bodily image and presentation. She argues that ugly, fat, non-white, and elderly bodies are inadmissible in societies that valorize an idealized white, slim, young, unwrinkled, and typically heterosexualized body. Bodies that do not conform to this ideal are out of place in the interactive sales/advice-giving industries and occupations that increasingly dominate in advanced industrial societies. Ideas of inequality and social justice at work must now include a great deal more than access to jobs and pay rates. In the final section, I explore the ways in which service sector growth and gendered norms interact at work in three different workspaces.

PERFORMING WORK: THREE CASE STUDIES

Masculinity, femininity and deference: working in fast food

Here, I show how embodied gendered performance and ideas about gendered and sexualized identities and idealized bodies are used to include some but exclude others as potential employees, as well as to regulate acceptable workplace performances. As mentioned earlier, Robin Leidner (1993) is the author of a book called *Fast Food Fast Talk* which is based on an examination of the training policies of the insurance and fast food industries. She became an observer at the McDonalds Training Centre and watched how the trainers produced and reproduced workers, drilling trainees to produce a standardized set of responses to customers as well as becoming part of an extreme division of labour as tasks are broken down into small components that have to be performed in a particular order within tight time limits. This Fordist division of labour, in which jobs are broken down into a series of repetitive tasks, has become standard practice in the fast food industry. This leads Yannis Gabriel (1988) to argue that fast food is, in many ways and, despite its location in the consumer service sector of a post-Fordist economy, a classic example of Fordism. Indeed, as he argued, 'the hamburger, the industry's acclaimed Model T, is carefully planned to appeal to the world market' (p. 93). In its employment policies, however, McDonalds and other fast food outlets operate a numerically flexible policy par excellence. Staff are recruited as casual and part-time workers. They are usually young, often students, and rates of labour turnover are extremely high as wages are low and conditions poor. As Gabriel (1998), in his study of fast food outlets, Leidner, and Katherine Newman (1999), in her interesting book, *There's No Shame In My Game,* all document, working for McDonalds is extremely hard. Youth and vigour are essential attributes of recruitment policies.

McDonalds has come to stand for the growth of bottom end, poorly remunerated and exploitative service sector work – indeed these kinds of entry level jobs are often collectively termed 'McJobs' (Ritzer, 2002), despite demanding close attention to an accurate workplace performance, as well as attention to maintaining an acceptable bodily image, to presentation and the maintenance of an acceptable set of workplace clothes. But attitudes, as well as bodily presentation, are also a key element in the performance of service work. The attitudinal and embodied attributes of deference and servility, as well as empathy with other's needs, required in these expanding low status 'servicing' jobs, where engagement with the public as well as colleagues is an essential attribute of the work, have often been associated with the social characteristics of femininity. As a consequence, men, and especially working class young men, who have developed a particular version of a tough, aggressive, sexualized street credibility that is inappropriate to servicing types of work, are socially constructed as out of place in many workplaces. Newman (1999) described how young male workers in fast food outlets in New York City found these demands conflicted with their sense of masculinity and their desire for 'respect' from co-workers and customers. This conflict between an idealized version of working class masculinity and a deferential workplace performance often led to disciplinary issues with management and to young men losing their jobs (see also Bourgois, 1995).

Newman's research was undertaken in New York City. I have worked in Sheffield and Cambridge, exploring the job prospects for unskilled young white men as they left school (McDowell, 2003). I found that many young men had clear views about the types of work they were prepared to consider, regarding most service sector work as 'women's work' and so beneath their dignity. Even if they were prepared to consider employment in the shops, clubs and fast food outlets that were the main types of work open to unqualified school leavers in these cities,

they often disqualified themselves as potential employees by their appearance and their attitudes during the recruitment process. Employers read the surface signals of bodily demeanour, dress and language as inappropriate for service employees. If the young men did find work, their sexualized, aggressive embodied interactions, especially with women co-workers and superiors, often became a problem (Bourgois, 1995). Many of the men I interviewed also found it hard to perform the deferential servility required in the service economy. Young women, on the other hand, are more experienced in presenting a modest demeanour and deferential attitudes to adult authority, as well as more able to defuse difficult situations. Leidner (1993) found that for these reasons, men were often cooking at the back rather than in jobs that involved direct contact with customers. Sexuality and service with a smile is important even in 'disembodied' jobs in, for example, call centres where clients and sellers are invisible to each other and yet a sale depends on the rapid establishment of social relations of trust and intimacy. Here, the allure and intimacy of the voice and the ability to establish a rapid and empathetic connection with the caller is important, whether the product is double glazing or sexual fantasies.

Although men, and typically young men, seem to be disadvantaged in bottom end service work, Leidner found that in some jobs both men and women are able to interpret the skills need in different jobs in ways that are congruent with their own gendered identities. In her case study of an insurance company she found that both women and men were recruited to undertake what is known in the trade as cold calling – that is calling on householders with no warning to persuade them to take out new policies. As Leidner notes, the attributes needed to do this work successfully – empathy, persuasiveness, an unthreatening appearance and sociable manner – all seem to line up with socially constructed characteristics of femininity and growing numbers of women were being recruited by the organization. Indeed, the women who were being trained learned to present themselves as unthreatening. Male sellers, however, found such a presentation of self problematic, and instead emphasized characteristics of the job that they believed matched their sense of themselves as masculine. They talked about the dangers involved in the urban streets, and being street-wise and able to protect themselves, and about the need to overcome people's resistance through the 'hard sell'. As women sales workers were both more successful and were paid lower wages, they were increasing their share in the sales teams. In the UK, too, gendered attributes have been used to restructure insurance selling by banks. Male-dominated cold calling teams typically have been replaced by women, sitting at desks in the front of the banking hall to attract the attention of bank customers as they come in to do other business by their smart attractive appearance, their smiling welcome and their accessibility (Halford et al., 1997). However, as Leyshon et al. (2006) have shown, cold calling is still common in money lending although it too is dominated by women. Through this gender transfer, banks and other money lending agencies are able to increase profits as feminization is typically associated with lower wages.

Data entry: dressing up for back office work

The second example draws on Carla Freeman's (2000) study of women data process entry workers in Barbados in the Caribbean in which she combined an analysis of globalization with an ethnographic study of the workplace. New technologies increasingly have made offshore data entry possible for large global corporations, linking workers in disparate locations to their headquarters in the US and UK. At the same time, labour relations in the Caribbean and elsewhere are being transformed by the new back office jobs. For example, Freeman (2000: 2) has

described the nature of this new form of work and the ways in which women employees represent themselves:

> [M]arking the latest version of high-tech rationalization of the labour process, this rapidly expanding new industry, known as informatics, represents a massive and transnational commodification of information. Its forms include airline tickets and consumer warranty cards, as well as academic texts, literary classics, pornographic novels, and specialized scientific articles . . . [D]espite the industry's highly regimented and disciplined labour process, closely resembling factory assembly work, informatics workers adopt a language and set of behaviours for describing and enacting themselves as 'professional' nonfactory workers that effectively demarcates them from traditional industrial labourers.

The women who work in these processing 'factories', in which their labour is highly routinized and monitored, both by supervisors and managers and by the 'hidden gaze' of the machines on which they work which calculate every key stroke, nevertheless take a degree of pride and experience pleasure in the presentation of themselves as professional women workers. Freeman's aim was to explore women's construction of self arguing that understandings of contemporary labour markets and their transformation through globalization must involve an intersection of political economy and cultural studies. She argues that an understanding of how work structures identity, desires and aspirations must be as much part of the analysis as labour routines and salary levels. The informatics industry is feminized, not only because the labour force is almost entirely constituted by women but also because, like the servicing industries that are expanding in the 'first world', 'the work process itself is imbued with notions of appropriate femininity, which include a quiet, responsible demeanour along with meticulous attention to detail and a quick and accurate keyboard technique' (pp. 3–4). As one manager of a small data entry company said when justifying his employment policy: 'typing is a skill that somehow seemed to fit into a female society' (p. 116).

But it is more than this conventional association, Freeman argues, that links the work to the construction of a particular version of femininity. Like the women bankers to be discussed next, these women data process workers, 'dress to impress' but in this case it is to impress their co-workers and themselves rather than clients, who are not co-present in the workplace. Thus, 'the particular appearance of informatics workers – the boldly adorned skirt suits and polished high heels – and the physical space they inhabit as workers – the air-conditioned and office-like settings – are integral to women's experience of these jobs and ultimately to their emergent identities' (p. 4).

These identities are part of what Freeman terms 'a new pink collar service class' (p. 22) that is emerging as a significant part of the global division of labour which takes a specific form in the Caribbean-based data processing industry. Here it is based on the coincidence of locally-specific notions of acceptable feminine identities and a Caribbean concept of respectability that does not construct women's waged work and family responsibilities as mutually exclusive. Thus, 'what emerges from this global/local conjuncture is that women's identities, as feminine members of the working class, become refashioned through a set of gendered practices encoded in the concept of 'professionalism', enacted on the production floor, as well as in the modes of consumption associated with the new informatics industry' (p. 23). These relations, excavated by combining an ethnographic analysis of the performance of identities with the analysis of structural economic change, bring together both the workplace and the home and an understanding of economic change and cultural representations in ways that are as yet atypical in analyses of globalization.

Maintaining masculine dominance of up-market financial advice

In the final example, the focus is on high status employment where dress and appearance is also important. Although research on

performance initially emphasized the 'servicing' end of the service sector it is clear that in the top end, high status jobs bodily images and embodied performances are also a key part of interactions between clients and employees and among employees. In my work in investment banks in the City of London (McDowell, 1997) I found that the sexualized body was a significant part of everyday working practices and that banks were saturated with sexualized language as well as idealized and sexualized performances. As feminist theorists have emphasized, jobs themselves embody idealized aspects of masculinity and femininity, as well as the active construction of masculinity and femininity of employees in the workplace. Workers do not enter their place of employment with their gender firmly fixed in place, rather gender is a fluid and multiple performance which varies according to type of work and its location. What might be suitable behaviour or a suitable appearance in one place is not in another.

In my study of investment banking sector in the early to mid-1990s, I explored whether the traditional associations of corporate banking with a bourgeois, cerebral masculinity and of trading with an embodied 'barrow boy' masculinity were disrupted as the City of London expanded and changed in the 1980s and 1990s, especially after the Financial Services Act in 1987, as men and women from a wider range of social and educational backgrounds were recruited. Interviews with high status and well-paid employees made it clear that workers in many of the occupations in merchant banking saw their everyday lives in terms of a performance or a game. Here, for example, is a male analyst talking about his job:

It's not just the quality of your work that matters, although that is important. It's only one of the things that is considered . . . I mean, I think that one of the strongest characteristics of someone in this business must be the ability to talk convincingly to their clients, and in a way it's almost a politician's job because if you really analyse it what are you doing? You're selling someone the idea that you know better than them. (McDowell, 1997: 98)

Banking is a sector marked by the rise of what Ulrich Beck (1994) has termed individualization and Scott Lash and John Urry (1994) characterized as a dematerialized or a culturalized labour process in which workers emphasize the uniquenesss, variety and individuality of their work. Lash has further argued that work in knowledge-based industries is 'reflexive', based on the development of relations of trust between workers, and between workers and clients based on shared identities. These notions dominate banking where recruitment and promotion are still based on criteria such as 'social fit' and a great deal of the work involves the construction and maintenance of personal networks. It is also, however, a world that remains based on binary distinctions between men and women, in which women are seen as less trustworthy and, less suitable. The everyday performance of women is often regarded as out of place, as overly-feminine/embodied, and so as unsuited to the rational cerebral and disembodied world of banking.

I wanted to assess Acker's argument that women tend to succeed in male-dominated organizations and corporations only if they adopt an unsexed, masculinized performance in the workplace: 'to be successful women have to become honorary men' (Acker, 1990: 140). Based on interviews with women bankers in high status jobs, I found that this performance of masculinity was often attempted, but was ultimately seen as impossible. Many of the women whom I interviewed argued that they remain tied to and excluded by the traditional associations of 'woman', by male beliefs in a version of 'natural' embodiment that make women unacceptable in 'rational' workplaces and by the social construction of femininity on the basis of sexualized attributes.

The conventional methods that women bankers adopted to construct a masculinized and a sexual performance at work ranged from the adoption of sombre clothing, the disguise of explicitly female conditions or interests, such as pregnancy and mothering, to the development of masculine mannerisms such as the aggressive use of language or dominating behaviour and attempting to become 'one of the boys' by joining in typically male after-work pursuits such as drinking.

Exaggerated forms of masculinized language and behaviour are commonplace in the trading and dealing arenas of banking. Here horse play, sexualized banter, loud and aggressive talk and forms of sexual harassment are common and women are often forced either into the position of unwilling arbiters of boundaries or less than willing participants in the sexualized banter. Examples of the first position are when women find that male colleagues stop talking when they join a group, or with exaggerated courtesy apologize for their language or ask for permission to continue. In the second case, women find that they too are, by choice or through a desire to fit into the accepted atmosphere, just as likely as their male colleagues to 'talk dirty'. But women in the main are visible on trading floors only by their absence. As one male trader told the *Independent on Sunday* in September 2002 (08/11/02) 'as I look around this floor, the only woman I can see is making my tea'.

On trading floors, especially in bull markets, an aggressive, hetero-sexualized masculine confidence in their own abilities creates an atmosphere inimical to many women and to gay men, and which might also lead to poor advice. In a recent study by investment bank Dresdner Kleinwort Wasserstein, analyst James Montier noted that 'much of the psychology behind markets has to do with the over-confidence of traders and the tendency to exaggerate their own abilities' and so under-estimate the impact of a falling market. According to Theodora Zenek, an asset manager in the City of London, men 'are aggressive buyers, but that either gives you staggering out-performance or staggering under-performance', in part because, as she noted, men have a 'tendency to fall in love with their investments' (quoted in the *Independent on Sunday* 08/11/02).

In the more conventional arenas of corporate banking, where interaction with business clients is a key part of the work, women tended to be treated with patriarchal courtesy and to be excluded through talk and interactions, based on networks of contacts that depend on 'the old school tie'. Even in this side of banking, however, the body mattered, despite its covering by pin-striped tailoring. Male interviewees emphasized the importance of the correct clothes – in quality and colour – as well as the importance of bodily hygiene and keeping weight within certain limits. In this world, a certain relatively youthful, male, bourgeois form of embodied performance based on a rigorously disciplined body was a key issue. Slenderness and an idealized image of youthful heterosexuality was most highly valorized and, through recruitment practices, tended to be largely reproduced from year to year. A casual glance at business pages in the broadsheet press is enough to confirm this hegemonic ideal.

I completed my empirical work in the mid-1990s as the City was beginning to boom again and recruitment was high. In this optimistic atmosphere women may have felt more able to take risks. Even so, women remained a tiny majority in the higher echelons of merchant banks. At the present time, however, the financial sector is once again experiencing redundancies, and although it may be inaccurate to draw a connection between women's experiences of discrimination and tense working conditions, it is noticeable that a number of high profile cases of harassment and unfair dismissal have recently reached the courts. Many of these cases involve discrimination in salaries but especially in performance related bonuses. But they also involve claimed discrimination on the basis of sexist behaviour and practice in the banks, including the hiring of escort girls for company parties or discriminating against women on the basis of their appearance.

Like bottom end service jobs, the world of banking is one of performance par excellence.

But this is still a world that is inimical to women rather than one in which discrimination in women's favour on the basis of supposed attributes of deference and empathy (but still paying low wages). High status service work – and similar case studies based on research among university teachers, lawyers and the police service would tell a similar story – remains a predominantly male world in its organizational culture and practices. Here there is little evidence of a 'crisis of masculinity' or a diminution of masculine power and privilege among its male employees. The general feminization of the service world of work has little impact here. However, the growing significance of women in the labour market, rising female participation rates in higher education and in professional employment, new working practices and types of work, recognition of the importance of emotions at work, and new organizational forms can and are gradually disrupting and modifying older practices. To paraphrase Judith Butler (1990), women in the workplace may constitute 'gender trouble' for organizations in the future. Certainly, large banks are finding women troublesome at present.

CONCLUSIONS

As I have suggested in this chapter, the social relations of employment in service-based economies emphasize the embodied nature of the exchange between the provider and purchaser of services, be they meals, massages, financial advice or different forms of health care. In this service economy, the attributes of masculinity and femininity are both mapped onto different categories of employment and are constructed and re-created through daily practices within the workplace as well as through the broader organizational structures of the economy. Gendered identities are not fixed and permanent; men and women do not enter the labour market with their sense of self already in place but instead workers 'do gender' (West and Zimmerman, 1987) at work. In the shift to labour markets dominated by service sector jobs and occupations, idealized notions of the preferred gender of employees change as new forms of working and new types of services become part of the cash nexus. In some areas of work, women seem to gain advantages from the association between certain attributes of femininity with sought-after employment characteristics and yet gender remains a significant axis of inequality. Despite their rising rates of educational attainment, women are still concentrated in the 'high touch' ends of the economy, performing caring and servicing work in jobs that tend to be less well-paid than 'high tech' and professional occupations. Further, as the empirical examples have demonstrated, employers continue to benefit from the social construction of women's labour as less valuable than that of men's. How to shift the vexed connections between gendered identities and labour market segmentation and the associated financial rewards remains an open question.

ACKNOWLEDGEMENT

This chapter is a revised and extended version of a chapter published in 2004. 'Sexuality, desire and embodied performances in the workplace' in Bainham, A. et al. (eds) *Sexuality Repositioned: Diversity and the Law.* Oxford: Hart. pp. 85–107.

REFERENCES

Acker, J. (1990) Hierarchies, jobs, bodies: A theory of gendered organizations. *Gender and Society,* 4: 139–58.

Adkins, L. (2004) Gender and the post structural social. In B. Marshall, and A. Witz (eds) *Engendering the Social: Feminist Encounters with Sociological Theory.* Maidenhead: Open University Press. pp. 139–54.

Adkins, L. and Lury, C. (2000) Making bodies, making people, making work. In L. McKie, and N. Watson (eds) *Organizing Bodies: Policy, Institutions and Work,* Basingstoke: Macmillan. pp. 151–65.

Beck, U. (1994) The reinvention of politics: Towards a theory of reflexive modernization. In U. Beck, A. Giddens, and S. Lash (eds) *Reflexive Modernization: Politics, Tradition and Modernization in the Modern Social Order.* Cambridge: Polity. pp. 1–55.

Bourgois, P. (1995) *In Search of Respect: Selling Crack in El Barrio.* Cambridge: Cambridge University Press.

Brush, L. (1999) Gender, work, who cares?! Production, reproduction, deindustrialisation and business as usual. In M.M. Ferree, J. Lorber, and B. Hess (eds) *Revisioning Gender.* London: SAGE. pp. 161–89.

Butler, J. (1990) *Gender Trouble.* London: Routledge.

Butler, J. (1993) *Bodies that Matter.* London: Routledge.

Butler, J. (2004) *Undoing Gender.* London: Routledge.

Castells, M. (2000) Materials for an exploratory theory of the network society. *British Journal of Sociology,* 51: 5–22.

Ferree, M.M., Lorber, J. and Hess, B.B. (eds) (1999) *Revisioning Gender.* London: SAGE.

Foucault, M. (1978) *The History of Sexuality Volume 1: An Introduction.* London: Allen Lane.

Freeman, C. (2000) *High Tech and High Heels in the Global Economy.* London: Duke University Press.

Gabriel, Y. (1988) *Working Lives in Catering.* London: Routledge.

Goffman, E. (1969) *The Presentation of Self in Everyday Life.* Harmondsworth: Penguin.

Goos, M. and Manning, A. (2003) McJobs and MacJobs: The growing polarisation of Jobs in the UK. In R. Dickens, P. Gregg, and J. Wadsworth (eds). *The Labour Market Under New Labour.* Basingstoke: Macmillan. pp. 70–85.

Halford, S., Savage, M. and Witz, A. (1997) *Gender, Careers and Organizations.* Basingstoke: Macmillan.

Hochschild, A. (1983) *The Managed Heart: The Commercialization of Human Feeling.* Berkeley: University of California Press.

Kanter, R.M. (1997) *Men and Women of the Corporation.* New York: Basic Books.

Lash, S. and Urry, J. (1994) *Economies of Signs and Space.* London: SAGE.

Leyshon, A., Signoretta, P., Knights, D., Alferoff, C., and Burton, D. (2006) Walking with money lenders: The ecology of the home-collected credit industry. *Urban Studies* 43: 161–86.

Liedner, R. (1993) *Fast Food, Fast Talk: Interactive Service Work and the Routinization of Everyday Life.* Berkeley: University of California Press.

McDowell, L. (1997) *Capital Culture: Gender at Work in the City*. Oxford: Blackwell.

McDowell, L. (2001) Father and Ford revisited: Gender, class and employment change in the new millennium. *Transactions of the Institute of British Geographers*, 24: 448–64

McDowell, L. (2003) *Redundant Masculinities? Employment Change and White Working Class Youth*. Oxford: Blackwell.

Newman, K. (1999) *No Shame in My Game: The Working Poor in the Inner City*. New York: Vintage Books and Russell Sage Foundation.

Pringle, R. (1988) *Secretaries Talk: Sexuality, Power and Work*. London: Verso.

Ritzer, G. (2002) *McDonaldization: The Reader*. Thousand Oaks, CA: Pine Forge Press.

Salih, S. (2002) *Judith Butler*. London: Routledge.

West, C. and Zimmerman, D. (1987) Doing gender. *Gender and Society,* 1: 125–51.

Wolkowitz, C. (2002) The social relations of body work. *Work, Employment and Society*, 16(3): 497–510.

Young, I. M. (1990) *Justice and the Politics of Difference*. Princeton: Princeton University Press.

PART 8

Rethinking the Economic

23

Feminist Economic Geographies

Louise Johnson

INTRODUCTION

If economic geography is primarily concerned with studying the generation and allocation of scarce resources across space, feminist intervention into this discourse has involved the inclusion of gender and the sexual division of labour as fundamental to the economy; critical evaluations of key concepts, assumptions, methods and studies; and their reformulation to create very different feminist economic geographies. Feminist economic geography therefore involves both critique and construct (Gunew, 1990). A feminist approach – putting women and their disadvantage relative to men central to analysis and ameliorative action – has been applied to the analysis of labour markets internationally, nationally and within cities, as well as to how workplaces, paid and unpaid, both create and construct gendered subjects. In so doing, notions such as 'the economy' and 'the labour market' as 'neutral' descriptors have been gendered, while the idea of 'work' has been broadened to include unpaid, voluntary, and other forms of labour, as well as waged

employment. Feminist economic geographers have thereby created different ways of understanding key concepts and economic spaces and generated alternative ways of thinking about the economy. In these activities, the counter-discourse has been nourished by broader feminist scholarship as well as by political activism that has questioned the ways in which apparently neutral economic concepts, policies and practices have differentially impacted on women and men. Feminist economic geography, therefore, has material foundations and effects, with gender relations, social justice and liberatory politics at its core.

This account will proceed chronologically but also thematically to highlight key empirical and theoretical developments in feminist economic geography. After contextualizing its emergence, the earliest critiques from Radical and Socialist Feminist perspectives in the 1970s will be summarized. From these critical beginnings, the sexual division of labour became the focal point of both descriptive and analytical accounts, as feminist economic geographers joined with other scholars to document and explain how new divisions of labour across international, regional and urban spaces in the 1980s intersected with and constituted gender relations. Often located within a Marxist problematic, these empirical studies reconfigured concepts such as class, labour power, social reproduction and value to variously theorize the connections between capitalism and patriarchy. Retaining a progressive commitment to social justice, feminist economic geographers subsequently engaged the 'Cultural Turn' in the discipline and new feminist perspectives on the body, power, scale, discourse and difference over the 1990s, to generate different ways of seeing how 'the economic' functions within places and across scales to constitute and be implicated by gender.

EMERGENCE OF FEMINIST ECONOMIC GEOGRAPHY

Feminist geography as a critical discourse has an ongoing relationship with feminism and a number of other progressive political movements that emerged in the 1960s. In the context of a long post war economic boom and mass higher education across the Western world, there were mobilizations of newly politicized young people calling for socially progressive change. In the United States there were claims for black and gay civil rights as well as an end to poverty, in Europe there were New Left inspired demands for student and worker rights, while voices across the world called for an end to imperialism and the Vietnam War. Entering higher education institutions *en masse*, enmeshed in movements for social justice, newly freed by the contraceptive pill from the connection of sexual activity to procreation, and participating in the paid workforce in ever larger numbers, *women* came to see themselves as a group that also experienced disadvantage (Morgan, 1970; Mitchell, 1971). Calls from radicals for women's liberation resonated

with many white suburban women who were asking of their pampered but limited lives: Is this all there is? (Friedan, 1963: 13). From this firmament, the Women's Liberation Movement defined women's oppression as the problem, identified men as the enemy, and the personal as political. Across Europe, England, North America and Australasia in the 1960s and 1970s, inspired by Marxism and Radical Feminism, middle and working class women mobilized to celebrate their sisterhood, demand equal pay for equal work, an end to male sexual violence, and dedicated policies, programmes and services. Middle class (and primarily white) women, agitated for and achieved a greater presence in the institutions of power, including the academy. Those disciplines which had significant numbers of women, engaged with the social and embraced a critical Marxism – such as sociology, anthropology and literature – were the first to adopt the feminist critique. Others, which had more of a scientific, masculinist orientation and fewer women – including geography and economics – came to feminism later. When those in the academy did embrace feminism, their focus was less on male violence and reproductive rights than on the sexual division of labour and women's role in the household. Critical to this orientation in the academy, was Marxist theory.

In what became known as the 'Domestic Labour Debate', participants variously grappled with the question of whether domestic labour encapsulated 'labour power' or was 'productive' and produced 'use values' in the Marxist sense. Further debate centred on whether women's confinement to the domestic sphere gave them a particular relation to the means of production which made them theoretically distinct from but also personally subservient to men (Benston, 1969; Seccomb, 1973; Coulson et al., 1975). This debate joined others on the nature of work and its theorization using Marxist categories to fill the pages of New Left and feminist publications over the 1970s and 1980s. These academic discussions served to highlight the value of domestic work to capital and, for some feminist analysts, numerous activists and women across the Western world, to men (see Delphy, 1984). Thus, one conclusion was that the sexual division of labour and women's domestic work were critical to the operation of capitalism. Another was that it was primarily men who benefitted. Practically, such work formed the basis of political campaigns demanding wages for housework and the enumeration of women's unpaid labour in national accounts (Dalla Costa and James, 1972; Waring, 1989).

The debate on domestic labour in the early 1970s did not translate directly into feminist economic geography; for the home and women's work within it did not become a site of widespread interest until a more relational view of paid and unpaid work emerged and paid labour was once again conducted within the home. Despite the early work of Pat Burnett (1973), there were few studies of mothers as workers until Jackie Tivers' work in the late 1970s (1978, 1985). But the mass entry of women into the paid workforce and, increasingly, into professional occupations meshed with new international migration flows to produce a new wave of paid domestic workers in the 1980s. With domestic space legitimated as a site for systematic study by feminist architects (such as Hayden, 1981, 1984; Rock et al., 1980), geographers too engaged with this space as a site for women's work – both paid and unpaid. Such studies proliferated with the burgeoning of paid home workers, with work on migrant house cleaners in Canada (Mackenzie, 1987; England and Stiell, 1997; Pratt, 2004) and nannies in Britain (Gregson and Lowe, 1994). More recently, feminist geographers have focused on the unpaid caring work that women do within the home (Dyck, 1990; England, 1997; Gardiner, 1997). The feminist and Marxist-inspired critique of the sexual division of labour thereby raised fundamental questions within geography about the nature and valuing of women's work, the vital economic role of unpaid domestic work, who

did such work – as labouring in the paid and unpaid spheres was increasingly shown to be highly gendered and interconnected – and, critically, who studied it.

In the context of the broader Women's Liberation Movement and with a growing presence of feminist women in the academy – as students and staff – a few women and some men began to critically examine the contents, methods and theories of the social sciences, including economics and geography, to document and demand changes in their demographics but also in the ways in which they engaged with gender, space and the economy. Thus, in 1973, in the pages of the new journal of 'radical geography', *Antipode*, Pat Burnett argued that existing models of urban form were static, conservative and assumed the sexual division of labour. She saw a Marxism enlivened by Radical Feminism as the alternative to an approach that ignored the structural relations between class, sex and race. In her framework, capitalism was built upon the family, an unequal gender division of labour and a 'male psychology of power' (Burnett, 1973). In her response, the economist Irene Bruegel (1973) argued for a need to re-centre the analysis on class and the Marxist framework, beginning a decade-long discussion on just how Socialist Feminists could remain true both to Marxist theoretical precepts *and* a woman-centred, feminist politics, to create a progressive feminist economic geography. In this exercise, the focus became the sexual division of labour, as it existed between homes and workplaces, as it structured the economy, cities and work spaces, and how it was changing across nations to become a New International Division of Labour. Such work drew on much that was occurring in disciplines outside of geography – such as sociology, economics and the emergent field of women's studies – and connected to the 1970s crisis of Western economies which saw the rapid de-industrialization of whole cities and regions.

MAPPING AND EXPLAINING THE SEXUAL DIVISIONS OF LABOUR

Over the 1970s and 1980s numerous studies investigated women's work and the gendered structuring of labour markets and workplaces across time and space. Building on the work of feminist historians and anthropologists (such as Lerner, 1971; Rosaldo and Lamphere, 1974; Spain, 1992; Shapiro, 1994) Domosh and Seager (2001) concluded that some version of the sexual division of labour is present in virtually all societies and throughout history. Across the Western world, scholars have documented the predominance of women in poorly paid, low status and dead end jobs – especially in the service sector and in arenas supposedly related to their 'natural' and domestic worlds of child care, education, sewing and inter-personal care. While women have entered the professions in ever larger numbers, studies confirm the continued existence of glass ceilings limiting women's advancement, the sex typing of women's and men's work within organizations and ongoing sex discrimination against women. Men in contrast are usually in charge, commanding the dizzy heights of corporate, government, business and service sector employment, though they are also associated with dirty, heavy and dangerous parts of manufacturing, transport, mining and agriculture (Game and Pringle, 1983). This gendering of work, skill and competencies was initially explained by the existence of sex roles, but then by the association of men with technology (Cockburn, 1983, 1985; Massey et al., 1992), by women's family obligations and biology (Pollert, 1981; Westwood, 1984) and more recently by deeper patterns of ascribed gender difference – whereby men's bodies are associated with being active and physical as well as cerebral and women's with weakness, emotion and intuition (McDowell, 2000). While countries differ in their detail and over time, an extraordinary pattern has been documented of an unequal sexual division of labour being at the core of industrial and corporate capitalism. The sexual division of labour was also shown to exist in newly developing countries by feminist development geographers, different from what existed in the developed world, but none the less pervasive and damaging to women.

In a groundbreaking book Esther Boserup (1970) looked at how such gendered views shaped the definition and practice of 'development', documented the centrality of women's paid and unpaid work to the well-being of households while also critiquing how interventions to facilitate economic growth tended to favour men and the masculine economy over women and their economic spaces. Such insights underpinned and continued to transform development geography which, as the work of Momson, Townsend and Kinnaid as well as Lawson (2007) indicates, continues to document the centrality of all aspects of women's work and details how they bear the brunt of current structural adjustment policies, extreme environmental degradation and deal with male bias in the rural development process (Momson and Townsend, 1987; Momson and Kincaid, 1993).

Why the sexual division of labour occurred and how it was manifested over space became a major focus for feminists in general as well as feminist economic geographers in particular. Theorizations built on Marxist and neoclassical studies of the productive economy see women located within the reserve army of labour, the dual labour market, and living at the intersection of the paid/productive and unpaid/reproductive realms. So, for example, Veronica Beechey argued that it was married women's place within the family – as child bearer and rearer and as a domestic labourer paid by the male wage to reproduce labour power – that shapes her utility to capital as a reserve army of labour and as a secondary workforce (Beechey, 1977). Anthias (1980), and Bland et al. (1978) question this formulation as ignoring the benefits that *men* gain from women's work. They argue that you cannot understand women's subordination only through the economic relations of capital but analyses have to examine the ways in which patriarchal relations between women and men are established outside paid work – in the home, community and in the semi-private sphere. That the paid and the unpaid work spheres – of production to social reproduction – were connected was a key insight of socialist feminists, and one that was subsequently incorporated into feminist economic geography.

Perceptive studies of 'skill' subsequently unpacked the ways in which the concept was gendered in such a way as to privilege men over women (Phillips and Taylor, 1980) while other studies of, for example, male printers (Cockburn, 1983), women bank, retail, factory, textile and clothing workers (Cavendish, 1982; Game and Pringle, 1983; Johnson, 1990) highlighted the connection of new technologies to male labour as well as the gendering of particular forms of paid work. Studies by sociologists, anthropologists, economists as well as geographers focused on how paid and unpaid work interconnected to produce particular work forces across space (Pollert, 1981; Westwood, 1984). From such work, the Australian sociologists Anne Game and Rosemary Pringle concluded that gender is fundamental to the way work is organized while work is central to the construction of gender. They argued that the sexual division of labour was not somehow 'functional' to capitalism but rather was a defining feature of it, as central as wage labour or surplus value (Game and Pringle, 1983: 14–15). Such patterns were subsequently mapped, explained and challenged by feminist economic geographers across cities, nations and internationally.

In geography, Suzanne Mackenzie set the scene in 1980 by calling for a new geography which examined how women shaped urban capitalism via the social relations of productive and reproductive work. In England, Linda McDowell (1984) pursued this approach in her historical analysis of British cities and their suburbs. She argued – following one line of socialist feminist theorizing – that production and reproduction were part of a single process which varied across space and time. She charted the development of

British suburbs as the outcome of a set of historically specific, contested and actively created relations between male and female paid work, housework and domestic ideologies. The result of these changing social relations was that suburbs were quite different in the 1950s compared to the 1960s and 1980s, as the nature of work and relations between paid and unpaid work as well as ideological constructions of gender roles, altered. Her work thereby linked the 'economic' as a discrete field of commercial work with other spheres and showed how the creation of a workplace as much as a suburb, was highly gendered and the outcome of complex interconnections between the domestic and the public, commercial economy.

In a series of Locality Studies funded across the United Kingdom (UK) in the 1980s, the relationships between productive and reproductive work were further studied by geographers, sociologists and economists (such as Lewis, 1984; Lancaster, Regionalism Group, 1985; Walby, 1986; Cooke, 1989; see also Cooke, 1984 for Europe). Along with a critique of Marxist-inspired studies of the capitalist labour process went a new approach to paid work, one which owed much to feminist theoretical and political interventions. Studies across the UK of manufacturing and mining decline detailed the ways in which this process impacted disproportionately on men but also how it was accompanied by a growth of new industries in green field sites where women were mobilized into paid labour. Explaining such patterns focused on how the sexual division of labour within the home, in paid work, within trade unions and in localities, was altering. Working with Linda McDowell, Doreen Massey subsequently examined how capitalism and patriarchy articulated to create a set of distinctive conditions for the maintenance of male dominance at various localities historically, be it in the mining villages of northern England, the Lancashire cotton towns, in the London rag trade or rural life in the Fens (McDowell and Massey, 1984; see also Mackenzie and Rose, 1983). McDowell and

Massey argued that capitalism presented patriarchy with different challenges across space which in turn shaped gender, class and labour relations, thereby prioritizing a key feminist term over those derived from Marxist theory. Other Locality Studies privileged capitalist over gender relations to echo a key debate in feminist scholarship – namely the theoretical relationship between capitalism and patriarchy. This problem was to be taken up in the mid-1980s by a number of geographers in what came to be known as 'the patriarchy debate'. Locality Studies also raised other issues which were subsequently explored further by feminist economic geographers – in particular, the complex relationship between place, paid and unpaid work as well as between localities and new international divisions of labour.

Doreen Massey in her *Spatial Divisions of Labour* (1984, 1995) was critical to further developing this approach to space, labour and gender, as she documented the fate of different industries, their international as well as their national and internal organization, in these terms. Here then was the sexual division of labour shaping the entire British spatial economy, influencing where and how work was created as well as where it was removed from across regions but also the world. Geraldine Pratt and Susan Hanson were to pursue this focus on localities in their detailed study of Worcester, Massachusetts. Here they argued that social and economic geographies are the media through which the segregation of large numbers of women into poorly paid jobs is produced and reproduced. *Gender, Work and Space* (1995) explores how boundaries are constructed between women and men, and among women living in different neighbourhoods. The focus is on work, the segregation of men and women into different occupations and variations in women's work experiences in different parts of the city. Building on earlier work on the relation of work to home and also on the different time-space budgets and journeys to work by women and men (Palm and Pred, 1974;

Hanson and Hanson, 1980; Palm, 1981; Pred, 1982), the book argues that these differences are grounded and constituted in and through space, place and situated social networks. The study establishes that many women, especially those with heavy household responsibilities, are dependent on local employment opportunities, such that social, economic and geographical boundaries are overlaid and intertwined. As employers locate firms and create labour forces with particular social characteristics, social and occupational differences are mapped on to place. Neighbourhood differences in community resources, occupational opportunities, labour processes, scheduling of work, and cultures of parenting affect the ways that families order their lives and how gender relations are enacted in daily life. By looking inside households, communities, *and* workplaces they draw together the insights of both feminist and industrial geographers to understand the 'dynamic dependencies' between employers and employees in creating local markets and labour market segmentation (Hanson and Pratt, 1995: 15). From such an understanding of how these boundaries – around labour markets, neighbourhoods, social networks, and specific gendered household arrangements are constructed – their hope is that women and men in Worcester (and elsewhere) will be able to move through and across them.

The fate and operation of engineering plants or electronics factories across England or the United States was not only strongly connected to gender relations within their localities by Massey, McDowell, Hanson and Pratt, but also to the international economy. And in their studies of trans-national companies, the mobility of capital investment and the development strategies of a number of what became Newly Industrialized Countries, feminist economists and geographers highlighted the vital role of gender in the creation of a New International Division of Labour. In the textile industry, for example, an early study by Froebel et al. (1980) detailed the ways in which German textile corporations moved over the 1960s and 1970s from central Europe to its various peripheries in search of ever higher profits. But it was feminist scholars and activists who pointed out the vital role of women's labour in such a move and detailed the ways in which an 'unskilled', 'docile', young and female workforce was mobilized to staff the textile and clothing workshops of South East Asia, Turkey and Mexico (Elson and Pearson, 1981a, b; Chapkis and Enloe, 1983; Enloe, 1983; Lim, 1983; Mitter, 1986; Nash and Fernandez-Kelly, 1983; War on Want, 1983). Here then was evidence of a gendered New International Division of Labour which formed the cornerstone of key industrial development strategies and was central to restoring the profitability of many multinational corporations. As Nagar, et al. (2002) conclude in their overview of globalization literatures, there is clearly a need not only to include feminist work on space, scale, the gendering of work, mobility and structural adjustment programmes in such large scale studies, but that global capitalism should be analysed as a set of social relations that are simultaneously mediated by hierarchies around gender, race and sexualities.

Through feminist scholarship the sexual division of labour was thereby shown to be central to the creation of workforces, to the operation of particular work places, to economic and regional restructuring and to new international divisions of labour. Feminist economists and economic geographers had therefore documented examples by which 'the economy' at a number of sites across the world was created through the intersection of gender, racism and class relations. How these new social relations were to be theorized continued the feminist focus on the relationship between patriarchy and capitalism but this was to be challenged by black and third world women and then broadened by post-structural thinking within geography.

THEORIZING CAPITALISM AND PATRIARCHY

The invocation of patriarchy – as a term signalling the dominance of men over women – and its complex relationship with capitalism and Marxist categories became the subject of discussion within feminist geography in the late 1980s. Such discussion culminated in 'the patriarchy debate' which raged over 1986 and 1987 in the pages of Antipode. Here was a core feminist concept, one derived primarily from a Radical Feminist agenda, that numerous feminist geographers were trying to connect in some meaningful way to their Marxism and to studies of space. In their opening essay Jo Foord and Nicky Gregson (1986) moved to reconceptualize patriarchy within a realist framework, isolating its necessary elements – the existence of men and women, biological reproduction and heterosexuality – from its contingent ones – patriarchy experienced at particular places and asserted within marriage and the nuclear family in 1980s Britain. It was primarily the consignment of heterosexuality and gender to the status of ahistorical universals that generated the most vehement responses as feminist geographers pointed to the dynamic, contested and locationally specific nature of gender and sexuality (see McDowell, 1986; Johnson, 1987; Knopp and Lauria, 1987).

The intensity of the patriarchy debate typified many of the dilemmas faced by feminist economic geographers as they tried to reconcile Marxist and feminist concepts as well as what often appeared to be divergent political priorities. At the time it mattered a great deal that Marxist categories would maintain their relevance and be meshed in a rigorous way to feminist views of the world. However, this urgency was to dissipate as east European communism crumbled and the end of ideology was trumpeted in the late 1980s. Before a rising cacophony of voices from minorities demanding to be heard, neo-liberals triumphed across the Western World, overseeing an economy, society and set of technologies now defined in terms of the modern and the post-modern rather than the capitalist and socialist. Feminist geographers too were increasingly engaged with these critiques and the very different approaches coming from post-modernity and post-colonialism. It was these new theoretical and political currents that were to inform subsequent feminist economic geographies.

CULTURAL ECONOMIC GEOGRAPHY

For many social observers, the 1980s were distinguished by a more pervasive globalization of Western economic, social and political relations, a shift from a Fordist form of mass production towards a disorganized, flexible or post-Fordist way of creating goods, and a change from manufacturing to service economies dominated by relations of consumption rather than production. Accompanying these structural economic shifts went changes in aesthetics and philosophy as accepted truths, certainties and frameworks derived from the Enlightenment, around rationality, the unified individual and science, were thrown into question. In their place was a sense of the world shaped by language and of bodies sculpted by words and images emanating from the mass media, medicine and popular psychology. Awareness of these discourses – statements with real effects articulated from particular positions of power by individuals or groups – was accompanied by techniques for deconstructing or articulating and questioning their operation. The elevation of cultural objects – texts and images – to the status of serious subjects with causal capacities, became part of what was subsequently labelled a 'cultural turn' in human geography, as places, activities, economic relations and people were approached in these terms.

In addition to the textual and cultural turn in social theory, went another which was more grounded in politics than the academy. For the focus on discourses also generated a crisis of European cultural authority – as universals were exposed as interested and limited – and those most often silenced, such as minorities and those from colonized countries, asserted their positions. In this critical milieu, feminism too was subjected to a post-colonial critique as its claims to speaking for all women were questioned and shown to be illegitimate (see, for example, Hooks, 1982; Mohanty, 1988; Minh-Ha, 1989). Responding to challenges of an 'imperial feminism' (Amos and Parmar, 1984), Michele Barrett and Mary McIntosh wrote their socialist feminist book on what they called *The Anti-Social Family* from an awareness of race and ethnicity (Barrett and McIntosh, 1982). However, despite acknowledging their own race and class privileges and seeing many core feminist concepts – including the sexual division of labour, the family and patriarchy – as negating the existence and experience of black women, their conflation of race with ethnicity and insistence on seeing patriarchy as universal, generated a heated response. As Hamidi Kazi observed: 'They have hidden the real issues of racism, sexism and the capitalist exploitation of black women behind ethnic characteristics' (1986: 90). Indeed, for black women such as Hazel Carby, families were all too often the sites of resistance to racial oppression. For Carby actions by the British state through policing and migration policies fractured immigrant families and lead many to fight for the maintenance of the family rather than to challenge its existence (Carby, 1982). In the face of such a critique – in this case of the socialist feminist view of the family as oppressive to women and a tool for capital – many other feminist claims and theories were seen as focusing on and representing the voices of white, Western, heterosexual and middle class women. Launched by minority and women of colour within the West as well as by women from Third World countries, this critique forced a new round of critical thinking as well as new approaches to the economy, forcing a more careful engagement with issues of social, racial and ethnic difference as well as the power relations emanating from colonial and post-colonial histories.

Within geography, the analysis and theorizing of post-modernity, globalization and late capitalism did not always engage with such vital concerns. Thus, the most 'important' works on the new era by, for example, David Harvey (1989) and Edward Soja (1989), did not acknowledge any debt to feminist or post-colonial thinking or even recognize the particular place of women in the new economic and social orders being created, be they in third world export processing zones or in the newly restructured industries and cultures of the first world. In this post-modern era, the new tool of textual deconstruction was turned upon such key works, while the complex ways in which cities, workplaces and workforces were discursively created was documented by feminist economic geographers newly sensitized to the complexities of race and ethnicity.

Thus, in a spirited engagement with these key post-modern theorists, Liz Bondi (1990), Rosalind Deutsche (1991), Doreen Massey (1991), Steve Pile and Gillian Rose (1992) noted how David Harvey's *Condition of Postmodernity* (1989) and Edward Soja's *Postmodern Geographies* (1989) were founded on an unexamined sexism which made their books partial and deeply limited. They variously argued that Harvey and Soja constructed a view of the post-modern condition that ignored women and feminism. Both failed to acknowledge that unequal gender relations and racism were fundamental aspects of oppression within both the modern and post-modern eras and that feminist, anti-racist and post-colonial struggles were significant in shaping these periods. Further, it was argued, neither author recognized their positions of discursive power as white, heterosexual, male geographers or acknowledged that they themselves were offering a totalizing framework rather than accepting the boundedness of their own positions.

If geographical knowledge was thereby subjected to a new round of politicized deconstruction, feminist economic geographers also applied these frameworks to the analysis of cities and workplaces. Thus, Linda McDowell engaged directly with the post-Fordist regime of production, highlighting the role of women as casualized and sexualized members of the rapidly expanding service industries (McDowell, 1991). She took this analysis further in later research which documented the importance of gender relations and, in particular, the construction of various forms of masculinity to the nature of London's banking and finance sector. In this work she drew not only on recent feminist work on the sexual division of labour but also feminist geographies on the discursively constituted body which is inscribed as gendered, sexualized and racialized in particular ways in work, shopping and other spaces (Longhurst, 2008). In *Capital Culture* (McDowell, 1997), the nature of the gendered body in space becomes critical, as dress codes, demeanour and the very nature of the work task becomes integrated into particular bodily types, activity patterns and looks. In later work, she explored the ways in which the social construction of masculinity excluded young unskilled men from the service sector (McDowell, 2003) (see Chapter 22).

Doreen Massey (1996) also utilizes the techniques of deconstruction and a broader focus on gender relations, to consider the mutual constitution of male identities and high technology workplaces in Cambridge, England. Building on a vibrant literature examining men and masculinities (such as Brod and Kaufman, 1994; Pease, 2001; Murphy, 2004), her research detailed how the work involved a particular attachment to and commitment to reason/science and transcendence, profoundly masculine ways of thinking that in turn devalued their opposite and feminized other. What is going on in and around these jobs is the construction and reinforcement of a particular kind of masculinity around research, being scientific, abstract thought and transcendence. It is a process which relates to some of the other dualisms in Western thought which have real and concrete effects on people's lives. Family commitments come second, with the job predicated on not having domestic responsibilities and even having someone looking after them. As Massey concludes:

> ... what is at issue here is not so much overt discrimination or sexism as deeply internalized dualisms which structure personal identities and daily lives, which have effects upon the lives of others through structuring the operation of social relations and dynamics, and which derive their masculine/feminine coding from the deep socio-philosophical underpinnings of Western society. (Massey, 1996: 117)

The characteristics Massey highlights are traits of masculinity, not of men. There is no simple homogeneity among the men studied, though dominant characteristics are embedded in the culture of high tech workplaces and individuals are drawn towards them. Some men embrace the culture, others modify it – by, for example, not taking work home – and a few resist it. Yet, for Massey, in this new post-Fordist and neo-liberal workspace, in the absence of collective resistance, legislative action or wider cultural shifts, individual attempts to deal with the conflicts and tensions result in a reinforcement of the dualisms which underpin it. Therefore, for Massey, her highly grounded study of men within one workplace, leads to a profound questioning of the dualisms which are still fundamental to Western society – work-home, reason-emotion, science-intuition, male-female – once more affirming the gendered, historical and relational nature of the economy and its conceptualization.

RETHINKING ECONOMIC GEOGRAPHIES

The long-dominant neo-classical view of economics is concerned with utility maximizing individuals, resource allocation, individual gratification and corporate profitability. Taking much from this form of economics,

economic geography has primarily been concerned with the spatial patterns associated with resource distribution, utilization, movement and consumption – be it on the land, in shops or industry, across cities, regions and national borders. Such specific sites have led to specialist sub-fields of economic geography – agricultural, industrial, retail, urban, regional, development and transport geographies. While the apolitical neo-classical position was questioned by Marxist economics in the 1970s, the entry of historical materialism and class analysis did not fundamentally unsettle its focus on resource location and allocation. The troubling of key concepts – such as the economy, resources, mobility and work – and ways of re-conceiving the sub-fields in economic geography had to await the emergence of new concepts and the feminist critique of the 1980s. Increasingly, these fields were seen as interconnected and overshadowed by notions such as post-Fordism, post-modernity and globalization. But these newer formulations of the economic landscape, as noted earlier, were also seen by feminist economic geographers to be in need of critique and reconceptualization.

As well as critiques of the classical formulation of post-modern economic geographies, feminist geographers have joined the critical interrogation of the post-Fordist (see McDowell, 1991) and globalization frameworks. Nagar et al. (2002) argued that the discourses of feminism and globalization need to better interconnect. Further, though, they also suggested that feminism should not just highlight women's mobility, paid and unpaid work but also rethink how globalization is conceptualized, studied and engaged with. While much globalization literature concentrates on the international and national scale, feminist work on households and localities has not only legitimated these sites, but highlighted the ways in which they are mutually constituted across a range of scales. A feminist politics also informs such an analysis, so that the objects of research become active subjects; actors with whom to collaborate rather than as victims of disembodied processes. As McDowell concludes elsewhere, the particularity of place is always constituted through the intersection of social processes at different scales and it is incorrect to assume that gender relations are local or that locally based research has spatially limited implications – they are all interconnected (2007: 63).

Similarly, Julie Graham (1992) observed how narratives of globalization are totalizing and exclusionary and, in line with a material conceptualization of discourse, further argued that such ways of thinking had real political effects. For in presenting an analysis where capitalism is the only pathway and globalization the only script, any sense of agency is removed and any resistance doomed from the start. Graham joined with Katherine Gibson to present not only a fundamental critique of this conceptualization of capitalism but to offer an alternative economic and social vision. Thus, their hybrid identity of Gibson-Graham wrote *The End of Capitalism (As We Knew It)* (1996) by deconstructing Marxist and post-modern theorizations. In this book and in their later *Postcapitalist Politics* (2006) they used feminist and other liberatory theorizing to construct an alternative economics. Beginning with a general concept of labour application and the appropriation of its products to isolate sites of economic activity – such as the home, the informal sector, crime, and exchange systems – in first and third world countries – they argue that these various sites are every bit as vital theoretically and practically as capitalist forms of production and exchange. Just as importantly for their political project, such non-capitalist forms of production and exchange are often less exploitative, violent and unstable and allow very different identities, alliances and economies to flourish. In examples drawn from abandoned industrial areas of Australia and the United States, they present cases where action research mobilizes cases of and desires for non-capitalist forms of becoming (2007). Here then is an alternative feminist economic geography, grounded in a progressive politics as well as in post-modern and post-colonial theorizing, one which is discursively powerful and politically mobilizing.

CONCLUSION: ALTERNATIVE FEMINIST ECONOMIC GEOGRAPHIES

Feminist economic geography emerged from the ferment of the Women's Liberation Movement in the 1960s. Drawing usefully from studies and theoretical work in feminist economics, women's studies, architecture and sociology, the earliest formulations grappled with the ways in which existing studies ignored the place of women and the theoretical marginalization of gender, while political activists highlighted the value of the personal, domestic labour and social reproduction. From such beginnings, feminist economic geography focused on mapping and explaining the sexual division of labour as it was constituted in developed and developing economies, regions, cities and workplaces. From the micro-politics of individual work sites to the New International Division of Labour, explanations drew on Marxist and radical feminist theory to focus on how skill, technology and particular jobs were gendered. Feminist economic geographers tended to focus their analyses on women and localities to unpack the ways in which place was mutually constituted through the gendering of paid and unpaid work. More recently, and engaging with the insights of deconstruction and returning to its liberatory roots, studies have examined the ways in which individual workplaces established their gendered cultures through constituting gendered, but also sexualized and racialized, male and female bodies, and also presented different ways of thinking about the economic and empowerment across scales.

Feminist economic geography has always been part of a much larger project to rethink and change the ways in which the economic has been conceptualized and lived. Feminists have noted how national accounts, for example, recorded only some aspects of the economy, indeed that primarily engaged in by men; with most labour, resource extraction, transformation and re-allocation work undertaken by women, ignored (Domosh and Seager, 2001). In the very definition of the economy, then, there are highly gendered assumptions at work, ones which have historically elevated the visibility and importance of men's activities over those of women. Even further than this, with its focus on the world of paid labour, public activity and the non-domestic spaces of production, exchange and consumption, the very constitution of *the economy* and its related geography, has been partial and sexist. Such views have had enormous implications not only for the recording of women's economic activity, but also in the formulation of social and economic policies.

Feminist economic geographers have been integral to movements to count all work that women do, exposing the ways in which notions such as 'development' as well as 'the economic' have privileged men's over women's activities and moved on to detail the ways in which domestic spaces, workplaces, neighbourhoods, regions, and international divisions of labour are highly gendered and racialized; with such dimensions fundamental to their constitution. Detailing the ways in which the sexual division of labour has been constituted and operated across time and space, has formed the foundation from which political campaigns for change have been launched – demanding wages for housework in the 1970s through to a recognition of informal but vital forms of labour exchange in developing countries in the 1980s and 1990s. Feminist economic geography has therefore always been about critique, reconstruction and alternative formulations of what constitutes 'the economic'.

REFERENCES

Amos, V. and Parmar, P. (1984) Challenging imperial feminism. *Feminist Review*, 17: 3–19.

Anthias, F. (1980) Women and the reserve army of labour: A critique of Veronica Beechey. *Capital and Class*, 10: 50–63.

Barrett, M. and McIntosh, M. (1982) *The Anti-social Family*. London: Verso.

Beechey, V. (1977) Some notes on female wage labour in capitalist production. *Capital and Class*, 3: 45–66.

Benston, M. (1969) The political economy of women's liberation. In E.H. Altback (ed.) *From Feminism to Liberation*. Cambridge, MA: Shenkman. pp.199–210.

Bland, L., Brunsdon, C., Hobson, D., and Winship, J. (1978) Women inside and outside the relations of production. In Women's Studies Group (eds) *Women Take Issue: Aspects of Women's Subordination*. London: Hutchinson Centre for Contemporary Cultural Studies. pp. 35–77.

Bondi, L. (1990) Feminism, postmodernism, and geography: Space for women? *Antipode*, 22(2): 156–67.

Boserup, E. (1970) *Women's Role in Economic Development*. New York: St Martin's Press.

Breugel, I. (1973) Cities, women and social class: A comment. *Antipode*, 5: 62–3.

Brod, A. and Kaufman, M. (1994) *Theorizing Masculinities*. Thousand Oaks, California: SAGE.

Burnett, P. (1973) Social change, the status of women and models of city form and development. *Antipode*, 5: 57–61.

Carby, H. (1982) White women listen! Black feminism and the boundaries of sisterhood. In *The Empire Strikes Back: Race and Racism in 70s Britain*. Centre for Contemporary Cultural Studies. London: Hutchison.

Cavendish, R. (1982) *Women on the Line*. London: Routledge and Kegan Paul.

Chapkis, W. and Enloe, C. (eds) (1983) *Of Common Cloth: Women in the Global Textile Industry*. Amsterdam: Transnational Institute.

Cockburn, C. (1983) *Brothers: Male Dominance and Technological Change*. London: Pluto.

Cockburn, C. (1985) *Machinery of Dominance: Women, Men and Technical Know-how*. London: Pluto Press.

Cooke, P. (1984) Region, class and gender: A European comparison. *Progress in Planning*, 22(2): 85–146.

Cooke, P. (1989) *Localities: The Changing Face of Urban Britain*. London: Unwin Hyman.

Coulson, M., Magas, B., and Wainwright, H. (1975) The housewife and her labour under capitalism: A critique. *New Left Review*, 89: 59–72.

Dalla Costa, M. and James, S. (1972) *The Power of Women and the Subversion of the Community*. London: Falling Wall Press.

Delphy, C. (1984) *Close to Home: A Materialist Analysis of Women's Oppression*. Hutchinson in association with the Explorations in Feminism Collective, London.

Deutsche, R. (1991) Boy's town. *Environment and Planning D: Society and Space*, 9: 9–30.

Domosh, M. and Seager, J. (2001) *Putting Women in Place. Feminist Geographers Make Sense of the World*. New York and London: Guildford Press.

Dyck, I. (1990) Space, time and renegotiating motherhood: An exploration of the domestic workplace. *Society and Space*, 8: 459–83.

Elson, D. and Pearson, R. (1981a) Nimble fingers make cheap workers: An analysis of women's employment in Third World manufacturing. *Feminist Review*, 7: 87–107.

Elson, D. and Pearson, R. (1981b) The subordination of women and the internationalisation of factory production. In K. Young, C. Wolkowicz, and R. McCullogh (eds) *Of Marriage and the Market: Women's Subordination in International Perspective*. London: CSE Books. pp. 144–66.

Enloe, C. (1983) Women textile workers and the militarization of Southeast Asia. In J. Nash and M.P. Fernandez-Kelly (eds) *Women, Men and the International Division of Labor*. Albany: State University of New York Press. pp. 407–25.

England, K. (1997) *Who Will Mind the Baby?: Geographies of Child Care and Working Mothers*. London: Routledge.

England, K. and Stiell, B. (1997) They think you're as stupid as your English is: Constructing foreign domestic workers in Toronto. *Environment and Planning A*, 29: 195–215.

Foord, J. and Gregson, N. (1986) Patriarchy: Towards a reconceptualisation. *Antipode* 18(2): 186–211.

Friedan, B. (1963) *The Feminine Mystique*. Harmondsworth: Penguin.

Froebel, F., Heinrichs, J. and Kreye, O. (eds) (1980) *The New International Division of Labour: Structural Unemployment in Industrialised Countries and Industrialisation in Developing Countries*. Cambridge: Cambridge University Press.

Game, A. and Pringle, R. (1983) *Gender at Work*. Sydney: George Allen and Unwin.

Gardiner, J. (1997) *Gender, Care and Economics*. Oxford: Clarendon Press.

Gibson-Graham, J.K. (1996) *The End of Capitalism (As We Knew It)*. Oxford/Cambridge: Blackwell.

Gibson-Graham, J.K. (2006) *A Postcapitalist Politics*. Minnesota: University of Minnesota Press.

Gibson-Graham, J.K. (2007) Cultivating subjects for a community economy. In A. Tickell, E. Sheppard, J. Peck, and T. Barnes (eds) *Politics and Practice in Economic Geography*. Los Angeles: SAGE. pp. 106–18.

Graham, J. (1992) Post-Fordism as politics: The political consequences of narratives on the left. *Environment and Planning D: Society and Space*, 10: 393–410.

Gregson, N. and Lowe, M. (1994) *Servicing the Middle Classes: Class, Gender and Waged Domestic Labour in Contemporary Britain*. London and New York: Routledge.

Gunew, S. (ed.) (1990) *Feminist Knowledge: Critique and Construct*. London: Routledge.

Hanson, S. and Hanson, P. (1980) Gender and urban activity patterns in Uppsala, Sweden. *Geographical Review*, 70: 291–99.

Hanson, S. and Pratt, G. (1995) *Women, Work and Space*. London and New York: Routledge.

Harvey, D. (1989) *The Condition of Postmodernity*. Oxford: Basil Blackwell.

Hayden, D. (1981) *The Grand Domestic Revolution: A History of Feminist Designs for American Homes*. Massachusetts and London: MIT Press.

Hayden, D. (1984) *Redesigning the American Dream: The Future of Housing, Work and Family Life*. New York: W.W. Norton.

Hooks, B. (1982) *Ain't I a Woman? Black Women and Feminism*. London: Pluto.

Johnson, L.C. (1987) (Un) realist perspectives: Patriarchy and feminist challenges in geography. *Antipode*, 19(2): 210–15.

Johnson, L.C. (1990) New patriarchal economies in the Australian textile industry. *Antipode*, 22(1): 1–32.

Kazi, H. (1986) The beginning of a debate now long overdue: Some observations on ethnocentrism and socialist feminist theory. *Feminist Review*, 22: 87–91.

Knopp, L. and Lauria, M. (1987) Gender relations as a particular form of social relations. *Antipode*, 19(1): 48–53.

Lancaster Regionalism Group (1985) *Localities, Class and Gender*. London: Pion.

Lawson, V. (2007) *Making Development Geography*. London: Oxford University Press.

Lerner, G. (1971) *The Woman in American History*. Menlo Park, California: Addison-Wesley.

Lewis, J. (1984) The role of female employment in the industrial restructuring and regional development of the United Kingdom. *Antipode*, 16: 47–59.

Lim, L. (1983) Capitalism, imperialism and patriarchy: The dilemma of third world women workers in multinational factories. In J. Nash and M.P. Fernandez-Kelly (eds) *Women, Men and the International Division of Labor*. Albany: State University of New York Press. pp. 70–91.

Longhurst, R. (2008) *Maternities: Gender, Bodies and Space*. New York: Routledge.

Mackenzie, S. (1987) Neglected spaces in peripheral places: Homeworkers and the creation of a new economic centre. *Cahiers de Geographie du Quebec*, 31: 247–60.

Mackenzie, S. and Rose, D. (1983) Industrial change, the domestic economy and home life. In J. Anderson, S., Duncan, and R. Hudson (eds) *Redundant spaces? Studies in Social Change and Industrial Decline.* London: Academic Press. pp. 155–200.

Massey, D. (1984/1995) *Spatial Divisions of Labour. Social Structures and the Geography of Production.* London: Macmillan.

Massey, D. (1991) Flexible sexism. *Environment and Planning D: Society and Space.* 9: 31–57.

Massey, D. (1996) Masculinity, dualisms and high technology. In N. Duncan (ed.) *BodySpace: Destablizing Geographies of Gender and Sexuality.* Routledge: London and New York. pp. 109–26.

Massey, D., Quintas, P. and Wield, D. (1992) *High Tech Fantasies: Science Parks in Society: Science and Space.* London: Routledge.

McDowell, L. (1984) Towards an understanding of the gender division of urban space. *Environment and Planning D: Society and Space.* 1: 59–72.

McDowell, L. (1986) Beyond patriarchy: A class-based explanation of women's subordination. *Antipode,* 18(3): 311–21.

McDowell, L. (1991) Life without father and Ford: The new gender order of post-Fordism. *Transactions of the Institute of British Geographers* N.S., 16: 400–19.

McDowell, L. (1997) *Capital Culture: Gender at Work in the City.* Oxford: Blackwell.

McDowell, L. (2000) Feminists rethink the economic: The economics of gender, the gender of economics. In G.E. Clark, M.P. Feldman, and M.S. Gertler (eds) *The Oxford Handbook of Economic Geography.* Oxford: Oxford University Press. pp. 497–517.

McDowell, L. (2003) *Redundant Masculinity?* Oxford: Blackwell.

McDowell, L. (2007) Sexing the economy, theorizing bodies. In A. Tickell, E. Sheppard, J. Peck, and T. Barnes (eds) *Politics and Practice in Economic Geography.* Los Angeles: SAGE. pp. 60–70.

McDowell, L. and Massey, D. (1984) A woman's place? In D. Massey, and J. Allen (eds) *Geography Matters! A Reader.* Cambridge: Cambridge University Press. pp. 128–47.

Minh-ha, T. (1989) *Woman, Native, Other.* Bloomington, IN: Indiana University Press.

Mitchell, J. (1971) *Woman's Estate.* New York: Vintage Books.

Mitter, S. (1986) *Common Fate, Common Bond: Women in the Global Economy.* London: Pluto.

Mohanty, C. (1988) Under Western eyes: Feminist scholarship and colonial discourse. *Feminist Review,* 30: 61–88.

Momson, J. and Townsend, J. (1987) *Geography of Gender in the Third World.* Albany: State University of New York.

Momsen, J. and Kincaid, V. (1993) *Different Places, Different Voices: Gender and Development in Africa, Asia and Latin America.* London: Routledge.

Morgan, R. (1970) *Sisterhood is Powerful.* Random House: New York.

Murphy, P.F. (2004) *Feminism and Masculinities.* Oxford: Oxford University Press.

Nagar, R., Lawson, V., McDowell, L. and Hanson, S. (2002) Locating globalization: Feminist (re)readings of the subjects and spaces of globalization. *Economic Geography,* 78: 257–84.

Nash J. and Fernandez-Kelly, M.P. (eds) (1983) *Women, Men and the International Division of Labor.* Albany: State University of New York Press.

Palm, R. (1981) Women in non-metropolitan areas: A time-budget survey. *Environment and Planning A.* 13: 373–78.

Palm, R. and Pred, A. (1974) *A Time-geographic Perspective on Problems of Inequality for Women.* Berkeley: University of California Geography Department Working Paper No. 236.

Pease, B. (2001) *Men and Gender Relations.* Croydon, Victoria: Tertiary Press.

Phillips, A. and Taylor, B. (1980) Sex and skill: Notes towards a feminist economics. *Feminist Review,* 6: 79–88.

Pile, S. and Rose, G. (1992) All or nothing? Politics and critiques in the modernism: Postmodernism debate. *Environment and Planning D: Society and Space,* 10: 123–36.

Pollert, A. (1981) *Girls, Wives and Factory Lives.* London: MacMillan.

Pratt, G. (2004) *Working Feminism.* Edinburgh: Edinburgh University Press.

Pred, A. (1982) Social reproduction and the time-geography of everyday life. In P. Gould and G. Olsson (eds) *A Search for Common Ground.* London: Pion. pp. 157–86.

Rosaldo, M.Z. and Lamphere, L. (1974) *Women, Culture and Society.* Stanford: Stanford University Press.

Rock, C., Torre, S. and Wright, G. (1980) The appropriation of the house: Changes in house design and concepts of domesticity. In G. Wekerle, R. Peterson, and D. Morley (eds) *New Space for Women.* Boulder, Colorado: Westview Press. pp. 83–100.

Seccombe, W. (1973) The housewife and her labour under capitalism. *New Left Review,* 83: 3–24.

Shapiro, A.L. (ed.) (1994) *Feminist Revision History.* New Brunswick and New York: Rutgers University Press.

Soja, E. (1989) *Postmodern Geographies: The Reassertion of Space in Critical Social Theory.* Cambridge, MA: Blackwell.

Spain, D. (1992) *Gendered Spaces*. Chapel Hill and London: University of North Carolina Press.

Tivers, J. (1978) How the other half lives: An historical study of women. *Area*, 10(4): 302–06.

Tivers, J. (1985) *Women Attached: The Daily Lives of Women with Young Children*. London: Croom Helm.

War on Want (1983) *Women Working Worldwide: The International Division of Labour in the Electronics, Clothing and Textile Industries*. London: War on Want.

Walby, S. (1986) *Patriarchy at Work*. Minneapolis: University of Minnesota Press.

Waring, M. (1989) *Counting for Nothing. What Men Value and What Women are Worth*. Wellington: Allen and Unwin.

Westwood, S. (1984) *All Day Every Day: Factory and Family in the Making of Women's Lives*. London: Pluto.

24

Ordinary Economic Geographies: Can Economic Geographies Be Non-Economic?

Roger Lee

INTRODUCTION

There are two apparently contradictory answers to the question posed in the sub-title of this chapter. At first sight, the answer is 'Of course not'. Insofar as they are involved in the consumption, production and circulation of value – which together constitute the materially inescapable relations in which people must necessarily engage if they are to make a living – economic geographies are irreducibly economic. But this vital materiality of economic geographies does not mean that they are necessarily driven *only* by a somehow separate and purely material set of economic logics. Indeed, both the potentially infinite variety of ways in which people may make their living across space and time (Lee, 2006) as well as the necessary non-economic relations involved in all economic activity (Massey, 1997; Sayer, 1997) point to the diverse influences of the non-economic. This variety stems from the social relations

of economy that shape their material form and dynamic. So the second answer to the question would seem to be 'Of course'. But how is this so?

This chapter is an attempt to answer that question. It does so first by re-emphasizing the critical social, environmental and political significance of economy. This significance has been laid bare in recent years by the growing recognition of the environmentally unsustainable trajectories of contemporary economic geographies and the economically and socially unsustainable practices of capitalist financial relations. But the significance of the economy is not merely of recent origin. The growing levels of inequality across the world economy since the late eighteenth century demonstrate that, for a significant minority, if not an actual majority of the world's population, contemporary economic geographies are not working, in that they deny access to the means of making a half-way decent living. The second section of the chapter considers economic geographies both as part of the problem and as possible solutions to this failure. This argument leads to the third section. Here the possibilities of diversity are set against a background both of what, it is argued, is an inescapable verity of economy – the need to reconcile the material verity of the production of a sufficient quantity and quality of value to sustain social life with the inherent diversity of the social constructions of value and the processes of evaluation within economic geographies. The fourth section considers the practices and discourses of diverse economies against the background of the historical geographies and ideas which give rise to them. The concluding comments in the fifth section return to the question of the geographies which shape the politics and possibilities of economic transformations.

THE EXCLUSION OF EVERYWHERE?

Economic geographies are socially purposive, meaningful and intentional. Thus, it is simply not possible to think of economic geographies only in material terms. The social relations that shape and guide them are a necessary component of their materiality and their trajectories. Social relations are, therefore, necessarily integral to the knowledgeable and hence effective (that is, critical as well as efficient) engagement of people in economic geographies. For example, asking why people should not simply resign themselves to the majority view of liberal-democratic capitalism as the best of worlds, the critical theorist, Slavoj Zizek has argued that '[T]he only *true* question today is: does global capitalism contain antagonisms strong enough to prevent its indefinite reproduction?' (2009: 53, original emphasis). The point of this formulation is that, if sense is to be made of economic geographies, it is the social relations of global *capitalism* and not merely the materialities

of a singular global *economy* that must be the objective of critique. And this formative inherency of social relations is true of all economic geographies.

For Zizek, the answer to 'the only true question' is unambiguous: Yes, capitalism does contain sufficient antagonisms that cast doubt over its long-term survival. And for four reasons: the contradictions involved in the privatization of (common) knowledge and the making of personal knowledge (for example, of individual bodies) available for commercial use; the drastic consequences of environmental change for 'external nature' (that is, the natural environment); the technologically induced genetic alienation of internal nature (that is human and more-than-human minds and bodies); and the gap between those people included and those excluded from ever being able to make even a minimal standard of living to ensure survival, or of gaining human legitimacy in an increasingly aggressive process of global socio-economic apartheid in which growing inequalities do not merely differentiate people but separate them into different social and economic worlds. Even taking national aggregate data as a means of comparison – aggregates which average out the major inequalities between people within nations – the ratio between richest and poorest is now about 30: 1. A fifth reason might also be added to this list: the continued absence, other than participation in markets, of ways through which people might make some kind of sense either of their economic predicament (that is, the imperative of being able to make a living) or of questions of identity in the face of the insistent norms of markets as moral arbiters in an 'era of market triumphalism' (Sandel, 2009) to which some commentators refer as neoliberalism (see, Harvey, 2005; Peck, 2008). Whilst the present may or may not represent the end of this era of market triumphalism it certainly does not represent the end of capitalism – liberal democratic or otherwise.

All of this matters because, in combination, these features of the 'best of worlds' contain the threat that:

> in contrast to the classic image of the proletarians who have 'nothing to lose but their chains', we are in danger of losing everything . . . dispossessed of all our symbolic content, with our genetic base manipulated, vegetating in an unliveable environment . . . excluded from nature as well as from our symbolic substance. (Zizek, 2009: 55).

In short, for Zizek, what is at stake is not just the 'marginalization of everywhere' (Lee, 2003) but of the whole of humanity. Notions of 'us' and 'them' are no longer relevant ideas in terms of economic marginalization. In the contemporary world we are, according to Zizek, all us and we are all excluded. Even if this case is overstated, the verities that lie behind it prompt the question how, and under what circumstances, can we act to prevent such an outcome? What kind of narrative is capable of addressing this condition of exclusion?

ECONOMIC GEOGRAPHIES AS PROBLEM AND SOLUTION

Whatever form a sustainable response to the contradictions outlined above might take, the significance of the economic geographies through which people continue to struggle to make a living remains a profound – perhaps even the most profound – influence upon social life. Certainly, the transformation of economic geographies must be central to any possible resolution of these contradictions. There are at least three reasons for this. First, economic geographies have shaped – maybe even determined – the circumstances of comprehensive (or even partial) marginalization spelled out by Zizek and must be a major feature of taking effective preventive action. But all economic geographies are socially constructed – they are made by people not just given to them – and so their reconstruction is both possible and may become part of the

solution rather than part of the problem in that their transformation may address at least some of the causes of this marginalization. However, contemporary economic geographies are increasingly dependent on highly specialized and complex divisions of labour, long-distance trade and investment and car-based urban regions. Further, capitalist economic geographies also reflect the power of mass markets to drive high levels of profitability and, thereby, to exclude both long-term sustainability in the design and layout of the built environments necessary to enable economic geographies to function. The contemporary built environments of retailing and housing for example, tend to force car use and to exclude the less mobile from contemporary consumption. Is there a way in which these high carbon geographies and the processes of production, circulation and consumption through which they take place might be transformed without a drastic reduction in living standards, especially for those already beyond the margins of global prosperity? Possibly.

The second reason for the significance of economic geographies in this context is that they are very difficult to change. As David Harvey (1978) pointed out long ago, the dynamics of capitalism create profound contradictions between the relative stasis of investments in the built environment and the dynamics of capitalist economic geographies (see also Chapters 8 and 17). The latter are dependent on the former to provide the infrastructure and facilities needed to take place and yet they are constantly constrained by them. The spaces through which economic geographies may take place are essential for economic activity but, once designed and built, they fix the geography of that activity in place no matter how dynamic its spatial form might be. This leads to increasing inefficiencies as economic geographies are forced to take place through inappropriate spaces which may, therefore, become redundant.

The veracity of this contradiction may be exemplified by policies adopted by the major clearing banks with respect to the geography of the closure of their bank branches, thereby contributing towards financial exclusion in the localities affected:

> changes in the social and economic geographies of British society have meant that for many financial institutions, a significant number of their branches are 'in the wrong place'. For them, closure programmes are part of a geographical restructuring exercise that seeks to ensure that their branch networks reflect these new social and economic geographies. This involves redirecting their assets away from economically struggling communities, where aggregate demand is falling, and towards new, more prosperous communities, where market opportunities are greater. (Leyshon et al., 2008: 460)

However, the issue is more complex than such single-minded seeking after markets and profitability. Built environments constructed primarily with capitalist accumulation and profitability rather than social needs or wants or environmental sustainability in mind, are also the places of daily social life. They are the places in which the rhythms and routines of all forms of sociability between individuals and amongst social groups are established, valued and take on a historical geography and socially reproductive path dependence of their own. As Denis Cosgrove (1989) argued, 'geography is everywhere' and shapes the histories and biographies of social life. So the question of changing the geography of the built environment involves not merely the replacement of economic redundancy by utility but the destruction of intimate social geographies. This raises serious questions about the relationship of the economic to social life.

Arguing with Margaret Thatcher that 'you can't buck the market' Tim Leunig (2008) extends this nonsensical proposition[1] to a grossly simplistic notion of geography: '[T]here's no altering geography, and some of our towns just aren't in the right place any more. . . . you can't buck geography either'.

> Cities such as Liverpool and Hull, for example, were perfectly placed for economic success in 1875 when Britain was a maritime nation, and imports, exports and even trade within Britain often went by sea. But today air, road and rail transport dominate, and suddenly places like Reading and Milton Keynes – awful locations in 1875 for business – beat our coastal cities hands down. No amount of regeneration spending can alter that basic reality.
>
> If we really want to give people in Liverpool, Sunderland, and so on the opportunities that people in most parts of the south-east take for granted, we need to let many of them move to the south-east. Just as the north-west was a great place for a textile industry in 1875, so the south-east is the best place for most high skilled service sector jobs – near to Europe, and (via Heathrow) the rest of the world.

There is a kind of logic to this argument of course[2] but it is a logic confined to the economic – and a very narrow and specific notion of the economic at that. To reduce places merely to their economic role assumes that a singular economic logic trumps everything. But these places are so much more than this. They are teeming with ordinary and extraordinary lives and relations. So, another solution is that an alternative economic geography might be put into place using different criteria of evaluation[3] which enables these lives and relations to continue to make a living.

Difficult though it is to address such critical issues, there is a third and even more profound influence of economic geographies on the possibilities for preventative action to counteract the trends towards generalized exclusion identified by Zizek. The contemporary social and material relations of economic geographies have also contributed to the decline of politics. Adam Smith (1759, 1776) believed that economic self-interest would translate itself via participation in markets into a desirable form of society. In the present day, the search for the good life and identity has come to be perceived as achievable almost exclusively through market-based consumption and identity. Participation in markets has displaced participation in politics. This reflects not merely a process of depoliticization but a widespread failure to see how politics might intervene to re-shape globalizing economic geographies rather than being shaped by them. Karl Polanyi (1944) referred to this apparent separation of the economic and the political as the 'disembedding' of economy from society (see Harvey and Metcalf, 2010) whereby economies are thought to be autonomous from the societies in which they operate. As such, they are presumed to be subject only to narrow economic logics. Any attempt to interfere with such logics is not only inappropriate but futile in that such interference will disrupt the economic logic and so reduce the effectiveness of economy. Under these circumstances, the contemporary relevance of a politics of economy is difficult to discern. 'There is no alternative' other than to accept and to follow the apparently predetermined economic logic.

Furthermore, the increasing globalization of economic geographies through flows of finance, people, commodities, and ideas has created an immensely powerful elite whose legitimacy both appeals to, and is based on, the logic of economy and which has an enormous reach beyond the comprehension of the ordinary citizen. Democratic politics is, thereby, being bypassed in a return to the elitist politics characteristic of pre-democracy (Crouch, 2004). What is more, as Madeleine Bunting (2009: 23) has argued, political-economic narratives such as communism and socialism

> laid claim to a . . . better world that would nurture a better human being. They were all narratives of redemption and salvation.

By contrast the narrative of exclusion is rather less than hopeful but, once again, answers have to lie in reconstructing economic geographies along very different socio-political lines from those that characterize the contemporary world. One way of going about the search for such answers is to reflect on the nature of economic geographies – what they are, what they do and how they function.

THE ORDINARY ECONOMY[4]

One of the most taken-for-granted features of social existence is that of economy (Lee, 2010a). A distinction may be made between economy as object and as practice (Sheppard, 2009). As *object*, economy refers to the idea that there is such a thing as *the* economy from which derive the kinds of argument which assume a separation and logic of economy mentioned above. As a set of *practices*, economy refers to the attempt to achieve the purposes of economic activity – consumption, production and exchange – with a minimum of effort. This relationship of economy and effort is a critical, universal feature of economies however it is that effort – or work – is valued or organized within them. Without a productive relationship between ends and means, economic practice could lead to the expenditure of greater economic effort than may be sustained by the output produced. This is a process of active underdevelopment which cannot long be sustained.

However, beyond this simple notion of material efficiency – which, in effect, relates to the capacity of economic activity materially to sustain people and societies – the range of criteria which may be applied in economic evaluation, and, thereby, shape economic geographies, is infinite (Lee, 2006; see, for example, Martin, 2009). These criteria – what I will call social relations of value – are socially constructed. They might – as in capitalism – stress profitability but, alternatively, they might stress environmental sustainability or social justice, for example. And social relations of value may emerge through some kind of democratic process, or they may be celebrated, grudgingly accepted or be forcibly imposed. In any event they are vital in giving direction to, and a means of communication about, economic geographies through the criteria of evaluation that they bring to bear upon them. Although for purposes of exposition, it is possible to imagine circuits of value as purely material relations and processes, all economies are necessarily and inherently social and material at the same time. The problem is that there isn't a word to express the indistinguishability of the social and the material in economic geographies. In his book *The Mental and the Material*, the anthropologist, Maurice Godelier (1986: 6) considers this issue:

> The difficulty derives from the fact that a society never exists by halves or in pieces. A society always exists as a whole – that is, as an articulated ensemble of relations and functions, all of which are *simultaneously necessary* for its existence as such, but whose importance for its reproduction is variable. That is why the reproduction of any given society cannot continue beyond certain variations or alterations in the social relations which constitute it and the material base upon which it depends.

Here Godelier struggles to find the words to make the material and the social indistinguishable and falls back on the analogy of the material 'base' and social 'superstructure' which all too easily can imply some kind of primacy one over the other. However, what follows makes it clear that he does not hold to this view:

> Social relations are not things. They do not exist without human intervention and action producing and reproducing them each day. . . . All relations are realities in flux and motion, and in this movement they are daily deformed, altered or eroded to a greater or lesser degree. . . . But since thought is not an instance separate from social relations, since a society has neither top nor bottom, since it does not consist of superimposed layers, we are forced to conclude that if the distinction between infrastructure and superstructures is to retain any meaning at all, it cannot be take as a distinction between levels or instances. . . . (Ibid., 18–19)

Thus, the notion of economy as object and as practice refers both to effective material relationships between ends and means and, simultaneously, to social relations of value which give direction to these material relationships. Economic geographies are, therefore, both social and material, and both are inseparable from one another. However, to illustrate these ideas, it is perhaps easiest to deal separately with the material and social relations of economic geographies.

Materialities

Economic geographies are constituted of definite sets of material practices – which I call circuits of value. Circuits of value may be represented as

$$- euv - C - elc - P - euv - C - elc - P - euv$$
$$| \qquad \qquad |$$
$$\text{--------- pC ---------}$$

where P is production, C is consumption, euv is the exchange of produced use values, elc is the exchange of labour power or other inputs into production, and pC is the productive consumption diverted from immediate consumption.

What this simple diagram shows is that economic geographies involve the circulation of value (that is, material and immaterial items of value, worth or use) from consumption, via various forms of exchange (for example, labour markets) to production. From there, again via processes of exchange such as the markets for goods and services, value flows back to consumption or, if instead it is directed to markets for the means of production such as property, machinery and infrastructure or the markets for finance which provide the investments necessary to enable production to take place once more, value flows directly back to production.

If societies are to be capable of material reproduction – if, that is, they are to be able to engage in the social and material struggles involved in making a living – people must be able to construct and to participate, actively or indirectly,[5] in circuits of value. And these circuits, in turn, must be capable of producing and exchanging at least as much material value as they consume. Such an engagement involves the transformation of nature in order that participants in circuits of value may produce, circulate and consume use values.[6]

Even in this elemental material sense, circuits of value are inherently geographical. For one thing, they involve the perpetual but forever changing movement of value through circuits of value from consumption via exchange to production, via exchange once more to consumption. Indeed, to be effective, circuits of value must be capable of reproduction and extension through time and across space. Economic geographies cannot consist merely of single moments in space or time. And for another, value itself is geographically specific. Value may be thought of as relations and things which, through the material and social practices of consumption, exchange and production, come to be regarded as useful, helpful, uplifting. But what is valued varies from place to place and from time to time. In this sense, then, economic diversity is inherent in circuits of value and in the economic geographies which are both enabled and created by them. It is possible to imagine circuits of value differentiated by what is valued (that is, by the social relations of value), and by the nature and organization of consumption, exchange and production that takes place in and through them. Indeed, it is not necessary to have to try to imagine such diversity as there are many contemporary and historical examples of diverse economic practices (Sheppard, 2009; see, for example Peck and Theodore, 2007).

Social relations of value

However, material diversity is one thing; the possibilities of diversity arising from social relations of value quite another. And it is primarily from these social relations of value that economic diversity derives. As indicated above, circuits of value are constituted materially through flows of value across space and time. But, the nature of value – the qualities that endow things and practices with worth or usefulness – is hardly straightforward. Value is itself socially constructed in and through the social experience of its consumption and production and in the transactions and exchanges involved in its circulation. Thus value can have no meaning outside an environmental, social and practical context in which it may be evaluated.

What is of value in one context may be valueless in another.

This is because value has an essentially practical dimension. If something serves some kind of purpose – even if only an intensely individual purpose such as the satisfaction that may be experienced from wearing a designer label or a piece of expensive jewellery – it is valuable (see Chapter 20). But such purposes are socially-determined: they are influenced to a greater or lesser extent by social norms and practices – the social relations of value. Thus, in attempting to understand the possibilities inherent in economic geographies, the goal must be 'to find out exactly how value is put upon things, processes, and even human beings, under the social conditions prevailing . . .' (Harvey, 2006: 38). To ask, in other words, how might value be constructed?

The origins of value may lie in desire which is psychologically and socially determined. But this does not mean that value is endowed in a purely individualistic fashion. Desire is not independent of the circumstances in which it may arise (see, for example, Miller, 2008). Value is valued for a reason – which may be nothing more than personal gratification – but even that is always influenced by wider sets of circumstances through which the bases of and need for gratification arise. No matter how sophisticated or 'new' – and hence desirable – software may be for example, it is of little value to anyone without the means either to recognize its wider significance (what it can do and the point of it so doing) or to make it do it.

More generally, value cannot be reduced to what individuals may take it to be. The reproductive requirements of circuits of value are themselves powerful influences and constraints on the nature and definition of value. From this perspective, value may be defined in terms of the sustenance of circuits of value. Sheppard and Barnes (1990) explain that the Marxian concept of social necessity has two meanings that link the evaluation of economic geographies to the material imperative of enabling sufficient value to be produced, circulated and exchanged in a circuit of value. First, it refers the value of a commodity as the labour *socially necessary* to produce that commodity. Second, it includes validation through exchange:

> Marx argued that the process of exchange plays a crucial role in coordinating the activities of individual capitalists . . . where the individual activities of many workers are confirmed as being socially useful because they produce commodities that are in demand, [they] may be regarded as a confirmation via exchange that the labour employed in production was useful. (Sheppard and Barnes, 1990: 37)

But the diverse geographies in and through which circuits of value take place – the historical geographies embodied in the economic as well as political and cultural processes operating on circuits of value in which labour produces value – are extremely influential in shaping what is socially necessary, what is efficient and, indeed, what is valuable. These geographies themselves give rise to diverse notions of value at the same time as they are themselves shaped by the circuits of value which flow through them. This is why struggles over the nature of value and of evaluation are profoundly political processes fundamental to the nature and shape of circuits of social reproduction. Thus, the sustenance of such circuits might well involve the forceful, even violent, imposition of particular norms of evaluation and the employment of systematic processes of socialization, such as education, to sustain them. This will certainly involve social struggle, not least over meanings, of the resultant social geographies of evaluation and understanding through which the social bases of value may be established. One of the most significant of such struggles arises over the distribution of value through society. Traditionally, the struggle between workers and employers is one of the most significant of such struggles but the global financial crisis which began in 2007 generalized such struggles to that between individuals, communities and nations and the capitalist financial system rightly perceived to be the cause of the crisis.

But this does not mean that different forms of value cannot co-exist and be co-present in circuits of value. They are rarely, if ever, singular. Indeed, a diversity of norms of value is necessary to sustain circuits of value if they are to be able to continue to work (Lee, 2006). For example, the response of Adair Turner (2009), chair of the UK Financial Services Authority to the financial crisis has been to claim that much financial activity is 'socially useless'. That is, it is lacking in value and, given that, to continue to promote the competitiveness of the City of London would merely contribute further to this inappropriate production of value. He proposes a series of regulatory measures to suppress this 'useless' activity. This response is hardly a critique of capitalism as a set of social relations of value. Nevertheless, it reveals that, even within capitalist social relations, the possibility of alternatives – here alternative notions of what is and what is not value – is always already co-present within such circuits and is also always necessary if they are to be sustainable.

Socialities of value: evaluation, coherence and difference

What is at issue here is the necessary simultaneity of social and material relations of value within circuits of value. But this simultaneity is not a mere 'natural' process. It is the outcome of social and political struggle and contestation over the shaping of the material practices, the social relations of value and the criteria of evaluation of circuits of value. Such struggles, and the geographies of value and of evaluation to which they give rise, reach the heart of the sustainability of economic geographies. They are manifest on a range of ways, from protests mounted around major economic events (like the G20 in London on 1 April 2009) to localized and more or less well-organized resistance to plant closures (for example, Hayter and Harvey, 1993), as well as the wide range of social movements around the world through which people struggle to transform the criteria of evaluation which shape the economic geographies and the livelihoods of those involved in such movements.

The process of such evaluation is necessarily continuous and involves the assessment of past and present trajectories of circuits of value thereby to propose and predict future trajectories against whatever evaluative norms emerge from political and discursive struggle. As a result of this open-ended political process, there arises the distinct possibility of economic incoherence, the reduction of the material effectiveness of circuits of value and the disruption of established relations of power. Attempts to ensure the coherence and effectiveness of circuits of value and their established power relations may be widely accepted, enforced or disrupted through struggles that take place over the nature of the social relations of value. But one thing is for sure: these social relations of value are far from simply given. Rather they are perpetually constructed and reconstructed in practice through political debate and contested discourses.

Thus economic geographies and the circuits of value of which they are constituted and enabled are, as Bob Jessop (1997) would put it, 'contingent necessities'. In other words, they are a condition of social survival and, as such, are constituted of certain necessary processes involving the establishment of social relations and the material practices of consumption, production and exchange, in order to sustain social life. Hence the stress on necessities. But the particular circumstances through which these necessities take place are not only geographically and socially variable and profoundly influential but also the outcome of political and social struggle. Hence the significance of contingency.

Commenting on 'contingent necessity', Ash Amin and Jerzy Hausner (1997: 4) suggest that:

[E]conomic activity is seen to be neither solely driven by abstract universal laws nor by economic agents behaving identically (e.g. *homo œconomicus*). Instead the social intermediation of the general necessities of economic reproduction (e.g. the wage relation, property rights, exchange relations, etc.), together with time- and place-specific patterns of economic behaviour, constitute a multiple set of non-universal determinants of economic activity.[7]

Thus economic geographies are the recursive effects of interactions and socially-articulated struggles between causal tendencies (including, in particular, those surrounding the material practices of circuits of value such as the formative power of finance capital) and counter tendencies (including alternative practices and criteria of evaluation of circuits of value such as proposals for the reform of finance). As a result, economic geographies which, to repeat, are circuits of value – that is, socially directed circuits of production, exchange and consumption – are neither singular nor an easily definable or containable sets of processes and practices. Certainly it is unlikely that they are capable of comprehension by abstract and abstracted economic models. This is because such models assume both a separation of the economic from the social and, within the economic, they assume rational behaviour on the part of economic actors. Rather, economic geographies are the dynamic and unstable effects of multiple and socially constructed networks of relations which combine in highly variable ways across space and through time.

As such, the construction of circuits of value and their economic geographies opens up a range of possibilities and so sets up a series of tensions between the multiplicity of possible alternative circuits of value. This complexity and these possibilities must be acknowledged as inherent within economic geographies. And yet, if circuits of value are to take place in a reasonably predictable and reliable fashion, they must (and this relates to the 'necessities' bit of 'contingent necessities') achieve some degree of 'systemic unity', as Amin and Hausner (1997: 7) would have it, or 'economic coherence', as Michael Storper and Robert Salais (1997: 21ff) suggest.

The point here is that people are recursively and reflexively involved in the construction of economic geographies and the circuits of value which form and flow through them. Whilst needing to ensure the material imperatives of circuits of value, those engaged in them are not merely passive in shaping their construction. In reflecting on the circuits in which they are engaged, people both influence and are influenced by circuits of value and adopt a particular stance (for example, a political stance) or set of stances towards them. So, the concrete-real practices of circuits of value are irreducible to simple causes and effects. They are the outcome of struggles between subversive moves towards multiple alternatives and the repression or harnessing of such tendencies to secure coherence.

An important determinant of the achievement (or lack of achievement) of such coherence and sustainability within economic geographies is the practical response of people to their experience of, and engagement in, circuits of value and their capacities to challenge existing practices and to formulate alternatives. Of particular significance is their understanding of whether circuits of value and the economic geographies through which they take place are, in practice, capable of doing the material business (consuming, producing and exchanging values) of making a living and of being able to do so repeatedly, across space and in socially- and environmentally-bearable or acceptable ways. Beyond this, the significance of economy for the construction of individual identity (in production, exchange and consumption) is a major factor in shaping the politics of economic geographies. The more that the economy works in an individualized fashion as a means of identity formation, especially perhaps through consumption, the less that politics involving any form of collective action is seen as either relevant or desirable. The potential for the loss of the chains that bind people to particular social and environmental forms of economic geographies is, apparently, a more potent political force than the

loss of everything which is, perhaps, too cataclysmic a possibility to generate a clear political response. Nevertheless, a constant feature of circuits of value is the political effort needed to sustain coherence against any inherent tendencies (such as may be embedded in 'socially useless' finance) towards incoherence. However, that the political is shoved out of the way by the powerful influence of the economic is itself problematic and opens up the wider possibilities for change.

DIVERSE ECONOMIES

Such arguments and the emergent geographies that lie behind them suggest that diverse economies are not merely possible but necessary if people's lives are not simply to be reduced to, and subsumed by, an economic logic apparently beyond their control. Indeed, if Zizek's arguments are even partially sustainable, then, unless it is possible for economic geographies to be non-economic in imagination and practice, little else may be possible. Such a realization is one reason for the growing recognition and widespread practice of diverse economies along with the conceptual ideas and theoretical framing of them that have become increasingly apparent over recent years. Thus, J.K. Gibson-Graham (2008: 613–614) suggests that

[A] new moment seems to be upon us, coinciding with the emergence of 'diverse economies' in geography. . . .
Projects of economic autonomy and experimentation are proliferating worldwide and there is a burgeoning cultural infrastructure of conferences, books, websites, blogs, films and other media to support and spread them.

She goes on to speak of 'the huge variety of economic transactions, labor practices and economic organizations . . . worldwide.'

But, perhaps even more hopeful, is the increasingly wide acceptance that diverse economies are not something exceptional. Rather, the mainstream view of economies recognizes that diversity is inherent. Eric Sheppard (2009: 185) puts it thus:

> Geographical economy is inseparable from and constituted through societal and biophysical processes, and is variegated rather than simply capitalist. There is no single economy applicable to all places, with advanced capitalism constituting a ubiquitous best practice for all, but room for geographically differentiated possibilities and imaginaries.

Thus, not only are diverse economies being widely practised, they are also being widely thought. It is this combination of practice and thought in response to the 'danger of losing everything', as Zizek puts it, which characterizes the current emergence of diverse economies. How has this come about?

Practices of economic diversity

The notion of economic diversity simply reflects the realization that economic geographies may be organized and driven in diverse ways; that they are not singular; and that they are not necessarily driven by one particular set of social norms and the objectives shaped by these norms. The social relations which shape the practices of these economic geographies and the ways in which practitioners come to understand them may take on a wide range of possibilities. This chapter does not – and indeed cannot – claim to point to a singular answer as to how these possibilities and imaginaries might or should be realized. But it does attempt to elucidate why economic geographies are so much more than mere spatial manifestations of a singular and autonomous economic logic. Hopefully, therefore, it thereby begins to throw a tiny chink of light on how they have come variously to be imagined and practised otherwise.

One explanation for the emergence of diverse economies[8] is that alternatives to mainstream economic activity and relations enable people to achieve their wider economic, social, environmental and political objectives (see, for example, North, 2006, 2008). Paradoxically,

the stimulus for such developments came not only from real and experienced contradictions of uneven development but also from the individualism of neo-liberal models of economy characteristic of the 1980s [and hence, in contradictory fashion, the notion of individual agency expressed – if uncertainly – in notions of post-fordism (Amin et al., 1994)] as well as from the radical critiques of capitalism and imperialism (Peet, 1977) through the 1970s following the end of the long post-war boom from the middle of the 1960s (Armstrong et al., 1984). The critical recognition that the fate of localities is bound up with geographically wider sets of economic relations which gave the lie to the notion that locality-based polices of development were sufficient to offset wider relations of uneven development (Massey, 1979; and see Chapters 11 and 17) pointed in the direction of alternative economic geographies – in effect bypassing these wider relations.

DISCOURSES OF DIVERSITY

But there is more to diversity than this. Agnès Humbert (2009: 33) tells of how she subverted economy as one way to publicize resistance to the Nazi occupation of Paris in 1941.

> On blue-and-white five-franc notes, I type in red letters: 'Vive le général de Gaulle'.[9] No one can afford to destroy a bank note, so they pass from hand to hand and my mission is accomplished.

Here the inseparability of economy and wider social relations is exemplified directly through the use of that most commonplace and mundane of economic symbols – paper money. The story shows how the everyday economy can be used to achieve particular social and political objectives.[10] Certainly it is a manifestation of economic diversity as it thinks, not just practises, economy differently. In other words, economic diversity is not limited to the manifestations of socially or organizationally alternative forms of economic geographies created outside the mainstream but, as Gibson-Graham (2008: 614–615) puts it, it involves 'performing new economies'.

This involves asking 'how theory and epistemology could advance what we [want] to do in the world'. For Gibson-Graham, this involves the adoption of 'an anti-essentialist approach, theorizing the contingency of social outcomes rather than the unfolding of structural logics'. Associated with this is a 'performative orientation to knowledge' which acknowledges that thought and knowledge production is not merely a reflection on what is but an active consideration of what might be opened up through thinking about the world differently. The goal is 'still to understand the world in order to change it, but with a post-structural twist – to change our understanding *is* to change the world' (original emphasis). This was achieved not by an even more though-going critique of capitalism, because critique is also a powerful form of legitimation, but by adopting an approach to economic activity similar to that followed in this chapter which is focused on what economic geographies do (rather than what they may appear to be).

Rather than thinking first about economic structures and laws of motion (for example, capitalism) the Gibson-Graham approach was to turn to an anti-essentialist form of Marxism (Resnick and Wolff, 1987) and to identify the diverse class relations of exploitation (independent, feudal, slave, communal and capitalist) within circuits of value. Gibson-Graham sought a way of thinking and a language for a diverse and heterogeneous economy:

> Wanting an economic politics that allowed us to think creatively and to start *now* and *here* to make new economies, we focused our attentions . . . on ways of thinking that distanced the economic from politics. These included the tendency to represent economy as a space of invariant logics and automatic unfolding that offered no field for intervention; the tendency to theorize economy as a stable and self-reproducing structure impervious to the proliferative and desultory wanderings of everyday politics; the tendency to constitute 'the' economy as a singular capitalist system or space rather than as a zone of cohabitation and contestation among

> multiple economic forms; and the tendency to lodge faith in accurate representation that guaranteed and stabilized the prevailing substantive framings. (Gibson-Graham, 2006, xxi–xxii)

> One of the goals of our 'language politics' has been to replace this impoverished conceptual ground with a rich diversity of economic practices and organizations – a heterogeneous set of transactions, forms of labor and remuneration, types of enterprise and modes of surplus appropriation and distribution. The language of the diverse economy brings into visibility a great variety of economic sites and practices in any particular location, constituting them as a resource for building community economies. (Ibid., 195)

> As we begin to conceptualize contingent relationships where invariant logics once reigned, the economy loses its character as an asocial body in lawful motion and instead becomes a space of recognition and negotiation. The economic certainties and generic stories of development discourse are effectively dislodged, as are the macronarratives of capitalist development (including most recently globalization) that loom in the vicinity of most social theorizing. (Ibid., xxx)

This opens up the possibility of theorizing new worlds (Gibson-Graham, 2006) – contributing to 'novel economic performances' and thereby repopulating 'the economic landscape as a proliferative space of difference' full of diverse economic geographies – rather than merely explaining existing worlds (see, for example, Lee et al., 2004).

CONCLUDING COMMENTS: TOWARDS A 'POST-CAPITALIST POLITICS'

The argument in this essay stresses above all that whilst materially imperative, economic geographies are, at the same time, social constructs and that, as such, they are subject to political challenge and to change. Change may be both intentional through attempts, for example, to replace one set of social relations with another or – and much more frequently – unintentional, emanating from frustrations with, or misunderstandings about, how circuits of value operate. So the struggle to make a living is not restricted merely to the material processes involved – notwithstanding their inescapable significance. It embraces the establishment of sustainable and coherent sets of social relations which then inform the ways in which these material processes are practised. And these social relations, in turn, both reflect and differentiate the nature of, and degree of access, to political power to shape circuits of value. But they also open up the possibility of constructing alternative economic geographies.

This chapter has tried to outline what is involved in this process (see also Lee, 2010 c, d). The issues go beyond the office, the factory, the industry, the sector, even the state – around which sites of economic geography political mobilization is relatively easy – to embrace the whole complex of circuits of value that make up the economic geographies of social life. In this context, one of the most remarkable features of the diverse economies project (Gibson-Graham, 1996, 2006) has been its insistence on practicality, engaging in and documenting 'a variety of paths toward differently imagined forms of social and economic development'. Further, '[E]ach has been treated as . . . an ethical and political space of decision in which negotiations over interdependence take place.' (Gibson-Graham, 2006: 192–193).

Gibson-Graham identifies four coordinates – meeting local needs directly, using any surplus value produced within economic geographies to strengthen community economies, recognizing consumption as a force for development rather than privileging investment, and enhancing the notion of commons as involving interdependence in pursuing routes to development by different means. To these four co-ordinates might be added a fifth: the recognition that the imperative of economy can be a force for liberation. This is because its very necessity does not countermand its social construction but rather necessitates the formulation of other/alternative ethical and political spaces through which sense may be made of the purpose of economic geographies, and preventative action of the kind called for by Zizek may be enabled.

Further, beginning from 'a fragmentary and incoherent starting place' and 'starting where you are' (Gibson-Graham, 2006: 195) also plays to the diversity of economic geographies necessary not merely to overcome the sheer size and complexity of the challenge of exclusion identified by Zizek but to imagine and enable accessible and meaningful responses by groups and individuals. From this might emerge 'a vision of global transformation through the accretion and interaction of small changes in place' (Gibson-Graham, 2006: 196). It is difficult to imagine a more realistic understanding of contemporary economic geographies[11] nor to conceive of a clearer endorsement of the centrality and power of economic geographies in building a new politics of preventative action.

ACKNOWLEDGEMENTS

I am heavily indebted to the perceptive reading of an earlier version of this paper undertaken by Andrew Leyshon and the pointed and supportively critical comments that he offered.

NOTES

1 One (of many) arguments that show that Thatcher's assertion is a nonsense is outlined in Lee (2006).

2 See, for example, Leunig, et al. (2007); Leyshon et al. (2008) provide qualitative evidence of the power of geography to shape profitability and hence the location of bank branches.

3 An account of economic geographies which points up the centrally significant role of evaluation may be found in Lee (2010b).

4 This section draws heavily on Lee (2006).

5 Not everyone is capable of engaging directly in circuits of value. The elderly, dependent children, the infirm, the imprisoned and those that consider (or are allowed to consider) themselves to be above and demeaned by work are all dependent upon other forms of access to circuits of value and hence to the values that they need to survive.

6 Use values may be defined quite simply as material or immaterial 'things which serve to satisfy needs of one kind or another' (Marx, 1976: 283). They are, in other words, items of value or worth.

7 Note the similarity between this description and that of Sheppard (2009) quoted above.

8 See Leyshon et al. (2003) and Fuller et al. (2010) for a range of examples of diverse economic practices.

9 De Gaulle was the then little-known leader of the Free French based in London.

10 See North (2007) for a sophisticated account of how economics and politics interweave and may be transformed through the emergence of diverse economic geographies.

11 Not least because 'where we are' is nearer than we may think to enabling transformation. It is important to remember that up to 50% of the GDP of most advanced economies is already sustained outside the private market-based economy (see also Chapters 13 and 22). Thus, although much of this value flows through thoroughly capitalist state systems, it represents a massive infrastructure already in place. What is more, it is arguable that at least as much value is produced outside the market economy in legal but unwaged and formally-unacknowledged economic activities as is produced within it. Again, it is hardly the case that alternatives need a thoroughgoing process of learning and restructuring. Alternatives are being practised day-to-day often at the very heart of capitalist economic practices (Lee, 2006).

REFERENCES

Amin, A. (ed) (1994) *Post-Fordism: A Reader.* Oxford and Cambridge MA: Blackwell.

Amin, A. and Hausner, J. (1997) Interactive governance and social complexity. Chapter 1 in A. Amin, and J. Hausner (eds) *Beyond Market and Hierarchy Interactive Governance and Social Complexity.* Cheltenham and Lyme, NH: Edward Elgar. pp. 1–31.

Armstrong, P. Glyn, A. and Harrison, J. (1984) *Capitalism Since World War II: The Making and Break Up of the Long Boom.* London: Fontana.

Bunting, M. (2009) Market dogma is exposed as myth: Where is the new vision to unite us? *The Guardian,* 29 June 23.

Cosgrove, D. (1989) Geography is everywhere: Culture and symbolism in human landscapes. Chapter 2.2 in D. Gregory, and R. Walford (eds) *Horizons in Human Geography.* London: Macmillan Hondmills. pp. 118–35.

Crouch, C. (2004) *Post-democracy.* Cambridge: Polity Press.

Fuller, D. Jonas, A. and Lee, R. (eds) (2010) *Interrogating Alterity.* Farnham: Ashgate.

Gibson-Graham, J.K. (1996/2006) *The End of Capitalism (As We Knew It): A Feminist Critique of Political Economy* (2nd edn). Minnesota: University of Minnesota Press.

Gibson-Graham, J.K. (2006) *A Post-capitalist Politics.* Minnesota: University of Minnesota Press.

Gibson-Graham, J.K. (2008) Diverse economies: Performative practices for 'other worlds'. *Progress in Human Geography,* 32(5): 613–32.

Godelier, M. (1986) *The Mental and the Material.* London: Verso.

Harvey, D. (1978) Urbanization under capitalism: A framework for analysis. *International Journal of Urban and Regional Research,* 2:101–31.

Harvey, D. (2005) *A Brief History of Neoliberalism.* Oxford: Oxford University Press.

Harvey, D. (2006) *The Limits to Capital.* London and New York: Verso.

Harvey, M. and Metcalfe, S. (2010) The ordering of change: Polanyi, Schumpeter and the nature of the market mechanism. Chapter 4 in M. Harvey (ed.) *Markets, Rules and Institutions of Exchange.* Manchester: Manchester University Press.

Hayter, T. and Harvey, D. (1993) *The Factory and the City: The Story of the Cowley Autoworkers in Oxford.* Brighton: Mansell.

Humbert, A. (2009) *Résistance Memoirs of Occupied France.* London: Bloomsbury Publishing.

Jessop, B. (1997) The governance of complexity and the complexity of governance: Preliminary remarks on some problems and limits of economic guidance. Chapter 5 in A. Amin, and J. Hausner (eds) *Beyond Market and Hierarchy: Interactive Governance and Social Complexity.* Cheltenham and Lyme, NH: Edward Elgar. pp. 95–128.

Lee, R. (2003) The marginalisation of everywhere?: Emerging geographies of emerging markets. Chapter 4 in J. Peck, and H. Wai-chung Yeung (eds) *Remaking the Global Economy: Economic-geographical Perspectives.* London, Thousand Oaks, New Delhi: SAGE. pp. 61–82.

Lee, R. (2006) The ordinary economy. *Transactions of the Institute of British Geographers*: 413–32.

Lee, R. (2010a) Economic society/social geography. Chapter 8 in S.J. Smith, R. Pain, S.A. Marston, and J.P. Jones III, (eds) *The SAGE Handbook of Social Geographies.* London, Thousand Oaks, New Delhi, Singapore: SAGE. pp. 205–21.

Lee, R. (2010b) Spaces of hegemony?: Circuits of value, finance capital and places of financial knowledge.

In J. Agnew, and D. Livingstone (eds) *Handbook of Geographical Knowledge*. London: SAGE.

Lee, R. (2010c) Spiders, bees or architects?: Imagination and the radical immanence of alternatives/diversity for political economic geographies. In D. Fuller, A. Jonas, and R. Lee, (eds) (2010) *Interrogating Alterity*. Farnham: Ashgate.

Lee, R. (2010d) Within and outwith/Material and political?: Local economic development and the spatialities of economic geographies. In A. Pike, A. Rodriguez- Pose, and J. Tomaney (eds) *A Handbook of Local and Regional Development*. London: Routledge.

Lee, R., Leyshon, A., Aldridge, T., Tooke, J., Williams, C., and Thrift, N. (2004) Making geographies and histories?: Constructing local circuits of value. *Environment and Planning D: Society and Space*, 22: 595–617.

Leunig, T. (2008) The regeneration game is up. *The Guardian* 13 August http://www.guardian.co.uk/commentisfree/2008/aug/13/regeneration.conservatives (accessed 7 July 2009).

Leunig, T., Swaffield, J. and Hartwich, O.M. (2007) *Cities Unlimited: Making Urban Regeneration Work*. London: Policy Exchange.

Leyshon, A., French, S., and Signoretta, P. (2008) Financial exclusion and the geography of bank and building society branch closure in Britain. *Transactions of the Institute of British Geographers*, 33: 447–65.

Leyshon, A., Lee, R., and Williams, C. (eds) (2003) *Alternative Economic Spaces*. London: SAGE.

Martin, K. (2009) Magic and myth of the rational market. *Financial Times*, 25 August 9. http://www.ft.com/cms/s/0/8f9efe98-90ec-11de-bc 99-00144feabdc0.html (accessed 8 September 2009).

Marx, K. (1976) *Capital*, vol. I. Harmondsworth: Penguin.

Massey, D. (1979) In what sense a regional problem? *Regional Studies*, 13: 233–43.

Massey, D. (1997) Economic/non-economic. Chapter 2 in R. Lee, and J. Wills (eds) *Geographies of Economies*. London: Arnold. pp. 27–36.

Miller, D. (2008) The uses of value. *Geoforum*, 39: 1122–32.

North, P. (2006) *Alternative Currencies as a Challenge to Globalisation?: A Case Study of Manchester's Local Currency Networks*. Farnham: Ashgate.

North, P. (2007) *Money and Liberation: The Micropolitics of Alternative Currency Movements*. Minneapolis: University of Minnesota Press.

North, P. (2008) Voices from the Trueque: Argentina's barter networks resisting neoliberalisation. In A. Smith, A., Stenning, and K. Willis (eds) *Social Justice and Neoliberalism: Global Perspectives*. London: Zed Books.

Peck, J. (2008) Remaking laissez-faire. *Progress in Human Geography*, 32: 13–43.

Peck, J, and Theodore N. (2007) Variegated capitalism. *Progress in Human Geography*, 31: 731–72.

Peet, R. (ed.) (1977) *Radical Geography: Alternative Viewpoints on Contemporary Social Issues*. London: Methuen.

Polanyi, K. (1944) *The Great Transformation: The Political and Economic Origins of Our Time*, 1957 edition. Boston: Beacon Press.

Resnick, S. A. and Wolff, R. D. (1987) *Knowledge and Class*. Chicago: University of Chicago Press.

Sandel, M. (2009) *BBC Reith Lectures*.

Sayer, A. (1997) The dialectic of culture and economy. Chapter 1 in R. Lee and J. Wills, (eds) *Geographies of Economies*. London: Arnold. pp.16–26.

Sheppard, E.S. (2009) Economy. In D. Gregory, R. Johnston, G. Pratt, M. Watts and J. Whatmore, (eds) *The Dictionary of Human Geography*. Malden MA, Oxford, Chichester: Wiley-Blackwell. pp.184–85.

Sheppard, E. and Barnes, T.J. (1990) *The Capitalist Space Economy: Geographical Analysis after Ricardo, Marx and Sraffa*. London: Unwin Hyman.

Smith, A. (1759) *The Theory of Moral Sentiments*, 2007 edition. Cosimo Inc.

Smith, A. (1776) *An Inquiry into the Nature and Causes of the Wealth of Nations*, 2001 edition. Adam Smith Institute.

Storper, M. and Salais, R. (1997) *Worlds of Production: The Action Frameworks of the Economy*. Cambridge, MA, London: Harvard University Press.

Turner, A. (2009) How to tame global finance. *Prospect*, 27th August, Issue 162. http://www.prospectmagazine.co.uk/2009/08/how-to-tame-global-finance/ (accessed 8 September 2009).

Zizek, S. (2009) How to begin from the beginning. *New Left Review*, 57: 43–55.

25

Towards a Non-Economic, Economic Geography? From Black Boxes to the Cultural Circuit of Capital in Economic Geographies of Firms and Managers

Andrew Leyshon

INTRODUCTION

This chapter attempts to show the ways in which facets of social action that once would have been seen as non-economic and unimportant have, over time, been recognized as significant in understanding the production of economic geographies. In particular, the chapter reflects upon the ways in which the sub-discipline of economic geography has gradually expanded its theoretical and conceptual repertoire. It considers the implications that this expansion has had for our understanding of the ways in which economies evolve, and the ways in which they ebb and flow in accordance with norms and practices that might escape a narrower frame of economic analysis. In order to do this, the chapter considers the ways in which economic geography has attempted to account for the role of powerful actors such as business corporations, as well as the managers and executives that run and embody them. Considerations of powerful business actors in understanding the geographical dynamics of the economy have been highly variable within the history of economic geography; managers and other powerful actors have for the most part been ignored, at times vilified, occasionally been celebrated and, in one example, purposely written out of the story altogether. Indeed, until relatively recently economic geographers even seemed reluctant to engage in critical discussion or attempt to define what a 'firm' might be. According to Maskell (2001), although the subject of the firm has appeared regularly within the texts and narratives developed within economic geography over many years, the firm 'remained a vague entity without a clearly defined form or function' (p. 329), with the result that for many years the firm remained something of a 'black box' that was left unexamined (Taylor and Asheim, 2001). In part, this was a legacy of the theoretical influences that the sub-discipline imported from neo-classical economics during the 1960s (see Chapter 1), where the firm was seen as device for rationally interpreting and acting upon price signals from the market. But, Maskell argues, it is also due to what he describes as economic geography's tendency to view the world as one made up of groups or populations rather than of individuals or agents; or, as Maskell himself describes it, geographers have demonstrated a preference for a phylogeneric ontology rather than an ontogenetic ontology (Maskell, 2001). This has meant that economic geography has tended to operate with a much better understanding of broader, macro-scale processes of change, relegating the analysis of micro-scale processes – such as the behaviour and performance of firms – to a secondary and merely supplemental interpretative status. This tendency is particularly evident in accounts rooted within Marxism or political economy, for example.

However, over time, as these influences within the sub-discipline have declined, so geographers have gradually been prepared to open up the black box and peer into the workings of firms and organizations, which have been revealed to be quite complex, flexible and often volatile entities, with often very fuzzy boundaries (Dicken and Malmberg, 2001; Maskell, 2001; Taylor and Asheim, 2001). Thus, the ways in which economic geographers have accounted for the role of firms and the people who run them – sometimes seeing them as unimportant and at other times important – has partly been a reflection of the theoretical positions and methodological practices that have been prevalent within the sub-discipline at different times, which have influenced the ways in which geographers have collectively seen the world, and the kinds of processes that produce it (Barnes et al., 2007; Clark, 1998). Recently, in line with a growing cultural turn within the discipline, the agency of firms and the managers that run them has been recognized as significant and informed by a broader system of ideas, knowledge and materials that has helped to formulate conventions and programmes of action and transformation, and that has had wide reaching consequences for the unfolding of economic life.

The remainder of this chapter examines the changing ways in which economic geography has addressed the role of firms and their managers and in understanding economic change over the course of its recent history. It does so in order to draw attention to the ways in which ideas and concepts have changed as economic geographers have responded to the economy's ability to change and mutate, and so escape their interpretative grasp, by shifting their theoretical position. The rest of the chapter is organized in four sections. The next section looks at the initial emergence of attempts to take firms and management seriously through the rise of corporate geography in the 1970s which made significant claims about the geographical presence or absence of managers and the parts of organizations that they inhabited in relation to uneven development. In contradistinction, the third section looks at the emergence of work on geographical industrialization in the 1980s which was informed by Marxism and political economy and which attempted to sound the death knell for such corporate geographies. The fourth section considers the implications of a growing interest in global commodity chains and the cultural turn in economic geography for the study of firms and their managers, and analyses in more detail work on the cultural circuit of capital. The fifth section concludes the chapter.

THE RISE OF CORPORATE GEOGRAPHY

Until the 1970s, economic geographers had a rather impoverished view of the role that firms and corporations played within processes of economic change. This was because of the strong influence that both spatial analysis and regional science exerted over the discipline in the 1950s and 1960s (Scott, 2000, and see Chapter 1). Spatial analysis constituted the leading edge of the quantitative revolution within the discipline as a whole, and drew inspiration from the industrial location models developed by Weber and Lösch and from Christaller's central place theory of settlement, all of which were based on undersocialized accounts of human behaviour that drew strongly on nineteenth century physics (Barnes, 1996) (see, in addition, Chapters 1 and 2). Meanwhile, regional science, which emerged in the 1950s as a hybrid discipline that combined elements of neoclassical economics with a geographical concern for the distribution of activities over space, sought 'to rewrite neoclassical competitive equilibrium theory in terms of spatial co-ordinates so that all demands, supplies and price variables could be expressed as an explicit function of location' (Scott, 2000: 486). The conceptual legacy of spatial analysis and regional science ensured that, under their influence, economic geography tended to under theorize the firm, which was often assumed to be an atomistic single plant entity, that resembled those described by Alfred Marshall in his analysis of industrial agglomerations in late nineteenth century Britain (Walker, 1989; Maskell, 2001). Neo-classical economics gave theoretical support for such a view by seeing the economy as a market made up of a set of contracts – including contracts for labour and assets and resources – within which the firm is just one agent among many, and not necessary a particularly significant agent at that. However, such 'complete contracts' economic theories are elegant but limited, not least because economic exchange is not a costless activity. Indeed,

exchange between independent economic actors generates transaction costs (such as legal costs, for example) which, if significant, will encourage firms to extend their boundaries to bring under their control transactions that were formerly contracted with external agents (Maskell, 2001). At the same time, there are limits to the size of firms, as management and organization becomes more problematic the bigger firms become, leading to problems of co-ordination and strategic direction. Therefore, firms tend to exist between the points where transaction costs become significant and where size and complexity leads to information overload (Maskell, 2001: 335).

Indeed, even by the time that Marshall was conducting his studies, large, multi-locational firms had begun to evolve and emerge as a force within the economy, being the organizational form pioneered by railway companies, first in Europe and then in North America. Railway companies necessarily operated across space and their existence, in combination with the rise of the telegraph and later the telephone, effectively reduced the amount of time it took to travel and send information across space, which encouraged other companies to expand their operations beyond a single location and take advantage of new markets and supplies of raw materials and labour (Leyshon, 1995).

By the middle of the twentieth century, the disjuncture between the rather antiquated treatment of the firm within economic geography and the material reality of a burgeoning international economy inhabited by multi-locational and, increasingly, multi-national firms could no longer be sustained, and was eventually rectified by the emergence of a body of research on the geography of corporations, which came into its own during the 1970s, although even here the nature of the firm remained relatively under theorized and taken for granted.

As is often the case, being a relatively open and porous discipline, as geographers turned their attention towards multi-locational corporations, they found inspiration in cognate social science disciplines. Pioneering business historian Alfred Chandler had charted the rise of the modern corporation in business history and reflected on its spatial implications, ideas that were taken further by heterodox economist Stephen Hymer who 'married Chandler to Marx in a highly-influential treatment of the multinational corporation and uneven development' (Walker, 1989: 44). In particular, Hymer drew attention to the ways in which the rise of the modern corporation was extending the social division of labour by increasing the scale and scope of production (Hymer, 1972). This necessitated the rise of a managerial class that was required to co-ordinate and organize production and administration as companies got larger and more complex. This extended social division of labour began to have geographical effects as corporations – and US corporations in particular – became first multi-locational and then multi-national. In so doing, these corporations began to influence the social division of labour within the countries in which they operated and fragmented the traditional international division of labour. Indeed, Hymer went so far as to argue that multi-nationals unified 'world capital and world labor into an interlocking system of cross penetration that completely changes the system of national economies that has characterized world capitalism for the past three hundred years' (1972: 92).

In this sense Hymer anticipated the process of economic expansion that would a decade later be described as globalization (see Chapter 5), and which in the 1970s was shortly to become known as the New International Division of Labour (NIDL) (Fröbel et al., 1980; Cohen, 1981). The 'old' international division of labour could be seen as 'horizontal', with different countries and global regions tending to specialize in different industries. However, a new international division of labour was seen to be emerging as the vertical division of labour characteristic of large corporations was transposed over space, leading to what Hymer described as a 'spatial division of labor' (1972: 104), within which there existed a 'correspondence

principle relating centralization of control within the corporation to centralization of control within the international economy' (Hymer, 1979: 63–64). Hymer argued that the internationalization of corporate-organized production resulted in the spatial redistribution of the internal functions of organizations across space, and in so doing added a spatial dimension to Chandler and Redlich's analysis of the development of corporate structure (1961). The highest level in the corporate hierarchy, Level I, comprised the senior management functions of goal determination and planning. Level II activities were those that coordinated the behaviours of managers at the lowest level, Level III. The role of management at Level III was to undertake tasks that are concerned with the day-to-day management of the firm within the established framework of the organization. The tasks of the bottom level were performed by people with relatively low pay and low status. Hymer translated this analysis into spatial terms by arguing that Level III functions were widely distributed in accordance with supplies of labour, markets and materials, while the higher levels of the corporate hierarchy were more spatially concentrated. Level I activities were the most concentrated and least dispersed because 'they must be located close to the capital market, the media, and the government . . . because of the need for face to face contact at higher levels of decision making' which means that 'one would expect to find the highest offices of the multinational corporations concentrated in the world's major cities' (Hymer, 1979: 64). In addition to foreshadowing the emergence of work on world cities and Sassen's argument about command and control functions (Beaverstock et al., 2000; and see Chapter 12), Hymer drew attention to the social and economic consequences of division of the labour process over space by multi-locational companies. The production of spatial divisions of labour has significant impacts, because of the way it contributes to the production of employment opportunities which has 'the most profound influence on people's lives' in that it 'imparts occupational skills, social contacts, work discipline and militancy, money for a certain standard of living and the like' (Storper and Walker, 1984). But given that spatial of divisions of labour tend to be geographically uneven, the rewards from such activities are unequally distributed.

Although from the perspective of the twenty-first century Hymer's understanding of the multi-national and multi-national corporation can be viewed as simplistic (Dicken and Malmberg, 2001), his concern with spatial divisions of labour, and the uneven distribution of jobs and functions along the occupational hierarchy that such divisions produce was pioneering and would be picked up throughout the 1970s and into the 1980s in work that shared his alignment with Marxism and political economy (see Chapter 17). However, the focus in this later research was less on the production of spatial divisions of labour on a global scale than the production of spatial divisions of labour within the space economies of industrialized countries, and in the US and the UK in particular, and which was initially couched in the language of regional development rather than that of global economic restructuring. Moreover, partly as a result of this focus, a good deal of this work was, initially at least, relatively unconcerned with broader theoretical explanatory frameworks and was more straightforwardly empirical and policy oriented, particularly in the attempt to identify and map out what was described as the branch plant economy (Watts, 1981). A key concern was to connect the existence of uneven regional development with the notion of 'external control', with the poor performance of lagging economic regions seen to be a result of them lacking higher level corporate and management functions and the autonomy and decision-making capacity assumed to be important in creating a vibrant and successful economic milieu (Britton, 1976; Britton, 1980; Goddard and Smith, 1978; McDermott, 1976; Westaway, 1974; Firn,

1975). This research sought to document the level of external ownership in regional (or national) economies as a measure of external control (Watts, 1981), and was concerned in particular with the way in which low levels of corporate autonomy might suppress interaction between firms in a region, which made such regions become 'dependent' on decisions made elsewhere (and to an extent was prescient of the concern with traded and non-traded interdependencies that was to be developed in work in economic geography on industrial districts and economic agglomerations during the 1980s (see Chapter 18)).

This research was concerned that high levels of external ownership, and the lack of managerial functions and jobs, would result in a preponderance of routinized production, effectively limiting the overall quality of work within an area. The nature of employment within production units at the lower levels of the corporate hierarchy is literally a pole apart from the high degree of autonomy, variety and remuneration associated with tasks at the higher end of the corporate hierarchy. The cumulative impact of differential levels of socio-economic reward associated with those occupations characteristic of either end of the production hierarchy was seen to produce uneven development. These impacts played out at both the macro- and micro-scale, although this strand of work was more concerned with the local economic impacts of external control, such as differential levels of remuneration, variable levels of job security and differing opportunities for career development within the jobs available in an area. In addition, the sub-division of internal labour markets over space was also considered to have important impacts upon the rate of new firm formation in an area.

The outcome of this work was to reveal the extent of uneven development within economies such as the UK and US, and the identification of the North–South Divide in the former, and the Rust Belt/Sun Belt divide in the former. Older industrial areas located in the North of the UK and north east of the US began to perform badly in relation to the rest of their economies, and studies in economic geography revealed that in the UK at least this seemed to be associated with a lack of functions towards the higher end of the corporate hierarchy as well as the nature of production located in those regions.

However, while work on the branch plant economy began to open up questions about the role of management and corporate power in producing economic geographies, they were never fully developed, and this particular research project began to falter in the 1980s. There were at least two reasons for this. The first was that although work of this kind was often based on painstaking empirical studies, the general absence of theoretical traction meant that although large volumes of data were produced on levels of external ownership and existence of branch plant economies (for example, McDermott, 1976; Firn, 1975), the purpose of documenting this phenomenon was never really justified any more clearly than a general sense that somehow ownership and control was 'good' if it was 'local' (although what was local was never really properly defined), and 'bad' if it was 'ex-local' (which was similarly loosely specified). The second and related reason was the failure of this work to become aligned with the dominant theoretical impulse of economic geography from the late 1970s to the mid-1980s, the restructuring school. This was surprising given that Doreen Massey's work on spatial divisions of labour was such a key impetus to the restructuring debate (Massey, 1984; Barnes, 1996), but significantly she was at pains to distinguish her political economy inspired investigations into the processes that cause uneven development from more empirically-driven audits of the level of external ownership and control. For example, having identified three examples of corporate spatial structures that might help produce uneven spatial divisions of labour, Massey was at pains to emphasize that these were heuristic tools and her 'intention [was] not to set off a search for them' (Massey, 1984: 76), for fear that this would stimulate even

more empirically-driven studies (see, also, Chapter 17). The weaknesses inherent in the branch plant economy approach, and the growing interest in phenomena such as industrial districts and agglomerations during the 1980s, where the naked power of large corporations was not so immediately obvious, encouraged the economic geographer Richard Walker (1989) to confidently declare the death of corporate geography at the end of that decade. This academic death notice is explored in more detail in the next section.

A REQUIEM FOR CORPORATE GEOGRAPHY?

Walker's criticism of what he considered to be economic geography's excessive focus on the large corporation (Walker, 1989) was part of his broader project to promote the concept of geographical industrialization, developed in conjunction with Michael Storper (Storper and Walker, 1989), which sought to extend the restructuring approach in a more analytically rigorous manner. Walker was highly critical of the empiricism of corporate geography, and took aim at the four pillars of the approach, namely; 'the spatial bias in location introduced by corporate calculation, the imprint of corporate structure on spatial divisions of labor, the impact of the corporate spatial division of labour on regional development, and the geographic expansion of corporate activities' (Walker, 1989: 46). Walker argued that corporate geographers overstated the significance of the power and agency of large corporations and the benefits they accrued from internal markets and internal division of labour, drawing attention to the growing propensity of corporations to run their sub-divisions as profit-centres that needed to operate in a solvent manner, which encouraged flexibility and responsibility, and the growing tendency to sub-contact and out-source increasing volumes of corporate business. It was not clear, Walker argued, what an analysis of the large firm in isolation actually contributed to an understanding of economic geography because of the failure of corporate geography to identify 'the causal force of the organization, *per se*, on location' (Walker, 1989: 47). An even more important factor in explaining the changing geographical composition of the economy, Walker argued, is the expanding social division of labour (see, in addition, Sayer and Walker, 1992), which caused new types of work and economic activities proliferate. The large corporation is better seen as a constituent component of this process rather than its cause. More significantly, Walker argues, corporate geography made the fatal mistake of moving against the tide of history in economic geographical history:

> The brashest advocates of corporate geography . . . were declaring an end to agglomeration economies (and hence cities) just in time to be swept away by a new wave of excitement over spatially concentrated 'flexible production complexes'. (Walker, 1989: 48) (See Chapter 18 for further discussion on agglomerations.)

The focus on the occupational hierarchy of the large firm to the exclusion of other factors in producing uneven divisions of labour was seen to be both reductionist and negligent. Walker argued that despite their size in relation to other firms and organizations within the economy, the agency and power of large corporations remained limited in relation to the wider, aggregated economy and the deeper forces of competition and regulation that drive the economy:

> The corporation is an effective instrument of capitalist development but not the essential cause of it; that lies deeper within the economic structure. Corporate geographers have circled around this conclusion but never quite grasped it because they lack a systematic understanding of capitalism . . . They introduce the large firm as an exogenous player that alters the rules of the industrial economy rather than one that raises and acts according to those rules. (*op. cit.*, p. 50)

Thus, Walker was critical of corporate geography, and its focus on the managerial

structures of organization, because it allocated a level of agency and autonomy to organizations, and the managers that run them, that they simply do not have. In this Walker was strongly influenced by Marxist ideas, and the notion that while actors have a capacity for action, it is strongly constrained and made in circumstances not of their own choosing. The more important forces are broader, deeper systemic social processes that push the economy along constrained paths of development, and from which, for most of the time, organizations are unable to stray if they wish to survive. As Walker argues, the size of corporations may afford them some protection 'from the exigencies of market for certain periods of time . . . but the grim reaper of competition ultimately brings them to heel too' (*op. cit.*, p. 46).

Walker's intervention was both powerful and persuasive. It revealed the theoretical paucity of what was generally referred to as 'industrial geography' which, at its extremes, seemed to be interested in mapping the geography of industry for its own sake, wrapped in the thinnest veneer of conceptual justification. Corporate geography was caught in a pincer movement, between two more theoretically rigorous movements: Marxist informed political economy on the one hand, and the more theoretically catholic body of work concerned with economic agglomerations on the other. (For useful illustrations of the kinds of work that was produced by studies in these two traditions see, for example, the edited collections by Cooke (1989) and Storper and Scott (1992)).

However, reports of the death of corporate geography were greatly exaggerated. For some critics, Walker's requiem was simply overblown, and that while he managed to deliver some telling critiques of the problems that beset certain aspects of industrial geography during the 1980s – not least a tendency to consider firms in isolation from the wider institutional and cultural contents within which they operated – his attempt to drive out any possibility for agency in the unfolding of economy took 'a sound criticism to the point of caricature' (Dicken and Thrift, 1992: 280). In particular, Dicken and Thrift argued that Walker's account was a revisionist history: while he may have been justified in his attempts to rein in the focus on organization and to draw attention to the significance of the wider mode of production within which corporations operate, Dicken and Thrift argued that Walker travelled too far along this road and produced what came perilously close to being an already pre-programmed account of economic change. They also made it clear that just as Walker accused corporate geographers of being on the wrong side of history, he too was in danger of arguing against the grain in as much as his denial of the role of organization was in flat contradiction to a growing number of studies from the late 1980s onwards that drew attention to the significance of organizational culture in understanding economic change. The next section of the chapter considers two bodies of work that cast new light on the role of organizations and, in so doing, began to move towards a more culturally sensitive reading of economic change. I begin with a brief consideration of work on global commodity chains before focusing on the idea of the 'discursive firm' and the cultural circuit of capital.

GLOBAL PRODUCTION NETWORKS, THE 'DISCURSIVE FIRM' AND THE CULTURAL CIRCUIT OF CAPITAL

The focus on inter-firm relations and networks that emerged within the work on agglomeration and clusters was a feature of a body of work that emerged during the 1990s which looked at the organization of production and services on a global scale. This work explored the organization of global commodity chains and followed the flow of production and value over geographical space from origins to destinations (and back again) (Gereffi and Korzeniewicz, 1994; Gereffi, 1999). Although these approaches were ini-

tially concerned with the functional organization of production rather than their geography, they shared a similar concern with earlier work on branch plant economies about the impact of external control on local economic growth (Smith et al., 2002). Although not unproblematic, such approaches were seen as valuable in contributing to an understanding of the interrelationship between corporate organization and the global geographies of production and consumption (Hartwick, 1998; Leslie and Reimer, 1999; Hughes, 2000; Hughes and Reimer, 2004). Here, firms were seen as 'networks within networks', in complex production networks which linked regions and cities across the world (Coe et al., 2004; Dicken et al., 2001; Dicken and Malmberg, 2001).

Meanwhile, across a wide range of economic-facing social science disciplines, such as economic sociology and management and business studies, there was a growing recognition of the way in which what we understand as 'the economic' was constituted through a range of cultural, social and political practices (Block, 1991). Studies in these disciplines focused attention upon the possibility of agency, and the ability of powerful actors such as managers to intervene within the unfolding of the economy, albeit within a broader economic context. As Dicken and Thrift (1992) insist, while it is important to consider the dynamics and trajectories of industries in the way that Walker suggests, explanation will be deficient unless it also takes into account a corporate metric which is sensitive to issues such as culture and the emergence of 'conventions' of behaviour at particular times and places. Or, in other words, the time and place in which corporate managers make their decisions affects their views of the world (Schoenberger, 1997).

As the 1990s unfolded, more studies began to emerge which took the agency of management seriously, doing so as part of a body of work that constituted a wider cultural turn within social studies of the economic. Many of these were, unsurprisingly, within the burgeoning field of management and business studies (Knights and Murray, 1994; Clegg, 1996; Kerfoot and Knights, 1998; Kerfoot, and Knights, 1993; Knights, 1992; Knights and Morgan, 1995; Knights et al., 1993) but also within fields such as sociology (du Gay, 1996). These studies engaged strongly with the cultural turn, focusing on the significance of a managerial 'discourse', the circulation of a set of ideas and forms of language to which managers can refer to make sense of what they do, both to themselves and to others. Many of these studies argued that since the 1980s a new kind of manager had emerged, who now had to cope with the heightened levels of uncertainty and volatility that had been unleashed on the world economy following the progressive embrace of a market logic across many economies as a part of a process of neoliberalization (Peck and Tickell, 2002) and the continued advance of globalization.

Geographers, influenced by such ideas, also began to explore the processes by which managers were constructed, the kinds of managerial discourses that flowed through organizations, and the consequences of this for the production of economic geographies. These studies ranged from considerations of attempts to create subject formations through acts of training that might create appropriate managerial actors (Hinchliffe, 2000), the gendered nature of management practices (McDowell 2001, 1997), and the ways in which once powerful companies and industries can fail through the inability of their managerial cultures to bring about organizational change necessary within fast-moving and highly competitive markets (Schoenberger, 1997; O'Neill, 2001; O'Neill and Gibson-Graham, 1999). In addition, there emerged a body of work that focused explicitly on capitalist elites, which became particularly significant from the 1990s onwards, as they were rewarded in ever more spectacular ways (Cormode and Hughes, 1996, 1999; Hughes and Cormode, 1998).

These ideas were amalgamated and developed further by Thrift (2005) under what he described as the cultural circuit of capital, which he claimed had emerged in response to chronic uncertainty and doubt within the 'controlling heights' of the economy. Thrift's concept of the cultural circuit of capital has interesting parallels with a similar theory about the power of ideas which was developed more or less contemporaneously to it. *Virtualism*, developed by the anthropologist Danny Miller and the economic historian James Carrier (Carrier and Miller, 1998), was an attempt to account for the purchase that abstract economic theory has upon the material reality of economic and social life:

> Economic practice shapes economic thought. Moreover . . . economic thought shapes economic practice. This is because people are driven by ideas and idealism, the desire to make the world conform to the image. (Carrier, 1998: 5)

As a result, so Carrier argues, 'in many important ways the economic realm is becoming more abstracted from its pre-existing social and political contexts, even if types of social and institutional context remain important' (1998: 19). This tendency is due in part to the growing power of the discipline of economics within the world, which has colonized a number of key institutions:

> What had been a rather arcane academic discipline, made visible by the presence of occasional representatives who, like Keynes, engaged in public debate, has become more prestigious and pervasive. Not only is there now a Nobel prize awarded in economics (the only social science so treated); economists who have won that prize, together with their less exalted fellows, write columns in popular periodicals (for example Becker . . .) and lecture the public on the fallacies of government policy (for example Krugman . . .). Similarly, economists have increasingly visible and powerful positions in a range of organizations that deal with money. The World Bank is a striking example, an institution that appears to be dominated in important ways not by bankers but by economists . . . a situation analogous to having an aircraft design company dominated not by aerodynamic engineers but by physicists. (Carrier, 1998: 7)

Carrier and Miller argued that economic thought had an important, but hitherto underreported, impact on economic practice. Because of the power of certain kinds of economic theory, particularly associated with neoliberal economics, the economic realm has become more abstracted from its pre-existing social and political contexts (Miller, 1998, 2000, 2003).

While the cultural circuit of capital has similarities to the concept of virtualism, it is different in a number of respects, not least in the fact that virtualism tends to focus on the power of academic ideas, whereas the cultural circuit of capital has a more catholic approach to the origin of ideas and recognizes that important economic ideas can also come from economic practice and the places associated with it. In this respect, the cultural circuit of capital has more in common with theories about the performativity of economic ideas, which have emanated in particular from a branch of science and technology studies focused on social studies of finance, and have looked at the ways in which they unfold in particular circumstances and arenas (MacKenzie, 2006; MacKenzie et al., 2007; Callon, 1998; Callon et al., 2002; Zaloom, 2006). The cultural circuit of capital is defined by Thrift as a self organizing network for the production and distribution of management knowledge, the size of which has increased markedly in recent years. This knowledge is produced by three main institutions: business schools; management consultants; and management gurus (Thrift, 2005). Business schools, based for the most part in universities, have become important crucibles of new business knowledge in the past half-century or so, with the number of business schools in the US having grown fivefold since the late 1950s. Management consultants have also become important players within the contemporary economy, being representative of the expanding social division of labour referred to earlier, and who generate fee income by producing ideas and solutions for business clients. Moreover, their alumni have been particularly successful in locating themselves at the key sites of economic and political power during this

time (Micklethwait and Wooldridge, 1997; O'Shea and Madigan, 1998; Huczynski, 1996). Management consultants both generate new and package existing ideas and concepts to make management knowledge generic and easily transferable between organizations and industries. Management gurus are a third group responsible for animating the cultural circuit of capital, and are individuals who have placed themselves in the position of influence either through the power of their rhetoric or the marketing of their image (or both). They include academic gurus, consultant gurus and so-called 'hero managers'; that is, chief executive officers who have earned celebrity either through remarkable feat of industrial transformation or through media related promotion of their ideas and management capability (Thrift, 2005).

Once produced, this management knowledge is disseminated through the rest of the economy in a number of ways. First, it is disseminated through lectures and seminars within Business Schools, and is then taken out into the rest of the economy through successive waves of Business School graduates. Second, this knowledge is disseminated through business media, which has proliferated in recent years to include specialist magazines, the business sections of newspapers, the 'business books' that are available at airports and service stations and in the dedicated spaces within bookshops, television and radio programmes and even media dedicated to business (such as CNBC and Bloomberg for example). Third, there are set-piece management seminars, wherein a leading management figure speaks to a mass audience made up of both the willing and the conscripted ranks of the business classes.

Thrift argues that there is an audience for this material because managers want and need new ideas, to better cope with uncertainty and the anxieties of their jobs. Indeed, he makes a bolder claim in arguing that the demand for knowledge has increased due to a perception that the economic environment in which managers operate has become ever more unstable. Thrift characterizes the management culture of the period following the Second World War up to the breakdown of the Bretton Woods system of stable exchange rates in the early 1970s as one in which a series of 'stable spaces' abounded. In turn, these stable spaces produced more stable and hierarchical organizational and managerial forms. The relative predictability of the economic environment encouraged the emergence of bureaucratic corporations that could aspire to organize the world, and employed people who conformed to such an environmental and organizational milieu. As Thrift points out, the world prior to the 1970s was, in truth, probably not as controllable as managerial elites might have believed, but the fact that they did believe it might have encouraged the development of appropriately stable institutions.

With the collapse of the Bretton Woods system, and the shift to floating and volatile exchange rates in the 1970s, followed by the embrace of the market associated with neoliberal political systems in the 1980s, there has been a recognition that the economy is very different to the stable entity it was once imagined to be. This, in turn, led to a recognition that new ways were needed to understand it and describe it. Thrift argues that, as a result, there has been a concerted attempt to grasp a new understanding of the economic world, which has involved producing new metaphors and ways of thinking in order to achieve this. These metaphors and ways of thinking share a concern with looser organizational forms which are more able to 'go with the flow', and are more open to a world which is perceived as more complex and ambiguous than hitherto. It is also involved attempting to inculcate new kinds of knowledge among employees in order to foster new subject positions – the kinds of people they are, in other words – which are seen a more appropriate to be successful in this more volatile and competitive economic environment. To illustrate this, Thrift (2005) identifies a number of companies and organisations that now employ a wide range of training

courses, often involving unusual and seemingly bizarre subjects and techniques, to push employees in new directions and to create new ways of thinking, often drawing on emotions. Many of these involve 'New Age' thinking, which has become popular in informing management training because of the eclectic nature of its world view and the fact that 'its emphasis on personal development fits with the rise of 'soft skills' light leadership, intuition, vision and the like' (Thrift, 2005: 41):

> In Britain, New Age training . . . crops up . . . in unlikely places. For example, the Bank of England, British Gas, Ernst and Whinney, Mars, and Legal and General have all sent executives to be taught how to do the Whirling Dervish dance, so as to allow their top managers to find inner peace and increase their business potential. Then again, 'The Scottish Office sent thousands of its employees on "new-age thinking" courses run by Louis Tice of the Pacific Institute which aimed to train the minds of workers to make them "high-performance people" in their work and private lives' . . . meanwhile decision development, a British new-age training company, was offering to boost the spiritual, emotional and creative powers of clients. The company uses the American Indian medicine wheel 'to take managers on a journey to discover their spiritual, emotional and creative self. The wheel allegedly enables trainees to access their inner selves by examining their dreams and fantasies'.

The managers are sent on these courses in order to give them the cultural resources to cope in an economic world that is uncertain, unpredictable and volatile. The 'skill sets' required of managers in the twenty-first-century are seen to be very different to those needed in more stable economic eras; whereas in the past managers needed to be skilled in the administration and negotiation of bureaucracy, the contemporary normative expectation is that business leaders be skilled in 'change management'.

To be sure, this interpretation needs to be qualified given its Eurocentric focus, although it is the case that the cultural circuit of capital has been putting down roots in Asia, not least through the rapid growth of Business Schools in that region (Thrift and Olds, 2005). Nevertheless, the rise of a new managerialist discourse produced under the influence of the cultural circuit of capital has had some important consequences. First, the focus on flexibility and adaptability has been extended out beyond the individual to embrace the kinds of organizations that are seen to be appropriate in the contemporary economy, which are looser and more flexible institutions than was previously the case. Second, the degree of training given to managers and other employees in changing their own subject positions carries with it an expectation that responsibility for career outcomes and continued employment is as much the responsibility of the individual as it is of the employer. The focus on volatility and uncertainty makes change in organizations become the norm, with severe consequences for job security. This encourages employees to work harder, and commit themselves fully to the organization or bear the (inevitable) consequences.

Thrift argues that this culturally inflected way of analysing capitalism has considerable advantages over the kind of political economy analyses favoured by critics such as Walker, for example. In this regard Thrift echoes criticisms developed by Gibson-Graham (Gibson-Graham, 1996) who argues that political economy criticisms of capitalism afford it more order and power than it really has, and in doing so construct a confident and super organized juggernaut that it makes practically challenging it a rather daunting prospect (see Chapter 24). However, a closer, cultural appreciation of the life of corporations reveals that far from being the all conquering beasts they are sometime depicted to be, they may be less in control than they would like. A growing number of studies in economic geography have begun to draw on the idea of the cultural circuit of capital to explain the power of ideas in bringing about economic change, ranging from studies of the London financial services district, through to analyses of the geography of the new economy, to studies of more traditional sectors like the coal industry in central Europe (Hall, 2007; Leyshon, et al.,

2005; Swain, 2006). Moreover, while the cultural circuit of capital may appear to offer capitalist elites a panacea for the uncertainty that they face, it may be better understood as a placebo. Despite their greater attention to knowledge and information, Thrift argues that he is not 'at all convinced that the managers of capitalist firms – jointly or severally – know what they are doing for quite a lot of the time' (2005: 2). Indeed, one only has to look at how close the financial system came to total collapse in the late 2000s and, in particular, the ways in which of some of the world's leading financial instructions were mismanaged in the run up to the financial crisis, to gain empirical support for such a view. It is quite clear in retrospect that many of the people running these large organizations – a fair number of whom subsequently lost their jobs – believed that they were running sound and viable businesses up until events demonstrated that they were clearly not (Lewis, 2010).

CONCLUSIONS

This chapter has considered the ways in which economic geographers have approached the issue of the role of management within the production of economic geographies. In doing so it has provided a slice through the history of the sub-discipline, which in this case has moved from episodes of empiricism, through a concern with political economy, to the rise of a growing attention to a wider range of social and cultural structures, processes and practices in analysing economic events. It shows how research undertaken at particular periods are informed both by the current theories circulating within the discipline, as well as by the material changes that are taking place within the economy as a whole. It also illustrates that work in one period is often used as a platform to develop research that moves in new and often very different directions. This makes it possible to look at the same problem from different viewpoints, even though reconciling these viewpoints may be difficult.

Moreover, it is important to point out that newer ideas are not necessarily 'better', even though they may draw attention to weaknesses in earlier positions. For example, while the earlier work on branch plant economies was empirically rich, its atheoretical nature meant that as a body of work it lacked cohesion compared to work in political economy, and in particular the latter's ability to explain uneven development. In turn, the focus on the underlying dynamics within capitalism that produced uneven development tended to downplay the possibilities of agency and the role of culture within processes of economic change, which was the point of departure for approaches such as the cultural circuit of capital. Indeed, criticisms of the cultural turn in economic geography in general, and of the cultural circuit of capital in particular, have already emerged (on the latter, see Sayer, 2007). No doubt new approaches based on based on criticisms of the cultural economy approach are already being written, and will produce new ways of apprehending economic geography.

ACKNOWLEDGEMENTS

I am very grateful for the helpful comments of Roger Lee and Linda McDowell in helping me to overcome oversights and omissions in earlier versions of this chapter. The responsibility for the remaining errors of argument and content are mine.

REFERENCES

Barnes, T., Peck, J., Sheppard, E., and Tickell, A. (2007) Methods matter: Transformations in economic geography. In A. Tickell, E. Sheppard, J. Peck, and T. Barnes (eds). *Politics and Practice in Economic Geography.* London: SAGE. 1–24.

Barnes, T.J. (1996) *Logics of Dislocation: Models, Metaphors, and Meanings of Economic Space.* New York: Guilford.

Beaverstock, J.V., Smith, R.G., and Taylor, P.J. (2000) World city network: A new metageography? *Annals of the Association of American Geographers,* 90: 123–34.

Block, F. (1991) *Postindustrial Possibilities: A Critique of Economic Discourse.* Berkeley: University of California Press.

Britton, J.N.H. (1976) Influence of corporate organization and ownership on linkages of industrial plants: Canadian inquiry. *Economic Geography,* 52: 311–24.

Britton, J.N.H. (1980) Industrial dependence and technological development: Canadian consequences of foreign direct-investment. *Regional Studies,* 14: 181–99.

Callon, M. (1998) The laws of the markets. In: *Sociological Review Monograph Series.* Oxford: Blackwell.

Callon, M., Meadel, C., and Rabeharisoa, V. (2002) The economy of qualities. *Economy and Society,* 31: 194–217.

Carrier, J.G. (1998) Introduction. In J.G. Carreier and D. Miller (ed) *Virtualism: A New Political Economy,* Oxford: Berg. 1–24.

Carrier, J.G. and Miller, D. (1998) *Virtualism: A New Political Economy.* Oxford: Berg. p. 222.

Chandler, A. and Redlich, F. (1961) Recent developments in American business administration and their conceptualization. *Business History Review,* Spring, pp. 103–28.

Clark, G.L. (1998) Stylized facts and close dialogue: Methodology in economic geography. *Annals of the Association of American Geographers,* 88: 73–87.

Clegg, S. (1996) Postmodern management. In G. Palmer and S. Clegg (eds). *Constituting Management: Markets, Meanings and Identities.* Berlin: Walter De Gruyter.

Coe, N.M., Hess, M., Yeung, H.W.C., Dicken, P., and Henderson, J. (2004) 'Globalizing' regional development: A global production networks perspective. *Transactions of the Institute of British Geographers,* 29: 468–84.

Cohen, R.B. (1981). The new international division of labor, multinational corporations and urban hierarchy. In M. J. Dear and A. J. Scott (eds). *Urbanization and Urban Planning in Capitalist Society.* London: Routledge. pp. 287–318.

Cooke, P. (1989). *Localities: The Changing Face of Urban Britain.* London: Routledge.

Cormode, L. and Hughes, A. (1996) Methodological issues in studying elites. *Area,* 28: 281–83.

Cormode, L. and Hughes, A. (1999) The economic geographer as a situated researcher of elites. *Geoforum,* 30: 299–300.

Dicken, P. and Malmberg, A. (2001) Firms in territories: A relational perspective. *Economic Geography,* 77: 345–63.

Dicken, P. and Thrift, N. (1992) The organization of production and the production of organization: Why business enterprises matter in the study of geographical industrialization. *Transactions of the Institute of British Geographers*, 17: 279–91.

Dicken, P., Kelly, P.F., Olds, K. and Yeung, H.W.-C. (2001) Chains and networks, territories and scales: Towards a relational framework for analyzing the global economy. *Global Networks*, 1: 89–112.

du Gay, P. (1996) Making up managers: Enterprise and the ethos of bureacracy. In S. Clegg and G. Palmer (eds). *The Politics of Managment Knowledge*. London: SAGE. pp. 19–35.

Firn, J. (1975) External control and regional development. *Environment and Planning A*, 7: 393–414.

Fröbel, F., Heinrichs, J., and O. Kreye (1980) *The New International Division of Labour: Structural Unemployment in Industrialised Countries and Industrialisation in Developing Countries*. Cambridge: Cambridge University Press.

Gereffi, G. (1999) International trade and industrial upgrading in the apparel commodity chain. *Journal of International Economics*, 48: 37–70.

Gereffi, G. and M. Korzeniewicz (1994) *Commodity Chains and Global Capitalism*. Westport, CT: Greenwoods.

Gibson-Graham, J.K. (1996) *The End of Capitalism (As We Knew It): A Feminist Critique of Political Economy*. Oxford: Blackwell.

Goddard, J.B. and Smith, I.J. (1978) Changes in corporate control in the British urban system, 1972–1977. *Environment and Planning A*, 10: 1073–84.

Hall, S. (2007) Geographies of business education: MBA programmes, reflexive business schools and the cultural circuit of capital. In *103rd Annual Conference of the Association-of-American-Geographers*: San Francisco, CA. pp. 27–41.

Hartwick, E.R. (1998) Geographies of consumption: A commodity chain approach. *Environment and Planning D: Society and Space*, 16: 423–37.

Hinchliffe, S. (2000) Performance and experimental knowledge: Outdoor management training and the end of epistemology. *Environment and Planning D: Society and Space*, 18: 575–95.

Huczynski, A.A. (1996). *Management Gurus: What Makes Them and How to Become One*. London: International Thomson Business Press.

Hughes, A. (2000) Retailers, knowledges and changing commodity networks: The case of the cut flower trade. *Geoforum*, 31: 175–90.

Hughes, A. and Cormode, L. (1998) Researching elites and elite spaces. *Environment and Planning A*, 30: 2098–2100.

Hughes, A. and Reimer, S. (2004) Introduction. In A. Hughes and S. Reimer (eds). *Geographies of Commodity Chains*. London: Routledge. pp. 1–16.

Hymer, S. (1972) Internationalization of capital. *Journal of Economic Issues*, 6: 91–111.

Hymer, S. (1979) The multinational corporations and the law of uneven development. In R.B. Cohen, N. Felton, M. Nkosi, V. Liere and N. Dennis (eds). *The Multinational Corporation: A Radical Approach*. Cambridge: Cambridge University Press. pp. 54–74.

Kerfoot, D. and Knights, D. (1993) Management, masculinity and manipulation: From paternalism to corporate strategy in financial services in Britain. *Journal of Management Studies*, 30: 0020–2380.

Kerfoot, D. and Knights, D. (1998) Managing masculinity in contemporary organizational life: A 'Man'agerial Project. *Organization*, 5: 7–26.

Knights, D. (1992) Changing spaces: The disruptive impact of a new epistemological location for the study of management. *Academy of Management Review*, 17: 514–36.

Knights, D. and Morgan, G. (1995) Strategy under the microscope: Strategic management and IT in financial services. *Journal of Management Studies*, 32: 191–214.

Knights, D. and Murray, F. (1994). *Managers Divided: Organisation Politics and Information Technology Management*. London: John Wiley.

Knights, D., Morgan, G., and Sturdy, A. (1993) Quality for the consumer in bancassurance? *Consumer Policy Review*, 3: 232–40.

Leslie, D. and Reimer, S. (1999) Spatializing commodity chains. *Progress in Human Geography*, 23: 401–20.

Lewis, M. (2010) *The Big Short: Inside the Doomsday Madchine*. London: Allen lane.

Leyshon, A. (1995) Annihilating space?: The speed-up of communications. In J. Allen and C. Hamnett (eds). *A Shrinking World?: Global Uneveness and Inequality*. Oxford: Oxford University Press. pp. 11–54.

Leyshon, A., French, S., Thrift, N., Crewe, L., and Webb, P. (2005) Accounting for e-commerce: Abstractions, virtualism and the cultural circuit of capital. *Economy and Society*, 34: 428–50.

MacKenzie, D. (2006) *An Engine, Not a Camera: How Financial Models Shape Markets*. Cambridge, MA: MIT Press.

MacKenzie, D., Muniesa, F. and, L. (2007) *Do Economists Make Markets?* Princeton: Princeton University Press.

Maskell, P. (2001) The firm in economic geography. *Economic Geography*, 77: 329–44.

Massey, D. (1984) *Spatial Divisions of Labour: Social Structures of the Geography of Production*. London: Macmillan.

McDermott, P.J. (1976) Ownership, organization and regional dependence in the Scottish electronics industry. *Regional Studies*, 10: 319–35.

McDowell, L. (1997) *Capital Culture: Gender at Work in the City*. Oxford: Blackwell.

McDowell, L. (2001) Men, management and multiple masculinities in organisations. *Geoforum*, 32: 181–98.

Micklethwait, J. and Wooldridge, A. (1997). *The Witch Doctors: What the Management Gurus are Saying, Why it Matters and How to Make Sense of it*. London: Mandarin.

Miller, D. (1998). Conclusion: A theory of virtualism. In J.G. Carrier and D. Miller (eds). *Virtualism: A New Political Economy*. Oxford: Berg. pp. 187–215.

Miller, D. (2000) Virtualism: The culture of political economy. In I. Cook, D. Crouch, S. Naylor and J. R. Ryan (eds). *Cultural Turns/Geographical Turns: Perspectives on Cultural Geography*. Harlow: Prentice Hall. pp. 196–213.

Miller, D. (2003) The virtual moment. *Journal of the Royal Anthropological Institute*, 9: 57–75.

O'Neill, P. (2001) Financial narratives of the modern corporation. *Journal of Economic Geography*, 1: 181–99.

O'Neill, P. and Gibson-Graham, J.K. (1999) Enterprise discourse and executive talk: Stories that destabilize the company. *Transactions of the Institute of British Geographers*, 24: 11–22.

O'Shea, J. and Madigan, C. (1998) *Dangerous Company: The Consulting Powerhouses and the Businesses They Save and Ruin*. London: Nicholas Brealey Publishing.

Peck, J.A. and Tickell, A. (2002) Neoliberalizing space. *Antipode*, 34: 380–404.

Sayer, A. (2007) Knowing capitalism. *Economic Geography*, 83, 97–98.

Sayer, A. and Walker, R. (1992) *The New Social Economy*. Oxford: Blackwell.

Schoenberger, E. (1997) *The Cultural Crisis of the Firm*. Oxford: Blackwell.

Scott, A.J. (2000) Economic geography: The great half-century. *Cambridge Journal of Economics*, 24: 483–504.

Smith, A. and Rainnie, Dunford, M., Hardy, J., Hudson, R., and Sadler, D. (2002) Networks of value, commodities and regions: Reworking divisions of labour in macro-regional economies. *Progress in Human Geography*, 26: 41–63.

Storper, M. and Scott. A.J. (1992). *Pathways to Industrialization and Regional Development*. London: Routledge.

Storper, M. and Walker, R. (1984). The spatial division of labor: Labor and the location of industries. In W. Tabb and L. Sawers (eds). *Sunbelt-Frostbelt: The Political Economy of Regional Restructuring*, New York: Oxford University Press. pp. 19–47.

Storper, M. and Walker, R. (1989) *The Capitalist Imperative: Territory, Technology and Industrial Growth*. London: Blackwell.

Swain, A. (2006) Soft capitalism and a hard industry: Virtualism, the 'transition industry' and the restructuring of the Ukrainian coal industry. *Transactions of the Institute of British Geographers*, 31: 208–23.

Taylor, M. and Asheim, B. (2001) The concept of the firm in economic geography. *Economic Geography*, 77: 315–28.

Thrift, N. (2005). *Knowing Capitalism*. London: SAGE.

Thrift, N. J. and Olds., K. (2005). Cultures on the brink: Re-engineering the soul of capitalism – on a global scale. In A. Ong and S. Collins (eds). *Global Assemblages: Technology, Politics, and Ethics as Anthropological Problems*. Oxford: Wiley-Blackwell. pp. 27–290.

Walker, R. (1989) A requiem for corporate geography: New directions in industrial organization, the production of place and the uneven development. *Geografiska Annaler Series B – Human Geography*, 71: 43–68.

Watts, H.D. (1981) *The Branch Plant Economy: A Study of External Control*. London: Longman.

Westaway, J. (1974) The spatial hierachy of business organizations and its implications for the British urban system. *Regional Studies*, 8: 145–55.

Zaloom, C. (2006) *Out of the Pits: Traders and Technology from Chicago to London*. Chicago: University of Chicago Press.

Author Index

Subject Index

LIBRARY, UNIVERSITY OF CHESTER